OF CONSUMING INTERESTS

The Style of Life in the Eighteenth Century

D0144894

PERSPECTIVES ON THE AMERICAN REVOLUTION
Ronald Hoffman and Peter J. Albert, Editors

Diplomacy and Revolution: The Franco-American Alliance of 1778

Sovereign States in an Age of Uncertainty

Slavery and Freedom in the Age of the American Revolution

Arms and Independence: The Military Character of the American Revolution

An Uncivil War: The Southern Backcountry during the American Revolution

Peace and the Peacemakers: The Treaty of 1783

The Economy of Early America: The Revolutionary Period, 1763–1790

Women in the Age of the American Revolution

"To Form a More Perfect Union": The Critical Ideas of the Constitution

Religion in a Revolutionary Age

Of Consuming Interests: The Style of Life in the Eighteenth Century

Of Consuming Interests

The Style of Life
in the Eighteenth Century

Edited by CARY CARSON
RONALD HOFFMAN
and PETER J. ALBERT

Published for the

UNITED STATES CAPITOL HISTORICAL SOCIETY

BY THE UNIVERSITY PRESS OF VIRGINIA

Charlottesville and London

THE UNIVERSITY PRESS OF VIRGINIA
Copyright © 1994 by the Rector and Visitors
of the University of Virginia

First Published 1994

Library of Congress Cataloging-in-Publication Data

Of consuming interests : the style of life in the eighteenth century /
edited by Cary Carson, Ronald Hoffman, and Peter J. Albert.
p.   cm. — (Perspectives on the American Revolution)
Includes bibliographical references and index.
ISBN 0–8139–1413–2 (cloth). — ISBN 0–8139–1473–6 (paper)
1. United States—Social life and customs—To 1775.   2. Consumer
behavior—United States—History—18th century.   3. United States—
Social life and customs—1783–1865.   I. Carson, Cary.
II. Hoffman, Ronald, 1941–   .   III. Albert, Peter J.   IV. United
States Capitol Historical Society.   V. Series.
E162.03   1994

973.2—dc20   94–17526
                                                                                 CIP

Printed in the United States of America

Contents

Contents

Preface

ON MAY 30, 1744, at 11:00 in the morning, the Scottish physician Dr. Alexander Hamilton set out from Annapolis on an amazing journey through the northern regions of British North America that lasted nearly four months. Fortunately for scholars of the style of life in the eighteenth century, Dr. Hamilton recorded his observations of the people he encountered and the places he visited in a document he called his *Itinerarium*.

Two themes emerge from Hamilton's impressions. First, his experiences reflect a pervading sense of class. Wherever he went, the doctor found men and women who shared his notions of decorum and dress, and, as a result, he could enjoy the congenial and familiar society of equally well-bred people whether he was in Philadelphia, Newport, Albany, or Boston. Such people to whom he carried letters of introduction and with whom he felt immediately at ease formed an intercolonial network of civility that deeply impressed Hamilton and inspired him to end his *Itinerarium* with the following paragraph: "In this itineration I compleated, by land and water together, a course of 1624 miles. The northern parts I found in generall much better settled than the southern. As to politeness and humanity, they are much alike except in the great towns where the inhabitants are more civilized, especially att Boston."[1]

Besides reflecting his bonds with others of his class, Hamilton's observations also portray the opinions the well-bred shared about how they differed from the lower orders of mankind. He looked with particular distaste, for example, upon the susceptibility of what he called "vulgar minds" to the machinations of preachers associated with the Great

[1] Carl Bridenbaugh, ed., *Gentleman's Progress: The Itinerarium of Dr. Alexander Hamilton, 1744* (Chapel Hill, N.C., 1948), p. 199.

Awakening's religious revivalism, and he viewed with similar opprobrium any ordinary folk who showed signs of trying to rise above their appointed station in life. On one occasion, Hamilton and an equally genteel fellow traveler found themselves in the abode of a poor man and his wife whose seven "wild and rustick" children were unabashedly "amazed" by the doctor's "laced hat and sword." Hamilton's critically observant companion quickly noted that there were "severall superfluous things" in the home "which showed an inclination to finery," among them "a looking glass with a painted frame, half a dozen pewter spoons and as many plates, old and wore out but bright and clean, a set of stone tea dishes, and a tea pot." Such items, the gentleman sniffed superciliously, were "too splendid for such a cottage, and therefor they ought to be sold to buy wool to make yarn." Instead of putting on airs inappropriate to their rank, the couple ought to content themselves with "a little water in a wooden pail" for a looking glass and an entirely serviceable set of wooden plates and spoons. Of the family's meager possessions, the "tea equipage" gave the travelers the greatest offense, while they deemed the man's musket the most "usefull . . . piece of furniture" in the house.[2]

While Hamilton's observations and those of other eighteenth-century travelers suggest how the diffusion of genteel culture and the ideal of cultivation shaped and imparted a certain uniformity to the colonists' class prejudices and sensibilities, these accounts also reveal that within the subtle and complex process of social and cultural evolution in British North America there existed as many differences as similarities. As the *Itinerarium* makes abundantly clear, the doctor's travels across a wide geographic area made him just as aware of the influence of distinct regional traits and characteristics as of common assumptions and values. To his consternation and dismay, Hamilton discovered while in the company of some fashionable Bostonians that a man's hometown habits could very well make him appear foolish to the genteel company of another region:

[2] Ibid., pp. 54–55.

I dined with Mr. Fletcher in the company of two Philadelphians, who could not be easy because for sooth they were in their night-caps seeing every body else in full dress with powdered wigs; it not being customary in Boston to go to dine or appear upon Change in caps as they do in other parts of America. What strange creatures we are, and what triffles make us uneasy! It is no mean jest that such worthless things as caps and wigs should disturb our tranquility and disorder our thoughts when we imagin they are wore out of season. I was my self much in the same state of uneasiness with these Philadelphians, for I had got a great hole in the lappet of my coat, to hide which employed so much of my thoughts in company that, for want of attention, I could not give a pertinent answer when I was spoke to.[3]

Some thirty years later, on the eve of the meeting of the First Continental Congress, such concerns still prevailed. Illustrative of the point is the delightful story about Samuel Adams recounted by Richard L. Bushman in an essay entitled "American High-Style and Vernacular Cultures." It seems that Adams's friends were so alarmed about the adverse effect that his personal disregard of dress might have on the reception accorded the Massachusetts delegation in Philadelphia that they procured Sam a new wardrobe and wigs and saw to it that he and the other Massachusetts representatives traveled to Congress in a splendid coach and four, complete with liveried servants and retainers.[4]

Once the delegates from the thirteen colonies had assembled in Philadelphia, however, they found the potentially unifying experience of belonging to the same social class fractured by some very deep-seated differences in the ways various geographic sections defined that group. For instance, some of the southern delegates had traveled in Europe or had been educated abroad, but many of the others—the Adams cousins included—had not previously ventured beyond the confines of their own provinces. In fact, according to the late

[3] Ibid., p. 134.

[4] Richard L. Bushman, "American High-Style and Vernacular Cultures," in Jack P. Greene and J. R. Pole, eds., *Colonial British America: Essays in the New History of the Early Modern Era* (Baltimore, 1984), pp. 359–60.

Preface

Merrill Jensen, the Adamses' trip to Philadelphia in 1774 marked the first time that John had ever ventured beyond the borders of Massachusetts, and Sam had never even been out of Boston, except to cross the Charles River to attend Harvard![5] Moreover, each region's delegates considered themselves superior to everyone else, and they took cold comfort from the fact that they were all supposed to be gentlemen. Indeed, they were not even sure that all of them were! John Adams once observed that in all of New York he had not "seen one real gentleman, one well bred man," and that civil conversation was not to be had in that province: "They talk very loud, very fast, and all together. If they ask you a question, before you can utter three words of your answer, they will break out upon you, again—and talk away."[6] Neither did Philadelphia really pass muster, in Adams's opinion, when compared to Boston, and in a fit of Massachusetts chauvinism, he confided to his diary that "the Morals of our people are much better, their manners are more polite, and agreeable— they are purer English. Our language is better, our persons are handsomer, our spirit is greater, our laws are wiser, our religion is superior, our education is better.'[7] He might justifiably have added "and our egos are larger"! The South fared worst of all, for Adams considered that an area inhabited by "the dons, the bashaws, the grandees, the patricians, the sachems, [and] the nabobs."[8] Not surprisingly, Edward Rutledge of South Carolina, one of the grandest of the grandees, held an equally unflattering opinion of New Englanders, which he expressed rather graphically in a letter to John Jay: "I dread their low cunning, and those levelling principles which men without character and without fortune in general possess."[9]

[5] Merrill Jensen, "The Sovereign States: Their Antagonisms and Rivalries and Some Consequences," in Ronald Hoffman and Peter J. Albert, eds., *Sovereign States in an Age of Uncertainty* (Charlottesville, Va., 1981), p. 232.

[6] Quoted ibid.

[7] Quoted ibid., p. 233.

[8] Quoted ibid., p. 235.

[9] Quoted ibid.

x

Two other factors should be kept in mind when considering the influence of culture and class on the style of life: the role of individuality and the opinions of American society expressed by visitors from abroad. In the first instance it is instructive to note the intraclass disparity exhibited by persons like the Virginia planter William Byrd III and his Maryland counterpart Charles Carroll of Annapolis. Two more different attitudes about the style of life can hardly be imagined. Byrd enjoyed living in an ostentatious, self-indulgent way, and by the eve of the American Revolution, he had managed to accumulate an incredible debt of nearly £100,000 sterling. By contrast, Charles Carroll of Annapolis, who possessed a substantial fortune worth nearly as much as Byrd owed, regarded any form of show and finery as reprehensible and did not hesitate to make his views on that subject quite explicit. Advising his son and daughter-in-law not to send to England "for any Superfluities," he warned that "to do so at any time is foolish." In Carroll's view, "What is decent & Convenient, You ought to Have, there is no end to a desier for finery of any sort. . . . Be content with what is neat Clean & Necessary."[10] This firm conviction sprang from Carroll's fundamental belief that a family's first order of business must always be to provide for the next generation. "Can fine furniture Clothes &c be put in Competition with a provision for Children?" he wrote his son Charles Carroll of Carrollton. "Pride & Vanity are not to be indulged in at their Expence, nor are You to be fools because many are So. . . . The Sumptuosity of Princes leaves roome for desier, I wish Yours & Mollys to be governed by Reason."[11]

Because the inhabitants of Britain's North American colonies were in large measure attempting to replicate in the New World the social customs and modes of behavior that had regulated life in the Old, it is not surprising that foreign observers frequently evaluated and commented upon their efforts. As might be expected, the advances in which upper-class colo-

[10]Charles Carroll of Annapolis to Charles Carroll of Carrollton, Nov. 30, 1770, Carroll Papers, MS 206, no. 151, Maryland Historical Society, Baltimore.

[11]Ibid.

nials took great pride often appeared as mere pretensions to gentility to the jaundiced eyes of foreign visitors who tended to render negative rather than positive assessments. Thus, an Englishman visiting Yorktown in 1736 commented disdainfully that "Almost every considerable Man Keeps an Equipage, tho' they have no Concern about the different Colours of their Coach Horses, driving frequently black, white, and chesnut, in the same Harness."[12] And another traveler, this one from France, reported with similar condescension of the same Virginia planters that they "do not understand the use of napkins, that they wear silk scarves, and that instead of using handkerchiefs they blow their noses with their fingers, or with a silk handkerchief which serves as a cravat, napkin, etc."[13]

Even if the inhabitants of eighteenth-century British North America did not always enjoy the approval of their Old World contemporaries, their customs and their style of life intrigued and fascinated the Europeans of that day as much as they intrigue and fascinate us. While this volume will greatly increase our knowledge of their style of life, it will also serve to whet our interest in the way they were, an interest that I expect is destined to remain as lively and unsatisfied as ever.

The editors would like to thank the commentators at the U.S. Capitol Historical Society's symposium Of Consuming Interests: The Style of Life in the Eighteenth Century, Loretta Valtz Mannucci and Michael W. Zuckerman, for their valuable criticisms. We would also like to acknowledge the help of Angeline Polites, Katherine Morin, and Aileen Arnold for their assistance in the editing and typing of this manuscript.

RONALD HOFFMAN

[12]Quoted in T. H. Breen, *Tobacco Culture: The Mentality of the Great Tidewater Planters on the Eve of Revolution* (Princeton, 1985), p. 37.

[13]Quoted in Arthur M. Schlesinger, Sr., *Learning How to Behave: A Historical Study of American Etiquette Books* (New York, 1946), p. 7.

OF CONSUMING INTERESTS

The Style of Life in the Eighteenth Century

KEVIN M. SWEENEY

High-Style
Vernacular:
Lifestyles of
the Colonial Elite

DURING HIS LIFETIME George Washington helped launch two
revolutions. His leadership during the American Revolution
earned him a place "first in war, first in peace, first in the
hearts of his countrymen." Even more important to Col.
Light-Horse Harry Lee, who proclaimed Washington's primacy in the new nation's public life, was the fact that Washington "was second to none in the humble and endearing scenes
of private life."[1] A rereading of Lee's complete sentence—
"First in war, first in peace, first in the hearts of his countrymen, he was second to none in the humble and endearing
scenes of private life"—makes clear that the eulogist placed
his emphasis on the second half of the sentence, on the domestic Washington, on the builder of Mount Vernon. Washington spent almost a lifetime fashioning his mansion into a
retreat for a wealthy planter, an elegant stage for the country's
most eminent citizen, and, ultimately, his personal monument. The reshaping and furnishing of his mansion also
made it an enduring monument to the consumer revolution
and to the pursuit of gentility and power that affected the
lives of many of the Virginian's contemporaries.

I want to thank Cary Carson, Carol Clark, Robert F. Dalzell, Jr., Margaret
Hunt, Gloria L. Main, and Robert Paynter for their comments and David
Barquist, Deborah Federhen, Elizabeth Donaghy Garrett, Susan Mackie-
wicz, and Beth Ann Twiss-Garrity for sharing material with me.

[1] Quoted in Gerald W. Johnson, *Mount Vernon: The Story of a Shrine* (Mount
Vernon, Va., 1953), p. 1.

1

Washington lived in an age when growing numbers of new consumer goods, essentially bourgeois luxuries, became available to those with means. Homes and furnishings acquired a heightened role in the lives of the upper classes—that 5 to 7 percent of the colonial population formed by the families of leading merchants, high government officials, wealthy southern planters, well-to-do professionals, and moderately well-off rural gentlemen. Their houses became embodiments of power, and goods that had once been exotic and unavailable became essential parts of genteel lifestyles and reinforced the claims of social status and political leadership of the colonies' essentially bourgeois upper classes.[2] But like the political revolution that began with America's War for Independence, the cultural transformations that accompanied upper-class participation in the consumer revolution were incomplete, for the lifestyles of the colonies' social and economic elite were shaped by local conditions and vernacular traditions as well as by English goods and the pursuit of gentility.

A close look at the mansions and household furnishings of wealthy Americans and the social and cultural aspirations that these material statements embodied helps reveal the contradictions in the eighteenth-century consumer revolution, the mediated reception of Georgian architecture, and the bourgeois nature of colonial gentility. Such an examination also helps refine contemporary colonial historians' concept of "Anglicization." Finally, this essay seeks to periodize the changing character of the relationship of the upper classes to the consumer revolution and stylistic changes.

Beginning in the late 1600s and early 1700s, ambitious and wealthy individuals throughout England's mainland colonies strove to attain, legitimize, and render inheritable positions of social and political prominence. Steady economic growth (often sustained by imperial wars) and the elaboration of po-

[2]On the bourgeois characteristics of colonial elites, see Carl Bridenbaugh, *Myths and Realities: Societies of the Colonial South* (New York, 1963), p. 53; T. H. Breen, *Tobacco Culture: The Mentality of the Great Tidewater Planters on the Eve of Revolution* (Princeton, 1985), pp. 17–23, 32–37; Frederick B. Tolles, *Meeting House and Counting House: The Quaker Merchants of Colonial Philadelphia, 1682–1763* (Chapel Hill, N.C., 1948), pp. 85–143, 161–204.

litical and military establishments provided structures upon which provincial oligarchies grew like intertwining vines. Before the colonial era ended, Virginia would have its hundred first families, twenty-five families would lead Connecticut during the eighteenth century, and in New Hampshire one family, the Wentworths, would attain unchallenged ascendancy.[3]

These upper-class families stood between, occasionally rather uneasily between, the governors and other royal officials at the apex of the colonies' political and social hierarchies and the vast majority of the population, free and slave. They also usually served as critical links in marketing networks that ran from colonial farms and plantations to England or the West Indies and back again. In 1700 few of these families could claim titled or distinguished pedigrees. They owed their positions to wealth and their wealth to a combination of entrepreneurial activity, commercial farming, and in some instances government service. Members of these aspiring families remained subject to the economic system that they had employed to rise in the world, and, like the price of crops, anything that had risen in the marketplace could just as easily fall. Throughout the colonial period, the bourgeois origins and commercially "tainted" occupations of most wealthy and socially prominent colonists stood in contradiction to their efforts to establish and legitimize a hierarchical, aristocratic social and political order based on family. Skillful use of material culture offered these elite families one set of tools for mediating between imperial officials and local dependents and between their bourgeois origins and aristocratic aspirations.[4]

At the beginning of the eighteenth century, wealthier

---

[3]John M. Murrin, "Political Development," in Jack P. Greene and J. R. Pole, eds., *Colonial British America: Essays in the New History of the Early Modern Era* (Baltimore, 1984), pp. 416–55; Leonard W. Labaree, *Conservatism in Early American History* (Ithaca, N.Y., 1948), pp. 1–31; David W. Jordan, "Political Stability and the Emergence of a Native Elite," in Thad W. Tate and David L. Ammerman, eds., *The Chesapeake in the Seventeenth Century: Essays on Anglo-American Society* (New York, 1979), pp. 269–70, 267; Gloria L. Main, *Tobacco Colony: Life in Early Maryland, 1650–1720* (Princeton, 1982), pp. 260–63; Tolles, *Meeting House and Counting House*, pp. 109–23.

[4]Jack P. Greene, "Search for Identity: An Interpretation of the Meaning of Selected Patterns of Social Response in Eighteenth-Century America,"

Americans usually lived simply and owned few possessions that differed from those found in the homes of their humbler neighbors.[5] Even wealthy planters of the Chesapeake often shared the life of "rude simplicity" that characterized most households in the region in the late seventeenth and early eighteenth centuries.[6] As late as the 1720s, the overwhelming majority—perhaps 80 percent—of Virginia's wealthiest residents lived in two-room, one- or one-and-a-half story houses.[7] A foreign visitor was surprised to discover in 1715 that wealthy planter Robert Beverley "lives well; but though rich, he has nothing in or about his house but what is necessary. He hath good beds in his house, but no curtains; and instead of cane chairs, he hath stools made of wood."[8] The situation in the middle colonies and in New England may have been somewhat less "rude" or crude. Still, the homes of the wealthy were more likely to be distinguished by a greater number of rooms and greater quantities of goods than by the character or quality of the furnishings.[9]

Journal of Social History 3 (1970):206–10; Carter L. Hudgins, "Patrician Culture, Public Ritual, and Political Authority in Virginia, 1680–1740," Ph.D. diss., College of William and Mary, 1984, pp. 22–23, 99–138; Carole Shammas, "English-Born and Creole Elites in Turn-of-the-Century Virginia," in Tate and Ammerman, eds., *Chesapeake in the Seventeenth Century*, pp. 284–94; Kevin M. Sweeney, "Mansion People: Kinship, Class, and Architecture in Western Massachusetts in the Mid-Eighteenth Century," *Winterthur Portfolio* 19 (1984): 231–55.

[5]Lois Green Carr and Lorena S. Walsh, "Changing Lifestyles and Consumer Behavior in the Colonial Chesapeake," in this volume; Main, *Tobacco Colony*, pp. 206, 239; Rhys Isaac, *The Transformation of Virginia, 1740–1790* (Chapel Hill, N.C., 1982), p. 73.

[6]Aubrey C. Land, "The Planters of Colonial Maryland," *Maryland Historical Magazine* 67 (1972):122.

[7]Carole Shammas, *The Pre-Industrial Consumer in England and America* (New York, 1990), p. 166.

[8]John Fontaine (1715), quoted in W. G. Standard, "Major Robert Beverley and His Descendants," *Virginia Magazine of History and Biography* 3 (1895):171.

[9]Isaac, *Transformation of Virginia*, p. 73; Main, *Tobacco Colony*, pp. 153–55, 159–62, 213–14; Kevin M. Sweeney, "Furniture and the Domestic Environ-

This situation began to change in many areas in the late 1710s and the 1720s. Wealthy colonists adopted a common strategy employed by intermediate social groups that involved imitating superiors to differentiate themselves from subordinates.[10] To distance themselves more obviously from their less wealthy neighbors and to impress royal officials and English merchants with their stature and "Englishness," these families began to cultivate a style of life that was qualitatively different and distinctive.[11] Domestic furnishings—imported goods and locally produced furniture and silver—played an important role in expressing a cultivated gentility. Previously unknown quantities and varieties of chairs and tables, imported textiles, and the like served as markers of status just as expensive and relatively rare possessions had during the 1600s and 1500s. Eighteenth-century goods were distinguished, however, by motifs inspired by the Orient, by a robust baroque classicism coupled with a new emphasis on smooth surfaces, and by the introduction of new forms expressing and facilitating leisure and convenience.[12]

These furnishings—in an early baroque style today referred to as William and Mary—were more obviously cosmopolitan and more obviously the products of intense manipulation and transformation of materials. In furniture design, craftsmen sought to transcend the limits that seventeenth-century construction techniques had placed on

---

ment in Wethersfield, Connecticut, 1639–1800," in Robert Blair St. George, ed., *Material Life in America, 1600–1860* (Boston, 1988), pp. 263–76.

[10]Grant McCracken, *Culture and Consumption: New Approaches to the Symbolic Character of Consumer Goods and Activities* (Bloomington, Ind., 1988), p. 94.

[11]Shammas, "English-Born and Creole Elites," pp. 285–89; Hudgins, "Patrician Culture," pp. 22–23, 99–113. The process may have begun a little earlier in Boston. See Barbara McLean Ward, "The Edwards Family and the Silversmithing Trade in Boston, 1692–1762," in Francis J. Puig and Michael Conforti, eds., *The American Craftsman and the European Tradition 1620–1820* (Minneapolis, 1989), pp. 67–72.

[12]Philip M. Johnston, "The William and Mary Style in America," in Reiner Baarsen et al., *Courts and Colonies: The William and Mary Style in Holland, England, and America* (New York, 1988), pp. 62–79.

design. As design moved away from the rectilinear forms popular in the previous century, craftsmen began to explore the potential of new materials and techniques. In high-style English furniture and colonial adaptations, boards became wider but thinner, methods of joining wood became more delicate and less visible, and surfaces became more highly polished. Chairs changed most dramatically as curved legs and backs shaped by more laborious techniques of sawing, carving, and offset turning replaced straight legs and back posts (fig. 1). Upholstered cushion or slip seats eventually replaced separate cushions. All of these changes resulted in more elegant, occasionally more comfortable, but invariably more labor-intensive and expensive-looking furnishings. Such expressions bespoke more clearly an owner's ability to command labor and materials of a larger world beyond the immediate locale, and they simultaneously reinforced the owner's ability to command labor and materials in the smaller world in which he held sway.[13]

The shining surfaces of walnut or mahogany tea tables and other specialized tables, sets of chairs, oriental and English ceramics, imported wineglasses, and dozens of other new furnishings did more than mark status. These goods also served to convey character.[14] In eighteenth-century America possessions became tools for actively cultivating a distinctive, genteel style of life that set off "polite society" from the "meaner sort." New patterns of personal deportment—of language and of movement—became critical expressions of character and gentility. In England and in America, manners and education bolstered the claims of social status based solely on the possession of wealth. Calculated but seemingly effortless demonstrations of control, moderation, grace, and polite learning distinguished genteel people.

[13] Ibid.

[14] Colin Campbell, *The Romantic Ethic and the Spirit of Modern Consumerism* (Oxford, 1987), esp. pp. 138–60; J. H. Plumb, *Georgian Delights* (Boston, 1980), pp. 146–47; Richard L. Bushman, "American High-Style and Vernacular Cultures," in Greene and Pole, eds., *Colonial British America*, pp. 352–60; Jack P. Greene, *Pursuits of Happiness: The Social Development of Early Modern British Colonies and the Formation of American Culture* (Chapel Hill, N.C., 1988), p. 107.

Figure 1. Side chair, Boston, 1689–1705. International in its design sources and materials—which can be traced back to Asia (the use of cane) and the Mediterranean (the scrolls)—this particular chair is an American-produced example of the distinctive high-backed English cane chairs that were exported by the thousands to other parts of Europe, the colonies, and elsewhere. Stylish, even exotic, these mass-produced chairs were aimed at an upper middle class, as opposed to aristocratic, market. (Courtesy, Winterthur Museum)

Occasions to eat, drink, play cards, dance, and just converse offered opportunities for displaying these qualities, and material goods played important roles in most genteel social gatherings (fig. 2). Matched sets of chairs, of glasses, and of plates, rounded, less hierarchical tables, individual eating utensils, and individual drinking vessels facilitated these gatherings. The sets of chairs and utensils helped turn eating into dining. New forms and increased quantities of glass and ceramic drinking vessels provided the proper containers for such imported beverages as claret, port, sherry, and Madeira. The combination of fine wines and imported glass elevated the act of drinking.[15]

Sets of chairs encouraged social calls and conversation among equals. Ideally, a "select company" or "picked company" provided the best place to display the requisite attributes of refinement.[16] Some anthropologists and historians have viewed the appearance of individualized eating utensils as announcing the birth of modern individualism and in doing so have slighted the role these objects played in defining and bonding peer groups, particularly elite peer groups.[17] For members of prominent families, sets of goods encouraged a cultivated individuation, not an unfettered individualism, and furthered, instead of undermined, a vision of a traditional, hierarchical order with its social and political elite.

By the 1720s tea drinking at home had established itself as the preeminent genteel ritual (fig. 3). It was a relatively new event featuring an exotic new beverage. Preparing, serving,

[15]Cary Carson and Lorena S. Walsh, "The Material Life of the Early American Housewife," *Winterthur Portfolio* (forthcoming); Main, *Tobacco Colony*, p. 248; Carr and Walsh, "Changing Lifestyles and Consumer Behavior"; Mark R. Wenger, "The Dining Room in Early Virginia," in Thomas Carter and Bernard L. Herman, eds., *Perspectives in Vernacular Architecture, III* (Columbia, Mo., 1989), p. 153; Shammas, *Pre-Industrial Consumer*, pp. 181, 183, 186.

[16]Mark A. DeWolf Howe, ed., "Journal of Josiah Quincy, Junior, 1773," Massachusetts Historical Society *Proceedings* 49 (1915–16):459, 472; William Eddis, *Letters from America*, ed. Aubrey C. Land (Cambridge, Mass., 1969), p. 20. For a discussion see Bushman, "American High-Style," pp. 352–53.

[17]James J. F. Deetz, *In Small Things Forgotten: The Archaeology of Early American Life* (Garden City, N.Y., 1977), pp. 59–60.

Figure 2. Parlor Scene. *Artist unknown, 1733. The picture shows a "select group" of males seated in cane chairs around a small square table. They are drinking from imported wineglasses and what may be a German stoneware mug, demonstrating the growing use of both expensive and inexpensive individual drinking vessels. (From William Winstanley,* A New Help to Discourse *[London, 1733]; photo by permission of the British Library)*

and consuming tea required new containers and utensils and new skills to use them successfully and gracefully. Ideally, this act of pouring boiled water on dried leaves and drinking the resulting liquid called for a tea kettle, a teapot (preferably of silver or porcelain), tea caddies, a tea strainer, a sugar bowl, sugar tongs, a creamer or milk pot, teacups and saucers, teaspoons, a spoon tray, a slop bowl, and a tea table. This proliferation of highly specialized artifacts offered new opportunities for consumption and display, but, more importantly, these objects turned tea drinking into a ritual. As participants moved and conversed, they evaluated potential business partners, potential marriage partners, and possible political allies. Through their participation in these ceremon-

Figure 3. Family Group. *Gawen Hamilton, England, c. 1730. Tea was most likely to be consumed by mixed groups of men and women, including family groups like the one pictured here. The tea equipage in this scene includes ceramic teacups and saucers, sugar bowl and creamer or milk pot, sugar tongs and spoons, and tea table. (Colonial Williamsburg Foundation)*

ies they also convinced others, and themselves, of their own gentility and status. Until the mid-1700s, few outside of the colonial elite could join this select company of frequent tea drinkers.[18]

The goods that supported such rituals were inherently fragile, usually new, and commercially available to others with similar aspirations and growing means.[19] To sustain and legitimize their positions, socially and politically prominent colo-

[18]Rodris Roth, *Tea Drinking in Eighteenth-Century America: Its Etiquette and Equipage,* U.S. National Museum Bulletin 225 (Washington, D.C., 1961), pp. 61–91.

[19]Carole Shammas recently categorized these goods as "semidurables" (see Shammas, *Pre-Industrial Consumer,* pp. 293, 297).

nists needed a more durable material culture that expressed stability as well as gentility. They required objects that would in time acquire a patina of age, a traditional basis for material claims to family pedigree.[20] Only a house—the traditional aristocratic embodiment of the cult of lineage—could offer upper-class colonial families an enduring material expression of their status and aspirations.

During the second quarter of the eighteenth century, wealthy southern planters, urban merchants, New England country squires, and other wealthy colonists began building mansion houses (fig. 4). This development, historian Roger G. Kennedy has argued, marked a critical transition from a colonial to a "truly provincial architecture" and simultaneously marked the "appearance of the first American landed aristocracy."[21] These houses drew their inspiration primarily from small, vernacular brick houses built in provincial England in the late 1600s and early 1700s.[22] Though often called "Wren Baroque" or "Early Georgian," houses of this form took shape before the coronation of George I and owed little in plan to academic architecture or professional architects such as Sir Christopher Wren. Instead, the skills of artisans and the needs of middle-class patrons shaped the English prototypes. This particular combination of artisans and patrons grafted classical decorative details onto evolving vernacular house forms in England and America.

Between 1720 and 1750 these new house forms were not derived from pattern books, but were shaped primarily by the experiences and aspirations of patrons and the skills and ideas of the builders.[23] In the Chesapeake the erection of brick mansion houses with central halls owed much to local house forms and patterns of living and to the social segregation and

[20] McCracken, *Culture and Consumption*, pp. 31–43.

[21] Roger G. Kennedy, *Architecture and Money in America, 1600–1860* (New York, 1985), p. 97. See also Bushman, "American High-Style," pp. 349–50.

[22] Daniel D. Reiff, *Small Georgian Houses in England and Virginia: Origins and Development through the 1750s* (Newark, Del., 1986), esp. pp. 221–315.

[23] In many discussions of Georgian architecture, emphasis is placed on the determining role of pattern books. See for example, Deetz, *Small Things Forgotten*, p. 112.

Figure 4. Westover, river front facade, James City County, Virginia, c. 1750; photograph c. 1909. Westover exhibits a number of features found on the new colonial mansion houses built between 1720 and 1750: brick construction, symmetrical facade, high hip roof, London-style sash windows with large panes of glass, and elaborate doorway, in this instance made of imported Portland stone. While the house is richly ornamented, it does eschew some high-style embellishments such as corner quoins found on comparable English houses. (Colonial Williamsburg Foundation)

distancing that had begun to develop by the late 1600s.[24] In urban and rural New England the development of mansion houses and a provincial high style was "characterized by the independent elaboration of indigenous ideas and forms introduced from elsewhere."[25] Despite their Georgian appearance,

[24]Reiff, *Small Georgian Houses*, p. 207, and Dell Upton, "Vernacular Domestic Architecture in Eighteenth-Century Virginia," *Winterthur Portfolio* 17 (1982):95–119.

[25]James L. Garvin, "Academic Architecture and the Building Trades in the Piscataqua Region of New Hampshire and Maine, 1715–1815," Ph.D.

brick town houses built during the 1720s by Philadelphia's leading citizens owed much to earlier vernacular building traditions, not pattern books.[26]

This is not to say that these houses represented an unaffected evolution of local architecture with an embellishment of academic architectural details. Still, upper-class colonists responded to English architecture by acting as filters, not sponges, and by making selective appropriations of imported goods and ideas. The houses were hybrids in their design, layout, furnishing, and use. They embodied the desire of wealthy and prominent colonists to balance public and private space, evoke hierarchy while permitting individuation, and wed genteel elegance to a rational order. And they contained within them the families' provincial conflict of loyalty between metropolitan ideals and local norms.[27]

The houses built by wealthy colonists between 1720 and 1750 stood out in the landscape. Their size, their elegance, their symmetrical facades, and sometimes their materials distinguished these houses from those of people farther down the social scale and from most of the homes of wealthy seventeenth-century colonists. In a century when typical dwelling houses ranged in size from approximately 320 square feet in the Chesapeake region to 800 square feet in New England, William Byrd's Westover covered 2,500 square feet and the more modest, wooden mansion houses of the New England

---

diss., Boston University, 1983, p. 1. Garvin is speaking of high-style provincial architecture in the Portsmouth, New Hampshire, area, but the process was similar in other regions such as the Connecticut Valley. See also William N. Hosley, Jr., "Architecture," in Gerald W. R. Ward and William N. Hosley, Jr., eds., *The Great River: Art and Society of the Connecticut Valley, 1635–1820* (Hartford, Conn., 1985), pp. 66–69.

[26]Susan Mackiewicz, "'Property Is the Great Idol of Mankind, However They May Profess Their Regard for Liberty and Religion': The Material Lives of Philadelphia Elites, 1700–1775" (Paper presented at the University of Delaware Seminar on Material Culture, Spring 1985), pp. 5–6.

[27]Upton, "Vernacular Domestic Architecture," p. 95; idem, *Holy Things and Profane: Anglican Parish Churches in Colonial Virginia* (Cambridge, Mass., 1986), pp. 27–28.

McGEE HOUSE *c.1790*
INDIAN RIVER HUNDRED, DELAWARE

0 FEET   50

HALL AND PARLOR HOUSE *c.1720*
CONNECTICUT VALLEY

WILLIAM HANCOCK HOUSE *1734*
HANCOCK'S BRIDGE, NEW JERSEY

SETH WETMORE HOUSE *c.1750*
MIDDLETOWN, CONNECTICUT

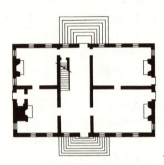

WESTOVER *c.1750*
CHARLES CITY COUNTY, VIRGINIA

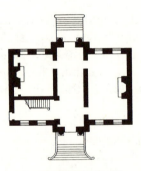

MOUNT PLEASANT *After 1761*
PHILADELPHIA, PENNSYLVANIA

CLIVEDEN *After 1763*
GERMANTOWN, PENNSYLVANIA

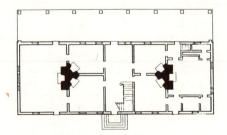

MOUNT VERNON *After 1787*
FAIRFAX COUNTY, VIRGINIA

14

gentry covered 1,200 to 1,600 square feet (fig. 5).[28] Unlike most colonial dwellings, the homes of wealthy southern planters and the New England gentry usually stood two or two and a half stories tall. The hip or gambrel roofs often found on these houses added to their height and the effect of grandeur (figs. 4 and 12).

The materials used often enhanced the effect. Cut stone proved to be difficult to obtain and too expensive if available. Brick therefore became the preferred material, especially in the Chesapeake and in urban areas. The choice of brick suggested material permanence and family stability. One Virginian, Lewis Burwell, purposefully laid out "great sums of money in building a mansion-house, and other out-houses, and in making gardens, and other considerable improvements . . . intending the same for the seat of the eldest son of the family."[29] Such a claim of permanence was particularly striking amidst the impermanent landscape of the Chesa-

[28] Mechel Sobel, *The World They Made Together: Black and White Values in Eighteenth-Century Virginia* (Princeton, 1987), p. 104; Michael Steinitz, "Rethinking Geographical Approaches to the Common House: The Evidence from Eighteenth-Century Massachusetts," in Carter and Herman, eds., *Perspectives in Architecture, III*, pp. 20–21.

[29] Quoted in William M. Kelso, *Kingsmill Plantations, 1619–1800: Archaeology of Country Life in Colonial Virginia* (Orlando, Fla., 1984), p. 44.

Figure 5. Eighteenth-century mansion houses. The differences in size and plan reflect variations in building traditions and wealth much more than changes over time. Note the use of central halls and the location of staircases as well as the asymmetry of the interior plans which reflected functional concerns. (Based on plans in Bernard L. Herman, The Stolen House *[Charlottesville, 1992], p. 177; Kevin M. Sweeney, "Mansion People: Kinship, Class, and Architecture in Western Massachusetts in the Mid-Eighteenth Century,* Winterthur Portfolio *19 [1984]:237, 241; Richard Pillsbury, "Patterns in the Folk and Vernacular House Forms of the Pennsylvania Culture Region,"* Pioneer America *9 [1977]:17; Fiske Kimball,* Domestic Architecture of the American Colonies and the Early Republic *[1922; reprint ed., New York, 1966], pp. 73, 74, 77; Thomas Tileston Waterman,* The Mansions of Virginia 1706–1776 *[Chapel Hill, N.C., 1945], p. 298, drawing, Jeffrey Bostetta and Cary Carson).*

peake.[30] To the north, in areas like southern New Jersey, the erection of a brick mansion house also made a particularly strong statement, one that was proclaimed in the initials and dates set in patterned brick in the gable ends of the well-known houses along Alloways Creek (fig. 6). Here, as in Virginia, "family institutions" were what these brick houses with any pretensions were "about."[31]

Most of the mansion houses erected by wealthier colonists were in fact built of framed wood. But in many instances owners had builders transform the wooden facades. Occasionally the houses were covered with planks grooved to imitate the appearance of ashlar blocks (fig. 7). Paint mixed with sand gave the wood a texture suggesting stone. While this particular treatment appears to have been relatively rare, the use of paint on the wood frame mansion houses of wealthier colonists was more widespread and distinguished these homes from the unpainted dwellings in which most colonial Americans lived.[32]

The application of architectural ornament could further dignify a wooden or brick mansion house. Classically inspired details, possibly drawn from English pattern books, but before 1750 more likely copied from other structures, enhanced the entrances to many of these colonial Georgian houses (fig. 4). In certain instances these architectural details, as well as other features such as materials, roof line, or fenestration, made reference to public buildings in the colonies. The English baroque interpretation of classical architecture established itself as the ornamental code for upper-class colonists

[30]Camille Wells, "The Eighteenth-Century Landscape of Virginia's Northern Neck," *Northern Neck of Virginia Historical Magazine* 37 (1987):4245.

[31]Alan Gowans, "The Mansions of Alloways Creek," in Dell Upton and John Michael Vlach, eds., *Common Places: Readings in American Vernacular Architecture* (Athens, Ga., 1986), p. 381; see also Kelso, *Kingsmill Plantations*, pp. 44, 199.

[32]Hugh Morrison, *Early American Architecture: From the First Colonial Settlements to the National Period* (New York, 1952), pp. 304–6; Sweeney, "Mansion People," pp. 243–44.

Figure 6. William Hancock house, Hancock's Bridge, New Jersey, 1734. This house is one of approximately one hundred eighteenth-century houses in the area that feature elaborate brickwork in the gable ends. A close look at the house's plan—fig. 5—reveals that the exterior symmetry masks an asymmetrical interior plan. The house and its plan represent a rural adaption of a vernacular urban house-plan found in Philadelphia and Restoration London. (Photo, Historic American Buildings Survey)

who often served on building committees for churches, meetinghouses, and other public buildings.[33]

The mansion houses of upper-class Americans shared with public buildings a relatively lavish use of imported window glass. Robert Beverley, writing about the architectural changes visible in the early eighteenth century, emphasized two things: the increased height of buildings and the intro-

[33] Upton, *Holy Things and Profane*, pp. 27–29, 101–62; Sweeney, "Mansion People," pp. 242–43; Hudgins, "Patrician Culture," pp. 253–54; Mackiewicz, "'Property Is the Great Idol,'" p. 26.

Figure 7. Mount Vernon, Fairfax County, Virginia, after 1787. The original house was a story and one-half high. The house was raised in 1757–58 and lengthened in 1776–79. The pediment was added in 1778 and the cupola finial in 1787. Note the scored wooden planks imitating ashlar stone and the asymmetry of the window placement in the central block. (Photo, courtesy of the Mount Vernon Ladies' Association)

duction of large sash windows with crystal glass.[34] The numbers of windows and of panes remained a noteworthy feature of these houses as late as 1798, the year of the Federal Direct Tax, or so-called window tax.[35] The windows of mansion houses let in more light, making interior spaces brighter, more inviting, and more elegant and genteel. At the same time, these windows served to articulate the symmetry of the facade, an important feature that imparted elegance to the exterior of even the simplest wooden mansion house (fig. 4).[36]

The emphasis on the facade's symmetry and proportion ex-

[34]Robert Beverley, *The History and Present State of Virginia* (1705), ed. Louis B. Wright (Chapel Hill, N.C., 1947), p. 289.

[35]This was a "strongly progressive tax" based on housing, taking into account the number and size of windows. See Lee Soltow, *Distribution of Wealth and Income in the United States in 1798* (Pittsburgh, 1989), p. 4.

[36]Morrison, *Early American Architecture*, pp. 303–4.

pressed the desire for order of the people who dwelt within. The homes of the elite were houses in motion, usually containing large families, employing servants, and witnessing constant comings and goings of kin, visitors, tradesmen, and others. The central hall or passageway with its stairway formed the dynamic core of these mansion houses (fig. 5). It functioned as the fulcrum that balanced the family's growing desire for privacy with these houses' primary role as a center for social power.[37]

The hall or passage, which had apparently evolved independently as part of vernacular architectural traditions in English cities and in the Chesapeake, created a more formal front entry and provided regulated access to most rooms in the house. Servants could greet visitors in this intermediary space, learn their business, and direct them according to their master's or mistress's instruction. The hall enabled guests, servants, and family members to move throughout the house without intruding upon other spaces, thus turning walls into true boundaries and barriers.[38]

The central hall served as a conduit as well as a baffle. Regulated movement could heighten the drama of social interaction as a visitor passed abruptly from one type of space to another. The most dramatic movements could involve the of-

[37] Elizabeth Donaghy Garrett, "The American Home, Part I, 'Center and Circumference': The American Domestic Scene in the Age of Enlightenment," *Antiques* 123 (1983):214–19; Hugh Morrison sees the Georgian house as a structure shaped by a style concerned with motion (*Early American Architecture*, p. 300). For more on motion and style see Upton, *Holy Things and Profane*, pp. 199–218. For suggestive reflections on Georgian houses see Witold Rybczynski, *Home: A Short History of an Idea* (New York, 1986), pp. 108–12.

[38] Deetz, *Small Things Forgotten*, pp. 115–17; Reiff, *Small Georgian Houses*, pp. 139–40; Henry Glassie, *Folk Housing in Middle Virginia: A Structural Analysis of Historic Artifacts* (Knoxville, Tenn., 1975), pp. 121–22; Hudgins, "Patrician Culture," p. 208; Isaac, *Transformation of Virginia*, p. 75; Sweeney, "Mansion People," p. 245; Beth Ann Twiss-Garrity, "Getting the Comfortable Fit: House Forms and Furnishings in Rural Delaware, 1780–1820," M.A. thesis, University of Delaware, 1983, pp. 40–49; Mark R. Wenger, "The Central Passage in Virginia: Evolution of an Eighteenth-Century Living Space," in Camille Wells, ed., *Perspectives in Vernacular Architecture, II* (Columbia, Mo., 1986), pp. 137–49.

ten grand stairway located in central halls. The master or mistress of the house could greet guests by gracefully descending the stairs. Alternatively, a servant could with due ceremony lead guests up the stairs and into more intimate regions of the house.[39]

In both northern and southern colonies the central passage also came to function as additional leisure space, especially during the warm days of summer. The introduction of the central passage in southern architecture has traditionally been explained by the need to move air through the house. Though it now appears that the passage's origin lay in the region's social climate instead of its weather, abundant evidence confirms that the passage came to be used as a summer sitting room, or "hall," as early as the 1730s.[40] Even in northern New York, residents of mansion houses took advantage of their central halls in the summer, furnishing them with "chairs and pictures like a summer parlor."[41]

The location of rooms in relation to the central passage and main stairway that formed a mansion house's core determined the dignity and character of the rooms. The genteel house functioned to a degree as a theatrical stage setting with front and back regions. Doors near the front of the passage led into parlors usually intended solely for formal entertainment. The practice of placing beds in prominent front rooms fell into disfavor among the wealthy as the century progressed. Back rooms on the first floor provided spaces for more informal sitting rooms, perhaps as a study for the mas-

[39] For all their interest in central halls or passages, recent students of eighteenth-century architecture have generally ignored the staircases usually found in them. Observations in the following works are suggestive: Morrison, *Early American Architecture*, pp. 300, 489, 499; Mark Girouard, *Life in the English Country House: A Social and Architectural History* (New Haven, 1978), pp. 198–99; George B. Tatum, *Philadelphia Georgian: The City House of Samuel Powel and Some of Its Eighteenth-Century Neighbors* (Middletown, Conn., 1976), pp. 67–72; and William M. S. Rasmussen, "Sabine Hall, a Classical Villa in Virginia," *Journal of the Society of Architectural Historians* 39 (1980):293.

[40] Wenger, "The Central Passage," p. 139.

[41] Anne Grant, *Memoirs of an American Lady*, 2 vols. in 1 (New York, 1909), 1:165–66.

ter of the house, a kitchen in the northern colonies, and, along with attic spaces, quarters for servants or slaves. Upstairs chambers were usually reserved for sleeping and the entertainment of especially favored guests. When present, secondary stairs enabled domestic servants to move throughout the house to deliver food, clean, and remove waste.[42]

Architectural finishes and furnishings articulated and reinforced this hierarchy of spaces. As Moreau de St. Méry discovered, "[The] decoration of the houses is only to be found in the rooms which a visitor is likely to see in any particular house; for everything that is normally out of sight is very ugly and very little cared for."[43] The particular color or lack of paint, the quality or outright absence of plaster, the character of the furniture, and the quality or absence of textiles immediately signaled a room's use and prominence. The greatest expenditure of resources was lavished on the formal entertaining spaces: the parlor or drawing room, and dining room, if there was one. As another French visitor familiar with the homes of Virginia's elite families and their priorities concluded: "All they want in a house is a bed, a dining room, and a drawing room for company."[44]

Conspicuous expenditures of resources on skilled labor, imported paints, or textiles created highly unified and artificial interiors in parlors and drawing rooms. Elaborately joined paneling, used alone or in combination with plaster, gave

[42] Hudgins, "Patrician Culture," p. 259; Sweeney, "Mansion People," pp. 245, 247; Tatum, *Philadelphia Georgian*, pp. 67–108; Twiss-Garrity, "Getting the Comfortable Fit," pp. 41–54; Nicholas B. Wainwright, *Colonial Grandeur in Philadelphia: The House and Furniture of General John Cadwalader* (Philadelphia, 1964), pp. 142, 145, 150; Wenger, "The Central Passage," p. 150; marquis de Chastellux, *Travels in North America in the Years 1780, 1781, and 1782*, ed. Howard C. Rice, Jr., 2 vols. (Chapel Hill, N.C., 1963), 2:514; Rasmussen, "Sabine Hall," p. 293; Grant, *Memoirs*, 1:170; Beverley, *History and Present State of Virginia*, p. 290; *Moreau de St. Méry's American Journey, 1793–1798*, trans. and ed. Kenneth Roberts and Anna M. Roberts (Garden City, N.Y., 1947), p. 101.

[43] *St. Méry's American Journey*, p. 264.

[44] Chastellux, *Travels in North America*, 2:441; see also Thomas Anburey, *Travels through the Interior Parts of America*, 2 vols. (1789; reprint ed., Boston, 1923), 2:208.

Figure 8. Parlor fireplace wall, Seth Wetmore house, Middletown, Connecticut, c. 1750. The paneling, including the built-in shell cupboard, has been cedar grained, and the pilasters flanking of the fireplace have been marbleized. The overmantel painting appears to be an idealized pastoral scene. (Wadsworth Atheneum, Hartford, Conn: The Ella Gallup Sumner and Mary Catlin Sumner Collection and the H. Hilliard Smith Fund)

these formal rooms a uniformity of finish that complemented the polished surfaces of the period's high-style furniture (fig. 8). In even relatively modest mansion houses, built-in cupboards constructed as integral components of the parlor served as focal points for conspicuous display of such consumer goods as wineglasses, punch bowls, and tea dishes. These often elaborately carved cupboards bespoke the intention of conspicuous display in architectural design as well as the marriage of space with new consumer goods and the genteel social rituals in which they were used.[45]

[45]J. Frederick Kelly, *Early Domestic Architecture of Connecticut* (1924; reprint ed., New York, 1963), pp. 167–72.

The uniformity and self-conscious contrivance could be enhanced by painting the room a single color, or the drama could be heightened by painting architectural details a contrasting color. In some instances the effect was carried further by using paint to grain, marbleize, or japan the wood (fig. 8).[46] New kinds of textiles also contributed to the general effect. During the eighteenth century upper-class Americans began finishing rooms en suite with matching textiles, thus pressing a traditional mode of display into the service of the drive for order characteristic of the period. Washington was typical of contemporaries in believing this effect to be "uniformly handsome and genteel."[47]

Colonial elites placed their furniture in parlors and drawing rooms to reinforce a sense of elegant order and heightened artificiality. When a room was not in use, the furniture was lined up against the wall. This practice facilitated a flexible use of space and made a powerful statement of both control and repetitive consumption as sets of chairs stood arrayed in a row. Here again, sets of goods, especially chairs, played a role by stressing uniformity. The effect could be carried further if tables and case pieces in the room exhibited similar finishes, stylistic motifs, and carved decoration. Just as important, these tables, chairs, and case pieces delineated the primary function of the room and facilitated social rituals.[48]

While these mansion houses were distinguished by the elaboration of space for entertaining, other spaces such as back regions and chambers provided places where some degree of family intimacy, solitude, or creature comforts could be found. Little dining rooms that accommodated family

[46]Garrett, "'Center and Circumference,'" pp. 219–21; idem, "The American Home, Part III: The Bedchamber," *Antiques* 123 (1983): 619; Edgar de N. Mayhew and Minor Myers, Jr., *A Documentary History of American Interiors from the Colonial Era to 1915* (New York, 1980), pp. 39–43, 68–72.

[47]Garrett, "'Center and Circumference,'" p. 221; idem, "The Bedchamber," pp. 617–18; "Invoice of Sundry Goods to Be Ship'd by Robt. Cary, Esq., and Company for the Use of George Washington," May 1759, in John C. Fitzpatrick, ed., *The Writings of George Washington from the Original Manuscript Sources, 1745–1799*, 39 vols. (Washington, D.C., 1931–44), 2:319–20.

[48]Garrett, "'Center and Circumference,'" pp. 221–22; Tatum, *Philadelphia Georgian*, pp. 108–18.

meals offered retreats from increasingly formal spaces.[49] Smaller back parlors "afforded a refuge to the family during the rigors of winter, when the spacious summer rooms would have been intolerably cold, and the smoke of prodigious wood fires would have sullied the elegantly clean furniture."[50] Second floor bed chambers, which tended to be smaller and easier to heat, offered additional places to chat with intimates and could be a welcome retreat on a cold wintry day.[51] Smaller fireplaces and, in some areas, stoves, as well as smaller rooms and screens, enhanced the comforts of such settings, and as the century progressed commentators increasingly commended a genteel house for its "comforts as well as its elegancies."[52]

Such improvements in comfort, though still relatively limited in the mid-1700s, document the bourgeois concerns with privacy and domesticity that lay behind the often aggressively aristocratic facades of Georgian mansion houses.[53] At the same time, the emphasis that some commentators came to place on the enjoyment of comforts—a less morally and socially threatening category of goods than "elegancies" or luxuries—revealed a growing uneasiness with consumption among wealthy and genteel Americans.[54]

Developments during the 1760s and 1770s presented challenges to the status of upper-class families whose mem-

[49] Wenger, "The Dining Room," p. 155.

[50] Grant, *Memoirs*, 1:170.

[51] Nancy Tomes, "The Quaker Connection," in Michael Zuckerman, ed., *Friends and Neighbors: Group Life in America's First Plural Society* (Philadelphia, 1982), p. 179; Alice Morse Earle, ed., *Diary of Anna Green Winslow* (Boston, 1894), p. 23.

[52] Eddis, *Letters*, pp. 16, 19; Rybczynski, *Home*, pp. 90–91.

[53] Rybczynski, *Home*, pp. 77, 85–87, 119–20.

[54] I am indebted to Joyce Appleby for her reflections on the use of the word *comfort* in the 1790s. My reading of sources suggests that the strategic use of *comfort* and *comforts* to avoid the aristocratic associations of the word *luxury* and the straightened circumstances associated with the word *necessities* began earlier around the time of the American Revolution. See Joyce Appleby, *Capitalism and a New Social Order: The Republican Vision of the 1790s* (New York, 1984), p. 90.

bers had attained their positions during the first half of the century. Dramatically increased government spending, resulting from military operations during the 1750s and early 1760s, and the growth of intercolonial trade created new opportunities for ambitious colonists and immigrants. These developments also indirectly financed increased consumer expenditures. Throughout the colonies, newly arrived royal officials and military officers, and Scots, Irish, English, and West Indies merchants who immigrated to cash in on the commercial boom usually set the standards for conspicuous consumption.[55]

Urban areas witnessed the greatest changes and displays of wealth and luxury. William Smith, Jr., of New York observed in the mid-1750s that "our affluence, during the late war, introduced a degree of luxury in tables, dress, and furniture, with which we were before unacquainted." Despite this he believed that New York still lagged behind "our neighbours in Boston and several of the Southern colonies."[56] In Philadelphia the number of taxpayers claiming to be "gentlemen" or "esquires" tripled between 1756 and 1772.[57] Mount Pleasant, built in 1761 for Scots merchant John MacPherson, and Port Royal, built in 1762 for Edward Stiles, a merchant and planter from the West Indies, stood as monuments to two immigrants' wealth, awareness of fashion, and claims to status (fig. 9).[58] Even the Quakers of Philadelphia were affected, and observers claimed that, while their luxury was "of a less noticeable sort," it was still noticeable.[59]

Throughout the colonies, the annual value of British imports rose by almost 100 percent from £1.1 million annually

[55] John Clive and Bernard Bailyn, "England's Cultural Provinces: Scotland and America," *William and Mary Quarterly,* 3d ser. 11 (1954):207–8.

[56] William Smith, Jr., *The History of the Province of New-York . . . to . . . 1732* (1757), ed. Michael G. Kammen, 2 vols. (Cambridge, Mass., 1972), 1:226.

[57] Billy G. Smith, "Inequality in Late Colonial Philadelphia: A Note on Its Nature and Growth," *William and Mary Quarterly,* 3d ser. 41 (1984):643.

[58] Ibid., pp. 641–43; Carl Bridenbaugh, *Cities in Revolt: Urban Life in America, 1743–1776* (New York, 1955), p. 338.

[59] Charles H. Sherrill, *French Memories of Eighteenth-Century America* (New York, 1915), p. 56.

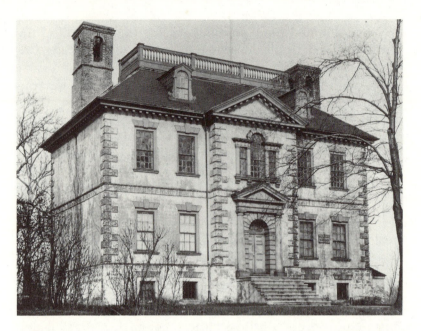

Figure 9. Mount Pleasant (west elevation), Fairmont Park, Philadelphia, 1761–62. The projecting pavilion, palladian window, and elaborate doorway with fanlight were features first found on houses built early in the third quarter of the eighteenth century. These features combine with the balustrade, heavy cornice, and corner quoins to create a heavily ornamented, more exuberant facade than that found on earlier eighteenth-century mansion houses. (Photo, courtesy of the Philadelphia Museum of Art)

in 1750 to £2.1 million in 1760.[60] The expanding capacity of English factories turned out increasing quantities of textiles, ceramics, cutlery, and other consumer goods. English entrepreneurs like Josiah Wedgwood used increasingly sophisticated marketing techniques to manipulate and promote products intended to encourage social imitation and emulative spending.[61] Though they occasionally felt manipulated by

[60] James A. Henretta and Gregory H. Nobles, *Evolution and Revolution: American Society, 1600–1820* (Lexington, Mass., 1987), p. 118.

[61] Neil McKendrick, "The Commercialization of Fashion," in Neil McKendrick, John Brewer, and J. H. Plumb, *The Birth of a Consumer Society: The Commercialization of Eighteenth-Century England* (Bloomington, Ind., 1982), p. 43.

the fashion system, wealthy consumers could overcome their misgivings as Benjamin Franklin did when he sent his wife four London-made silver salt ladles in the "newest, but ugliest, Fashion."[62] An English resident of Annapolis, William Eddis, claimed, probably with some hyperbole, that "a new fashion is adopted earlier by the polished and affluent American than by many opulent persons in the great metropolis."[63]

Statements by contemporary observers like Eddis and studies by architectural, economic, and cultural historians argue that among the very wealthy, fashion assumed new importance during the third quarter of the eighteenth century.[64] The latest style in furniture—today called the Chippendale after the influential English cabinetmaker Thomas Chippendale—was more a series of "decorative options" than a radically new style, especially suited to fashionable manipulation.[65] Aristocratic and even regal associations added to the appeal.[66] First appearing in the mid-1750s, the style with its "gothick," "chinese," and "modern" (or what is now called rococo) decorative motifs saw its full flowering in the 1760s and 1770s.[67] While the basic furniture forms often remained baroque in their massing, they could be ornamented with fanciful and intricate profusions of gothic tracery, oriental-looking

[62]Benjamin Franklin to Deborah Franklin, Feb. 19, 1758, Leonard W. Labaree et al., eds., *The Papers of Benjamin Franklin,* 28 vols. to date (New Haven, 1959–), 7:381.

[63]Eddis, *Letters,* pp. 57–58.

[64]McKendrick, "Commercialization of Fashion," p. 54; Upton, *Holy Things and Profane,* p. 229; Carr and Walsh, "Changing Lifestyles and Consumer Behavior."

[65]I am indebted to Gerry Ward for the observation and the term *decorative options* (Gerald W. R. Ward, "Reflections on the Rococo: New Visions and Future Directions," Lecture given at the Metropolitan Museum of Art symposium on the American Rococo, Jan. 24, 1992). For an excellent discussion of the customizing of Philadelphia Chippendale chairs, see Philip D. Zimmerman, "Workmanship as Evidence: A Model for Object Study" *Winterthur Portfolio* 16 (1981):289–307.

[66]Rybczynski, *Home,* pp. 98, 106.

[67]Morrison H. Heckscher and Leslie Greene Bowman, *American Rococo, 1750–1775: Elegance in Ornament* (New York, 1992), pp. 5–18.

fretwork, and naturalistic rococo motifs such as shells, vines, leaves, and flowers. In Philadelphia, chairmakers offered a range of options in the shape of crest rails, splats, and legs, and the amount and type of carved ornamentation (figs. 10 and 11).[68] Elaborate rococo ornamentation could also be found on silver—Franklin's salt ladles in the "newest, but ugliest, Fashion" were no doubt rococo—and in architectural interiors as the growing availability of English design sources and specialized English-trained craftsmen capable of executing the designs made available a range of options for those who wanted fashionable appointments.[69] In cities such as Williamsburg, Philadelphia, and Portsmouth, New Hampshire, the direct influence of English designs on locally produced furniture became pronounced in the 1760s.[70]

Such competitive consumption could blur rather than strengthen class distinctions and posed a threat to the position of more established upper-class colonial families, who had relied on goods, homes, and other material props to express their genteel status.[71] Possessions such as tableknives, glassware, and tea equipage that had once been found only in the

[68]Zimmerman, "Workmanship as Evidence," pp. 289–307.

[69]Heckscher and Bowman, *American Rococo*, pp. 5–9. On the dramatic influx of English craftsmen during this period see Bernard Bailyn, *The Peopling of British North America: An Introduction* (New York, 1986), pp. 63–64.

[70]Wallace B. Gusler, "The Anthony Hay Shop and the English Tradition," and Morrison H. Heckscher, "Philadelphia Furniture, 1760–90: Native-Born and London-Trained Craftsmen," in Puig and Conforti, eds., *American Craftsman and European Tradition*, pp. 42–65, 92–111; Brock Jobe, "An Introduction to Portsmouth Furniture of the Mid-Eighteenth Century," in *Old Time New England* 72 (1987):192.

[71]For suggestive comments on midcentury challenges to the material culture of established members of the upper classes, see Gordon S. Wood, *The Radicalism of the American Revolution* (New York, 1992), pp. 134–36; David E. Shi, *The Simple Life: Plain Living and High Thinking in American Culture* (New York, 1985), p. 51; Gloria L. Main, "The Distribution of Consumer Goods in Colonial New England: A Subregional Approach," in Peter Benes, ed., *Early American Probate Inventories* (Boston, 1989), p. 166; Upton, *Holy Things and Profane*, p. 229; Mark P. Leone and Paul A. Shackle, "Forks, Clocks, and Power," in Daniel W. Ingersoll, Jr., and Gordon Bronitsky, eds., *Mirror and Metaphor: Material and Social Constructions of Reality* (Lanham, Md., 1987), p. 54.

Figure 10. Side chair, Philadelphia, 1760–80. Chairs in figs. 10 and 11 represent two versions of Chippendale chairs available from the same Philadelphia shop. This chair has Marlborough legs, a "gothick" style splat, and Chinese-inspired brackets at the knees. The fluting on the back, the type of splat, and the brackets probably added 13 shillings to the base price of £1 12s. (Courtesy, Winterthur Museum)

Figure 11. Side chair, Philadelphia, 1760–80. The base price of this chair—approximately £1 14s.—was more than that of the chair in fig. 10 because this one has "crooked legs." The basic cost has been increased to approximately £2 10s by the selection of a "cut-through" splat (2 shillings), "claw feet" (4 shillings), "leaves on the knees" (6 shillings), and fluted backs (4 shillings). The "claw feet" popularly associated with Chippendale-style furniture in America were first used in England in the 1720s and considered outmoded when Chippendale published his Directory. *(Gift of Mr. and Mrs. Maxim Karolik; M. & M. Karolick Collection of Eighteenth-Century American Arts. Courtesy, Museum of Fine Arts, Boston)*

homes of the elite became "mass consumption goods" available to all classes.[72] Existing codes of genteel and elite consumption had become goals that a wider spectrum of the population strove to attain and that some could even surpass. As one disapproving New York City resident lamented: "Furniture and expenses of every tradesman now equal those of the merchant formerly; those of the merchant surpass those of the first rate gentleman; those of the gentleman, the old lords."[73] Though tea drinking still retained genteel associations, the inmates of Philadelphia's poorhouse demanded the beverage in the 1750s and insisted on the best variety, Bohea.[74] New rituals, such as more elaborate dinners, replaced old ones, and new goods displaced or competed with older props of gentility.[75] By the 1760s achievement of distinction in furnishing and lifestyle could cost £500 to £1,000 sterling annually, more than the net worth of many country gentlemen.[76]

Established upper-class consumers of British goods and of English ideas of gentility and polite taste responded in differing ways to the heightened role of fashion and the expense of competing. Three responses or strategies are discernible: some upper-class families clung to older elite modes and refused to be drawn in, others chose to compete and consume with varying degrees of conviction, and some of the very wealthiest came to argue for an aesthetic of simplicity and restraint in consumption. In certain instances the behavior and statements of an entire group of elites can be summarized

[72] Shammas, *Pre-Industrial Consumer,* pp. 183–85.

[73] Quoted in Esther Singleton, *Social New York under the Georges, 1714–1776* (New York, 1902), p. 375.

[74] T. H. Breen, "An Empire of Goods: The Anglicization of Colonial America, 1690–1776," *Journal of British Studies* 25 (1986):488.

[75] Wenger, "The Dining Room," p. 157.

[76] Lyman H. Butterfield, ed., *Diary and Autobiography of John Adams,* 4 vols. (Cambridge, Mass., 1961), 1:294; Thomas M. Doerflinger, *A Vigorous Spirit of Enterprise: Merchants and Economic Development in Revolutionary Philadelphia* (Chapel Hill, N.C., 1986), pp. 36–37 n. 23; Jackson Turner Main, *The Social Structure of Revolutionary America* (Princeton, 1965), pp. 123, 161; Sweeney, "Mansion People," p. 255.

with a degree of accuracy by reference to a particular strategy. Other cases are not so clear-cut. Not surprisingly, some individuals and some groups appear to have pursued more than one strategy.

Many of the gentry in rural New England, the ordinary or middling planters in the southern colonies, and working merchants in coastal ports could not or would not participate in the quickening pace and escalating costs of competitive consumption. The country gentry of the northeastern colonies had limited resources to expend on houses and furnishings. A foreign visitor was struck by the contrast between "the state of simplicity and even scarcity in which these people [gentry families on Long Island] live, their small and miserable houses, without ornament or the least comfort" and the "lofty ideas that dwell in their minds."[77] Their wooden frame mansion houses, which could present a more ambitious, occasionally painted, face to their neighbors, often hid a shabby gentility within, which was evident to outsiders (fig. 12). Usually there would be tea equipage, some silver perhaps adorned with an appropriated coat of arms, sets of chairs, and specialized tables. But the chairs were usually turned with flag-bottom seats, and the more elegant furniture forms were more likely made of pine, maple, or cherry than of mahogany.[78] A traveling Harvard student commented in 1760: "The Painting and Utensils, and Furniture in the Houses, do not equal [the] outward Appearances of their Houses."[79] Even the Albany mansion of Philip Schuyler held furniture "not very well chosen or assorted."[80]

A restrained vision as well as relatively limited resources

[77] John S. Ezell, ed., *The New Democracy in America: Travels of Francisco de Miranda in the United States, 1783–1784*, trans. Judson P. Wood (Norman, Okla., 1963), p. 130.

[78] Sweeney, "Mansion People," pp. 249–50; Peter Benes, *Old Town and the Waterside: Two Hundred Years of Tradition and Change in Newbury, Newburyport, and West Newbury, 1635–1835* (Newburyport, Mass., 1986), pp. 17–19, 23–25.

[79] Paul Coffin, "Memoir and Journals: Journal of a Tour from Wells to the Connecticut River," Maine Historical Society *Collections* 4 (1856):264.

[80] Grant, *Memoirs*, 1:166.

*Figure 12. Overmantel, Moses Marcy house, Southbridge, Massachu-
setts, c. 1760. The prominence given the imported wineglass and
punch bowl in the foreground and the large gambrel-roof, central-hall
mansion house pictured in the middle ground suggests an ideal of a
genteel style of life that dates back to the 1720s. While such emblems
of gentility were somewhat dated by the 1760s, the possession of such
goods and a large house distinguished the gentry of rural New England from their yeoman neighbors. (Photo, Henry E. Peach, neg. no.
B19942, Old Sturbridge Village)*

curbed the excesses of members of many rural gentry families. While making use of certain design ideas and purchasing some imported goods, they rejected alternatives that would have produced too foreign a statement. Local leaders who wished to have followers had to strike a balance between expressions of cosmopolitan awareness and affirmations of loyalty to locally recognized cultural norms. In rural New England the persistent strength of the Reformed Protestant tradition made unbridled consumption suspect even among the gentry. By the late 1760s and 1770s others with fewer scruples and more resources outbuilt and outspent the more established rural gentry families who remained wedded to older modes of genteel material culture that were usually more dependent on form than fashion.[81]

For the ordinary or middling Virginia planters who were George Washington's neighbors, the fashionableness of consumer goods and furnishings usually played a decidedly secondary role in defining a genteel lifestyle. While economic uncertainties and criticism from religious Dissenters could challenge efforts by the Chesapeake's ordinary planters to project a genteel lifestyle, social distance separating even the middling planters from their yeoman neighbors, tenants, indentured servants, and black slaves remained great. Imported consumer goods played a role in maintaining this distance, but the character of these particular material claims to status often left outside observers unimpressed. European visitors noted disapprovingly the modest size of the houses of ordinary planters and their indulgence in "tawdry luxury."[82] An English resident of Williamsburg in 1770 also found

[81] Kevin M. Sweeney, "River Gods and Related Minor Deities: The Williams Family and the Connecticut River Valley, 1637–1790," Ph.D. diss., Yale University, 1986, pp. 628–717. See also Gloria L. Main, "The Standard of Living in Southern New England, 1640–1773," *William and Mary Quarterly*, 3d ser. 45 (1988):129.

[82] Ezell, ed., *Travels of Miranda*, p. 8; *St. Méry's American Journey*, p. 121; J. P. Brissot de Warville, *New Travels in the United States of America, 1788*, ed. Durand Echeverria, trans. Mara Soceanu Vamos and Durand Echeverria (Cambridge, Mass., 1964), p. 347.

"much of [their] furniture is of an hundred years date, so it would serve an hundred years hence."[83]

The definition and expression of the middling planters' position lay in the forms and quantity of goods and the finish or relative size of their houses, which were often modest, one- or two-room frame structures with little architectural embellishment (fig. 13).[84] The seeming modesty of these houses has led some investigators to classify them as "folk houses,"[85] but "plain folk" did not dwell in them, and subtle details communicated this fact. The order of the surrounding quarters, the finish of the exteriors, the number of windows, the presence of some interior paneling, and the use of plaster usually distinguished these houses from their more ramshackle neighbors. They stood out in what has been characterized as a landscape of "rough and ready fences, tar-covered agricultural buildings," and very small, impermanent dwelling houses.[86]

Active traders and working merchants in Boston, New York, and Philadelphia also lacked the funds, economic security, and sometimes the inclination to participate fully in fashionable consumption patterns. One moderately wealthy Philadelphia merchant calculated that in 1772 a small family required £500 annually to live "genteely." Significantly, he claimed that it had cost much less ten years earlier when "luxuries were fewer."[87] A substantial portion of Philadelphia's merchants did own slaves, horses, silver plate, and fine furniture, and some owned light carriages, but most merchants lived in houses that differed little from those inhabited by middling artisans. In such homes, privacy was at a premium

[83] Quoted in Mayhew and Myers, *American Interiors,* pp. 60–61.

[84] Wells, "Eighteenth-Century Landscape," p. 4240; Upton, "Vernacular Domestic Architecture," pp. 114–15; Bernard L. Herman, *The Stolen House* (Charlottesville, Va., 1992), pp. 177–83, 199–200, 206–8, 218–19.

[85] Glassie, *Folk Housing.*

[86] Wells, "Eighteenth-Century Landscape," p. 4246; Sobel, *World They Made Together,* p. 90.

[87] Doerflinger, *Vigorous Spirit,* pp. 36–37 n. 23.

Figure 13. Rochester house, Westmoreland County, Virginia, eigh-teenth century. Despite its modest size, this one-room dwelling is distin-guished by the chimney's patterned brickwork, tiled chimney corners, glazed windows, and paneled door. This was probably the home of a well-to-do family. (Photo, Edward A. Chappell, Colonial Wil-liamsburg Foundation)

and less emphasis was placed on rooms for entertaining. The economic distance separating these merchants from the city's poorer artisans and common laborers was actually growing during this period, but so too was the distance between 90 percent of Philadelphia's merchants and traders and the city's true moneyed and landed elite, who got wealthier during the period.[88] Throughout the colonies, merchants favored a con-servative style in architecture and furniture that contempo-raries saw as a combination of elegance and simplicity, and that subsequent architectural historians have labeled *retarda-taire*.[89]

[88] Ibid., pp. 11–69.

[89] Alan Gowans, *Images of American Living: Four Centuries of Architecture and Furniture as Cultural Expression* (Philadelphia, 1964), p. 199.

Those upper-class colonists who continued to follow British fashions embraced new styles in goods and deportment during the 1760s and 1770s. Expensive consumer goods imported from England added to the comfort and distinction of genteel interiors. Substantial floor coverings, rare before midcentury, and wallpapers became necessary appointments of a rich interior.[90] Even though the availability of these goods grew with an expanding factory system in England, they were not inexpensive, and certain varieties became particularly desirable. Washington, Franklin, Miles Brewton of Charleston, Robert Beverley, Robert Carter, Thomas Jefferson, and Governor Botetourt of Virginia all ordered blue papers with gilt borders.[91] Elite codes could find expression even in the products of factories.

Carriages, some imported from England, joined floor coverings, wallpaper, and fine mahogany furniture as badges of distinction that set apart the very rich from the merely wealthy.[92] In Philadelphia and elsewhere the "first class" of society was "composed of carriage folk," and "almost all these gentry, whatever their origin, [had] their coats of arms painted upon their carriage-doors."[93] These expensive consumer goods, which usually were taxed as luxuries throughout the colonies, expressed the genteel ideal of graceful, effortless movement through the landscape. Ideally, it would

[90]Audrey Michie, "The Fashion for Carpets in South Carolina, 1736–1820," *Journal of Early Southern Decorative Arts* 8 (1982):25–28; Mayhew and Myers, *American Interiors*, pp. 61–62. Shammas concludes that such furnishings were found in at most only 10 percent of households. Shammas, *Pre-Industrial Consumer*, pp. 172, 191.

[91]Barbara G. Carson, *The Governor's Palace: The Williamsburg Residence of Virginia's Royal Governor* (Williamsburg, 1987), p. 78; Graham Hood, "Early Neoclassicism in America" 140 *Antiques* (1991):981–82; Mayhew and Myers, *American Interiors*, p. 68; Howe, ed., "Journal of Quincy," pp. 444–45.

[92]Bridenbaugh, *Cities in Revolt*, pp. 146, 341–42; Tolles, *Meeting House and Counting House*, pp. 130–31; Shammas, *Pre-Industrial Consumer*, pp. 169, 172, 209; Soltow, *Distribution of Wealth and Income*, p. 72; Alan D. Watson, "Luxury Vehicles and Elitism in Colonial North Carolina," *Southern Studies* 19 (1980):147–55.

[93]Sherrill, *French Memories*, p. 47.

be movement from a town house to a country seat or from one country seat to another. But unlike a fine horse carrying a single gentleman, the carriage provided a mode of travel for the entire family. One French visitor claimed that American women "especially desire them to a degree that approaches delirium; and a woman who owns one is very certain that no other woman who lacks a carriage will ever be considered, or ever become, her equal."[94] Carriages thus played an important role in the circulation of gentry families that was necessary to maintain family ties and forge new ones through suitable marriages.[95]

But houses still embodied the most expensive and expressive element in a fashionable, genteel style of life. Though the basic massing and exterior architectural treatments of mansions remained within the Georgian style, houses grew in size while more labor and money was expended on interior woodwork, decorative plaster, and other details. After 1760 spending on houses reached levels never witnessed before. The Schuyler mansion in Albany cost £1,400, the house begun in Annapolis by Samuel Chase and completed by Edward Lloyd IV, cost from £3,000 to £6,000, the Annapolis home of Daniel Dulaney cost £10,000, the Miles Brewton house in Charleston reportedly cost £8,000, and the Jeremiah Lee mansion in Marblehead, Massachusetts, reputedly cost £10,000.[96] Wealthy New Yorkers collectively spent hundreds of thousands of pounds of their newly acquired fortunes constructing mansions and laying out gardens.[97] Philadelphia, where a good town house could cost £2,000 to £4,000, experienced a similar boom after midcentury, leading one commentator to declare, "Tis one eternal scene of pulling down and putting

[94] St. Méry's American Journey, p. 334.

[95] See Barbara G. Carson, "Early American Tourists and the Commercialization of Leisure," in this volume; Smith, "Inequality in Late Colonial Philadelphia," p. 643.

[96] Mayhew and Meyers, American Interiors, p. 54; Howe, ed., "Journal of Quincy," pp. 444–45; Morrison, Early American Architecture, p. 358; Eddis, Letters, p. xiv.

[97] Bridenbaugh, Cities in Revolt, p. 339.

up."[98] For the first time the cost of houses approached expenditures by the minor gentry in England.[99]

After midcentury the Georgian-style houses of the wealthiest colonists began to resemble English models more closely in architectural detail, and occasionally in plan.[100] Imported pattern books and migrating craftsmen and architects like John Ariss and William Buckland facilitated this process. The results, however, were not always felicitous. Architectural historian Hugh Morrison has observed that in their zeal to display their English culture, colonial patrons and craftsmen "not only went too much by the book, but threw its whole content on their walls."[101] Yet a close examination of houses such as Mount Vernon, the Lee mansion, Tuckahoe Plantation, and others reveals that the location of walls upon which this academic ornament was thrown could be determined by existing conditions and local traditions. It is misleading to view even the more seemingly academic Georgian houses as being forms primarily derived from books instead of the minds of patrons and builders. Washington's Mount Vernon, with its asymmetrical fenestration and grand piazza, which owes little or nothing to pattern books and academic architecture, is best understood as a large, academically enhanced vernacular dwelling (figs. 7 and 14).[102] Several architectural historians have concluded that the adaptations of English architectural ideas during the third quarter of the eighteenth century fundamentally represented a "momentary correspondence of academic form with local priorities."[103]

Local taste and local craftsmen modified renderings of aca-

---

[98] Quoted in Carl Bridenbaugh and Jessica Bridenbaugh, *Rebels and Gentlemen: Philadelphia in the Age of Franklin* (New York, 1968), p. 181.

[99] Lawrence Stone and Jeanne C. Fawtier Stone, *An Open Elite? England, 1540–1880,* abridged ed. (New York, 1986), p. 250.

[100] Reiff, *Small Georgian Houses,* p. 272.

[101] Morrison, *Early American Architecture,* p. 493.

[102] Kennedy, *Architecture and Money,* p. 122; Morrison, *Early American Architecture,* pp. 357–60.

[103] Wenger, "The Central Passage," p. 144; Upton, *Holy Things and Profane,* pp. 27–28.

Figure 14. Mount Vernon, river front, Fairfax County, Virginia, after 1785. Despite its monumental character, the large veranda or piazza probably had its origin in vernacular building traditions. (Photo, courtesy of the Mount Vernon Ladies' Association)

demic ornament. Precise copies of pattern book designs were relatively rare, and the deviations, which are found even in urban and urbane settings, cannot be uniformly explained by a lack of skill or awareness. Even in fashionable Charleston, rococo carving exhibited a strong tendency toward symmetrical composition and a less dynamic, more ponderous execution than English models.[104] Local craftsmen's sense of fitness often determined the character of architectural detail and the final appearance of objects.

The form and decoration of large pieces of storage furniture also document the influence of the local patrons' taste and the creative role played by colonial craftsmen.[105] In Boston, blockfronting, introduced possibly from England in the

[104] John Bivins, Jr., "Charleston Rococo Interiors, 1765–1775: The 'Sommers' Carvers," *Journal of Early Southern Decorative Arts* 12 (1986):15–17; Garvin, "Academic Architecture," p. 27.

[105] For a continuing preference for older forms in silver, see Ward, "Edwards Family and Silversmithing," p. 75.

1730s, and the swelled shapes of bombé furniture initially copied from an English chest-on-chest in the early 1750s, remained popular into the 1780s (fig. 15). These "bourgeois baroque" expressions, like the striking block and shell desks and bookcases and chest-on-chests produced in Rhode Island and neighboring eastern Connecticut, continued to be popular with local elites but rarely made significant concessions to the Chippendale style.[106] The pedimented high chest—today's highboy—was probably a colonial innovation of the 1730s. In rural New England and urban Philadelphia, the form continued to evolve independently and respond cautiously to English stylistic influences until well into the 1780s (fig. 16). Rococo carving often made such chests more fashionable in decorative vocabulary, but by the 1760s the basic form and silhouette owed little if anything to contemporary English design.[107] Virginians, New Yorkers, and South Carolinians did embrace the more up-to-date clothes press that was usually executed in an understated "neat and plain" style (fig. 17).[108] For wealthy consumers in Virginia and Charleston these preferences probably expressed an emulation of the taste of London's upper middle class, while in New York and neighboring northern New Jersey the form may have represented a stylistically fashionable embodiment of a traditional Dutch preference for hanging clothes in a *kas* (fig. 18).[109]

[106]Margaretta M. Lovell, "Boston Blockfront Furniture," and Gilbert T. Vincent, "The Bombé Furniture of Boston," in Walter Muir Whitehill and Brock Jobe, eds., *Boston Furniture of the Eighteenth Century: A Conference Held by the Colonial Society of Massachusetts, 11 and 12 May, 1972* (Boston, 1974), pp. 77–135 and 137–96; Robert F. Trent, "The Colchester School of Cabinetmaking, 1750–1800," in Puig and Conforti, eds., *American Craftsman and European Tradition*, pp. 112–35. The term *bourgeois baroque* is from Lovell, "Boston Blockfront Furniture," p. 78.

[107]Charles F. Montgomery, "Regional Preferences and Characteristics in American Decorative Arts: 1750–1800," in Charles F. Montgomery and Patricia E. Kane, eds., *American Art, 1750–1800: Towards Independence* (Boston, 1976), p. 60.

[108]Trent, "Colchester School of Cabinetmaking," p. 125.

[109]Roderic H. Blackburn, *Cherry Hill: The History and Collections of a Van Rensselaer Family* (Albany, 1976), p. 77.

Figure 15. Chest-on-chest, Marblehead, Massachusetts, 1760–90. Probably English in origin, the blockfront treatment of the facades of casepieces experienced a popularity and longevity in parts of New England unknown in England. The only concessions to the Chippendale mode in this chest-on-chest were the "claw feet," which would have been regarded as old-fashioned in England. (Bequest of Mrs. Sarah W. Whitman. Courtesy, Museum of Fine Arts, Boston)

Figure 16. High chest of drawers, Philadelphia, 1769. Like an automobile today, a high chest could be purchased stripped or loaded. This one is loaded with rococo-style carving that has added at least £8 to the basic price of £13. The purchaser has paid extra for the "claw feet," "leaves on the knees," shell drawer, quarter columns, finials, scroll pediment, and carved work. (Courtesy, Winterthur Museum)

Figure 17. Clothes press, Petersburg, Richmond, or Norfolk, Virginia, c. 1785. In its up-to-date form, restrained decoration, and superior construction, this Virginia-made clothes press embodied the qualities found in contemporary London furniture. The flat panels of the doors and the delicate dentils of the cornice are features that would have been found on later neoclassical or federal-style furniture. (Colonial Williamsburg Foundation)

*Figure 18. Linen press cupboard, New York, 1787–95. A form simi-
lar to that in fig. 17, this press's appearance and associations suggest
its New York origin. The press has "claw feet" and carved gadrooning
on its skirt. The press served the same function as the old kas form so
prevalent in New York and New Jersey. (Collection of Historic Cherry
Hill, Albany, N.Y.)*

Such choices, in some cases conscious and in many instances undoubtedly unconscious, provided both patron and craftsman a measure of release from servile conformity to fashionable taste.[110] Charles F. Montgomery probably overstated the revolutionary character of these actions when he argued that "in the 1750s and 1760s many Americans began to assert their independence by adopting the highboy and the blockfront as their own and by continuing to use porringers and tankards."[111] It is more appropriate to view these actions as a creative wrestling with the central contradiction in the genteel style of even the most fashionable American consumers: the dual loyalty to both the academic high style of England and the local vernacular material culture.[112] The exercise of choice in the design and ornamentation of houses and furniture allowed the owner or purchaser some latitude to act as a fashion-conscious patron instead of a manipulated consumer and provided the craftsman with a more creative challenge than "mere" copying. Even non-English cultural preferences could reside within or beneath a very English furniture form like the New York clothes press (fig. 18).

Though they rarely divorced themselves completely from some grounding in vernacular traditions, local taste, and colonial social conditions, fashionable and luxurious modes of consumption and building drew increasing criticism. There was a long tradition of celebrating the virtues of simplicity in the Chesapeake,[113] and New Englanders had their own religiously imbued traditions of restraint and moderation on which they could call. Latter-day Puritans like Samuel Adams of Boston had no use for the Boston merchant class and their

[110] On the idea of an "interlude of release," see George A. Kubler, "The Arts: Fine and Plain," in Ian M. G. Quimby and Scott T. Swank, eds., *Perspectives on American Folk Art* (New York, 1980), p. 237.

[111] Montgomery, "Regional Preferences and Characteristics," p. 64.

[112] On this see Upton, *Holy Things and Profane*, pp. 27–28.

[113] Shammas, "English-Born and Creole Elites," p. 288; Hudgins, "Patrician Culture," pp. 341–42.

"Decorations of the Parlor, the shining Boards of Plate, the costly Piles of China."[114] Pointed criticism also came from radical evangelicals or Quaker reformers like Anthony Benezet and John Woolman.[115] During the 1760s some of these critics with political agendas pointed specifically to the corrupting influence of England and "the Baubles of Britain."[116]

Wealthy consumers, who were often the targets of this criticism, expressed similar reservations and criticisms. When Pennsylvania Chief Justice Benjamin Chew ordered urns for his country seat, Cliveden, he instructed his English agent that they should have "little or no carve work as most suitable to the plainness of my building" (fig. 19).[117] Rebecca Shoemaker of nearby Philadelphia advised her daughter to buy chairs that were "plain, even if carved were the same price."[118] Further south, Charles Carroll of Annapolis, one of the wealthiest men in America, urged his heir to "lay out as little money as Possible in dress furniture & shew of any Sort, decency is the only Point to be aimed at."[119] His son apparently heeded his advice. When ordering gifts for his fiancée, Charles Carroll of Carrollton informed his correspondent that "every Lady should strive to be, what the *Spectator* finely expresses, *elegantly neat:* magnificence and finery in Cloaths is

[114]Quoted in Shi, *Simple Life,* p. 61.

[115]Ibid., p. 53.

[116]Ibid., pp. 50–68; Edmund S. Morgan, "The Puritan Ethic and the American Revolution," *William and Mary Quarterly,* 3d ser. 24 (1967):8–18. See also T. H. Breen "'Baubles of Britain': The American and Consumer Revolutions of the Eighteenth Century," in this volume.

[117]Quoted in Raymond V. Shepard, "Cliveden and Its Philadelphia-Chippendale Furniture: A Documented History," *American Art Journal* 8 (1976):2.

[118]Quoted in David Barquest, "'The Honours of a Court, the Severity of Virtue': Household Furnishings and Cultural Aspirations in Philadelphia, 1750–1800" (Paper presented at the Winterthur Conference on Shaping a National Culture: The Philadelphia Experience, 1750–1800, Winterthur, Del., Nov. 6–7, 1987), p. 9.

[119]Charles Carroll of Annapolis to Charles Carroll of Carrollton, June 1, 1772, in *Antiques* 103 (1973):1188.

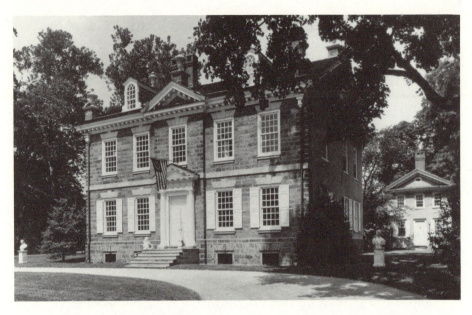

Figure 19. Cliveden, Germantown, Pennsylvania, after 1763. The plainness or simplicity of Benjamin Chew's imported urns contributes to an overall effect that is rich though perhaps somewhat less ornate than Mount Pleasant with its balustrade, corner quoins, palladian window, and more elaborate doorway. (Photo, Jack Boucher, Historic American Buildings Survey)

neither mine nor the lady's taste: she would chuse them decent, handsome and genteel." [120]

In some circles during the later 1760s and 1770s simplicity became a code, a code signaling gentility and fashionability in furniture and architecture as well as in clothing.[121] In 1765 Philip Livingston of New York advised his son-in-law, Stephen Van Rensselaer, against putting stucco work on the ceiling of his hall for "a Plain Ceiling is now Esteemed the most Genteel."[122] The ceiling, which is today part of the American Wing

[120]Quoted in Pauline Maier, *The Old Revolutionaries: Political Lives in the Age of Samuel Adams* (New York, 1980), p. 211.

[121]On the association of fashion with simplicity during this period see Elizabeth Donaghy Garrett, *At Home: The American Family, 1750–1870* (New York, 1990), p. 47, and Karin Calvert, "The Function of Fashion in Eighteenth-Century America," in this volume.

[122]Heckscher and Bowman, *American Rococo*, p. 25.

of the Metropolitan Museum, never received the decorative stucco work. Virginian Robert Beverley who desired to fit up his new house "in a plain neat Manner . . . willingly consult[ed] the present Fashion."[123] When Peter Manigault of Charleston ordered furniture from England in 1771, he desired "the plainer the better so that they are fashionable."[124] In part because of this "neat and plain" ideal of fashionability, individuals saw no contradiction between their rhetoric and consumption, no contradiction between politically virtuous avowals of denial and the increased importation of British goods during the early 1770s.

In the 1770s and 1780s, foreign visitors' descriptions of the homes of fashionable colonial elites were filled with comments on their simplicity and their elegance, beauty, and magnificence.[125] While some objects in the new neoclassical style appeared in the colonies before the Revolution,[126] most colonists desiring a plainer aesthetic usually settled for simplified expressions in the Chippendale or Georgian mode during the later 1760s and 1770s (fig. 20). A fashionable desire for simplicity may very well explain the persistence of such earlier unadorned baroque forms as blockfront chests and desks and bookcases in New England and the restrained Chippendale furniture that was so popular in Virginia in the 1770s (figs. 15 and 18).[127]

By the late 1780s and 1790s silver and furniture and occasionally houses for the urban elite conformed to the new neo-

[123] Quoted in Hood, "Early Neoclassicism in America," p. 981.

[124] Quoted in George C. Rogers, Jr., "Changes in Taste in the Eighteenth Century: A Shift from the Useful to the Ornamental," *Journal of Early Southern Decorative Arts* 8 (1982):20.

[125] Brissot de Warville, *New Travels*, p. 342; Sherrill, *French Memories*, pp. 93–94; Chastellux, *Travels in North America*, 2:491.

[126] Hood, "Early Neoclassicism in America," pp. 978–85.

[127] Trent, "Colchester School of Cabinetmaking," pp. 112–35; Wallace B. Gusler, *Furniture of Williamsburg and Eastern Virginia, 1710–1790* (Richmond, 1979), pp. 115–37; For a slightly different reading see Margaretta M. Lovell, "'Such Furniture as Will Be Most Profitable': The Business of Cabinetmaking in Eighteenth-Century Newport," *Winterthur Portfolio* 26 (1991):32–33, 49–50.

Figure 20. Side chair, England, 1755–75. This chair may be from a set of twelve chairs Charles Carroll of Carrollton ordered with a "fashionable Sopha" to match in 1771. The chair is a good example of the fashionable but "neat and plain" interpretation of the Chippendale mode favored by some consumers in the 1770s. (Courtesy, the Maryland Historical Society, Baltimore)

classical style or as it is sometimes called today in America, the federal style. The style, which had gained popularity in England during the 1760s and 1770s, provided an obvious mode for those Americans who sought to communicate status and wealth with an understated style. Because of the emphasis on plain and planar surfaces, rectilinear forms, and restrained use of carving, neoclassical interiors, furniture and metalwares were invariably described as "neat and plain."[128] Furniture in particular embodied dramatic changes in form which became lighter and rectilinear and in ornamentation which eschewed heavy carving in favor of clean surfaces with rich veneers and intricate inlays. The resulting chairs, which lacked stretchers, and tables, which had extremely slender legs, appeared to sacrifice durability to fashion (figs. 21 and 22). During this period, furnishings "in the latest taste" challenged the appeal of those "made to endure."[129]

The underlying value system and patterns of consumption, however, remained unchanged. Neoclassical simplicity became an integral part of design and thus of consumption.[130] The visual rhetoric of austerity and restraint was accommodated to the dictates of fashion. For those who could read the new stylistic code, the austerity, restraint, and seeming simplicity of these objects also communicated wealth, luxury, and cosmopolitan taste.[131] As informed consumers of furnishings and architectural embellishments in the "neat and plain" neoclassical style undoubtedly knew, the style was aristocratic in its origins and very English in its initial American expressions. Though sometimes associated with Roman republicanism, the neoclassical style was hardly antiaristocratic nor even nec-

[128] Hood, "Early Neoclassicism in America," p. 981.

[129] Garrett, *At Home*, p. 255.

[130] Hood, "Early Neoclassicism in America," p. 984.

[131] For two slightly different treatments of the neoclassical style and the rhetoric of virtue and restraint, see Neil Harris, "The Making of an American Culture: 1750–1800," and Jules David Prown, "Style in American Art: 1750–1800," in Montgomery and Kane, eds., *American Art*, pp. 22–39. I believe that neoclassicism is the answer to the question posed by Harris: "How could the nation consume objects of luxury and proclaim its allegiance to restraint?" (p. 30).

*Figure 21. Card table, Boston, 1785–1815. This "neat and plain"
card table avoids carving in favor of delicate inlays. The urns and the
eagle inlays also make evident the classical and nationalistic associations of the neoclassical style in America. Still, the rich figure of the
mahogany veneer, the delicacy of the legs that proclaims the triumph of
fashion over durability, and the table's function make it at best an ambiguous statement of republican simplicity. (Courtesy of the Yale University Art Gallery, Yale University, New Haven, Conn., the Mabel
Brady Garvan Collection)*

essarily antimonarchical.[132] In both England and France, aristocratic patrons, as well as artists and architects, associated the
style with patriotic support for monarchy. Robert Adam, one
of the leading English proponents of the neoclassical style,
dedicated his influential 1764 volume, *The Ruins of Spalato,* to
George III, while in Virginia Norborne Berkeley, baron de
Botetourt, the royal governor from 1768 to 1770, was one of

---

[132]Hugh Honour, *Neo-classicism* (New York, 1968), pp. 22–27, 69–80.

Figure 22. Side chair, New York, c. 1800. This chair is based on plate 36, no. 1, of Thomas Sheraton's The Cabinet-Maker and Upholsterer's Drawing Book *(London, 1793). (Photo, Helga Studios; courtesy of Historic Deerfield, Inc.)*

the earliest patrons of the neoclassical style in the colonies.[133] After the American Revolution, British craftsmen such as John and Thomas Seymour and Duncan Phyfe and English pattern books by George Hepplewhite, Thomas Sheraton, and Thomas Shearer strongly influenced the design of American neoclassical furniture. If anything, American expressions in the neoclassical mode in the 1790s and early 1800s often followed English prototypes more closely than American expressions in the Chippendale style had (fig. 22).[134]

American critics who saw such indulgence in the new English fashion as a threat to republican virtue attacked this stylistic subterfuge and the baneful influence of the continued role of English fashion.[135] One newspaper commentator who rejected "the light, costly, and the flimsy ornaments of the drawing room" yearned for the "old-fashioned, yet ponderous furniture" presumably in the Chippendale style with its characteristically "high backed mahogany chairs, the heavy carved mirrors, the bed and durable curtains."[136] The Philadelphia house built by William Bingham in the new neoclassical style in 1786 disturbed the Boston architect Charles Bulfinch, who saw in the house's restrained luxury "an elegance of construction" and "magnificence of decoration" that made it "a palace . . . far *too* rich for *any* man in this country" (fig. 23).[137] The

[133]Ibid., p. 29, and Hood, "Early Neoclassicism in America," pp. 981–83.

[134]Gregory R. Weidman, "Baltimore Federal Furniture: In the English Tradition," in Puig and Conforti, eds., *American Craftsman and European Tradition*, pp. 256–81.

[135]Louis B. Wright and Marion Tinling, eds., *Quebec to Carolina in 1785–1786; Being the Travel Diary and Observations of Robert Hunter, Jr., a Young Merchant of London* (San Marino, Calif., 1943), pp. 135, 226; Henry Wansey, *The Journal of an Excursion to the United States of America in the Summer of 1794* (1796; reprint ed., New York, 1969), p. 123; Drew R. McCoy, *The Elusive Republic: Political Economy in Jeffersonian America* (Chapel Hill, N.C., 1980), pp. 21–23, 95–104, 176–84.

[136]*Camden Gazette* (South Carolina), Sept. 9, 1819. I want to thank the staff at the Museum of Southern Decorative Arts for bringing this quotation to my attention.

[137]Charles Bulfinch to his parents, Apr. 2, 1789, Ellen Susan Bulfinch, ed., *The Life and Letters of Charles Bulfinch, Architect, with Other Family Papers* (Boston and New York, 1896), pp. 75–76.

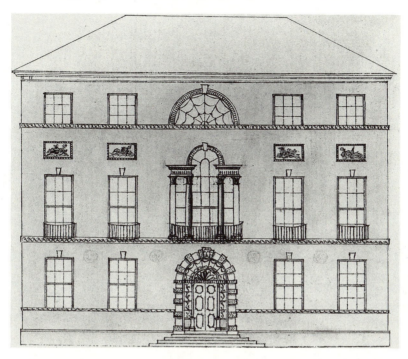

Figure 23. William Bingham house. *Charles Bulfinch, c. 1789. Though the magnificence of William Bingham's house may have shocked Charles Bulfinch, he drew its facade and used it as the basis for his design for the first Harrison Gray Otis house built in Boston between 1795 and 1796. (Courtesy, Library of Congress)*

richness and novelty of the house's new style and plan struck Philadelphian Ann Warder as being "very ungenteel."[138] Warder's comment suggests that the new neoclassical style went beyond previously established stylistic boundaries shared by both elite and vernacular culture, a sharing which had been integral to the colonial definition of gentility. The extent of the style's departure from previous architectural conventions was even more obvious in the massing of rectilinear and curvilinear shapes, smooth stuccoed surfaces, and geometric room designs of the neoclassical house produced by William Hamilton's 1787–89 remodeling of The Woodlands, his country seat outside of Philadelphia (fig. 24)[139]

[138]Quoted in Barquest, "'Honours of a Court,'" p. 20.

[139]Richard J. Betts, "The Woodlands," *Winterthur Portfolio* 14 (1979):213–34.

Figure 24. The Woodlands. *William Birch. After its 1787–89 al-
terations, shown here, The Woodlands represented a radical departure
in massing and plan from previous American mansion houses.
Thomas Jefferson proclaimed it to be "the only rival I have known in
America to what may be seen in England." (From William Birch,*
Country Seats of the United States of North America

Other members of the new republic's upper classes followed the lead of men like Bingham and Hamilton. Bingham's friend and sometime partner, Gen. Henry Knox,
informed the builder of his house, Montpelier, that he wanted
"a well built house, yet I am also desirous of having it plain
without carving or other expensive ornaments."[140] The finished house, which may have been based on a plan by Bulfinch, was described as being "a very fine one and the whole

[140]Quoted in Carolyn S. Parsons, "'Bordering on Magnificence': Urban
Domestic Planning in the Maine Woods," in Charles E. Clark, James S.
Leamon, and Karen Bowden, eds., *Maine in the Early Republic* (Hanover,
N.H., 1988), p. 70.

of his stile rather bordering on magnificence."[141] The Boston area saw the construction of similar country seats and neoclassical town houses as Bulfinch overcame his initial assessment of the inappropriateness of such buildings. These houses in the neoclassical style were among the most austere and most expensive in America.[142] The neoclassical austerity and restrained decoration can be seen as privatized statements of classical civic virtue that belied the personal ambition and devotion to wealth that the houses embodied.

Foreign visitors during the late 1700s were shocked to discover that residents of the new republic—including those who embraced the neoclassical style—did not exhibit "the austerity of early Roman customs." Instead visitors like the French poet Chateaubriand were scandalized to find "on all sides elegance of attire, luxury of equipages, frivolity of conversation, inequality of fortune."[143] Wealth and custom established in society "more decided lines than elsewhere,"[144] and differences in housing and furnishings played obvious roles in marking off and expressing these lines.[145] To the English-born architect Benjamin Latrobe, the neoclassical homes of the new nation's elite were not "neat and plain" expressions of republican simplicity but "structures copied from the palaces of the corrupt age of Diocletian, or the still more absurd and debased taste of Louis the XIV" (fig. 24).[146]

[141] Quoted ibid., p. 69.

[142] Harold Kirker, *The Architecture of Charles Bulfinch* (Cambridge, Mass., 1969), pp. 45–53, 74–76, 93–100, 118–39; Lee Soltow, "Egalitarian America and Its Inegalitarian Housing in the Federal Period," *Social Science History* 9 (1985):201, 210–11.

[143] Sherrill, *French Memories*, p. 55.

[144] Ibid., p. 48.

[145] Soltow, *Distribution of Wealth and Income*, pp. 49–59, 73, 141–74, 244.

[146] Quoted in Kenneth C. Hafertepe, "The Enlightened Sensibility: Scottish Philosophy in American Art and Architecture," Ph.D. diss., University of Texas at Austin, 1986, p. 225. Hafertepe interprets this remark as "clear references to the Adam style of 'The Woodlands,' the estate of William Hamilton just across the Schuylkill, and to Pierre Charles L'Enfant's house for Robert Morris, in Philadelphia proper" (pp. 225–26).

What has been identified as the "most complete and dramatic stylistic change in the entire history of American art" did not alter the patterns of consumption and display of wealthy Americans.[147] If anything, the change in style reinforced these patterns as the new neoclassical style initially distanced elite artifacts and their possessors from the vernacular traditions that had often remained embedded in Georgian modes of elite expressions in housing and furnishing. Despite the words of critics, the purchases and stylistic preferences of wealthy Americans continued to demonstrate that the fashion system remained integral to their efforts at self-definition and social distancing. This drive, which was given substance and shape by the consumer revolution of the eighteenth century, was not interrupted by the political revolution of the 1770s or by any subsequent development.

[147] Prown, "Style in American Art," p. 32.

LOIS GREEN CARR
LORENA S. WALSH

Changing Lifestyles and Consumer Behavior in the Colonial Chesapeake

A MARYLAND OR VIRGINIA household in the 1770s was very different from what it had been a hundred years earlier. Over the course of a century standards of life in the colonial Chesapeake changed remarkably, and the lifestyles of the rich were transformed. To some degree these changes paralleled changes taking place in England. There had generally been a considerable time lag between the appearance of new goods or modes of behavior in the mother country and their adoption in the colonies. But by the time of the American Revo-

The research for this essay was funded by the Historic St. Mary's City Commission, by grants to the Commission from the National Science Foundation (GS-32272) and the National Endowment for the Humanities (RO-228-72-468, RO-10585-74-267, RS-23687-76-431, and RS-20199-81-1955), and by a post-doctoral fellowship given to Lorena S. Walsh by the Regional Economic History Research Center, Eleutherian Mills-Hagley Foundation. The authors wish to express thanks for this support.
    Our solutions to technical problems in using probate inventories, which provide most of the data for the essay, are discussed in Appendix A. All tables and graphs are based on data from our computerized inventory files. We have grouped the data into three- and four-year segments for some purposes and combined these segment into nine-, eleven-, and twelve-year groups for others. All tables and graphs in this essay are based on the large year groups. Graphs in figures 1 through 11 and 13 through 17 are presented in semilogarithmic form to emphasize rates of increase.

lution new European fashions appeared in rich planter households almost as soon as they appeared in London. A rising standard of consumption was underway on both sides of the Atlantic, and it brought changes in behavior even among people too poor to participate, except in token amounts.

We are not talking here of essentials—sufficiency of food, shelter, clothing. Chesapeake settlers, after the very first years, never suffered famine in a land where a few days' labor could yield a maize crop that would feed a man for a year and a few pigs in the forest could supply his meat. The forests provided timber for housing and firewood. Exported tobacco crops purchased basic tools and clothing. Rather, we are talking of the nonessentials—things that made life more comfortable or inspired awe or envy in those who did not possess them. To be sure, these items usually did not include other kinds of equipment that today we would consider essential to well-being: items for cleanliness or sanitation. Not until the early nineteenth century did cleanliness become socially important. Until then, these changes concerned increasing attractiveness and elegance in living quarters and dress, greater individual use of space and utensils, and increased emphasis on manners and social ceremony. In the eighteenth century these could be summed up in the word *gentility*.[1]

[1] For a general discussion of changes in material life, see Fernand Braudel, *Capitalism and Material Life, 1400–1800,* trans. Miriam Kochan (New York, 1974); idem, *Civilization and Capitalism, 15th–18th Century,* trans. Siân Reynolds, 3 vols. (New York, 1981–84). For Great Britain, see Lorna Weatherill, *Consumer Behaviour and Material Culture in Britain, 1660–1760* (London, 1988); idem, "Consumer Behaviour and Social Status in England, 1660–1750," *Continuity and Change* 1 (1986):191–216; A. H. John, "Aspects of English Economic Growth in the First Half of the Eighteenth Century," in E. M. Carus-Wilson, ed., *Essays in Economic History,* 3 vols. (London, 1954–62), 2:360–73; idem, "Agricultural Productivity and Economic Growth in England, 1700–1760," *Journal of Economic History* 25 (1965):19–34; F. J. Fisher, "The Development of London as a Center of Conspicuous Consumption in the Sixteenth and Seventeenth Centuries," in Carus-Wilson, ed., *Essays in Economic History,* 2:197–207; Neil McKendrick, "Josiah Wedgwood: An Eighteenth-Century Entrepreneur in Salesmanship and Marketing Techniques," in Carus-Wilson, ed., *Essays in Economic History,* 3:353–79; idem, "Home Demand and Economic Growth: A New View of the Role of Women and Children in the Industrial Revolution," in Neil McKendrick, ed., *Historical Perspectives: Studies in English*

The culture of gentility became a means of emphasizing social differences and fueling social competition. Members of the seventeenth-century planter elite had signified their positions with large holdings of land and labor, the sources of their wealth, and these remained basic elements of hierarchical distinctions. But near the turn of the century colonial men of wealth and power began to signal their rank through elegance in lifestyle. By the 1760s the social position of anyone could be gauged not just by wealth or offices held but by their dress, household arrangements, and social ceremonies.

————

Thought and Society in Honour of J. H. Plumb (London, 1974), pp. 150–210; Charles Wilson, *England's Apprenticeship, 1603–1763* (New York, 1965); Phyllis Deane and W. A. Cole, *British Economic Growth, 1688–1959* (Cambridge, 1967); D. E. C. Eversley, "The Home Market and Economic Growth in England, 1750–1780," in Eric L. Jones and G. E. Mingay, eds., *Land, Labour, and Population in the Industrial Revolution: Essays Presented to J. D. Chambers* (London, 1967), pp. 216–59; L. A. Clarkson, *The Pre-Industrial Economy in England, 1500–1750* (New York, 1972); Penelope J. Corfield, "A Provincial Capital in the Late Seventeenth Century: The Case of Norwich," in Peter Clark and Paul Slack, eds., *Crisis and Order in English Towns, 1500–1700* (Toronto, 1972); Eric L. Jones, "The Fashion Manipulators: Consumer Tastes and British Industries, 1660–1800," in Louis P. Cain and Paul J. Uselding, eds., *Business Enterprise and Economic Change: Essays in Honor of Harold F. Williamson* (Kent, Ohio, 1973), pp. 198–226; Eric L. Jones, *Agriculture and the Industrial Revolution* (Oxford, 1974), chaps. 3–4; Jan De Vries, *The Economy of Europe in an Age of Crisis, 1600–1750* (Cambridge, 1976), chap. 6; Joel Mokyr, "Demand vs. Supply in the Industrial Revolution," *Journal of Economic History* 37 (1977):981–1008; Joan Thirsk, *Economic Policy and Projects: The Development of a Consumer Society in Early Modern England* (Oxford, 1978); Carole Shammas, "The Domestic Environment in Early Modern England and America," *Journal of Social History* 14 (1980):3–24; idem, *The Pre-Industrial Consumer in England and America* (Oxford, 1990); Neil McKendrick, John Brewer, and J. H. Plumb, *The Birth of a Consumer Society: The Commercialization of Eighteenth-Century England* (Bloomington, Ind., 1982); Maxine Berg, *The Age of Manufactures: Industry, Innovation, and Work in Britain, 1700–1820* (Oxford, 1985); Ian Mitchell, "The Development of Urban Retailing, 1700–1815," in Peter Clark, ed., *The Transformation of English Provincial Towns, 1600–1800* (London, 1984), pp. 259–83; Witold Rybczynski, *Home: A Short History of an Idea* (New York, 1986); C. G. A. Clay, *Economic Expansion and Social Change: England, 1500–1700*, 2 vols. (London, 1984), 2:22–43. On ideas for conceptualizing consumer behavior, see Carole Shammas, "Explaining Past Changes in Consumption and Consumer Behavior, *Historical Methods* 22 (1989):61–67.

When areas were first settled, most colonists possessed little in the way of household goods, although some of the rich had luxury items that they had brought with them, prized possessions from another world.[2] As more new households were formed by planters who had come with nothing but their labor, a relatively uniform lifestyle emerged that required a minimum of domestic or architectural props for its support.

Until the second quarter of the eighteenth century, settlers below the level of the economic elite put a high priority on basic household equipment: a good mattress (feather if possible), a few cooking pots, plates or bowls for food, a chest or two for storing goods, and a gun for hunting. Even after farms were well established, chairs, tables, bedsteads to keep mattresses off the floor, sheets, chamber pots, and interior lighting were among the ordinary—to us—amenities without which many people managed to function very well. Such

[2]Other studies dealing with consumer behavior in the Chesapeake include Gloria L. Main, *Tobacco Colony: Life in Early Maryland, 1650–1720* (Princeton, 1982); idem, "The Standard of Living in Maryland and Massachusetts, 1656–1719," and Barbara G. Carson, "Living Habits in Seventeenth-Century Maryland" (Papers presented at the Third Hall of Records Conference in Maryland History, "Maryland: A Product of Two Worlds," St. Mary's City, May 1984); Barbara G. Carson and Cary Carson, "Styles and Standards of Living in Southern Maryland, 1670–1752" (Paper presented at the Forty-second Annual Meeting of the Southern Historical Association, Atlanta, Nov. 1976); and James P. P. Horn, "Adapting to a New World: A Comparative Study of Local Society in England and Maryland, 1650–1700," in Lois Green Carr, Philip D. Morgan, and Jean B. Russo, eds., *Colonial Chesapeake Society* (Chapel Hill, N.C., 1988), pp. 133–75. The discussion that follows is further elaborated and documented in Lois Green Carr and Lorena S. Walsh, "How Colonial Tobacco Planters Lived: Consumption in St. Mary's County, Maryland, 1658–1777," (Paper presented at the Forty-second Annual Meeting of the Southern Historical Association, Atlanta, Nov. 1976); idem, "Changing Life-Styles in Colonial St. Mary's County," *Working Papers from the Regional Economic History Research Center* 1 (1978):73–118; Lorena S. Walsh, "A Culture of 'Rude Sufficiency': Life-Styles on Maryland's Lower Western Shore between 1658 and 1720" (Paper presented at the Twelfth Annual Meeting of the Society for Historical Archaeology, Nashville, Jan. 1979); idem, "Urban Amenities and Rural Sufficiency: Living Standards and Consumer Behavior in the Colonial Chesapeake, 1643–1777," *Journal of Economic History* 43 (1983):109–17; Cary Carson and Lorena S. Walsh, "The Material Life of the Early American Housewife," *Winterthur Portfolio* (forthcoming).

items were more common among middling landowning families but still were far from universally standard equipment. Living largely in crude, one- or two-room dwellings where chambers functioned simultaneously as bedroom, sitting room, work space, kitchen, and dining hall, ordinary families found that a few pieces of easily moved or multipurpose furniture and a small store of communal vessels best served their needs. They rolled mattresses into corners during the day. They sat on chests. They ate from common dishes.

The rich had more, but more meant more comfort rather than distinction. Their houses were larger but because of extremely high labor costs were so "meane and Little" by English standards that newcomers found them to be unreliable guides to the owners' social position.[3] The early planter elite built modestly and then established social distance from servants and slaves by relegating such workers—and some workplaces, like kitchens—to flimsy outbuildings. Within the dwelling of the white family, living and work spaces remained intermixed. The parlor might boast a cupboard and curtained bed, but it was likely also to house bales of trade goods, tools, horse gear, and stored foodstuffs.

Being rich meant using candles after dark, owning more pewter dining and drinking vessels than poorer people, sleeping in better beds with linens, bedsteads, and hangings, using a greater variety of cooking equipment, and having now and then a picture or looking glass. Once one got beyond the beds, sheets, and candlesticks, however, there was no agreed-upon assemblage of goods that indicated a truly distinctive upper-class style of life nor even consensus that more than mere sufficiency was necessary. A poor man might sit on benches, chests, or overturned casks. A rich man might have chairs. But his chairs would not be the elegant works of craftsmanship found in such households by the time of the American Revolution. A seventeenth-century poor man might pass a mug or pewter tankard from hand to hand; a rich man's tankard might be fashioned from silver, but he might not see

[3]Charles, Lord Baltimore, to the Lords of Trade, Mar. 26, 1678, William Hand Browne et al., eds., *Archives of Maryland,* 72 vols. to date (Baltimore, 1883–), 5:265–66.

the need for individual drinking vessels for every person, such as are found in later households. As late as 1715 a foreigner expressed surprise that Robert Beverley, a prominent Virginian, "lives well, but though rich, he has nothing in or about his house but what is necessary. He hath good beds in his house, but no curtains; and instead of cane chairs, he hath stools made of wood."[4] While by that time others of high status lived somewhat more elaborately, Beverley's case is instructive in that it shows that plain living was still acceptable in the highest circles.

What we find, then, in the seventeenth century, is not simply a brief reversion to primitive and spartan conditions on a frontier but a broadly shared material condition and cultural attitude that was distinctly premodern. The work of James P. P. Horn, Lorna Weatherill, and others suggests that the same was still true in England in social groups below aristocrats and the upper gentry.[5] The colonists' standards of sufficiency (or comfort) and of luxury were not simply more modest versions of the dictates of the mid-eighteenth century with which we are so much more familiar. They were different standards altogether. The fact that most seventeenth-century Chesapeake colonists, even many who got rich, were English immigrants from the ranks below the gentry undoubtedly contributed to the prevalence of these premodern attitudes at all social levels.[6] Doubtless there were subtle ways in which some wealthy families used their larger stocks of relatively commonplace possessions to set themselves off from their social inferiors. Nevertheless, what struck the eyes of contemporary aristocratic European observers was the general lack of

[4]W. G. Stanard, "Major Robert Beverley and His Descendants," *Virginia Magazine of History and Biography* 3 (1895):171.

[5]Horn, "Adapting to a New World," pp. 151–64; Weatherill, *Consumer Behaviour and Material Culture*, chaps. 1, 3.

[6]On the social origins of Chesapeake immigrants and their social mobility, see David W. Galenson, *White Servitude in Colonial America: An Economic Analysis* (Cambridge, 1981); Mildred Campbell, "Social Origins of Some Early Americans," in James Morton Smith, ed., *Seventeenth-Century America* (Chapel Hill, N.C., 1959), pp. 63–89; Russell R. Menard, "From Servant to Freeholder: Status Mobility and Property Accumulation in Seventeenth-Century Maryland," *William and Mary Quarterly*, 3d ser. 30 (1973):37–64.

distinction between wealth groups and the peculiar homoge-
neity of seventeenth- and early eighteenth-century Tidewater
Chesapeake culture.[7]

While the material culture of the seventeenth century was
most remarkable for its sameness, changes can be seen at the
very top beginning about the mid-1680s. The region's wealthiest men and women had not yet adopted an integrated lifestyle set off from that of other groups. Still, by 1700 they
could be distinguished from others far more readily than in
the 1660s. Estates of more than £490 usually contained most
of the available comforts or one or two luxuries—say, pictures, watches and clocks, large looking glasses, or window
curtains—and a few showed signs of taking up newer fashions, such as more widespread use of table knives and forks,
the acquisition of a few pieces of imported fine furniture, and,
most consistently, increasingly larger quantities of elaborately
wrought silver plate.[8]

Consider, for example, the house of Henrietta Maria Lloyd,
the grand dame of seventeenth-century Maryland. An inventory of her house taken in 1697 shows that she lived very comfortably for her time, with ample beds, chairs, linen, and
pewter. Her hall and parlor were free of beds, although not
of storage. Exceptional items were two chests of drawers (one
of rare olivewood), some caned chairs (a new fashion), a clock,
several large "seeing glasses," and a few shillings worth of
earthenware described as "fine." In addition she proclaimed

[7]See Barbara G. Carson, "Living Habits." The following show similar
conditions in this early period in Massachusetts and Pennsylvania: Main,
"Standard of Living"; Gloria L. Main and Jackson T. Main, "Economic
Growth and the Standard of Living in Southern New England, 1640–
1774," *Journal of Economic History* 48 (1988):27–46; Kevin M. Sweeney, "Furniture and the Domestic Environment in Wethersfield, Connecticut,
1639–1800," *Connecticut Antiquarian* 36 (1984):10–39; Jack Michel, "'In a
Manner and Fashion Suitable to Their Degree': A Preliminary Investigation
of the Material Culture of Early Rural Pennsylvania," *Working Papers from
the Regional Economic History Research Center* 5 (1981).

[8]One can form a good idea of the lifestyle of the most luxury-conscious
elite at the turn of the century from Richard Beale Davis, ed., *William Fitzhugh and His Chesapeake World, 1676–1701: The Fitzhugh Letters and Other Documents* (Chapel Hill, N.C., 1963).

her position with silver plate worth £88, magnificent silk gowns, and pearl and diamond jewelry. Most of her furnishings, however, were of a kind and value that could be found in middling households. There simply were more of them. Nor were there signs of the elaborate etiquette of tea drinking and dining that later generations would embrace.

Over the first quarter of the eighteenth century change accelerated in the households of the rich and powerful. They began to acquire a greater array of material goods that permitted a style of living truly different from that of more ordinary people. The households of John and Thomas Addison, father and son and both longtime members of the Maryland Council, illustrate the transformation. The father died about 1706 in a house only somewhat less spartan than Robert Beverley's. He had comfortable curtained beds, some "russia leather" chairs, an oval table, and plenty of bed and table linen. Perhaps because he lived on the frontier, where few of his peers would visit, he had no silver plate and his equipment for dining must have been included in his forty pounds of pewter worth less than £2. By contrast, Thomas, at his death in 1727, had a house that would appear well appointed today. A parlor and a "Back Room" were furnished exclusively for social intercourse, with pictures and mirrors in gilded frames, glass candelabra, "easy" chairs, a backgammon table, tea tables, china tea sets, and copper coffee pots. Utensils for dining included a dozen china plates, two china punch bowls, four dozen "drinking glasses," decanters, and case knives and forks, some hafted with horn, others with silver. Every bedroom had window curtains, and the best bed, with its silk hangings, was worth nearly £50, equal to the value of all the movable property in the majority of Maryland households. No one had lived at this scale in the 1690s. Thomas's visit to England in 1709–10 may well have transformed his view of how a councillor should live.

By the 1760s many of these notions of comfort and ways of using objects to advertise status appeared not only in wealthy but in middling households, and even the poor were participating to some degree. The luxuries of the Addisons became widespread in wealthy Chesapeake households. Matched china place settings, mahogany furniture (Addison's was walnut), specialized beverage glasses and serving dishes, candelabra, tea and coffee services—to name just a few examples—began to fill up larger, more formal dwellings that now boasted separate drawing and dining rooms. Social spaces became divorced from workplaces, storerooms, and sleeping quarters. Conspicuous consumption of the kind described by Thorstein Veblen was beginning to appear, although not to the degree practiced by the English aristocracy.[9]

At the lowest levels of wealth, some planters were acquiring more of the ordinary amenities that had been missing in equivalent seventeenth-century households: chairs, bedsteads, individual knives and forks, bed and table linens, and inexpensive ceramic tableware. They also were acquiring a taste for that symbolic luxury, tea. Middling families moved beyond commonplace amenities, substituting a piece of case furniture for plain, utilitarian chests and trunks, setting tables with full ceramic place settings, preparing more varied and elaborate meals with a burgeoning variety of cookware, and drinking tea in full, ritual fashion. Neat, orderly domestic furnishings that afforded comfort with an appropriate touch of elegance here and there—and of course manners to match—were becoming one of the chief means of conveying a family's status and respectability.

How thoroughgoing these changes were can be seen in a 1762 letter of Virginia planter Robert Beverley, grandson of the Robert Beverley whose spartan household had evoked comment in 1715. The younger Beverley had spent some years in England acquiring an education, but his decision to marry a local heiress meant, as he explained to a London fac-

[9]Inventories and Accounts 15:198–212, 29:193–98, Inventories 12:295–313, Maryland State Archives, Annapolis. See also Richard L. Bushman, "The Gentrification of Kent County, Delaware, 1740–1776" (Paper presented at the Washington Area Seminar in Early American History, April 1987); Thomas M. Doerflinger, "Farmers and Dry Goods in the Philadelphia Market Area, 1750–1800," in Ronald Hoffman, John J. McCusker, Russell R. Menard, and Peter J. Albert, eds., *The Economy of Early America: The Revolutionary Period, 1763–1790* (Charlottesville, Va., 1988), pp. 166–95; Sweeney, "Furniture and Domestic Environment," pp. 10–39; Main and Main, "Economic Growth," pp. 27–46.

tor, that he probably would spend the rest of his life in Virginia. As Providence had put him in affluent circumstances, "I shall always desire to make it as commodious as the Place [will] admit of." Setting up a proper household meant acquiring the proper equipment. Beverley was especially anxious to start out with a set of china "of the most fashionable sort . . . sufficient for 2 Genteel Courses of Victuals," along with various pieces of mahogany furniture. Just nine years later, he found it necessary to reoutfit his house completely. As he explained to another London agent, "I w[oul]d willingly consult the present Fashion for you know that foolish Passion has made its bray, even into this remote region." This time Beverley's invoice included requests for marble chimney pieces and wallpaper like that the newly arrived royal governor used to decorate his palace in Williamsburg.[10] Beverley's grandfather would have been shocked at such display.

For the most part, one does not learn of such changes in lifestyle from letters, diaries, or other personal records. Such documents do not abound in the Chesapeake, and where they do exist they tell us much more about the rich than the poor. One finds most of the relevant information in probate records: wills and inventories. In the Chesapeake region of the British colonies, inventories list in great detail all the movable possessions (including debts owed to the estate) of men and women whose estates went through probate. The range of households represented is wide, from the very poor to the very rich. For this reason it is possible to observe the behavior of people in a variety of social groups.[11]

This study is based on some 7,500 inventories from four Tidewater Chesapeake counties selected for differing characteristics. Two counties, Anne Arundel in Maryland and York

[10]Robert Beverley to [John Bland], Dec. 27, 1762; Beverley to Samuel Athawes, Apr. 15, July 16, 1771, Robert Beverley Letterbook, 1761–93, Library of Congress.

[11]In this region land and its improvements were not inventoried. For a general discussion of our methods, see Lois Green Carr and Lorena S. Walsh, "Inventories and the Analysis of Wealth and Consumption Patterns in St. Mary's County, Maryland, 1658–1777," *Historical Methods* 13 (1980):81–104. For a discussion of problems particular to this paper, see Appendix A, below.

in Virginia, were the seats of provincial capitals, Annapolis and Williamsburg, and offered urban-rural contrasts. Planters in both counties grew tobacco as their primary crop, but men of York concentrated on the more valuable sweetscented variety, whereas those of Anne Arundel grew oronoco; planters in both eventually added corn to tobacco as a crop for export. St. Mary's County, Maryland, also was a center for growing oronoco, but of poorer quality than that of Anne Arundel. Planters here concentrated more exclusively on tobacco than did those in the other sample counties. Finally, Somerset County, on Maryland's lower Eastern Shore, had less good tobacco soil than the other areas and early developed a much more diversified economy.[12]

In using these inventories to study change in lifestyle, we have experimented with a variety of measures. We have counted the quantities and values of basic kinds of furnishings. We have tabulated the total value of all consumer goods. And we have developed a method for scoring the appearance of selected amenities in what we call an "amenities index." The picture of change can be seen most easily in movements in these amenities scores. We selected twelve items and noted their presence or absence in each inventory. These items were: coarse earthenware and bed or table linen for convenience and sanitation; table knives, forks, and fine earthenware for refinements in convenience and for increasing elegance at the table; spices for variety in diet (using signs of spice use, such as pepper boxes or nutmeg graters, as well as stocks of spices); books—religious and secular—for education and perhaps some use of leisure time; and wigs, watches or clocks, pictures, and silver plate for signs of luxury and display. The number of categories present was the score for each inventory, with a range from 0 to 12.

Figure 1 shows overall progress in acquisition of these amenities based on mean scores throughout the period 1643–1777. Mean scores are the added scores of all estates for each time division divided by the number of estates. The graph

[12]Lois Green Carr, "Diversification in the Colonial Chesapeake: Somerset County, Maryland, in Comparative Perspective," in Carr, Morgan, and Russo, eds., *Colonial Chesapeake Society,* pp. 342–88. See also Appendix A, below.

demonstrates that there was little change in the acquisition of amenities during the seventeenth century; the mean remained at about two items. After the turn of the century mean scores increased steadily until they approached five items in the 1770s. Amenities scores increased two and a half times.

The graph also shows that these changes were regionwide. Shifts in mean scores occurred at about the same time in all the counties studied, regardless of differing local resources and marketing connections or of peculiar characteristics of local populations. This rise in scores might simply reflect an upward shift in the structure of inventoried wealth that does not necessarily indicate improvement in living conditions for all planters. Figures 2 through 7, however, make clear that inhabitants at all levels of wealth were improving their standard of consumption. The rich, those with more than £225 in movable wealth, moved soonest and achieved the highest scores; but even people with estates worth less than £50 were showing progress by the 1730s.[13]

[13]All values have been put into constant pounds, using a commodity price index created with prices from the inventories. In our original study, which focused on St. Mary's County, we selected cutting points for wealth as follows: at £50 (close to the median until the 1730s), at £225 (amenities scores jumped at this point across the whole colonial period), and at £490 (inventoried wealthholders worth more were the top 5 to 10 percent over the whole period). Decedents worth less than £50 seldom owned slaves; many were landowners. Those worth £50–225 increasingly owned slaves and usually land. Those worth more than £225 generally owned land and slaves; many were officeholders. We have found these wealth divisions in

NOTE: *These figures and those that follow, except for fig. 12, use a semilogarithmic scale to show rates of change. Points are the center points of year groups. The year groups differ from county to county before 1677. For York, they are 1636–48 (this year group includes one inventory from 1652; we found no other York inventories for the years 1649–57), 1658–64, 1665–77; for St. Mary's, 1658–64, 1665–77; for Somerset, 1665–77; for Anne Arundel, 1658–77. Thereafter the year groups are as follows: 1678–87, 1688–99, 1700–1709, 1710–22, 1723–32, 1733–44, 1745–54, 1755–67, 1768–77. Data sources are the St. Mary's City Commission Inventory Files, Maryland State Archives, Annapolis.*

Figure 1.   Mean value of consumer durables (pounds, constant value) and mean amenities scores, four counties, all estates, 1636-1777

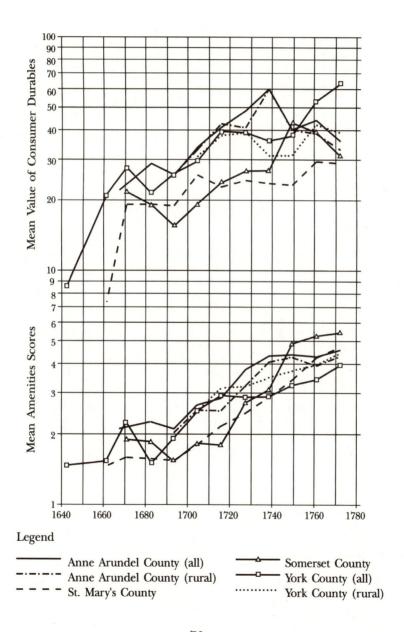

Legend

—————— Anne Arundel County (all)	—△— Somerset County
—·—··—·· Anne Arundel County (rural)	—□— York County (all)
– – – – St. Mary's County	·········· York County (rural)

Figure 2. Mean amenities scores and mean value of consumer durables (pounds, constant value), 1658-1777, rural Anne Arundel County and St. Mary's County: all wealth groups and wealthiest group

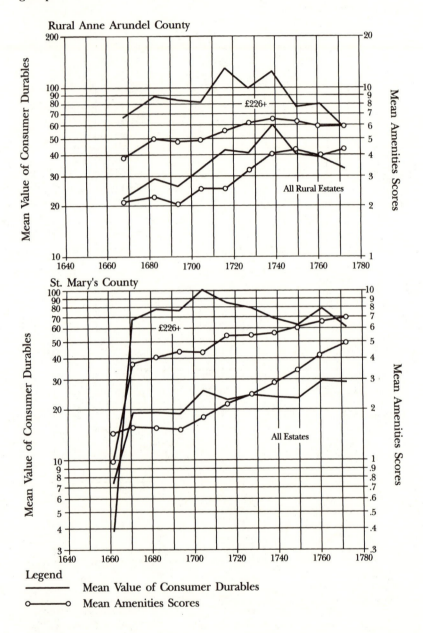

Legend

———— Mean Value of Consumer Durables

o————o Mean Amenities Scores

NOTE: For information about construction of the figure and about sources, see note to fig. 1.

Figure 3. Mean amenities scores and mean value of consumer durables (pounds, constant value), 1636-1777, rural York County and Somerset County: all wealth groups and wealthiest group

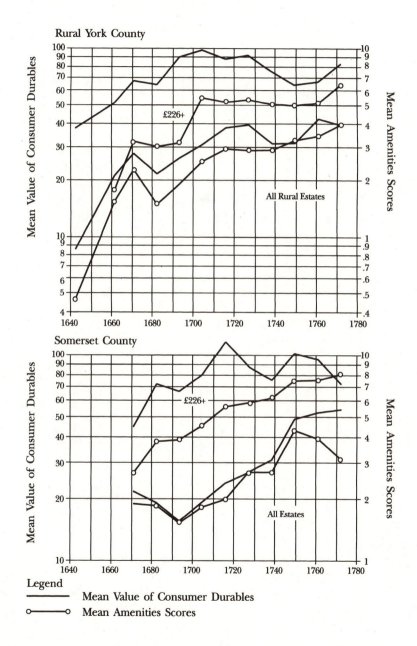

Legend

———— Mean Value of Consumer Durables

o————o Mean Amenities Scores

NOTE: For information about construction of the figure and about sources, see note to fig. 1.

Figure 4. Mean amenities scores and mean value of consumer durables (pounds, constant value), 1658-1777, rural Anne Arundel County: lower wealth groups

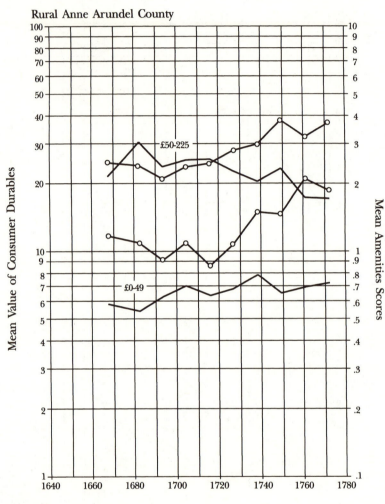

NOTE: For information about construction of the figure and about sources, see note to fig. 1.

Figure 5. Mean amenities scores and mean value of consumer durables (pounds, constant value), 1636-1777, rural York County: lower wealth groups

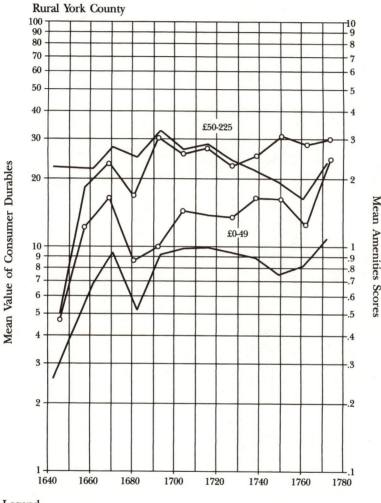

Legend

——————— Mean Value of Consumer Durables
o————o Mean Amenities Scores

NOTE: For information about construction of the figure and about sources, see note to fig. 1.

Figure 6. Mean amenities scores and mean value of consumer durables (pounds, constant value), 1658-1777, St. Mary's County: lower wealth groups

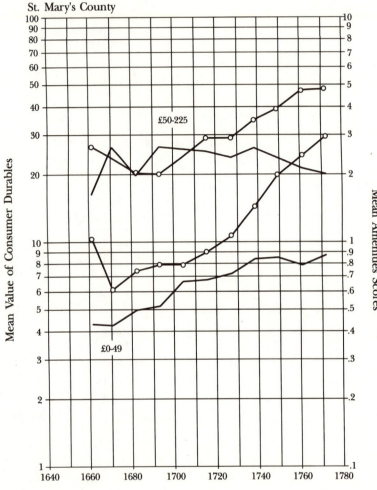

St. Mary's County

£50-225

£0-49

Mean Value of Consumer Durables

Mean Amenities Scores

Legend
———— Mean Value of Consumer Durables
o———o Mean Amenities Scores

NOTE: For information about construction of the figure and about sources, see note to fig. 1.

Figure 7. Mean amenities scores and mean value of consumer durables (pounds, constant value), 1665-1777, Somerset County: lower wealth groups

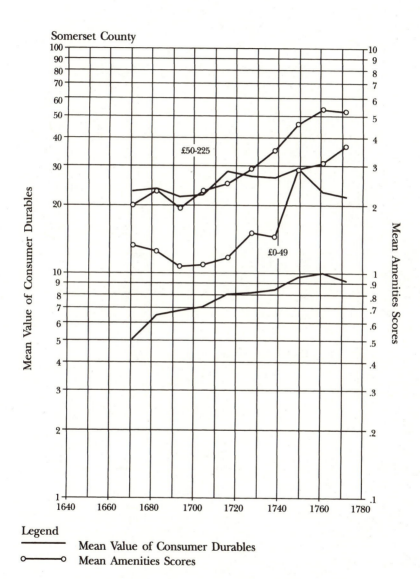

Legend

—————— Mean Value of Consumer Durables
o—————o Mean Amenities Scores

NOTE: For information about construction of the figure and about sources, see note to fig. 1.

Table 1. Incidence of selected consumer items, Anne Arundel County (rural)

Total estate value	1655–64 N = 8	1665–77 N = 103	1678–87 N = 100	1688–99 N = 157	1700–1709 N = 163	1710–22 N = 199	1723–32 N = 115	1733–44 N = 215	1745–54 N = 167	1755–67 N = 251	1768–77 N = 181
Coarse earthenware											
£ 0–49	50%	34%	35%	25%	34%	28%	32%	45%	50%	53%	47%
£ 50–94	0	39	55	41	44	48	42	52	75	81	60
£ 95–225	0	53	71	49	68	63	88	63	92	80	90
£ 226–490	0	60	83	77	64	59	79	84	95	84	93
£ 491+	—	67	86	82	83	81	95	93	96	94	95
Bed or table linen											
£ 0–49	75	26	24	19	15	9	11	9	8	23	22
£ 50–94	100	70	73	44	30	41	32	28	29	19	32
£ 95–225	50	87	75	76	79	66	79	53	67	46	48
£ 226–490	0	93	83	100	84	82	93	78	83	70	76
£ 491+	—	67	86	100	94	100	100	91	96	96	90
Table knives											
£ 0–49	0	11	0	5	9	7	5	19	18	37	31
£ 50–94	0	17	0	9	4	15	16	32	50	48	56
£ 95–225	0	27	11	3	18	16	25	35	59	62	68
£ 226–490	0	47	33	8	20	32	57	73	63	64	76
£ 491+	—	33	43	55	72	69	55	84	92	85	82
Table forks											
£ 0–49	0	0	0	5	5	7	5	17	16	37	31
£ 50–94	0	0	0	3	0	11	16	32	50	48	56
£ 95–225	0	0	0	3	7	11	25	33	59	62	63
£ 226–490	0	0	0	8	12	27	57	73	59	64	76
£ 491+	—	0	0	27	50	65	55	84	88	83	82

		C1	C2	C3	C4	C5	C6	C7	C8	C9	C10	C11
Fine earthenware												
£	0–49	0	0	0	3	2	0	3	4	3	7	6
£	50–94	0	0	0	0	0	4	0	16	8	10	12
£	95–225	0	7	0	0	0	5	8	8	21	14	35
£	226–490	0	0	0	0	8	14	21	38	32	28	46
£	491+	—	0	14	9	22	27	30	51	80	68	62
Spices												
£	0–49	25	4	5	3	2	1	3	6	8	8	11
£	50–94	100	17	14	6	4	7	5	12	13	7	12
£	95–225	50	27	18	22	21	16	17	35	18	18	23
£	226–490	100	53	17	15	48	14	43	47	29	32	32
£	491+	—	67	43	55	78	62	50	65	64	55	33
Books: religious												
£	0–49	75	23	30	19	23	20	32	28	24	33	25
£	50–94	100	30	46	34	48	59	42	44	58	39	48
£	95–225	100	60	50	57	68	42	67	51	69	52	63
£	226–490	0	53	83	62	72	68	79	71	83	66	66
£	491+	—	100	57	73	94	85	85	86	92	85	82
Books: secular												
£	0–49	0	2	0	2	5	0	5	0	3	1	3
£	50–94	0	0	0	3	7	0	0	4	0	0	0
£	95–225	0	0	7	3	0	5	0	2	5	2	5
£	226–490	0	0	0	0	0	5	0	16	0	2	0
£	491+	—	0	0	36	6	4	20	14	8	4	5
Wigs												
£	0–49	0	2	5	3	3	6	5	4	0	0	0
£	50–94	0	0	5	0	7	0	5	0	0	0	0
£	95–225	0	7	0	3	4	11	4	4	0	2	0
£	226–490	0	0	0	0	4	23	0	2	7	4	2
£	491+	—	0	29	9	11	23	20	9	0	0	3

Table 1. (continued)

Total estate value	1655–64 N = 8	1665–77 N = 103	1678–87 N = 100	1688–99 N = 157	1700–1709 N = 163	1710–22 N = 199	1723–32 N = 115	1733–44 N = 215	1745–54 N = 167	1755–67 N = 251	1768–77 N = 181
Clocks and watches											
£ 0–49	0	0	3	0	2	0	0	2	0	1	3
£ 50–94	0	0	0	0	4	0	0	0	0	3	4
£ 95–225	0	0	0	0	4	5	4	10	10	4	13
£ 226–490	100	0	33	15	0	14	14	13	20	8	10
£ 491+	—	0	43	27	44	42	55	61	60	43	39
Pictures											
£ 0–49	0	0	0	0	2	0	3	0	3	0	0
£ 50–94	0	4	0	0	4	0	0	0	4	0	0
£ 95–225	0	7	7	0	4	5	8	6	3	2	5
£ 226–490	0	0	33	0	0	9	7	7	10	10	12
£ 491+	—	67	29	27	11	19	30	23	24	15	18
Silver plate											
£ 0–49	25	0	3	5	2	4	0	6	11	3	6
£ 50–94	0	4	5	3	4	15	11	4	13	0	16
£ 95–225	100	13	21	35	29	11	25	25	18	10	13
£ 226–490	100	47	67	69	28	50	36	38	44	32	37
£ 491+	—	67	86	91	83	89	85	70	80	79	54
Tea and teaware											
£ 0–49	0	0	3	0	2	0	0	0	11	21	28
£ 50–94	0	0	0	0	0	0	5	4	13	7	40
£ 95–225	0	0	0	0	0	3	4	14	31	50	58
£ 226–490	0	0	0	0	0	5	0	36	54	52	83
£ 491+	—	0	0	0	0	19	45	58	84	85	85

SOURCE: Maryland History Computer Files, Historic St. Mary's City Commission, Maryland State Archives, Annapolis.

NOTE: Tea and teaware are not included in the twelve-item index. Silver plate is included only if valued at £1 or more.

When broken down by item, the index also tells us something about consumer choices. Table 1 shows the data for Anne Arundel County. Some kinds of objects were always luxuries confined primarily to the households of the rich; those selected included timepieces, pictures, and silver plate. On the other hand, table knives and forks and fine earthenware, the social props for genteel dining, were confined to the rich at first, but by the 1770s they were considered desirable and affordable by some well down on the economic scale. In addition, tea and teaware, not included in the index but shown in the table, were nonessential items that showed major increases even in estates worth less than £50. Evidently the social definition of what was a luxury had changed. Of the remaining items—coarse ceramics, linens, books, and spices—the first three were the most likely to appear in the inventories of the poor. All show differences across wealth, but only the ceramics show increases over time. An interesting point here is that in the poorest group, while, predictably, coarse earthenware appeared most often, religious books came next. A fifth to a third of these poor decedents had at least a Bible.

The other three counties show similar results, except among the poor (see tables 2–4); the poor show regional differences. In St. Mary's and Somerset, the appearance not only of coarse ceramics but of linens, spices, and books increased over time. In St. Mary's this increase brought the poor to the

---

other counties as well. However, in Anne Arundel and York, proportionally fewer poor men were inventoried than in St. Mary's and Somerset, creating a range for the groups worth more than £490 of from 7 to 20 percent of inventoried wealthholders. In some parts of the analysis we divided the middle group into two subgroups, £50–94 and £95–225. After 1700, these middle groups generally included from 30 to 48 percent of inventoried wealthholders, with three exceptions (Somerset, 1723–32, 52 percent; York, 1745–54 and 1768–77, below 30 percent).

At various points in the eighteenth century, depending upon the county, the poorest group began to diminish proportionally, the groups worth over £226 and over £490 grew larger, and mean inventoried wealth began to rise. Although there were local variations in the propensity to leave an inventory, local reporting rates did not change except in York, where they improved about 1700 (see Appendix A, below). These results suggest a rise in mean wealth per household in the living population.

Table 2. Incidence of selected consumer items, St. Mary's County

Total estate value	1655–64 N = 33	1665–77 N = 183	1678–87 N = 143	1688–99 N = 179	1700–1709 N = 160	1710–22 N = 359	1723–32 N = 241	1733–44 N = 361	1745–54 N = 301	1755–67 N = 367	1768–77 N = 255
Coarse earthenware											
£ 0–49	24%	24%	31%	25%	22%	39%	41%	52%	71%	61%	71%
£ 50–94	67	49	54	28	41	48	71	80	80	83	74
£ 95–225	100	67	62	65	68	62	80	89	83	86	94
£ 226–490	0	46	55	80	43	77	90	86	95	89	92
£ 491+	—	63	75	75	75	87	100	91	92	91	92
Bed or table linen											
£ 0–49	20	12	15	13	17	9	12	17	13	22	25
£ 50–94	17	33	43	28	48	47	51	49	35	58	60
£ 95–225	100	67	54	78	50	75	77	70	59	86	71
£ 226–490	100	62	73	80	93	90	100	89	87	87	90
£ 491+	—	100	75	88	88	93	100	91	92	86	96
Table knives											
£ 0–49	4	0	1	1	2	6	8	14	28	44	45
£ 50–94	0	6	4	3	10	18	18	35	47	65	74
£ 95–225	0	7	15	9	18	30	23	45	71	79	68
£ 226–490	0	8	36	10	36	40	55	60	82	83	86
£ 491+	—	38	38	38	25	47	43	82	92	83	96
Table forks											
£ 0–49	4	0	0	1	1	4	7	10	24	39	43
£ 50–94	0	0	0	0	3	13	15	31	43	62	76
£ 95–225	0	0	0	0	14	27	23	45	67	76	68
£ 226–490	0	8	0	0	14	40	52	60	74	83	86
£ 491+	—	0	13	13	13	40	29	73	75	80	96

	1	2	3	4	5	6	7	8	9	10	11
Fine earthenware											
£ 0–49	0	1	0	1	2	1	2	5	7	14	24
£ 50–94	0	6	0	0	3	2	4	9	27	28	41
£ 95–225	0	7	8	13	5	15	10	26	30	48	39
£ 226–490	0	0	9	20	0	17	31	34	63	69	72
£ 491+	—	25	38	25	38	40	43	64	58	80	89
Spices											
£ 0–49	12	2	5	3	3	4	3	7	10	22	23
£ 50–94	17	12	11	3	3	16	26	6	25	38	24
£ 95–225	33	27	23	22	18	25	23	14	14	43	39
£ 226–490	0	31	27	20	29	33	38	34	47	64	44
£ 491+	—	75	50	50	25	67	71	64	50	69	62
Books: religious											
£ 0–49	32	15	16	21	21	25	23	28	35	33	44
£ 50–94	67	30	25	28	59	52	53	58	51	51	69
£ 95–225	67	53	54	70	50	55	57	61	65	73	71
£ 226–490	0	54	36	50	79	87	76	66	63	81	78
£ 491+	—	50	75	75	100	73	86	91	92	74	85
Books: secular											
£ 0–49	0	2	0	2	2	2	1	0	1	1	1
£ 50–94	0	0	0	0	3	2	0	4	4	4	10
£ 95–225	33	17	8	4	0	2	5	4	5	3	5
£ 226–490	0	0	18	0	14	0	10	0	8	19	16
£ 491+	—	0	13	13	13	7	14	18	0	14	15
Wigs											
£ 0–49	0	0	0	7	2	2	5	4	2	1	3
£ 50–94	0	3	7	6	10	7	0	5	0	2	0
£ 95–225	0	0	8	4	14	12	5	7	6	0	0
£ 226–490	0	0	0	30	0	17	7	6	5	2	2
£ 491+	—	13	13	13	25	33	29	46	8	14	8

Table 2. *(continued)*

Total estate value	1655–64 N = 33	1665–77 N = 183	1678–87 N = 143	1688–99 N = 179	1700–1709 N = 160	1710–22 N = 359	1723–32 N = 241	1733–44 N = 361	1745–54 N = 301	1755–67 N = 367	1768–77 N = 255
Clocks and watches											
£ 0–49	0	0	1	0	0	1	0	1	0	0	3
£ 50–94	0	0	4	0	0	2	2	5	0	1	7
£ 95–225	0	17	8	4	0	13	5	5	2	2	8
£ 226–490	0	31	9	20	0	13	17	17	8	14	18
£ 491+	—	25	13	38	25	33	57	27	33	43	62
Pictures											
£ 0–49	4	0	0	1	1	2	2	1	0	0	4
£ 50–94	17	15	0	3	7	3	4	6	10	1	5
£ 95–225	0	7	8	9	18	12	5	4	6	11	3
£ 226–490	0	15	9	30	14	13	10	11	13	8	14
£ 491+	—	38	50	13	0	40	43	36	58	26	35
Silver plate											
£ 0–49	0	1	2	3	0	2	2	3	4	1	4
£ 50–94	0	6	11	13	7	10	6	7	4	3	7
£ 95–225	67	30	15	26	23	27	18	22	14	18	15
£ 226–490	0	54	36	50	71	50	38	51	37	40	46
£ 491+	—	75	88	63	100	73	86	64	75	80	85

SOURCE: Maryland History Computer Files, Historic St. Mary's City Commission, Maryland State Archives, Annapolis.
NOTE: Silver plate is included only if valued at £1 or more.

Table 3. Incidence of selected consumer items, Somerset County

Total estate value	1665–77 N = 18	1678–87 N = 48	1688–99 N = 139	1700–1709 N = 208	1710–22 N = 386	1723–32 N = 237	1733–44 N = 329	1745–54 N = 195	1755–67 N = 261	1768–77 N = 261
Coarse earthenware										
£ 0–49	40%	11%	20%	27%	34%	42%	43%	71%	72%	64%
£ 50–94	43	13	30	46	53	82	63	61	82	78
£ 95–225	33	63	44	58	64	82	84	87	90	77
£ 226–490	0	50	50	46	82	79	93	85	87	97
£ 491+	—	100	67	75	100	78	92	93	93	100
Bed or table linen										
£ 0–49	20	33	21	21	22	24	24	37	66	53
£ 50–94	57	50	56	56	45	61	48	53	75	69
£ 95–225	100	100	72	58	74	64	75	72	82	74
£ 226–490	100	100	83	77	91	95	93	87	87	87
£ 491+	100	100	67	75	100	78	92	100	96	100
Table knives										
£ 0–49	0	7	7	8	5	12	17	41	48	51
£ 50–94	14	0	4	10	8	14	38	58	73	69
£ 95–225	0	38	6	23	15	18	55	75	84	77
£ 226–490	67	25	17	31	23	79	58	85	89	90
£ 491+	—	0	33	25	88	33	75	93	89	85
Table forks										
£ 0–49	0	0	0	7	4	11	15	36	45	51
£ 50–94	0	0	0	0	8	13	35	58	71	69
£ 95–225	0	0	0	12	15	14	54	72	82	77
£ 226–490	0	0	0	23	23	79	55	85	83	90
£ 491+	—	0	0	25	75	33	75	93	82	89

Table 3. *(continued)*

Total estate value	1665–77 N = 18	1678–87 N = 48	1688–99 N = 139	1700–1709 N = 208	1710–22 N = 386	1723–32 N = 237	1733–44 N = 329	1745–54 N = 195	1755–67 N = 261	1768–77 N = 261
Fine earthenware										
£ 0–49	20	0	2	0	0	0	5	7	17	25
£ 50–94	14	13	4	0	0	1	4	14	25	43
£ 95–225	0	0	0	4	5	9	15	43	47	50
£ 226–490	0	25	0	31	5	32	33	51	63	79
£ 491+	—	100	33	0	88	22	50	93	85	96
Spices										
£ 0–49	0	0	4	3	2	4	3	5	22	25
£ 50–94	14	0	15	10	6	14	4	22	36	39
£ 95–225	33	25	0	8	7	16	21	36	55	40
£ 226–490	33	50	17	31	23	26	30	64	61	74
£ 491+	—	100	67	38	38	67	83	64	63	82
Books: religious										
£ 0–49	20	33	36	25	37	41	45	66	67	66
£ 50–94	29	38	30	51	60	61	68	78	84	82
£ 95–225	67	63	67	69	61	61	72	79	77	84
£ 226–490	33	100	67	69	86	95	90	95	93	90
£ 491+	—	100	100	100	100	78	92	93	93	96
Books: secular										
£ 0–49	0	7	5	6	2	5	1	3	4	11
£ 50–94	0	0	0	5	3	8	7	0	23	4
£ 95–225	33	13	11	12	5	7	6	6	5	11
£ 226–490	0	0	17	0	0	21	10	21	26	21
£ 491+	—	100	0	13	63	11	33	50	59	44
Wigs										
£ 0–49	0	0	1	3	2	4	2	5	1	4
£ 50–94	0	0	0	0	4	0	4	6	0	2
£ 95–225	0	0	6	8	7	9	12	13	5	5
£ 226–490	0	0	0	23	14	16	15	21	20	24
£ 491+	—	0	33	13	63	22	17	57	30	33

Clocks and watches

£ 0–49	0	0	1	0	0	1	0	1	2
£ 50–94	0	0	0	0	0	1	0	0	0
£ 95–225	0	0	4	5	2	3	2	3	7
£ 226–490	0	0	15	5	5	10	10	13	16
£ 491+	0	33	25	38	22	58	50	52	48

Pictures

£ 0–49	4	0	2	1	1	2	3	0	0
£ 50–94	0	0	0	1	0	4	6	0	2
£ 95–225	0	17	0	5	0	2	0	5	3
£ 226–490	0	0	23	23	11	15	15	17	11
£ 491+	—	33	13	88	22	42	57	33	41

Silver plate

£ 0–49	4	5	2	3	1	5	5	7	6
£ 50–94	0	4	5	14	10	9	17	2	2
£ 95–225	13	33	23	26	23	6	21	15	26
£ 226–490	25	67	69	46	53	45	56	35	45
£ 491+	0	33	75	100	67	83	93	74	78

Tea and teaware

£ 0–49	0	0	0	0	0	0	7	21	32
£ 50–94	0	0	0	0	0	1	19	30	43
£ 95–225	0	0	0	0	0	10	32	44	57
£ 226–490	0	0	0	0	16	20	64	67	76
£ 491+	—	0	0	63	11	42	93	85	89

SOURCE: Maryland History Computer Files, Historic St. Mary's City Commission, Maryland State Archives, Annapolis.
NOTE: Tea and teaware are not included in the twelve-item index. Silver plate is included only if valued at £1 or more.

Table 4. Incidence of selected consumer items, York County (rural)

Total estate value	1643–54 N = 23	1655–64 N = 19	1665–77 N = 38	1678–87 N = 51	1688–99 N = 60	1700–09 N = 62	1710–22 N = 146	1723–32 N = 77	1733–44 N = 117	1745–54 N = 107	1755–67 N = 106	1768–77 N = 73
Coarse earthenware												
£ 0–49	0%	11%	27%	14%	29%	53%	51%	44%	42%	41%	38%	50%
£ 50–94	0	33	44	29	63	57	70	50	60	60	53	70
£ 95–225	0	33	46	30	64	33	66	61	81	50	62	73
£ 226–490	0	0	100	33	0	71	81	87	90	72	70	80
£ 491+	—	33	33	33	50	100	91	86	90	86	82	93
Bed or table linen												
£ 0–49	0	22	55	24	35	31	28	26	17	28	14	29
£ 50–94	0	33	44	57	75	71	78	36	35	40	53	30
£ 95–225	25	67	77	30	73	83	66	56	50	50	19	60
£ 226–490	0	100	100	100	80	100	88	87	79	76	60	90
£ 491+	—	0	100	100	50	100	91	100	100	93	96	93
Table knives												
£ 0–49	0	0	0	5	0	3	6	4	17	23	14	25
£ 50–94	0	0	0	0	13	0	11	7	15	33	65	40
£ 95–225	0	0	8	0	0	25	11	28	31	50	54	47
£ 226–490	0	0	50	0	0	43	27	60	47	48	65	50
£ 491+	—	0	0	0	50	50	73	71	70	71	64	79
Table forks												
£ 0–49	0	0	0	0	0	3	6	4	11	21	5	25
£ 50–94	0	0	0	0	0	0	11	7	15	33	41	30
£ 95–225	0	0	0	0	0	8	9	28	34	50	42	47
£ 226–490	0	0	0	0	0	29	23	53	42	44	60	50
£ 491+	—	0	0	0	0	50	73	71	70	71	64	79
Fine earthenware												
£ 0–49	0	0	0	0	0	0	0	4	6	0	5	13
£ 50–94	0	0	0	0	0	0	4	0	5	0	6	30
£ 95–225	0	0	0	0	0	0	3	6	13	14	12	20
£ 226–490	0	0	0	0	0	14	15	33	5	32	35	70
£ 491	—	0	0	0	0	25	18	29	50	43	55	93

Spices

£												
0–49	0	11	0	5	3	6	11	4	17	10	10	8
50–94	0	0	0	14	13	14	11	0	5	7	18	0
95–225	0	0	15	20	36	17	23	22	6	36	15	7
226–490	0	100	50	33	0	29	27	20	21	12	25	10
491+	—	0	0	0	100	50	64	43	20	7	14	14

Books: religious

£												
0–49	41	22	55	24	24	31	26	22	31	28	19	33
50–94	0	67	44	14	50	43	44	43	40	40	41	30
95–225	25	67	62	50	73	50	66	61	50	64	54	53
226–490	0	100	100	100	60	71	81	67	84	68	55	90
491+	—	0	33	67	50	100	82	100	80	64	73	79

Books: secular

£												
0–49	6	0	9	0	0	0	0	0	3	0	0	4
50–94	0	0	11	0	13	0	0	0	0	7	0	10
95–225	0	0	0	0	9	8	3	0	0	0	4	0
226–490	0	0	0	0	0	29	8	0	5	4	5	10
491+	—	33	0	0	0	0	0	0	30	21	18	27

Wigs

£												
0–49	0	0	0	5	0	0	6	4	8	3	5	8
50–94	0	0	0	7	0	0	11	0	0	13	6	10
95–225	0	0	0	0	0	0	3	0	6	0	4	0
226–490	0	0	0	0	0	0	11	0	0	12	5	0
491+	—	0	0	0	0	0	27	0	0	7	5	0

Clocks and watches

£												
0–49	0	11	0	0	0	0	0	4	3	0	5	21
50–94	0	0	22	0	0	0	0	0	0	13	6	0
95–225	0	0	8	0	9	8	0	0	3	14	0	0
226–490	0	0	0	0	40	14	15	20	16	28	15	20
491+	—	0	0	0	50	75	64	29	30	29	27	57

Table 4. (*continued*)

Total estate value	1643–54 N = 23	1655–64 N = 19	1665–77 N = 38	1678–87 N = 51	1688–99 N = 60	1700–09 N = 62	1710–22 N = 146	1723–32 N = 77	1733–44 N = 117	1745–54 N = 107	1755–67 N = 106	1768–77 N = 73
Pictures												
£ 0–49	0	0	9	0	0	3	0	4	0	0	5	0
£ 50–94	0	33	0	0	0	14	4	0	5	0	0	0
£ 95–225	0	0	8	0	9	0	3	0	0	7	0	7
£ 226–490	0	0	0	0	0	14	0	13	11	16	0	0
£ 491+	—	0	0	0	50	25	46	29	20	14	14	29
Silver plate												
£ 0–49	100	22	9	0	0	0	2	4	6	3	5	17
£ 50–94	100	33	22	8	38	14	19	7	0	7	0	10
£ 95–225	100	0	15	40	18	17	20	11	16	29	12	7
£ 226–490	100	0	50	67	60	57	46	47	32	52	50	46
£ 491+	—	67	67	67	50	100	91	57	60	53	54	92
Tea and teaware												
£ 0–49	0	0	0	0	0	0	0	4	3	8	19	25
£ 50–94	0	0	0	0	0	0	7	0	10	7	29	30
£ 95–225	0	0	0	0	0	0	3	0	6	29	23	60
£ 226–490	0	0	0	0	0	0	0	33	11	52	45	50
£ 491+	—	0	0	0	0	0	36	29	80	71	73	86

SOURCE: Maryland History Computer Files, Historic St. Mary's City Commission, Maryland State Archives, Annapolis.
NOTE: Percentages for York County after 1755 represent a minimum, since some inventories are partially mutilated. Tea and teaware are not included in the twelve-item index. Silver plate is included only if valued at £1 or more. For the years 1636–42 (N=3), 100% had bed or table linen in the £0–94 group and 50% had silver plate in the £0–49 group. Otherwise none of the consumer items appeared.

level of rural Anne Arundel and rural York, but Somerset was different. This was an area where home industries in spinning yarn and weaving cloth developed early, and it was also the focus of a substantial population of Quakers and Presbyterians, groups that emphasized Bible reading. Here religious books and linens ultimately reached between half and two-thirds of poor estates, twice the level found anywhere else. Indeed, these items became more prevalent in Somerset than elsewhere in all wealth groups, even the highest.[14]

The index has also enabled us to summarize differences between urban and rural lifestyles. Figures 8 through 11 show that at all levels of wealth, people who died in Annapolis, Williamsburg, and Yorktown scored higher than did country dwellers. The reasons, of course, are not far to seek. Town living revolved more around clock time and offered many more opportunities for social intercourse than country living did. In tables 5 and 6 we can see that even town dwellers with property of less than £50 had watches, table knives, forks, good china, table linen, and teaware more often than did their country counterparts. With the exception of timepieces, all inventoried estates among the very rich in Annapolis—those worth more than £490—had these items by the 1770s and Virginia's urban inhabitants were not far behind.

More detailed examination of household goods bears out what this scoring indicates.[15] Townspeople spent proportion-

[14]Similarly, Lorna Weatherill found relatively high book ownership in northwest England, an area where there were religious Dissenters, although ownership of other goods was low relative to more economically advanced regions (*Consumer Behaviour and Material Culture*, pp. 49, 55–56). On home industries in Somerset, see Carr, "Diversification in the Colonial Chesapeake," pp. 355, 371, 373, 376, 380–81; on the religious character of Somerset, see Lois Green Carr and David W. Jordan, *Maryland's Revolution of Government, 1689–1692* (Ithaca, N.Y., 1974), p. 34, and Clayton Torrence, *Old Somerset on the Eastern Shore of Maryland: A Study in Foundations and Founders* (1935; reprint ed., Baltimore, 1966).

[15]See especially table 1 printed in Walsh, "Urban Amenities and Rural Sufficiency," pp. 114–15, which shows value of various categories of consumer durables as proportions of total noncapital value. For similar differences between urban and rural households in Britain, see Weatherill, *Consumer Behaviour and Material Culture*, chaps. 3, 4, and 8. However, she found more clocks in the countryside than we did (pp. 79–84).

Figure 8. Urban and rural mean value of consumer durables (pounds, constant value) and mean amenities scores, Anne Arundel County, 1700-1777: all wealth groups and wealthiest group

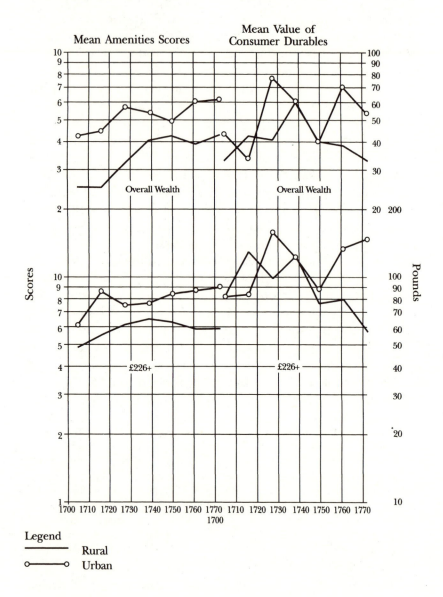

NOTE: For information about construction of the figure and about sources, see note to fig. 1.

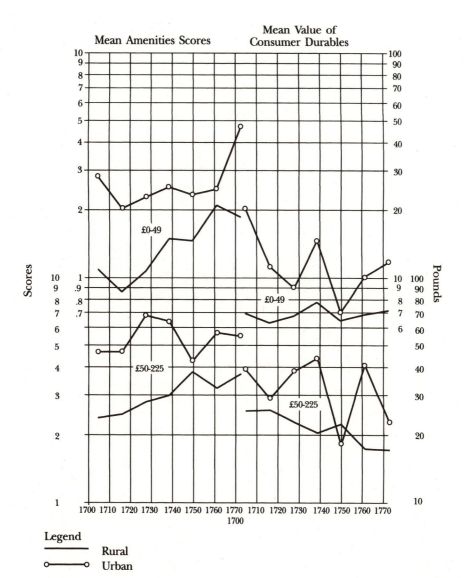

Figure 9.   Urban and rural mean value of consumer durables (pounds, constant value) and mean amenities scores, Anne Arundel County, 1700-1777: lower wealth groups

Mean Amenities Scores

Mean Value of
Consumer Durables

£0-49

£50-225

£0-49

£50-225

Scores

Pounds

1700 1710 1720 1730 1740 1750 1760 1770 1710 1720 1730 1740 1750 1760 1770
1700

Legend

—————— Rural
o————o Urban

NOTE: For information about construction of the figure and about sources,
   see note to fig. 1.

Figure 10. Urban and rural mean value of consumer durables (pounds, constant value) and mean amenities scores, York County, 1700-1777: all wealth groups and wealthiest group

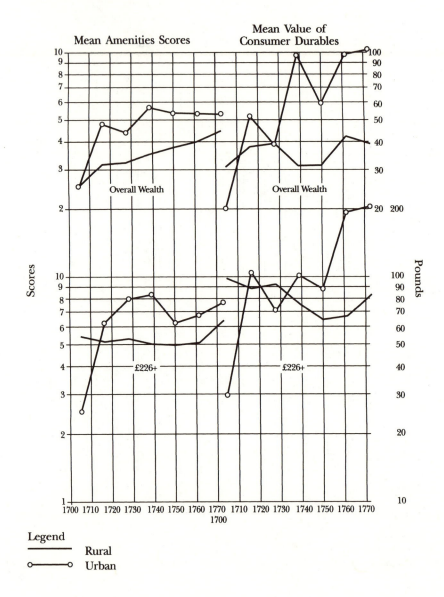

NOTE: For information about construction of the figure and about sources, see note to fig. 1.

Figure 11. Urban and rural mean value of consumer durables (pounds, constant value) and mean amenities scores, York County, 1700-1777: lower wealth groups

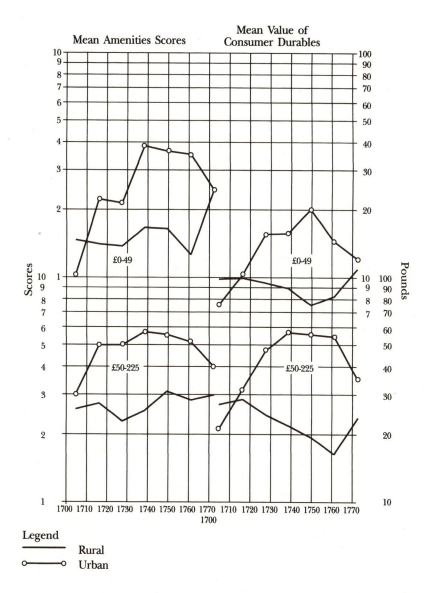

NOTE: For information about construction of the figure and about sources, see note to fig. 1.

Table 5. Incidence of selected consumer items, Anne Arundel County (urban)

Total estate value	1688–99 N = 4	1700–1709 N = 13	1710–22 N = 40	1723–32 N = 33	1733–44 N = 51	1745–54 N = 31	1755–67 N = 53	1768–77 N = 30
Coarse earthenware								
£ 0–49	67%	50%	27%	50%	32%	40%	43%	44%
£ 50–94	—	100	64	50	100	0	50	80
£ 95–225	—	100	67	83	67	67	75	88
£ 226–490	100	100	60	86	100	75	75	100
£ 491+	—	0	100	83	90	100	92	83
Bed or table linen								
£ 0–49	67	50	40	40	42	27	36	67
£ 50–94	—	100	82	75	50	100	83	80
£ 95–225	—	50	67	83	92	67	92	88
£ 226–490	100	100	80	100	100	100	75	100
£ 491+	—	100	100	100	70	88	100	100
Table knives								
£ 0–49	67	0	0	20	21	27	36	57
£ 50–94	—	100	36	75	0	0	50	0
£ 95–225	—	50	17	83	58	67	50	75
£ 226–490	100	67	40	71	100	75	75	100
£ 491+	—	0	100	67	70	100	100	100
Table forks								
£ 0–49	0	0	0	20	21	27	36	56
£ 50–94	—	0	36	75	0	0	50	0
£ 95–225	—	50	17	83	50	67	50	75
£ 226–490	100	0	60	71	100	75	75	100
£ 491+	—	0	100	67	60	100	100	100

Fine earthenware

£ 0–49	0	0	13	10	21	27	29	44
£ 50–94	—	0	18	25	0	0	50	60
£ 95–225	—	0	0	83	67	67	67	63
£ 226–490	0	0	60	86	88	100	75	50
£ 491+	—	0	100	67	80	100	100	100

Spices

£ 0–49	33	0	7	10	0	0	0	11
£ 50–94	—	0	27	0	0	0	17	20
£ 95–225	—	50	33	33	33	0	0	0
£ 226–490	100	100	60	71	13	0	75	0
£ 491+	—	0	67	67	60	75	77	83

Books: religious

£ 0–49	33	67	47	40	26	33	14	67
£ 50–94	—	0	91	75	100	0	50	60
£ 95–225	—	100	67	67	92	0	67	75
£ 226–490	100	100	80	72	63	50	75	50
£ 491+	—	100	33	67	70	88	85	83

Books: secular

£ 0–49	0	33	0	0	5	0	0	11
£ 50–94	—	0	9	0	0	0	0	0
£ 95–225	—	0	0	17	8	0	0	0
£ 226–490	0	0	80	14	13	25	13	100
£ 491+	—	0	67	33	40	25	23	0

Wigs

£ 0–49	33	33	20	10	5	0	0	11
£ 50–94	—	0	27	50	0	0	33	20
£ 95–225	—	50	33	33	33	0	17	0
£ 226–490	100	0	80	29	0	0	13	0
£ 491+	—	100	33	33	10	13	8	0

Table 5. (continued)

Total estate value	1688–99 N = 4	1700–1709 N = 13	1710–22 N = 40	1723–32 N = 33	1733–44 N = 51	1745–54 N = 31	1755–67 N = 53	1768–77 N = 30
Clocks and watches								
£ 0–49	0	0	7	0	11	7	14	33
£ 50–94	—	0	9	25	0	0	0	40
£ 95–225	—	0	33	50	67	67	50	50
£ 226–490	100	0	100	29	88	75	63	50
£ 491+	—	100	67	50	60	63	92	67
Pictures								
£ 0–49	0	17	20	10	32	7	0	22
£ 50–94	—	0	36	25	50	0	17	40
£ 95–225	—	0	33	67	42	67	33	0
£ 226–490	100	67	60	43	100	50	50	50
£ 491+	—	100	33	67	30	63	69	100
Silver plate								
£ 0–49	0	17	20	0	26	40	36	44
£ 50–94	—	100	27	25	0	100	50	60
£ 95–225	—	50	83	100	58	33	92	75
£ 226–490	100	67	100	71	75	100	100	100
£ 491+	—	100	100	67	90	100	100	100
Tea and teaware								
£ 0–49	0	0	0	0	16	40	57	67
£ 50–94	—	0	27	50	0	0	83	80
£ 95–225	—	0	17	67	58	33	83	63
£ 226–490	0	0	40	71	75	50	88	100
£ 491+	—	0	100	67	70	100	92	100

SOURCE: Maryland History Computer Files, Historic St. Mary's City Commission, Maryland State Archives, Annapolis.
NOTE: Tea and teaware are not included in the twelve-item index. Silver plate is included only if valued at £1 or more.

Table 6. Incidence of selected consumer items, York County (urban)

Total estate value	1700–1709 N = 9	1710–22 N = 20	1723–32 N = 22	1733–44 N = 33	1745–54 N = 32	1755–67 N = 44	1768–77 N = 44
Coarse earthenware							
£ 0–49	0%	20%	22%	36%	25%	64%	20%
£ 50–94	50	100	80	33	25	67	80
£ 95–225	100	80	100	56	100	50	70
£ 226–490	0	80	67	100	57	75	100
£ 491+	100	100	100	100	80	70	86
Bed or table linen							
£ 0–49	50	20	44	55	50	29	40
£ 50–94	75	100	40	83	50	33	40
£ 95–225	100	80	100	56	75	83	40
£ 226–490	0	80	100	100	71	75	100
£ 491+	100	100	100	100	80	90	93
Table knives							
£ 0–49	0	20	0	46	38	36	10
£ 50–94	0	67	0	50	0	50	20
£ 95–225	0	40	75	44	75	17	50
£ 226–490	0	60	100	83	43	50	80
£ 491+	0	100	100	100	60	80	71
Table forks							
£ 0–49	0	20	0	46	38	36	10
£ 50–94	0	33	0	50	0	50	20
£ 95–225	0	40	75	44	75	17	40
£ 226–490	0	60	100	83	43	50	80
£ 491+	0	100	100	100	60	80	64

Table 6. (continued)

Total estate value	1700–1709 N = 9	1710–22 N = 20	1723–32 N = 22	1733–44 N = 33	1745–54 N = 32	1755–67 N = 44	1768–77 N = 44
Fine earthenware							
£ 0–49	0	0	11	18	13	29	40
£ 50–94	0	0	20	33	0	67	20
£ 95–225	0	40	25	44	75	50	50
£ 226–490	0	60	67	67	57	63	80
£ 491+	0	50	100	100	60	70	86
Spices							
£ 0–49	0	20	11	18	13	14	0
£ 50–94	0	0	20	17	25	0	0
£ 95–225	100	0	0	22	13	17	0
£ 226–490	0	0	0	50	14	13	20
£ 491+	0	50	0	0	20	20	29
Books: religious							
£ 0–49	0	60	44	55	0	57	30
£ 50–94	50	67	40	83	50	67	80
£ 95–225	0	60	50	78	75	50	30
£ 226–490	0	60	100	83	57	75	100
£ 491+	0	50	0	100	40	60	79
Books: secular							
£ 0–49	0	0	0	0	13	7	10
£ 50–94	0	0	20	33	50	17	40
£ 95–225	100	0	50	44	0	33	0
£ 226–490	0	0	33	0	29	62	20
£ 491+	0	50	0	100	20	0	21
Wigs							
£ 0–49	0	20	33	18	50	21	10
£ 50–94	0	0	40	17	50	33	40
£ 95–225	100	0	0	44	38	50	0
£ 226–490	0	40	33	67	29	13	0
£ 491+	0	0	0	0	40	20	0

Clocks and watches

£ 0–49	0	0	11	27	38	21	10
£ 50–94	0	0	40	33	25	33	40
£ 95–225	100	0	50	78	50	50	0
£ 226–490	0	20	100	50	57	38	60
£ 491+	100	50	100	100	80	70	64

Pictures

£ 0–49	0	0	22	27	13	7	20
£ 50–94	0	67	40	33	0	17	20
£ 95–225	0	60	50	22	50	67	50
£ 226–490	0	0	0	50	57	75	60
£ 491+	100	100	100	100	80	60	86

Silver plate

£ 0–49	0	0	0	36	50	21	20
£ 50–94	25	67	60	50	25	50	60
£ 95–225	0	80	50	89	63	83	40
£ 226–490	0	80	100	67	71	75	100
£ 491+	100	100	100	100	100	70	93

Tea and teaware

£ 0–49	0	0	22	36	50	64	60
£ 50–94	0	0	0	33	50	83	100
£ 95–225	0	80	100	56	88	83	90
£ 226–490	0	0	33	83	57	88	100
£ 491+	0	100	0	100	80	90	86

SOURCE: Maryland History Computer Files, Historic St. Mary's City Commission, Maryland State Archives, Annapolis.

NOTE: Percentages for York County after 1755 represent a minimum, since some inventories for these years are partially mutilated. Tea and teaware are not included in the twelve-item index. Silver plate is included only if valued at £1 or more.

ately more of their noncapital resources than did country dwellers on social equipment—elaborate dining ware, gaming tables, toilet articles, lighting devices, tea services, secular books, and a multitude of highly specialized chairs and tables. Whatever their level of wealth, town residents owned, on the average, twice as many chairs and at least three times as many tables and candlesticks as did country cousins of similar means. Town life encouraged a proliferation of supporting props that even gentry hospitality in the country did not require. Other differences in spending and acquisition patterns also reflect characteristics of town life. There was less equipment for dairying, butchering, and corn milling than in the countryside, where outlying farmers performed these services.

All told, town living encouraged a level of conspicuous consumption never matched in the country. Prominent officeholders and bureaucrats stocked newly built, elegant town houses with the latest in fashionable imports, showing an abandon that some thought verged on decadence. The local artisans and laborers who served their rich neighbors purchased amenities and minor luxuries on a scale far exceeding that of other county residents at similar levels of wealth. Indeed, in town, keeping up with the Joneses meant spending ever greater proportions of total movable wealth on consumer goods.[16]

Did these urban developments eventually encourage the spread of amenities in the countryside? Figures 2 through 7 suggest not. In all wealth groups the entirely rural counties reached higher scores than did the rural parts of York and Anne Arundel, where such efforts should be most noticeable. The local towns were too sparsely populated and had too few

[16]Gordon S. Wood, *The Creation of the American Republic, 1776–1787* (Chapel Hill, N.C., 1969), pp. 108–18; Edmund S. Morgan, "The Puritan Ethic and the American Revolution," *William and Mary Quarterly*, 3d ser. 24 (1967):3–43; T. H. Breen, "'Baubles of Britain': The American and Consumer Revolutions of the Eighteenth Century," in this volume. Ann Morgan Smart, "The Urban/Rural Dichotomy of Status Consumption: Tidewater Virginia, 1815," M.A. thesis, College of William and Mary, 1986, shows that urban-rural differences became more pronounced with the passage of time.

commercial connections with a hinterland to be a main source of influence. English merchants took their wares directly to scattered country landings, where they purchased the tobacco that paid for the goods. Urban shopkeepers, furthermore, demanded payment in cash, a condition that resident officials, bureaucrats, and laborers whose wages were paid in coin could easily meet, but one that discouraged large-scale purchases by visiting planters, who were accustomed to buying imports with commodities.[17]

If urban consumption habits had any influence in the immediate countryside, this was most likely reflected in the quality and style of their furnishings rather than in the amount and kinds of rural domestic equipment. Inventories suggest this possibility, although too few exist in sufficient detail to prove the point conclusively. For example, where appraisers bothered to list the material from which furniture was made, walnut and mahogany appear the woods of choice among York County consumers.[18] These woods were particularly suited to the kinds of elaborate shaping and carving that were increasingly in high fashion after the 1730s. Since many York County tobacco growers dealt especially on the London consignment market, they were in an excellent position to obtain currently fashionable English imports like those fancied in Williamsburg and Yorktown. Alternatively, they may have turned as well to local craftsmen, for these same woods also were favored by Williamsburg cabinetmakers. Surviving examples of the chairs, tables, and case furniture these artisans turned out are all of high-style urban English design and construction.[19]

[17]Edward C. Papenfuse, *In Pursuit of Profit: The Annapolis Merchants in the Era of the American Revolution, 1763–1805* (Baltimore, 1975), chap. 1.

[18]A few appraisers described the material of which all major furnishings were made; many more gave no descriptions at all. Others listed only the material of the most valuable pieces. While one cannot determine the composition of most furniture from inventory descriptions, one can get an idea of what sorts of materials were considered most desirable in a given area (see Michel, "'In a Manner and Fashion'").

[19]Wallace B. Gusler, *Furniture of Williamsburg and Eastern Virginia, 1710–1790* (Richmond, 1979).

In contrast, mahogany furniture rarely appears in inventories in backwater Somerset County, where there were no style-setting towns and where most planters sold their low-grade tobacco directly to country merchants, who dealt with the English outports. There, too, consumers bought some choice pieces fashioned from walnut—probably reflecting a combination of imports and locally made pieces—but, unlike York County residents, Somerset families largely equipped their homes with pine furniture, most of which surely was locally made. Surviving pieces known to have been made on the Eastern Shore are almost all fashioned from pine, are more simply and economically constructed than the Williamsburg pieces, and reflect provincial English design.[20]

York County planters, then, may indeed have responded to influences from Williamsburg. Further study of the limited descriptions of household furnishings found in inventories, combined with surveys of surviving examples of period furniture, may well confirm that in some subregions, colonial Chesapeake planters were making efforts to emulate town dwellers, using very subtle trade-offs between quantity, quality (value), and style that our preliminary explorations have missed. The analysis so far has concentrated on the most readily measurable indicators: number of objects reported in inventories and proportions of movable personal wealth allocated to various categories of consumer durables. At this level, differences between rural and urban consumer behavior continue to stand out.

What caused the escalation in living standards, which, regardless of urban-rural differences, appeared everywhere in the Tidewater? Of primary importance were changes taking place in England, changes both in social behavior and in the English economy. Neil McKendrick and others have described the explosion of fashion and luxury spending by the English upper classes and the imitations becoming evident

[20]Ibid.; James R. Melchor, N. Gordon Lohr, and Marilyn S. Melchor, *Eastern Shore, Virginia, Raised Panel Furniture, 1730–1830* (Norfolk, Va., 1982). Gregory R. Weidman, *Furniture in Maryland, 1740–1940: The Collection of the Maryland Historical Society* (Baltimore, 1984), discusses the origins and construction of surviving Maryland pieces.

among lower groups as the eighteenth century progressed.[21]
The Chesapeake gentry had a model to which they could aspire, and they, in turn, could provide models for middling
planters. If one regards England as the metropolis, then metropolitan standards were influencing Chesapeake inhabitants
and, indeed, all inhabitants of the English world.

Equally important, new methods of English manufacture
and improved transportation networks that helped create
marketing efficiencies were making a variety of goods more
plentiful and often cheaper than before.[22] In consequence, a
variety of products came within reach of far more people than
they had earlier. One of the most striking examples was the
increase in the available quantities of good ceramics, the result of technological advances in English potteries near midcentury. Earthenware cost much less per piece than did
pewter, although the fact that pewter could be recycled made
it less expensive in the long run. The result was a rapid rise
in the proportion of Chesapeake inventories containing
crockery, including upscale items like delft bowls, creamware
dishes, and tea sets.[23]

In the Chesapeake the availability of such goods was related

[21] See especially McKendrick, Brewer, and Plumb, *Birth of a Consumer Society.*

[22] Deane and Cole, *British Economic Growth,* pp. 50–63; Wilson, *England's
Apprenticeship,* chap. 14; B. A. Holderness, *Pre-Industrial England: Economy
and Society, 1500–1750* (London, 1976); Lorna Weatherill, *The Pottery Trade
and North Staffordshire, 1660–1760* (Manchester, 1971); idem, "The Business
of Middleman in the English Pottery Trade before 1780," *Business History*
28 (July 1986):51–76; idem, *Consumer Behaviour and Material Culture,* chaps.
2, 5; Clay, *Economic Expansion and Social Change,* 2:28–43.

[23] Lorna Weatherill shows that ceramic tableware was much less expensive than pewter (*Consumer Behaviour and Material Culture,* p. 110). However,
not all ceramic goods were becoming cheaper. Neil McKendrick has shown
that after midcentury Josiah Wedgwood raised rather than lowered his
prices to give snob appeal to his wares, and Weatherill points out that china
merchants of an earlier period had also taken this tack (see McKendrick,
"Josiah Wedgwood" and "Josiah Wedgwood and the Commercialization of
the Potteries," in McKendrick, Brewer, and Plumb, *Birth of a Consumer Society,* pp. 100–108; Weatherill, "The Business of Middleman," pp. 61–63). It
has not been possible to make a price series from Chesapeake inventories.
Price series for any manufactured goods are hard to construct because of

not only to better supplies from England but also to local marketing opportunities. In the seventeenth century low population densities had discouraged permanent stores. The number of families living within three to five miles of any location—an hour's walk or horseback ride—was too few to support a store year-round. Merchants sent enough goods to purchase a shipload of tobacco, and when the goods were all sold, people had to wait until the next crop brought more ships. Planters stocked up at once to ensure sufficient supplies and concentrated on those goods their families were sure to need. In consequence, English merchants and their factors did not venture many nonessentials and imported only those items that they were certain of selling, offering planters a limited range of "coarse goods such as are usefull for the Country. . . . nails, hoes, axes, kersey, Cotton & other coarse goods." [24] Only large growers who sent their tobacco to England on consignment and ordered manufactures through metropolitan factors could count on procuring nonessentials, and even they had to wait nearly a year for their orders to arrive. But as neighborhoods became more densely populated, more families lived within easy distance of a merchant. The merchant could more readily afford to keep a year-round store and stock it with a greater variety of goods. Planters could buy goods as needed and could risk spending a shilling or two on teacups without having to fear a future shortage of stockings. Merchants, in turn, could afford to stock the teacups along with the cloth, haberdashery, nails, tools, salt, sugar, and rum that continued to dominate the store inventories. [25]

Other kinds of changes also contributed to making amenities more available. Advances in methods of packing and as-

---

the difficulty of finding items of uniform quality or size to follow. Our prices for manufactures are confined to pewter, which was inventoried by the pound, and a very coarse cloth called osnaburg. For further discussion see n. 40, below.

[24] Davis, ed., *William Fitzhugh*, pp. 143, 339.

[25] Lois Green Carr, " 'The Metropolis of Maryland': A Comment on Town Development along the Tobacco Coast," *Maryland Historical Magazine*" 69 (1974):142–43.

sembling cargoes of tobacco greatly reduced turn-around time for ships in the region, and merchants began to send goods more frequently. By the 1760s there were not just one, but two major annual shipments. Spring and summer goods arrived in February or March, and a second shipment, of fall and winter goods, came in late summer or early fall. Thus waiting time for orders was cut in half.[26]

All these changes produced new methods of merchandizing. In the rough-and-ready trade of the seventeenth and early eighteenth centuries, merchants had no need to display their wares in order to entice customers to buy. The most transient factors dispensed with store buildings altogether, exposing their goods to view and concluding bargains on the decks of their vessels. Others located some structure available for rent, unloaded their merchandise, and "kept store" until the goods ran out or stocks were so depleted that the residue had to be passed on to smaller traders living in more remote areas. A few of the largest resident merchants put up buildings especially intended for storing and retailing goods, and some of these were equipped with niceties such as a counter and a few shelves. But even so, most of the merchandise was kept out of sight, stored in boxes, chests, and trunks, tucked away in lofts, or locked up in other, smaller outbuildings. Often only bulky goods were kept in the "store," while for greater security the merchant kept more valuable items—such as fine cloth or sugar, which could be readily pilfered or damaged by moths or rats—in the principal rooms of his dwelling. Entertainments were of a kind appropriate to the circumstances; expenses similar to an entry of £12 in a factor's account of 1716 for "Rumm Sugar and Lime Juyce Expended in Treating Customers as is usual" appeared in many merchants' records.[27]

By the 1730s the number of stores began to grow rapidly

[26]James F. Shepherd and Gary M. Walton, *Shipping, Maritime Trade, and the Economic Development of Colonial North America* (Cambridge, 1972), chap. 5.

[27]Provincial Court Judgments VD 2:106–13, Md. State Arch. For an account of the operations of a merchant of this period, see Jacob M. Price, "*Sheffield* v. *Starke:* Institutional Experimentation in the London-Maryland Trade, c. 1696–1706," *Business History* 28 (July 1986):19–39.

and more of them stocked goods year-round. Changes in the tobacco trade encouraged the proliferation of stores. First outport and then Scottish merchants began to purchase ever larger amounts of ordinary grades of tobacco directly from planters through chains of rural stores. By the early 1740s competition became intense in older areas. The experience of Virginia merchant Francis Jerdone was repeated throughout the Tidewater. In 1743 Jerdone noted that "there are 25 stores within 18 miles round [in lower Hanover County, Virginia] which is 13 more than at Mr. Johnson's death [in 1740] and 4 or 5 more expected next year from some of the outports."[28]

This competition benefited colonial consumers. It kept the prices of goods low in the colonies, forcing British merchants to buy manufactures more efficiently at home or to accept lower profit margins.[29] Competitors also were finding Chesapeake customers insisting that merchants maintain a reasonable stock of basic items. By the middle of the century resident factors increasingly and more urgently reminded their British principals of the necessity of keeping a "well sorted" store inventory in order to retain customers. Others tried to compete by assembling separate cargoes for each store. This gave "a better Gloss in the Eye of the Planter who is always apt to

[28]Francis Jerdone to Neil Buchanan, Aug. 4, 1743, Francis Jerdone Account and Letterbooks, 1736–37, 1738–44, College of William and Mary, Williamsburg. Also see Jerdone to Buchanan, May 7, 1739: "This river at present is so crowded with stores that its very difficult to make a purchase, and every year grows worse & worse," Jerdone to Messrs. Buchanan and Wilson, Sept. 8, 1740, ibid., and Henry Callister to Foster Cunliffe, Jan. 10, 1743, Callister Papers, Maryland Diocesan Library, Maryland Historical Society, Baltimore.

[29]Callister to Cunliffe, Aug. 6, 1747, Callister Papers. For studies of the eighteenth-century Chesapeake merchants, see Calvin Brewster Coulter, Jr., "The Virginia Merchant," Ph.D. diss., Princeton University, 1944; Robert Polk Thompson, "The Merchant in Virginia, 1700–1775," Ph.D. diss., University of Wisconsin, 1955; John W. Tyler, "Foster Cunliffe and Sons: Liverpool Merchants in the Maryland Tobacco Trade, 1738–1765," *Maryland Historical Magazine* 73 (1978):246–79; Jacob M. Price, "The Rise of Glasgow in the Chesapeake Tobacco Trade, 1707–1775," *William and Mary Quarterly*, 3d ser. 11 (1954):179–99; idem, "The Economic Growth of the Chesapeake and the European Market, 1697–1775," *Journal of Economic*

imagine that one store made out of another must be made up of Remnants or refused Goods."[30]

By the 1740s, Chesapeake merchants had to cope not only with competition but also with better-informed colonial consumers. More and more sons of the local gentry returned to Britain to get an education, one that included knowledge of current metropolitan fashions and prices. Doubtless some of this news was passed on to provincial friends and neighbors. The proliferation of country merchants supplied another channel for information about products and prices. In 1749 one factor informed a prospective English trader that "the [large] Planters here are all Merchants & most of the Croppers [smaller growers who produced enough tobacco to make up one or more full hogsheads and who sometimes marketed their crops on consignment] know the Cost of Goods as well as the English Country Merchant so that to buy up at a bad hand would certainly come to a bad acco[un]t."[31] If by midcentury the range of goods that ordinary planters wanted still remained somewhat limited, they had nonetheless learned to a degree of painful accuracy what these items ought to sell for.

Although demand for cheap, durable goods remained strong, concerns about price and practicality were increasingly coupled with the planters' insistence that what they bought be both new and fashionable. Factors reported that secondhand goods were virtually unsalable, and even ready-made items, aside from stockings, shoes, hats, and the like, were "slighted."[32] Consequently storekeepers found it increasingly advantageous to appeal to the consumers' eyes as well as to their pocketbooks. Francis Jerdone observed in

---

History 24 (1964):496–511; idem, Introduction to *Joshua Johnson's Letterbook, 1771–1774: Letters from a Merchant in London to His Partners in Maryland* (London, 1979); Paul G. E. Clemens, "The Rise of Liverpool, 1665–1750," *Economic History Review*, 2d ser. 29 (1976):211–25; James H. Soltow, *The Economic Role of Williamsburg* (Williamsburg, 1965); and Shepherd and Walton, *Shipping, Trade, and Development.*

[30]Callister to Cunliffe, Oct. 2, 1750, Callister Papers.

[31]Henry Callister to Evan Callister, Nov. 12, 1749, ibid.

[32]Henry Callister to Charles Craven, Aug. 21, 1746, ibid.

1742 that "the planters are so very *humorous,* they will not sell their Tobacco but where they see everything before them."[33] Similarly, in 1749, a Maryland factor, Henry Callister, spoke of cargoes "suited to the situation of the Store and *Fancy* of the Customers."[34] Merchants were discovering that attractive display of goods was another way to lure prospective customers. In 1748 Callister secured a new house that would display his goods to better advantage and aggressively courted patrons. "You know the influence of the Wives upon their Husbands, & it is but a trifle that wins 'em over, they must be taken notice of or there will be nothing done with them."[35] A few years later some merchants were building substantial brick store buildings equipped with more elaborate shelves and counters for display, and chairs, tables, glassware, and teaware for the genteel entertainment of customers.[36]

An attractive display of wares was not the only bait required, for the supply of imported dry goods periodically outstripped local demand. Cash payments for crops and extension of credit also were necessary lures. To secure "tip top Crops," merchants had to pay cash in full for the weed. To best a competitor for more ordinary tobacco, they often had to pay small growers more percentage in cash, instead of offering only merchandise, and almost always had to extend more credit. As Francis Jerdone explained, "So soon as they pay off their old acc[oun]t they imediatly are in want & run in again and such we look on as good pay its true its a great advance of mon[e]y but theirs no carrying bussiness such as yours otherwise."[37] The majority of planters would more likely than not use much of this windfall to buy slaves or land. Nevertheless, more credit did tempt families to buy some ex-

[33]Jerdone to Buchanan, Mar. 24, 1742, Jerdone Account and Letterbooks. Italics ours.

[34]Henry Callister to Craven, Nov. 12, 1749, Callister Papers. Italics ours.

[35]Henry Callister to Robert Morris, [June] 1747, ibid.

[36]Harold B. Gill, unpublished manuscript on eighteenth-century Virginia stores, Colonial Williamsburg Foundation, Williamsburg. See also T. H. Breen, "An Empire of Goods: The Anglicization of Colonial America, 1690–1776," *Journal of British Studies* 25 (1986):467–99.

[37]Jerdone to Buchanan, Oct. 4, 1739, Jerdone Account and Letterbooks.

tra goods from the storekeepers to whom they sold their tobacco in barter, while cash payments allowed them to buy from more than one store.[38]

Thus marketing strategies had effects on consumer wants. To bring in customers, storekeepers stocked a greater and greater variety of goods, and the proliferation of stores helped to keep prices competitive. As a result, these goods began to reach people at lower and lower levels of wealth. Amenities thought little of in 1700 were widespread by 1775, and merchandising in the modern sense had helped to bring this about.

Underlying these purchases of goods, of course, was the ability to buy, and this depended on the structure of wealth. Had Chesapeake society consisted only of two sorts of persons—very rich people with the remainder very poor—demand for goods would have been insufficient to induce merchants to import the amenities that were changing lifestyles. However, the spread of wealth as revealed by inventories does not show great gaps between the rich and those less well off. Furthermore, the middle wealth groups—those that ranged from £50 to £225—were a sizable portion of the inventoried population, ranging from about 30 to 45 percent. While the proportion of this group in the living population was undoubtedly smaller, these planters, in combination with those who were rich, had enough spare income for nonessentials to provide merchants with an attractive market. And once such goods became widespread, many of the poor began to acquire them, even if only in token amounts.[39]

[38] Marc Egnal, "The Economic Development of the Thirteen Continental Colonies, 1720–1775," *William and Mary Quarterly*, 3d ser. 32 (1975):216; Marc Egnal and Joseph A. Ernst, "An Economic Interpretation of the American Revolution," *William and Mary Quarterly* 29 (1972):25–27; Jacob M. Price, *Capital and Credit in British Overseas Trade: The View from the Chesapeake, 1700–1776* (Cambridge, Mass., 1980); Samuel M. Rosenblatt, "The Significance of Credit in the Tobacco Consignment Trade: A Study of John Norton & Sons, 1768–1775," *William and Mary Quarterly*, 3d ser. 19 (1962):383–99; Coulter, "Virginia Merchant"; Thompson, "Merchant in Virginia."

[39] For wealth groups, see n. 13, above. Neil McKendrick discusses the effect on consumption in England of the "closely packed social structure" (McKendrick, Brewer, and Plumb, *Birth of a Consumer Society*, pp. 19–20).

The terms of trade also may have had an impact on planters' purchases of comforts or luxuries. When tobacco prices
were high in relation to prices of imports, planters had more
expendable income. However, they may have invested in
slaves or made other outlays in capital at such times. Unfortunately we have not been able to devise a method of testing
these propositions. There is no way to tell when planters purchased the goods their inventories list and thus compare the
movements of prices with the patterns of acquisition. Nevertheless, it seems reasonable to suppose that more expendable
income did lead to at least some spending for consumer
goods. Figure 12 suggests that the effects, if any, should have
been particularly important in the Maryland counties after
1749 and continuous in York from the time that increases in
the appearance of amenities began.[40] Figures 2 through 7,
which show amenities scores by wealth, suggest that the poor
may have benefited especially, although less in Virginia than
in Maryland.

Of more certain importance to the rising standard of amenities was the fact that planters could change their consumption habits without much alteration in their spending
patterns. Shifts in consumer behavior were not necessarily accompanied by greatly increased expenditures for consumer
goods, or at least for goods durable enough to appear as a
stock in an inventory. Our best proxy for the value of all inventoried consumer durables is the residual obtained by sub-
tracting from the total estate value the value of all capital
goods, which we defined as goods used for the production of
income. Among the rich, as seen in figures 2 and 3, the value
of consumer durables had begun to level out or decline everywhere by 1720; yet, except in rural York County, amenities

[40] In Carr and Walsh, "Inventories and Wealth," p. 93 and fig. 5, we show
that unexchanged prices for imported manufactures as seen in pewter and
cloth prices taken from inventories rose until the late 1740s and then began
to fall until the American Revolution. However, our data show that *sterling*
prices for the same goods fell until about 1749 in Maryland and until 1760
in Virginia and then rose until 1776. These differences do not affect the
terms of trade, which remain as shown in fig. 12. It is the terms of trade,
what planters could buy for their tobacco, whether figured in sterling or
local currency, that matters to the argument.

Figure 12. Terms of trade, by three- and four-year groups, three areas, 1658-1777

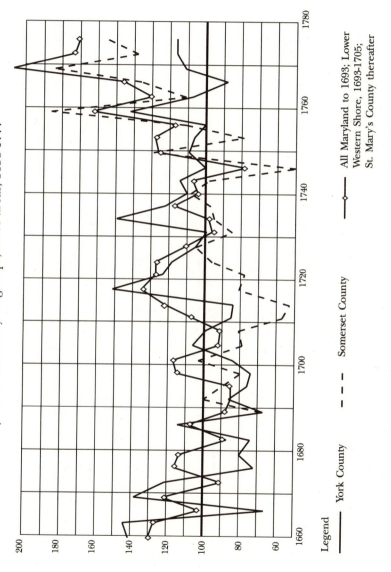

Legend

——— York County

– – – Somerset County

——— All Maryland to 1693; Lower
Western Shore, 1693-1705;
St. Mary's County thereafter

SOURCE: St. Mary's City Commission price files, Maryland State Archives, Annapolis.

NOTE: Terms of trade are calculated by dividing a tobacco price index by an imports price index and multiplying by 100.
Above a score of 100, terms are favorable.

scores continued to rise. These advances, furthermore, are to some degree minimized by the scoring device, since no allowance is made for the introduction of new kinds of luxuries, such as riding chairs or carriages.[41] A decade later a similar pattern had started among the bottom and middle groups (see figs. 4 through 7). Into the 1770s rural people at these levels in all four counties steadily raised their standard of consumption, in most cases substantially. Yet their inventories show level, decreasing, or only slightly rising value in stocks of consumer goods. Poor and middling planter families were all the more readily drawn into nonessential expenditures precisely because they could do so without spending more on consumer assets.

The finding that standards of consumption rose is affected, in part at least, by the scoring method, which measures only entry into acquisition of consumption items, not the amount or quality of the goods. One tin fork in an inventory counts as much as several cases of silver forks. This very aspect of our method has an advantage, however. It highlights the fact that families did not have to make significant changes in the way they allocated basic resources to adopt new ways of enjoying life. A poor planter might pay 4d. for a knife and fork, a shilling for a Bible, or 9d. for a delft mug, all indicators of changes in behavior or taste, without noticeably increasing the overall value of the family's consumer durables.

Even if Chesapeake planters were not escalating total expenditures on consumer goods, were they in fact increasing the proportion of total wealth they put into beds or teacups? If so, were they reducing their accumulation of capital goods and possibly their capacity to produce? Table 7 indicates not. Over the seventeenth and early eighteenth centuries, consumer goods as a proportion of inventoried wealth rose some-

[41] In order to see whether this was a major problem, we also tried out a twenty-four-item index that added to the original index twelve eighteenth-century luxuries including carriages, gaming tables, and specialized serving dishes. For rural areas the shape and even the level of this expanded index was quite similar to that of the original index because such goods did not appear often enough to have much effect on mean scores. For town dwellers, however, the expanded index did show greater advances among wealthier decedents.

Table 7. Mean value of consumer durables as percent of mean total estate value, four counties, 1658–1777

	Anne Arundel		St. Mary's	Somerset	York	
	All	Rural			All	Rural
	%	%	%	%	%	%
1658–64	8.7	8.7	24.8		28.7	28.7
1665–77	23.7	23.7	24.5	23.9	28.7	28.7
1678–87	26.2	26.2	23.4	22.8	29.0	29.0
1688–99	25.2	24.9	25.4	24.7	34.7	34.7
1700–1709	27.1	25.3	26.1	25.6	31.1	31.9
1710–22	27.5	25.8	26.9	30.8	29.6	28.8
1723–32	26.0	22.8	27.3	31.7	32.2	26.4
1733–44	22.9	19.5	29.6	29.8	30.0	25.3
1745–54	20.4	18.7	26.5	28.1	29.4	25.2
1755–67	22.0	19.2	25.3	24.9	27.5	19.2
1768–77	19.0	16.2	23.1	23.9	30.1	27.2

SOURCE: Maryland History Computer Files, Historic St. Mary's City Commission, Maryland State Archives, Annapolis.

NOTE: Mean percentages are higher in York County than elsewhere, not necessarily because these Virginians were more willing to invest in consumer goods, but because information about debts (part of an inventoried estate) in York inventories is much less complete than in those of Maryland.

On ways in which table 7 differs from table IV in Lois Green Carr and Lorena S. Walsh, "The Standard of Living in the Colonial Chesapeake," *William and Mary Quarterly,* 3d ser. 45 (1988):150, see n. 42.

what, a not surprising result in a society where most people started with very little property of any kind; but the rate of increase in the mean percentage was slight, and between the 1690s and 1740s, depending upon the county, increase turned into decline. Planters did not sacrifice investment in productive goods as they joined in the pursuit of comfort, fashion, and genteel display.[42]

[42]Table 7 differs from table 4 in Lois Green Carr and Lorena S. Walsh, "The Standard of Living in the Colonial Chesapeake," *William and Mary Quarterly,* 3d ser. 45 (1988):150, in that it computes stocks of consumer goods as a percentage of total inventoried wealth inventory by inventory and shows the mean percentage for each area and time period. The earlier table shows the mean value of all consumer goods as a percentage of all total estate value for each region. It shows region-wide change in this per-

In some degree, the finding that Chesapeake inhabitants acquired amenities and luxuries without escalating expenditures may be a result of the insensitivity of our measure—appearance in inventories—to the costs of replacing goods. For example, ceramics generally were cheaper than metals. As ceramic tableware became available, planters could outfit their dining rooms with crockery instead of pewter and at a lower cost, unless they were indulging in expensive porcelain. But crockery breaks and cannot be recycled. Pewter is more durable and can be melted down and refashioned. Over a lifetime one planter might spend more on tableware by using crockery than would another who used pewter for an equal number of similar utensils; but at the moment an inventory was taken, the planter with crockery would show less value in his tableware than would the planter with pewter. Other kinds of substitutions—say, comfortable for more durable clothing—may have had similar effects. Of course, some influences may have worked in the other direction. If products, such as shoes, came to be better made they may have lasted longer, thereby lowering cumulative replacement costs.[43]

Although inventories cannot tell us about lifetime expenditures for consumer durables or, indeed, durables of any kind, these listings do reflect accumulation over many years of acquisition. If we could measure all expenditures on durable goods for each decedent, perhaps the mean value over time of consumer goods would show an increase. But on the basis of the evidence we have, it seems unlikely that the increase would match that shown for appearance of amenities or would much affect consumer goods as a percentage of total wealth. Eighteenth-century Chesapeake inhabitants changed

centage and makes clear that in every region by 1720 consumer goods as a proportion of total inventoried wealth began to fall. The present table takes into account differences in the behavior of planters in various wealth groups. Poor planters necessarily had a larger proportion of their wealth in consumer goods than did the rich and increased this proportion over a longer period.

[43]On ceramic vs. pewter tableware, see Weatherill, *Consumer Behaviour and Material Culture*, p. 110. Carole Shammas has a good discussion of the effects of substitution in *Pre-Industrial Consumer*, chap. 4.

social habits without changing the priorities their predecessors had set for investment in producer goods.

Continuity in rural patterns of consumption expenditure is increasingly apparent when consumer durables are broken down by basic household functions such as sleeping, cooking, dining, seating, and storage. From the early eighteenth century, when the value of consumer durables in the estates of middling planters leveled out, the proportion of value in various categories of their domestic equipment also achieved stability. By midcentury, the poor, who took longer to reach stable levels of overall value, were allocating their resources much as middling groups did. Only among the rural elite did a growing taste for coaches, expensive timepieces, decorative objects, and sets of fine china bring about some shifts in spending priorities for consumer items. For the majority of the population nothing replaced the good feather bed as the most desirable of all household equipment. Improvements in the sleeping arrangements of the master and mistress and later of other family members continued to absorb about a third of noncapital wealth. Utensils for cooking food and eating it remained second in importance, although across time more was spent on dining ware than on cooking equipment! Most rural families were able to fulfill basic needs, fill them more comfortably, and still acquire some nonessentials without greatly changing spending patterns inherited from a time when artifacts mattered much less.[44]

Availability of new kinds of goods, including many that were inexpensive, new marketing strategies, and perhaps fluctuating improvements in the terms of trade combined to help Chesapeake inhabitants keep abreast of the changes in lifestyle occurring in England without forcing shifts in allocation of basic resources; but economic, demographic, and cultural changes more internal to Chesapeake society also had effects. In Appendix B we discuss a set of regressions that uses such evidence for these changes as is measurable to help explain

[44]See Walsh, "Urban Amenities and Rural Sufficiency," pp. 112–13 and table 1.

consumer behavior. Here we will avoid technical discussion but set out the conclusions these regressions permit.

Overall wealth, of course, was far and away the most important determinant of where a planter would rank on the consumption scale; hence increasing mean wealth undoubtedly helped produce a rise in mean consumption scores. The timing of increases varied from area to area (see fig. 13), but the contributions of mean wealth to improving scores were certainly prevalent over most of the eighteenth century.[45] True, during periods of rising wealth, the value of consumer durables often did not keep up; planters were investing more in slaves and other capital assets—or in ephemerals—than in household furnishings. Nevertheless, as people grew richer they chose new styles of living that required new kinds of products.

In York and Anne Arundel counties—the counties with towns—another important element that explains consumer behavior was urban or rural location, but this observation contributes little to explanations of change. Already we have seen both that town dwellers at all wealth levels outdistanced their country neighbors and that urban behavior did not visibly influence rural areas. Rising consumption scores in the countryside probably owe little to the growth of towns.

Shifts in the structure of the Chesapeake economy had more influence. Economic activity, concentrated at first in the tobacco industry, eventually diversified. To measure diversification we developed an index that uses a variety of tools and crops as indicators.[46] When put in the regressions on consumption scores, diversification showed significant impact, and the parts of the index that measured craft activity and home industry also had large effects.

Movement toward diversification began late in the seven-

[45] Differences from county to county in levels of mean wealth are affected by the inventory reporting rate and do not necessarily indicate differences in prosperity. See Appendix A, below.

[46] This index is described in Carr, "Diversification in the Colonial Chesapeake," p. 388.

Figure 13. Mean total estate value (pounds, constant value) four counties, 1636-1777

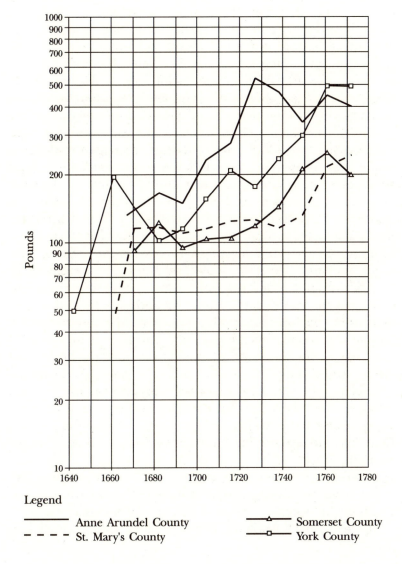

Legend

——————— Anne Arundel County   —△— Somerset County

– – – – St. Mary's County   —□— York County

NOTE: For information about construction of the figure and about sources, see note to fig. 1.

teenth century (see fig. 14).[47] Until then Chesapeake planters concentrated on raising corn and livestock for food and tobacco for export. It was most cost-effective to import all manufactures and pay for them with tobacco. The only craftsmen this economy encouraged were carpenters and coopers, who made housing for people and crops and hogsheads for shipping tobacco. But toward 1700 several changes began to multiply the ways men and women made their living and provided themselves with food, clothing, tools, and other needs. First, the 1680s and 1690s saw exceptionally low tobacco prices for long periods. In these circumstances planters got less for their tobacco than before. In addition, European wars disrupted trade. Of necessity families began to develop home industries—spinning and weaving cloth and making shoes. Second, as more and more families completed the basic requirements of farm building—clearing land, constructing houses and fences, planting orchards—they had time not formerly available for other activities, many of which encouraged local craftsmen. Men began to remove stumps from their fields, making it possible to plow and thus more easily plant wheat, rye, and other English grains. These new crops encouraged the use of carts, and carts and plows together created the need for blacksmiths, wheelwrights, and additional carpenters to make such equipment and keep it functioning. Similarly, women took more time to turn milk into butter and cheese and to help make fruit into cider and perry, thereby producing a demand for casks and tubs and further encouraging woodworkers. In addition, more women were available for spinning and dairying and processing fruit as the population became predominantly native-born and sex ratios evened out.

Diversification began first among the wealthy, who had more labor to divert to new activities, but by 1700 it had reached the poorest groups. Thereafter it increased steadily at all wealth levels until at least midcentury. Index scores then

[47]For the next four paragraphs, see ibid., pp. 342–88, and Jean B. Russo, "Self-Sufficiency and Local Exchange: Free Craftsmen in the Rural Chesapeake Economy," in Carr, Morgan, and Russo, eds., *Colonial Chesapeake Society*, pp. 389–432.

Figure 14. Total diversificatión scores, four counties, 1658-1777, all estates

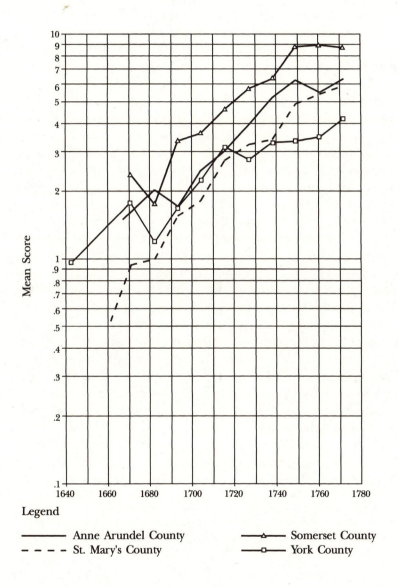

Legend

—————— Anne Arundel County   ——△—— Somerset County
– – – – St. Mary's County   ——□—— York County

NOTE: For composition of the diversification index, see reference in n. 46. For information about construction of the figure and about sources, see note to fig. 1.

leveled out in Somerset and Anne Arundel counties but continued to rise in the others.

This growing diversification did not mean that plantations were simply more self-sufficient; rather it meant more local exchange. Planters sold surpluses of grain, meat, butter, and cider in a local market—although by the mid-eighteenth century they were also exporting grains—and cloth making necessarily entailed local exchange. The number of spinning wheels rose phenomenally, but looms were far less prevalent. Spinners took their product to weavers and accepted payment in cloth, produce, tobacco, or cash. Shoemakers, tanners, blacksmiths, and other craftsmen all served local neighborhoods. Local networks of exchange were achieving more and more importance in the developing Chesapeake economy.

The results for consumption were twofold. First, diversification, generally, provided a hedge against the vagaries of the tobacco market and thus encouraged a more stable local economy. In turn, greater economic stability surely encouraged planters to spend income on more than necessities, however necessities were defined at various economic levels. Second, crafts and home industries could supply some of the necessities that formerly had been imported, such as shoes or clothing, thereby freeing income for purchase of nonessentials. Finally, these activities produced both homemade amenities, such as linens, and extra income from salable surpluses. Such income could supplement returns from field crops to make possible the purchase of extras.[48]

What is particularly interesting about the contribution of home industries is that it was largely the work of women.[49] Women worked the dairy, helped make the cider, spun all the

[48]Joan Thirsk has shown how in sixteenth- and early seventeenth-century England, small additions to disposable income from a variety of economic activities could make a big difference (*Economic Policy and Projects*, esp. chap. 7).

[49]On these points, see Lois Green Carr and Lorena S. Walsh, "Economic Diversification and Labor Organization in the Chesapeake, 1650–1820," in Stephen Innes, ed., *Work and Labor in Early America* (Chapel Hill, N.C., 1988), pp. 172–75.

yarn, and wove some of the cloth. Cloth-related home industry in itself contributed substantially to consumption scores.
Had women not put more time and labor into carding, hack-
ling, spinning, and weaving, the standard of consumption
would have been measurably lower. This must have been especially true for households in the lower two wealth groups,
where income from home industries must have been a larger
proportion of total income than in households of the rich.
Somerset County provides an excellent illustration. There the
investment of women's labor in cloth production was especially high, and, as we have seen, table 3 shows that in these
wealth groups many more households had linens than did
their equivalents in other counties.[50]

Another positive effect on consumption as seen in the regressions was the size of a planter's bound labor force. On
scores the effect appeared only in St. Mary's County regressions run separately for the seventeenth century, but why it
turned up at all is a puzzle. Since families with many servants
or slaves also were very rich, the relationship of labor force
to increasing amenities is probably actually related to wealth.
More predictable was the effect, everywhere apparent, on the
value of consumer durables. The more servants and slaves
there were on a plantation, the more household equipment
was necessary for their support.

Demographic changes also account for some of the changes
in consumer behavior. We have alluded already to the effects
of population growth on the development of year-round
stores and how the presence of more women affected home
production and improved the standard of consumption.
Changes in family structure also had effects, although the regression models indicate these were usually small. We divided
inventoried men and women into four life-cycle groups: those
who were single, those whose children were minors, those
who had some adult children, and those whose children were
all adults (see table 8). Men who were married or who had
survived their wives had more in household goods than did

[50]On the Somerset cloth industry, see Carr, "Diversification in the Colonial Chesapeake," pp. 355, 375–76, 380–81.

Table 8. Proportions of decedents by life cycle for four counties

Years	N	(1) Unmarried	(2) Married minor children only	(3) Married minor and adult children	(4) Married all adult children	(5) Some adult children	(6) Unknown
Anne Arundel County							
1658–64	8	38%	62%	0%	0%	0%	0%
1665–77	103	26	51	7	16	23	0
1678–87	100	23	53	10	14	25	0
1688–99	161	26	50	11	13	24	0
1700–1709	176	24	47	11	18	29	0
1710–22	239	22	47	13	18	31	.4
1723–32	148	20	39	12	28	40	0
1733–44	266	17	34	18	32	50	0
1745–54	198	18	27	27	29	56	0
1755–67	304	21	28	23	29	52	.3
1768–77	211	17	26	21	36	57	0
St. Mary's County							
1658–64	35	34	40	17	0	20	6
1665–77	183	31	57	6	3	10	2
1678–87	143	30	46	6	4	10	13
1688–99	179	19	42	7	6	15	25
1700–1709	160	15	29	17	9	31	26
1710–22	359	18	28	12	14	31	24
1723–32	241	16	38	17	8	29	17
1733–44	361	15	45	22	8	33	8
1745–54	301	18	37	23	11	37	7
1755–67	367	14	31	22	16	41	14
1768–77	255	10	30	19	10	35	25

Somerset County

1665–77	18	17	6	72	0	6	6
1678–87	48	25	19	40	8	33	2
1688–99	139	13	14	44	12	31	12
1700–1709	208	26	13	33	7	26	15
1710–22	386	20	21	26	12	41	12
1723–32	237	12	21	39	14	42	7
1733–44	329	18	24	39	11	39	5
1745–54	195	10	26	43	13	44	3
1755–67	261	8	31	34	13	54	4
1768–77	261	17	22	25	15	49	9

York County

1655–64	19	32	5	47	10	16	5
1665–77	38	10	8	68	3	13	8
1678–87	51	10	10	43	2	18	29
1688–99	60	5	10	38	8	27	30
1700–1709	71	11	13	46	10	30	13
1710–22	164	16	15	46	9	27	10
1723–32	99	13	16	44	7	25	17
1733–44	149	20	18	47	6	27	7
1745–54	139	21	18	34	12	32	13
1755–67	150	17	12	47	12	27	9
1768–77	117	21	11	40	23	36	3

SOURCE: Maryland History Computer Files, Historic St. Mary's City Commission, Maryland State Archives, Annapolis.
NOTE: Percentages across rows do not add up to 100 because column 5 contains all decedents in columns 3 and 4 plus some additional decedents for whom we know only that they had at least one adult child.

bachelors, a result one would expect.[51] Without a wife, a man would need less in household furnishings than his married counterparts, and if he were an inmate of the household of another, he would own few consumer goods beyond his clothing. In consequence, a decline in the proportion of inventoried bachelors would contribute to a rise in the value of consumer durables.

In the overall population of the Chesapeake, such a decline occurred early in the eighteenth century.[52] Sex ratios were even among the native-born but highly skewed toward males among immigrants. In the predominantly immigrant population of the seventeenth century, a large proportion of men had died as bachelors, whereas opportunity to marry improved as sex ratios evened out. Inventoried bachelors became proportionately less numerous in all the counties studied, beginning in the decades before and after 1700, and there is every reason to suppose that the same was true in the general population (see table 8). This change in population structure coincided with the years over which value of consumer durables rose. The increase in the proportion of married men must have had an impact on the standard of consumption.[53]

Once a man was married, would the age of his children affect household consumption habits? Men and women who died without children of age would have had less time to ac-

---

[51]The regression for seventeenth-century St. Mary's County shows that marriage had no significant effect on scored amenities such as appeared elsewhere, but did on value of consumer durables.

[52]On these population changes, see Russell R. Menard, "Immigrants and Their Increase: The Process of Population Growth in Early Colonial Maryland," in Aubrey C. Land, Lois Green Carr, and Edward C. Papenfuse, eds., *Law, Society, and Politics in Early Maryland* (Baltimore, 1977), pp. 88–110.

[53]Table 8 shows that in Somerset and St. Mary's counties the decline in the number of bachelors was initially abrupt and then continued slowly. In Anne Arundel County the change was less strong. Unfortunately, in York County, the large number of unknowns makes the data less reliable and judgment of the timing and strength of the change less easy to assess. The most that can be said is that this demographic shift may have begun earlier in York than elsewhere, a likely reflection of the area's earlier date of settlement.

quire consumer goods than would those who had older children. The regression model indicates, however, that older children did not increase accumulation of consumer durables. Probably children leaving the household to marry took at least part of their future portions with them.

Changes in family age structure affected the value of consumer goods in predictable ways, but behavior as seen in scored amenities is less easy to interpret. One might expect that a man without wife or children would be less likely than others to own linens, season his food, or concern himself with appearances at table, even if he headed a household, and clearly this was true to some degree. Everywhere mean scores for men (or widows) with only minor children were higher than for bachelors (or spinsters). However, in two of the four counties, York and Somerset, the inventoried who had children of age did no better than those who were unmarried. This seems too drastic a result to be explained by practices of giving portions at marriage. The findings for Anne Arundel and St. Mary's are easier to explain. There, mean scores for all ever-married people were higher than for those who were single. Still, men with adult children scored less well than those who had only minor children. Presumably some items, such as pictures or ceramics, went with married children into new households or could not be replaced when worn out because of the drain that providing portions put on family resources.

The failure of scores to rise through stages in the married life-cycle allows an interesting inference. Perhaps couples brought to their marriages already-formed standards of comfort and gentility. Doubtless these standards were created in part by the goods that families of the parents' generation had acquired, but perhaps quite recent changes in standards of consumption were stronger influences. If very early in the marriage couples either inherited or purchased token amounts of the goods that could symbolize these standards, scored amenities would change little with the length of the marriage.[54]

[54]Lorna Weatherill's analysis of expenditures over the life cycle of individuals in early eighteenth-century Britain suggests that spending for fur-

Nevertheless, family structure probably had more effect than is revealed through our index, which is too crude to capture nuances of behavior. Older children, especially older daughters, would provide additional help and create time for social ceremonies, such as drinking tea. Indeed, changing age structures in the slave population also may have had an effect, since women too young or too old for field work could be used to advantage at the house. For example, in 1712 George Gale, one of the richest men who lived in Somerset County during the colonial period, died with a comfortably furnished house but no signs of elegant uses of leisure. By contrast, Isaac Handy, a far less wealthy man, albeit richer than most of his neighbors and a powerful officeholder, died in Somerset in 1761 owning china in a glassfront cupboard, tea tables, and other signs of social ceremony.[55] Betty Gale was a busy woman with little household help and no older children. The slaves that made up the plantation labor force included two women, but both were young and were inventoried as field hands. Madame Gale had no time for the tea ceremony and no equipment for it, although by that time women of her status in England had both. Mrs. Handy, on the other hand, had a daughter of marriageable age who was available to help run the house. In addition, the family slaves included two older women who probably worked at the house at least part time. In this home there was both time for social ceremony and a need to create social opportunities for a marriageable daugh-

---

niture and utensils was high in the first year of a marriage and small and irregular thereafter (*Consumer Behaviour and Material Culture*, chap. 6). By the third quarter of the eighteenth century members of the Chesapeake gentry often upgraded furnishings—at least for the more public spaces of their homes—once, and in some cases more than that, after marriage. Families at lower levels of wealth surely made fewer alterations to their initial stock of household goods. However, by this time even laboring men and women had expanded their ideas of what constituted the minimal equipment necessary to take up housekeeping over the norms of earlier years. See, for example, James P. P. Horn, "The Letters of William Roberts of All Hallows Parish, Anne Arundel County, Maryland, 1756–1769," *Maryland Historical Magazine* 74 (1979):117–32.

[55] Inventories and Accounts 34:131; Inventories 81:303; Wills 31:942, Md. State Arch.

ter. Throughout Chesapeake society, the appearance of older children, or at least daughters, in the household, perhaps combined with a more varied age structure in the slave population, must have provided encouragement for these changes in ways of living.

The shift to a native-born population brought more than change in family structure; the native-born were much more likely than were immigrants to start with an inheritance. Seventeenth-century settlers mostly arrived as indentured servants, unable even to pay for their passage except with hard labor. Once free to establish their own households, they had first to acquire essentials. Their children, on the other hand, probably started with at least some necessities—a cow or a pig, a bed and a pot—by gift or inheritance from parents. One might suppose that starting with a stock of such items enabled the poor to acquire comforts like ceramics or linens and generally increase their consumer goods. Among the richer, inheritance would free resources for more luxurious consumption.

We tested this proposition in Anne Arundel County, the only place where information about immigrant or native-born status was sufficient, with surprising results. The effects of inheritance were slight. True, planters who had arrived as servants did worse in value of consumer durables than did the first generation of native-born. But results were positive and significant for the second generation only when agricultural items and crafts not connected with cloth making were eliminated from the diversification index. Thereafter the effects of inheritance disappeared entirely. Furthermore, generation had no significant effect on scores. This is an especially interesting finding. Evidently planters who started without an inheritance had managed by the time they died to supply themselves with at least token amounts of the linens, ceramics, table forks, or books that others might have inherited or been able to purchase sooner. Once more, there is a suggestion that couples acquired a desire for status items early and procured as quickly as possible at least enough to show that they recognized the standard.

Clearly, cultural as well as economic and demographic changes were at work as lifestyles changed. The only cultural element we could directly introduce into our regression model was literacy, and once more information was sufficient only in Anne Arundel County. There literacy made a positive although slight difference in consumption scores, although not on value of consumer durables. All other things being equal, planters with some education were more likely than others to acquire amenities, and the proportion of the literate rose from the early eighteenth century until the 1730s (see table 9). The effect on rising mean consumption scores was felt especially across that period.

Other cultural changes are not so easily inferred from statistical measurement. The artifacts are easy enough to trace, but almost undocumented is the blending of appointment, ritual, and manner that must have been part of the process. Families not only bought more personal possessions, these increasingly were individualized. People sat on chairs, one to a person, instead of sharing benches; they ate from individual plates instead of common dishes; they drank from individual glasses instead of passing the tankard. These new possessions also needed to be used to best effect. Parents had to school the children in their use to communicate the "liberality of sentiment and genuine hospitality"[56] that became the hallmarks of the Chesapeake gentry and that increasingly established a standard toward which middling planter families also aspired.

Evidence from all sources suggests that the middle decades of the eighteenth century were the time for changes in social rituals and the use of leisure. Articles associated with eating, drinking, and entertaining became extremely attractive to almost all consumers.[57] The proliferation of tea drinking and teaware was especially striking and penetrated into every social group (see tables 1–6).[58] Social rituals, furthermore, were

[56]William Eddis, *Letters from America*, ed. Aubrey C. Land (Cambridge, Mass., 1969), p. 57.

[57]Shammas, "Domestic Environment," pp. 3–24, and Weatherill, *Consumer Behaviour and Material Culture*, chap. 7, also address this development.

[58]Similar changes were occurring in England, where tea consumption had been rising steadily as prices there began to fall dramatically from the 1720s. Tea prices (presumably in the colonies as well as in England) were especially low between 1765 and 1775, just when usage was rapidly increas-

Table 9. Signature literacy in Anne Arundel County, 1658–1777

Years	N	Unknown	Cannot sign	Can sign	Signature and / or evidence of more education
1658–64	8	37.5%	0%	25.0%	62.5%
1665–77	103	44.7	26.2	22.3	29.0
1678–87	100	50.0	19.0	23.0	31.0
1688–99	161	54.0	19.9	19.3	26.1
1700–1709	176	49.4	14.2	27.3	36.4
1710–22	239	48.1	13.8	19.7	38.1
1723–32	148	52.0	4.7	4.7	43.3
1733–44	266	56.0	4.5	4.5	39.5
1745–54	198	60.6	4.0	8.1	35.4
1755–67	384	54.3	3.9	36.8	41.7
1768–77	211	52.1	0.9	44.1	47.0

SOURCE: Maryland History Computer Files, Historic St. Mary's City Commission, Maryland State Archives, Annapolis.

reinforced by an increasingly widespread commitment to fashion among the upper social groups. Only occasionally had the invoices of more privileged planters of the seventeenth century included requests for anything that was not eminently "useful for this country"; by the mid-eighteenth century imported clothing or furnishings had above all to be "fashionable." While some disgruntled customers complained that they ended up with shopworn or outdated goods, it was the timeliness of the imports that struck English observers. In 1771 William Eddis wrote from Annapolis, "The quick importation of fashions from the mother country is really astonishing. I am almost inclined to believe that a new fashion is adopted earlier by the polished and affluent American than by many opulent persons in the great metropolis." Even in distant rural areas he encountered "elegance as well as comfort . . . in very many of the habitations."[59]

The increasing spread of amenities is clear; nevertheless,

---

ing among poorer consumers (Wilson, *England's Apprenticeship*, chap. 14; Deane and Cole, *British Economic Growth*, p. 84; Rodris Roth, *Tea Drinking in Eighteenth-Century America: Its Etiquette and Equipage*, U.S. National Museum Bulletin 225 [Washington, D.C., 1961], pp. 61–91).

[59] Eddis, *Letters*, pp. 19, 57–58.

the overall impact of these changes should not be exaggerated. At the end of the colonial period, a sizable proportion—at least 40 percent and probably much more—of the propertied population had less than £50 of movable wealth.[60] While planters at this level had increased their amenities score, the mean was still less than three items out of twelve. Such families still lived in small, poorly equipped houses with at most two rooms, a loft, and a wooden chimney.[61] Family members might enjoy a cup of tea and eat with a fork, luxuries unknown to their grandparents, but living conditions for large numbers of inhabitants were still primitive.

On the other hand, forks and tea are indications of changes in cultural attitudes that were permeating all society. At all levels Chesapeake planters were learning to use personal possessions to make increasingly sophisticated and elaborate social statements. Their choices were not made just for comfort or even beauty. Families at the top of the social ladder attempted to establish their superiority by adopting the refinements and sophistications of English gentry, although the lifestyles of the top nobility were not within reach. At the same time, the lower orders increasingly aimed at achieving some aspects of the lifestyles of their betters. Families at various levels were using artifacts both to create social distance from those below them and to bridge the gap separating them from those above.

The great proliferation of new goods that accompanied these changes raises another question. Did Chesapeake families add items of comfort or convenience as they became more

[60]Although inventories suggest that over time wealthholders with movable assets worth less than £50 were a decreasing proportion of the total, by the 1770s in all four counties they were still 30 percent of all, and those worth less than £95 were 38 to 45 percent. Since poor people were less likely than the rich to go through probate, the proportions of all people who died in these wealth groups were larger, and given the age bias of the dying, wealthholders at these levels were a still larger proportion in the living population.

[61]On housing, see Cary Carson, Norman F. Barka, William M. Kelso, Garry Wheeler Stone, and Dell Upton, "Impermanent Architecture in the Southern American Colonies," *Winterthur Portfolio* 16 (1981):145–96.

available or affordable, or did cultural change—attitudes toward class hierarchy and appropriate or desirable social observances—most influence the choice of goods? In an effort to answer this question we devised a second index, which we call the "modern index." For this we selected ten items that most westerners now consider the basic household equipment needed to ensure a minimum of comfort and cleanliness: a mattress, a bedstead, some bed linen, a table, one or more chairs, pots for boiling food, other utensils for food preparation, some coarse ceramics, table forks, and some means of interior lighting. Figures 15 through 17 show that acquisition of this combination of rudimentary "modern" household equipment was of much greater concern to the affluent than to the poor, but even among the very rich not every household had all of them. Families with movables worth less than £95—close to half of all inventoried decedents and a much larger group in the living population—either could not afford half or more of these items or still considered them unnecessary. Nor, after the early eighteenth century, was there much change in the likelihood that planters in any wealth group would improve their position. Yet inventoried planters of all wealth levels increased acquisition of other kinds of nonessentials. The proliferation of teaware, as shown in tables 1 to 6, is one of the striking examples. The reasons for these purchases cannot lie in less availability or much greater costs of most of the modern index items as opposed to those of the amenities index. The choices must have reflected the demands of gentility, a cultural change that did not reach many kinds of available conveniences we now think essential.

Counts of additional goods, especially those connected with cleanliness, bear out this conclusion. The rich were more likely than the poor to own chamber pots, washtubs, smoothing irons, brooms, and scrub brushes, but these were far from standard even in gentry households. Nor did the appearance of such equipment increase much across time, with the possible exception of laundry equipment in the households of the well-to-do (see table 10). There was also no sign of a desire to increase privacy and reduce crowding by acquiring separate beds for most family members. Richer households were usu-

ally larger than poorer ones, and from the beginning the rich
had more beds than others did. But as table 11 indicates, the
mean number of beds per householding inventory did not
increase across time in any wealth group. During the eighteenth century all groups continued to spend more on bedding than on any other functional grouping of equipment.
What was desired, however, was better beds, not more of
them.[62] These were not yet the areas of cultural change. It
probably took the merging of concerns about genteel appearances with a growing awareness of the connection between
dirt and disease to produce the interest in cleanliness and sanitation that appeared in the early nineteenth century.[63]

The question remains: What fueled the movement toward
gentility, the pursuit of fashion, and the escalation of luxury
that underlay these beginnings of a consumer society? The
pursuit of fashion and luxury had its roots in marketing techniques that appealed to drives for social emulation and competition. There was nothing new in either emulation or
competition, of course. What was new was the availability of
new kinds of goods, a distribution system that enabled them
to reach broad markets, and discoveries of how to advertise
and display these goods in ways that appealed to buyers. If
these changes combine with the drive for emulation, fashion
and even luxury can become social criteria for status. Since
changing fashions create new markets, creating fashions becomes part of entrepreneurship and the process becomes self-
perpetuating. Neil McKendrick and others have shown how
this process got underway in eighteenth-century England.
The evidence offered here shows the extension of the process
to the Chesapeake colonies.

Insofar as this argument depends on emulation, there are
negative voices to be heard. Lorna Weatherill, in her study of

[62] For percentage of consumer durables spent on various kinds of equipment, see Walsh, "Urban Amenities and Rural Sufficiency," pp. 114–15.

[63] Bushman has most persuasively linked the pursuit of other genteel values in "Gentrification of Kent County." Richard L. Bushman and Claudia
L. Bushman, "The Early History of Cleanliness in America," *Journal of
American History* 74 (1988):1213–38, argues that a growing commitment to
cleanliness in the nineteenth century resulted from the intermingling of
cultural, medical, and moral concerns.

Figure 15. Modern index, York County householders, 1636-1777

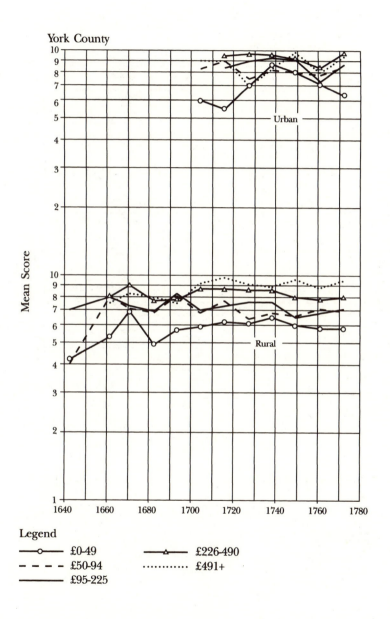

York County

Mean Score

Urban

Rural

1640   1660   1680   1700   1720   1740   1760   1780

Legend

———o——— £0-49   ———△——— £226-490
– – – – £50-94   ············ £491+
——————— £95-225

NOTE: For composition of the index, see text. For information about
construction of the figure and about sources, see note to fig. 1.

Figure 16. Modern index, Anne Arundel County householders, 1658-1777

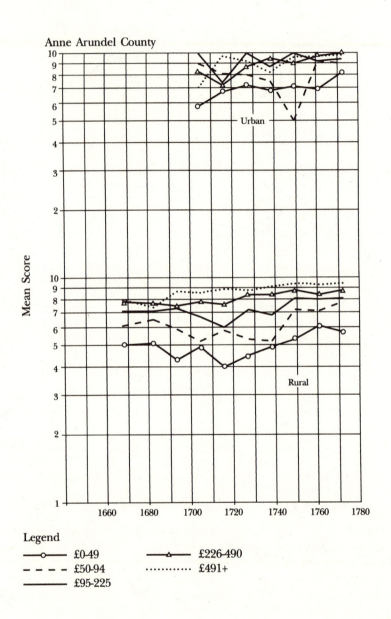

Anne Arundel County

Mean Score

Urban

Rural

Legend

—o— £0-49
– – – £50-94
——— £95-225

—△— £226-490
············ £491+

NOTE: For composition of the index, see text. For information about construction of the figure and about sources, see note to fig. 1.

Figure 17. Modern index, Somerset County householders, 1665-1777

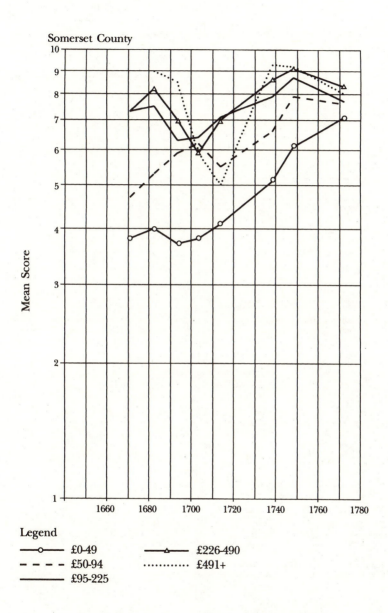

Somerset County

Mean Score

Legend

———o——— £0-49   ———△——— £226-490
– – – – £50-94   .... £491+
——————— £95-225

NOTE: For information about construction of the figure and about sources, see note to fig. 1. Because in Somerset County only selective years were coded for modern index items, the year groups are as follows: 1665-77, 1678-87, 1688-99, 1700-1706, 1713-15, 1733-44, 1745-51, 1768-77.

Table 10. Incidence of selected equipment for cleanliness, by wealth

Years	Estates N	Sanitary* %	Laundry† %	Vermin control‡ %	Cleaning§ %
			York County		
			£0–49		
1700–1709	24	17	38	0	0
1710–22	30	7	13	0	0
1723–32	17	0	18	0	0
1733–44	30	3	27	3	0
1745–54	34	0	6	0	0
1755–67	25	20	40	0	12
1768–77	27	4	30	0	4
			£50–94		
1700–1709	10	50	10	0	0
1710–22	26	19	35	0	0
1723–32	15	7	27	0	0
1733–44	22	23	0	4	0
1745–54	13	15	23	0	0
1755–67	20	15	45	0	5
1768–77	11	9	54	0	0
			£95–225		
1700–1709	9	44	22	0	0
1710–22	39	33	28	0	0
1723–32	19	16	21	0	5
1733–44	34	15	21	6	0
1745–54	22	46	46	14	18
1755–67	25	32	56	4	4
1768–77	19	32	63	5	10
			£226–490		
1700–1709	7	71	43	0	14
1710–22	23	30	22	0	4
1723–32	15	20	13	7	0
1733–44	22	27	27	9	4
1745–54	29	21	38	3	3
1755–67	19	32	58	0	5
1768–77	16	38	75	12	12
			£491+		
1700–1709	5	100	40	20	20
1710–22	11	73	64	27	9
1723–32	8	75	25	0	12
1733–44	10	60	50	0	0
1745–54	18	50	39	22	11
1755–67	31	39	55	3	19
1768–77	27	63	96	16	30

Table 10.   *(continued)*

Years	Estates N	Sanitary* %	Laundry† %	Vermin control‡ %	Cleaning§ %
		Somerset County			
		£0–49			
1700–1706	50	8	20	0	0
1713–15	28	11	32	0	0
1733–44	98	5	10	0	0
1745–51	37	3	14	0	0
1768–74	67	12	22	0	2
		£50–94			
1700–1706	24	17	25	0	0
1713–15	6	17	17	0	0
1733–44	67	6	18	0	0
1745–51	23	4	22	4	0
1768–74	38	16	42	3	3
		£95–225			
1700–1706	10	10	10	0	0
1713–15	8	0	12	0	0
1733–44	61	12	13	2	0
1745–51	35	20	43	0	0
1768–74	50	28	50	4	2
		£226–490			
1700–1706	7	0	57	0	0
1713–15	3	0	33	0	0
1733–44	38	26	32	3	3
1745–51	35	29	43	0	3
1768–74	31	58	68	10	3
		£491+			
1700–1706	5	0	20	0	0
1713–15	1	100	0	0	0
1733–44	12	33	25	8	17
1745–51	12	58	42	0	25
1768–74	20	85	70	15	10

SOURCE: Maryland History Computer Files, Historic St. Mary's City Commission, Maryland State Archives, Annapolis.

*Close stools, chamber pots
†Wash tubs, irons, soap, clothes horses
‡Mosquito nets, rat and mouse traps
§Brooms, mops, scrub brushes

Table 11. Mean numbers of selected consumer items per inventory, York County, Virginia, and Somerset County, Maryland

Years	N	Chairs	Tables	Beds†	Bedsteads	Desks	Case furniture*
York County							
£0–49							
1643–54	8	0.3	0.1	0.8	0	0	0
1655–64	4	1.5	0.2	1.5	0.2	0	0
1665–77	8	4.7	0.8	3.0	1.2	0.1	0
1678–87	16	1.7	0.6	2.2	0.4	0.1	0.2
1688–99	26	2.1	0.9	2.4	1.0	<0.1	0.3
1700–1709	24	2.0	1.1	2.6	0.7	<0.1	0.1
1710–22	30	4.5	0.8	2.2	1.0	<0.1	0.1
1723–32	17	5.7	1.2	2.7	1.8	0	0.1
1733–44	30	5.0	1.6	2.2	1.4	0.1	0.3
1745–54	34	4.3	1.1	2.1	0.8	0.1	0.4
1755–67	25	7.4	1.8	1.9	0.9	0.1	0.7
1768–77	27	5.0	1.6	1.6	0.5	0.3	0.4
£50–94							
1636–42	1	0	0	1.0	0	0	0
1643–54	1	2.0	1.0	3.0	0	0	0
1655–64	2	2.0	1.5	5.0	2.5	0	0
1665–77	9	6.2	1.6	4.4	1.6	0	0.2
1678–87	12	4.0	1.5	4.1	1.9	0	0.3
1688–99	8	7.1	2.0	3.9	2.2	0.1	0.6
1700–1709	10	3.8	1.5	3.3	1.6	0	0.4
1710–22	26	6.3	2.6	3.0	1.8	<0.1	0.3
1723–32	15	4.6	1.7	2.7	1.7	0.2	0.5
1733–44	22	9.2	1.9	3.0	1.3	0.2	0.5
1745–54	13	7.5	1.5	2.3	0.9	0	0.3
1755–67	20	9.2	2.4	2.4	1.6	0.4	0.4
1768–77	11	9.2	2.0	2.8	1.5	0.5	1.1

£95–225

1643–54	3	6.7	3.7	5.7	3.0	0.3	1.0
1655–64	2	6.0	1.5	4.0	2.0	0	0.5
1665–77	12	7.3	1.3	5.0	2.1	0.2	0.5
1678–87	10	7.7	2.1	5.0	2.3	0.2	0.6
1688–99	10	10.1	2.4	5.1	2.1	0	1.2
1700–1709	9	7.3	1.2	3.7	1.3	0.1	0.6
1710–22	39	12.4	2.7	3.5	1.8	0.1	0.4
1723–32	19	10.5	2.3	3.5	1.8	0.2	0.7
1733–44	34	10.9	2.4	3.5	2.1	0.4	0.6
1745–54	22	11.3	3.2	3.2	2.0	0.7	1.2
1755–67	25	10.1	2.6	3.0	1.5	0.3	0.5
1768–77	19	16.6	3.9	4.1	2.6	0.8	0.9

£226–490

1655–64	1	7.0	1.0	7.0	4.0	0	0
1665–77	2	10.0	2.0	6.0	3.5	0	1.0
1678–87	3	23.3	3.3	5.0	4.7	0.3	1.3
1688–99	4	22.5	4.8	6.8	2.8	0	1.8
1700–1709	7	13.7	2.9	6.0	3.6	0.4	0.9
1710–22	23	17.3	3.3	4.7	2.2	0.2	0.5
1723–32	15	20.7	3.7	5.1	2.3	0.5	0.8
1733–44	22	18.9	4.4	4.9	2.8	0.5	0.9
1745–54	29	15.1	3.9	4.1	2.2	0.8	0.9
1755–67	19	13.6	3.5	3.4	2.2	0.8	0.6
1768–77	16	18.2	4.9	4.2	1.8	1.1	1.1

Table 11. (continued)

Years	N	Chairs	Tables	Beds	Bedsteads	Desks	Case furniture*
				£491+			
1655–64	2	7.5	3.0	3.5	2.5	0.5	1.0
1665–77	3	18.7	3.7	8.0	5.0	0.3	2.0
1678–87	3	13.7	2.0	6.7	2.7	0	1.0
1688–99	2	31.0	5.5	10.0	5.5	0.5	3.0
1700–1709	5	39.2	8.0	11.2	6.4	0.2	1.8
1710–22	11	42.2	8.0	10.5	6.0	0.6	2.2
1723–32	8	26.1	4.5	5.2	2.8	0.2	0.9
1733–44	10	31.4	5.8	7.8	3.8	0.8	1.0
1745–54	18	31.3	7.3	7.9	4.7	1.2	1.7
1755–67	31	25.0	5.2	6.1	4.1	1.3	1.3
1768–77	27	32.9	8.5	8.1	6.0	1.5	2.3
			Somerset County‡				
				£0–49			
1665–77	4	0.5	0	1.0	0	0	0
1678–87	17	1.6	0.8	2.3	0.5	0.1	0.1
1688–99	62	1.9	0.5	2.0	0.5	0.1	<0.1
1700–1706	50	2.3	0.7	1.8	0.4	0.1	<0.1
1713–15	28	3.3	0.5	1.6	1.2	<0.1	<0.1
1733–44	98	3.2	0.8	2.2	1.1	<0.1	0.1
1745–51	37	4.2	1.4	2.3	1.3	0.1	0.1
1768–74	67	4.3	1.8	1.9	1.6	0.1	0.1
				£50–94			
1665–77	5	3.0	0.4	5.2	0.8	0	0
1678–87	7	3.1	1.0	3.1	0.4	0	0
1688–99	27	4.4	1.0	3.7	0.7	<0.1	0.1
1700–1706	24	4.8	1.2	3.3	1.2	0	0.2
1713–15	6	5.8	1.3	2.7	1.2	0	0.2
1733–44	67	4.7	1.5	3.3	1.8	0.1	0.2
1745–51	23	7.1	1.8	3.3	2.0	0.3	0.5
1768–74	38	7.8	1.9	3.4	2.7	0.4	0.3

£95–225						
1665–77	3	3.0	5.0	5.3	2.7	0	0.7
1678–87	7	13.1	2.1	7.6	2.7	0	0.7
1688–99	16	7.9	1.9	4.7	1.9	0.1	0.5
1700–1706	10	6.3	1.3	4.4	0.4	0	0.3
1713–15	8	13.0	2.1	4.6	1.5	0.1	0.6
1733–44	61	10.1	2.3	4.7	2.6	0.2	0.3
1745–51	35	9.9	3.2	4.2	2.7	0.5	0.4
1768–74	50	9.6	2.7	3.6	2.6	0.7	0.7

£226–490						
1665–77	3	18.0	2.0	7.3	2.3	0	0.3
1678–87	4	8.2	1.8	5.2	2.2	0	0.2
1688–99	6	12.8	1.7	7.3	2.2	0.2	0.8
1700–1706	7	10.4	2.3	6.9	3.4	0.4	1.0
1713–15	3	23.0	3.7	6.3	2.7	0	0.7
1733–44	38	12.2	3.0	5.4	3.3	0.7	0.8
1745–51	35	16.1	3.4	5.6	4.1	1.0	1.3
1768–74	31	14.1	3.8	5.2	4.6	1.1	1.3

£491+						
1678–87	1	24.0	3.0	15.0	4.0	0	0
1688–99	3	29.0	4.3	8.0	3.3	0	0.7
1700–1706	5	15.8	2.8	9.6	4.4	0.6	0.4
1713–15	1	23.0	4.0	6.0	0	1.0	0.4
1733–44	12	26.9	5.2	7.1	3.9	1.2	1.0
1745–51	12	37.4	6.3	9.6	7.8	2.1	1.5
1768–74	20	19.1	5.6	5.6	4.6	1.4	2.2

SOURCE: Maryland History Computer Files, Historic St. Mary's City Commission, Maryland State Archives, Annapolis.

*Includes chests of drawers, cupboards, presses, and safes.

†Figures after 1755 represent a minimum because some inventories are partially mutilated.

‡Dates represent years for which data were coded.

consumer behavior in England from 1660 to 1760, points out that the hierarchy of expenditure on consumer goods was not the same as the social hierarchy. For example, merchants and tradesmen often had more upscale goods than did the minor gentry. At the same time she finds evidence that middling groups in general may not have entirely approved of or copied the spending habits of people of higher rank. However, a consumption hierarchy is all that our argument needs. In the Chesapeake, furthermore, wealth and status were more directly connected than in England, where trading was not a gentleman's role.[64]

Colin Campbell makes a different argument. He suggests that the rapid changes in fashion that increasingly underlay the proliferation of goods would not have been possible without moral legitimation and, in his view, the forces of emulation and manipulation (advertising) cannot explain moral acceptance of continuous novelty. Campbell offers a complex solution related to changes in western middle-class consciousness that began with the Protestant Reformation and underwent a variety of transformations, ultimately becoming the romantic ethic.[65] We cannot evaluate his argument here. But he has raised a question that will not go away: How did the pursuit of fashion become morally acceptable?[66]

The roots of gentility are equally obscure. Pursuit of fashion and luxury, the economic and technological changes that encouraged them, and the social emulation and competition that underlay them all played a role in spreading the culture of gentility. But these do not explain the social choices that

[64] Weatherill, *Consumer Behaviour and Material Culture*, pp. 38–40.

[65] Colin Campbell, *The Romantic Ethic and the Spirit of Modern Consumerism* (Oxford, 1987).

[66] Among the difficulties that Campbell's argument presents to us are, first, its failure to examine the kinds of goods that people were acquiring, and, second, problems of timing. In England, Lorna Weatherill finds major changes in the character and quantities of domestic furnishings over the period 1670–1725 (*Consumer Behaviour and Material Culture*, chap. 2); moreover, the rate of increase in the appearance of amenities in the Chesapeake was rapid after 1700 (see fig. 1). This is early for major effects from the cultural transformations Campbell describes, if one accepts them as true.

gentility represented—the emphasis on individualized furnishings used for social purposes, the elaboration of social
equipment, the more specialized uses of space, and the new
forms of social ritual like the tea ceremony. Since notions of
gentility appeared earlier in England than in the colonies, the
answers doubtless lie in cultural changes that were transferred across the Atlantic. Demographic and economic developments—the appearance of more families, a more
diversified economy, the willingness of merchants to risk
nonessentials in Chesapeake markets—provided the necessary ingredients for eighteenth-century Chesapeake society to
move forward to gentility. But why Englishmen, either at
home or in the colonies, developed the particular sets of attitudes toward household artifacts and their uses that gentility
required, or accepted the dictates of ever-changing fashions
in pursuing it, is a question that needs much greater understanding than we currently have of how and why cultural
change occurs.[67]

By the 1770s Chesapeake planters were well along the road
toward the consumer society. They enjoyed comforts unknown to earlier generations, they were using artifacts and
social rituals to advertise social position, those who could afford them were insisting on the newest fashions, and storekeepers were catering to these needs with increasingly
elaborate displays of merchandise aimed at attracting buyers.
The poor shared less than others in these changes, but even
they paid attention to comfort and ceremony in ways their
seventeenth-century predecessors had never thought of doing. The world of the seventeenth century in both Europe
and America is difficult for the twentieth-century mind to
comprehend; in the famous phrase of Peter Laslett, it is
"the world we have lost." The world of the 1770s contained
the cultural foundations for consumer demand that was to
help fuel industrialization; it is a world that we can recognize.

[67] Grant McCracken, *Culture and Consumption: New Approaches to the Symbolic Character of Consumer Goods and Activities* (Bloomington, Ind., 1988),
published after this essay was written, offers a discussion of these problems.

APPENDIX A

Biases in Inventory Data

This essay is part of a larger project in which we have been collaborating with P. M. G. Harris of Temple University and Russell R. Menard of the University of Minnesota. Together, all of us have faced a number of special problems that accompany the use of inventories for social and economic analysis. We reported basic strategies in our article analyzing inventories and wealth in St. Mary's County, Maryland.[1] Since then we have extended the procedures to other areas.

Two aspects of these procedures are particularly important for this study. It was necessary to standardize inventory values over both time and place with a Maryland-Virginia commodity price index. Details of its construction can be obtained from the authors. Tests for discovering whether and when reporting rates changed within a county were equally essential. If reporting rates did not change, shifts that inventories show in the distribution of wealth and its components can be trusted, even though one may not know what the actual size of the distributions are in the living population. If reporting changes occurred, one must determine which kinds of estates were dropping in or out before trying to interpret what inventories reveal. Comparison of numbers of inventories with numbers of taxables, making allowances for slaves, generally shows little long-term variation in the counties examined for this project, although short-term variations can be large. P. M. G. Harris has found that in Anne Arundel, St. Mary's,

[1] Lois Green Carr and Lorena S. Walsh, "Inventories and the Analysis of Wealth and Consumption Patterns in St. Mary's County, Maryland, 1658–1777," *Historical Methods* 13 (1980):81–104. For other discussions of inventory bias, see Alice Hanson Jones, "Wealth Estimates for the American Middle Colonies, 1774," *Economic Development and Cultural Change* 18 (1970):109–21; Gloria L. Main, "The Correction of Biases in Colonial American Probate Records," *Historical Methods Newsletter* 8 (1974):10–28; and Daniel Scott Smith, "Under-registration and Bias in Probate Records: An Analysis of Data from Eighteenth-Century Hingham, Massachusetts," *William and Mary Quarterly*, 3d ser. 32 (1975):100–110.

Charles, Prince George's, and Somerset counties servants appeared in inventories, and free immigrants and native-born appeared among decedents in patterns that fit predicted growth curves.[2] This finding confirms the notion that in these places reporting rates varied little over the long run. Consequently, large changes in the distribution of wealth that appear in inventories can be trusted. True, in parts of Somerset there is some evidence that reporting rates dropped in the 1720s and 1750s. But tax lists for this county for many of the years from 1723 to 1759 have permitted the testing of economic groups in the inventories against similar groups in the living population. The results show that the drop in reporting was across all wealth groups, not only among the poor, so adjustments for the change in reporting need not be made.

Information on population growth and composition needed for this kind of analysis is still insufficient for York County. But since the evidence from other counties indicates that on the whole the propensity of various kinds of people to be inventoried does not vary so much over time that gross changes shown in wealth cannot be accepted, we and our colleagues believe that information from York inventories can also be trusted.[3]

Changes in the age structure of the inventoried population are a third source of bias in inventory data. We have followed these in the body of the essay and used them in interpreting the findings.

[2] P. M. G. Harris, "The Nativity, Migration, and Landowning Characteristics of Anne Arundel County Decedents in Comparative Perspective," unpublished manuscript in possession of the authors.

[3] In this essay we have concentrated on patterns of change rather than variations in consumption from county to county; hence we do not present here our findings about differing levels of inventory reporting that might create spurious regional differences. Lois Green Carr has presented preliminary results on regional differences in levels of reporting in "Diversification in the Colonial Chesapeake: Somerset County, Maryland, in Comparative Perspective," in Lois Green Carr, Philip D. Morgan, and Jean B. Russo, eds., *Colonial Chesapeake Society* (Chapel Hill, N.C., 1988), Appendix 1.

APPENDIX B

The Regressions

Our earlier studies gave us a general idea of what kinds of changes might be influencing consumption habits. In this essay we have used regression models to test these ideas further, using consumption scores and value of consumer durables as the dependent variables.[1] We selected the following independent variables from our inventory files.

1. Total estate value. This includes all physical and financial assets except land, which in the Chesapeake was not inventoried. This variable was not used when value of consumer durables was the dependent variable.

2. Membership in three wealth groups: less than £50, £50–225, and over £225. The rationale for these groups is laid out in note 13 of the essay. Zero class is less than £50.

3. Urban-rural location in Anne Arundel and York counties, already established as a variable of importance.

4. Amount of diversification of economic activity as measured by a twenty-seven-item index of tools, other equipment, and agricultural products, and by two of its subdivisions. A craft index contains twelve of the twenty-seven items and an index of cloth-related activities contains four of the twelve craft items. We wished to test three ideas: that diversification, by increasing economic stability, contributed generally to expenditure on consumption; that crafts and home industries—stronger indicators of local exchange than the agricultural part of the diversification index—in themselves promoted consumption; and that home industries enabled women to earn additional income that could purchase consumption amenities. Regressions were run separately for each index.

It can be argued that the crops and products that the diversification indices represent, either directly or by tools used in production, appear on both sides of our regression equations. Bed and table linen may have been made with the cards,

[1] We wish to give special thanks to Helen M. Hunter of Bryn Mawr College for help in constructing the regression models.

hackles, spinning wheels, and looms that appear in the cloth index; besides, linens, kitchenware such as pots, and furniture such as tables or chairs, which are valued as consumer durables, may be the product of various craft tools. This may be true in some households, but we believe the index measures not self-sufficiency but local exchange, as more kinds of products or tools appear. Men who acquired the necessary skills and equipment for blacksmithing and woodjoining (as opposed to simple carpentry) used them to produce income, not just family comfort. Furthermore, the number of blacksmiths and joiners in the population was always very small.[2] When it comes to cloth, except in Somerset County, less than 10 percent of inventories had looms before the late 1750s, and thereafter the figure rose only to about 15 percent. (In Somerset this proportion admittedly reached one half.) Processing fibers was much more common than weaving as a household industry, by the 1750s reaching half or more of inventories (90 percent in Somerset). We think the cloth-making indicators have importance as a measure of local exchange rather than of self-sufficiency in cloth. Further support for this idea comes from the fact that over the whole colonial period less than 0.5 percent of Anne Arundel and York county inventories had both looms and country-made cloth (which in bolt was always identified). Even in Somerset the figure was only 5.2 percent. (Country cloth appeared so infrequently in St. Mary's County that it was not coded there.) It may be that in Somerset more households than elsewhere had homemade linens that appear in the amenities scores. But we also believe that even in Somerset the value of homemade items constituted a percentage of the value of consumer durables too small to account for any important amount of the rise in this variable.

5. Amount of diversification by time periods: before 1705, 1705–49, and after 1749. The first half of the century was the period of the most rapid growth of diversification, which be-

---

[2] Tables to show the incidence of blacksmiths' tools can be obtained from the authors. Joiners were not coded separately from carpenters, but we do not doubt that they were small in number.

gan to level out in some areas in the 1750s. The time-break
dates represent the midpoints of the year groups 1700–1709
and 1745–54. Zero class was the period before 1705.

6. Time. This captures changes we have not otherwise been
able to specify. It may include changes in marketing and merchandising that we believe affected consumption.

7. Marital status and age structure of the decedent's family,
if married. Here we looked for effects of demographic
changes. We established four life cycles: single, married with
no children or only minor children, married with some children of age, and married with all children of age. Zero class
was single.

8. Immigrant or native-born status and native-born generation (Anne Arundel County only). We wished to test the effect
of inheritance. Zero class was servant immigrant.

9. Size of bound labor force. This variable seemed likely to
affect value of consumer durables.

10. Education (Anne Arundel County only). Education
seemed likely to affect tastes.

The regressions are laid out in appendix tables 1–4. In St.
Mary's County (table 2) there are two regressions, one to 1702
and one beginning in 1703, because the computer files split
there and the variables were sufficiently different to make a
merge impractical. Among the independent variables, total
estate value and size of labor force are logged. Beyond a certain point more wealth or more labor is likely to have a dimin-
ishing effect on consumption, and in any case the broad range
of wealth was out of scale with the other variables. Value of
consumer durables and the amenities index, the two dependent variables, also were logged to eliminate heteroskedacity,
which showed in the residuals when these variables were not
so transformed. Since some variables were logged, we have
included in the tables the standardized B coefficients, the Be-
tas, to show the relative importance of the variables.

The most important variables were wealth, location, and,
usually, diversification. Other things being equal, wealth everywhere had the strongest effect on consumption scores, a
result that is no surprise. Equally expected was the domi-
nating effect of wealth class, especially the top group, on value
of consumer durables. On consumption scores, wealth class

was insignificant, with two exceptions; in St. Mary's County an acceleration of the scores occurred as estates rose on the scale of wealth, and in Anne Arundel County estates in the wealthiest group accelerated more than others.

In Anne Arundel County, urban versus rural location was second in positive influence on consumption scores in two of the three regressions, once Annapolis came into existence; in York this variable came third. However, location was less important in its effect on value of consumer durables, another reasonable outcome. Town life required a style of living different from that of country life, but not necessarily more value in consumer assets. It may also be that absence of field laborers in town households cut back on the amount and value of consumer assets.

For both measures, the diversification indices were usually next, following wealth directly in counties without towns. There were exceptions, however. In seventeenth-century St. Mary's County diversification was downgraded for both sets of regressions, reflecting the absence of diversified activities before 1702. Had the other county regressions been divided at this point, the outcome would have been the same.[3] In Anne Arundel County, life-cycle variables had more effect than diversification on value of consumer durables, and in Somerset County time had more effect on scored amenities. Nevertheless, the progress of diversification over the eighteenth century was a structural shift in the Chesapeake economy that was clearly one of the most important generators of changes in consumption. Equally important, diversification into crafts and female-based home industry had the importance we anticipated.

We expected diversification to have its most important effects over the period of its most rapid development, from 1700 to 1750. In scores this proved to be untrue. Time breaks were not significant and we eliminated them from these regressions. Other things being equal, however, the effect of diversification on value of consumer durables everywhere

---

[3] We ran regressions for Anne Arundel County to 1702 and obtained the same results.

Appendix table 1. Anne Arundel County regressions (N = 1,914)

	A. With total divers. index (27 indicators)			B. With craft index (12 indicators)			C. With cloth index (4 indicators)		
I. Regressions on amenities scores (12 indicators, logged)[a]									
	B	Beta	T	B	Beta	T	B	Beta	T
Total estate value [1][b]	.19	.41	8.50	.21	.44	9.27	.22	.46	9.66
Diversification	.05	.31	13.38	.10	.23	12.21	.17	.20	10.40
Urban-rural location [2][c]	.58	.27	15.39	.51	.23	13.74	.51	.24	13.64
Wealth group 3 (£226+) [1,3][d]							.25	.12	16.40
Married children 0 or minors [2]	.17	.11	5.31	.17	.11	5.09	.18	.12	5.32
Married some children of age [2]							.09	.05	2.18
Married all children of age [2]	.08	.05	.229	.10	.06	2.74	.11	.06	2.81
Time				.001	.05	2.30			
Education	.11	.04	2.76	.10	.04	2.53	.11	.04	2.79
Free immigrant [2]	.13	.04	2.61	.12	.04	2.46	.13	.04	2.55
Constant	-.23		-2.94	-.27		-3.42	-.28		-3.60
R²	.56			.56			.55		
Standard error of estimate	.49			.49			.50		
Mean value, dep. variable	ln1.28			ln1.28			ln1.28		
Durbin-Watson	1.97			1.95			1.96		

II. Regressions on value of consumer durables (logged)[e]

	A. With total divers. index (27 indicators)			B. With craft index (12 indicators)			C. With cloth index (4 indicators)		
	B	Beta	T	B	Beta	T	B	Beta	T
Wealth group 3 (£226+) [2]	1.46	.51	19.06	1.60	.55	20.88	1.63	.57	21.11
Wealth group 2 (£50–225) [2]	.87	.31	17.99	.91	.33	18.66	.92	.33	18.68
Diversification, 1658–1749	.08	.26	12.30	.14	.17	9.02	.18	.12	5.82
Size of labor force	.25	.21	8.79	.28	.24	10.03	.30	.25	10.57
Urban-rural location [2]	.77	.20	13.17	.67	.17	11.53	.65	.17	11.08
Married children 0 or minors [2]	.46	.17	9.17	.47	.17	9.15	.49	.18	9.51
Married all children of age [2]	.40	.13	6.90	.44	.14	7.54	.46	.15	7.80
Married some children of age [2]	.40	.11	6.13	.45	.13	6.96	.50	.14	7.53
Time	-.004	-.08	-4.34	-.003	-.08	-4.01	-.004	-.08	-4.12
Free immigrant [2]	.35	.06	4.50	.33	.06	4.25	.33	.06	4.16
Diversification, 1750+	.05	.05	7.14	.07	.03	4.12	.07	.02	2.26
Native born, 1st gen. [2]	.09	.03	1.904[f]	.10	.14	2.24	.11	.04	2.39
Native born, 2d gen. [2]							.13	.04	1.98
Constant	1.31		16.27	1.33		16.43	1.34		16.34
R²	.68			.67			.66		
Standard error of estimate	.76			.78			.78		
Mean value, dep. variable	ln2.89			ln2.89			ln2.89		
Durbin-Watson	1.86			1.85			1.86		

Appendix table 1. *(continued)*

SOURCE: Maryland History Computer Files, Historic St. Mary's City Commission, Maryland State Archives, Annapolis.

NOTES: For wealth groups, 0 class is less than £50; for life cycles, single; for generation, servant immigrant. The dependent variables are logged with natural logarithms. Except as noted, all variables are significant at the .05 level.

[a]Variables omitted because not significant: size of labor force; all native-born generations; wealth group 2 (£50–225); wealth group 3 (£226+) in regressions with total and craft diversification indices; married, some children of age in regressions with total and craft diversification indices; time in regressions with total and cloth indices.

[b][1] logged with natural logarithms.

[c][2] dummy variable, 0 or 1.

[d][3] dummy variable applied to a continuous variable.

[e]Variables omitted because not significant: education; native-born, third generation or more; native-born, second generation in regressions that include total and craft diversification indices.

[f]Significant at .0571 level.

Appendix table 2. St. Mary's County regressions

| | I. Regressions on amenities scores (12 indicators, logged), 1658–1702 (N = 632)[a] | | | | | | | | |
| | A. With total divers. index (27 indicators) | | | B. With craft index (12 indicators) | | | C. With cloth index (4 indicators) | | |
	B	Beta	T	B	Beta	T	B	Beta	T
Total estate value [1][b]	.19	.38	5.61	.19	.39	5.73	.19	.29	5.77
Size of labor force	.13	.15	3.42	.13	.16	3.58	.14	.16	3.64
Wealth group 2 (£50–225) [1,3][c]	.23	.08	9.20	.23	.08	9.20	.23	.08	9.20
Diversification	.04	.12	3.34	.06	.08	2.50	.12	.09	3.01
Constant	−.12		−1.20	−.13		−1.29	−.13		−1.27
R²	.45			.45			.45		
Standard error of estimate	.49			.49			.49		
Mean value, dep. variable	*b.*77			*b.*77			*b.*77		
Durbin-Watson	2.07			2.06			2.06		

Appendix table 2. (continued)

II. Regressions on amenities scores (12 indicators, logged), 1703–77 (N = 1,914)[d]

	A. With total divers. index (27 indicators)			B. With craft index (12 indicators)			C. With cloth index (4 indicators)		
	B	Beta	T	B	Beta	T	B	Beta	T
Total estate value	.21	.38	9.65	.23	.42	10.62	.23	.32	10.93
Diversification	.05	.24	12.37	.08	.19	10.37	.10	.17	9.64
Time	.007	.19	11.62	.007	.21	12.73	.007	.20	11.83
Wealth group 3 (£226+) [1,3]	.25	.11	14.71	.28	.13	17.50	.28	.13	17.50
Wealth group 2 (£50–225) [1,3]	.25	.08	14.71	.26	.08	16.88	.27	.09	16.25
Married children 0 or minors [2][e]	.11	.08	4.14	.11	.07	3.93	.11	.07	3.71
Married all children of age [2]	.11	.05	2.93	.14	.06	3.47	.13	.06	4.29
Married some children of age [2]	.07	.04	2.32	.07	.04	2.12	.08	.05	2.42
Constant	−.27		−4.107	−.32		−4.83	−.32		−4.84
R²	.55			.54			.54		
Standard error of estimate	.48			.48			.48		
Mean value, dep. variable	ℓ_n1.22			ℓ_n1.22			ℓ_n1.22		
Durbin-Watson	1.99			1.98			1.99		

III. Regressions on value of consumer durables (logged), 1658–1702 (N = 632)[f]

	A. With total divers. index (27 indicators)			B. With craft index (12 indicators)			C. With cloth index (4 indicators)		
	B	Beta	T	B	Beta	T	B	Beta	T
Wealth group 2 (£50–225) [2]	1.27	.42	14.25	1.32	.44	14.54	1.31	.43	14.55
Wealth group 3 (£226+) [2]	1.60	.36	4.90	1.77	.40	10.97	1.76	.39	10.92
Size of labor force [1]	.40	.22	6.16	.44	.24	6.65	.44	.24	6.69
Diversification	.13	.15	5.24				.18	.07	2.49
Married children 0 or minors [2]	.26	.09	3.12	.28	.10	3.33	.29	.10	3.36
Time	.01	.09	3.42	.01	.12	4.27	.01	.11	4.26
Married some children of age [2]	.40	.08	2.90	.45	.10	3.25	.45	.10	3.24
Married all children of age [2]	.35	.05	2.02	.36	.05	1.99	.38	.06	2.14
Constant	.69		6.72	.67		6.42	.68		6.53
R²	.60			.58			.58		
Standard error of estimate	.89			.91			.91		
Mean value, dep. variable	ℓℓ2.07			ℓℓ2.07			ℓℓ2.07		
Durbin-Watson	2.02			2.02			2.02		

Appendix table 2. (*continued*)

IV. Regressions on value of consumer durables (logged), 1703–77 (N = 1,914)[g]

	A. With total divers. index (27 indicators)			B. With craft index (12 indicators)			C. With cloth index (4 indicators)		
	B	Beta	T	B	Beta	T	B	Beta	T
Wealth group 3 (£226+) [2]	1.47	.49	17.53	.60	.53	19.12	1.66	.55	19.72
Wealth group 2 (£50–225) [2]	.86	.36	19.59	.95	.40	21.66	.98	.41	22.24
Diversification, 1703–49	.10	.29	13.33	.14	.21	10.15	.16	.17	8.13
Married children 0 or minors [2]	.34	.14	8.49	.35	.14	8.35	.35	.14	8.35
Married some children of age [2]	.40	.14	8.58	.40	.15	8.44	.43	.16	9.05
Size of labor force [1]	.16	.13	5.29	.17	.14	5.44	.18	.15	5.66
Married all children of age [2]	.40	.11	7.00	.44	.12	7.66	.44	.12	7.61
Diversification, 1750+	.06	.05	8.57	.09	.08	6.42	.10	.08	5.00
Time							-.002	-.04	-2.05
Constant	1.36		28.48	1.44		30.67	1.47		31.39
R²	.63			.62			.61		
Standard error of estimate	.70			.72			.72		
Mean value, dep. variable	2.62			2.62			2.62		
Durbin-Watson	1.59			1.58			1.58		

SOURCE: Maryland History Computer Files, Historic St. Mary's City Commission, Maryland State Archives, Annapolis.

[a]Variables omitted because not significant: wealth group 3 (£226+); all life cycle variables; time.

[b][1] logged with natural logarithms.

[c][3] dummy variable applied to a continuous variable.

[d]Variable omitted because not significant: size of labor force.

[e][2] dummy variable, 0 or 1.

[f]Variables omitted because not significant: diversification in regression with craft index.

[g]Variables omitted because not significant: time in regressions with total diversification and craft indices.

Appendix table 3. Somerset County regressions (N = 2,082)

| | I. Regressions on amenities scores (12 indicators, logged)[a] | | | | | | | | |
| | A. With total divers. index (27 indicators) | | | B. With craft index (12 indicators) | | | C. With cloth index (4 indicators) | | |
	B	Beta	T	B	Beta	T	B	Beta	T
Total estate value	.22	.39	10.24	.24	.42	10.92	.24	.42	11.10
Time	.008	.28	16.42	.008	.30	18.52	.009	.30	18.87
Diversification	.04	.27	11.94	.07	.23	11.81	.10	.21	11.28
Married children 0 or minors [2][b]	.11	.07	3.67	.11	.07	3.60	.10	.07	3.19
Constant	-.52		-7.34	-.59		-8.45	-.62		-8.81
R²	.56			.56			.55		
Standard error of estimate	.48			.48			.48		
Mean value, dep. variable	log 1.24			log 1.24			log 1.24		
Durbin-Watson	1.88			1.90			1.87		

II. Regressions on value of consumer durables (logged)[c]

	A. With total divers. index (27 indicators)			B. With craft index (12 indicators)			C. With cloth index (4 indicators)		
	B	Beta	T	B	Beta	T	B	Beta	T
Wealth group 3 (£226+) [2]	1.35	.42	17.62	1.51	.47	19.86	1.57	.49	20.63
Diversification, 1665–1749	.09	.34	16.61	.13	.25	14.02	.18	.22	12.87
Wealth group 2 (£50–225) [2]	.75	.32	18.68	.84	.35	20.82	.86	.36	21.42
Size of labor force [1][d]	.19	.15	6.66	.21	.16	7.27	.23	.18	8.02
Married children 0 or minors [2]	.34	.14	7.80	.38	.15	8.45	.37	.15	8.16
Married some children of age [2]	.36	.14	7.66	.40	.16	8.43	.40	.15	8.20
Married all children of age [2]	.35	.10	6.18	.41	.11	7.07	.39	.11	6.56
Diversification, 1750+	.06	.06	5.00	.07	.07	5.83	.11	.10	6.11
Time							.002	.04	2.12
Constant	1.27		22.16	1.24		21.32	1.23		20.98
R^2	.65			.64			.64		
Standard error of estimate	.69			.70			.71		
Mean value, dep. variable	ℓ2.70			ℓ2.70			ℓ2.70		
Durbin-Watson	1.94			1.95			1.96		

SOURCE: Maryland History Computer Files, Historic St. Mary's City Commission, Maryland State Archives, Annapolis.

NOTES: For wealth groups, 0 class is less than £50; for life cycles, single. The dependent variables are logged with natural logarithms.

[a] Variables omitted because not significant: wealth groups 2 (£50–225) and 3 (£226+); size of labor force; married, some children of age; married, all children of age.

[b] [2] dummy variable, 0 or 1.

[c] Variables omitted because not significant: time in regressions with total diversification and craft indices.

[d] [1] logged with natural logarithms.

Appendix table 4. York County regressions (N = 1,097)

| | I. Regressions on amenities scores (12 indicators, logged)[a] | | | | | | | | |
| | A. With total divers. index (27 indicators) | | | B. With craft index (12 indicators) | | | C. With cloth index (4 indicators) | | |
	B	Beta	T	B	Beta	T	B	Beta	T
Total estate value	.19	.40	5.95	.20	.41	6.19	.21	.44	6.47
Diversification	.06	.28	9.60	.11	.24	9.05	.11	.17	6.40
Urban-rural location [2][b]	.49	.23	9.34	.47	.22	9.02	.47	.22	8.62
Time	.002	.08	2.95	.002	.07	2.59	.002	.07	2.51
Married children 0 or minors [2]	.11	.07	2.75	.11	.07	2.67	.11	.07	2.64
Constant	-.05		-.51	-.06		-.55	-.07		-.69
R²	.42			.41			.39		
Standard error of estimate	.55			.55			.56		
Mean value, dep. variable	$\ln$1.213			$\ln$1.213			$\ln$1.213		
Durbin-Watson	1.94			1.92			1.92		

II. Regressions on value of consumer durables (logged)[c]

	A. With total divers. index (27 indicators)			B. With craft index (12 indicators)			C. With cloth index (4 indicators)		
	B	Beta	T	B	Beta	T	B	Beta	T
Wealth group 3 (£226+) [2]	.97	.32	8.40	1.07	.36	9.20	1.11	.37	9.44
Diversification, 1658–1749	.13	.31	10.59	.20	.24	8.86	.22	.19	6.75
Size of labor force [1][d]	.28	.23	6.69	.32	.26	7.76	.35	.29	8.30
Urban-rural location [2]	.85	.22	9.89	.81	.21	9.40	.80	.21	8.89
Wealth group 2 (£50–225) [2]	.52	.19	6.97	.55	.20	7.22	.58	.21	7.47
Married children 0 or minors [2]	.35	.12	5.16	.36	.13	5.24	.37	.13	5.22
Diversification, 1750+	.09	.10	6.43				.13	.14	3.33
Married some children of age [2]	.34	.09	3.82	.38	.10	4.20	.41	.11	4.52
Constant	1.56		13.21	1.64		13.79	1.63		13.44
R²	.54			.53			.51		
Standard error of estimate	.91			.92			.94		
Mean value, dep. variable	ℓ2.91			ℓ2.91			ℓ2.91		
Durbin-Watson	1.84			1.46			1.85		

SOURCE: Maryland History Computer Files, Historic St. Mary's City Commission, Maryland State Archives, Annapolis.

NOTES: For wealth groups, 0 class is less than £50; for life cycles, single. The dependent variables are logged with natural logarithms.

[a]Variables omitted because not significant: wealth groups 2 (£50–225) and 3 (£226+); size of labor force; married, some children of age; married, all children of age.

[b][2] dummy variable, 0 or 1.

[c]Variables omitted because not significant: time; married, all children of age; diversification, 1750+ for regression with craft index.

[d][1] logged with natural logarithms.

declined afer 1750. The earlier additions to planters' economic activities had indeed had the most effect, although beginning in 1658, not in 1705.

The remaining variables showed greater change from
county to county. Time preceded diversification in predicting
the appearance of amenities in Somerset County but elsewhere had less effect than diversification on this measure. Not
surprisingly, time was insignificant in seventeenth-century St.
Mary's County, where consumption scores had barely started
to grow by 1702; if the other counties had been divided at the
same date, the result would have been similar.[4] Time had little
or no influence anywhere on value of consumer durables.

Life-cycle variables had mostly small effects. Except in
eighteenth-century St. Mary's, only Life Cycle 2 was significant for scores, but the positive influence of being married
was clear.[5] All married life cycles were significant and positive
in all the regressions for value of consumer durables except
one. In York County, Life Cycle 4 was insignificant. Why this
difference appeared is unclear.

The regressions for Anne Arundel County are the only
ones that test for the effects of inheritance. To our surprise,
although the first native-born generation was significant for
scores, it was negative, and with a minor exception all native-
born variables were insignificant for value of consumer durables. The exception was the regression that included the cloth
index, which showed a small effect from being second generation of native-born. Apart from this, other things being equal,
only status as a free immigrant predicted more value in consumer assets than those who were servant immigrants. Inheritance had little importance for consumer behavior.

Size of the bound labor force was included for its likely positive effect on value of consumer durables. The results showed
considerable variation. Sometimes this variable followed diversification and preceded life cycle, and sometimes the re-

[4]The regressions for Anne Arundel County to 1702 produced the same
result.

[5]In Anne Arundel County we ran the regressions on scores with single
vs. married as an independent variable. Marriage was significant, although
last in importance, after literacy.

verse was true. In the seventeenth century, as shown in St. Mary's County, the number of bound laborers may have had greater importance than later. There was little diversification anywhere in the Chesapeake, and unmarried decedents were a far larger proportion of the inventoried population than they were after 1700. What appeared unexpectedly in seventeenth-century St. Mary's was a significant and positive effect of the number of laborers on consumption scores. This probably was a byproduct of wealth, and in any case was always small.

Like the inheritance variables, education could be tested only in Anne Arundel County. Mainly this was a test for signature literacy—that is, whether a person could sign a document with his or her name, rather than with a mark. In the regressions for scored amenities, literacy was significant and positive, but the effects were the least of any variable. Literacy was insignificant for value of consumer durables.

We attempted unsuccessfully to find a way to include the terms of trade in the regression equation. The problem arose from the fact that our measure for terms of trade is a comparison of annual price relatives[6] of tobacco and imported manufactures, whereas consumer durables were accumulated over a period of years. One is a flow, the other a stock. We have no way to determine when a planter purchased his amenities or other consumer durables. We tried taking only planters in Life Cycle 2—those married or widowed with no children of age, who probably had not been householders for more than fifteen years. We then lagged the price relatives for one to ten years but had no significant results for any period of lag. One could interpret this to mean that planters did not purchase amenities with the increased disposable income that came when the price of tobacco rose relative to the prices of imports. Since diversification correlated positively to rising scores, one might conclude that internal economic development rather than events in the export sector was primarily responsible for changes in consumer behavior. However, it

[6]To obtain price relatives one chooses a base year or years and divides each price by the price for the base year or years. This form of standardization enables one to compare price movements of different kinds of goods.

seemed too uncertain that our measure had corrected the stock-flow problem to draw such a conclusion from a totally negative result. We finally abandoned the effort to include the terms of trade among the independent variables.

The meaning of these results for changes in consumption is discussed in the text.

We owe thanks to many friends and colleagues. Jean B. Russo and Helen M. Hunter provided essential assistance with the preparation of the essay, and Robert J. Brugger, Richard L. Bushman, Cary Carson, Stanley Engerman, Robert Gallman, Gloria L. Main, Jackson T. Main, and Carole Shammas made helpful comments. The essay also has benefited from presentation to the Washington Area Seminar in Early American History and the Seminar of the Philadelphia Center for Early American Studies. In addition, we express our gratitude to David Bohmer and Billy G. Smith, who participated in the early phases of this research, and to the valiant coders who made possible the collection of the data: Emily Kutler, Marianne Braun, Susan Collins, Victoria Allan, Christopher Allan, Elizabeth Blistein, Janice Watson, Nancy Baker, and Dreama Greaves. This research is part of a larger study of Chesapeake economy and society in which we are collaborating with P. M. G. Harris and Russell R. Menard. They have provided invaluable advice and support. No one in this army of collaborators and advisors is responsible for our errors.

EDWARD A. CHAPPELL

Housing a Nation: The Transformation of Living Standards in Early America

FOR ALL ITS present-day allure, eighteenth-century life was not just a simplified version of our own existence, dignified by the soothing presence of Copleys, creamware, and chintz. Each new scholarly excursion into the preindustrial past seems to remove the lives of ordinary people further from our own. The diets of these people were poorer, their clothing meaner, and their personal habits ruder and more violent than most historians once imagined.[1] Earliest European-Americans could be an ill-smelling, eye-gouging horde, squatting for want of chairs, eating communally for lack of individual utensils and vessels. The majority offered little portent of dawning bourgeois sensibilities.

The notion of a consumer revolution now figures prominently in attempts to explain when and how this world was

For their assistance in the preparation of this essay the author wishes to thank Barbara G. Carson and Cary Carson, B. D. Cotton, Willie Graham, Bernard L. Herman, Kevin Kelly, Carl R. Lounsbury, Vanessa Patrick, Orlando Ridout V, Helen Tate, Dell Upton, and Mark R. Wenger. Research and writing were supported by a fellowship from the Virginia Foundation for the Humanities.

[1] Billy G. Smith, The "Lower Sort": Philadelphia's Laboring People, 1750–1800 (Ithaca, N.Y., 1990); Gloria L. Main, Tobacco Colony: Life in Early Maryland, 1650–1720 (Princeton, 1982); Norbert Elias, The Civilizing Process: The Development of Manners, vol. 1, trans. Edmund Jephcott (New York, 1978); Robert Darnton, The Great Cat Massacre and Other Episodes in French Cultural History (New York, 1984).

transformed. English and American historians have argued that by the latter half of the eighteenth century great numbers of people were able to purchase a wide variety of goods. An accelerated economy permitted large-scale advances in access to durable goods, ostensibly for working people as well as the rich, and by the last quarter of the eighteenth century, material accommodation for English men and women had changed profoundly. These were early stages of what was to be a sustained revolution.[2]

Yet one must ask how accurately this rosy and Whiggish view reflects the realities of life in eighteenth-century America. What *was* the extent of the consumer revolution in America? Was the recasting of material culture in the colonies and early republic as thorough and pervasive as we have been led to believe? If so, was it essentially concurrent with developments in England, and who were affected? How great was the advance in use of material goods, *in terms of economic class and category of things consumed?* To put it differently, how much did the change affect the living standards of ordinary people?

As containers for people's goods and activities, houses have obvious relevance to these questions. They are the ultimate consumer object. Houses embody attitudes toward material life and are shaped by new domestic activities and changing economic conditions.[3] While many people live their lives without building or significantly altering their houses, those who do demonstrate much about social relations and perceived domestic needs. Degrees of permanence, size, allowance for privacy, and finish employed in rooms for specialized domestic activity all reveal people's priorities as well as their ability to pay. Ideas about light, cleanliness, and warmth are of special

[2] Neil McKendrick, John Brewer, and J. H. Plumb, *The Birth of a Consumer Society: The Commercialization of Eighteenth-Century England* (Bloomington, Ind., 1982).

[3] James J. F. Deetz, "Ceramics from Plymouth, 1635–1835: The Archaeological Evidence," in Ian M. G. Quimby, ed., *Ceramics in America* (Charlottesville, Va., 1973), pp. 15–40. Nineteenth-century critics saw this in broad moral terms. Landscape architect and popular advisor on household design A. J. Downing observed that "much of the character of every man may be read in his house" (Downing, *The Architecture of Country Houses* [New York, 1850], p. 25).

significance. Costly and resistant to easy modification, housing is more essential to standards of living than objects easily acquired and discarded. Broad shifts in housing may be, then, more reliable measures of how life changed than chamber pots and dressing boxes.

A broad segment of the eighteenth-century American population lived in houses without plaster walls, wood floors, or glass windows. Dwellings often consisted of no more than a single heated room. Our most basic middle- and working-class expectations about housing would have appeared extravagant and foreign to these Americans—people for whom it was not so remarkable to urinate through broken windows or dance in rooms where snow had drifted on the floor.[4] Using houses as a criterion, I propose to investigate the bounds of new consumption. What were the social limits of good housing, and how did those limits change?

Certainly the consumer revolution brought significant innovations to some English houses,[5] changes that went beyond the earlier improvements of inserted fireplaces, floored halls,

---

[4]The cost of labor and materials, for example, made glazed window sash a luxury affordable only to the relatively affluent. Even among those occupying buildings with glazed windows, concern for soundness of sash appears to have been somewhat less than our own. In 1772 the eternally unhappy Landon Carter fretted about his daughter's attending a dance held at a tavern where, according to his sources, sufficient snow had blown through broken windows to form drifts in the ballroom. Twenty-five years later, Louis-Philippe recorded American males' practice of urinating through broken panes, a custom he supposedly embraced until he found himself in a room with openings too high to reach. Upon complaining of this difficulty, he was brought a cooking pot. Similar ambivalence existed about the soundness of chimneys. Wooden chimneys remained common in some regions throughout the colonial period and beyond, and some people survived with even less. In 1788, one John McFarguhar, a resident of Petersburg, Virginia, was charged with "keeping a fire in his sellar without a chimney contrary to the bye laws of our corporation" (Jack P. Greene, ed., *The Diary of Colonel Landon Carter of Sabine Hall, 1752–1778*, 2 vols. [Charlottesville, Va., 1965], 2:659; Louis-Philippe, *Diary of My Travels in America*, trans. Stephen Becker [New York, 1977], pp. 60–61; Petersburg Husting Court Minutes, 1 [1784–91], Virginia State Library, Richmond, pp. 221 [Mar. 5, 1788], 227 [May 7, 1788]).

[5]The essential treatments of the earlier "great rebuilding" are: W. G. Hoskins, "The Rebuilding of Rural England, 1570–1640," *Past and Present*

and separate withdrawing rooms. Few English landscapes eluded transformation in the eighteenth century. Enclosures, transportation projects, and estate planning altered the look of the land, while builders provided newly formalized interior spaces that segregated household activities by function and social class. In conspicuous ways, many new houses as well as renovated old ones offered improved accommodation in smoothly plastered, handsomely trimmed rooms arranged behind well-ordered facades.[6] Large, symmetrically deployed windows illuminated the rational spaces that succeeded low, dimly lit interiors with nonclassical woodwork. If the sixteenth- and seventeenth-century great rebuilding created the private house, with multiple spaces allowing individuals separation from the extended family and community, the Georgian rebuilding created the *refined house*. Yet just what

---

4 (1953):44–89; J. T. Smith, "The Evolution of the English Peasant House to the Late Seventeenth Century: The Evidence of the Buildings," *Journal of the British Archaeological Association,* 3d ser. 33 (1970):122–47; R. Machin, "The Great Rebuilding: A Reassessment," *Past and Present* 77 (1977):33–56; and idem, *The Houses of Yetminster [Dorset]* (Bristol, 1978). On Georgian change, see Michael Reed, *The Georgian Triumph, 1700–1830* (London, 1983); Penelope J. Corfield, *The Impact of English Towns, 1700–1800* (Oxford, 1982); C. W. Chalkin, *The Provincial Towns of Georgian England: A Study of the Building Process, 1740–1820* (London, 1974); Peter Borsay, *The English Urban Renaissance: Culture and Society in the Provincial Town, 1660–1770* (Oxford, 1989), pp. 3–113.

[6]The modern concept of Georgianization as a reordering of people's material world has been more broadly considered in the United States than Britain. See Henry Glassie, *Folk Housing in Middle Virginia: A Structural Analysis of Historic Artifacts* (Knoxville, Tenn., 1975); idem, "Meaningful Things and Appropriate Myths: The Artifact's Place in American Studies," in *Prospects: An Annual of American Cultural Studies,* ed. Jack Salzman, vol. 3 (1977), pp. 1–49; idem, "Eighteenth-Century Cultural Process in Delaware Valley Folk Building," *Winterthur Portfolio* 7 (1972):29–57; James J. F. Deetz, *In Small Things Forgotten: The Archaeology of Early American Life* (Garden City, N.Y., 1977); and, less closely tied to the evidence, Mark P. Leone, "The Georgian Order as the Order of Merchant Capitalism in Annapolis, Maryland," in Mark P. Leone and Parker B. Potter, Jr., eds., *The Recovery of Meaning: Historical Archaeology in the Eastern United States* (Washington, D.C., 1988), pp. 235–61.

segment of the English population was Georgianized remains an unanswered question.[7]

For some eighteenth-century Americans, the quality of housing improved markedly, but for most it changed modestly if at all. In architectural terms, the eighteenth century saw a growing disparity between kinds of people rather than a general advance in the quality of life. The disparity perhaps is not surprising, although the inferior quality of so much eighteenth-century housing may disappoint expectations raised by Neil McKendrick and J. H. Plumb. What is *unex-pected*, but resoundingly demonstrated by the buildings themselves, is that the housing change most relevant to the present topic took place in the decades following the American Revolution, not before. Even this transformation appears to have been largely confined to the upper reaches of rural and urban society. Yet it is the closest thing we find to a housing revolution in early America. Ultimately, reasons for the change call for explanation.

In the seventeenth-century Chesapeake, buildings were overwhelmingly poor in quality. Archaeologist Garry Wheeler Stone's observation that "the roof leaked, but the price was right" is an apt description of housing conditions for almost everyone in the first century of settlement.[8] Much earth has

[7]Art and architectural historians have attended to the process of genteel change in accommodation largely ignored by their vernacular colleagues, but most of the work was focused on such a rarefied level that it is of peripheral interest to those who search for demographics. The best work is Mark Girouard's popular *Life in the English Country House: A Social and Architectural History* (New Haven, 1978) and Dan Cruickshank and Neil Burton's *Life in the Georgian City* (London, 1990). Also see Peter Thornton, *Seventeenth-Century Interior Decoration in England, France, and Holland* (New Haven, 1978); John Fowler and John Cornforth, *English Decoration in the 18th Century* (London, 1974).

[8]Cary Carson, Norman F. Barka, William M. Kelso, Garry Wheeler Stone, and Dell Upton, "Impermanent Architecture in the Southern American Colonies," *Winterthur Portfolio* 16 (1981):135–96. Dell Upton was the first scholar fully to recognize and deal with the poor quality of much early Chesapeake building. See Upton, "Early Vernacular Architecture in Southeastern Virginia," Ph.D. diss., Brown University, 1980; idem, "Board

been moved in Maryland and Virginia to reveal the fact, unrecognized by earlier historians, that *durable* seventeenth-century houses were exceptional.[9] Bacon's Castle is one of the few that remain in Virginia, not because the land was laid waste by nineteenth-century economics and war, but because multistory brick houses were always rare in the colony. A single house in Maryland is thought to predate 1700, and despite several claimants none appear to survive in the Carolinas. Rich seventeenth-century Virginians and Marylanders might have indulged in costly clothing and tablewares, but their houses were generally frame structures without masonry foundations. For social as well as structural reasons such houses did not survive many generations.

There were exceptions, of course, including a striking frame house of manorial character apparently built for Sir George Yeardley or Abraham Peirsey before 1630 on the south side of the James River and long since lost.[10] There

Roofing in Tidewater Virginia," *APT Bulletin* 8 (1976):22–43; idem, "New Views of the Virginia Landscape," *Virginia Magazine of History and Biography* 96 (1988):421–25. Garry Wheeler Stone, "The Roof Leaked, but the Price Was Right: The Virginia House Reconsidered" (Paper presented at the Annual Meeting of the Society for Historical Archaeology, Williamsburg, Jan. 1984).

[9]The majority of the sites remain individually unpublished, though Carson et al., "Impermanent Architecture," provides a concise summary of most of those excavated before 1981. Also see William M. Kelso, *Kingsmill Plantations 1619–1800: Archaeology of Country Life in Colonial Virginia* (Orlando, Fla., 1984); Garry Wheeler Stone, "St. John's Archaeological Questions and Answers," *Maryland Historical Magazine* 69 (1974):146–68; idem, "Society, Housing, and Architecture in Early Maryland: John Lewger's St. John's," Ph.D. diss., University of Pennsylvania, 1982; Robert W. Keller, "The Homelot on the Seventeenth-Century Chesapeake Tidewater Frontier," Ph.D. diss., University of Oregon, 1978; William T. Buchanan and Edward F. Heite, "The Hallowes Site: A Seventeenth-Century Yeoman's Cottage in Virginia," *Historical Archaeology* 5 (1971):38–48.

[10]The Flowerdew Hundred house began as a forty-one by twenty-four-foot structure with an off-center projection perhaps too large solely for a stair block. That this was a three-unit house is a reasonable assumption, the hall and inner room both being provided with five-foot fireplaces. The house was enlarged with sheds and a large attached workroom before coming down around midcentury (Norman F. Barka, "The Archaeology of

were also at least three substantial groups of row houses and several freestanding houses of high quality and splashy design built at Jamestown in the last half of the seventeenth century. It is evident that the rooms in these buildings were well-finished with plaster and trim, as well as being sufficient in number to allow for generous division of functions and provision of personal space. In fact, one may see some evidence of improvement in the quality of the best Virginia houses late in the century—for example in the presence of well-built roofs covered with tiles or imported slate at Jamestown and on houses of some rich planters like Thomas Swann's across the James in Surry. Also built in the last quarter, an impressive double-pile brick house measuring a surprising fifty-four by forty-four feet and standing at least two stories high was built by John Custis at Arlington on the southern tip of the Virginia Eastern Shore. But for Gov. William Berkeley's Greenspring, Arlington represents the largest private house we know of from the seventeenth-century Chesapeake. Together with the Jamestown edifices, it was so unusual as to be atypical of even the most affluent Virginians' housing.[11]

Flowerdew Hundred Plantation: The Stone House Foundation Site—An Interim Report," unpublished manuscript, 1976, Southside Historical Sites, Inc., Hopewell, Va.; Carson et al., "Impermanent Architecture," pp. 152, 182).

[11] Excavations carried out on Jamestown Island from 1901 until 1957 revealed the solid brick foundations of as many as a dozen relatively substantial houses, all apparently outside the old town. Probably most lavish was a large U-shaped building constructed of brick and containing at least one public room richly decorated with high-relief plasterwork. The good room was located in one of the projecting wings; paving suggests that the opposite wing contained service space. Unfortunately, this was among the most poorly excavated buildings (John L. Cotter, *Archaeological Excavations at Jamestown, Virginia* [Washington, D. C., 1958]; Kathleen J. Bragdon, Cary Carson, Edward A. Chappell, and Willie Graham, "The Range of Building Styles in Late Seventeenth-Century Jamestown" [Paper presented at the Annual Meeting of the Archaeological Society of Virginia, Hampton, Oct. 1988]). Related plasterwork was found in 1991 in the cellar of The Mount, a lost fifty-foot by twenty-three-foot brick house built about 1696 near Port Royal, Caroline County. The foundations of the Arlington house were recently discovered in the midst of a housing development and partially excavated by the James River Institute for Archaeology. Those foundations

More representative was the "manner house" at the Clifts Plantation on the Potomac River, constructed around 1670 by means of posts stuck directly into the earth; the same was true of the James City County houses of Thomas Pettus, a member of the governor's council, and William Drummond, also a member of the colony's elite, who was executed for his support of Nathaniel Bacon.[12] Lesser Virginians and Marylanders occupied small dwellings with earthfast frame walls that required periodic shoring in order to survive for a decade or two.[13]

Until recently, lower death rates and the substantial middling status of some seventeenth-century New Englanders have been interpreted as cause for the building of durable two-room and larger houses within one or two generations of settlement.[14] Accepting inventories and surviving buildings at

---

suggest that the main elevations were symmetrical, but it is likely that they did not enclose a central stair passage running the depth of the building. Other recent excavations at Curles Neck in Henrico County, Virginia, have located the remains of a single-room-plan house of multiple stories, built about 1675 against an existing frame structure. The new house had walls decorated with richly molded bricks and was covered with a tile roof. It has been argued that this is the house occupied briefly by Nathaniel Bacon before Bacon's Rebellion in 1676 (excavation by Daniel Mouer, Archaeological Research Center, Virginia Commonwealth University, Richmond).

[12] Fraser Neiman, "Domestic Architecture at the Clifts Plantation: The Social Context of Early Virginia Building," *Northern Neck of Virginia Historical Magazine* 28 (1978):3096–4128; idem, *The "Manner House" before Stratford (Discovering the "Clift's Plantation")* (Stratford, Va., 1980); Kelso, *Kingsmill Plantations*, pp. 76–80. Drummond excavation by Alain C. Outlaw, Division of Historic Landmarks, Richmond.

[13] The archaeological remains of several more modest earthfast Virginia houses are discussed and the economic status of their occupants considered in Nicholas M. Luccketti, "Archaeology at Bennett Farm: The Life Style of a Seventeenth-Century Middling Planter in York County, Virginia," M.A. thesis, College of William and Mary, 1990.

[14] Abbott Lowell Cummings, *The Framed Houses of Massachusetts Bay, 1625–1725* (Cambridge, Mass., 1979), esp. pp. 203–4; Robert Blair St. George, "'Set Thine House in Order': The Domestication of the Yeomanry in Seventeenth-Century New England," in Jonathan L. Fairbanks and Robert F. Trent, eds., *New England Begins: The Seventeenth Century*, 3 vols. (Boston, 1982), 2:159–87. St. George's 145 two- to six-room houses enumerated in

face value, scholars have portrayed seventeenth-century New England as a land of comparative prosperity and physical comfort. But recent work there and in the Mid-Atlantic states suggests that conditions in these areas were more primitive for longer periods of time than previously supposed. Archaeological discoveries of buildings with earthfast frames in Massachusetts have been confined so far to sites occupied before about 1660, leading their excavators to see impermanent building as primarily a characteristic of the settlement period.[15] Maine archaeologists have recently found posthole remnants and cellars of impermanent buildings dating from the 1630s to the 1730s, and evidence of an earthfast frame farmhouse and outbuilding with plank-lined cellar dating as late as 1816 has just appeared near Burlington, Vermont.[16]

New England inventories before 1701 are impressive, though one assumes these houses were highly unrepresentative at the time they were inventoried (p. 168). Also see Anthony N. B. Garvan, *Architecture and Town Planning in Colonial Connecticut* (New Haven, 1951); Dell Upton, "Architectural Change in Colonial Rhode Island: The Mott House as a Case Study," *Old-Time New England* 69 (1979):18–23; William N. Hosley, Jr., "Architecture," in Gerald W. R. Ward and William N. Hosley, Jr., eds., *The Great River: Art and Society of the Connecticut Valley, 1635–1820* (Hartford, 1985), pp. 63–66, 73–74.

[15] James J. F. Deetz, "Plymouth Colony Architecture: Archaeological Evidence from the Seventeenth Century," in Abbott Lowell Cummings, ed., *Architecture in Colonial Massachusetts* (Boston, 1979), pp. 43–59; Steven R. Pendery, "Impermanent Architecture in Early New England" (Paper presented at the Annual Meeting of the Society for Historical Archaeology, Williamsburg, Jan. 1984); idem, "Symbols of Community: Status Differences and the Archaeological Record in Charlestown, Massachusetts, 1630–1760," Ph.D. diss., Harvard University, 1987. The large numbers of earthfast buildings found by Chesapeake archaeologists in the last two decades have not been paralleled by New England discoveries, but much of this imbalance may be due to the greater extent of excavation to the south, as some of the impermanent structures—like the 1638 James Garrett House in Charlestown—were of relatively high status.

[16] Emerson W. Baker, Robert L. Bradley, Leon Cranmer, and Neill DePaoli, "Earthfast Architecture in Early Maine" (Paper presented at the Annual Meeting of the Vernacular Architecture Forum, Portsmouth, N. H., May 1992); Leon Cranmer, *Cushnoc: The History and Archaeology of Plymouth Colony Traders on the Kennebec* (Augusta, Maine, 1990); Robert L. Bradley, "Was the Plantation Despicable? The Archaeology of the Phips Site, ca.

Archaeologists excavating the site of Snowtown, a free black and poor white neighborhood beside the tidal basin in Providence, Rhode Island, found the remains of two houses supported on posts and an outbuilding with wood-lined cellar, all damaged by the "Great Gale" of 1815. Cellars of similar nature were constructed at the Providence site again after the hurricane.[17]

Likewise, the excavation of plank-lined cellars of what New York state archaeologist Paul R. Huey calls "perishable" buildings in the Hudson Valley dating from early Dutch settlement into the second half of the eighteenth century suggests that the proper world one might imagine from the 1670 Castello plan of New Amsterdam had significant limits.[18] What a decade ago seemed a radical portrait of unsavory life in seventeenth-century Virginia and Maryland now appears to represent more the norm throughout the East Coast.

Portions of Massachusetts Bay may provide only New England exceptions, with a relatively large number of surviving "first period" buildings in Essex County and circumstantial evidence for similar structures built by rich inhabitants of Boston and its environs. Among New England's current vernacular architecture scholars, the consensus is that not a single seventeenth-century house survives in Maine, only a handful in New Hampshire, and at most several dozen in

---

1646–1676," *Kennebec Proprietor* 6 (1990):11–17. Excavation at Essex, Vermont, by Robert A. Sloma, The Consulting Archaeological Program, University of Vermont.

[17]Myron O. Stachiw, "Impermanent Architecture in the City: Examples from Nineteenth-Century New England" (Paper presented at the Annual Meeting of the Vernacular Architecture Forum, Port Penn, Del., May 1984); Janice Artemel et al., *Providence Cove Lands: Phase III Report* (Washington, D.C., 1984).

[18]Paul R. Huey, "Archeological Evidence of Dutch Wooden Cellars and Perishable Wooden Structures at Seventeenth and Eighteenth Century Sites in the Upper Hudson Valley," in Roderic H. Blackburn and Nancy A. Kelley, *New World Dutch Studies: Dutch Arts and Culture in Colonial America, 1609–1776* (Albany, 1987), pp. 13–35; idem, "Aspects of Continuity and Change in Colonial Dutch Material Culture at Fort Orange, 1624–1664," Ph.D. diss., University of Pennsylvania, 1988.

Rhode Island, Connecticut, and old Plymouth.[19] The sturdy stone-enders long thought characteristic of life in early Rhode Island are now viewed as exotics stationed at the upper end of the colony's late seventeenth-century accommodation.

Polite housing came late and only for a few. Even among the wealthiest East Coast gentry, substantial mansions were generally not built until the first half, usually the second quarter, of the eighteenth century.[20] The best were constructed of brick, two or sometimes three stories high, and had rooms

[19]"First Period Buildings in Eastern Massachusetts: A Thematic Survey Report, Phase 1: Essex, Suffolk, and Middlesex Counties," comp. Richard M. Candee, unpublished report, n.d., Preservation Studies Program and American & New England Studies Program, Boston University; idem, "A Documentary History of Plymouth Colony Architecture, 1620–1700," *Old-Time New England* 59 (1969):58–71, 105–11; vol. 60 (1969):36–53; idem, "The Architecture of Maine's Settlement: Vernacular Architecture to About 1720," in Deborah Thompson, ed., *Maine Forms of American Architecture* (Waterville, Maine, 1976), pp. 15–44; idem, "Wooden Building in Early Maine and New Hampshire: A Technological and Cultural History, 1600–1720," Ph.D. diss., University of Pennsylvania, 1976; Robert L. Bradley, *Maine's First Buildings: The Architecture of Settlement, 1604–1700* (Augusta, Maine, n.d.); Robert Blair St. George, "Retreat from the Wilderness: Pattern in the Domestic Environments of Southeastern New England, 1630–1730," Ph.D. diss., University of Pennsylvania, 1982.

[20]Robert Carter's Corotoman in Lancaster County, Virginia, provides a useful benchmark for high gentry housing in the early Chesapeake. Carter, thought to be the richest Virginian living in the first quarter of the eighteenth century, built himself a mansion in about 1720, at the height of his financial career. The house burned in 1729, while still occupied by Carter, and its site was excavated in 1977–78. What archaeologists found was not a double-pile building like Custis's Arlington or later Georgian houses, but an overscaled single-pile center-passage house with large closets beyond the fireplaces of two first-floor rooms and a substantial porch running the length of the house. Despite its impressive size (ninety feet by twenty-five feet without the porch), the house offered few rooms for differentiated social activity. The windows seem to have held casements rather than sliding sash (see Carter L. Hudgins, "Archaeology in the 'King's' Realm: A Summary Report of a 1977 Survey at Corotoman with a Proposal for the 1979 Season," unpublished report, Virginia Research Center for Archaeology, Williamsburg, 1979, esp. pp. 22–28; idem, "Archaeology in the 'King's' Realm: Excavations at Robert Carter's Corotoman," unpublished report, Virginia Research Center for Archaeology, Yorktown, 1982). The majority of the great Georgian houses in the Chesapeake were not built until the

arranged two deep. Principal facades were balanced, and circulation patterns almost universally allowed independent access to entertainment rooms and bedchambers. Plaster and wainscoting were costly additions that carried connotations of wealth and position, and varying degrees of finish clarified the relative social importance of different rooms.[21] Such distinctions were very important, since one of the chief motivations for the new type of house was the creation of public spaces specifically intended for entertainment. Sometimes oversized but often not, these rooms were the focus of architectural decoration comparable to the best matched furniture and ceramics used or displayed there.[22] Builders of fancy housing increasingly moved domestic work areas away from the public spaces—into rear rooms in the North and into separate outbuildings in the South.

middle of the eighteenth century, though many of them have been mistaken for earlier houses. Perhaps the earliest surviving English-American house roughly conforming to what has come to be called Georgian planning is Verdmont, well off the east coast in Bermuda, a colony that developed a lively maritime economy in the seventeenth century and became the site of a sizable number of Bacon's Castle–like houses by the early eighteenth century. Verdmont dates between about 1700 and 1714.

[21]Dell Upton draws a contrast between "style" as a community-wide language of design and "mode" as a means of creating social distinctions. Employing Upton's terminology, we can see variation in quality of finish as modish behavior. Of course, scale as well as detail has generally played a role in defining social divisions. Upton observes that by building churches that resembled their houses in size and finish, the eighteenth-century Virginia elite suggested an inevitability to their status and a position closer to God than to their neighbors (Dell Upton, *Holy Things and Profane: Anglican Parish Churches in Colonial Virginia* [Cambridge, Mass., 1986], esp. pp. 101–73; idem, "Form and User: Style, Mode, Fashion and the Artifact," in Gerald L. Pocius, ed., *Living in the Material World: Canadian and American Approaches to the Material Culture* [St. Johns, Newfoundland, 1991], pp. 156–69).

[22]Mark. R. Wenger, "The Central Passage in Virginia: Evolution of an Eighteenth-Century Living Space," in Camille Wells, ed., *Perspectives in Vernacular Architecture, II* (Columbia, Mo., 1986), pp. 137–49; idem, "The Dining Room in Early Virginia," in Thomas Carter and Bernard L. Herman, eds., *Perspectives in Vernacular Architecture, III* (Columbia, Mo., 1989), pp. 149–59; Edward A. Chappell, "Looking at Buildings," *Fresh Advices: A Research Supplement to the Colonial Williamsburg Interpreter* 5 (1984):i–vi.

If traditional construction dates are roughly correct, a series of grand houses built by merchants in Boston and Portsmouth and the richest rice planters of the South Carolina lowcountry in the first two decades of the eighteenth century were among the earliest expressions of great conspicuous consumption in the mainland colonies.[23] At the same time a costly and assertive house for Virginia governors was being slowly constructed in Williamsburg.[24] This edifice must have affected the gentry perception of proper housing—at least in Virginia—in terms of scale, level of finish, and segregation of spaces. However, few gentry houses in Virginia or elsewhere in the colonies were based on any specific American model. Such houses were generally related to the sizable merchant or minor gentry houses in provincial British towns, but planned in response to local notions of what constituted a

[23] Abbott Lowell Cummings, "The Beginnings of Provincial Renaissance Architecture in Boston, 1690–1725," *Journal of the Society of Architectural Historians* 42 (1983):43–53; Richard M. Candee, "'An Old Town by the Sea': Urban Landscapes and Vernacular Building in Portsmouth, N.H., 1660–1990," (Field Guide for the Annual Meeting of the Vernacular Architecture Forum, Portsmouth, May 1992), pp. 40–44; Mills Lane, *Architecture of the Old South: South Carolina* (Savannah, 1984), pp. 14–32; Samuel Gaillard Stoney, *Plantations of the South Carolina Low Country,* ed. Albert Simons and Samuel Lapham, Jr. (Charleston, 1938). With the exception of the fanciful brick house called Mulberry, the most extraordinary of the early South Carolina mansions have been lost, making investigation of their long-accepted dates more difficult. One would like to see dendrochronological investigation done at Mulberry and archaeology at some of the other seemingly early gentry house sites. The advanced skeptic might also question whether the mansion that Thomas Hutchinson fled in the face of a 1767 Boston mob had reached its well-developed state in 1690–92, but be forewarned the extensive evidence has already been carefully weighed (see Abbott Lowell Cummings, "The Foster-Hutchinson House," *Old-Time New England* 54 [1964]:59–76). The house was pulled down in 1833, but a stone capital with pendants and garland reminiscent of the late seventeenth-century plasterwork from Jamestown and The Mount (n. 11, above) survives in the care of the Society for the Preservation of New England Antiquities.

[24] Marcus Whiffen, *The Public Buildings of Williamsburg* (Williamsburg, 1958), pp. 53–66, 88–95; Barbara G. Carson, *The Governor's Palace: The Williamsburg Residence of Virginia's Royal Governor* (Williamsburg, 1987); Mark R. Wenger, "Reconstruction of the Governor's Palace," unpublished report, 1980, Colonial Williamsburg Foundation, Williamsburg.

proper genteel environment.[25] Certainly this was the case with the brick houses built by affluent southern New Jersey farmers in the earliest decades of the century, as well as the better-known frame houses built in Connecticut and western Massachusetts forty and fifty years later.[26]

Lacking edifices of aristocratic scale, the late colonial American landscape was characterized nonetheless by vastly different grades of housing.[27] A revolution in taste transformed the kinds of houses that the most affluent would build, and yet the majority of people still lived in strikingly rustic homes. One of the more representative portraits of eighteenth-century Chesapeake buildings is provided by orphans court records maintained to ensure that guardians respected the property of minors. Large segments of the Maryland Or-

[25]Dell Upton, "Vernacular Domestic Architecture in Eighteenth-Century Virginia," *Winterthur Portfolio* 17 (1982):95–119, and idem, "Toward a Performance Theory of Vernacular Architecture: Early Tidewater Virginia as a Case Study," *Folklore Forum* 12 (1979):173–96. For a rather overwrought exposition on the British merchant connection, see Daniel D. Reiff, *Small Georgian Houses in England and Virginia: Origins and Development through the 1750s* (Newark, Del., 1986). Reiff accepts without question implausibly early dates for houses like Jamestown's Ambler mansion and proceeds to build a confused evolution on this faulty information. Although Thomas Tileston Waterman's *The Mansions of Virginia, 1706–1776* (Chapel Hill, N.C., 1945), is largely descriptive rather than analytical, and some of its date and designer attributions are now recognized as too optimistic, the book remains the chief available product of conscientious fieldwork among eighteenth-century American gentry houses.

[26]New Jersey fieldwork is now being pursued by Bernard L. Herman. The two venerable treatments of early Connecticut building are Norman M. Isham and Albert F. Brown, *Early Connecticut Houses: An Historical and Architectural Study* (1900; reprint ed., New York, 1965), and J. Frederick Kelly, *The Early Domestic Architecture of Connecticut* (1924; reprint ed., New York, 1963). Also, see Hosley, "Architecture," pp. 66–68, 98–102, and Kevin M. Sweeney, "Mansion People: Kinship, Class, and Architecture in Western Massachusetts in the Mid-Eighteenth Century," *Winterthur Portfolio* 19 (1984):231–55.

[27]Dell Upton, "Black and White Landscapes of Eighteenth-Century Virginia," *Places* 2 (1985):59–72; idem, *Holy Things and Profane*, pp. 110–14; Camille Wells, "The Eighteenth-Century Landscape of Virginia's Northern Neck," *Northern Neck of Virginia Historical Magazine* 37 (1987):4217–55.

phans Court records survive, and they describe an extraordinary variety of poor housing. The Maryland manuscripts suggest that most landowners were living in small houses having one or two rooms on the first floor and a loft above, all with simple finish, and generally with one and sometimes two brick chimneys.[28] Some tenants lived in well-finished two-room plan houses, but most occupied smaller dwellings with little or no trim, plaster, or paint. Such buildings were covered primarily with riven clapboards rather than sawn weatherboards and rounded shingles, and had minimal glazing. Slave housing was so inferior that most of it escaped detailed description. In short, orphans court records suggest a Chesapeake much like that portrayed by Rhys Isaac: a few large gentry mansions and some well-built lesser gentry and glebe

[28]Here is a representative, nicely detailed example. On May 20, 1744, two appraisers visited the Dorchester County property of John Rider Nevett. The "Indian Town lands" occupied by tenant Joseph Thompson had "one logged dwelling house 20 by 15 feet, old and not worth repairing." A more valuable piece of property was rented to James Layton, who occupied "one dwelling house of hewed logs 20 by 16 feet with an 8 foot shed, one brick chimney and another to the shed, plank floors above and below and a clapboard roof" and "one kitchen of round logs 26 by 12 feet with a clapboard roof and a wooden chimney." In addition to a barn and two corncribs, Layton's holding had "one logged quarter 16 by 12 feet covered with clapboards" and presumably either with a wooden chimney or none at all. The better of two dwellings available to a third tenant, James Jones, was "one hewed logged dwelling house 20 by 15 feet, an indifferent plank floor below, none above [that is, there was no usable loft], and a wooden chimney, the whole in but indifferent repair." Despite the seeming inferiority of Jones's housing, he had a separate kitchen: "one round logged kitchen 20 by 15 feet in but middling repair," and a quarter: "about 15 by 10 feet not worth repairing." Land on Hunting Creek was rented to Richard Stanford, who had "one old dwelling house 20 by 16 feet with a wooden chimney the whole very ordinary and not worth repairing," but no separate kitchen (Orphans Court Evaluation, Dorchester County, Maryland, typescript in the files of St. Mary's City Commission, St. Mary's, Maryland). How poor such housing was is revealed by comparing it with much superior buildings that nevertheless are the simplest survivors from eighteenth-century Maryland, as in J. Richard Rivoire, *Homeplaces: Traditional Domestic Architecture of Charles County, Maryland* (La Plata, Md., 1990), pp. 98–105. Also see Gregory A. Stiverson, *Poverty in a Land of Plenty: Tenancy in Eighteenth Century Maryland* (Baltimore, 1977), pp. 56–84.

houses starkly contrasting with the small and shoddy dwell-ings of poor people and middling sorts.[29]

Eighteenth-century housing standards seem to have been somewhat better in parts of New England, where more people of middling status lived in hall-parlor houses with cen-tral chimneys, lobby entries, and service rooms contained in a rear lean-to. Yet the spaces in most of the houses were much smaller than those we know from the standard publications. With principal rooms of ten by twelve or twelve feet square, it would require three of these houses to fill the kind of upper crust dwellings that are today's house museums. Collaborat-ing with other promoters of Yankee regionalism, museums have obscured the reality that—outside the coastal ports and a few inland towns—most colonial New Englanders lived in low one- and two-room houses bereft of the charms they as-sumed in the nineteenth century.[30] In virtually every region of British North America, the image of a pre-Revolutionary landscape dominated by starched and pressed yeoman farms is a product of nineteenth-century improvement and twentieth-century imagination.[31]

On the other hand, contemporary views of American cities show dense concentrations of sizable houses, implying a strong middling affluence and penchant for costly building. Great ranges of surviving moderately substantial housing in Phil-adelphia and their detached counterparts in Charleston rein-force this impression, though these all need sober analysis.[32]

[29]Rhys Isaac, *The Transformation of Virginia, 1740–1790* (Chapel Hill, N.C., 1982). Also see Ebenezer Hazard's remark about the two classes of people in Revolutionary Virginia, in Fred Shelley, ed., "The Journal of Ebe-nezer Hazard in Virginia, 1777," *Virginia Magazine of History and Biography* 62 (1954):414.

[30]J. S. Wood and M. Steinitz, "A World We Have Gained: House, Com-mon, and Village in New England," *Journal of Historical Geography* 18 (1992):105–20.

[31]Thomas C. Hubka, *Big House, Little House, Back House, Barn: The Con-nected Farm Buildings of New England* (Hanover, N.H., 1984).

[32]See, for example, Robert F. Looney, *Old Philadelphia in Early Photo-graphs, 1839–1914: 215 Prints from the Collection of the Free Library of Philadel-phia* (New York, 1976), and Samuel Gaillard Stoney, *This Is Charleston: A Survey of the Architectural Heritage of a Unique American City*, 3d ed. (Charles-

While much of the earliest surviving urban housing appears post-Revolutionary, it is clear that central Philadelphia contained large numbers of brick houses by the middle of the eighteenth century, not just the few mansions built by successful merchants like Joshua Carpenter and Jonathan Dickinson early in the century. For many affluent Philadelphians below the gentry and rich merchant classes, brick houses with circulation spaces and multiple rooms in each story became a statement of personal status. By the advent of the Revolution, such houses were occupied by successful tradesmen and shopkeepers as well as lucky merchants. In fact, ironmongers, coachmakers, tailors, and their peers may have occupied more than half the solid middling housing that cost from £500 to £750 in the inflated Philadelphia house market, though most could afford far less.[33]

While the immediacy of its commercial culture and the sometimes impersonal nature of urban life might spur greater expenditure on housing and other status-related property, substantial middling houses were not entirely confined to city streets.[34] Certain middling eighteenth-century farmers with rich land in southeastern Pennsylvania and southern and western New Jersey built rural houses approaching in scale and finish those of up-and-coming Philadelphia tradesmen.

---

ton, 1964). Early houses of differing quality are briefly treated in William John Murtagh, "The Philadelphia Row House," *Journal of the Society of Architectural Historians* 16 (1957):8–13.

[33]Thomas M. Doerflinger's *A Vigorous Spirit of Enterprise: Merchants and Economic Development in Revolutionary Philadelphia* (Chapel Hill, N.C., 1986), offers a useful picture of commercial life in late eighteenth-century Philadelphia, although the reader should observe the degree to which the analysis of housing is drawn from post-Revolutionary records. Also see Stuart M. Blumin, *The Emergence of the Middle Class: Social Experience in the American City, 1760–1900* (Cambridge, Mass., 1989); Smith, *The "Lower Sort"*; Susan Mackiewicz, "Philadelphia Flourishing: The Material World of Philadelphians, 1682–1760," Ph.D. diss., University of Delaware, 1988; Sam Bass Warner, Jr., *The Private City: Philadelphia in Three Periods of Its Growth* (Philadelphia, 1968).

[34]As a caution against viewing eighteenth-century urban life as too impersonal, however, read Gary B. Nash's treatment of face-to-face relations in *The Urban Crucible: Social Change, Political Consciousness, and the Origins of the American Revolution* (Cambridge, Mass., 1979).

A few farmhouses on both sides of the lower Delaware River were left to us by landholders without servants or slaves but with desire to build confident exteriors and socially-differentiated rooms. Often these combined old-fashioned plans with elaborated decoration—what Bernard L. Herman has called "the perfection of the yeoman house."[35]

Even in the Chesapeake there were exceptions to the rule of poor subgentry housing. Williamsburg offers a striking contradiction—or intriguing complexity—to the pattern of house survival we see emerging in the rural Chesapeake. An administrative center and synodical gathering place for the gentry rather than a port, Williamsburg lacked Philadelphia's biggest financial risk-takers and its thoroughly urban housing. While Philadelphia was characterized by density and hardness of streetscape, Williamsburg was never more than a collection of mostly rural houses dropped into an elongated grid, often on combined lots, however punctuated the composition was by public edifices. Among predictable buildings in the town, the house bought by Councillor Robert Carter for £650 in 1761 and occupied by his family until 1773 approximates what one would expect of a rather high-gentry dwelling. Each of two full stories had three rooms (two of 310 to 330 square feet and another of about 190), all sufficiently refined for reception rooms, and all accessible from a pair of L-shaped stair passages. Several comparable houses were built in Williamsburg at an early date, such as the one now thought to have been put up by William Robertson in 1716,

[35] Julie Riesenweber, "Order in Domestic Space: House Plans and Room Use in the Vernacular Dwellings of Salem County, New Jersey, 1700–1774," M.A. thesis, University of Delaware, 1984; Alan Gowans, "The Mansions of Alloways Creek," in Dell Upton and John Michael Vlach, eds., *Common Places: Readings in American Vernacular Architecture* (Athens, Ga., 1986), pp. 367–93; Michael J. Chiarappa, "The Social Context of Eighteenth-Century West New Jersey Brick Artisanry," in Thomas Carter and Bernard L. Herman, eds., *Perspectives in Vernacular Architecture, IV* (Columbia, Mo., 1991), pp. 31–43; Jack Michel, "'In a Manner and Fashion Suitable to Their Degree': A Preliminary Investigation of the Material Culture of Early Rural Pennsylvania," *Working Papers from the Regional Economic History Research Center* 5 (1981); Bernard L. Herman, *Architecture and Rural Life in Central Delaware, 1700–1900* (Knoxville, 1987).

which had three well-finished rooms and a corner passage on each of two full floors.[36] Robertson was clerk of the governor's council for thirty-eight years, and his house represents an upper level of urban gentry accommodation in the early eighteenth-century Chesapeake. His rooms were smaller (four were about 210 square feet, the other two about 170), and the smaller ones had no direct access to the modest passage. Robertson's and Carter's houses were built of frame, not brick.

What is more interesting in Williamsburg is the majority of houses owned, not by great landholders, but by successful tradesmen. Most seem to date to the third quarter of the century, like the house purchased by wigmaker and tavern keeper Edward Charlton for £240 in 1772 and a similar house built ten years earlier by thirty-one-year-old silversmith and silver retailer James Geddy II. Both are well finished, with sawn and beaded siding, large sliding sash windows, decorative modillion cornices, and a variety of carefully plastered and trimmed rooms. Both are also two stories high, with three rooms on the first floor accessible from a central passage. A similar combination of spaces was packaged in a smaller story-and-a-half house on the eastern margin of town. Apparently owned by bricklayer Humphrey Harwood, the dwelling had first-floor rooms with finish resembling that at the Geddy house.[37] The three rooms are arranged quite

[36]Marcus Whiffen, *The Eighteenth-Century Houses of Williamsburg*, rev. ed. (Williamsburg, 1984), pp. 170–73, 190–94. Willie Graham, "Building an Image: An Architectural Report on the Peyton Randolph Site," unpublished report, 1985, Col. Williamsburg Found. While passages were adopted very slowly in the eighteenth-century Chesapeake, there are a number of indications that these circulation spaces were utilized early in the century at Williamsburg. Whiffen does not consider questions of accommodation or function, but the book is a useful source of available documentation and plans for the Williamsburg houses discussed here.

[37]Whiffen, *Houses*, pp. 162–64, 186–89; Herman J. Heikkenen, "The Years of Construction for Eight Historical Structures in Colonial Williamsburg, Virginia, as Derived by the Key-Year Dendrochronology Technique," unpublished report, 1984, American Institute of Dendrochronology, Blacksburg, Va., pp. 37–39.

differently in each case, but the particular configuration is less important than the components, which in houses such as these were usually called hall or parlor, dining room, and chamber.[38]

In the third quarter of the century, it became increasingly important to Americans with available capital and social pretensions to have at least one room that was large and well finished.[39] The principal room might be used either as a parlor or as a rather grand dining room (there is evidence for both), but a requisite feature of a fashionable house was the large entertaining room. Mayor Samuel Powel's residence in Philadelphia had a lavish example (costing him more than Edward Charlton's whole house) on the second floor, as did slave trader Miles Brewton's in Charleston.[40] A fine paneled parlor was among the additions made by John Mawdsley to the seventeenth-century Bull house in Newport in 1760, about the time fellow merchant Metcalf Bowler enlarged the Vernon house and placed similar paneling over painted plaster in its old parlor.[41] When the richest Annapolis merchants built their grand houses in the quarter-century before the Revolution, none planned a room as impressive as Gov. Thomas Bladen had attempted at the center of his ill-fated "Bladen's Folly." Yet all included richly decorated rooms, many of which enclosed more space than other Marylanders

[38] Upton, "Vernacular Domestic Architecture."

[39] Edward A. Chappell, "Gentry Houses Late in the Life of the Thirteen Colonies: Selected Fieldwork," unpublished report, 1989, Col. Williamsburg Found.

[40] Samuel Powel paid Robert Smith £268 for remodeling his principal room, and wealthier neighbor John Cadwalader paid more for enrichment of several entertaining rooms (George B. Tatum, *Philadelphia Georgian: The City House of Samuel Powel and Some of Its Eighteenth-Century Neighbors* [Middletown, Conn., 1976]; Nicholas B. Wainwright, *Colonial Grandeur in Philadelphia: The House and Furniture of General John Cadwalader* [Philadelphia, 1964]; Lane, *Architecture of the Old South: South Carolina,* pp. 60–68; Caroline Wyche Dixon, "The Miles Brewton House: Ezra Waite's Architectural Books and Other Possible Design Sources," *South Carolina Historical and Genealogical Magazine* 82 [1981]:118–42).

[41] Antoinette F. Downing and Vincent J. Scully, Jr., *The Architectural Heritage of Newport, Rhode Island,* 2d ed. (New York, 1967), pp. 453–54, 456–57.

had in their entire dwellings.[42] A great ballroom wing was added to the rear of the Virginia governor's house in 1751, and around that time Peyton Randolph extended the old Robertson house with a broad stair passage, a large dining room with walnut trim and a marble mantel, and a sizable new chamber above. Within a decade or two, and on a much more modest scale, jurist Benjamin Waller and probably John Blair added larger rooms with marble mantels to their middling-size houses in Williamsburg.[43] It is clear that by the Revolution the building choices of middling artisan-merchants, as well as the very wealthy elite, could be powerfully motivated by a perceived need for particular kinds of socially charged rooms. At the same time, a general conspicuous consumption of architecture—long symmetrical facades, fussy brickwork, acres of flat plaster, and flashy decorative details—were not restricted to the most affluent.

Sometimes the houses suggest a gentility that masked financial realities. About 1751–52 Williamsburg tailor and merchant Robert Nicolson built a well-detailed wooden house with two rooms, probably a hall and bedchamber, located to one side of a first-floor passage. About fifteen years later he added an entertaining room and chamber on the opposite side of the passage. Together these new spaces were larger than the old rooms, and the new front room was fitted with a well-crafted mantel. The building seems then to have followed a familiar pattern, with two superior rooms set aside for entertaining. What the edifice itself does not tell us is that

[42] Andrew Burnaby, *Travels through the Middle Settlements in North-America in the Years 1759 and 1760*, 2d ed. (Ithaca, N.Y., 1960), p. 47. Despite their glamor and fame, the houses of Annapolis have received little serious attention in print. For the people and the town, see Edward C. Papenfuse, *In Pursuit of Profit: The Annapolis Merchants in the Era of the American Revolution, 1763–1805* (Baltimore, 1975); Rosamond Randall Beirne and John Henry Scarff, *William Buckland, 1734–1774,* 2d ed. (Lorton, Va., 1958); Deering Davis, *Annapolis Houses, 1700–1775* (New York, 1947).

[43] Edward A. Chappell, "Reconsidered Splendor: The [Virginia Governor's] Palace Addition of 1751," unpublished report, 1985, Col. Williamsburg Found.; idem, "Williamsburg Architecture as Social Space," *Fresh Advices: A Research Supplement to the Colonial Williamsburg Interpreter* 2 (1981):i–iv; Whiffen, *Houses*, pp. 133–35, 151–54, and 190–94.

throughout much of the period Nicolson kept lodgers in his house and advertised for new tenants. Apparently some of the nicely plastered and wainscoted rooms were employed not only for entertaining guests and enjoying private domestic pursuits, but also as rental space in which an itinerant music teacher and others slept and perhaps plied their trades.[44]

This is no surprise. Improved housing often requires financial overextension. Mortgaging one's career to pay for too good a house has been a common Western activity for three centuries.[45] Nevertheless, it is significant that towns like Williamsburg, not to mention cities with more activity in trade than government, fostered sizable numbers of upwardly-mobile tradesmen who spent substantial amounts of money on well-built housing that featured rooms set aside for profitable entertainment. Their expansive style could be ridiculed. Coachmaker Elkanah Deane, who paid £700 for his house and town lots in 1772, was labeled "an Hibernian Cottager" and the "Palace Street Puffer" by a rival tradesman.[46] One characteristic of urban life since the Middle Ages is, of course, the presence of merchant capital and the houses it built looming over more modest neighbors. Presumably most of the larger houses in seventeenth-century Boston as well as Jamestown were occupied by successful merchants, like their counterparts in contemporary English government centers and market towns. But Charlton, Geddy, Harwood, Nicolson, and Deane represent a different crowd, perhaps best seen as entrepreneurial tradesmen, a group that increasingly defined itself as a capitalized estate with respectable housing as well as other material distinctions.

[44]*Virginia Gazette* (Purdie and Dixon), Sept. 12, 1766, p. 3; ibid. (Hunter), Mar. 28, 1755, p. 4. Music teacher Cuthbert Ogle died there in 1755, leaving his harpsichord and only a few other worldly belongings, suggesting that he probably taught keyboard music at Nicolson's house. In 1777 Nicolson advertised that he would no longer be taking lodgers (Mark R. Wenger, "The Robert Nicolson House, Block 7, Building 12: A Social and Architectural Study," unpublished report, 1986, Col. Williamsburg Found.).

[45]Compare Bernard L. Herman, "Multiple Materials, Multiple Meanings: The Fortunes of Thomas Mendenhall," *Winterthur Portfolio* 19 (1984):67–86. Mark Girouard discusses the great gambles of aristocratic house building in *Life in the Country House*.

[46]*Virginia Gazette* (Rind), Nov. 11, 1773, p. 2.

Few historians would view such preindustrial figures as middle class. Perhaps the most thoughtful assessment of the creation of the Anglo-American middle class is provided by Stuart M. Blumin. Though Blumin's middle class is a mid-nineteenth-century urban creation, his observation that classes are formed "through the convergence of relevant experience" rather than solely by development of ideological consciousness has relevance to these successful businessmen.[47] While they may not have used their well-built houses to distinguish themselves as a self-conscious *class,* their refined buildings, furnishings, dress, and manners represented a body of shared expectations. These were applied toward the purchase of entry into an existing genteel culture rather than formation of a new social tier. Houses like Nicolson's were virtually identical to neighboring houses of gentlemen like John Tayloe. These artisans were united by their aspirations to become gentlemen—as wheelwright and house carpenter Benjamin Powell ultimately did. On the other hand, their dependence on the gentry, as tradesmen and creditors, could create awkwardness, particularly when pressing for payments on services long rendered.[48]

What about the less capitalized, less socially mobile townspeople, who could not build a three-room-plan house and who would not likely be invited into one for dinner and conversation? Clearly, the few known small Williamsburg houses would not have provided the collective accommodation needed for these people.[49] It is increasingly evident that many, perhaps most, people of middling status in pre-

[47] Blumin, *Emergence of the Middle Class,* p. 11.

[48] Powell played the game well, with a refined house and gentleman's accoutrements like wine bottles sealed with his initials. Toward the end of his life, he sat as a local justice and city councilman and was called "gent" by clerks in the county court records. Artisan families with comparable motivations may have built houses with entertaining rooms and respectable finish in New England towns like Marblehead and Salem before their Chesapeake counterparts began to resemble gentlefolk, but the houses and their owners need more systematic analysis.

[49] Among the surviving small Williamsburg houses are the original single-room sections of the Wray tenement and the James Galt house, as well as the later "Quarter," all located on back streets.

Revolutionary Williamsburg were tenants, renting all or parts of houses.[50] Families involved in trade could combine their work and domestic lives in one- or two-room tenements like those that flanked Henry Wetherburn's tavern, buildings less specialized than the prim shops now lining the streets of Williamsburg and other museums. On the other hand, tradesmen sometimes rented and shared with laborers buildings that resembled substantial houses. William Rind and later his widow Clementina published their *Virginia Gazette* from the impressive Ludwell mansion in the early 1770s, ostensibly with their presses set up in a room one now would expect to contain teawares and fine furniture.

Tenancy was even more the rule in large urban centers. Sam Bass Warner, Jr., has calculated from tax records that in 1774 only 19 percent of Philadelphia families owned houses and that 89 percent of the taxable property was owned by the richest tenth of the taxpaying households. For Philadelphia's affluent Middle Ward, the 1774 tax list includes 80 homeowners, 266 house renters, and 102 taxpayers living with other families.[51] Less than one in ten workers owned a house.

[50]The inventories of thirty-three decedents in Williamsburg between 1765 and 1775 indicate a value of inventoried local property (total property, no rural land or urban lots) ranging from Mary Lewis at £7 to merchant William Prentis at £9,498 and merchant-tailor Thomas Hornsby at £10,773. The mean appraisal is £1,170 (£592 if Prentis and Hornsby are omitted), and the median is £294 (£272 without Prentis and Hornsby.) Within this small list of inventory values, there is a very precise point at which people begin to own a Williamsburg lot: between plasterer Simon Whitaker at £603 and John Coke at £773. Only Mary Prentis in the top twelve (36 percent) did not own a lot, and only three people— Elizabeth Balsom, Joanna McKenzie, and cabinetmaker John Jergitts—in the lower twenty-one (64 percent) owned lots (Kevin Kelly, "The Demographic and Social Character of Williamsburg on the Eve of the Revolution," unpublished report, 1979, Col. Williamsburg Found.; Emma L. Powers, "Landlords, Tenants, and Rental Property in Williamsburg and Yorktown, 1730–80," unpublished report, 1990, Col. Williamsburg Found.).

[51]Warner, *The Private City*, pp. 9 and 15. Warner conceived of common artisans' and shopkeepers' housing in the Middle Ward on the eve of the American Revolution as measuring roughly seventeen feet wide and twenty-five feet deep, with the larger front room serving as work or sales space, and bedchambers in the attic. With riches came a full second floor

Most laboring Philadelphians lived as boarders or tenants, and the small houses in the center of blocks and at the edges of the city were often shared by two or more families. William Smith's house in Harmony Alley was fairly typical. Smith, his wife, three children, and two boarders lived in a two-story frame house, eighteen feet square, without a detached kitchen. Other laborers' houses were smaller, such as the eleven-by-fourteen-foot single-story house occupied by the family of mariner Richard Crips.[52] Particularly in the northern port cities, such people were growing in numbers while often declining in relative wealth. The widening gulf of living conditions sharpened their group consciousness as well. Using things to distinguish oneself from those of inferior circumstance reflected and fostered urban class formation, by turn, for those with and without money.

Slave housing throughout the eighteenth century was markedly inferior to those familiar cabins of the antebellum period, small and mean though the latter were. In Williamsburg, where half the population was enslaved, there is no evidence of separate buildings constructed specifically to house blacks. Urban blacks often lived in secondary spaces of principal dwellings and work buildings, such as rooms formed by crude clapboard partitions in unfinished and un-

---

and a rear ell housing a kitchen. Much of the workers' housing was crowded into alleys dividing city blocks and on rear yards (pp. 15, 17–19). Sharon V. Salinger and Charles Weatherell have found evidence for widespread use of meaner houses: some 30 percent of renters paid £10 or less in annual rent for single-story houses of roughly twelve feet by eighteen, and another 20 or 30 percent paid less than £18 for only slightly larger abodes. Yet renting and poverty were not synonymous. Salinger and Weatherell argue for income being more important than property holding. The 1769 Philadelphia County Provincial Tax list shows the ranks of the city's renters included people of substantial income, such as Quaker merchant Henry Drinker, who was able to pay £90 rent for his house and Carter John Knees, who paid £54 ("Wealth and Renting in Prerevolutionary Philadelphia," *Journal of American History* 71 [1985]:834, 836. Compare with the more optimistic interpretation of house ownership in Boston: G. B. Warden, "The Distribution of Property in Boston, 1692–1775," *Perspectives in American History* 10 [1976]:81–128).

[52]Smith, *The "Lower Sort,"* pp. 158–63.

ventilated attics. As late as 1823 a correspondent wrote to Alexander Galt complaining that Williamsburg houses lacked separate quarters, so that servants "have to stay in the basement or the garret rooms."[53] At best, these were small, simply finished rooms like those in the nine-by-seventeen-foot addition to Thomas Everard's brick kitchen and in its unfinished attic, spaces that offered some potential for the creation of a relatively independent domestic environment. Others were no more than poor shelters in which to rest. A 1770 *Virginia Gazette* advertisement for the sale of Market Square Tavern lists a variety of associated buildings, including "a large and strong smokehouse, at one end of it a place for people to sleep in."[54]

Very little housing built exclusively for slaves in the eighteenth century survives in the South. There are rare exceptions, such as the twelve-by-sixteen-foot core of a house, which was enlarged in the nineteenth century, at Sir Peyton Skipwith's Prestwould in Mecklenburg County, Virginia. Like the houses of many whites, its spindly frame was covered with riven clapboards on the exterior and largely exposed inside. Doors were small (that on the rear being only eighteen inches wide) and the few small windows had sliding shutters and no glass. Unlike most eighteenth-century slaves, the occupants of the Prestwould house had a wooden lower floor and an attic, which though confined and poorly ventilated, offered a separate space for sleeping. Several eighteenth-century buildings associated with grand Charleston mansions also retain evidence of use as slave accommodations, but recognizable slave housing there and elsewhere dates almost entirely from the mid-nineteenth century.[55]

In sum, the housing of eighteenth-century Americans was marked by radical diversity. The dwellings of gentry landowners and affluent merchants ranged from simply built and

[53] Mary [Browne] to Dr. A. D. Galt, Sept. 13, 1832, Galt Family Papers, Swem Library, College of William and Mary, Williamsburg, Va.

[54] *Virginia Gazette* (Purdie and Dixon), Aug. 30, 1770, p. 3.

[55] Edward A. Chappell, "Architectural Recording and the American Open-Air Museum: A View from the Field," in Wells, ed., *Perspectives in Architecture, II*, pp. 30, 32–34.

well-finished hall-parlor houses to grand mansions much like those occupied by successful merchants in Britain. In cities and sizable towns, prosperous tradesmen and merchants occupied buildings that approach modern middle-class standards, while their more humble and numerous counterparts usually conducted both work and domestic activities in modest, poorly finished, and dimly lighted houses with few rooms. A very small, rich minority lived in lavish multistory double-pile edifices, while the majority of people occupied one or more rooms in tenements or their own houses. Urban blacks inhabited buildings used for other purposes, some in rooms especially arranged for them and probably many more in unfinished and undifferentiated spaces. At main plantation houses and nearby quarters in the South, rural slaves were in much the same situation, occupying a room above the kitchen or a corner of a work or storage building. Enslaved agricultural workers and most free blacks were housed in very mean log or hole-set frame structures between garden plots and capital-producing fields. In families or other groups, they shared a single small space, possibly with a wooden chimney and almost certainly without glazed windows or wooden floors. Most rural whites lived in one- and two-room-plan houses with a minimum of finish and privacy, often little different from the homes of their black neighbors. Inferior to most surviving small eighteenth-century buildings, these houses were often covered with riven boards and left unplastered and unsheathed inside, without insulation. Again, dirt floors, wooden chimneys, and unglazed windows were a common sight. Only among the wealthy, for the most part, was substantial decoration part of the building process. Paint, too, was a reflection of affluence, not convention.

Innovation in British-American housing did indeed occur in the eighteenth century, a change in building design that reflected increased desire for visual order and functional separation, if not segregation in the modern sense. This change was more than a stylistic shift.[56] It involved the same quest for social esteem that encouraged people to read novels, buy

[56] Deetz, *In Small Things Forgotten;* Glassie, *Folk Housing.*

large matched sets of ceramics and glassware, follow rules of etiquette, and travel for pleasure to out-of-the-way places with bad-smelling water. Symmetrical facades, circulation passages, fully plastered rooms, and specialized spaces for entertaining provided acceptability and enforced social inequalities, as did mezzotints and foppish poses. The revolution reached every corner of the English speaking world.[57] It was a mile wide and an inch—no, a foot—deep. Most people were touched by the change, if only in the way they were treated by their social superiors. Just as clearly, many people did not take part in the architectural transformation.

American buildings themselves testify to a major historical event that is generally overlooked by historians and not fully revealed in the records. Beginning in the late eighteenth century and continuing into the nineteenth century, American housing underwent a dramatic rebuilding. Close examination of almost any area of the East Coast reveals that the great majority of standing early houses below the gentry level are post-Revolutionary. The transformation of middling housing varied considerably by region, but the general pattern of this republican rebuilding is pervasive and undeniable. It is true of both urban and rural houses.

The degree to which the sizes of houses or numbers of rooms grew is difficult to know. What is very evident is that more people made the shift from impermanent to durable housing, and from rudely finished to more refined—at least *partially* refined—housing, and toward increased division of activities, particularly segregation of work and social endeavor.

While side-passage row houses with service spaces behind or below had been largely confined to a few intensely occupied colonial cities, they became a staple of fine and middling urban housing in the new republic, in towns as well as thriving cities. Unlike their British counterparts running the length of blocks, the American houses were often built as pairs and flanked by alleys at right angles to the streets. The old mode of living above the shop took on new character as many

[57]Richard L. Bushman, "American High-Style and Vernacular Cultures," in Jack P. Greene and J. R. Pole, eds., *Colonial British America: Essays in the New History of the Early Modern Era* (Baltimore, 1984), pp. 345–83.

urban buildings were constructed with shops on the lower floor and elaborate housing above. Occupants renting the elevated apartments were often unrelated to those running the shops below them: a duplex shop-house might provide the developer with rent from two shopkeepers and two different families. The upper floors were normally reached with stairs rising in passages accessible from the front, side, or even rear, independent of entrances to the commercial establishments. Commonly the second floor was expensively finished as a pair of entertaining rooms, and bedchambers were housed in the lower, plainer rooms on the third and sometimes fourth floors. The problem of where to place kitchens and other workrooms met with various solutions, including placement directly behind or even below the shop. It is evident by comparing the workmanship of such buildings with that of conventional homes of similar scale built in less densely populated neighborhoods developed contemporaneously nearby that the new apartments were intended as stylish accommodation, whatever the inconveniences of their use.

New York City's extraordinary building boom that began soon after the War of 1812 resulted in thousands of new row houses in the old city and on additional streets extending up Manhattan Island. Few recognizable Dutch buildings survived by the time James Fenimore Cooper's fictitious traveling bachelor walked these streets in 1828. In increasingly segregated "mechanic wards," tradesmen and laborers let floors or single rooms, often above ground-floor workshops. The best of the new houses dispensed with shops and counting rooms and had their principal spaces raised above a service cellar reached by steps descending from sidewalk to walled and fenced "areas." Here as well as elsewhere, two entertaining rooms were paired on opposite sides of large folding or sliding doors, so that partygoers could easily circulate between spaces of comparably good finish. Often these were both treated as parlors, resulting in demotion of dining to a cellar room. More modest New Yorkers employed taverns and the streets as their social space.[58]

[58]Elizabeth Blackmar, *Manhattan for Rent, 1785–1850* (Ithaca, N.Y., 1982); Charles Lockwood, *Bricks and Brownstone: The New York Row House,*

In rural New England a variety of Georgian house elements joined the lobby-entrance plan as acceptable alternatives for middling clients. Two-story single-pile houses with multiple chimneys on interior or rear walls were first built in large numbers in the 1790s, as were houses with two rooms front to back on one side of a stair passage. The venerable lobby-entrance house also continued to be built into the 1830s. None of these forms were entirely new; the *change* was in the size and numbers in which they were built, and the kinds of people who occupied them.[59] Notable in its absence is that staple of the republican rebuilding south of New York: the two-story I house, with single rooms disposed symmetrically on both sides of a through passage.[60]

In southeastern Pennsylvania and the areas of western Maryland and the Shenandoah Valley settled by German-speaking people, post-Revolutionary buildings for a time held to forms that were recognizably deviant from British-American houses. Such culturally distinct housing was built in

1783–1929 (New York, 1972); Barbara G. Carson, *Ambitious Appetites: Dining, Behavior, and Patterns of Consumption in Federal Washington* (Washington, D.C., 1990); Mark R. Wenger and Willie Graham, "Battersea and the Double Parlor in Early America" (Paper delivered at the Annual Meeting of the Vernacular Architecture Forum, Lexington, Ky., May 1990). For glimpses of the various teas, sibling conversations, poetry readings, servant reprimands, and solitary reflection for which an affluent Philadelphia Quaker family used its front and rear parlors, see Elaine Forman Crane, ed., *The Diary of Elizabeth Drinker,* 3 vols. (Boston, 1991).

[59]The longevity of the lobby-entrance house is most striking. Hosley has observed, for example, that while archaic jettied versions are generally thought to represent seventeenth-century architecture in the rich Connecticut Valley, even these continued to be built there until the last decade of the eighteenth century (Hosley, "Architecture," pp. 75, 102–3). An eccentric Edenton, North Carolina, house with jetty ostensibly influenced by New England building traditions has recently been dated by dendrochronologist Herman Heikkenen to 1758.

[60]Symmetrical two-story single-pile houses with central passages were a familiar southern and midwestern building choice throughout the nineteenth century. They are now called I houses, a term of modern convenience (Henry Glassie, *Pattern in the Material Folk Culture of the Eastern United States* [Philadelphia, 1968]).

the decade or so on either side of 1800, but increasingly it was transformed in strange, somewhat schizophrenic ways to resemble British-American, or if you will, Georgian planning. Vestiges of this distinctive mixture survived until the mid-nineteenth century in southeastern Pennsylvania, but in the Shenandoah Valley, affluent middling farmers entirely abandoned the old and confusing forms in favor of the symmetrical, respectable, two-story, center-passage houses constructed of materials preferred by the affluent English speakers: brick or weatherboarded frame, not log or stone. The new forms now vastly outnumber the old; today it is no easy task to find a recognizable Germanic house south of Pennsylvania. Throughout the ascendance of the big symmetrical house in the German areas of the Shenandoah Valley, less affluent farmers and tenants built smaller log dwellings. Those that survive are the best of these, often with two full floors and two first-floor rooms.[61]

Fieldwork in Delaware has revealed that, while sizable center-passage houses were built by wealthy merchants as early as the 1740s, most of these were changed by the early Federal period and are now far outnumbered by houses built between 1790 and 1830. In southern Newcastle County, only about half a dozen eighteenth-century interiors survive, and almost all the early houses have service wings that were added in the second quarter of the nineteenth century. For example, the Christopher Vandergrift House, inland from the Delaware River, was constructed as a one-room-plan house in the

[61] Glassie, "Delaware Valley Folk Building"; Edward A. Chappell, "Acculturation in the Shenandoah Valley: Rhenish Houses of the Massanutten Settlement," *Proceedings of the American Philosophical Society* 124 (1980):55–89; idem, "Germans and Swiss," in Dell Upton, ed., *America's Architectural Roots: Ethnic Groups That Built America* (Washington, D. C., 1986), pp. 68–73. Most surviving distinctive and sizable eighteenth-century German-American houses were substantially altered in the nineteenth century for both aesthetic and functional reasons. The exceptions are largely the result of their being replaced by a more acceptable nineteenth-century house and being reduced in status to that of a secondary dwelling on the property. Fort Zeller in Pennsylvania and Fort Egypt in Virginia are two prominent examples. Measured drawings of both are available in the Historic American Buildings Survey Collection, Prints and Photographs Division, Library of Congress.

middle of the eighteenth century, but in the nineteenth century it sustained as many as eight successive additions. Other buildings had their trim upgraded, with new mantels and window sash, for example.[62]

Settlement had barely begun in Kentucky and Tennessee when the post-Revolutionary rebuilding started to transform the landscape of the East Coast. Very soon the richest sections of these frontier areas acquired an architectural personality that was regionally distinctive, although it paralleled the national pattern to some degree. The pace of settlement was very rapid and the land division ruthless. It took only ten to twenty years, rather than an entire century, for an extremely hierarchical society to find full expression in permanent houses. By the second quarter of the nineteenth century, ordinary people in central Kentucky were living in frame or log houses much like those of their counterparts to the east, that is, with one or two first-floor rooms and very often an unfinished attic. The winners from the litigious early years at first built sedate stone hall-and-chamber houses, but soon developed a taste for strikingly imaginative plans, rich wood interior decoration, and good brickwork. In some ways neat brickwork with regular joints is like good teeth—it has social as well as practical value. Even today, the early brick ruling-class houses of Kentucky constitute an extraordinary group, with great fanlighted doorways piercing gable-fronted blocks, with Palladian windows strung across three- and five-part facades in an unruly manner that must have seemed astounding and impudent at the time. One would like to know something about the choices in ceramics these people made. Interestingly, conventional central-passage houses did not come to dominate until the 1840s, when much of the excitement had moved farther west and a new conservatism made the first-generation devices seem old-fashioned and unacceptable for new construction.[63]

[62]Herman, *Architecture and Life in Delaware;* idem, "Delaware Vernacular: Folk Housing in Three Counties," in Camille Wells, ed., *Perspectives in Vernacular Architecture* (Annapolis, 1982), pp. 179–93.

[63]As in most states, there has been little deep analysis of the changing essential character of housing in Kentucky and Tennessee. There have been, however, extensive recording and publication about central Ken-

In Georgia, on the other hand, late antebellum houses often surpassed those of the Federal era, both in scale and in the inventiveness of their bids for attention. Such southern bourgeois buildings were far fewer in number than the more modestly scaled Greek houses in some areas of New York state, for example. Yet the richness of housing for affluent antebellum Georgians contrasts sharply with the absence of survivals from before the Revolution, which is surprising given the English occupation of the colony since 1733.[64]

In North Carolina, too, despite its early settlement, housing in general was poor throughout the eighteenth century. New Bern, where Tryon Palace surpassed the Virginia governor's house, retains a few late colonial houses, but in most eighteenth-century North Carolina towns the earliest substantial private buildings date from the Federal period. These are predominantly two-story, two- and three-room-plan houses with expressive woodwork in the public rooms. Across the state most people lived in small, mostly log houses through the first half of the nineteenth century. In 1842 Englishman James Silk Buckingham described what he saw in the eastern Piedmont: "There were a few decent houses but the greatest number of these were miserable-looking dwellings, rude and dirty without, and bare and comfortless within. The broken panes of glass being more numerous than those that were whole, and everything bespeaking the indolence and dirty habits of the occupants."[65] Buckingham indulged in stereo-

---

tucky. See Clay Lancaster, *Ante Bellum Houses of the Bluegrass: The Development of Residential Architecture in Fayette County, Kentucky* (Lexington, Ky., 1961); Rexford Newcomb, *Architecture in Old Kentucky* (Urbana, Ill., 1953); Camille Wells, *Fleming County: An Architectural Survey* (Frankfort, Ky., 1979); Anthony O. James, David Morgan, Carolyn Torma, and A. Camille Wells, *Survey of Historic Sites in Kentucky: Clark County* (Frankfort, Ky., 1979); Kenneth T. Gibbs, *Historic Architecture of Green County, Kentucky* (Greensburg, Ky., 1983). Also James Patrick, *Architecture in Tennessee, 1768–1897* (Knoxville, Tenn., 1981).

[64] John Linley, *The Georgia Catalog: Historic American Buildings Survey* (Athens, Ga., 1982); Frederick Doveton Nichols, *The Architecture of Georgia*, ed. Mills Lane (Savannah, 1976).

[65] Peter B. Sandbeck, *The Historic Architecture of New Bern and Craven County, North Carolina* (New Bern, 1988); James Silk Buckingham, *The Slave*

types, but there is little doubt that the level of most housing remained unremittingly poor. In 1810, a series of local correspondents from eastern and Piedmont counties described their localities for the *Raleigh Star.* Almost always they characterized local housing as snug and comfortable, never elegant.[66] There was a housing revolution of sorts in early nineteenth-century North Carolina, but it consisted primarily of modest upgrading and of the building by a very small minority of two-story houses with passages and two or three rooms on a floor. The humbleness of building in the region is starkly illustrated by the paucity of surviving buildings today. In some areas of eastern North Carolina literally no buildings survive from before the Civil War.[67]

The Chesapeake again provides a useful perspective because of intensive architectural surveys done during the last fifteen years, together with the availability of related though fragmentary documentation. Through most of Tidewater and Piedmont Virginia and Maryland, houses of the Federal period vastly outnumber everything built before the late eighteenth century. Naturally, local economic circumstance affected the housing revolution to varying degrees: the rapid

---

States in America, 2 vols. (London, 1842), 2:198. Reconstructions such as that of Tryon Palace can confuse perceptions about the nature of a sometimes modest predecessor. However, architect John Hawk's drawings and his recently discovered 1783 letter to Francisco de Miranda reveal that the scale and lavish first-floor finish of Tryon Palace were extraordinary in the context of the American colonies, not to mention in North Carolina (memorandum, Hawks on the Design of the Governor's House in New Bern, July 12, 1783, Archive de Francisco de Miranda, 5, pp. 95–97, Academia Nacional de la Historia, Caracas, Venezuela; copies of drawings and letter on file at Tryon Palace office, New Bern, N.C.).

[66] For a useful treatment of North Carolina buildings over more than three centuries, see Catherine W. Bishir, Charlotte V. Brown, Carl R. Lounsbury, and Ernest H. Wood III, *Architects and Builders in North Carolina: A History of the Practice of Building* (Chapel Hill, N.C., 1990). The *Raleigh Star* survey is mentioned on pp. 53–54.

[67] Edward A. Chappell, "A Report on the Architectural Resources of Buckingham, Fluvanna, Mecklenburg, and Greensville Counties in Virginia, and Bertie County in North Carolina," unpublished report, 1984, Envirosphere Co., New York City, part 3: Bertie County.

growth of truck farms near Baltimore would not be reflected in the deep southern Piedmont or in the counties in easternmost Virginia. Nevertheless, housing for some people improved significantly from the conditions already described, despite immediate local conditions. Some new houses rivaled the old high-gentry mansions, fitted with sensuously curving stairs and chic Adamesque woodwork, and insured by their owners for as much as $10,000 with organizations like the Mutual Assurance Company in Richmond and the Baltimore Fire Insurance Company. But these were rare in both the cities and the countryside. The best house in any rural locality would more often be a big single-pile or small Georgian-plan house, the sort of building that was likely to be insured for $1,000 to $4,000.[68] More important for the purposes of our inquiry, the *average* house of the era ranged from a single-room dwelling to a small two-story, central-passage house, with the numbers weighted toward the lower end. Most surviving single-room-plan and hall-and-chamber houses were trimmed out much like their larger contemporaries and worth anywhere from $200 to $1,000 when built. Sleeping lofts were often left unfinished, but first floors generally featured plastered or sheathed walls, glazed sash windows, and well executed if not lively woodwork—the kinds of details that clearly distinguished them from the rudely built and poorly maintained houses of comparable scale that tax assessors commonly estimated as worth less than $100.[69]

The larger houses reflect a conscious attempt at functional separation, and passages were even used with some single-room plans. Servants were channeled into ever less visible

---

[68] Mutual Assurance Company Collection, Virginia State Library, Richmond; Baltimore Fire Insurance Company Records, vol. 2, Maryland Historical Society, Baltimore. While they never represent the full spectrum of housing, post-Revolutionary insurance policies are informative about forms, materials, and values. They offer one means of judging how literal the values assigned in tax assessments were (also see Franklin Insurance Company Collection, Pennsylvania Historical Society, Philadelphia, and Insurance Company of North America Records, Cigna Archives, Philadelphia).

[69] The spectrum of surviving houses is illustrated by Upton, "Vernacular Architecture in Southeastern Virginia"; John G. Zehmer, Jr., "The Early

locations and the space given solely to entertainment was expanded, with more and larger rooms. Yet the forms of big new houses were essentially those of their colonial predecessors. Seldom did builders and buyers experiment with radical new plans and spatial relationships, the Kentucky effervescence notwithstanding. Old assumptions about the best places to work, sleep, and entertain were relied on again and again. The same was true of construction techniques. The early nineteenth-century manner of framing buildings in the Chesapeake region displays greater regularity of joinery and specialization of scantling size, but the essential eighteenth-century system for assembling a frame changed insignificantly before the Civil War.[70] Only in nonstructural elaboration were there significant departures from buildings of comparable size built in, say, 1765. Consequently, new houses in most Chesapeake regions closely resembled their colonial predecessors in form and in technology. The change was not so much in the houses themselves as in their numbers, and by extension, in the number of people they sheltered.

County records provide some crucial connections between these houses and the economic status of their occupants.

Domestic Architecture of Dinwiddie County, Virginia," M.A. thesis, University of Virginia, 1970; Jeffrey Marshall O'Dell, *Inventory of Early Architecture and Historic Sites* (Henrico, Va., 1976); idem, *Chesterfield County: Early Architecture and Historic Sites* (Chesterfield, Va., 1983); *Inventory of Historic Sites in Calvert County, Charles County, and St. Mary's County,* rev. ed. (Annapolis, 1980); Christopher Weeks, ed., *Between the Nanticoke and the Choptank: An Architectural History of Dorchester County, Maryland* (Baltimore, 1984); idem, ed., *Where Land and Water Intertwine: An Architectural History of Talbot County, Maryland* (Baltimore, 1984); Rivoire, *Homeplaces;* Paul Baker Touart, *Somerset: An Architectural History* (Annapolis, 1990). Most of the many architectural surveys carried out in the Chesapeake by state historic preservation offices remain unpublished. Tax assessments did not necessarily reflect full value, but houses assessed at $100 or less were predominantly inferior to the simplest surviving houses from the early national period.

[70]Dell Upton, "Traditional Timber Framing," in Brooke Hindle, ed., *Material Culture of the Wooden Age* (Tarrytown, N.Y., 1981), pp. 35–93; Whiffen, *Houses,* pp. 89–98; Paul E. Buchanan, "The Eighteenth-Century Frame Houses of Tidewater Virginia," in Charles E. Peterson, ed., *Building Early America: Contributions toward the History of a Great Industry* (Radnor, Pa., 1976), pp. 60–68.

Again, in most Virginia counties, a majority of surviving pre–Civil War houses date from the period of post-Revolutionary rebuilding or later. In Southampton and Isle of Wight counties south of the James River, the *poorest* of these (that is, one-room houses measuring eighteen feet square, sixteen by eighteen, or sixteen by twenty, with brick chimneys and elevated wood floors but only modestly finished, sometimes unplastered) were the homes of well-to-do farmers. With few exceptions, the occupants had at least 100 acres of land, placing them in the top 35 to 40 percent of the landowning population.[71]

This evidence indicates that rebuilding in southeastern Virginia after the Revolutionary War represented significant improvement in the housing standards of affluent people, but even at this level most houses remained small and simple. Improvement for a moderately successful farmer might include a well finished house with a carefully hewn and sawed frame on a raised brick foundation. Its walls could be covered with sawed weatherboards outside and plaster within, and the whole lighted with glazed sash windows. The chief improvement could well have been one of craftsmanship and durability rather than size. The new house might have provided a room in which to take tea after the proper fashion, or in which guests could admire some bit of amusing mantel-joiners art. Just as likely, this was the same space in which meals were taken, meetings held, domestic work accom-

[71] Since 1981, the Department of Architectural Research at Colonial Williamsburg has recorded a broad range of early buildings in the Chesapeake, most of them threatened with demolition or decay. When available, county records have been used to reconstruct a scale of wealth invested in property in order to define the position of the buildings' occupants among property owners in their districts. Dell Upton used a similar technique with much the same results in a study for the National Museum of American History show "After the Revolution" (Upton, "The Virginia Parlor, National Museum of American History, Smithsonian Institution: A Report on the Henry Saunders House and Its Occupants," unpublished report, 1981, Smithsonian Institution, Washington, D.C.). For a popular account, see Barbara Clark Smith, *After the Revolution: The Smithsonian History of Everyday Life in the Eighteenth Century* [New York, 1985], pp. 89–137). For related findings in Delaware, see Bernard L. Herman, "Architectural Renewal and the Maintenance of Customary Relationships," *Material Culture* 19 (1987):85–99.

plished, and some members of the family bedded down at night. Cooking probably was removed to a detached building. This practice was already a hundred or more years old in the region, though many small eighteenth-century houses still incorporated the kitchen into the main structure.

Well-appointed or not, a house with a single room on each floor could not offer much real privacy, even if the loft was fitted out as a bedroom and nonfamily members of the household were quartered in separate buildings. Princeton-educated Presbyterian minister Philip Fithian expressed embarrassment at the lack of privacy while at the same time acknowledging the reputability of a small central Pennsylvania house where he lodged in August 1775: "Cleanliness & Smartness are visible in our little Hamlet. All is suitable but this going to Bed & rising in the same Room, & in full view, of the whole Family—This, to be sure, puts me often to the Blush." Five months later he was traveling in the upper Shenandoah Valley. Again he recorded his social discomfort with the intimacies of a respectable but small house: "Here at Mr. Davis's, as last Summer, I am to sleep in the same Room with a large Family, mostly Women; Do my best, I am abashed!"[72] Living in the multiroom houses in New Jersey and Tidewater Virginia, Fithian had developed a standard of privacy different from that of his hosts, who could feel equally respectable while sharing limited space. Their less delicate standard was informed by the one-room houses of their neighbors, as much the result of choice as economic opportunity.

As one fieldworker has observed about recent black housing in Maryland, single spaces of this sort can still support

[72]Fithian spent many of his traveling nights in similar circumstances. He was also on the Pennsylvania frontier in July 1775, when he recorded in his journal: "One thing here I dont like—in almost all these rural Cots I am under the Necessity of sleeping in the same Room with all the Family—It seems indelicate, at least new, to strip, surrounded by different Ages & Sexes, & rise in the Morning, in the Blaze of Day, with the Eyes of, at least, one blinking Irish Female, searching out Subjects for Remark." Two nights later, conditions had not improved: "Fleas biting!—Bugs crawling!—On a hard Board, surrounded by a snoring Family!" (Robert Greenhalgh Albion and Leonidas Dodson, eds., *Philip Vickers Fithian: Journal, 1775–1776, Written on the Virginia-Pennsylvania Frontier and in the Army around New York* [Princeton, 1934], pp. 95, 166, 67–68).

clearly defined zones of activity.[73] Perhaps dwellers of single-room houses once created mental divisions that allowed them to feel a degree of seclusion within the household as well as a sense of practical order. Such imaginary walls might organize interior space very effectively for the residents of a small dwelling and yet go wholly unperceived by guests.

In one of the more colorful and unlikely glimpses of domestic intimacies in late eighteenth-century America, the future king of France recorded an experience that he and his three brothers purported to have had in a single-room house belonging to a Captain Chapman north of Nashville in 1797:

> There were only two beds in the one room that was the house's entire living area, and we were granted only what they call here house-room, that is, permission to spread our blankets on the rough planks of the floor, with our bedding arranged so that all four of us lay abreast with our feet to the fire, between the two beds. Captain Chapman got into one bed with his wife, which seemed perfectly straightforward to us. A rather pretty girl who we knew was unmarried got into the other, and that too seemed perfectly straightforward. A strapping young man of about 20 or 22 arrived shortly afterward, while we were settling into our bedding; not standing on ceremony, he undressed and plunked himself into the girl's bed; and while that was indubitably natural, it occasioned a certain surprise on our part. It had no such effect on the captain, who, to relax from the day's fatigues, was enjoying a prose with his wife of which we (though present) were the topic, and in the course of which he found us odd fellows, to leave our home and undergo all the travail of a painful journey to see deserts, savages, and a thousand other things that a man might reasonably think not worth all the trouble. Nor was he distressed by the young man's intimate manner with his daughter. His other daughter blew out the candle and slipped into the young people's bed, so that the young man was in the middle. That seemed to us even more extraordinary; but the flow of matrimonial conversation abated not a whit. We four paid close at-

[73] George W. McDaniel, *Hearth and Home: Preserving a People's Culture* (Philadelphia, 1982). Also see Michael Ann Williams, "The Little 'Big House': The Use and Meaning of the Single-Pen Dwelling," in Wells, ed., *Perspectives in Architecture, II*, pp. 133–35, and Robert R. Madden and T. Russell Jones, *Mountain Home: The Walker Family Farmstead, Great Smoky Mountains National Park* (Washington, D.C., 1977), pp. 19–23, 27.

tention to these goings-on, and saw to our left, by the gleam of the fire, the young man and the first daughter get up and settle again at the foot of the bed; in a word, we saw all that one can see while the paternal word-mill continued to grind away as before.[74]

Communal sleeping was, in fact, a common part of premodern experience in most of the Western world, but the descriptions that have descended to us come largely from privileged or foreign observers, who regarded it with distaste or amusement.[75]

The 1798 Federal Direct Tax lists provide an unusually precise portrait of the size and character of American buildings at an early point in the post-Revolutionary rebuilding. They catch the building revolution in midstream and, in so doing, graphically illustrate the variety of housing standards within various communities and the continued use by many people of small, unimproved houses. Working with the 1798 tax lists and orphans court records, Orlando Ridout V has shown that about 1800 almost two-thirds of the principal houses in rural Queen Anne's County on Maryland's Eastern Shore contained less than 500 square feet; the most common size was sixteen feet by twenty feet. The pattern of buildings that survive from 1798 is also informative. In the three studied districts of Queen Anne's County, slightly less than 10 percent of the principal dwellings remained standing in 1982. Only about 2.5 percent of the enumerated houses with less than 500 square feet on the first floor survived; of those containing from 500 to 1,000 square feet, an impressive 40 percent did. The poorest houses, valued at less than $100, were not included since none survived.[76]

[74]Louis-Philippe, *Diary of My Travels in America*, pp. 113–14.

[75]Jean-Louis Flandrin, *Families in Former Times: Kinship, Household and Sexuality* (Cambridge, 1979), pp. 98–102.

[76]Orlando Ridout V, "Re-editing the Past: A Comparison of Surviving Documentary and Physical Evidence" (Paper presented at the Annual Meeting of the Society of Architectural Historians, New Haven, Apr. 1982). Also Garry Wheeler Stone, "Artifacts Are Not Enough," *The Conference on Historic Site Archaeology Papers* 2 (1977):43–63.

Many houses were, of course, worth considerably less. The 1798 Direct Tax assessment for King George's and Grubb Hundreds in rural Prince George's County, Maryland, included forty-three subsidiary dwellings, other than slave quarters, for which individual values were given. These tenements, overseers' houses, and various "old and crazy" houses ranged in assessed value from $20 to $96, with an average value of $55, and sizes from twelve feet square to sixteen by thirty-six. The thirty-six comparable houses listed in the Horsepen and Patuxent Hundred assessments were thought to be of slightly lower value: from $15 to $80, with an average of $37. The smallest tenant house was ten feet by twelve, and the largest was twenty-four by thirty-two.[77]

While the Chesapeake may represent the low end of the spectrum for all but the rich both before and after the Revolution, similar patterns of limited post-Revolutionary improvement can be found elsewhere. In Worcester County in central Massachusetts there was substantial new building in the 1790s, but most of the houses remained small. Out of a sample of nearly 2,300 houses in fourteen Worcester County towns in 1798, 14 percent of the buildings had less than 500 square feet and 24 percent less than 600. The most common dwelling there in 1798 incorporated approximately 600 square feet in a two-room plan. Assessed house values ranged from $4 for a twenty-eight-foot by eighteen-foot log house to $3,000 for a mansion in Brookfield. Nevertheless the $4 dwelling was considered to be worth more than twice that of "one poor little miserable low house, no window, no glass" in Boxborough. Most were valued at less than $350, generally between $100 and $150. A broader sampling of contemporary tax lists from Massachusetts towns indicates that although two-story houses predominate among surviving eighteenth-century structures, they equaled or surpassed single-story houses only in a few long-settled and prosperous communities. Most middling farmers living in Massachusetts towns in 1798 occupied single-story houses of two or three

[77] 1798 Direct Tax, Prince George's Co., Md., Maryland State Archives, Annapolis.

rooms, and less than 10 percent of these remain serviceable to the present day.[78]

Common house values drawn from the 1798 tax lists for Mifflin County and Delaware County in Pennsylvania vary considerably, but most houses were mean and cheap. Sixty-eight percent of the recorded houses in Mifflin County were valued at $100 or less and 28 percent at $101 to $500. Houses valued at more than $501 constituted only 4 percent of the group. The housing stock in Delaware County was significantly better: 26.2 percent of its dwellings were valued at $100 or less, 49.7 percent at $101 to $500, and 24.1 percent at over $500.[79]

Interpreting the 1798 tax lists is complex because they straddle two eras. Examination of the buildings themselves makes it clear that a major rebuilding was underway by 1798. At the same time, the tax lists describe many pre-Revolutionary buildings. The lists also refer to great numbers of new houses, many of them just as poor as their predecessors. It is no great revelation that one can find bad houses in the era of a building boom. The same was true in the late 1940s. What is important is that during the era of the most extensive housing renewal in the first two centuries of British-American settlement—an era that postdated the one when the English consumer mania is said to have "reached revolutionary proportions"[80]—most Americans were still living in small, mean, vernacular houses. Despite the improved stan-

[78]Michael Steinitz, "Rethinking Geographical Approaches to the Common House: The Evidence from Eighteenth-Century Massachusetts," in Carter and Herman, eds., *Perspectives in Architecture, III,* and Myron O. Stachiw and Nora Pat Small, "Tradition and Transformation: Rural Society and Architectural Change in Nineteenth-Century Central Massachusetts," in Carter and Herman, eds., *Perspectives in Architecture, III.* Kevin Sweeney finds that while large houses dominate the tax lists for affluent Connecticut River towns, dwellings in the hill towns were predominately "log huts" and other relatively mean buildings (Sweeney, "Mansion People," pp. 242–44; Hosley, "Architecture," pp. 65, 133).

[79]Lee Soltow, "Housing Characteristics on the Pennsylvania Frontier: Mifflin County Dwelling Values in 1798," *Pennsylvania History* 46 (1980):57–70.

[80]McKendrick, Brewer, and Plumb, *Birth of a Consumer Society,* p. 9.

dards recorded in the federal tax lists and elsewhere, one is not aware of a consumer revolution having transformed the material lives of most people as represented by their dwellings. Manners, taste in ceramics, and holiday destinations may have changed dramatically, but broad-based changes are not so evident in the listings of that principal artifact, the house.

Be that as it may, the picture must not be oversimplified. Conditions were changing in rich cities of the new republic, and urban housing stock was clearly different in 1825 from what it had been early in the era of rebuilding. Both tax lists and surviving fabric show that housing had improved dramatically for those with excess capital or credit and some people in their employ. By 1814 there were laboring Wilmingtonians who rented multiroom masonry houses on streets where the best houses were occupied by prosperous Delaware businessmen.[81] By 1832 well over half the houses in the central Massachusetts community of Shirley had two full stories, a significant increase in their numbers in the short space of three decades.[82] Even houses belonging to slaves and free workers saw some improvement in the second quarter century. These advances are most evident in the mill villages of New England. They can also still be seen in the old industrial areas of cities like Petersburg, Virginia, and on substantial farms across much of the South. Workers' housing remained undecorated and small in both size and number of rooms. Yet its advantages over much rural housing were significant enough to help lure poor whites away from their traditional occupations and ensure that, as investments, some slaves were relatively well protected from the elements. Within the slave system, housing was conspicuously inequitable, the inequality serving as a means of control unavailable to those who provided consistently poor housing. Nevertheless, superior accommodations for laborers were rare. In fact, most rural laborers' housing was of such poor quality that it could not

[81] Herman, "Thomas Mendenhall," pp. 73–75.

[82] Jack Larkin, "Inequality, Economic Transformation, and the Changing Domestic Environment" (Paper presented at the Winterthur Conference "Everyday Life in the Early Republic, 1789–1828," Winterthur, Del., Nov. 1988).

survive for more than a generation or two. Not until late in the nineteenth century, when cheap, mass-produced materials became available, were permanent tenant houses built in large numbers.[83]

Racism made housing especially difficult for free blacks to find, and many people crowded into congested, unhealthy multifamily tenements in alleys, courts, and backs of lots in cities like Cincinnati and Albany. At its worst, such tenements were like those recorded in New York and at the edge of Philadelphia in the 1840s: six-foot-square hovels packed together on two and three levels and served by catwalks that, when they didn't collapse, kept people above the animal and human waste.[84] Throughout the antebellum period some more fortunate urban free blacks built and occupied their own frame houses with one to two rooms on each of one or more floors. Multiple rooms commonly allowed owners to rent space to other blacks, free or enslaved. Some such Brooklyn and Richmond houses, well framed, solidly underpinned, and provided with glazed windows, have been sufficiently acceptable to attract public-funded preservation or white gentrification in recent years.[85] Black housing of this kind is, of course, virtually undistinguishable, without the aid of tax lists and city direc-

[83]A few rich Georgia and South Carolina lowcountry planters built improved three-room houses for some slave families toward the middle of the century. Groups of these houses survive at Silver Hill in Georgetown County, McLeod Plantation in Charleston County, and Hobonny in Beaufort County, South Carolina (Gary Stanton, Edward A. Chappell, and Willie Graham, "One Man's Home Is Another Man's Castle: Extant Slave Housing in South Carolina" [Paper presented at the Annual Meeting of the American Folklore Society, Albuquerque, N.M., Oct. 1987]). Meager though it was, such housing for workers was very rare before the Civil War throughout the South. In affluent areas of central Kentucky, for example, thousands of modest two- and three-room houses built for tenant farmers in the last third of the nineteenth century are still occupied, but one seldom finds more than an occasional remaining single- or two-room duplex slave house there. Houses comparable to the three-room Georgia and South Carolina quarters seem entirely absent in the upper South.

[84]Leonard P. Curry, *The Free Black in Urban America, 1800–1850: The Shadow of the Dream* (Chicago, 1981), pp. 49–54.

[85]Marie Tyler-McGraw and Gregg D. Kimball, *In Bondage and Freedom: Antebellum Black Life in Richmond, Virginia* (Richmond, 1988); Luther Porter

tories, from that owned and let by whites. Urban neighborhoods were rarely sorted by race to the degree they are today, though the first half of the nineteenth century saw a general decline in the racial mix of wards in large American cities.[86]

In the competitive real estate environments of Philadelphia and New York City, post-Revolutionary change in the system of property management led to an actual decline in housing standards for much of the population. While the domestic expectations of some affluent nineteenth-century New Yorkers rose with the appearance of increasingly grand ready-to-wear middle-class housing, a whole class of workers was forced to make do in ever smaller divisions of buildings originally intended to house a single family. New methods of financing construction and the subdivision of old houses, coupled with the growth of middle-class desire for social exclusivity, encouraged the creation of class divisions by neighborhood, an altogether alien concept in the "walking cities" of the eighteenth century.[87]

Even in the era of cheap but lasting two- and three-room tenant-farmer houses, much of the rural poor occupied buildings that were little different from those described in the eighteenth-century orphans court records.[88] Late nineteenth-

---

Jackson, *Free Negro Labor and Property-Holding in Virginia* (New York, 1942); Joan Maynard, "The Weeksville Project," *CRM* 15 (1992):4–5. For now, we assume that such substantial free black housing was rare, and that most American free blacks lived in far less secure environments. Compare Stachiw, "Impermanent Architecture," and Pamela J. Cressey, "Alexandria, Virginia City-Site: Archaeology in an Afro-American Neighborhood, 1830–1910," Ph.D. diss., University of Iowa, 1985.

[86]Curry, *Free Black*, pp. 54–80.

[87]Betsy Blackmar, "Rewalking the 'Walking City': Housing and Property Relations in New York City, 1780–1840," *Radical History Review* 21 (1979):131–48; idem, *Manhattan for Rent;* Warner, *The Private City.*

[88]Orville Vernon Burton suggests that in Edgefield, South Carolina, north of Augusta, Georgia, housing conditions actually worsened for ex-slaves after the Civil War because of the unwillingness of whites to allow many blacks to build on their land or occupy old housing stock (*In My Father's House Are Many Mansions: Family and Community in Edgefield, South Carolina* [Chapel Hill, N.C., 1985], pp. 274–77).

century photographers in pursuit of picturesque poverty as well as those employed by the Historic American Buildings Survey and the Works Projects Administration in the 1930s recorded countless laborers and mountain farm families living in houses of the same size and relative absence of finish.[89] The frame and log walls of their houses commonly remained unsheathed and unplastered, and recycled newspapers and magazines were the normal choice of wallpaper. Southerners with memories of the 1910s and 1920s can recall the use of wooden chimneys and clay floors, and sizable numbers of surviving rural buildings used to house workers still have windows fitted with shutters rather than sash. Most remaining duplex slave houses were converted into multiroom residences for single families of workers by the 1920s. Other poor people continued to occupy buildings with a single first-floor room and an attic. Urban workers were crowded into equally small parts of apartment buildings in most American cities in the second half of the nineteenth century.

Although the disparities in quality of housing remained great in the early national period, increasing numbers of people could afford improved housing and chose to spend their money on it. Reasons for this as well as the more limited changes of the preceding half century call for consideration. It has been suggested that more specialized and environmentally secure farming methods and the shift to crops like grain provided a new level of financial security; therefore, more people below the gentry level could partake of the new sufficiency in housing.[90] Certainly agricultural specialization made

[89]See, for example, Carl Lounsbury, "Vernacular Construction in the Survey," in C. Ford Peatross, ed., *Historic America: Buildings, Structures, and Sites Recorded by the Historic American Buildings Survey and the Historic American Engineering Record* (Washington, D.C., 1983), pp. 182–95; A. Lawrence Kocher and Howard Dearstyne, *Shadows in Silver* (New York, 1954), pp. 90, 217–19; Henry Glassie, "The Types of the Southern Mountain Cabin," in Jan Harold Brunvard, *The Study of American Folklore: An Introduction* (New York, 1968), pp. 338–70.

[90]Carson et al., "Impermanent Architecture"; Steinitz, "Rethinking Geographical Approaches"; Paul G. E. Clemens, *The Atlantic Economy and Colonial Maryland's Eastern Shore: From Tobacco to Grain* (Ithaca, N.Y., 1980).

more capital available for building, and arguably the same improvement-minded course of action that led to rotation, manuring, and liming of fields may have encouraged the building of houses that put one's domestic world into better order. Yet the shift from tobacco to grain had brought certain stability to the finances of the richest Chesapeake farmers nearly half a century before the housing revolution began, the shift was often spotty, and the simple presence of more capital does not explain the motivation for change.[91] Both the rise in consumption of movable goods and improvement in housing standards reflect a pattern that existed outside local economic circumstances. As a result, the pattern is evident in both urban and rural settings.

From our own perspective, eighteenth- and nineteenth-century desire for improvements in domestic comfort, privacy, and sanitation seems only normal and healthy, an almost predictable response to any opportunity for change.[92] Development of a market economy simply made the change possible. If we accept Norbert Elias's analysis of the early modern advance in the frontiers of personal decorum or

---

[91] Stiverson, *Poverty in a Land of Plenty.*

[92] An eighteenth-century American staying in London, for example, might expect a room with window, fireplace, and a good bed, but finding these amenities for an affordable price was not inevitable. In 1728 a relative living in Chelsea wrote to Elizabeth Jones in Virginia: "Because you wrote soe pressingly for one answer about Takeing Lodgings for you; accordingly I went to Severall Streets but could find no Lodgings to be Lett but what was two story high; and yt at Six Shillings [per] week; in Gracious Street I went to a widdow woman a Quaker and a Milliner by trade with whom I was Acquainted; She shew me a room up one pr. of stairs; their was an Indifferent good bed in it the room is a Chamber that fronts the main Street—but the furniture in it was mean and the price at Six Shilings [per] week but their is no Chimne in the room. . . . I went to Mr. William Pooles in Bishopgate Street; I agreed with him for a Chamber up one pr: of Stairs, where their was a good Large bed and good Large Closet a fireplace Convenient and the rest of ye. Furniture Indifferent, good all at 5 Shillings per week." An invoice dated Dec. 23 from William Poole shows that Jones and a sister occupied the latter room for five weeks at 18 *sh.* per week, including board, and that their servant stayed either in the same room or elsewhere in Poole's house (Jones Family Papers, Library of Congress, items 357 and 372).

delicacy, though, we may recognize even these seemingly natural yearnings as part of a great shift in expectations, a shift that defines certain essential characteristics of the modern era.[93]

More important to the explanation for widespread housing change is its role in the increasing use of material distinctions to maintain and modify social relations within communities and individual households. Counterposed to this motivation, moreover, was a growing concern about minimum housing standards for others, however much housing fell short of those standards. Finally, and perhaps more surprising, the role of architectural fashion in rejection of existing social codes deserves attention. Much of this is indeed related to development of a market economy and growth of a bourgeois class, but it precedes classic suburban middle-class life and more than construction of social boundaries was at work.

An essential factor in consumption was the increasing desire for the material distinction of the individual, a sentiment that ultimately may not have been shared equally by British and American people. Much of the housing improvement for affluent Americans in the second and third quarters of the eighteenth century and at lower social levels soon thereafter was driven by what Richard L. Bushman sees as a quest for gentility.[94] Eighteenth-century Americans, like their contemporaries in Europe, were increasingly concerned that in a relatively mobile world their positions be maintained and advanced. Status directly affected political and economic fate and was, to judge from both the words and buildings left to us, an obsession of the age. The concern may often have been not so much to rise swiftly through the ranks as to present oneself as worthy and acceptable, to be placed above the rabble—a sentiment expressed continually, for example, by travelers seeking satisfactory accommodation. Goods might

---

[93] Elias, *Civilizing Process.* Also see Roger Chartier, ed., *A History of Private Life,* vol. 3, *Passions of the Renaissance* (Cambridge, Mass., 1989); John F. Kasson, *Rudeness and Civility: Manners in Nineteenth-Century Urban America* (New York, 1990); Arlie Russell Hochschild, *The Managed Heart: Commercialization of Human Feeling* (Berkeley, 1983); and Flandrin, *Families in Former Times.*

[94] Bushman, "American High-Style."

be used to more immediate social advantage in America, but even the British system could be manipulated by a nice suit of clothes or, one suspects, a pretty facade.[95] Both in Britain and the colonies, refined behavior and accoutrement became necessary aids in the pursuit of success.

To survive and prosper in the broader European world, one had to engage skillfully and gracefully in social activities, the rules of which evolved and were elaborated in the eighteenth century. Following the dictates of courtesy in eating by not touching anything others might eat is one example; as French historian Jean-Louis Flandrin observes, "every diner was surrounded by an invisible cage." Such delicate processes require certain artifacts. People were judged by their skills in using socially charged objects as well as in conversation and movement, and simply by what they owned.[96] As early as 1688 William Fitzhugh mused on the simple advantages of owning silver dinnerware: "I esteem it as well politic as reputable, to furnish my self with an handsom Cupboard of plate which gives my self the present use & Credit, [and] is a sure friend at a dead lift."[97] Sizable rooms with fine furnishings and finish

[95] Beverly Lemire cites this evocative observation from Bernard Mandeville's *Fable of the Bees* (London, 1714): "People, where they are not known, are generally honour'd according to their Clothes and other Accoutrements. . . . It is this which encourages every Body, who is conscious of his little Merit, if he is any ways able, to wear Clothes above his Rank, especially in large and populous Cities, where obscure Men may hourly meet with fifty Strangers to one Acquaintance, and consequently have the Pleasure of beeing esteem'd by a vast Majority, not as what they are, but what they appear to be" (Lemire, "Consumerism in Preindustrial and Early Industrial England: The Trade in Secondhand Clothes," *Journal of British Studies* 27 [1988]:5).

[96] Jean-Louis Flandrin, "Distinction through Taste," in Chartier, *Passions of the Renaissance*, p. 266; Rodris Roth, *Tea-Drinking in Eighteenth-Century America: Its Etiquette and Equipage*, U.S. National Museum Bulletin 225 (Washington, D.C., 1961), pp. 61–91. Diana diZerega Wall, "Family Dinners and Social Teas: Ceramics and Domestic Rituals" (Paper presented at the Winterthur Conference "Everyday Life in the Early Republic, 1789–1828," Winterthur, Del., Nov. 1988).

[97] William Fitzhugh to Nicholas Hayward, June 1, 1688, in Richard Beale Davis, ed., *William Fitzhugh and His Chesapeake World, 1676–1701: The Fitzhugh Letters and Other Documents* (Chapel Hill, N.C., 1963), p. 246.

were essential settings for meaningful entertainment, just as, in the most basic sense, the size and character of a person's house clarified his or her position in the community. But Fitzhugh was after more than sheer bulk for display. The items he mentioned served a specific and necessary function in the newly formalized conduct of meals.

Increasingly in the eighteenth century, the procurement and use of new *things*—matched sets of china, chairs, pictures, and such—and investment in conspicuously superior domestic architecture together created a reciprocal process in which the acquisition of one encouraged pursuit of another. In 1752 Williamsburg apothecary George Gilmer spoke of entertainment paraphernalia with a wry remark on the use of such trappings by one of his profession. Writing to Bristol merchant Walter King, he observed: "Mrs Gilmer is perfectly satisfied with your conduct about her China and desires you will take your own time. I have just finished a closet for her to put it in as agreed on before you left us. I am wainscoting my dining room, which with a handsome marble chimney piece &c with glass over it, will make a tolerable room for an Apothecary."[98]

Gilmer's new ceramics and new room finish were both parts of a social strategy that he apparently used with skill, since he was eventually elected to two terms as mayor of Williamsburg. In his seemingly modest way, Gilmer is representative of many affluent eighteenth-century Anglo-Americans who invested in a combination of architecture and artifacts as a means of personal advancement. By the end of the colonial era, the recently consolidated social order was already under considerable duress.[99] In the early republic, the scramble to establish financial and political advantage was intense, and the British class structure exerted even less influence. More than ever before, appearances could affect success.

For some eighteenth-century Americans, differences in quality of material things were used to define intended social

[98] George Gilmer to Walter King, Aug. 6, 1752, copied into Brock Manuscript Notebook, p. 154, Huntington Library, San Marino, Calif.

[99] Isaac, *Transformation of Virginia;* Upton, *Holy Things and Profane;* Nash, *Urban Crucible.*

relationships within households as well as communities. In rich people's houses, gradations among architectural finish and furnishings constantly reminded owners, guests, and workers of where they happened to be in the household, spatially and socially. Objects carried explicit signals for how people should feel and act.[100] Degrees to which these cues were actually heeded are now harder to know.

The best woodwork and textiles in a grand eighteenth-century house were concentrated in the rooms intended for conversation and dining. Subtle distinctions were commonly made even among adjoining entertaining rooms, bedchambers, or passages, and much clearer distinctions were created between such groups.[101] Details as individually inconsequential as panel moldings and sometimes as invisible as different methods of joining floorboards were used to delineate hierarchies of space.[102] Some of the visual cues remain opaque to us,

[100] David Harvey, *The Urban Experience* (Baltimore, 1989), p. 187.

[101] Walking into Councillor Robert Carter's house today, it is difficult to recognize which of the six principal rooms were his "three parlours" and which were bedchambers. There would have been no uncertainty, however, after his remodeling of 1762, when the walls of the reception rooms were hung with paper. He ordered a good crimson paper for the first parlor, a better white paper with large green leaves for the second, and the best blue paper with large yellow flowers for the third, which was probably the destination for yellow silk and worsted damask curtains and eighteen chairs covered with the same material. At least several of the wallpapered rooms had their trim painted a fashionable off-white. The passages were also hung with paper, but most of the bedchambers appear to have been left with plain plaster walls and woodwork painted in darker hues (Robert Carter to Thomas Bladen, Feb. 16, 1762, Robert Carter Letterbook, 1761–65, Col. Williamsburg Found. Paint analysis by Frank S. Welsh, 1992).

[102] Chappell, "Looking at Buildings"; Upton, *Holy Things and Profane*, p. 110. Attention to variations in the quality of different parts of a building is generally absent from early American construction contracts. However, much of the spectrum of quality found in the best Philadelphia houses at the end of the eighteenth century, as well as the costs inherent in the elaboration, is carefully enumerated in the surveys done for the (Philadelphia) Mutual Assurance Company and Franklin Insurance Company (Anthony N. B. Garvan, Cynthia Koch, Donald Arbuckle, and Deborah Hart, eds., *The Mutual Assurance Company Papers*, vol. 1, *The Architectural Surveys, 1784–1794* [Philadelphia, 1976]). Also see Charles E. Peterson, ed., *The Rules of Work of the Carpenters' Company of the City and County of Philadelphia, 1786* (Philadelphia, 1971), pp. 10–11, for different grades of flooring, and pp.

and many may have been ambiguous when first created. It is clear, though, that decisions about relative quality were commonly made to emphasize the importance of rooms in which public entertainment took place. Circulation spaces, even those that led to these rooms, were less important. Bedchambers, too, were generally treated as secondary, declining perceptibly in quality as one moved up toward the garret or out toward a domestic wing.[103]

Drawing on the work of Erving Goffman and later sociologists, Lorna Weatherill makes a distinction between "front stage" and "back stage" in the treatment of British houses.[104] Here as well as there, though, the line between public and private space was not always sharply drawn. In the best eighteenth-century houses it was common to find a richly finished bedchamber on the same floor as the entertaining room, sometimes intentionally not connected to it. More commonly, all chambers intended for family and guests were *decently* finished. Even in the attic bedchambers at Shirley on the James River or Mount Pleasant on the Schuylkill, there are plaster walls and ceilings, if not everywhere wainscoting and mantels. It is significant that genteel accoutrements were not confined to public rooms. By the mid-eighteenth century, rich people's houses consistently promoted the proposition that domestic gentility extended into the private realm.

It did not extend to service areas. Despite their proximity to public rooms, and whether or not they were frequented by the property owners, the areas in which cooking, washing,

---

18–19 for paneling. For different grades of carpenters' and joiners' work with English prices, see William Salmon, *Palladio Londinensis*, 3d ed. (London, 1748), pp. 41–50.

[103]The 1773 specifications for a rather costly (£653) brick, two-story glebe house and outbuildings in Fairfax County, Virginia, for example, calls for the doors on the first floor to have six panels, brass locks, and "double architraves" as frames, while those on the upper floor were to have four panels, painted iron locks, and simpler frames (Fairfax Parish Vestry Book, 1765–1843, Va. St. Libr., pp. 55–58).

[104]Lorna Weatherill, *Consumer Behaviour and Material Culture in Britain, 1660–1760* (London, 1988); Erving Goffman, *The Presentation of Self in Everyday Life* (New York, 1959).

and other heavy work was done were treated quite differently, usually with bare masonry walls, stone or unplaned wood floors, and little light.[105] The nearby spaces in which servants and slaves lived were generally worse rather than better. The borders of genteel space were made evident to all involved.[106]

Zones of gentility were, of course, far more limited in the houses of affluent but less grand colonial Americans. For many, there was an essential difference in quality between first-floor rooms, where entertaining and family activities took place, and the sleeping space above. The former could have all the requisite features of plaster walls, nicely planed wood trim, glazed windows, and fireplaces finished with mantels—the proper environment for polite behavior. Climbing the stairs to sleep, as much of the family, boarders, and perhaps guests would do, though, one would encounter a space little different from the loft of a barn, with small shuttered windows, the roof frame and covering exposed, and no comforting fireplaces. No three-quarter length mirrors or dressing tables here, in the low, dark space where wind whistled through the shingles and dirt daubers built their nests. Environments in which the decorous and the crude intersected were normal, expected even by most who had access to well-trimmed parlors. Fully unfinished houses seem easier for us to comprehend then these hybrid settings, where people decided to plaster and wainscot some rooms while leaving others completely unfinished. The pervasive coexistence of rudeness and civility belies the suggestion of conformity implicit in most explanations of early modern consumer practice.

[105] In English-settled areas south of New England, detached kitchens became common by the eighteenth century. There was a growing and important distinction between households with detached kitchens and those—in much of eighteenth-century Britain and Germanic areas of the American colonies, for example—that commonly incorporated cooking into the center of the house. It seems particularly important for those households in which most or all of the cooking was done by women family members, not slaves or servants. Given the central emotional as well as productive role that cooking plays in households, its removal to separate and distinctly inferior space has powerful implications for gender relations and familial succor, in an era when open expression of affection and relative equality within the family ostensibly was increasing.

[106] Upton, "White and Black Landscapes."

It is important to recognize some element of *choice* as well as financial limits in the absence of refined housing. Whether in house building or the enjoyment of blood sports, some Americans as well as their European counterparts consciously resisted progressive notions of propriety. There remained, well into the nineteenth century, elements of the opposition E. P. Thompson labeled "patrician society, plebian culture,"[107] so that some people chose to occupy houses that to us seem partially or entirely unfinished. Arguments for a consumer revolution are strongest when they avoid the tendency to become a new consensus history, portraying populations with more the character of lemmings than real people with varied individual and group sensibilities.[108] Most eighteenth- and early nineteenth-century Americans were not uncritical, insatiable consumers of furnishings or architecture. Much reluctance lingered in what became the working class, though it was never confined there. The half-finished houses of the Chesapeake were homes for distinctly middling families. Other factors affected choice. Republican ideals in some communities could, for example, circumscribe the rarified taste of ruling-class consumers. The rich James C. Johnston, who built a lavish house called Hayes near Edenton, North Carolina, underscored the point when ordering furniture for Hayes from New York in 1817. He wrote, "It is unnecessary for me to say that I wish them of the plainest and neatest kind and not in the extreme of the fashion but what would suit a moderate liver in New York. A man by appearing very different from his neighbors is more apt to excite their ridicule and perhaps envy than their esteem & respect."[109]

[107]E. P. Thompson, *The Making of the English Working Class* (London, 1963); idem, *Customs in Common: Studies in Traditional Popular Culture* (New York, 1991).

[108]The uncritical tendency in characterizing early modern consumption dates to Thorstein Veblen, *The Theory of the Leisure Class: An Economic Study of Institutions* (London, 1925). There are promising recent exceptions, like Weatherill, *Consumer Behaviour and Material Culture,* and Carole Shammas, *The Pre-Industrial Consumer in England and America* (Oxford, 1990).

[109]Hayes Collection, Southern Historical Collection, University of North Carolina Library, Chapel Hill, N.C.

Still, the first half of the nineteenth century saw increasing numbers of Americans moving from unfinished rooms into something roughly akin in quality to bedchambers in surviving gentry houses. In some of the housing built by the rich for their workers and by the state for the deviant, dependent, or handicapped, we can observe a shift from unmitigated concern for creating architectural distinctions among people and activities to a modest but nevertheless increased concern for a minimum standard of what we might call decency. As already suggested, by the 1820s it was no longer unusual for a millowner to build multiple housing with solid walls, workmanlike joinery, and sizable glass windows. Along with more efficient technological means of employing labor came the return of more excess capital to maintain the workers—or at least *some* workers.

The pattern extended beyond concerns for the successful management of labor, reflecting new reformist attitudes about the form, finish, and cleanliness of domestic space. The change in popular attitudes toward what people required in order to lead respectable lives is nicely illustrated by various kinds of multiple housing. For their growing numbers of members, communal societies like the Shakers and Harmonists constructed dormitories with rooms offering simple but respectable and consistent finish in plaster and trim. Comparable rooms of striking consistency filled collegiate dormitories across the land. In the same era, governments built schools for the deaf and blind with reasonably well-crafted interiors and some classical ornamentation. Most informative perhaps are contemporary insane asylums, where adequate, domesticlike environments were considered necessary, even central factors in returning their inmates to sanity. In an extraordinary show of faith in the curative powers of decent housing, hospitals like Bloomingdale Asylum in New York, the Nashville Lunatic Asylum, and St. Elizabeth's in Washington encompassed literally hundreds of rooms finished to resemble what had come to be viewed as acceptable American bedrooms. When not involved in rigorous work or group activities, patients occupied rooms finished with white walls, simple neoclassical trim, and paneled doors designed to minimize the frightening appearance of apparatus for security and observation.[110]

One should not suggest that the concern was unconditionally humanitarian or all-pervasive. Control was at least as important as succor. Decorous boardinghouses representing corporate paternalism were used to regulate rigidly the off-duty lives of factory laborers. Workhouses were often intentionally planned as abusive environments in order to discourage indolence, and many domestic workers labored in the completely unfinished and unheated rooms inside stylish wings of great houses.[111] This, too, was the era of rapidly growing social segregation, when neighborhoods became increasingly distinct economically, and servants were more vigorously routed away from the public parts of large houses. The rapid growth in numbers of people removed to asylums is, of course, a telling social expression of the age of institutional expansion and nascent reform.

Especially in Britain, degree of wealth and the quantity of material goods owned were not always synonymous with class. Communities recognized some members with few worldly goods as gentry, while others with more goods were clearly not members of this group.[112] Time was a factor in allowing money to buy veneration, and in Britain the time required by the process extended to generations. Anthropologist Grant McCracken suggests that the formation of patina on expensive household objects was employed as an indicator of superior status. Patina conferred social meaning that the objects lacked when new. Essential change came in the eighteenth century, McCracken argues, when fashion replaced patina as "status gatekeeper," and the successful assimilation of new fashions rather than lineage became a common standard for

[110]David J. Rothman, *The Discovery of the Asylum: Social Order and Disorder in the New Republic* (Boston, 1971).

[111]Mary C. Beaudry, "The Lowell Boot Mills Complex and Its Housing: Material Expressions of Corporate Ideology," *Journal of the Society for Historical Archaeology* 23 (1989):19–32. On the building of poorhouses and the intentional humiliation of the poor in late colonial Virginia, see Upton, *Holy Things and Profane*, pp. 220–22.

[112]Weatherill, *Consumer Behaviour and Material Culture*, pp. 166–89.

judging status.[113] However optimistic this perception of eighteenth-century social mobility, there can be no doubting that the pace of European stylistic change quickened in the eighteenth century, and its power as an incentive for popular consumption grew dramatically on both sides of the Atlantic.

Fashion was a relatively minor factor in the changes housing underwent in colonial America, but it played a greater role in the building boom of the young republic. Most obviously, neoclassical taste affected the planning of grand houses, especially in the reshaping of principal rooms or whole buildings to reflect new fascination with geometric shapes. Houses that employ ovals and polygons, even those that are essentially familiar vernacular buildings with unfamiliar shapes dropped into the plan, never numbered more than a handful outside a few cities like Boston, Philadelphia, and Charleston.[114] More common is woodwork and plaster that employs the use of neoclassical motifs. A minority of high-style houses had mantels and doorways little different from those of a Robert Adam town house, with Wedgwood-like putti tumbling across friezes that ride on svelte columns or pilasters.[115] Far

[113]Grant McCracken, *Culture and Consumption: New Approaches to the Symbolic Character of Consumer Goods and Activities* (Bloomington, Ind., 1988), pp. 31–43.

[114]Fiske Kimball, *Domestic Architecture of the American Colonies and of the Early Republic* (New York, 1922), pp. 145–78; Harold Kirker, *The Architecture of Charles Bulfinch* (Cambridge, Mass., 1969); Richard Hubbard Howland and Eleanor Patterson Spencer, *The Architecture of Baltimore* (Baltimore, 1953), pp. 8–9, 13–14, 24, 26; Orlando Ridout V, *Building the Octagon* (Washington, D.C., 1989); Mary Wingfield Scott, *Houses of Old Richmond* (Richmond, 1941), pp. 54–61, 68–78, 84–88, 100–105; Albert Simons and Samuel Lapham, Jr., *Charleston, South Carolina,* The Octagon Library of Early American Architecture, vol. 1 (New York, 1927), pp. 113–15, 120–25, 138.

[115]William D. Shipman, "The Federal Style: From about 1790 to 1825," in Thompson, ed., *Maine Forms,* p. 78; Frank Cousins and Phil M. Riley, *The Woodcarver of Salem: Samuel McIntire, His Life and Work* (Boston, 1916); Charles Morse Stotz, *The Early Architecture of Western Pennsylvania* (New York, 1936), pp. 164–66; George Fletcher Bennett, *Early Architecture of Delaware* (Wilmington, Del., 1932), pp. 104–7, 111–30; Michael F. Trostel, *Mount Clare; Being on Account of the Seat Built by Charles Carroll, Barrister, upon His Lands at Patapsco* (Baltimore, 1981), pp. 81–82, 110–11; Francis Benjamin

more often, though, strict neoclassical design criteria were subordinated to a simple fascination with individuality and whimsy. In almost all regions, clients and artisans took apparent pleasure in seeing how many ways reeding, fluting, or gouging could be used to create imaginative designs that still bore some resemblance to a mantel. Together they conspired to flout the old artistic conventions. In northeastern Ohio, fanlike rows of tapered reeding were hung over openings like the wings of giant bats, while in central North Carolina moldings were piled on one another in fantastic, anticlassical heaps.[116] The elaboration was often enhanced with polychrome paint schemes that were, themselves, a form of entertainment.

We should not confuse an international style of decoration with a robust folk aesthetic in backwoods America. The point is that after the Revolution, American means of visually elaborating both buildings and furniture changed significantly, often by employing neoclassical motifs in very lively and unconventional ways. When rooms in earlier eighteenth-century houses were decorated, the principal sentiment

---

Johnson and Thomas Tileston Waterman, *The Early Architecture of North Carolina* (Chapel Hill, N.C., 1941), pp. 108–10, 134, 226.

[116]The geographic as well as visual range of such woodwork is modestly suggested by the following samples: Denys Peter Myers, *Maine Catalog: Historic American Buildings Survey* (Augusta, Maine, 1974), p. 49; I. T. Frary, *Early American Doorways* (Richmond, 1937), pp. 50–52, 57–59, for New York; Margaret Berwind Schiffer, *Survey of Chester County, Pennsylvania, Architecture* (Exton, Pa., 1976), pp. 112–13; William B. Bassett, *Historic American Buildings Survey of New Jersey* (Newark, N.J., 1977), pp. 34, 120, 127, 144, 152, 173; Rodris Roth, "Interior Decoration of City Houses in Baltimore: The Federal Period," *Winterthur Portfolio* 5 (1969):75, 80–82; Mills Lane, *Architecture of the Old South: Virginia* (Savannah, 1987), pp. 139, 162; idem, *Architecture of the Old South: North Carolina* (Savannah, 1985), pp. 109, 117, 133–34, 140–43, 159; Nichols and Johnson, *Architecture of Georgia*, pp. 147–51, 161–67; I. T. Frary, *Early Houses of Ohio* (Richmond, 1936), pp. 52, 254–55; Walter C. Kidney, *Historic Buildings of Ohio* (Pittsburgh, 1972), pp. 41, 61; Helen C. Powell, ed., *Historic Sites of Harrodsburg and Mercer County, Kentucky* (Harrodsburg, 1988), pp. 9, 18, 37, 41, 43, 195; Thomas B. Brumbaugh, Martha I. Strayhorn, and Gary B. Gore, eds., *Architecture of Middle Tennessee: The Historic American Buildings Survey* (Nashville, 1974), p. 129; Milly McGehee, "Auburn in Natchez," *Antiques* 111 (1977):546–53.

seems to have been a desire for respectability. Fielded paneling was endlessly employed to establish the relative importance of various rooms, and while its configuration and the
details of its joinery offered modest opportunity for creativity,
the limits of one's imagination were rarely tested. Mantels
were essentially architraves, classical moldings carried around
the fireplace opening, sometimes supporting an equally doc-
trinaire frieze and shelf, and occasionally embellished with
pilasters or overmantels. Only in the grandest gentry houses
were the elements enriched with very much carving, and almost all of these follow predictable models.[117]

The quest for respectability did not lessen in the early republic. Judging from the growing quantities of fastidious
brickwork and plaster, it affected a much wider segment of
the population than previously. Yet the many ways in which
new motifs were assembled also suggest the widespread presence of new criteria, those of diversity and, at least to
twentieth-century eyes, amusement.[118] For many, architectural
decoration ceased to be merely a matter of getting it right. In
the new age of hallucinogenic Adamesque, a woodworker
might experiment with just how many ways he could use a
sunburst motif to decorate not just friezes and spandrels of
a door, say, but even its radically twisted cornices and thin,
exaggerated columns. The shift reflects more than a development of decorative style. It suggests a significant change in
attitude about decoration, and about building in general.[119]

In the decades after the Revolution, economic expansion
and republican individualism found expression in increasing

[117]The prominent exceptions draped with flamboyant carving are relatively few. See especially the Gov. Benning Wentworth House in Little Harbor, New Hampshire, the Blackwell House once in Philadelphia, and
Gunston Hall near Lorton, Virginia. A taste for restraint in furniture and
ceramics as well as interior architecture is nicely illustrated by the frequency
with which affluent Americans used the adjective "neat" in describing
their desires.

[118]McKendrick gives a central position to the role of novelty in fashion:
"novelty became an irresistible drug" (McKendrick, Brewer, and Plumb,
Birth of a Consumer Society, p. 10).

[119]A similar shift in taste can be seen in the change in the ceramics produced by English industrialists for the American market, from a restrained

numbers of permanent dwellings with masonry foundations and chimneys, wood floors, glazed windows, and multiple rooms. More pointedly, that individualism was revealed in the extraordinary growth of affection for fashionable and idiosyncratic decoration—decoration that suggested both affluence and independence from social and visual convention. Employment of the unruly new fashion was not undertaken in emulation of traditional superiors. Rather, it suggested new kinds of people in the community, ones who saw themselves as financially and socially muscular and standing more in opposition to traditional patinated status than in emulation of it.[120] The growing ranks of new American home consumers bring to mind Alexis de Tocqueville's characterization of the individualism that American democracy created: "Individualism is a calm and considered feeling which disposes each citizen to isolate himself from the mass of his fellows and withdraw into the circle of family and friends; with this little society formed to his taste, he gladly leaves the rest of society to take care of itself."[121] Tocqueville's view coincides with the evidence that, widespread and energetic as the American housing revolution was, it remained an expression for the winners—not for everyone, not even for a modest majority.[122] Most Americans continued to lack anything approaching genteel housing, whatever their choice of clothing and flatware.

There is irony in the apparent development of both a soci-

---

and relatively limited choice of saltglaze and creamware patterns to the flamboyant banded, transfer printed, marbled, and spattered pearlwares and creamwares of the post-Revolutionary period. It would be worth investigating the degree to which these imports varied from what was produced for the domestic English market.

[120]Such new republicans might be usefully contrasted with many owners of old, outmoded colonial mansions who, feeling little need to replace sedate old woodwork with fashionable new creations, left their houses unaltered.

[121]Alexis de Tocqueville, *Democracy in America*, 2 vols., ed. George Lawrence (New York, 1969), 2:506–7.

[122]The perceptions as well as the realities of economic inequality in the era after Tocqueville wrote are addressed in Lawrence Frederick Kohl, *The

ety absorbed with creation of its own home-centered material-ism and apparent concern over standards for domestic environments for some who were unable to meet those standards alone. Historian Gillian Brown makes the seeming paradox more comprehensible with her analysis of the broader social aims underlying domesticity in the writings of Beecher, Stowe, and Hawthorne.[123] Brown sees these and other mid-century writers as promoting amelioration of society's ills through the influence of female-dominated households and corollary architectural settings. Actual buildings on the other hand, particularly those intended to house communal populations, demonstrate a substantial belief in the importance of physical respectability before the midcentury reformers began to write about the power of domesticity. By the middle of the nineteenth century the notion that home was the locus from which one's family, if not all society, must be nurtured had become an article of middle-class faith with stronger marketing attraction than the social rituals of the eighteenth century.

By considering the causes that quickened consumption in certain categories of objects and stasis in others, we can recognize the limitations of current explanations about the consumer revolution. It is evident that new consumption of both movable goods and housing reflects formation of self-conscious middling rank, with available capital and a new list of needs on which to spend it. By the middle of the nineteenth century, increased consumption was a chief characteristic of the new middle class. Yet acquisition of both movable goods and housing affected people above and below this class. Certain eighteenth-century slaves acquired English tablewares, and improved yet mean housing was available to some of their late antebellum descendants. By this time students, communalist religious adherents, and asylum inmates occupied plastered, painted, heated, and well-lighted rooms. Also, many of

---

Politics of Individualism: Parties and the American Character in the Jacksonian Era (New York, 1989).

[123]Gillian Brown, *Domestic Individualism: Imagining Self in Nineteenth-Century America* (Berkeley, 1990).

the improved post-Revolutionary American houses were built for relatively successful craftsworkers, northern agriculturalists, and slaveholding farmers, none of them middle class in the conventional sense. Most of the new homeowners were, however, suppliers for or otherwise associated with a developing capitalist system of manufacturing and export. In turning part of their profits to the improvement of workers' material conditions, owners responded as much to new managerial strategies for raising profits as to the kind of sensibilities that encouraged public funding of progressive asylums and improvement of space and finish in their own houses.

Further, managers' and workers' use of imported ceramics had as much to do with successful mass production and marketing as with their own domestic aspirations. Mass production makes some things more available, and others less so. Objects recently found at late colonial slave quarters illustrate how large-scale manufacturing diminished the market for locally made wares. Neil McKendrick observes that increased consumption of fashionable, portable goods was encouraged by promotion as well as growth in production. Consumers were not left to recognize their own stirrings of affection for new fashion. Rather they were actively seduced into pursuing the pleasures of stylistic philandery.[124] Long before McKendrick, Marx argued that, in capitalist societies, manufacturers increase or sustain their profits by creating new markets for their goods. Or, as interpreted by Henri Lefebvre, "a mass of available money gives rise to a corresponding mass of commodities; a cycle is set up, the cycle of the market."[125] Philadelphia hatters and Parisian harpsichord makers as well as Staffordshire potters cultivated markets in a way that builders and designers did not successfully do in eighteenth- and early nineteenth-century America. Architecture, by its very nature,

---

[124]McKendrick, Brewer, and Plumb, *Birth of a Consumer Society;* McKendrick, "Josiah Wedgwood: An Eighteenth-Century Entrepreneur in Salesmanship and Marketing Techniques," *Economic History Review,* 2d ser. 12 (1960):408–33.

[125]Karl Marx, *Capital,* 3 vols. (New York, 1967); Henri Lefebvre, *The Survival of Capitalism* (New York, 1976), p. 9. Also see Harvey, *Urban Experience.*

exhibited a certain inertia. Speculative builders provided much of the housing in nineteenth-century cities—perhaps as much as 99 percent in London, it has been estimated.[126] Both contractors and architects worked at making space an interchangeable and therefore negotiable commodity in post-Revolutionary urban America,[127] but only in certain hothouse economic environments did they promote superior and more costly housing sufficient to significantly change living standards. Ready-made house frames were sometimes available in the eighteenth-century colonies and the new republic, but it was not until the second half of the next century that house designs and components were purchased by a sizable middle class.[128] It was only late in the nineteenth century that either financiers or builders found themselves in a position to court actively sizable parts of the American population. In short, many consumer goods were purchasable and promotable in eighteenth-century America. For most people, refined housing was not. Available choices were made when portable goods, mass-produced in Europe and pitched with increasing efficiency, were within reach. Costly housing, inescapably local and laborious in creation, remained beyond most people's grasp. It is likely that home-ownership or the maintenance of a prim household was once less important an element in defining oneself than it has since become.[129]

Ever attuned to the ironies of American social practice,

[126]Stefan Muthesius, *The English Terraced House* (New Haven, 1982), p. 19; H. J. Dyos, *Victorian Suburb: A Study of the Growth of Camberwell* (Leicester, 1961).

[127]Dell Upton, "Urban Cultural Landscapes in Early Republican Philadelphia" (Paper presented at the Commonwealth Center, College of William and Mary, Williamsburg, Mar. 1989).

[128]For example, see *South Carolina Gazette*, May 29, 1742, p. 3; July 14, 1767, p. 3; *Columbia Mirror and Alexandria Gazette*, Dec. 27, 1796, p. 1, Feb. 27, 1798, p. 1. John Barber advertised in the Dec. 27, 1796, *Mirror and Gazette:* "House frames of the following dimensions, 24 by 18 feet square, two stories—14 by 18 do 14 by 18 single story 12 by 16 story and a half 12 by 16, and some 12 by 14 feet square, one story."

[129]Salinger and Wetherell, "Wealth and Renting," pp. 826–40.

Frances Trollope provides an evocative—if caricatured—example of homes in which refinement had made only partial inroads, changing manners and a few objects, but little affecting the domestic setting. She took tea with a Maryland slaveholding family on their three-hundred-acre farm about 1830: "The house was built of wood, and looked as if the three slaves might have overturned it, had they pushed hard against the gable end. It contained one room, of about twelve feet square, and another adjoining it, hardly larger than a closet; this second chamber was the lodging-room of the white part of the family. Above these rooms was a loft, without windows, where I was told the 'staying company' who visited them, were lodged. Near this mansion was a 'shanty,' a black hole, without any window, which served as kitchen and all other offices, and also as the lodging of the blacks." Rustic food served on "the coarsest blue ware" by slaves "considerably more than half naked" also fell short of Trollope's expectations. She mused over the stark contrast with well-prepared teas she had enjoyed in poor but clean and respectable tenant farmhouses in England. What made the Maryland scene absurd to Trollope was the degree of social pretense displayed in the midst of sloth and material deprivation. "The lady I now visited . . . greatly surpassed my quondam friends in the refinement of her conversation. She ambled through the whole time the visit lasted, in a sort of elegantly mincing familiar style of gossip, which, I think, she was imitating from some novel, for I was told she was a great novel reader, and left all household occupations to be performed by her slaves." But what was feeble imitation of genteel behavior to a middle-class English traveler in search of American vulgarity could be successful presentation to those enacting their roles. Trollope saw the seriousness with which the participants perceived the meal, even one of the young boys serving her, to which the hostess's command "'Attend to your young master, Lycurgus,' must have been heard to be conceived in the full extent of its mock heroic."[130] The Maryland hostess so unlucky as to entertain Mrs. Trollope had embraced some of gentility's trappings, but

[130] Frances Trollope, *Domestic Manners of the Americans* (1832; reprint ed. Gloucester, Mass., 1974), pp. 241–43.

major aspects of her life remained wholly untouched by the revolution in question.

Ultimately, the great age of elaborated American housing was the second half of the nineteenth century, for successful farmers, small-town elites, and city-dwellers alike. This came with the emergence of a large middle class and the dominance of its values toward material well-being and importance of nurturance in the well-cared-for home, as well as with expanded systems of producing and transporting building parts, while employing technology to diminish the numbers of skilled craftsworkers necessary to produce them. One of the most useful observations the buildings make evident is that some change in middling housing was underway in the eighteenth century, and that the more pervasive change in republican America extended to middling farmers as well as successful urban tradesmen and merchants.

If a notion that the housing revolution simply bolstered political dominance is naive, so too is a smooth trickle-down theory of mass consumerism in eighteenth-century America. Eighteenth- and nineteenth-century change in housing standards, like the contemporary advance in the use of portable consumer goods, is part of the process of change in European life generally driven by development of a new market economy and a growing bourgeois class beginning in the late sixteenth century. Just how regionally diverse this could be, depending on when certain changes took place, is illustrated by the degree to which some European cities are richly endowed with preindustrial housing while others took on most of their architectural permanence only in the last hundred and fifty years. For all its regional and class diversity, early nineteenth-century housing here is distinctly American, in decorative details as well as spatial means of serving its occupants. Whether standing on the Mississippi River or the Hudson, one seldom is uncertain of the country in which the houses were built.

Successful nineteenth-century middle-class families increasingly used their capital to enhance their comfort, cultivate their domestic lives, and distance themselves from lesser sorts, both spatially and materially. Indeed they flourished and marked their status on the land to an extent and with such permanence so as to confound Marxist predictions of the class's demise. While vastly advanced production brought better housing to some workers, the increasing disparity of accommodation can be seen as a factor encouraging development of working-class identity as well.[131]

In preindustrial America, and in Europe as well, chronically bad housing was among the factors, like limited diet and clothing, that defined the universe of possibilities.[132] Through the seventeenth century and beyond, the boundaries of possibility were expanding upward. In some realms of eighteenth-century material life, they changed so rapidly that the resulting shift in ways of life can be called a revolution. In the midst of this revolution though, most Americans continued to dwell in houses that by our standards were very poor. There was advance in housing, in terms of comfort and privacy as well as show. Yet even with the increasing consumerism of the early republic, change in quality of housing did not parallel the apparent rise in people's ability and desire to obtain lesser goods. Early American consumers may have lined up for fine earthenwares like claim stakers at an Oklahoma land rush, but not for new housing.

By the era of Levittown, there may have seemed no limit to the accessibility of middle-class housing. But today it is brutally evident that the simple quickening of consumerism can widen gulfs between different kinds of people rather than bring revolutionary improvement to most.

[131]The formation of American working-class identity ·is addressed in Nash, *The Urban Crucible;* Sean Wilentz, *Chants Democratic: New York City and the Rise of the American Working Class, 1788–1850* (New York, 1984); and Herbert G. Gutman, *Work, Culture, and Society in Industrializing America: Essays in American Working-Class and Social History* (New York, 1976), all of which owe a debt to E. P. Thompson's *The Making of the English Working Class.* It should be said that these historians do not necessarily see improvement in the housing of capitalist workers.

[132]Fernand Braudel, *Civilization and Capitalism, 15th-18th Century,* vol. 1, *The Structures of Everyday Life: The Limits of the Possible,* trans. Siān Reynolds (New York, 1981); idem, *Afterthoughts on Material Civilization and Capitalism,* trans. Patricia M. Ranum (Baltimore, 1977).

RICHARD L. BUSHMAN

Shopping and Advertising in Colonial America

RESEARCH IN COLONIAL America, England, France, and Friesland has established the fact that in the first half of the eighteenth century amenities and luxuries began to dot the probate inventories of the upper and middling groups in society with far greater frequency than ever before. Sets of ceramic plates, tea sets, books, musical instruments, mahogany tables, and matched sets of chairs appeared in great number among the wealthiest group; lower in the social scale cheaper versions of many of the same items turned up along with lesser amenities like spices and knives and forks.[1]

One of the questions this assemblage of new goods raises is how they arrived in the consumer's household. The sheer number of objects that spread downward through the social structure implies the existence of an elaborate commercial system. Looking glasses in the houses of a tiny elite can easily be accounted for. The great planters added mirrors to their English orders and, in due time, the mirrors arrived. But as we move down in the social scale the number of participating households multiplies rapidly, and a single teacup in each one amounts to a large number in the whole. By the middle of the eighteenth century there must have been thousands and thousands of teacups in colonial America, the bulk of which had arrived in the previous three decades. In that volume, teacups require further explanation. How did they get from

[1] For a summary and evaluation of the current literature on imports and consumption, see John J. McCusker and Russell R. Menard, *The Economy of British America, 1607–1789* (Chapel Hill, N.C., 1985), pp. 277–94.

the port cities to rural towns and finally to individual farm households?

The histories of eighteenth-century commerce have little to say about the commercial infrastructure that carried this burden of goods. The economic histories describe at length the wholesale trade from England but neglect retail trade almost entirely. We know how the goods got to the American shore but not how they went from the merchants' warehouses in the port cities to consumers in the countryside where most Americans lived. We can deduce from the presence of more goods in the inventories that the system, whatever it was, must have grown immensely in the course of the eighteenth century, but we cannot say just how it worked.

We have a clearer picture of how retailing developed in Europe. Markets and fairs, once the primary mechanism for relaying goods to the countryside, faded away and were replaced by permanent shops in market towns. Traditionally, small traders from the country towns came together at the market cross at the appointed time with the sundries the villagers could not make among themselves. At the same time, the eggs, butter, vegetables, and animals with which the villagers made payment were gathered up for transport to the larger places where they had a market. In the eighteenth century the local fairs and markets diminished in importance, and shops in the little market towns took over the business of distributing goods to the countryside and collecting the surplus farm production.

At first glance it appears that American development was almost the reverse of Europe's. The first American settlers arrived with the expectation of organizing town markets. The assemblies ordered them, and town charters frequently granted the privilege, but usually to no avail. Boston's market seems to have come to nothing in the 1600s, judging from the fact that efforts to revive it were made near the end of the century. Philadelphia's market also was primarily an eighteenth-century institution.[2] In the smaller towns in the

[2] Philip Alexander Bruce, *Economic History of Virginia in the Seventeenth Century: An Inquiry into the Material Condition of the People Based upon Original and Contemporaneous Records*, 2 vols. (New York, 1895), 2:389–91; Darrett R. Rutman, "The Traditional World in an American Setting" (Paper presented

backcountry, there seems to have been no pretense at all of formalizing a market. All in all, it appears that there were no markets in seventeenth-century America to be displaced by shops; indeed, there were shops but no markets, the reverse of the European pattern. If anything, markets grew stronger rather than weaker in the eighteenth century, when weekly or twice-weekly markets appeared and then flourished in New York, Charleston, Philadelphia, and Boston along with fairs in smaller towns.[3]

But the changes in America were not truly a reversal of the European pattern, for shops did grow in importance just as in Europe; there were more shops and new kinds of them. Moreover, the shop came to play a different role in colonial society. In the eighteenth century, shopkeepers advertised for the first time in the sense of promoting their goods through their ads, not merely listing items for sale, and their advertising copy offers us a clue to the interplay of commerce and culture in late colonial society. The ads help us see that shops went from being places for obtaining supplies to places for realizing aspirations. Customers encountered and were invited to adopt a more refined style of life. Stocked with fashionable items flowing in from Europe, shops shaped the desires of consumers not for goods alone but for a new social identity.

The modes of commercial exchange in the seventeenth-century colonies can be grouped roughly into three categories: barter among neighbors, orders on account from Europe, and the activities of a much more diverse collection of mercantile figures who can be called storekeepers, though they ranged from great merchants in port towns to planters who offered a small stock of goods from time to time for their rural neighbors' consumption. All three modes persisted into

---

at a conference on "The Social World of Britain and America, 1600–1820: A Comparison from the Perspective of Social History," Williamsburg, Va., Sept. 1985), pp. 21–22.

[3]Claudia L. Bushman, "Fairs and Markets," in Claudia L. Bushman, ed., *Views of Newark* (Newark, Del., 1985).

the eighteenth century and beyond. George Washington's correspondence in the 1760s gives ample evidence of the first two, barter and European orders. Washington's neighbors came to him for smithing, wagonage, leather, meat, grain, and salt, and repaid with whatever they had at hand—eggs, a cow, old iron, land, cattle, and wine. Among those who so traded were Lord Fairfax, the Reverend Charles Green, and other local gentry who depended on the local exchanges to augment their resources as much as less affluent people did. At the same time, Washington was writing to Robert Cary and Company and to Richard Washington in London for mahogany tables, fashionable locks, wallpaper, and shoes.[4] Like so many of his great planter contemporaries and like the commercial magnates in the North, Washington thought of the London he had never visited as a place to shop for fine goods.

Storekeeping, a more protean category in the first place, persisted through the seventeenth and eighteenth centuries, but it took on a different cast in the eighteenth. In the earlier period shops in the North were located primarily in the port towns. Samuel Maverick described Boston to be "full of good shopps well furnished with all kinds of Merchandise." The 1652 probate inventory of Capt. Bozone Allen, Boston "shopkeeper," listed fabric in many varieties, pins, buttons, lace, hinges, handsaws, hourglasses, candlesticks, scissors, combs, and sundry other items. In the same years there were comparable shops in lesser places along the coast such as Salem and Roxbury.[5] Besides these formal undertakings, to the south and probably elsewhere large planters customarily kept a store of goods for sale and exchange. In 1687 it was said that ten to thirty planters on each of the navigable streams flowing into the Chesapeake provided this service. In a sample of Maryland inventories dating from 1660 to 1719, 80 percent

[4]Douglas Southall Freeman, *George Washington: A Biography*, vol. 3, *Planter and Patriot* (New York, 1951), pp. 64–66; John C. Fitzpatrick, ed., *The Writings of George Washington from the Original Manuscript Sources, 1745–1799*, 39 vols. (Washington, D.C., 1931–44), 2:23, 331, 340, 350–52.

[5]George Francis Dow, *Everyday Life in the Massachusetts Bay Colony* (1935; reprint ed., New York, 1977), pp. 242–45, 258–69; Carl Bridenbaugh, *Cities in the Wilderness: The First Century of Urban Life in America, 1625–1742* (New York, 1938), pp. 40–42.

of the top 4 percent of planters showed a store. In the next lower 16 percent roughly a quarter to a third did.[6]

In the eighteenth century, city shops multiplied in number and kind and grew ever more specialized, while planter stores dwindled. In the city a host of smaller shops run by middlemen appeared alongside the retail outlets of great merchants. In Boston many were retail groceries carrying sugar, tea, coffee, spices, and molasses. A few shops specialized in books, musical instruments, or glassware. By midcentury the number and variety had increased prodigiously. There were tobacco shops, cork shops, glove shops, and millinery shops. Richard Waddington, couturier, made garments after the "neatest and most fashionable Manner, according to the Court of Great Britain." The same expansion occurred in the other cities. Philadelphia had just twenty-nine shopkeepers in 1690; in May and June of 1717 alone, twenty-eight new shopkeepers requested the freedom of the Corporation. New York lagged behind Boston and Philadelphia, yet after 1750 there were said to be two hundred shop windows in the city. One man, formerly the governor's gardener, sold seeds, roots, and plants. Secondary towns like Hartford had merchants with elaborate selections of luxury goods such as knives and forks with ivory handles, along with an amazing selection of buttons; one shop had forty bags of them.[7]

The planter stores, while not entirely eliminated, gave way steadily before the extension of the city network into the countryside. Already in the early years of the eighteenth cen-

[6] Bruce, *Economic History of Virginia*, 2:377–78, 381; Gloria L. Main, *Tobacco Colony: Life in Early Maryland, 1650–1720* (Princeton, 1982), p. 161. The figures on planters with stores are derived from inventories that give room-by-room breakdowns. In the storeroom at his home in Middlesex County, Virginia, Tobias Mickleburrough from the 1680s until his death in 1703 kept on hand sundry items worth about £20: nails, cloth, thread, buttons, combs, mirrors, pewter, gunpowder, locks, hinges, and window glass. Mickleburrough, in turn, as Darrett and Anita Rutman have explained, obtained his goods from a larger Middlesex merchant, William Churchill, who imported goods from London via various merchant houses that honored his credit (Darrett B. Rutman and Anita H. Rutman, *A Place in Time: Middlesex County, Virginia, 1650–1750* [New York, 1984], pp. 205–8).

[7] Bridenbaugh, *Cities in the Wilderness*, pp. 42, 188–89, 341–44, quotation on p. 342; idem, *Cities in Revolt: Urban Life in America, 1743–1776* (1955;

tury, as Darrett and Anita Rutman have told us, an established store began to displace the planter-storekeepers in Middlesex County, Virginia. From 1704 on, traders offered goods for sale in the little town auspiciously named Urbanna that grew up along Rosegill Creek near the Rappahannock. The merchant firms that formed and reformed in the flow of trade through Urbanna gradually took business away from the planters who had previously supplied local needs. Urbanna storekeepers offered easier credit but also attracted customers with a broader selection of wares. The stock on hand was both more dependable and more varied. William Gordon and Company sold pewter, indigo, calico curtains and valances, Madeira, pictures, flowerpots, eyeglasses, and, like the Hartford merchants, coat buttons in great profusion; forty-four dozen were in stock when Gordon died in 1720. For this new group of merchants, trade was not ancillary to other occupations as it was with the seventeenth-century planter-storekeepers. The Urbanna merchants owned land and slaves, but their plantations grew out of their trading rather than the other way around.[8]

The great Glasgow firms trading for tobacco in the Chesapeake sprinkled the countryside with similar stores. Some set up their own retail outlets; others, like Buchanan and Simson, dealt almost entirely in wholesale lots. Firms like Buchanan and Simson implied the existence of large numbers of independent dealers who collected the tobacco and retailed cargoes of British manufactured goods for the wholesalers. Considering both the Glasgow storekeepers and the independents, we must multiply the Urbanna merchants many times over and distribute them all about the Chesapeake to envisage properly the eighteenth-century retail system in the South.[9]

reprint ed., New York, 1971), p. 275; Barbara McLean Ward, "Metalwares," in Gerald W. R. Ward and William N. Hosley, Jr., eds., *The Great River: Art and Society of the Connecticut Valley, 1635–1820* (Hartford, 1985), p. 274.

[8]Rutman and Rutman, *A Place in Time*, pp. 225, 228–31.

[9]Jacob M. Price, "Buchanan and Simson, 1759–1763: A Different Kind of Glasgow Firm Trading to the Chesapeake," *William and Mary Quarterly*, 3d ser. 40 (1983): 3–41.

Tax data permit us to survey Massachusetts storekeeping on the eve of the Revolution more systematically than elsewhere and provide a sharp focus on the retail system in one colony. The tax valuation lists for 1771 include returns for 152 Massachusetts towns, half the total. Among the categories listed, along with agricultural possessions such as pasture and tillage, was value of merchandise. The incidence of taxables with merchandise provides a rough measure of people who retailed goods in sufficiently large quantities to keep an inventory on hand. Small artisans producing custom work would not be included.

Plotting the incidence of storekeepers on a map of Massachusetts gives a concrete idea of how far the commercial network had penetrated the countryside by 1771. Such a map shows that most of the older towns had a store by that date. Of the towns east of Worcester, roughly the midpoint of the province, 80 percent (66 of 82) had at least one store. To the west, in the mountainous and poorer region, the picture was quite different. Excluding the wealthier towns immediately adjacent to the Connecticut River, just 42 percent (17 of 40) had stores. Along the river, the proportion was like that to the east: 83 percent (10 of 12) of the towns had stores.[10] The crucial factor in the strength of retailing was the prosperity of the town's agricultural sector. As Bettye Hobbs Pruitt has shown in her analysis of these tax data, the value of merchandise per poll in country towns was not related to the number of mills or artisans or other businesses but to a high level of agricultural wealth distributed broadly through the population. Distance from navigable streams did not prevent the commercial network from reaching a village. Nor was general development of the economy a prerequisite to commercial growth. What mattered was the presence of farmers with a surplus that enabled them to purchase imported goods.[11]

The 1771 evaluation list also emphasizes the importance of

[10]The figures in this and subsequent paragraphs are tabulated from Bettye Hobbs Pruitt, ed., *The Massachusetts Tax Valuation List of 1771* (Boston, 1978).

[11]Pruitt, "Agriculture and Society in the Towns of Massachusetts, 1771: A Statistical Analysis," Ph.D. diss., Boston University, 1981, pp. 131, 158–61.

coastal ports—not just Boston but also the so-called outports. Boston had 519 taxables listed with merchandise, which comprised 23 percent of all taxables on the valuation list. Their combined inventories were worth £188,453. But the presence of that great mart did not overshadow other trading centers almost immediately adjacent. Charlestown, just across the Charles River, had 99 stores, Roxbury, immediately to the south, 60, and Medford, just to the north, 34. Traffic to Boston benefited the city's immediate neighbors. The same was true for the north shore. Salem was the province's second largest trade center, with 172 stores and merchandise valued at £102,310, but Gloucester, a few miles farther north, had 93 merchants, Marblehead had 34, and a little farther up the coast, Ipswich had 42, and Newburyport 96. These towns, along with Plymouth on the south, comprised the province's major trading centers. In the Connecticut Valley, by comparison, Springfield, a major western market town, had only 26 merchants with total merchandise worth just £2,110, and Worcester, near the center, had 12 storekeepers with combined inventories valued at £2,792.[12] The fact that country storekeepers bought their stock from the large wholesale houses in the ports partly accounts for the high volume of trade there. But the large number of stores and the value of merchandise also suggests that much of the retail trade in finer goods still centered in the coastal cities.

City shops and country stores provided only a portion of the goods flowing into colonial households in the early eighteenth century. In his study of Friesland at the end of the seventeenth century, Jan De Vries found that small local producers satisfied most of the growing peasant demand. There is every indication that colonial artisans filled the same function in America. No systematic data exist for all the trades, but those studied in the greatest detail—furniture making and silversmithing—mushroomed in the eighteenth century, especially in the larger towns. Fewer than a dozen silversmiths worked in New York City in all of the seventeenth century, but in 1720 thirteen were following their occupations at the same time. In Boston, 40 furniture makers practiced in

[12] Figures tabulated from Pruitt, ed., *Massachusetts Tax Valuation List.*

the first decade of the eighteenth century; in the second there were 121. Like the shops, the tradesmen grew in variety as well as number, especially among the luxury crafts. In Boston after 1720 there were jewellers, spectacle makers, cleaning and dyeing establishments, milliners, barber shops, coach makers, looking glass makers, clock makers, upholsterers, and peruke makers.[13]

The craftsmen were not confined to the cities, though they were always more concentrated there. They began to distribute themselves more widely as the markets for their wares developed in the backcountry. The first silversmith in the Connecticut Valley, John Potwine, moved to Hartford in 1737, where he received commissions for church objects and made hollowware for wealthy families. Local farmers with a modicum of skill also saw the opportunities and began to engage in craft production. It is estimated that by midcentury one-quarter of Hartford County's adult males were practicing a craft of some sort.[14]

Some tradesmen settled in the towns where they believed local demand would support them; others kept moving to find or make their markets. The best-known examples of itinerant tradesmen at the high end of the economic scale were the portrait painters. Few American towns could keep a portrait painter busy all the time year after year. The best of them moved from place to place, setting up temporary studios and advertising their services. They met the demand of the mo-

[13]Jan De Vries, "Peasant Demand Patterns and Economic Development: Friesland, 1550–1750," in William N. Parker and Eric L. Jones, eds., *European Peasants and Their Markets: Essays in Agrarian Economic History*, p. 236; Bridenbaugh, *Cities in the Wilderness*, pp. 191, 345–47; idem, *Cities in Revolt*, pp. 272–73. The figures on Boston furniture makers are tabulated from Myrna Kaye, "Eighteenth-Century Boston Furniture Craftsmen," in Walter Muir Whitehill and Brock Jobe, eds., *Boston Furniture of the Eighteenth Century: A Conference Held by the Colonial Society of Massachusetts, 11 and 12 May, 1972* (Boston, 1974), pp. 267–302. Potteries and silversmiths before and after the Revolution are mapped in Lester J. Cappon, Barbara Bartz Petchenik, and John Hamilton Long, eds., *Atlas of Early American History: The Revolutionary Era, 1760–1790* (Princeton, 1976), pp. 28, 30–31.

[14]Ward, "Metalwares," p. 275; Kevin M. Sweeney, "From Wilderness to Arcadian Vale: Material Life in the Connecticut River Valley, 1635–1760," in Ward and Hosley, eds., *Great River*, p. 23.

ment and moved on, perhaps returning later when demand had built up again. Theater companies and dancing masters fall into the same category. Lower on the economic scale came cobblers and tailors. The peddlers, whose presence is known from the eighteenth-century legislation limiting their activities, were also among the producers and shopkeepers who recognized a dispersed demand that could be turned to gain by traveling to find the customers. The demand for amenities brought into being a new group of transients, moving about the countryside in search of markets.

All told, the eighteenth-century American, whether in city or country, had far more opportunities to buy goods than his compatriot of a century earlier. In the larger cities he saw a great many more shops and tradesmen—street after street lined with places of business—offering a far greater variety of goods and services than before. Farmers who once had to visit Boston, Newport, New York, Philadelphia, or Charleston now were likely to have a country store within fifteen or twenty miles of their homes. By midcentury a host of secondary centers such as Hartford, Lancaster, Pennsylvania, Chestertown, Maryland, and Alexandria, Virginia, presented to visitors an array of shops and specialized craftsmen that a hundred years earlier would have rivaled those in the cities. From time to time, tradesmen and peddlers brought a selection of pins, buttons, fabrics, nails, and other sundries right into the farmyard itself. Commerce had extended the retailing network in one form or another into nearly every corner of the land.

But that is not the whole story. The changes in the colonial retailing system cannot be summed up in the increased number of stores and their closer proximity to purchasers. To understand all that was happening, we must keep in mind the meaning of purchasing and how it differed from item to item and store to store. Going back to George Washington's neighborly exchanges, we see at once that barter encompassed a quite different range of goods from his orders to London. In the one case he received eggs, a cow, old iron, a pair of knit socks; in the other he bought mahogany chairs, papier-mâché for the ceiling of his rooms, a marble chimney piece, and dessert glasses.[15] The two groups of goods were related to quite different segments of Washington's life, to different locations in his house and estate, and to different sorts of people engaged in sharply contrasting activities. Barter was associated with the farm servants, the barn, the kitchen, and the back parts of the house, with rough clothes and possibly rough talk. English orders flowed into drawing room and dining room, rooms with cornices, pediments, sconces, and mirrors. English goods were brought into use on grand occasions, with genteel neighbors dressed in silks and fine woolens, where talk was of politics, distant places, and grand schemes.

The word *fashionable* separated one group of commodities from the other. Not everything ordered from London was meant to be fashionable; Washington bought strong work shoes and coarse fabric from Robert Cary in London. But he told Richard Washington in 1757 that where price was not a major consideration, the goods were always to be fashionable and neat. *Fashionable* in one of its meanings signified up-to-date. Washington complained to Robert Cary that "instead of getting things good and fashionable in their several kinds we often have Articles sent Us that coud only have been usd by our Forefathers in the days of yore."[16] He did not wish to fall behind the times in his apparel or furnishings. But fashion also meant a social group, as in "people of fashion," the stylish circle of distinguished people who made it their business to know and to set the fashions. The point of requiring fashionable door locks was not simply to be au courant but to claim membership in that circle.

It was of immense importance to Washington to be considered a gentleman, and in the eighteenth century that claim depended on wearing fashionable clothes and filling Mount Vernon with fashionable furnishings, whatever the fashion happened to be. His London orders were a crucial element in Washington's most fundamental social identity. He complained endlessly of poorly fitting shoes, inferior materials

[15] Fitzpatrick, ed., *Writings of Washington*, 2:23, 331, 340, 350–52.

[16] George Washington to Robert Cary and Co., Sept. 28, 1760, ibid., p. 350.

and workmanship, of London tradesmen who passed off shoddy goods to the bumpkins in the American provinces, and yet the orders did not stop.[17] In 1768, buried in debt to his English correspondents and turning every way he could to extricate himself through initiation of a host of new ventures, Washington collected unexpectedly on an old debt of £300. Did the money go to Robert Cary and Company to reduce what was owed? Apparently without a second thought, Washington ordered a new chariot and a handsome suit.[18] Although he saw planters on every side crumpling under the burden of their debts, Washington had to keep fashionable goods flowing from London as if they were his life's blood.

In the 1760s Washington did not consider New York or Philadelphia shops adequate for his fashionable needs. He placed an order with Beverley Robinson in New York in 1762, but it was for sugar, candles, biscuits, and apples.[19] Nonetheless, during the previous half-century American shops had developed pretensions to serve the fashionable world. When they began to advertise more liberally in the 1720s, the storekeepers announced that they had the latest from London for sale. Virtually every item Washington ordered from Robert Cary could be purchased in Philadelphia in the 1760s, though perhaps not always to meet Washington's standards. Both local artisan production and imports from England and France marketed in American cities aspired to meet the very needs Washington felt. Rural gentry who were down a notch from Washington recognized this fact and placed their orders on Philadelphia, New York, or Boston as he ordered from London.

The existence of fashionable shops, along with the vastly increased and extended retailing network used merely for supplies, prompts us to reconsider the nature of the purchasing experience in the eighteenth century and its effects on the lives and values of the purchasers. In the seventeenth century the possessions of the middling and lower orders had primar-

[17]Ibid., pp. 340, 350, 352, 363, 429.

[18]Freeman, *Planter and Patriot*, p. 207.

[19]Washington to Beverley Robinson, Sept. 27, 1762, Fitzpatrick, ed., *Writings of Washington*, 2:383.

ily utilitarian purposes. The reason for buying a pot, or carpenter's tools, or firearms was instrumental: to obtain an implement useful in the household or farm economy. Suitability to function matched against price was the primary basis for a decision regarding purchase. A century later, households contained more objects valued for their aesthetic or representational qualities: pictures, books, looking glasses, tea sets, buckles, suits, and silverware. Besides judging function and price, the purchaser had to evaluate the object's beauty and its fashionableness. Did it make the right impression as well as perform its proper function? The presentational or symbolic uses of the object added a new dimension to purchases. The choice was all the greater because there were so many ways to make the proper impression, not all of which were within the buyer's financial reach. Should he buy more chairs for his house, or a tea set, or silver buckles for his shoes, or better linens for his table, or silverware, or ceramics, or pictures for the walls? All exuded the desired gentility, but few buyers could afford them all. Choices had to be made.

Customers seemed to desire more choices, as if fashionable purchases were best made where there was a wide selection. In the advertisements that tradesmen placed in newspapers, a frequent claim on behalf of the shop's merchandise was the size of the inventory. Merchants told the world of their "complete" assortment of goods. A Connecticut Valley merchant advertised that he had "now on hand and daily expecting, perhaps, the most universal assortment of goods, that can be found at any one store in the Commonwealth." One of the primary reasons for Urbanna's competitive edge over the planter stores was the broad choice of goods. At the Principio Iron Works in Elkton, Maryland, the company store offered seven varieties of male headgear, ranging in cost from three shillings to seven. Obviously more than mere function was at stake. Buyers had a choice to make in quality and style. Wherever one turns, the element of choice entered into the act of buying as never before, altering the meaning of eighteenth-century purchasing.[20]

[20] Margaret E. Martin, *Merchants and Trade of the Connecticut River Valley, 1750–1820* (Northampton, Mass., 1939), pp. 148–49; Rutman and Rutman, *A Place in Time*, p. 230; David A. Oliver, "Urban Culture and Economy

Perhaps it is safe to say that the increased emphasis on personal decision in the selection of goods introduced people of that era to what we call shopping. Shopping today involves more than merely laying in supplies. It includes the survey of a broad range of goods, mentally or actually trying them on for fit and suitability, deciding if this or that item truly meets our desires—or if it can arouse a desire. Shopping differs from buying. It is possible to shop for many hours without ever actually making a purchase. People derive pleasure from the mere acts of surveying and evaluating. With the assistance of elaborate retailing systems, twentieth-century people have raised the act of shopping to a fine art, far beyond the capacities of eighteenth-century retailers or customers. But by the middle of the eighteenth century the retailing system and the cultural needs of the populace had arrived at the point where purchasing had become at least a rudimentary form of shopping.

The tradesmen themselves attempted to envelop the act of buying in its own distinctive atmosphere. We can recover something of the eighteenth-century shop mentality from newspaper advertisements. Not every tradesman and merchant advertised. In Philip Freneau's poem "The Village Merchant," the countryman in pursuit of goods to stock his store found prices too high along the main street of the city and turned on to a side street "where humbler shop-men from the crowd retreat."[21] These lesser shopkeepers could not afford advertisements, and perhaps their customers could not afford newspapers. Only a small fraction of the 519 storeowners in Boston in 1771 ever advertised. Among those who did, some merely listed the items available. Another substantial group, however, addressed their prospective customers, appealed to them, and attempted to establish a relationship through the

in the Countryside: Three Towns at the Head of the Chesapeake Bay, 1710–1786," M.A. thesis, University of Delaware, 1983, pp. 43–44; George Francis Dow, comp., *The Arts and Crafts in New England, 1704–1775: Gleanings from Boston Newspapers* (Topsfield, Mass., 1927), pp. 77–78, 81, 87, 94–95, 101, 132, 138 142.

[21][Philip Freneau], *The Village Merchant: A Poem* (Philadelphia, 1794), p. 7.

medium of advertising copy. From this large group of advertisements we can recapture the shopkeepers' personas, that
is, their manner of presenting themselves on the public stage,
and the personas of the idealized purchasers.

The characterization of the shopkeepers began with the
characterization of their customers. The advertisements almost invariably spoke of prospective customers as "gentlemen
and ladies." Substantial advertisements appear for the first
time in the 1720s, and in those years the word *gentlemen* frequently was used alone. By the 1750s, it was much more common to refer to both gentlemen and ladies, usually naming
the gentlemen first. The other words for readers were *customers,* or *friends,* or *the publick.* But in some instances, the word
publick did not actually enlarge the audience. In 1768, William
Axson begged leave in the *South Carolina Gazette* "to inform
the public in general, and his friends in particular, That he
carries on the Cabinet-Makers business in all its branches."
The word *publick* implied that Axson addressed a broad clientele. But in the next sentence he added that "those Ladies
and Gentlemen that please to employ him, may depend upon
his utmost endeavours to give them satisfaction." Presumably
his friends and the public all were properly addressed as ladies and gentlemen.[22] Rather than reaching a broader group,
Axson spoke as if ladies and gentlemen were the public.

The terminology did not change when the shopkeepers addressed customers in the country. City shopkeepers were fully
aware of how much business came in from outside the city
and made efforts to win the country trade, but they had the
rural gentry in mind, not the common farmer. In 1768
George Killcup, Jr., informed "the Gentlemen and Ladies in
town and Country" through the *Boston News-Letter* "that he
Paints Carpets & other Articles, and Papers Rooms in the
neatest manner."[23] Artisans promised quick delivery and
sometimes offered to pay transportation charges to obtain

[22]Alfred Coxe Prime, comp., *The Arts and Crafts in Philadelphia, Maryland,
and South Carolina, 1721–1785: Gleanings from Newspapers,* 1st ser. (1929; reprint ed., New York, 1969), p. 159. For the usage concerning ladies and
gentlemen, see pp. 162–63, and Dow, comp., *Arts and Crafts in New England,*
pp. 6, 12, 15, 26, 134, 137, 139–40, 142, 144, 152–53, 283, 285–89, 296.

[23]Dow, comp., *Arts and Crafts in New England,* p. 153.

country business, but always that of the gentlemen and ladies.

The terms *gentlemen and ladies* became so debased in the nineteenth century that we may easily misread the eighteenth-century meaning. "The gentlemen of the place," a common phrase in all kinds of writing, referred to a specific group and not to all the males of whatever class, as it did later. Though in individual instances borderline cases might be hard to define, gentlemen were persons of superior wealth, perhaps claiming some education, often vested with public responsibilities in the courts, who managed a style of life above the ordinary. In time of war they became officers, while the rest were enlisted men. In speaking to gentlemen and ladies, the advertisements addressed a defined group, and one far more limited in size than implied in the modern usage of those words.

The limitation may have reflected economic reality. Shopkeepers who advertised may in fact have sold mainly to the gentry. Surely that was true for most painters, silversmiths, paperhangers, clock makers, and even pewterers. The mass market for genteel goods was still in the making. The English gentry had long been a primary market for most of the luxury trades, and the same was likely true in the colonies. The advertisements rightly addressed their primary market as gentlemen and ladies.

But the shopkeepers were not above flattering their customers. The tradesman did not require a demonstration of gentility before selling a silver spoon. The silversmith sold his teapots to any customer with adequate means. If some fell below the level of gentlemen and ladies more rigorously defined, that fact did not stop the silversmith from addressing his advertisements to the gentry. For business purposes, the shopkeeper willingly absorbed all of his customers into the gentry class. He in effect defined "ladies and gentlemen" by claiming implicitly that all of his customers were gentry. By that definition, one became a lady or a gentleman by trading in his store. Though perhaps marginal gentry at best in every other setting, in the shop the purchaser was accepted without question as a gentleman or a lady.

In view of the titles given to customers, the shopkeeper's implied relationship is surprising in one respect, the matter of price. Along with a complete assortment and the assurance of up-to-the-minute fashion, the advertisements promised the most reasonable rates, or "very cheap." Samuel Whitney of Boston offered "Curtains ready made . . . as cheap as can be bought in Town." "A neat assortment of Indian China Ware" was to be sold "exceeding low for Cash, much cheaper than they are usually sold."[24] Presumably the gentry did not favor extravagance and considered it desirable to get the best buy for the money, even in luxury goods. The pursuit of the best quality at the lowest price, one of the excitements of modern shopping as well, suggests that the shopkeeper's ladies and gentlemen were not above polite haggling. In the language of the ads, genteel customers were considered to be sharp buyers, aware of the best values and demanding the lowest price.[25]

More in keeping with the expected treatment of gentlemen and ladies was shopkeeper complaisance. Complaisance, the desire to please, was a valued trait among the gentry themselves; Lord Chesterfield strongly recommended it to his son. It implied an effort to delight and to serve others. Silversmiths, portrait painters, and other tradesmen who dealt almost exclusively with the upper reaches of society indulged most heavily in the rhetoric of complaisance. John Anthony Beau, a Genevan who did chasing work in gold and silver, adopted the conventional words for recommending himself. "All persons who will honour him with their employment in any such work, may be assured that he will use his utmost endeavours to give them universal satisfaction."[26] The sentiments underlying shopkeeper complaisance were the promise to give satisfaction and gratitude for the honor of the customer's business. The tradesman promised "to perform his work, with all the care, dispatch and nicety that can be required," to deliver it punctually, and in general to work "to the full satisfaction of his employers." In his public persona, the tradesman felt honored and grateful for the business. The

[24] Ibid., pp. 129, 95.

[25] For the emphasis on price, see ibid., pp. 2, 15–17, 21, 76–77, 89, 95, 118, 129, 134–35, 137, 141, 151, 156.

[26] Prime, comp., *Arts and Crafts,* p. 47

common phrases were "grateful acknowledgment" and "return his thanks for all past favors." A South Carolina cabinet-maker promised the most satisfactory work to "gentlemen and ladies that please to favor him with commands."[27] The word *commands,* which played a large part in the advertisements, now transformed into our word *orders,* still bore something of the relationship of master to servant. The word placed the giver of the commands in the superior position, and the tradesman in the role of inferior striving to please. The purchaser was the patron whose business transformed the tradesman into a client with an obligation, out of gratitude, to serve and please.[28]

The tradesman's role of client apparently contradicted his other role as tutor and guide. The shopkeeper had to apprise his customers of the latest London fashions that his goods were meant to represent. He was the one in touch with the polite world, and he was expected to know what was best for his customers. Yet his role, as described in the advertisements, was to comply with the customers' *commands.* Some knew their wants precisely; others did not. Country people and marginal gentry required guidance. They followed the tradesman's lead while still giving the orders. Conversely, the shopkeeper tactfully directed his customers while always remaining subservient. The shopkeeper was both tutor and servant.

To step inside such a shop thus involved a prospective purchaser in a complex relationship. To be there at all implied commitment to some form of gentility. The customer already was, or aspired to be, a gentleman or a lady. The shopkeeper, though doubtless able to size the visitor up at a glance, for business purposes vested his customers with that status. As one reviewed the merchandise, trying it on mentally, the relationship with the shopkeeper attending to the customer's needs presumably sustained the promise in the advertisements. The tradesman sought to please, to produce the best work at the lowest price, punctually and neatly, and showed humble gratitude for the pleasure. For the duration of the

[27] Ibid., pp. 46–47, 49, 169.

[28] For complaisant usage in general, see ibid., pp. 4–5, 8, 12, 50, 52, 59–60, 109–11, 128–29, 167–75, 177, 275, 277–79; Dow, comp., *Arts and Crafts in New England,* pp. 2, 285.

transaction, the customer became a patron bestowing his favors on a grateful and compliant client.

Not every shop so exalted its customers. Even in the cities only a few shops achieved this polish. The country storekeeper fell far short of the standard. But it *was* a standard and an ideal. Freneau's village merchant reclaimed a smokehouse for his store. In it he built shelves and a counter and put out the best of his pottery to make the right impression.[29] There were many rude village equivalents of the urbane city shop.

The eighteenth-century retail network thus conveyed more to the American provinces than a few additional personal amenities. The retail system brought into being a new person, the shopkeeper, who for his own purposes extended society an invitation. Overtly it was an invitation to buy, but implicit in the act of purchasing was a transforming relationship. Within the walls of the shop, the purchaser became a gentleman or a lady. The goods themselves held that promise in the first place; they were meant to dignify the person, or the house, or social rituals in the house, by conferring gentility. But beyond the goods themselves, the shopkeeper treated customers as ladies or gentlemen, for the moment transforming their social identities into more exalted ones.

People secure in their position among the gentry expected nothing less. But such treatment was vastly more stimulating to the greater number of marginal people on the edges of gentility. Shopping gave them a delicious taste of a superior culture. Selecting furnishings for a new brick house, purchasing fabric for a dress, or picking out knives and forks for a dining room were part of a thrilling initiation. For those few moments in the shopkeeper's presence, the customer became genteel. In the very act of seeking and serving customers, shopkeepers recruited for a cultural style. Somewhere in their makeup, even small shops bore the seeds of mighty changes. Each one speeded the process by which a great body of Americans made gentility their own, turning themselves into the people who in time would comprise a recognizable middle class.

[29][Freneau], *Village Merchant*, p. 4.

KARIN CALVERT

The Function
of Fashion in
Eighteenth-Century
America

ON A FALL DAY in 1774 the prosperous Virginia planter Robert
Carter took his young son and his clerk, a Mr. Randolph, on
a visit to one of his mills. While they were there, a poor farmer
from Maryland with grain to grind approached the boy and
asked which of the two gentlemen was the master. Young Bob,
with the impudence of youth and position, pointed out Randolph, who was dressed in a fine scarlet coat. When asked the
identity of the second gentleman, the man in the dark coat
and "frowsled wig," Bob replied that he was his father's clerk.[1]
The joke, of course, was on the gullible farmer dazzled by the
clerk's penchant for finery and color, but such a joke was only
possible in a society where the rules of genteel dress had
changed so radically and recently that unsophisticated men
could no longer trust their own judgment to distinguish men
of rank by sight. To the poor Marylander, the clerk in his scarlet coat looked more like a gentleman than did the drably
dressed but wealthy planter. Such profound and, to the uninitiated, such confusing changes were only one manifestation
of a general reorganization of society that evolved over the
course of the eighteenth century.

In traditional Western culture, costume had been an elaborate and fairly precise visual code, communicating such useful
information as the wearer's gender, marital status, age, mili-

[1]John Rogers Williams, ed., *Philip Vickers Fithian's Journal and Letters,
1767–1774* (Princeton, 1900), p.235.

tary rank, religious or political office, occupation, and social position. Virtually all members of the society could identify a chain or badge of office, religious habit, servant's livery, scholar's gown, widow's weeds, farmer's smock, or the brand upon the face of a felon. This visual system of classification immediately identified any stranger, distinguishing countrymen from foreigners and gentlemen from vagabonds, and it ensured that each could be accorded his due. Indeed, there were direct cultural and linguistic links between the correct dress and address accorded each position in society. Costume thus helped to define the social order and to organize the world. There was comfort in knowing that, at least in theory, everyone was what they appeared to be; that, in terms of social position, anyone could be taken at face value with some degree of confidence. Understandably then, society traditionally had been particularly severe with the individual who failed to conform, punishing, for example, the unsanctioned use of religious habit or the woman in male dress, and treating the spy more severely than the clearly distinguishable enemy soldier.

By the second half of the eighteenth century, however, the rules of costume had been radically altered, and what made the poor Marylander at the mill the butt of young Bob Carter's joke was precisely the fact that he did not know how to interpret the sartorial code of his betters. The Marylander, confused by the ongoing reformulation of taste and fashion, had hoped to rely on a knowledgeable informant and his own understanding of the traditional codes of dress to identify the men he saw at the mill. Both had led him astray. In his eyes, the past certainly must have seemed a simpler time.

Throughout the seventeenth century, colonists had brought with them to America, in the clothing they wore, established and recognizable patterns of social stratification. In a society where the interaction between individuals was dependent upon the social position of each, any code of dress needed to be both hierarchical and comprehensible to all members of the society. A humble laborer, for example, had to be able immediately to identify a gentleman as a gentleman in order to assume the expected attitude of deference. There would have been no point in devising a code too subtle or vague for easy recognition—the intended message would have been lost on some of the participants. Therefore, in the traditional European societies of the sixteenth and seventeenth centuries (from which colonial American culture derived), where consumer goods were scarce and most people owned little more than a rudimentary set of clothing, a simple and straightforward sartorial language operated, one that could be understood by all. A gentleman announced his wealth and position through the direct display of wealth, manifested in his house, his carriage, his servants, and his clothes. The equation was direct and impossible to misinterpret: a man of wealth could be identified by the wealth he displayed and an important part of that display was costume.

Perhaps the most vivid example of this traditional approach to costume is evident in the famous 1540 portrait of Henry VIII by Hans Holbein—an extreme case to be sure, but useful since it combines all contemporary manifestations of social position on one figure and therefore serves as something of a sartorial glossary.[2] Textile production in the sixteenth century was extremely slow and laborious, making fabric comparatively more expensive than, say, furniture. For his portrait Henry not only wore multiple layers of the most expensive textiles (silks, velvets, and brocades), but all of the rich fabrics were gathered, padded, and stiffened to give them additional volume and Henry a more commanding and formidable presence. The heavily padded shoulders, wadded doublet, and protruding codpiece deliberately and blatantly underscored an image of royal strength and virility greater than that of ordinary mortals. The costly textiles had been further enriched with the expensive dyes necessary to produce the brilliant colors of yellow, gold, and crimson, and then given even greater sparkle with an overlay of gold embroidery. Small white puffs of Henry's linen shirt protruded from the dozens of slashes made in the sleeves and body of his doublet, an example of Veblenesque conspicuous waste since the more a fabric is cut, the more it is weakened and the sooner it will

[2]See Hans Holbein's portrait of Henry VIII, 1540, Walker Art Gallery, Liverpool.

fray and tear.³ Finally, all of the rich fabrics served as a background to exotic furs and ostrich feathers, and to gold and bejewelled pins, pendants, hatpins, chains, and finger rings. The sartorial message of power, prestige, and wealth is unmistakable. Henry VIII wore his treasure like an Algerian bride decked in the silver coins of her dowry.

This custom of representing wealth and position by wearing goods of great intrinsic value still held strong among American colonists in the seventeenth century, differing from Henry in degree, of course, but not in kind. The wealthier citizens of the colonies, such as Daniel Parke of Virginia, wore gold and silver lace, knots and roses of silk ribbon, intricately embroidered velvets, slashed sleeves, and gold and silver rings, chains, and buttons (fig. 1). Equally expensive fabrics and perhaps even finer lace appeared in early New York. The portrait of Mrs. John Rolfe of Virginia, painted upon her arrival in England in 1616, reveals a striking young woman dressed in the accepted accoutrements of her new station, including a gold-embroidered doublet with gold buttons, lace collar, beaver hat with gold hatband, pearl earrings, and a gold-handled ostrich-feather fan.⁴ Whether Mrs. Rolfe actually possessed all the depicted finery is, of course, uncertain, since artists could and did embellish portraits to please their patrons. For the most part, however, the finery present in a portrait represents what was commonly viewed as acceptable or desirable for a particular social class and therefore tells us more perhaps about men or women of that social station in the aggregate than about the particular individual.⁵ And indeed, throughout the colonies, the fashionable wore gold or silver hatbands, girdles, buckles, brooches, and finger rings as visible confirmation of their rightful social preeminence.

³Thorstein Veblen, *The Theory of the Leisure Class* (1899; reprint ed., New York, 1953), pp. 60–80.

⁴See the anonymous portrait of Mrs. John Rolfe, 1616, National Portrait Gallery, Smithsonian Institution, Washington, D.C.

⁵Nathaniel B. Shurtleff, ed., *Records of the Governor and Company of the Massachusetts Bay in New England*, 5 vols. (Boston, 1853–54), 1:124, 261, 3:311, vol. 4, pt. 1, p. 57; Max von Boehn, *Modes and Manners*, vol. 3, *The Seventeenth Century*, trans. Joan Joshua (1932; reprint ed., Philadelphia, 1963), p. 170.

Figure 1. Portrait of Daniel Parke. John Closterman, c. 1705. (Courtesy of the Virginia Historical Society, Richmond)

Such conspicuous display in an orderly world would have distinguished, and for the most part did distinguish, the elite from their more ordinary fellow citizens. The transatlantic community of the seventeenth century, however, was not an orderly world. Unsettling events, including the English Civil War, the establishment of the American colonies, and the opening of new foreign markets brought with them economic opportunities and pitfalls and a resultant reshuffling of wealth and power for some families. Enough men of the middle classes prospered to create a general climate of optimism and expectation. Men of ambition felt it not unreasonable to aspire to the status of gentlemen and, with that in mind, to assume the prerogatives and privileges of that station. To the consternation of their betters, some among the general public procured for themselves what finery they could, albeit often secondhand, and in the process they confounded the accepted assumptions of place and the privileges of rank. In every colony a few ordinary citizens found the means to dress in the richness of silk, lace, and gold. One Jamestown cowkeeper wore scarlet silk on Sundays, and the wife of an ex-collier flaunted a beaver hat with a pearl hatband.[6] In the second quarter of the eighteenth century, Dr. Alexander Hamilton was astounded to meet two Mohawk Indians on horseback on the road from Boston to Cambridge "dressed *à la mode Francois* with laced hats, full trimmed coats, and ruffled shirts."[7] Anyone with discretionary funds enough could choose to spend their money on fashionable clothing.

America, however, was far from unique in experiencing a strong challenge to the accepted exclusivity of expensive finery. In Europe, pressure from an ambitious middle class increased markedly in the seventeenth century, leading one German gentleman to complain that "display in dress has reached such a pitch that it is impossible to distinguish artisan from nobleman or nobleman from prince."[8] The resulting

[6]Alice Morse Earle, *Costume of Colonial Times* (1894; reprint ed., New York, 1924), p. 5.

[7]Carl Bridenbaugh, ed., *Gentleman's Progress: The Itinerarium of Dr. Alexander Hamilton, 1744* (1948; reprint ed., Westport, Conn., 1973), p. 141.

[8]Boehn, *The Seventeenth Century*, p. 173.

confusion of being and seeming threatened established assumptions of legitimacy and authenticity. Anyone, it appeared, could usurp the appearance of a gentleman by acquiring the accoutrements of a gentleman, and such goods could be had with a simple exchange of money. The considerable expense of a lace collar or pearl earring was enough to keep such items beyond the reach of most colonists, but the barrier of great cost was not a perfect defense against the determined and aspiring. The growing consumer demand for fine clothes challenged traditional prerogatives, and the elite on both sides of the Atlantic retaliated against what they perceived as an attack on their legitimacy by passing sumptuary laws limiting to themselves the right of conspicuous display.

The governments of Europe had sporadically attempted to legislate dress at least since the fourteenth century. Each time the attempt failed. Only within controlled and closed institutions where there is a precise and fixed system of rank—the church or the military, for example—have sumptuary laws proved effective. Nonetheless, in a flurry of codes and prohibitions the nations of Europe in the seventeenth century made one last attempt to legislate rules of dress. The American colonies, from New England to Virginia, devised similar legislation of their own. For example, in 1651 the General Court of Massachusetts Bay declared "our utter detestation and dislike that men and women of meane condition, education and callings should take upon them the garbe of Gentlemen," and therefore prohibited the wearing of costly finery for all but those with estates in excess of £200. For the General Court, the ideal sartorial code was simple and straightforward: wealth worn represented, or should represent, greater wealth possessed.

The members of the court were men of the world, however, and realized that their society was not as tidy as they might have liked. Therefore they gave exemptions to bona fide gentlemen who had fallen on hard times, "any others whose education and employments have been above the ordinary degree," and military officers. Not surprisingly, the legislators also exempted themselves, their wives, and their children.[9]

[9]Shurtleff, *Records*, vol. 4, pt. 1, p. 57.

On the one hand, the exemptions clearly demonstrated how difficult it was to define gentility and to identify those who possessed it. On the other, the loopholes proved large enough that most people who could afford to purchase forbidden finery could stretch one exemption or another to serve as justification. The courts recognized Ruth Halfield of Ipswich and Alice Flint of Salem as exempt, when charges were brought against them for dressing above their station, since both women could point to fathers worth more than £200. The wives of Richard Cory, Hugh March, John Whipple, Richard Knight, and Nicholas Noyes proved to the satisfaction of the Ipswich court that their husbands either met one of the exemptions or that they held or would inherit estates in excess of the stipulated £200. Charges against Thomas Harris, Thomas Wayre, and Edward Browne were dismissed on evidence of a superior education or genteel upbringing. In fact, it is difficult to find anyone in the court records who was prosecuted successfully under the statute. By September 1653 the colony's courts had given up and declined to hear further cases.[10] The opinion of the burgomaster of Berlin concerning the failure of a similar attempt to enforce sumptuary laws in the Old World—that "it had no effect and did no good"—proved equally true in the New World.[11] Although such legislation has appeared sporadically since, the attempts of the seventeenth century proved to be the last concerted effort to legislate class distinctions in dress.

It is commonly assumed that these sumptuary laws failed because the growing middle-class demand for consumer goods could not be denied while the means to procure them were available. Since colonists had increasing access to the necessary goods and services—imported and local fabrics and notions, as well as tailors, milliners, and seamstresses—it would appear that the middling sort succeeded, despite the grumbling of their betters, in adopting genteel fashions modified to accommodate a lighter purse. It was, apparently, a victory for egalitarianism and free enterprise. Such conclusions are oversimplifications on two counts. First, the middling sort

[10]"Apparel of the First Settlers," *Essex Antiquarian* 10 (1906): 49–54.

[11]Boehn, *The Seventeenth Century*, p. 170.

were by no means fighting for a leveling of the dress code. Rather, ambitious individuals within the middle class sought to gain entrance into genteel society in part by assuming elite prerogatives of dress and display. This was not an attempt to destroy the social hierarchy but to move up within it. Second, when sumptuary laws proved ineffective, the fashionable elite gradually developed an entirely new code of correct dress that did not require legislation to protect its exclusivity. By changing the rules, the elite quite effectively blocked the shortcuts to advancement previously used by the aspiring, without resorting to legislation.

By the early eighteenth century the traditional sartorial code of privilege had lost much of its effectiveness because, in an increasingly prosperous society, it had become too easily accessible. The display of precious goods no longer could carry quite the same aura of exclusivity and legitimacy. Around the turn of the century, the fashionable elite, having failed to legislate their traditional prerogatives, turned to the negative strategies of discretion and understatement. They abandoned what now amounted to the debased coinage of traditional flamboyance and gradually devised a new code of genteel dress that was more complex, subtler, and more difficult for the uninitiated to master. The ideal of the gentleman turned from an image of excess in dress, manner, speech, and habits to one of restraint, refinement, and control. The raw force of a bellowing Henry VIII gave way to the calculated control of Lord Chesterfield. The test of a gentleman was not that he could afford luxuries but that he could afford the greater luxury of leisure time in which to absorb the mounting intricacies of taste, grace, fashion, and elegance. An aesthetic of austerity and subtlety proved harder for aspiring colonists to emulate than an aesthetic of opulence and bravado.

The emerging image of the eighteenth-century gentleman required that he dress in accordance with his station, which involved considerable expense, but without overstepping into the newly defined excesses of ostentatious or pretentious display. Men continued to wear gold or silver buckles, but they rejected most other forms of jewelry. They dressed in rich fabrics, but wore less of them and in increasingly drabber colors.

Instead of rich and garish costumes, they concentrated their attention on the subtleties of fine tailoring and the privileged esoterica of an intricately knotted cravat. The process was very gradual; new strategies came forward, were tried, and sometimes abandoned. The new code of genteel dress begun about 1700 did not reach its full elaboration until the 1820s.

Beginning in about the first decade of the eighteenth century, gentlemen abandoned the doublet with slashed sleeves, silk roses and knots, and wide lace collars for a costume whose major elements would remain standard for the next two centuries. A gentleman wore a white linen shirt, breeches, stockings and shoes, a coat, waistcoat, and cravat. The breeches, coat, and waistcoat could be en suite of a single cloth, or of different fabrics and colors. Throughout the century fabrics from Europe remained very expensive and hard to procure, and even the cost of domestically manufactured linens and woolens was considerable. Clothing was prized enough that individual garments were sometimes worn for twenty or thirty years, willed to heirs, sold, or stolen from wash lines and unguarded luggage.[12]

During the first half of the century, suits were made of linen, wool, silk, velvet, and brocade in colors from green and scarlet to rose and lilac. The coat and waistcoat were cut along very ample lines with full skirts reaching below the knee. Wire or stiff padding in the skirts held them out from the body, increasing the impression of mass.[13] Huge cuffs, or bag sleeves, on the coat extended up to the elbow, further emphasizing the sense of monumentality and importance and requiring even more of the expensive fabric. Gold, silver, or silk embroidery could appear on either coat, and buttons and buckles of silver or pewter embellished coats, knees, and shoes (fig. 2). For the first time, however, men of means eschewed other forms of jewelry, including rings, brooches, chains, and hatbands, thus abandoning nonfunctional jewelry

[12]Claudia B. Kidwell, "Bicentennial Outlook: Riches, Rags, and In-Between," *Historic Preservation* 28 (1976):28–33; Bridenbaugh, ed., *Gentleman's Progress,* p. 29.

[13]Max von Boehn, *Modes and Manners,* vol. 4, *The Eighteenth Century,* trans. Joan Joshua (1932; reprint ed., Philadelphia, 1963), p. 29.

Figure 2. Portrait of Brigadier General Samuel Waldo. Robert Feke, c. 1748. (Courtesy of the Bowdoin College Museum of Art, Brunswick, Maine. Bequest of Mrs. Lucy Flucker Knox Thatcher)

as the most obvious symbol of wealth. But even without the precious baubles of previous eras, a gentleman of the early eighteenth century still cut an impressive figure. Dr. Hamilton awed the common folk on his travels through the colonies in 1744 with his dark silk coat, hat trimmed in lace, sword, and pistols, though he himself admitted the decrees of fashion could sometimes prove trying. While reaching for a mug of beer at dinner one evening, the voluminous bag sleeve of his coat caught the handle of a dish and "unfortunately overset the clams, at which the landlady was a little ruffled."[14] Some years later, a Mr. Lane, a young graduate of Princeton with good prospects and the heart of a dandy, could array himself—to the admiration of his friends—in "black superfine broadcloth, gold-laced hat, lace ruffles and black silk stockings." Most colonists, however, could not afford such fashionable dress.[15] The need for easy mobility to carry out the activities of daily life and the very high cost of fabric forced most men to modify the long full skirts and wide sleeves of fashionable coats. Men of modest means wore coats with little or no cuff and with skirts that extended only to mid-thigh (fig. 3). The skimpier the cut, the lighter the purse.

Perhaps the most formal and artificial manifestation of the eighteenth-century preoccupation with social order was the popularity of the new fashion of wearing wigs. A fine head of hair had long been a mark of masculine beauty and gentility. In the seventeenth century men of position wore their own hair, curled and perfumed, cascading onto their shoulders. By the early eighteenth century, gentlemen took to shaving their heads and wore elaborate and expensive wigs. The new fashion met with opposition at first, not because of the expense or implicit vanity, but because the best wigs were made of women's hair. "Women's hair," admonished Nicholas Noyes in 1700, "when on their own heads, is a token of subjection—how comes it to cease to be a token of subjection when men wear it?"[16] The display of beautiful hair was regarded as

[14] Bridenbaugh, ed., *Gentleman's Progress,* pp. 40, 55, 80.

[15] Williams, ed., *Fithian's Journal,* p. 113.

[16] Nicholas Noyes, "Reasons against Wearing Periwigs," (1700), *Publications of the Colonial Society of Massachusetts* 20 (1917–19):120–28.

Figure 3. Sea Captains Carousing in Surinam. *John Greenwood, c. 1775. (Courtesy of the Saint Louis Art Museum)*

a male prerogative associated with virility and power. Traditionally women submissively had coiled their hair up and covered it with hoods or caps. As the status of women changed over the eighteenth century, they permitted more and more of their hair to show until, by the 1770s, fashionable women proudly displayed huge, elaborately teased, and powdered hairstyles. American women, however, never adopted wigs. That extravagance was limited, for the most part, to the ladies of the courts of Europe.

American merchants offered wigs made of human hair, wool, and horse and goat hair, in dozens of different styles. By 1764 the *Encyclopédie Perruquière* recognized 115 styles, each designed for a particular social position, profession, or activity. A man of importance and prominence wore a full-bottomed peruke of human hair that rose in peaks on each side of a center part and cascaded in masses of curls well below his shoulders (fig. 1). In 1715 such magnificence could cost as much as £20 and usually was reserved for men of mature years and solid position.[17] When, therefore, only months after inheriting one of the largest fortunes in New England, the youthful Isaac Royall commissioned a group portrait of his family, including himself in a handsome red coat and full-bottomed peruke, he was, in very clear terms, demonstrating his newly acquired importance.[18]

Specific wig styles became associated with particular professions. Many doctors ministered in a physick's wig, which had a woolly, teased appearance known as a natty bob, while clergymen and scholars wore variations of the parson's wig, with its rows of neat curls.[19] A popular style with American merchants was a version of the natty bob with curled ends that can be seen in many of the portraits by John Singleton Copley (fig. 4). So strong was the association between particular wigs and professions that in 1775 one author described the odd dress of one individual as being "as improper as a physician

[17] Anne Buck, *Dress in Eighteenth-Century England* (London, 1979), p. 29.

[18] See Robert Feke's *Isaac Royall and His Family,* 1741, Harvard Law Art Collection, Harvard University, Cambridge, Mass.

[19] Richard Corson, *Fashions in Hair: The First Five Thousand Years* (London, 1965), p. 275.

Figure 4. Daniel Hubbard. *John Singleton Copley, 1764. (The Art Institute of Chicago Purchase Fund 1947.27. Courtesy of the Art Institute of Chicago. Photograph © 1991, the Art Institute of Chicago. All Rights Reserved)*

266

would seem ridiculous prescribing in a bag-wig." [20] Where traditional dress had drawn a direct, if crude, equation between the display of precious goods and the wealth of the wearer, the wig was part of a new artificial code whose complexity and subtlety offered greater precision in distinguishing rank.

In the privacy of his home or in an informal public setting, a gentleman removed his wig—which was hot, heavy, made the head itch, and could so cover the ears as seriously to impair hearing—and covered his shaved head with a soft nightcap. This was a cap commonly worn in the evenings and is not to be mistaken for a bedcap (fig. 5). Precisely when it was permissible for a gentleman to forego the wig varied from colony to colony and city to city. Dr. Hamilton described dining in Boston "in the company of two Philadelphians, who could not be easy because forsooth they were in their nightcaps seeing every body else in full dress with powdered wigs; it not being customary in Boston to go to dine . . . in caps as they do in other parts of America." [21] The two Philadelphians were nonetheless accepted as gentlemen by their dress, manner, and shaved heads, as opposed to common folk "having their own hair." [22]

There were subtle variations within the general formula. Convention dictated that craftsmen, as men who worked with their hands, usually appeared in their own hair regardless of their social position. This category included artists. The self-portraits of John Smibert, Robert Feke, Benjamin West, and even Charles Willson Peale who "has Vanity—loves Finery—wears a sword—gold lace—speaks French," all depict the artist wearing his own hair. [23] Scholars and scientists, men of the mind who customarily worked in the privacy of the study or laboratory, frequently chose to have themselves presented in a portrait wearing a banyan (a loose dressing gown) and nightcap. This more informal at-home costume became the

[20] *Connoisseur,* Apr. 24, 1775, p. 23.

[21] Bridenbaugh, ed., *Gentleman's Progress,* p. 134.

[22] Ibid., p. 93.

[23] John Adams to Abigail Adams, Aug. 21, 1776, Lyman H. Butterfield et al., eds., *The Book of Abigail and John: Selected Letters of the Adams Family, 1762–1784* (Cambridge, Mass., 1975), p. 157.

Figure 5. Thomas Boylston, Jr. *John Singleton Copley, c. 1767.*
(Courtesy of the Harvard University Portrait Collection, Harvard
University, Cambridge, Mass.)

recognized uniform of the contemplative life and is visible in portraits of, among others, the scientist David Rittenhouse and Benjamin Franklin when he was portrayed in his role as scientist. Conversely, servants of the wealthy sometimes wore wigs (specific wigs being associated with footmen, coachmen, and the like), which, like livery, reflected the importance of their master's position.

As a general rule, a wig carried more prestige than one's own hair, and a powdered wig more than a natural-colored one, all of which meant that the necessary grooming was a messy and tedious process. First the hair of the wig had to be smeared with pomatum, a grease made of animal fat, then teased or curled with a hot iron and rolled in papers, rubbed with more pomatum, positioned firmly on the head of the wearer, and blown with powder from a small tube. The powder could consist of flour, white earth, kaolin, or a mixture of starch and plaster of paris. Whatever the components, the powder and pomatum solidified to the point that regrooming usually was not necessary for some time, though a fresh dusting of powder was applied at each wearing.[24] On at least one evening, Philip Vickers Fithian, a tutor at the plantation of Robert Carter in the 1770s, decided it was less troublesome to go without dinner than to submit to having his head dressed for the occasion.[25] Unlike the gold hatband or pearl earring of an earlier era, a wig represented not only a considerable initial cost but also a continuing investment of skill, patience, and time for its maintenance. The additional requirements of time proved particularly burdensome for anyone who worked for a living.

Wearing a wig required as much attention and practice as grooming one. While clothes of the first half of the eighteenth century tended to be loose and the fit approximate, a wig permitted much less tolerance; too big and it could slide askew, too tight and it perched precariously above the natural hairline. Either way the wearer not only looked ridiculous but risked the greater embarrassment of having it fall off al-

[24]Corson, *Fashions in Hair*, p. 275.

[25]Williams, ed., *Fithian's Journal*, p. 180.

together.[26] The ill-fitting wig failed one of the primary rules of gentility in the eighteenth century, which was to make artifice seem completely natural and the difficult appear effortless. A powdered wig offered further pitfalls for the uninitiated. Any sudden movement, such as a sneeze or a jerk of the head, could send flying a shower of loose powder. A dusting of powder on the shoulders betrayed the socially inept, for a true gentleman knew how to walk, turn, and bow with fluid grace. A gentleman's appearance had come to depend as much on how he wore clothes as on what he wore, and that meant time had to be spent acquiring specific skills, mannerisms, and rules of behavior.

Unfortunately, even the acquisition of correct manners was not in itself enough. Genteel behavior was not merely a matter of knowing what to do but of performing the prescribed activity with an air of spontaneity and nonchalance. The fundamental issue in the eighteenth-century concept of gentility was the claim of legitimacy that separated those with a recognized right to position from those who consciously set out to acquire it. Legitimacy was predicated on knowing, not learning, the self-confidence and casual attitude of the man who had absorbed the intricacies of etiquette from childhood rather than the intensity and self-consciousness of the man determined to learn the rules. "I would have a man know everything," wrote Antoine Gombaud in a description of the ideal gentleman, "and yet, by his manner of speaking, not be convicted of having studied."[27]

Gentility required an elegance and refinement of movement, manners, and speech developed through practice and attention but delivered with an easy grace which persuaded that such were the most natural of actions. In his widely read book of letters, Lord Chesterfield warned his son "that all the talents in the world still want their lustre if they are not adorned with that easy good-breeding, that engaging man-

[26]Corson, *Fashions in Hair*, p. 280.

[27]Antoine Gombaud, chevalier de Mere, *De la conversation* (Paris, 1681), as quoted in Pierre Bourdieu, *Distinction: A Social Critique of the Judgement of Taste*, trans. Richard Nice (Cambridge, Mass., 1984), p. 71.

ner, and those graces, which seduce and prepossess people in your favor at first sight."[28]

To assure that his son would master the intricacies of what should appear as effortless grace, he sent the boy into European society under the guidance of a private tutor and dancing master. To be awkward invited ridicule, no matter how fine the mind, the costume, or the fortune. Conversely, grace went far to overcome any material shortcomings. A man of humble origin could move up in society and be respected as a gentleman, but it required more than the accumulation of wealth, land, or power. It meant acquiring the esoteric knowledge, the poise, and the confidence of the elite.

While living in Europe, John Adams noted that "our New England people are awkward and bashful . . . which excites ridicule and disgust." Like many other middle-class Americans, Adams realized that respect and acceptance in society meant acquiring "the exterior and superficial accomplishments of gentlemen upon which the world has foolishly set so high a value."[29] Now a man was judged not just by the elegance of his appearance, but by the way he carried himself, doffed his hat, handled a fork, and entered into conversation. Middle-class Americans proved an eager audience for books that promised to guide them through the growing labyrinth of genteel taste and etiquette. American editions of *The Whole Duty of Man, The Compleat Gentleman, The School of Good Manners, The English Dancing Master, The Courtier,* and, of course, Chesterfield's *Letters to His Son* remained popular and profitable throughout the century.[30] Ironically, the very zeal of the middling sort to learn the rules of genteel behavior, and the seriousness with which they approached their own self-

[28] Earl of Chesterfield, *Letters to His Son on the Fine Art of Becoming a Man of the World and a Gentleman* (1761; reprint ed., New York, 1965), p. 40.

[29] John Adams to Abigail Adams, Aug. 4, 1776, Butterfield et al., eds., *Book of Abigail and John,* pp. 149–50.

[30] Arthur M. Schlesinger, Sr., *Learning How to Behave: A Historical Study of American Etiquette Books* (New York, 1946), pp. 1–26; Gerald Carson, *The Polite Americans* (New York, 1966), pp. 20–50; William Ivensen, *O the Times, O the Manners* (New York, 1965), p. 202.

improvement, set them apart from the elite, who had absorbed the intricacies of genteel behavior from childhood and casually accepted its forms as natural to themselves. The "air of ease which comes from a fortunate birth and an excellent habit is one of the amenities of a gentleman," warned Gombaud, and one that tended to separate the gentleman by birth from his emulators.[31] Men could and did rise through the ranks of colonial society, but to do so required a good deal more than the wherewithal for the proper accoutrements and an understanding of the rules of etiquette. It also demanded grace—that is, an ease and confidence in the role—that was much more difficult, though not impossible, to counterfeit.

For the eighteenth-century gentleman, the moment when his costume, manner, grace, ease, and mastery of the general accomplishments would most likely and most often come under public scrutiny was on the dance floor. Philip Fithian warned an acquaintance from New Jersey who planned a trip to Virginia that "any young gentleman travelling through the colony is presumed to be acquainted with Dancing."[32] Fithian, in fact, went to considerable lengths to keep his own inability to dance a secret for fear of losing the respect of Virginia society. Dancing in the eighteenth century had become both the school and the ultimate test of the genteel graces. To dance was crucial, and to dance badly was perhaps worse than not dancing at all. A young member of the Lee family confided to her journal with the thoughtless cruelty of youth that she looked forward to attending a particular dance for the opportunity to observe one Captain Grigg, a notoriously poor dancer. To her delight the hapless captain met her expectations. "I don't think I ever laugh't so much in my life as I did last night at Captain Grigg's minuet," she wrote the next day. "It is really the most ludicrous thing I ever saw; and what makes it more so is, he thinks he dances a most delightful one."[33]

[31] Bourdieu, *Distinction*, p. 71.

[32] Philip Vickers Fithian to John Peck, Aug. 12, 1774, Williams, ed., *Fithian's Journal*, p. 287.

[33] Lucinda Lee Orr, *Journal of a Young Lady of Virginia, 1782* (Baltimore, 1871), pp. 36–37.

Dancing meant above all learning the complex and ever-changing minuet. Essentially the minuet set to music the stately promenade, aristocratic bearing, and courtly bows and curtsies of a formal reception. It required not only learning the intricate patterns, but also how to execute the stilted steps and gestures with a fluid grace that made the ritualized movements appear completely effortless and natural. Captain Grigg probably had learned the correct steps, but he bungled the execution. Success required style as well as substance. Thus a conscientious gentleman like William Byrd of Westover began each day by reading Greek and practicing his dance, exercising mind and body in the esoteric skills of privilege and gentility.

While still a young man, John Adams faced the importance of social skills when he wrote his brother-in-law, Richard Crench, upon the birth of "another fine child," that now "there must be Dancing Schools and Boarding Schools and all that, or else, you know, we shall not give them polite Educations, and they will better not have been born you know than not have polite Educations."[34] More seriously, he encouraged his own son years later to acquire grace through dancing, riding, and ice skating.[35]

Americans turned to dancing masters to acquire the polish and grace required in all areas of life. Gen. Friedrich von Steuben recommended that dancing be made a required course for military cadets at West Point, since officers also were expected to be gentlemen.[36] Besides the rules of dancing itself, dancing masters taught the highly stylized and artificial way to walk, sit, stand, turn, and bow regularly adopted by genteel society. Correct posture for a gentleman entailed holding the head erect, chest out, back straight, and heels together with toes pointed out, then keeping the knees straight and toes out while walking. The stately glide thus achieved helped ensure, among other things, that the wig and its powder stayed in place. So accepted was this posture that Sir

[34] John Adams to Richard Crench, Sept. 23, 1767, Butterfield et al., eds., *Book of Abigail and John*, p. 48.

[35] John Adams to John Quincy Adams, Dec. 28, 1780, ibid., p. 284.

[36] Ivensen, *O the Times*, p. 205.

Joshua Reynolds was astonished when a professor of anatomy was able to prove to him that such a posture was "contrary to nature."[37] The five basic positions of ballet were merely formalized versions of already formal genteel posture, and countless gentlemen stood for their portraits in a fairly good approximation of the classic first and second positions.

Costume accommodated the expectations of genteel bearing. Coats were cut narrow across the back and more amply across the chest to hang correctly when the shoulders were drawn sharply back.[38] So ingrained was the connection between erect bearing and gentility that the word *upright* referred both to physical and moral stature, and a *slouch* meant both someone who was round-shouldered and a lazy ne'er-do-well. White silk stockings showed to advantage the graceful curves of legs developed through the genteel pastimes of dancing, riding, and fencing. Like a fine head of hair, a well-turned leg was considered one of the best features of a gentleman, so much so that false calves of wool were available for those less amply endowed. A man's carriage and physique revealed his social position as clearly as his costume, and his costume was meant to emphasize his genteel bearing.

As gentility became more a matter of manner, society placed less emphasis on material display. Over the last half of the eighteenth century, gentlemen eschewed most of the obvious trappings of wealth in their manner of dress. The imposing baroque presence of the first half of the century in full-bodied wig, huge bag sleeves, and coats with voluminous full skirts gave way to a darker, slimmer ideal. The proportions of the coats shrank, requiring less material but better tailoring. Sleeves became tight fitting, pocket flaps and cuffs disappeared, the skirts of the frock coat became slimmer and receded toward the sides, and the skirts of the waistcoat gradually disappeared altogether. At the same time men took to wearing only a light queue wig or simply powdering their own hair (fig. 6). After 1750 fashionable men also gradually

[37] Sir Joshua Reynolds, *Discourses on Art* (1783; reprint ed., San Marino, Calif., 1959), p. 48.

[38] Kidwell, "Bicentennial Outlook," pp. 28–33.

abandoned bright colors and rich fabrics for sober broadcloth suits in drab or neutral colors.

By the last decade of the eighteenth century gentlemen had given up virtually all manner of sartorial display as ostentatious or self-indulgent. Silks and satins, bright colors and pastels, lace and jewelry became, by default, almost exclusively objects of feminine adornment. A wide variety of fabrics, colors, and ornamentation that earlier had been worn by both men and women came to be firmly regarded as by nature feminine and would remain so well into the twentieth century. Where previously most goods had been equally available with few gender restrictions (and those applying more to women than men), now all aspects of clothing were becoming rigidly gender-specific with more prohibitions on men than women. The developing aesthetic of understatement that delineated the negative boundary of ostentation also established the pejorative concept of effeminate.

Under these circumstances, the aspiring middle class found itself at a decided disadvantage. People could turn to etiquette books, dancing masters, and tailors for assistance, but, for the most part, they lacked sufficient free time to master the subtleties of genteel manner and fashion. Even then their determination and seriousness often separated their studied efforts from the casual facility of the born elite. The subtleties and complexities of the new aesthetic succeeded in keeping the uninitiated, such as the poor Marylander cited at the beginning of this essay, off guard and at a disadvantage.

Overzealousness, a desire to please or impress, and a failure to appreciate an aesthetic of understatement led many to err on the side of ostentation. "The poor Doctor thought his clothes were not good enough to wait upon us," wrote Sarah Miles in her journal of 1773, "therefore he delays his visit until he gets fitted up in Macaronia I suppose."[39] The new code of genteel dress did not require a man merely to wear the finest he could afford. Instead he was obliged to identify a fairly narrow band of correct dress located on a spectrum that ranged from plain, worn, or out-of-date clothing unworthy of

[39] Elisabeth McClellan, *Historic Dress in America: 1607 to 1800* (Philadelphia, 1904), p. 241.

Figure 6. Daniel Boardman. *Ralph Earl, 1789. (Courtesy of the National Gallery of Art, Washington, D.C. Gift of Mrs. W. Murray Crane)*

a gentleman, to the very rich or elaborate goods now considered gaudy and ostentatious, and thus equally unworthy of a
gentleman. A code of nuances and refinements left the aspiring uncertain as to how successfully to emulate rules not
clearly understood. For the middling sort, there was the
vague disquiet that no matter what one did, it would somehow fail to hit the mark.

In their disdain for pedantry and their confidence in the
natural superiority of breeding, the elite, on the other hand,
permitted themselves the freedom deliberately to transgress
the rules of dress that bound lesser men.[40] An accepted
gentleman could hold himself above rules, since his position
was secure enough that he need not prove his right to it. "One
Mr. Lightfoot," for example, whom Dr. Hamilton met on his
journey through New England in 1744, was "a gentleman of
regular education, having been brought up att Oxford."
Nonetheless he arrived at the inn where Hamilton was staying wearing "a straw hat dyed black but no wig," explaining
to the curious gentlemen present "that he always rode in this
trim in hot weather." After observing the poise and confidence of his manner and the polish of his conversation, Hamilton declared Lightfoot "a man of good humour and
excellent sense," despite the "oddity of his dress."[41] The ultimate luxury enjoyed by gentlemen of the eighteenth century
was freedom—freedom from economic necessity that permitted them to employ their time mastering the erudite codes of
manners, dress, politics, and a classical education, and freedom from the need to justify themselves, confident in the absolute legitimacy of their position. Gentlemen made the rules
and reserved for themselves the right to transgress those rules
for their own convenience, always provided, of course, that
they did not go too far.

While individual gentlemen enjoyed the privilege of occasionally modifying or disregarding the rules of dress, a comprehensive system of transgression developed in England at
midcentury. This system gradually evolved into a new code
of genteel dress that spread rapidly throughout Europe and

[40] Bourdieu, *Distinction*, p. 255.

[41] Bridenbaugh, ed., *Gentleman's Progress*, pp. 104–5.

America. For the first half of the eighteenth century the French court had dominated fashion styles and standards. Urbane elegance reigned at the expense of comfort and practicality. By midcentury, however, a significant portion of the English gentry had turned their attention to their country estates and away from London and the Hanoverian court. They became caught up in rural activities such as strolling the grounds and parks, riding, hunting, and implementing new agricultural techniques and improved methods of animal husbandry.[42] Some commissioned paintings of their fields and estates and even individual portraits of their prize livestock.

The delicate fabrics and tight fit of court costume obviously were unsuited for the comparative rigors of country life. English country gentlemen adopted cut-away riding jackets, double-breasted shooting jackets, broad-brimmed farmer's hats, and high riding boots, all of sturdy material and workmanship, and with little or no superfluous ornamentation. Significantly, they also abandoned the most prominent badges of the gentleman, the wig and the sword.[43] During the last quarter of the century the fashion *à l'anglaise* was adopted by Londoners, young German romantics including Goethe, and eventually even the French court, at least for its more informal moments. In the process, the English redefined the concept of gentility. Where previously a gentleman had been a man free of the necessity to work, now he was free to take up work if he so chose. The practicality and simplicity of the new style admirably suited the need of the middle class on both sides of the Atlantic to reconcile physical activity and the appearance of respectability at a reasonable price. Professional men, such as Dr. William Glysson of Massachusetts, visited patients respectably attired in a riding coat and high boots. A very few men went further and, like Paul Revere—who significantly was a staunch revolutionary—posed for formal portraits in the informal shirtsleeves of a tradesman. Ironically, American patriots observing the embargo on English goods during the Revolutionary War found English country dress to

[42]See, for example, Mark Girouard, *Life in the English Country House: A Social and Architectural History* (New Haven, 1978), pp. 213–45.

[43]Boehn, *The Eighteenth Century,* pp. 230–36.

be the style most congenial for clothing made of homespun.[44] From English gentleman farmer to American professional to American craftsman, the idea of a working gentleman was no longer necessarily a contradiction in terms. What had begun as a deliberate transgression of the rules of correct dress became itself a formalized code.

At approximately the same time that American men adopted elements of the more informal English country fashions, they also permitted more freedom to their children. For most of the century, young children had worn several layers of full-skirted petticoats, tight bodices, and stiffened corsets, deliberately designed to restrict any expression of youthful exuberance and physically to enforce a sense of decorum. By the 1770s parents and child-rearing authorities gradually came to accept childhood as a natural stage in man's development, and play as the natural activity of the young. Parents began to heed the advice of John Locke, who, writing nearly one hundred years earlier, encouraged parents to dress their children loosely and lightly to permit greater freedom of movement.[45] Young children in the last decades of the eighteenth century dressed in light cotton frocks and low-heeled slippers.

Traditionally boys had remained in petticoats until the age of six or seven when they received their first pair of breeches, but in the last quarter of the century parents allowed boys to abandon petticoats by the age of three or four for a dramatically new costume of short jacket and long trousers (fig. 7). Called a hussar or skeleton suit, the new outfit derived from the long trousers traditionally worn by some sailors, soldiers, and peasants—that is from the costume of lower-class men. The skeleton suit permitted boys more freedom of movement, recognized their masculinity at an earlier age, yet at the same time indicated their subservience to their fathers who still wore the knee breeches of gentlemen. Gradually parents

[44]Abigail Adams to John Adams, June 3, 1776, Butterfield et al., eds., *Book of Abigail and John*, p. 136; Alice Morse Earle, ed., *Diary of Anna Green Winslow* (Boston, 1894), p. 92.

[45]John Locke, *Some Thoughts concerning Education* (1680; reprint ed., New York, 1910), pp. 152–68.

Figure 7. Nathan Hawley and Family. *William Wilkie, 1801.*
(Courtesy of the Albany Institute of History and Art, Albany, N.Y.)

extended the number of years that their children wore child-
ish dress well into adolescence.[46]

By the 1780s the last vestige of the eighteenth-century
gentleman, a well-turned leg shown to advantage in white silk
stockings, was rapidly disappearing. Already tall riding boots
in the English fashion were common, and there was a growing
interest in a romantic image of the American frontiersman in
native ornament and leather leggings—an image that formed
around such men as Ethan Allen, Daniel Boone, and Meri-
wether Lewis. In the early years of the nineteenth century,
young gentlemen retained for themselves the freedom that
their childhood clothing had permitted, and, like Nathan
Hawley in 1801 (fig. 7), continued to wear trousers as adults.

[46]Karin Calvert, "Children in American Family Portraiture, 1670 to
1810," *William and Mary Quarterly,* 3d ser. 39 (1982): 87–113.

At the same time, their wives continued to wear the simple white frocks of their childhood, free of petticoats, hoops, and corsets.

Dressed almost exclusively in black, grey, or buff, with white linen, the skirts of his coat now mere vestigial tails, a man of fashion cut a slender figure, lithe as an athlete and graceful as a dancer. His appearance relied on the skills of his tailor, the precision of his grooming, and his own taste and ability to project a sense of understated elegance. This seemingly effortless art, which actually required considerable skill, is highly apparent in the 1802 portrait of Aaron Burr by John Vanderlyn (fig. 8). Burr captivates, not with the splendor of his dress, but with its precision and his own aristocratic bearing and self-assurance. There is virtually nothing here in the way of material goods that could be protected by sumptuary laws. Wealth and position are encoded not in gold or velvet but in a sense of style both obvious and intangible. Dress had become a minimalistic art and an erudite science. In the process it had become extremely difficult to counterfeit.

At the close of the eighteenth century, men of the middle classes still emulated the fashions of the elite, while the elite, exercising their prerogative to transgress their own rules, borrowed practical and comfortable styles from peasants, sailors, and even little children. It should be noted that an individual from one class did not usually borrow from the class directly beneath him on the social scale, since this might be misinterpreted as downward social mobility, but members of the upper classes could with safety borrow from the lower classes since this was recognized as deliberate slumming, and, as such, carried little or no social stigma. Similarly, an individual could borrow from the group directly above him on the social scale, but not from one higher than that since this would be regarded as overweening ambition. Thus, on an oversimplistic social scale, the upper classes could appropriate elements of costume from the lower classes: these, in turn, could emulate the middling sort, who, in their turn, copied the fashions of the elite (including the bits inspired by working-class clothes).

As a result of this round robin, the basic elements of dress

Figure 8. Aaron Burr. *John Vanderlyn, 1802. (Courtesy of the Yale University Art Gallery, Yale University, New Haven, Conn. Bequest of Oliver Burr Jennings. Photo courtesy of the National Portrait Gallery, Smithsonian Institution)*

became more universal and visually egalitarian than ever before. The farmer's smock and the gentleman's knee breeches gave way to a basic costume of shirt, trousers, vest, and jacket for men of all classes. At the same time, the intricacies and nuances of the genteel code of fashion assured that few could successfully pass for gentlemen without actually becoming gentlemen, that is, without acquiring the speech, manners, and mien of gentlemen. The appearance of society was at once fundamentally egalitarian and markedly stratified. While the distance between the social strata appeared narrower, the difficulties in overcoming that distance had markedly increased.

MARGARETTA M. LOVELL

Painters and Their Customers: Aspects of Art and Money in Eighteenth-Century America

THE THEORY OF an eighteenth-century consumer revolution, one that predated and nourished the subsequent Industrial Revolution, suggests dramatically altered patterns of consumption, new populations of consumers, and ever-novel products. It also suggests subtler metamorphoses in older, long-established cultural patterns of making, vending, and using objects. Art objects, specifically paintings, representing a special category of production, were made and used in eighteenth-century America in ways that overlaid traditional usage with new purposes, ways that affected the producers, the consumers, and the products. These new patterns of production, marketing, and usage were not as immediately visible (or as profitable) as the technological and marketing innovations of such heroes of the English consumer revolution as Josiah Wedgwood and Matthew Boulton, but on close inspection they exhibit many of the same characteristics of market positioning on the part of the producers and a felt need on the part of the purchasers that we associate with more obvious consumer goods.

As a consumer product, a painting is eccentric. On the one hand it resists modern, profitable production techniques, retaining through the eighteenth, indeed the nineteenth century, the same basic materials and methods that had been established 300 years earlier. On the other hand, by its very nature a painting partakes of exactly that kind of alchemical straw-into-gold magic that is the admiration, in fact the goal, of the modern entrepreneur. As the English theoretician and painter Jonathan Richardson put it early in the eighteenth century: "I have observ'd heretofore, that there is no Artist [artisan] whatsoever, that produces a piece of work of a value so vastly above that of the Materials of Natures furnishing as the Painter does, nor consequently that can Enrich a Countrey in any Degree like Him."[1] The materials are negligible, common, and cheap; the product can be unique, soul-stirring, and immensely valuable. While there is, of course, an aesthetic dimension with economic value in all design, from the humblest earthenware teapot to the most exquisitely crafted cabinet, in a painting this ratio of aesthetic power to economic value exists in its purest form. And as the value of an object is determined not only by its craftsmanship and its desirability to a wide and economically empowered audience but also by its portability, paintings suggest themselves as logical, pleasurable, liquidatable investments, retaining the virtues and associations of handcraftsmanship but participating in newer patterns of economic behavior.

It is curious, then, that while the English gentry expanded the market and the role for painting in the eighteenth century, acquiring both modern and old masterworks in a wide variety of genres for personal pleasure, social display, and active investment, their American counterparts resisted this trend.[2] Not just a result of colonial remoteness from Europe or provincial pragmatism (indeed, Americans expended substantial fortunes on a wide variety of European luxury goods), this phenomenon suggests active choice, for painting did exist, in fact could be said to have flourished, in America during this period, although only within narrow confines. Americans bought portraits. They did not buy landscapes, still lifes, or

[1] Jonathan Richardson, *Two Discourses* (London, 1719), pt. 2, pp. 41–52.

[2] Ibid.; p. 47; see also Louise Lippincott, *Selling Art in Georgian London: The Rise of Arthur Pond* (New Haven, 1983), pp. 95–125.

genre scenes; they did not even branch out into portraits of horses or houses or conversation pieces. They focused solely—but enthusiastically—on portraits of individuals, couples, and, occasionally, families.

While this ready market for portraits generated a livelihood, even wealth, for a considerable number of painters in America, it represented a meager, in fact a negative, investment opportunity for the purchaser. Its cost was high (about that of a silver tankard or a teapot, or nine weeks' wages for a skilled journeyman artisan), but unlike the expense of a silver object or a landscape painting, its cost was unrecoverable. It had virtually no resale value. Given what we are told so often about the pragmatic nature of eighteenth-century Americans, what kind of cultural meaning can be ascribed to this widespread behavior? Why were so many so willing to spend so much to achieve—from an investment point of view—so little? And how, from the other point of view, did the artist-entrepreneur respond to this new and eager market? Or, to recast the question, what economic and cultural roles did painting play in eighteenth-century America, and how do these roles intersect with other evidence of a burgeoning consumer economy?

What, then, was a portraitist selling, besides an object that was expensive, effectively useless, and, as an exchange commodity, valueless? Clearly he was selling something both abstract and deeply rooted in the culture. Remarkably little has been written about the social functions of portraiture, especially in America. Surely it services a need deeper than personal vanity and more focused than a repeated hymn to the virtues of post-Renaissance individualism. Its impetus, we suspect, is also more complex and more interesting than that capsulized in the popular assumption that painters gave their subjects a better, more flattering view than the looking glass by adjusting their physiognomies closer to norms of beauty and by displaying the body in a pose and costume perhaps slightly above their station. Vanity, individualism, and flattery were not new in the eighteenth century, but wider distribution of wealth was. It seems more reasonable, therefore, to see the expanding market for portraiture in relation to family

substance rather than individual virtues or vices because portraiture—even of single individuals—is fundamentally a family matter.

The relationship between wealth and portraiture is not a
simple one of luxury expense requiring discretionary income
but rather a more subtle one involving the movement of
wealth between generations. Eighteenth-century small
tradesmen and journeymen artisans were infrequent patrons
of the portraitist, not because they could not afford his wares
(presumably they could if they forewent other small luxuries)
but because they did not *need* portraits. The need arises when
there is inheritable substance, and the consecutiveness of the
family line—the preservation of the "house" in the most medieval sense—is at stake.[3] It is for this reason that almost all
private portraits are made at the time of an individual's
achievement of majority, inheritance, marriage, or first issue—moments that mark the movement of family substance
in an orderly, prescribed manner. Portraits, then, are documents of the family line in operation, of the rules being followed, of chaos and litigation avoided, of family acquiescence
to a new order in the all-important arena of money. They are
generational documents with a diachronic as well as a syn-
chronic audience, not just celebrations of personal prerogative, beauty, charm, taste, or mere acquisition. Because there
was more inheritable wealth (as distinct from prosperity that
earns and consumes generously but equally) in more hands
with each passing decade of the eighteenth century in
America, there was an ever-increasing demand for portraits.
Therefore, while they represent an established, even an archaic, art form, and they document the vestiges of a semi-
feudal sense of the family, portraits participated in the
modern economy of the eighteenth century with as much en-

[3] Georges Duby, *The Knight, the Lady, and the Priest: The Making of Modern
Marriage in Medieval France,* trans. Barbara Bray (New York, 1983), pp.92–
95, 235–40; see also Lippincott, *Selling Art,* pp. 64–66. Prown estimates that
39 pecent of Copley's customers had an income between £100 and £500,
31 percent an income between £500 and £1,000, and 22 percent an income
over £1,000 (Jules David Prown, *John Singleton Copley,* 2 vols. [Cambridge,
Mass., 1966], 1:127).

ergy and power as the newer consumer products of Wedgwood or Boulton.

Such evidence as we have suggests that a family's portraits
were hung together, often in pairs (see figs. 1 and 2), in one
of the principal downstairs rooms.[4] Here they were observed
by visitors, but more frequently and perhaps more importantly, by the family members themselves. As Richardson remarked in his *Essay on the Theory of Painting*, "The Picture of an
absent Relation, or Friend, helps to keep up those Sentiments
which frequently languish by Absence and may be instrumental to maintain, and sometimes to augment Friendship, and
Paternal, Filial, and Conjugal Love, and Duty."[5] The portrait
acts as a mnemonic, it excites the bonds of affection but also,
more important, those of duty. It functions, even in the physical absence of the imaged personage, to cement the social
hierarchy and to remind family members of the facts of authority and duty. Such a group of portraits diagrams the vital
statistics not just of individual existences but also of the family's more abstract and therefore more vulnerable existence.
It insists on the social order within that microcosm of the state
which is the family.

Portraits of public figures (and prints after them) functioned similarly but in a larger arena. They documented the
victories of generals, the succession of monarchs, and the
memorable remarks of divines whose prerogatives and
achievements were a source of public pride and civic order.
These publicly displayed oil or widely distributed print portrait images simultaneously solicited admiration, respect, and,
in Richardson's terms, duty. But, unlike the individual family

[4]Richard Henry Saunders III, "John Smibert (1688–1751): Anglo-
American Portrait Painter," Ph.D. diss., Yale University, 1979, p. 166 n. 28;
Wayne Craven, *Colonial American Portraiture: The Economic, Religious, Social,
Cultural, Philosophical, Scientific and Aesthetic Foundations* (Cambridge, Mass.,
1986), pp. 183, 167 (a reference to family portraits inventoried explicitly in
pairs). Prown reports that 45 percent of Copley's business was for portraits
ordered in pairs (*Copley*, 1:135).

[5]Jonathan Richardson, *An Essay on the Theory of Painting*, 2d ed. (1725;
reprint ed., Manston, Yorkshire, 1971), pp. 13–14, cited in Richard H.
Saunders and Ellen G. Miles, *American Colonial Portraits: 1700–1776* (Washington, D.C., 1987), p. 45.

Figure 1. Mrs. James Bowdoin II (née Elizabeth Erving). *Robert Feke, 1748. (Courtesy of the Bowdoin College Museum of Art, Brunswick, Maine. Bequest of Mrs. Sarah Bowdoin Dearborn)*

Figure 2. James Bowdoin II. *Robert Feke, 1748. (Courtesy of the Bowdoin College Museum of Art, Brunswick, Maine. Bequest of Mrs. Sarah Bowdoin Dearborn)*

portraits, they were not commissioned by the imaged individual but by government entities or publishers (a book of sermons sold better with a portrait frontispiece), or they were executed as speculative ventures by artists who wished to tap the public interest in illustrious personages.

The ever-widening market for portraits provided opportunities for increasing numbers of artists, drawing numerous immigrant practitioners to America. They brought with them not only their training and technique but also their prints, copies of old master paintings, even plaster casts of the Venus de Medici.[6] They emigrated for a number of reasons. For example, we are told, according to his epitaph, that John Smibert, about whom we know more than most, "preferred [America] for health's sake." But English contemporaries reported perhaps more frankly that he found the profession as it was practiced in London too nasty ("he could not well relish, the false selfish griping, overreaching ways too commonly practiz'd here") and, having taken a measure of his talent, he "was not contented here, to be on a level with some of the best painters but desird to be were he might at the present, be lookt on as at the top [of] his profession."[7] For any individual there were probably a variety of complex, overlapping reasons to embark on such a venture. Whatever their rationale for coming, artists soon found that the American appetite for pictures, while keen, was considerably narrower than the British—focusing, as noted above, solely on portraits of persons—and that talent did not ensure success or even a suitable livelihood. Being a painter in America meant not only producing but actively marketing an expensive, rather singular commodity.

Like the immigrant painters, native-born artists were also, in a sense, strangers to the communities they came to serve, and this was a key factor in the struggles of both groups to secure patronage and market their wares. America's artists were self-recruited from artisan backgrounds, while portrait

[6]Henry Wilder Foote, *John Smibert, Painter* (Cambridge, Mass., 1950), p. 13.

[7]Ibid., pp. 106–7; George Vertue, *Note Books*, 6 vols., (Oxford, 1930–55), 3:36, 161, cited in Saunders, "John Smibert," pp. xxiii, 240.

purchasers—by definition members of families with inheritable substance—were overwhelmingly merchant and gentry-
class figures. America offered the artist no long-term courtly
patronage; indeed, this form of support for artists and poets
was virtually extinct in Europe by the mid-eighteenth century.
Yet the newly established patronage forum of the public exhibition was unknown in the colonies, leaving the artist somewhat adrift, but also nominally independent, in a risky,
competitive marketplace. In America the portrait painter and
the subject engaged in a contract that lasted only until the
painting was finished. Typically it involved the payment of
half the agreed-upon price at the time the painter accepted
the commission and half upon satisfactory completion of the
work. From the notebook of John Smibert early in the eighteenth century and the surviving accounts of John Singleton
Copley late in the colonial period, it is evident that successful
portraitists painted, on the average, one portrait every two
weeks (although production was often faster, especially during painting tours, and occasionally much slower, or intermit-
tent).[8] The business of the artist, however, as the careers of
these two best-known successful portraitists exhibit, involved
more than talent, training, orderly scheduling, and self-
presentation before an eager market. Hungry as they were
for the product, portrait patrons evidently were reluctant to
trust their pictorial immortality to any but an artist who would
be as sensitive to class-defined body language, fashion, and
taste as they. In a word, the artist had to present himself as
one of their own; for a portraitist, living like a gentleman was
not just the reward of success but it was also the criterion of
success.

Louise Lippincott, in her remarkable analysis of the account book of the successful London portraitist Arthur Pond,
has chronicled in detail the complex ingredients of his carefully constructed reputation.[9] We can see both Smibert and
Copley employing many of the same strategies for securing
and publicizing the accoutrements of gentility and the aura

[8]*The Notebook of John Smibert* (Boston, 1969), pp. 73–99; Prown, *Copley*,
1:36 n. 2, 128–29.

[9]Lippincott, *Selling Art*, pp. 32–34, 108.

of skill, taste, and success. Smibert, the son of a Scottish wool dyer, brought with him from Europe prints, copies of old masters, plaster casts after the antique, an association with George Berkeley's proposed university, and the reputation garnered in a short but successful portrait career in London. Copley, on the other hand, was a tobacco seller's son from Long Wharf in Boston. His stepfather, the mezzotint engraver Peter Pelham, was probably the key figure not only in his choice of vocation and early art education but also in his acquisition of the arts of gentility, for Pelham ran, among other enterprises, a finishing school for young gentry, and his lessons surely were not lost on the adolescent Copley.[10] Perhaps more important, both Smibert and Copley married well, that is, not only to their great financial advantage but also advantageously for their continued professional rise. Smibert's father-in-law built him a house, studio, and shop, while Copley's marriage resulted in his purchase of twenty acres on Beacon Hill, a choice property adjoining that of the immensely wealthy Hancock family.[11] And at least in part because their homes were their places of business, these artists lived well. Smibert's inventory, taken in 1752, is that of a wealthy gentleman and exhibits—with its silver-hilted sword, five looking glasses, forty-six chairs, and substantial real estate—a fivefold increase in luxury goods over the quite substantial furnishings with which he had equipped his London studio and dwelling three decades before.[12] Unlike post-romantic artists, who deliberately position themselves outside the establishment, creating works for an unknown speculative market with the assistance of merchant middlemen, eighteenth-century painters accepted and executed projects directly from and for the patron group in the very personal area of the portrait commission and therefore, necessarily, assumed the guise of the client group.

[10] Craven, *Colonial American Portraiture*, pp. 141, 149.

[11] Saunders, "John Smibert," pp. 175–76; George Vertue speaks of Smibert's wife, whom Smibert had married within months of his arrival in Boston, as "a woman of considerable fortune" (ibid., p. 240); Prown, *Copley*, pp. 62–65, figs. 224 and 225.

[12] Saunders, "John Smibert," pp. 254–55 n. 63; *Notebook of Smibert*, p. 77.

While in general the market for portraits was always good, even the successful portraitist-entrepreneur had a chronic problem: he had no repeat customers. Even Copley, whose genius was as apparent to his contemporaries as to subsequent generations, had only a 10 percent return rate for sitters.[13] Because portraits marked decisive moments in an individual's assumption of new roles in the family line (most often marriage), only one was needed in a lifetime. If subsequent portraits were called for, the new commission almost always went to a different artist for variety's sake.[14] And because it behooved the artist to act like a gentleman as well as live like one, he charged his customers not in pounds but in guineas, the medium of exchange among gentry and professionals, but suffered the disadvantage of necessary public reticence. Both Smibert and Copley, for instance, eschewed advertising their availability as portraitists in the newspapers, although they did advertise for a runaway slave or an offering of other merchandise such as prints. Other American artists advertised their portrait skills, but London artists did not, and the more upscale American artists did not.[15] Nor—with the conspicuous exception of Hogarth—did they hang out a sign. Consequently their need for a new circle of customers was chronic, but their guise as gentlemen working with gentry inhibited the more public announcements of availability. Instead, they depended on word of mouth or, in both the gentlemanly and artistic sense, reputation. And this went far, especially within the basic structure in which and for which portraiture flourished, the family. Bound by ties of interest, money, and genuine affection, eighteenth-century families were strong vehicles for the transmission of ideas, behavior, and goods, and so it is no surprise that we find strong kinship ties in the patron lists of portraitists. In his exhaustive study of Copley's patrons, Jules David Prown noted that 80 percent

[13] Prown, *Copley*, p. 137.

[14] There are portraits of Isaac Winslow, for instance, by both Joseph Blackburn and Copley at the Museum of Fine Arts, Boston; see also Lippincott, *Selling Art*, pp. 64–65, 69.

[15] For a discussion of some American portraitists who did advertise, see Saunders and Miles, *American Colonial Portraits*, pp. 12, 58–61.

of Copley's patrons over a quarter of a century fit onto just twenty-eight family trees.[16] This is not just evidence of the close-knit nature of colonial wealth and power but also an indication of the lines along which that amorphous but instrumental quality known as reputation flows.

While most scholars of American eighteenth-century painting are dismayed to find evidence of artists engaged in activities that drew them away from "full-time" painter status and see this as evidence of an inhospitable environment for art, one also might see these activities as conscious and useful forays into potential new customer groups. For example, in the "colour shop" adjacent to his studio, Smibert sold prints, professional equipment, and materials for amateurs such as fan paper and fan mounts for the then-fashionable activity of painting fans.[17] Just as Arthur Pond's drawing lessons for women amateurs gave him entré into court circles for portrait patronage, surely Smibert found among his print purchasers and fan enthusiasts leisured, moneyed gentlefolk who could easily note his primary offering: portraiture.[18]

Another strategy for locating new customers was the painting tour. Often interpreted as the plight of the itinerant hack whose hometown had few customers or whose talent was too modest to find ready buyers, the painting tour was used by such prominent artists as Smibert, Copley, and their London counterparts to locate new customers—usually with letters of introduction and a certain number of commissions presecured. Although it was a nuisance, the painting tour was—in cases best documented—highly profitable.[19]

Perhaps the most effective strategy for attracting new customers was the relatively novel device of the artist's signature. In the seventeenth century American painters did not sign their work, but in the eighteenth we find increasing numbers

[16] Prown, *Copley*, p. 139.

[17] Saunders, "John Smibert," pp. 175–76, 219, 227, 240–41; M. A. Flory, *A Book about Fans* (1895; reprint ed., Detroit, 1974), pp. 37–38, cited in Craven, *Colonial American Portraiture*, pp. 286, 428 n. 9.

[18] Lippincott, *Selling Art*, pp. 38, 30.

[19] Saunders, "John Smibert," pp. 211–15; Prown, *Copley*, pp. 79–82; Lippincott, *Selling Art*, pp. 36–38.

of artists signing their paintings clearly and systematically, usually in a lower corner where an observant visitor could note it easily. Usually attributed to burgeoning "pride," these signatures seem more likely to have been both guarantees of quality for the assurance of the purchaser—not unlike the silversmith's touchmark or the clockmaker's dial-imprinted name—as well as covert messages addressed to potential purchasers.[20] In a business that depended on personal contact, it was only logical that the eighteenth-century painter should attempt to extend his reach through whatever means appeared appropriate, profitable, and polite.

In John Smibert's notebook—a meticulous account of 175 paintings executed in London and 241 executed in America, in which he lists dates, sitters, canvas sizes, and costs—there is a single laconic entry made late in 1738 that reads "a vew of Boston."[21] It is the only entry in which there is no notation of canvas size or price, and one could surmise that it was that vacant right column, usually so plump with guineas, that warned him not to venture again beyond the comfortable world of commissions and portraits. From the perspective of the late twentieth century, it seems strange that Smibert did not indulge his interests and educate his patrons to this new taste. In 1743 he confided to Arthur Pond, his fellow artist and materials supplier, "You know I was always fond of Landskips," and in his last months he wrote, "I grow old, my eyes has been some time failing me, but . . . [I am] diverting myself with something in the Landskip way which you know I always liked."[22] Smibert died a very wealthy man, with lands, goods, and luxuries that bespeak the possibility of a discretionary use of time. Yet only these references and one landscape painting survive as testaments to his genre restlessness. His business was painting portraits, and both he and his customers were too habituated to this mode to venture into the painting of

[20]Saunders and Miles, *American Colonial Portraits*, p. 43; Margaretta M. Lovell, "'Such Furniture as Will Be Most Profitable': The Business of Cabinetmaking in Eighteenth-Century Newport," *Winterthur Portfolio* 26 (1991):44–48.

[21]*Notebook of Smibert*, p. 95.

[22]Saunders, "John Smibert," pp. 226, 237.

unbespoke artworks or the buying of expensive artworks they did not need, as they felt they needed portraits.

If Smibert grew wistful about his lot as a portraitist, Copley grew truculent, even rebellious. But while he also had enough of a financial cushion to experiment with alternative genres, he declined to do so, emigrating instead to England, where he knew there were established markets for a wide range of genres and a functioning forum—the Royal Academy exhibitions—in which artists with works done speculatively could offer them to potential customers. It was not until the very end of the century that a few artists gained the confidence (or forum) to offer uncommissioned paintings to a curious public in America.

While few painters ventured into the realm of speculative art production, printmakers discovered and began to exploit the market potential of anonymous retail sales from the mid-eighteenth century. By definition, a print is a multiple, and while it takes little time or money to make a single print, the investment involved in making the plate from which the prints are pulled is considerable. In order to be profitable, then, a print, with its modest per-item profit, must sell in volume. A few portrait prints of noted clergymen were made in America early in the eighteenth century, usually to serve as frontispieces to collections of sermons or tracts. Other prints of noted ministers were paid for by subscription. After mid-century, prints, especially mezzotints with their velvety texture and graduated values imitative of oil paintings, were made of secular public figures as well and increasingly as speculative ventures independent of both book publishing and the complications of subscription sales.[23] The most successful American print ventures were related to topical subjects and figures such as the Louisbourg campaign of 1745.[24] But even a popular issue (for example, the repeal of the Stamp Act) and the depiction of a well-known figure such as William Pitt could not ensure the financial success of Charles

[23] Wendy J. Shadwell, *American Printmaking: The First 150 Years* (Washington, D.C., 1969), pp. 16–21; Saunders and Miles, *American Colonial Portraits*, pp. 80, 90, 134–43, 151–52.

[24] Saunders and Miles, *American Colonial Portraits*, pp. 140–41.

Willson Peale's overcomplex and slightly bathetic *William Pitt*.[25] The decision to issue a print was a risky one and, like all speculation on public demand and taste, it involved the specter of loss as well as the promise of profit. Perhaps the best-known (and possibly worst-executed) eighteenth-century topical American print is *The Bloody Massacre* (1770 [fig. 3]) dramatizing the incident that has become known as the Boston Massacre; it is credited to Paul Revere but known to be plagiarized from Henry Pelham's design.[26] Revere's desire for profit here overcame his scruples; the fact that his reward has not been infamy but profit and fame indicates the value at which his contemporaries held entrepreneurship. The innovations in the area of prints during the eighteenth century included new subjects, expanding retail audiences, and, it seems, profits for which one might risk damnation.

If the painter's inescapable problem was the absence of repeat customers, the printmaker's was the competition of cheap and technically polished English and continental wares. Like other products of mechanical reproduction, European prints generally presented colonial makers with higher quality at lower cost than they could effectively challenge. One of the novel aspects of the eighteenth-century British art market, these widely available prints, especially mezzotints, usually reproduced paintings—cheaply and with reasonable accuracy—in black and white on a readily portable scale. In its volume, impersonality, and emphasis on novelty, this trade is more obviously linked to other aspects of the consumer revolution than is its parent art of painting.[27] While all kinds of artworks were reproduced in the London shops, including landscapes, views of Rome, and genre series (beginning with William Hogarth's *Harlot's Progress* in 1731), those which found the readiest market in America were images of famous personages. Unlike the artist who painted portraits on

[25] Wendy J. Shadwell, "The Portrait Engravings of Charles Willson Peale," in Joan D. Dolmetsch, ed., *Eighteenth-Century Prints in Colonial America: To Educate and Decorate* (Williamsburg, 1979), pp. 125–28.

[26] Shadwell, *American Printmaking*, figs. 33–35; Saunders and Miles, *American Colonial Portraits*, p. 308 n. 2.

[27] Lippincott, *Selling Art*, pp. 126–59.

Figure 3. The Bloody Massacre. *Paul Revere, 1770. (Courtesy, Winterthur Museum)*

commission, the mezzotint artist or publisher who produced a print from a painting elected his own subject, and he did so in response to a sense of what would sell in a spontaneous, anonymous, ready-made, rather than bespoke, marketplace. The audience in America bought prints of men who were illustrious by virtue of their aristocratic lineage or their military prowess, and women who were illustrious by virtue of their beauty. In making these purchases the colonials were consumers not just of the specific artwork but also of the "body rhetoric" such works imaged. We can assume that many purchasers studied these prints as models in the matter of costume, pose, gesture, accoutrements, even anatomy. We know the artists did so; they frequently based entire paintings on English mezzotint sources, mimicking the attitudes and finery, even the dogs and background trees of remote English aristocrats (see figs. 1 and 4).[28] This "borrowed body" syndrome is one of the most interesting aspects of colonial art, and it has been explained variously as timidity and self-education on the part of the colonial artist, or pseudoaristocratic ambition on the part of the sitters.[29] In fact it seems to point to the exploration and appropriation of ever-new concepts of the body by way of this novel commodity, the portrait print. For the human form and its management is as subject to fashion, signaled by patterns of emulation and change, as the clothes that adorn and display it.

While these conventionalized, print-inspired poses sometimes tell us less than they might about specific individual identities, they are solid evidence about cultural ideals and preoccupations.[30] For instance, we would have a good sense of the erotic focus of the eighteenth-century male gaze on female anatomy from the verses which James Bowdoin II (fig. 2) wrote concerning his wife (fig. 1). After a series of fa-

[28] For classic examples see Craven, *Colonial American Portraiture*, figs. 112 and 113, 123 and 124, 145 and 146; Saunders and Miles, *American Colonial Portraits*, figs. 75 and 79.

[29] Saunders and Miles, *American Colonial Portraits*, pp. 237–38, 247.

[30] Margaretta M. Lovell, "Reading Portraits: Social Images and Self-Images in Eighteenth-Century American Family Portraits," *Winterthur Portfolio* 22 (1987):46–71.

Figure 4. Princess Anne. *By Isaac Beckett after William Wissing, 1710–30. (Courtesy, Winterthur Museum)*

miliar conceits in which her neck is likened to a column, her glance to lightning, her cheeks to roses, he concludes:

> Her coral lips, whene'er she speaks disclose
> The finest iv'ry in concentric rows;
> Her tempting breasts in whiteness far outgo
> The op'ning lilly, and the new faln snow;
> Her tempting breasts the eyes of all command,
> And gently rising court the am'rous hand.[31]

We would have little sense of the limits of modesty in décolletage, however, without the portrait (fig. 1), or of the even more generous limits in earlier English court manners without the source print (fig. 4). Without this portrait, and many like it, we would not know (because the poets and behavior tracts do not mention it) the convention of female posture which almost invariably places a woman's legs and knees apart and insists on a horizontally generous lap area. Similarly, while several commentators remark on the importance of a well-rounded calf to a man's personal appearance and suggest ways of standing that will exhibit these assets appropriately, without the full-length portraits (fig. 5) we would have little idea of the insistence on simultaneous side and frontal calf elevations. These and other conventions concerning the body and its depiction in portraiture suggest that the consumption of body language, democratized through the mime of the inexpensive portrait print, was yet another, albeit abstract, commodity in the American marketplace. More than almost any other eighteenth-century commodity produced or sold in America, mezzotint engravings embody cultural paradox, bridging as they do disparate economic and social worlds. Imaging individuals, they were sold impersonally at booksellers; picturing aristocrats and their prerogatives, they were available to all; and asserting feudal relationships of mutual duty and obligation, they figured prominently in the rapid, cheap commodity production and exchange that characterized the ideology of capitalism. They operated both as endorsements

---

[31] Quoted in Marvin Sadik, *Colonial and Federal Portraits at Bowdoin College* (Brunswick, Maine, 1966), pp. 49, 51.

Figure 5. Colonel Nathanial Sparhawk. *John Singleton Copley, 1764. (Charles H. Bayley Picture and Paintings Fund. Courtesy, Museum of Fine Arts, Boston)*

of the status quo and as objects of democratization, injecting courtly body language and novel definitions of art into an eager and ever-broadening marketplace.

By the end of the colonial period, the artist in America had two potential careers and patronage relationships to choose from. The first was the realm of painted portraits, with its ever-widening circle of potential customers with inheritable wealth but with its limitations in genre and the solicitation of customers. Unprecedented escalation in wealth—from trade, land speculation, and production—ensured the portraitist a large and constantly growing population of consumer families, but simultaneously circumscribed his self-presentation and marketing mechanisms within somewhat archaic notions of gentility and personalized exchange. The depersonalized world of prints, on the other hand, was independent of notions of the family—its obligations, hierarchy, and consecutiveness—so intimately involved in portraiture. Prints presented both the artist and the consumer with newly discovered and rapidly exploited opportunities. They served a mnemonic function as surely as painted portraits did, but their message (even though many were portraits) was much less focused, more impersonal, and voluntary. They appealed to a wide range of political, ecclesiastical, aesthetic, even comic interests. Consumers seemed not only more willing to expend at the modest level of prints but also were eager for the impersonal exchange at the bookseller's or other retail outlets. Furthermore, the fact that the images were made speculatively and were presented to the customer as ready-made goods also seemed to concede to the print purchaser apparent control of the exchange.

Because of these rather dramatic differences between portrait production and the print enterprise, we find that they represent alternative career paths with little crossover. And this in spite of the fact that the eighteenth-century printmaker almost always worked from a painting—either one already available or, more often, one commissioned for the purpose. Copley's first known artwork was a print venture, and, as we have seen, Peale attempted to tap public sentiment with his *William Pitt.* But by and large, print production in America was in the hands of nonpainter specialists. Their greatest difficulty was the fact that—unlike portraitists—they worked in direct competition with English and continental printmakers whose imports found a ready market in America. For this reason, the subjects that were offered by American printmakers tended to focus on topical matters of primary concern to a wide North American audience.

While we know little about print purchasers in eighteenth-century America, it is clear from inventories that as the century drew to a close, prints occurred in ever-increasing numbers in an ever-broader spectrum of households. In many cases print purchasers were also portrait purchasers but with one dramatic difference: while the head of a family might commission portraits of several members, once this need had been fulfilled neither a change in fashion nor the arrival of a new portraitist usually impelled him to commission new images. Print purchasers, on the other hand, were almost invariably repeat customers. Because of their relative cheapness, their wide-ranging subjects, and frequently their topicality, prints were bought and gathered into what, in fact, could be termed collections.[32] Therefore, while they were sometimes made and sold by the same individuals and not infrequently bought by the same customers, the relationship of these two very different kinds of artworks to their culture is more one of difference than identity. That difference is graphically articulated in our acknowledgment that the purchaser of the portrait was a patron (a term summoning up archaic and entangled relationships), while the purchaser of the print was, in the most modern sense of the term, a consumer.

While developments in the world of art in eighteenth-century America do not present us with dramatic watersheds or remarkable moments of marketing or consuming invention and initiation, they do, on close inspection, give us some insight into new patterns of thinking and acting on the part of both the producers and purchasers of the pictorial arts. Prints, with their low cost, volume sales, and topicality, offered to an ever-widening depersonalized group of consumers a

[32] *Notebook of Smibert,* p. 10; Craven, *Colonial American Portraiture,* pp. 162, 183, 197, 291, 360.

broad range of visual experiences—from reproduction of old master paintings to military heroes and satirical comments on daily events. Painters, despite the restriction of the field to portraiture and the personalized nature of their trade, nevertheless exhibited resourceful responses to the problem of marketing themselves and their products to a willing but initially "foreign" and ever-new audience. Together, the novel strategies of eighteenth-century artists and their evolving relationships with customers represent not so much a consumer revolution as a producer-consumer awakening to the possibilities of an art marketplace.

CYNTHIA ADAMS HOOVER

Music and Theater in the Lives of Eighteenth-Century Americans

IN 1790 BENJAMIN RUSH offered encouragement to teachers of music in his *Information to Europeans Who Are Disposed to Migrate to the United States*. A taste for music, he wrote, "prevails very generally in our large cities, and eminent masters in that art who have arrived here since the peace have received considerable sums of money by exercising their profession among us."[1] In that same year, however, Boston musicians were organizing a concert of sacred music to relieve the impoverished William Billings—well known as a teacher of music in the singing school tradition, the most important native-born composer, with over 300 published sacred pieces to his credit, and, yet, from 1786 the holder of such menial part-time jobs as municipal "scavenger" or street cleaner, and hog-reeve or policer of hogs on the Boston streets.[2]

What was happening on the American musical scene that could give rise to two such disparate accounts of the rewards that might be possible to practitioners of music? Did two different standards exist—one for European-based music and one for less sophisticated and possibly home-grown traditions? And how much musical activity was there if not too many years later John Quincy Adams, when asked in Europe

[1]Lyman H. Butterfield, ed., *The Letters of Benjamin Rush*, 2 vols. (Princeton, 1951), 1:550.

[2]David P. McKay and Richard A. Crawford, *William Billings of Boston: Eighteenth-Century Composer* (Princeton, 1975), pp. 163, 158.

if there was "much taste for music in America," could reply that his countrymen were not "attached much to music"?[3]

Contrary to Adams's view, many Americans were avid music lovers, but there were competing traditions seeking their support and attention. America's split musical personality—variously described by scholars as cultivated-vernacular, urban-rural, or cosmopolitan-provincial—has loomed large in the musical marketplace throughout this country's history. The tension between the cultivated and the vernacular approaches to music and the theater was not unlike that found in other areas of eighteenth-century American culture discussed in this volume—in art, in the choice of reading material, in the furnishing of homes, and in the acquisition of social graces. As in these other spheres, trades and crafts developed to provide musical and theatrical goods and services for the emerging American audiences and practitioners of both traditions.

This essay considers how and where these contrasting strains developed, what audience and participants each approach attracted, what activities, teachers, performers, and musical goods were available, and what patterns were established during the early years of the new republic that have continued to influence America's musical scene down to the present day. It is thus a brief review of eighteenth-century American musical and theatrical life that merely sketches in the broad outlines. For fuller coverage, the excellent studies by Oscar G. Sonneck, Irving Lowens, Richard A. Crawford, and Kenneth Silverman are especially recommended.[4] Still,

[3]Charles Francis Adams, ed., *Memoirs of John Quincy Adams*, 12 vols. (New York, 1874–77), 1:98–99, cited in H. Earle Johnson, "The Adams Family and Good Listening," *Journal of the American Musicological Society* 11 (1958):172.

[4]Oscar G. Sonneck was a pioneer in documenting eighteenth-century American musical life. His most important works include *A Bibliography of Early Secular American Music* (1905–7, revised and enlarged by William Treat Upton, 1945; reprint ed., New York, 1964), *Francis Hopkinson and James Lyon* (1905; reprint ed., New York, 1967), *Early Concert-Life in America (1731–1800)* (1907; reprint ed., Wiesbaden, 1969), and *Early Opera in America* (1914; reprint ed., New York, 1963). Irving Lowens carried on pioneering work through many articles, the most important of them collected in his

the review can serve not only as an outline of events and trends but also as a vehicle to show, through pertinent illustrations, tangible evidence of the existence of music trades throughout the century. As in Great Britain, these trades used newspaper advertisements, broadsides, trade cards, and many other forms to make their existence known to the public.

MUSICAL ACTIVITY

It should come as no surprise that America, a British colony for most of the century, developed patterns of musical activity and consumerism similar to those in England. The major difference was one of scale: settlements here were small and isolated, and musical activities only began to increase, as Benjamin Franklin noted, once "the first cares of the necessaries of life" were satisfied and the communities grew large and wealthy enough to support the "embellishments."[5] For most of the century the majority of the colonists looked to London not only for advice in the latest fashion, music, and theater, but also as the source for music, musical instruments, and musicians.

Early in the century there were scattered newspaper advertisements of immigrant teachers and performers, primarily from England, who began to give lessons in dancing and other ornamental arts and to sell imported musical goods. In 1713 in Boston, George Brownell—an early teacher of Frank-

---

Music and Musicians in Early America (New York, 1964). Richard A. Crawford has published several excellent studies, including *Andrew Law, American Psalmodist* (Evanston, Ill., 1968), with David P. McKay, *William Billings of Boston: Eighteenth-Century Composer,* and, with Allen Perdue Britten and Irving Lowens, *Early American Sacred Imprints: A Bibliography* (Worcester, Mass., 1990). He has also published editions of music, numerous articles, and detailed record notes for the New World Records Bicentennial project. Kenneth Silverman's book *A Cultural History of the American Revolution: Painting, Music, Literature, and the Theatre . . . 1763–1789* (New York, 1976) provides many insights into the relationship of music to the other arts in America in the latter half of the eighteenth century.

[5] Benjamin Franklin to Mary Stevenson, Mar. 25, 1763, quoted in Oscar G. Sonneck, *Suum Cuique: Essays in Music* (New York, 1916), p. 77.

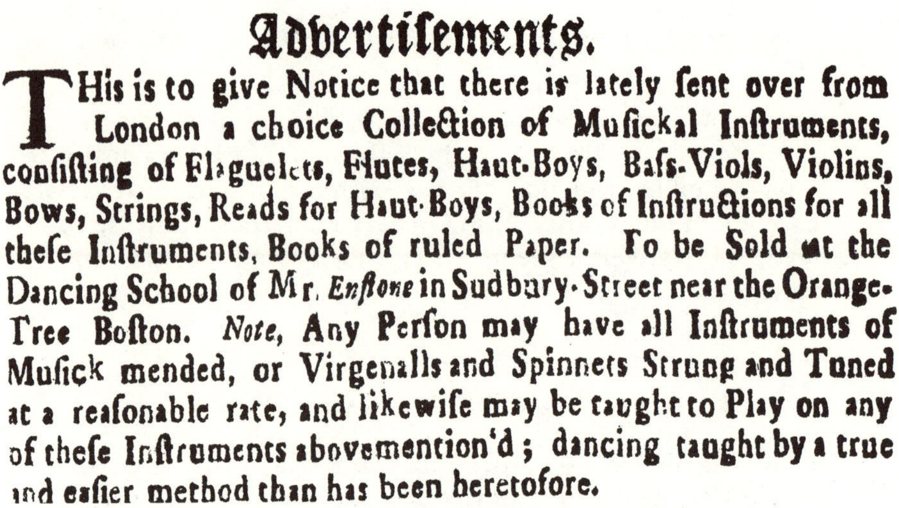

Advertisements.

THis is to give Notice that there is lately sent over from London a choice Collection of Musickal Instruments, consisting of Flaguelets, Flutes, Haut-Boys, Bass-Viols, Violins, Bows, Strings, Reads for Haut-Boys, Books of Instructions for all these Instruments, Books of ruled Paper. To be Sold at the Dancing School of Mr. *Enstone* in Sudbury-Street near the Orange-Tree Boston. *Note,* Any Person may have all Instruments of Musick mended, or Virgenalls and Spinnets Strung and Tuned at a reasonable rate, and likewise may be taught to Play on any of these Instruments abovemention'd ; dancing taught by a true and easier method than has been heretofore.

Figure 1. Advertisement by Edward Enstone, Sudbury Street, Boston. Boston News-Letter. Apr. 16, 1716. Typical of most eighteenth-century musicians, Enstone offers to sell musical goods and services and to teach music and dancing. (Courtesy, American Antiquarian Society)

lin—offered instruction in writing, cyphering, dancing, treble violin, flute, and spinet. In 1716 Edward Enstone listed himself as a music dealer and repairer and a teacher of instruments and dance (fig. 1). Enstone was attracted originally to this continent by the organist's position for the newly acquired instrument at King's Chapel, the Anglican church in Boston. As these advertisements from the Boston newspapers indicate, it was necessary from the beginning to combine various jobs to make a living.

The first known public concert in America was given in 1729 in Boston at a dancing school (very possibly Enstone's).[6] The participants, though not listed, were probably the few professional musicians like Enstone (and fellow organist and dancing instructor Peter Pelham) who combined forces with

[6] For more detail on this concert, see Cynthia Adams Hoover, "Secular Music in Early Massachusetts," in *Music in Colonial Massachusetts, 1630–1820: A Conference Held by the Colonial Society of Massachusetts, May 17 and 18, 1973,* 2 vols. (Boston, 1980–85), 2:802–4, and Henry Woodward, "February 18, 1729: A Neglected Date in Boston Concert Life," Music Library Association *Notes* 33 (1976):243–52.

Figure 2. Of the Theatre—Tuesday Club. *Attributed to Dr. Alexander Hamilton, Annapolis, c. 1745–56. The musicians in the orchestra appear to be playing a violoncello (or double bass), a violin, a bagpipe, and a bassoon. (Courtesy of the John Work Garrett Collection of The Johns Hopkins University Library)*

local gentlemen amateurs to make a workable ensemble, a performance practice common in England then and one that continues in small American communities today.[7] Particularly until after the Revolution, gentlemen amateurs joined with professionals and with musicians from military bands to make up the increasing number of concert and theatrical ensembles. One active group was the Tuesday Club of Annapolis, shown in a drawing made by Dr. Alexander Hamilton, one of its members, in the late 1740s (fig. 2). These men are thought to have been some of the "private gentlemen" who assisted with the first documented American performance—in 1752—of an opera accompanied by an orchestra.[8]

By the 1760s performances of instrumental and vocal music became available more frequently in the major towns—Philadelphia, New York, Boston, and Charleston—through subscriptions and membership in private clubs, though rarely by general admission.[9] Often the concerts sponsored by pri-

[7]For studies on the amateur tradition in England, see Neil Zaslaw, "The Compleat Orchestral Musician," *Early Music* 7 (1979): 46–57, and J. H. Plumb, *The Commercialisation of Leisure in Eighteenth-Century England* (Reading, 1973), p. 15.

[8]For more information about the Tuesday Club, see James Heintze, "Alexander Malcolm: Musician, Clergyman, and Schoolmaster," *Maryland Historical Magazine* 73 (1978): 226–35. The musical activity of several American gentleman amateurs is discussed in Cynthia Adams Hoover, "Instrumental Ensembles in Eighteenth-Century America" (Paper presented at the joint meetings of the Repertoire International d'Iconographie Musicale and the American Musical Instrument Society, Chicago, Apr. 1979).

[9]Sonneck, *Early Concert-Life*. For an analysis of Boston concerts, see Hoover, "Secular Music," pp. 802–27.

Figure 3. Sir Foplings Airs . . . *1710. Artist unknown, London? c. 1740. This example by an unknown artist shows, top to bottom, the tune of "Sir Foplings Airs," a fancy dress ball in progress, and the instructions for the dance. The instruments in the gallery include four strings, an oboe, and a bass. The illustration is very similar to the title page of the eighteenth edition of John Playford's* The Dancing Master *(London, c. 1728), a dance instruction book very popular in Great Britain and the colonies. (Courtesy, Winterthur Library: Joseph Downs Manuscript Collection, no. 63x71)*

For the Benefit of Mr. JOAN,
Will be performed,

A Grand CONCERT

Of VOCAL and INSTRUMENTAL MUSIC,
At Concert Hall, on Thursday the 1ſt of *March*,
To begin at Half after 6 o'Clock, P. M.
The Vocal Part, viz.

Two grand Choruſes for four Voices,
the Words well adapted to the preſent Times.
Two other excellent Songs.

TICKETS to be had of the Printers (at Half a
Dollar each) or of the ſaid JOAN, living at ſaid
Concert Hall, where he teaches the Violin, Ger-
man-Flute, and Baſſe Viol.

☞ ALL the Violins that ſhall be uſed in this
Concert, have been manufactured here by the ſaid
JOAN, who makes & ſells very cheap, Violins, Screw-
Bows and Caſes, Baſſe-Viols, &c. no ways inferior
to the beſt imported :—He alſo mends thoſe ſorts of
Inſtruments at a reaſonable Rate.

Figure 4. James Joan advertising a concert employing violins which he has made. Boston Evening Post, *Feb. 19, 1770. Mr. "Joan" arrived in Boston from Halifax in 1768. In 1770, when theater performances were not allowed in Boston, he "read" and sang all the parts from* The Beggar's Opera *and several other popular British theater pieces. Known also as James Juhan, he had settled in Virginia by 1787 as a maker of keyboard instruments. No instruments by Juhan (d. 1797) are known to survive.*

vate subscription were followed by dances where the wealthy could show off their training and their finery. The gatherings were not unlike that shown in "Sir Foplings Airs," an anonymous eighteenth-century watercolor (fig. 3). The performers in these events included the increasing number of immigrant musicians attracted by the promise of a decent living. Also arriving in the 1760s and 1770s were musical instrument

JOHN SHEYBLI,
ORGAN-BUILDER,
At Mr. Samuel Prince's, cabinet-maker, in Horse and
Cart-ftreet, New-York;

MAKES, repairs and tunes all forts of organs,
harpfichords, fpinnets and Fortepianoes, on the
moft reafonable terms.

N. B. He has now ready for fale, one neat chamber
organ, one hammer fpinnet, one common fpinnet.

Figure 5. Advertisement by John Sheybli, keyboard maker. New York
Gazette and the Weekly Mercury, *Oct. 17, 1774. This advertisement is one of the few showing the interior of an instrument maker's
workshop, which was apparently a portion of cabinetmaker Samuel
Prince's establishment. With the mention of "one hammer spinnet" for
sale, Sheybli may have published the earliest advertisement for a piano
completed by a maker in America. Of German stock, Sheybli (also
Sheiuble, Scheible, or Shively) was still making pianos and organs in
Lancaster County, Pennsylvania, at the time of his death in late
1792–early 1793.*

builders, the largest number of them German, with the English a close second. The expectations of these craftsmen for a
brisk trade were disappointed when their patrons turned
their attention to the revolt against Great Britain (figs. 4 and
5).[10] After the peace, the professors, builders, and performers

[10]A detailed study of the instrument trade is given in Cynthia Adams
Hoover, "The Manufacture and Sale of Musical Instruments in Eighteenth-

who began immigrating in the 1780s were successful enough to stay on to establish and dominate a healthy cosmopolitan musical tradition.

THE THEATER

Among those in the later wave of immigration were actors, actresses, and theater musicians recruited by managers who thought that at last there was support for the theater in America. Although stage productions were known in Williamsburg as early as 1716, in Charleston and New York by the 1730s, and in Philadelphia and Boston by the 1740s, few managers were able to establish a profitable, lasting company. The communities were still not large enough and, more importantly, the religious and moral opposition was too strong, although in times of war—such as the French and Indian War and the Revolution—"morals were loosened" and plays were staged for, and sometimes by, the visiting troops, who demanded the amusements they had become accustomed to in Europe.[11]

Despite laws to prevent theatrical entertainments, some itinerant troupes performed wherever they could find an audience, whether at a country fair probably not too different from one in York, Pennsylvania, in 1801 (fig. 6), in a converted warehouse as shown on the right in a 1749 rendition of Philadelphia (fig. 7), or in simple productions in modest theaters such as Southwark Theatre in Philadelphia or others in communities like Charleston and New York built in the 1760s and 1770s. But by the 1790s, with the building of handsome structures such as the Chestnut Street Theatre, which opened in Philadelphia in 1794 (fig. 8), and similar ones in New York and Boston, Americans made it clear that they would no longer be content to be deprived of their theatrical diversions.[12]

Century America" (Paper presented at the Third Annual Meeting of the Sonneck Society for American Music, Ann Arbor, Mich., Apr. 1978).

[11] Hoover, "Secular Music," pp. 836–44.

[12] For more details on the history of the theater in America, see William Dunlap, *History of the American Theatre* (1797; reprint ed., New York, 1963),

Figure 6. Yearly Market, or publick fare. Held in the Borough of York, June 9th 1801. *From Lewis Miller,* The Chronicle of York, 1799–1870. *Miller (1796–1882), folk artist and carpenter of York, Pennsylvania, recorded his memory of the entertainments at a public fair in York in 1801. By 1816 even these York fairs were prohibited because they caused "a common nuisance." George Washington is known to have attended in 1752 a theatrical performance by the traveling troupe of Keane and Murray at the June Fair in Fredericksburg, Virginia. (Courtesy of the Historical Society of York County, York, Pa.)*

The strong religious opposition to the theater came from Calvinist-oriented believers who knew, from their church fathers and from their own experience, how compelling was the

---

Julian Mates, *The American Musical Stage before 1800* (New Brunswick, N.J., 1962), Brooks McNamara, *The American Playhouse in the Eighteenth Century* (Cambridge, Mass., 1969), and Cynthia Adams Hoover, "Music in Eighteenth-Century American Theater," *American Music* 2 (1984):6–18.

Figure 7. William Plumstead's warehouse, the site of a theater in Philadelphia by 1749. Detail from George Heap and Nicholas Scull, An East Prospect of the City of Philadelphia *(1754). The English traveler the Rev. Andrew Burnaby wrote in 1760 of attending a performance in another makeshift theater in Upper Marlborough, Maryland, "a most neat, convenient tobacco-house, well-fitted for the purpose." (Courtesy, Winterthur Museum)*

power of music to move their hearts and control their senses.[13] The senses were not to be distracted, however, by "painted Strumpets" cutting capers on the stage or by frivolous lyrics, but were to be directed toward the contemplation of God through the singing of sacred texts.[14]

SINGING SCHOOLS: A VERNACULAR AND DEMOCRATIC TRADITION

Earlier in the century, several Puritan ministers in Boston, convinced that the power of the words was being weakened

[13]John Calvin, Foreword to the *Geneva Psalter* (1543), translated in Oliver Strunk, ed., *Source Readings in Music History*, 5 vols. (New York, 1965), 2:155–58, cited in Ruth Mack Wilson with the assistance of Kate Van Winkle Keller, *Connecticut's Music in the Revolutionary Era* (Hartford, 1979), pp. 13–14.

[14]*The American Magazine and Historical Chronicle* 3 (1746):356, quoted in full in Hoover, "Secular Music," p. 837.

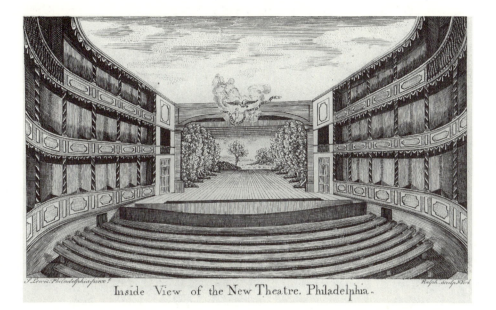

Inside View of the New Theatre. Philadelphia.

Figure 8. Inside view of the New Theatre, Chestnut Street Theatre, Philadelphia. New York Magazine, *April 1794. Engraved by J. Lewis. The elegant "New Theatre" in Philadelphia was highly praised by foreign and American visitors. Said to accommodate 1,155 patrons in the boxes and the pit, it had a total depth of 134 feet, a stage 71 feet deep and 36 feet wide at the apron, fitted with the usual five wings of scenery, and an orchestra pit that could hold thirty musicians in two rows facing each other. (Courtesy of the Cooper-Hewitt Museum, Smithsonian Institution/Art Resource, New York)*

by the low state to which congregational singing had fallen, set about to improve the "Jarrs & Discords" and "Howling" by teaching note reading and rudiments of music at singing schools.[15] It was, as Thomas Clap, president of Yale, maintained, "the duty of all persons to sing," and all who were "not idiots may learn to Read, or to Cypher" and to "learn to sing by Rule."[16] Thus, in New England and in other communities

[15] McKay and Crawford, *William Billings,* pp. 9–20; Alan Buechner, "Yankee Singing Schools and the Golden Age of Choral Music in New England, 1760–1800," Ph.D. diss., Harvard University, 1960.

[16] "Some Considerations Tending to Put an End to the Differences That Have Been about Singing," Beinecke Rare Book and Manuscript Library, Yale University, New Haven, cited in Wilson, *Connecticut's Music,* pp. 10–11.

Mr. L A W,

HAS OPENED A

Singing School,

In Mr. PAYNE's SCHOOL-ROOM, oppofite to the Rev. Mr. POPKINS's Meeting-Houfe,
two Evenings in the week—to wit :

TUESDAY and FRIDAY,

From fix o'clock till nine.

The terms are, Four Dollars per quarter ; Two Dollars to be paid at the time of entrance, and the other Two at the expiration of the Quarter.

Ladies and Gentlemen, defirous of placing themfelves or their children, under his Tuition, are refpectfully folicited to apply for entrance as foon as convenient.

If any Ladies prefer being taught in their own houfes, and will form into Societies for that purpofe, he will wait on them at fuch hours in the day as fhall be moft agreeable, provided they do not interfere with his Evening Schools.

Figure 9. Announcement by Andrew Law, Boston, c. 1805. This is a rare example of a broadside advertising a New England singing school. Classes were offered not only to children in the schoolroom but also to adults (especially ladies) in their own houses. Andrew Law (1749–1821) was very influential not only through his established singing schools in New England, Philadelphia, New York, and Charleston, but also through his pupils who taught in rural Maryland, Virginia, and the Carolinas and who used his many tunebook compilations and music primers. (Courtesy, American Antiquarian Society)

influenced by this religious outlook, music was to be learned and performed by everyone.

From the lively accounts of these singing schools, students from all levels of society gathered to learn to sing. Advertisements mention separate classes for children and youth (young ladies and gentlemen over age twelve) with the addition sometimes of "some old scattered singers," as the Rev. William Bentley noted in his Salem diary.[17] Rosters show the presence of students from the leading families of the community sitting next to a ropemaker, shipwright, baker, miner, cooper,

---

[17] *The Diary of William Bentley, D. D., Pastor of the East Church, Salem, Massachusetts,* 4 vols. (1905–14; reprint ed., Gloucester, Mass., 1962), 1:337, cited in Buechner, "Yankee Singing Schools," p. 174.

farmer, or boatbuilder.[18] Classes usually were held in school-rooms or taverns during the winter on one, two, or three nights a week, with as many as sixty students.[19] The classes were advertised through newspapers, announcements in churches and schools, and broadsides (fig. 9). Students at Yale found scholarly life bearable when they knew they could look forward to the weekly singing meeting, which they attended not only to make music but also to indulge, as one student wrote, "in some of the carnal Delights of the Flesh, such as kissing, squeezing, &c. &c."[20]

After midcentury, with the importation of English tune-books containing more elaborate music with imitative "fugu-ing" sections, the singers became more expert and began demanding to sit together in church. Not without contro-versy, special choirs began to appear after the mid-1760s, of-ten seated in the church gallery (fig. 10) and led by the singing master or one of their own group, as shown in the title page of Oliver Brownson's collection of 1783 (fig. 11). Later, players of the flute, clarinet, violin, and bass viol—taught in classes open to all—were known to join the singers in the gallery.[21] Thus, even within this tradition based on democratic principles, a hierarchy of prestige created through musical experience was emerging.

THE RISE AND FALL
OF THE YANKEE TUNESMITHS

The success of the schools and the spread of musical literacy created a demand for more tunes and more teachers. Many students, with no more training than a term of singing school, began to compose and advertise their own classes. According to statistics compiled by Richard Crawford, between 1770 and about 1790 there were hundreds of new sacred pieces com-posed by native-born psalmodists, engraved and published by

[18] Ibid., p. 176.

[19] Ibid., pp. 126–250

[20] Simeon E. Baldwin, *Life and Letters of Simeon Baldwin* (New Haven, 1919), p. 56, cited in Wilson, *Connecticut's Music*, p. 91.

[21] Buechner, "Yankee Singing Schools," pp. 277–87.

Figure 10. Title page from Oliver Brownson's Select Harmony *(Boston, 1783). The gallery choir, composed of women (left) and men (right), distanced itself from the congregation both through its musical expertise and its physical location. Brownson (1746–1815), active in Connecticut and New York state, included in* Select Harmony *compositions by British and American composers. (Courtesy, Library of Congress)*

Figure 11. Detail of fig. 10 showing singer with pitch pipe. The leader of the singers is shown using a small wooden pitch pipe, one of the first instruments to be allowed in the New England churches. Some pitch pipes were made in the size and shape of a tune book, the better to disguise their presence during the service.

themselves or by their local printer, and distributed to the singing school circuit.[22] It was a heady time. Over 300 psalm composers are known to have been active, some at a very young age.[23] At age seventeen, for example, Timothy Swan is said to have written his tune "Montague," a piece that became and remains one of the more popular tunes of the repertory.[24]

It was during this period that William Billings wrote and published most of his compositions. These were done in a lively style not confined, as he wrote, "to any Rules for Composition . . . ; it is best for every *Composer* to be his own *Carver.*"[25] His collections of choral works appealed to a wide audience. His first, *The New-England Psalm-Singer,* published in 1770 when he was twenty-four, was intended for Americans for liturgical and educational use (the choice of the words "New-England" in 1770 for patriot Billings was no accident). *The Singing Master's Assistant* (1778) includes material directed especially to the singing school; *The Psalm-Singer's Amusement* (1781) aimed more at concert and recreational singing (fig. 12).

Tunebook compilation was another occupation that emerged at this time to meet the demand for more music, with early compilers guided more by personal preference and public taste than by ecclesiastical authority in their selection of tunes.[26] By the 1790s, however, taste had changed and another reform had set in. The influx of many "good, musical

[22]McKay and Crawford, *William Billings*, pp. 21–24; Richard A. Crawford, ed., *The Core Repertory of Early American Psalmody* (Madison, Wis., 1984), and idem, "Connecticut Sacred Music Imprints, 1778–1810," *Notes* 27 (1971):445–52, 671–79.

[23]The estimate of the number of psalmodists is fromNym Cooke, whose dissertation ("American Psalmodists in Contact and Collaboration, 1770–1820," University of Michigan, 1990), provides much information on the activity of American psalmody.

[24]Crawford, *Core Repertory*, pp. xiv, 93–95.

[25]From the section "To All Musical Practitioners," in William Billings's Introduction to *The New-England Psalm-Singer*, available in a modern critical edition, Karl Kroeger et al., eds., *The Complete Works of William Billings*, 4 vols. (Charlottesville, Va., 1977–90), 1:32.

[26]McKay and Crawford, *William Billings*, p. 23.

Figure 12. Title page of William Billings's The Psalm-Singer's Amusement *(Boston, 1781). Engraved by John Norman, this title page shows a leader with a pitch pipe (center) and, at the corners, four different groups in what appear to be secular settings. Two of the groups are playing flutes and strings. The well-dressed ladies at the upper left seem to be spectators rather than performers.*

emigrants . . . daily seeking asylum in this country" caused many compilers, singers, and native psalmodists to question the indigenous musical style and to turn to compositional techniques and actual tunes from European sources.[27] The publishers' doors were no longer open to the American style. Billings's star fell as the "good taste" of European fashion gained control of America's sacred and secular music.

GOOD TASTE AND THE CULTIVATED TRADITION

Good taste dictated the acquisition of certain social graces and ornamental skills. In a family seeking acceptance in polite

[27] From *The Massachusetts Compiler of Theoretical and Practical Elements of Sacred Vocal Music . . . Chiefly Selected or Adapted from Modern European Publications,* compiled by immigrant Hans Gram and Americans Samuel Holyoke and Oliver Holden (Boston, 1795), p. [iii], cited in McKay and Crawford, *William Billings,* p. 29.

society, an educated woman was one accomplished in "needle-work, embroidery, drawing, music, dancing, dress, polite-ness" (fig. 13).[28] Courtesy books, which contained advice on education and etiquette and circulated widely in Britain and America, claimed that training for polite society "refines the Taste, polishes the Mind" and would preserve a woman "from the Rust of Idleness, the most pernicious Enemy to Virtue."[29] Women usually studied singing, English guitar (fig. 14), and keyboard instruments.

Young men were encouraged to acquire, in moderation, the skills of dancing (which taught "good Behaviour & decent Carriage"), drawing, and music.[30] They usually studied the violin or German flute (fig. 15). Too much interest in music could, as one observer wrote, "induce a suspicion of attention to this art, to the neglect of others."[31] But the courtesy books made it clear that more serious studies (that is, those that in-cluded Latin, Greek, mathematics, and history) were to come first. The ornaments for a man were, as one writer put it, mainly for "modish Address and a female Entertainment. Let a Man rather trim up his Mind, than his Body: Those Embellishments are more *noble* and *rich* that lie in the Brain,

[28]John Bennett, *Letters to a Young Lady,* first published in London in the early 1790s and then in Hartford by 1791, Newburyport by 1792, and in Philadelphia, New York, and Worcester before the decade was over, cited in Judith Tick, *American Women Composers before 1870* (Ann Arbor, Mich., 1983), p. 13. For the Isaiah Thomas version, see Clifford K. Shipton, ed., *Early American Imprints, 1639–1800* (microcard; Worcester, Mass., 1955–68), no. 33403.

[29]John Essex, *The Young Ladies' Conduct; or, Rules for Education, under Several Heads: With Instructions upon Dress, Both before and after Marriage, and Advice to Young Wives* (London, 1722), p. 85, cited in Richard D. Leppert, "Men, Women, and Music at Home: The Influence of Cultual Values on Musical Life in Eighteenth-Century England," *Imago Musicae* 2 (1985):83.

[30][Increase Mather et al.], *An Arrow against Profane and Promiscuous Dancing, Drawn Out of the Quiver of the Scriptures* (Boston, 1684 [probably 1686]), pp. 24–25, cited in Hoover, "Secular Music," p. 731.

[31]Hugh Henry Brackenridge, *Modern Chivalry,* 6 vols. (Philadelphia, 1792–1805), 2:56–57, cited in Nicholas E. Tawa, "Secular Music in the Late-Eighteenth-Century American Home," *Musical Quarterly* 61 (1975):514–15.

than those that sink into the Feet, or *perch* on the Finger's End."[32]

Throughout the century Americans viewed cultural embellishments with ambivalence. The arts, especially theater, were considered a threat to religion, morals, industry, and frugality, and were thought to encourage idleness, effeminacy, dissipation, and false gentility.[33] With the rise of a new nation they could become a threat to the republic and democracy, as many questioned how they could seek refinement without some cost to social equality.[34] For many then and now, the arts could be justified only if they could serve a useful purpose. Benjamin Rush could approve of singing, for example, because it was good for civilizing the mind and clearing the lungs.[35] Noah Webster considered music, because of its influence on the human mind, "an article of education, *useful* as well as ornamental."[36]

Other leading citizens, especially those removed geographically and by religion from pervading Puritan influences, were more relaxed about supporting the arts. Thomas Jefferson felt no constraint in calling music "the favorite passion" of his soul,[37] and George Washington found nothing "more agreeable and ornamental, than good music."[38] As they mingled with new company both here and abroad, provincial leaders who had formerly given them little thought saw how useful social graces and ornaments could be. This was especially true of New Englanders like John Adams who, once critical of airs

[32] William Darrell, *A Gentleman Instructed in the Conduct of a Virtuous and Happy Life* (London, 1704), cited in Leppert, "Music at Home," p. 72.

[33] Silverman, *Cultural History of the Revolution,* pp. 512, 545.

[34] Ibid., pp. 546–49.

[35] "On the Mode of Education Proper in a Republic" (1784), Dagobert D. Runes, ed., *The Selected Writings of Benjamin Rush* (New York, 1947), p. 92, cited in Silverman, *Cultural History of the Revolution,* p. 477.

[36] From an article attributed to Noah Webster, "On Music," *American Magazine* (June 1788):448, cited in Wilson, *Connecticut's Music,* pp. 95–96.

[37] Thomas Jefferson to an anonymous friend, June 8, 1778, cited in Sonneck, *Suum Cuique,* pp. 54–55.

[38] Judith S. Britt, *Nothing More Agreeable: Music in George Washington's Family* (Mount Vernon, Va., 1984), p. 101.

Figure 13. Harpsichord Recital at Count Rumford's, Concord, New Hampshire. *Benjamin Thompson (Count Rumford), c. 1800. The young lady seated at the left is playing what appears to be a two-manual harpsichord made by Baker Harris of London. It is possible that the seated young lady on the right is singing. Diaries and travel accounts of the period often mention informal musical performances by the women of the household following dinner or during tea. (Courtesy of the National Gallery of Art, Washington, D.C. Gift of Edgar William and Bernice Chrysler Garbisch)*

Figure 14. Julia Stockton *(Mrs. Benjamin Rush). Charles Willson Peale, Philadelphia, 1776. The English guitar appears in several portraits of American women, especially those from Pennsylvania (including Moravian count von Zinzendorf's daughter) and areas south. The instruments, fitted with ten wire strings arranged in pairs, were imported from England and were relatively easy to learn to play. Benjamin Rush, who married Julia Stockton in 1776 about the time this portrait was finished, in a letter to Lady Jane Belsch (Apr. 21, 1784) praised his wife for her beauty, temper, prudence, understanding, and excellent accomplishments. He confided that Julia, fourteen years younger than Rush, had won his heart through her singing of the song "The Birks of Endermay." (Courtesy, Winterthur Museum)*

Figure 15. Dr. Abraham Beekman. *Lawrence Kilburn, New York, c. 1761. Although trained as a physician, Beekman (1729–89) chose to portray himself at age thirty-two with a flute and an architectural column, symbols of leisure time and affluence. (Courtesy of the New-York Historical Society, New York City)*

and what he considered the frivolities of the social set, traveled in 1774 in a coach and four from Boston to the Continental Congress in Philadelphia. There he learned to admire the artistic talents of men such as Francis Hopkinson, and commented frequently in his letters and diary on the lack of these graces in his own life.[39] His children and their generation, with more leisure time, insisted that there be increased opportunities to enjoy the arts in America. An advocate of the theater in Boston reflected the attitude of this new generation when he wrote in 1792 that "head-work is now in more repute than hand-work and ease will not be exchanged for toil."[40]

OVERLAPPING OF VERNACULAR
AND CULTIVATED TRADITIONS

Even those who did "hand-work" sought more access to these pleasures. Certainly the working class frolicked at weddings (fig. 16), ship launchings,[41] quilting parties (fig. 17), and in taverns,[42] where they could share amusements with others. Especially in the South, they would have encountered the dancing and music of the slaves, such as the group of black musicians on a South Carolina plantation about 1800 shown in figure 18. Working people sang hymn tunes at the forge or

[39] For more on the spread of gentility, see Richard L. Bushman, "American High-Style and Vernacular Cultures," in Jack P. Greene and J. R. Pole, eds., *Colonial British America: Essays in the New History of the Early Modern Era* (Baltimore, 1984), pp. 345–83, esp. pp. 359–60. See also John Adams's advice on the education of his children and his reaction to meeting Francis Hopkinson (John Adams to Abigail Adams, Aug. 21, 1776, Lyman H. Butterfield, ed., *Adams Family Correspondence*, 4 vols. to date [Cambridge, Mass., 1963-], 1:104).

[40] William Haliburton, *Effects of the Stage on the Manners* (Boston, 1792), p.8 (Shipton, ed., *Early American Imprints*, no. 24371).

[41] John Adams describes a lively tavern celebration following a launching on Nov. 25, 1760. See Lyman H. Butterfield, ed., *Diary and Autobiography of John Adams*, 4 vols. (Cambridge, Mass., 1961), 1:172–73.

[42] "Extracts from Captain Francis Goelet's Journal," *New England Historical and Genealogical Register* 24 (1870):53, cited in Hoover, "Secular Music," p. 758.

Figure 16. The Wedding. *Artist unknown, American, c. 1805. The flute player at the left appears to be preparing to play for the dancing festivities to follow the wedding ceremony. (Courtesy of the Edgar William and Bernice Chrysler Garbisch Collection, Philadelphia Museum of Art)*

in the field and ballads on the street. Parades to mark important events included music by bands with British-trained players not unlike these shown in a London engraving of 1753 (fig. 19), or those from the local community, such as the ensemble marching in York, Pennsylvania, in 1799, in a funeral parade to honor George Washington (fig. 20). But the working classes wanted more. They especially wanted the theater, where all who could pay the price of the ticket could attend. A notice from a "mechanick" in a 1792 Boston newspaper gives one explanation for this: "From my situation in life, I am *virtually* debared from any of the *common amusements* of this town—I cannot attend the CONCERTS, ASSEMBLIES, OR CARD-PARTIES—I do not say, that their regulations exclude *mechanicks;* but then the *distance* that is always observed by those

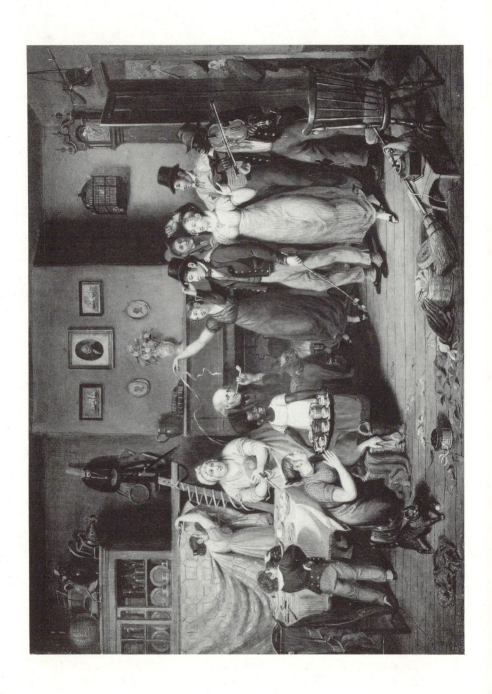

Figure 18. The Old Plantation. *Artist unknown, c. 1800. With the plantation in the background, the slaves, dressed in late eighteenth-century clothing, dance to instruments from Africa—a plucked string instrument (perhaps a molo) and possible precursor of the banjo, and a drum similar to the Yoruba dudugudu. Found in Columbia, South Carolina, this watercolor is thought to have been painted on a plantation between Charleston and Orangeburg. It was executed on paper with a watermark used by English papermaker James Whatman, Jr., between 1777 and 1794. (Courtesy of the Abby Aldrich Rockefeller Folk Art Center, Williamsburg)*

Figure 17. The Quilting Frolic. *John Lewis Krimmel, Pennsylvania, 1813. The group on the right (or perhaps just the men) seem to have arrived with a black fiddler who would play for the entertainment and dancing once those at the left moved their quilting materials and frame. Black fiddlers are known to have played for many occasions in eighteenth- and nineteenth-century America. (Courtesy, Winterthur Museum)*

Figure 19. A detail showing a Harmoniemusik *ensemble from* A View of Royal Building for the Majesty's Horse & Foot Guards. *Artist unknown, hand-colored engraving (London, 1753). Several British military bands arriving in America in the 1760s became the nucleus for concert activity before the Revolution. The eight musicians seem to be playing the typical grouping for bands at the time: two horns, two bassoons, two oboes, and two clarinets (not clearly shown). (Courtesy of the Raoul and Amy Camus Collection, Whitestone, N.Y.)*

who move in the higher sphere, and the *mortification* which I and my family must inevitably undergo, if we were with them, exclude us as much as if there was a solemn *act* of exclusion."[43]

Once established, the theater attracted an audience that included ladies and their beaux who came to be seen in the boxes, the "lewd leer of the pit"—a mix of local and visiting gentlemen and military officers who could be expected to be

[43]*Columbian Centinel,* Dec. 8, 1792.

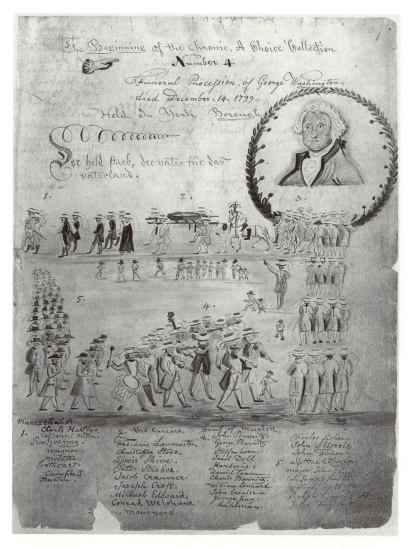

Figure 20. Funeral Procession of George Washington, died December 14, 1799 . . . Held In York Borough. *From Lewis Miller,* The Chronicle of York, 1799–1870. *This provincial band is not typical of the marching bands of the period with its several violins, about five flutes, and a double bass or violoncello. Miller lists the names of the band members at the bottom, under "band of Musick"; several of these appear in his other illustrations as brewers and other local townsmen. (Courtesy of the Historical Society of York County, York, Pa.)*

335

greeted by harlots at the pit entrances,[44] and the seamen, servants, and working classes in the balcony, where, as Washington Irving wrote, the gallery gods created a noise not unlike Noah's ark in their "imitation of the whistles and yells of every kind of animal."[45] To avoid flying missiles and riots, managers often had to acquiesce to the shouted requests from the gallery for tunes like *Roast Beef* or *Moll in the Wad,* or politically charged favorites like *The Marseilles* or *Yankee Doodle.*[46] The entrepreneurs scheduled many of the latest plays from London but, in order to attract working-class audiences, they frequently had to follow one of the operating principles of the famous London actor-manager David Garrick: "If you won't come to Lear and Hamlet, I must give you Harlequin."[47] And Harlequin it was, often danced by John Durang, along with William Dunlap, one of the few native-born performers allowed to join the European professionals who dominated the concert and theatrical scene. Programs also included entr'actes, songs, dances (much as Durang's hornpipe shown in figure 21), ropewalkers, and even the circus, the most famous being Rickett's Circus.

THE RISE OF MUSIC TRADES

The opening of major theaters was a further attraction to musical immigrants. With them came a core of trained musicians who began to establish America's musical professions: teachers, composers, performers, music publishers and distributors, managers, critics, and makers and sellers of musical

[44]Reference to the harlots is found in a verse printed in the *Freeman's Journal; or, the North-American Intelligencer,* Mar. 10, 1784, cited in Silverman, *Cultural History of the Revolution,* pp. 546–47.

[45]*Letters of Jonathan Oldstyle* (1824; reprint ed., New York, 1941), p. 18. Margaretta M. Lovell has suggested that the social hierarchy of seating at the theater reinforced and even replaced the ebbing power of church seating that had previously established community social structures.

[46]Irving Lowens, "Benjamin Carr's Federal Overture (1794)," in Lowens, *Music and Musicians,* pp. 89–114; Hoover, "Secular Music," pp. 855–56.

[47]Quoted by Anne Dhu Shapiro in "Action Music in American Pantomime and Melodrama, 1730–1913," *American Music* 2 (1984):50.

Figure 21. John Durang's Hornpipe. *John Durang, Pennsylvania, c. 1816. John Durang (1785–1816) painted this depiction of his appearance on stage performing the hornpipe for inclusion in his memoirs, which describe in lively detail his growing up in York and Philadelphia and his life as a minor character in the American theater and circus. (Courtesy of the Historical Society of York County, York, Pa.)*

goods.[48] Much work remains to be done in documenting America's musical trades, but a few observations can be made. Teaching served as a major source of support. Upon ar-

[48]These professional roles (except for managers) were singled out by Richard A. Crawford in his 1985 University of California Bloch lectures (*The American Musical Landscape* [Berkeley, 1993], chap. 2).

rival, most musicians announced their availability as teachers in addition to other offerings. Or they were attracted by musical positions. An organist, for example, might be paid £50 a year for his services and could earn two or three times that amount for private music instruction.[49] A prestigious professor like Alexander Reinagle, who was a leading composer, musical director of the Chestnut Street Theatre, and teacher of young ladies like Nelly Custis, commanded fees that were similar to those charged in London. Reinagle was making the "considerable sums of money" mentioned by Benjamin Rush.[50] Teachers offering both private lessons and psalmody spent a good deal of time traveling from one house to another in the city or from one plantation or community to another

[49]The organist's position itself at St. Philip's Church in Charleston in 1753 offered a salary of £50 and assured the candidate between 100 to 150 guineas per years for teaching harpsichord and spinet and an additonal 30 to 40 guineas for concerts of music to the "Gentlemen and Ladies of the Place." George Hartley, organist at St. Michael's in Charleston, was dismissed in 1776 because of his loyalist sympathies. His claims for compensation for lost earnings included £150 for his salary as organist, £80 as harpsichordist with the orchestra of the St. Cecilia Society, and £300 for his private music teaching (cited in Norman Benson, "The Itinerant Dancing and Music Masters of Eighteenth-Century America," Ph.D. diss., University of Minnesota, 1963, pp. 137–39, 167. Also discussed in Crawford, "Professions and Patronage," pp. 6–7).

[50]Although more information is needed to reconstruct Reinagle's total earnings from teaching, extant account book notations can give us some indication of his teaching income. In November 1790, he received £13.10 for three months of lessons for the Misses C. and N. Norton of Virginia (Francis Norton Mason, *John Norton & Sons, Merchants of London and Virginia* [Richmond, 1937], p. 501). The Washington accounts show the following payments to Reinagle: June 26, 1789—"Entrance money to instruct Miss Custis on the Piano Forte," £2.8.0; Oct. 16, 1789—"for teaching Miss Custis Music & furnishing books," £17; July 7, 1792—"pd. Mr. Reinagle on acct. of Miss Custis," $19 (cited in Robert Stevenson, "The Music That George Washington Knew: Neglected Phases," *Inter-American Music Review* 5 [1982]:41–42). The English scene is well documented in Richard D. Leppert's excellent article "Music Teachers of Upper-Class Amateur Musicians in Eighteenth-Century England," in Allan W. Atlas, ed., *Music in the Classic Period: Essays in Honor of Barry S. Brook* (New York, 1985), pp. 133–58.

in the country, and giving lessons at "any hour or any place," as one advertisement put it.[51]

Usually students were young men and women with enough time for lessons and practice and enough money to purchase expensive instruments such as the violin, harpsichord, or pianoforte. As more people aspired to be accepted socially, older gentlemen and ladies were offered classes in dancing, advertised to be held in "Utmost Secrecy" until the students were "capable of exhibiting in high Taste."[52] A typical weekly schedule for a young lady in New York acquiring the social graces was "four days to dancing school—three to drawing and . . . a music lesson three times a week." The latter was sometimes scheduled before breakfast so the music teacher, in this case another leading immigrant, James Hewitt, could move on to composing, rehearsing his new music at the Park Street Theatre, and publishing other music.[53]

Musical scores were acquired through copying by the teacher, by a hired copyist, or by the student, as the portrait of Catherine Browne of New York suggests (fig. 22).[54] Music

[51] Benson, "Itinerant Dancing and Music Masters," documents the activities of numerous itinerant musicians. One of them, P. Gaujean, offered to teach violin and German flute in Charleston "at any hour or any place, that may be appointed" (*South Carolina Gazette*, July 15, 1799).

[52] The *Boston Evening Post* (May 23, 30, June 6, 1774) includes dancing instructor William Turner's advertisement that ends with the following: "Mr Turner will attend two Days in the Week at any House from 6 o'clock in the Evening on grown Gentlemen and Ladies, & assures the utmost Secrecy shall be kept till they are capable of exhibiting in high Taste" (cited in *Music in Colonial Massachusetts*, Appendix C: "Music Masters in Colonial Boston," comp. Barbara Lambert, 2:1070).

[53] Harriet and Maria Trumbull, daughters of the governor of Connecticut, Jonathan Trumbull, Jr., spent three months in New York learning social graces and ornamental skills. Their letters to their parents are annotated and published in Helen M. Morgan, *A Season in New York, 1801: Letters of Harriet and Maria Trumbull* (Pittsburgh, 1969). Their weekly schedule is described in a letter from Maria dated Mar. 5, 1801, pp. 131–32. The activities of James Hewitt are summarized in John W. Wagner, "James Hewitt, 1770–1827," *Musical Quarterly* 58 (1972):259–76.

[54] A discussion of the manuscript music copied by Reinagle and Nelly Custis is found in Britt, *Nothing More Agreeable*, pp. 30–52. John Gualdo in

Figure 22. Catherine Browne. *Artist unknown, American?*
1800–1810. The subject sits in front of a harpsichord as she writes in
her book. Surviving music manuscripts bound in handsome leather
bindings attest to the frequent copying of music by students. The li-
brary of Nelly Custis includes impressive examples. (Courtesy, Winter-
thur Museum)

Figure 23. Trade card of Lewis Deblois, Boston, 1757. Engraved by Thomas Johnston. The Deblois family was involved with music and general trade in Boston from the late 1720s until the Revolution. For a time Gilbert and Lewis Deblois had their shop, Crown and Comb, on the ground floor of Concert Hall, which they opened in 1754. (Courtesy, Winterthur Library: Joseph Downs Manuscript Collection, no. 66x152)

published in Europe could be purchased from dealers, both those who sold a variety of goods (fig. 23) and those who specialized in musical items (fig. 24). Patrons could join circulating libraries that provided music on loan for three, six, or

---

Philadelphia offered a variety of musical services, including "in his house a German Gentleman, who teaches to play on the violin, violoncello and French horn, at Twenty Shillings per month—Likewise he has a servant boy who copies music; therefore if any gentleman or lady should want a particular song, sonata, trio, duet, solo, minuet or country dance, they may be supplied with [it], without buying the whole book, in which such song,

Imp ried, and to be fold by
MICHAEL HILLEGAS.

At his House in Second-ftreet, between Arch and Race ftreets,

A NEAT Affortment of Mufic and Mufical Inftruments. amongft which are, Solo's by Tartini, Hafs, Nofen, Alberti, Vincent, Carter, Miller, Ballicourt, Teffarini, Reed, Stanley, Viaci, Cervetto, Davis, Quantz, Martini, Wedeman, Helkendaal, Pepufh, Triemer, Woolzka, &c. Concerto's by Corelli, Stanley, Depuis, Avifon, Humphreys, Teffarini, Alcock, Fefting, Handel, Vivaldi, &c. Sonata's by Boyce, Ruge, Price, Burney, Ca ter, Fifher, Ferigo, Teffarini, Flackton, Hafs, Bates, Quants, Retzel, Benegger, B zozsi, Albinoni, Graun, Martini, Fritz, Baibella, Humphreys, Richter, Stamitz, Kieinecht, Lanpugnuni, Pafquali, M'Gibbon, &c. Duetts by Teffarini, Dottel, Gerard, Weidemen, Stechwey, Battino, Bates, Campioni, Claget, Martini, Agzell, Fefting, Noteri, Dottel, Fiylio, Diragini, &c. Voluntaries by Stanley, Walond, and Berg.-----La zetti's Solo's and Cervetto's Leffons for Violoncello. Noteri So'o, Shuman's Leffons; Mifs Stevenfon's Songs, &c. &c. for Guittar. Lessons by Kunzen, Purcel, Scarlatti, Handel, Smith, Barbandt, with Stanley's Concerto's, Haffe's Sonata's, Berg's Sonatina's, &c. for Harpfichord. The a'mired Clio and Euterpe, in 2 Vols. Apollo's Cabinet in 2 Vols. The Comic Tunes in Harlequin China, Harlequin Soccer, Queen Mab, Fair Fortunatus; great Variety of Song Books, Englifh and Italian, neweft Sheet Songs; Artaxe xes a new Opera, Beggar's Opera, with Mufic, in Quarto, the beft Edition ever publifhed; Opera of Eliza, Pafquali's Thorough Bafs, and Art of Fingering; Variety of Books of Minuets, Hornpipes, Dances, Marches, &c. Tutors for Violin, Harpfichord, Guittar, German Flute, Common Flute, &c. &c. together with a very large Variety of Violins of all Prices, fome of which made by the beft Hands in Europe, Spinnets, Violoncellos, little Violins, Kitts, Violin d'Amours, Pfalters, Guittars, great Variety of German Flutes, Common Flutes, Hautboys, Clarinets, Welch Harp, Monochords, Mutes or Sardines, Rozin, Boxes, Spinnet Hammers, Pritchers, Violin Cafes, Hautboy Reeds, a large Parcel of Guittar and Harpfichord Wire, Violin and Violoncello Strings; ruling Pens, ruled Paper, ruled Books, Violin Bows, Violin Bridges, &c. &c.   6 W.

N. B. The afcemed Cannon-ftoves are yet fold by him.

Figure 24. Advertisement for Michael Hillegas. Pennsylvania Gazette, *Jan. 5, 1764. This advertisement offers a wide variety of music and instruments for sale and is a valuable document of what Philadelphians had available to them before the Revolution. Michael Hillegas, a successful businessman who in 1777 became treasurer of the United States, ran the music shop from his home on Second Street from 1759 until the mid-1770s.*

Figure 25. Trade card for James Harrison, New York, c. 1793.
Based on a European model, Harrison and others like James Hewitt
offered musicians an opportunity to rent expensive and scarce music
from their collections of more than 1,000 pieces. It is thought that
many rented the music long enough to copy it in their manuscript
books. (Courtesy, American Antiquarian Society)

---

sonata, &c., might be printed—He adopts and composes music for every
kind of instrument, as usual" (*Pennsylvania Chronicle*, Feb. 8, 1769). In
Charleston Mr. Garnet of the West and Bignall theatrical troupe offered to
give lessons, tune harpsichords and pianos, and provide "music neatly copied or taken from the voice, and adapted for any instrument" (*Charleston
City Gazette*, Feb.14, 1794).

Figure 26. New-Plymouth *by William Billings. Printed typographically by Isaiah Thomas in* The Continental Harmony *(Boston, 1794). Typeset music is characterized by the distinct break in the staff lines between note clusters. The typical pithy style of William Billings can be seen in the comment at the bottom of the page.*

twelve months (fig. 25).[55] From the 1760s, engraved, oblong psalm books printed in America became readily available. In 1786 Isaiah Thomas, the successful Worcester printer, began using movable music type, which allowed sacred tunebooks to be produced more cheaply and to be distributed through the printer's already-established network of dealers (fig. 26).[56] Large, engraved sheets of the latest theater tunes or keyboard compositions (fig. 27), directed toward a cosmopolitan and wealthy audience, began to be published here in the late

[55] Richard J. Wolfe, *Early American Music Engraving and Printing* (Urbana, Ill., 1980), discusses musical circulating libraries (pp. 227–29) and illustrates two trade cards advertising circulating libraries (illustrations 5 and 6).

[56] See Richard A. Crawford and D. W. Krummel, "Early American Music Printing and Publishing," in William L. Joyce et al., eds., *Printing and Society in Early America* (Worcester, Mass., 1983), pp. 195–99, 215–21.

Figure 27. The Twins of Latona. *Sheet music issued by James Hewitt, New York, c. 1800. This piece is from the popular opera* The Poor Soldier. *The engraver indicated orchestral accompaniment by the insertion of the word* Horns *at the beginning. The quality of the engraving is not first-rate; note the unevenness of the letters in the song title and the insertion of a word above a line. (Courtesy, Library of Congress)*

1780s, with advice from musicians such as Reinagle, who possibly even provided the engraving tools.[57]

Until late in the century, most instruments were imported through dealers, or in the case of such people as Jefferson and Francis Hopkinson, through first-hand negotiations with

[57] Ibid., pp. 199–215; Wolfe, *Music Engraving and Printing*, pp. 41–42, 113–20.

345

Figure 28. Violin made by John Antes, Bethlehem, Pa., 1759. Pennsylvania-born John Antes (1740–1811) made at least seven string instruments while living in the Bethlehem Moravian community. By 1764 he had left Pennsylvania to spend the rest of his life as a missionary and sometime composer in Germany, Egypt, and England. (Courtesy of the Moravian Historical Society, Nazareth, Pa.)

346

Figure 29. Spinet made by Samuel Blyth, Salem, Mass., 1786. Blyth (1744–95) built only one musical instrument, this spinet based on English models for the daughter of Mrs. Margaret Barton in 1786 for the price of £18. Spending his entire life in Salem, Blyth ran a boarding school for girls, was a painter of ships, carriages, carpets, and cannisters, made Venetian blinds, and on occasion played the organ for St. Peter's Church between 1766 and 1783. (Courtesy of the Essex Institute, Salem, Mass.)

leading London builders.[58] Although many makers advertised their services, few instruments made in America before the 1790s survive. The few that do include several by American-born craftsmen or amateurs apparently meeting local needs: a 1759 violin made by John Antes in Bethlehem, Pennsylvania (fig. 28), a 1786 spinet made by Samuel Blyth in Salem, Massachusetts (fig. 29), of a 1794–95 cello or bass viol by amateur George Jewett in New England (fig. 30). After becoming associated with Boston theater musicians, another New England builder, Benjamin Crehore of Milton, Massa-

[58]See Raymond Russell, *The Harpsichord and the Clavichord,* Appendix Fifteen: "Letters between Hopkinson, Jefferson, and Burney" (London, 1959), pp. 177–82.

Figure 30. Folk cello made by George Jewett, Lebanon, Maine, 1794–95. The cello is fitted with a simple carved painted head in place of the usual scroll and with a tail-piece carved in the shape of a heart in which is carved "Pamele/1794" and below which is carved "J. Jewett/Fecit." Written in ink on the back is "George Jewett/A D 1795." Jewett, not familiar with wood bending techniques, made the sides from thick, molded cardboard. (Courtesy of the Smithsonian Institution, Division of Musical History, Washington, D.C.)

chusetts, made cellos and pianos more in the European tradition (figs. 31 and 32). In his shop he apprenticed several local craftsmen who later made important contributions to the American piano trade.[59]

[59]A more detailed study of buiders can be found in Hoover, "Manufacture and Sale of Instruments." For more detail on Crehore, see Darcy Kur-

Figure 31. Cello in its case made by Benjamin Crehore, Milton, Mass., c. 1795. Although Crehore (c. 1765–1831) spent most of his working life in Milton, he had much contact with the Boston musical scene. This instrument is of special interest because it still has a wooden carrying case typical of the period. (Courtesy of the Smithsonian Institution, Division of Musical History, Washington, D.C.)

In the 1790s a flood of immigrant builders, including Charles Albrecht in Philadelphia (fig. 33), began to establish shops and manufactories in the larger cities, claiming that instruments built here had an advantage over imports, for they were built to withstand America's climate.[60] This challenge to

onen, "The Musical Instruments of Benjamin Crehore," *Journal of the Museum of Fine Arts, Boston* 4 (1992): 52–79.

[60]The piano builders Dodds and Claus included the following lengthy notice in the New York newspaper *The Diary: or Loudon's Register* (Sept. 19, 1792, through 1794): "The Forte-Piano is become so exceedingly fashionable in Europe that few polite families are without it. This much esteemed instrument forms an agreeable accompaniment for the female voice, takes up but little room, may be moved with ease, and consequently kept in tune with little attention—so that it is on that account supperior to the harpsi-

Figure 32. Piano made by Benjamin Crehore, Milton, Mass., c. 1795–1800. Often called the founder of the New England piano industry, Crehore trained piano makers William and Adam Bent and Lewis and Alpheus Babcock (the latter the inventor of the one-piece iron frame). He formed a short partnership with Boston music dealer, teacher, and theater musician Peter van Hagen and agreed to make piano-organs in 1804 with organ maker William Goodrich. (Gift of Camilla Cunningham Blackman in memory of Lucy Clarendon Crehore. Courtesy, Museum of Fine Arts, Boston)

chord. The improvements which Messrs. Dodds and Claus have made in the Forte-Piano, has rendered it much more acceptable than those imported. The introduction of their new invented hammers, and dampers, is acknowledged to be a great improvement, as also the means they have taken to prepare their wood to stand the effect of our Climatte, which imported instruments never do, but are sure to suffer not only from the agitation of the vessel, but the saline qualities of the seas. One great advantage to the purchaser is, that Messrs. Dodds and Claus make it an invariable rule to repair any instrument that may prove defective in the workmanship, if applied to within 2 years after delivery. At this manufactory every kind of

Figure 33. Piano made by Charles Albrecht, Philadelphia, c. 1800. Albrecht (c. 1760–1848) came from Germany about 1785 and is known to have been making pianos by the late 1780s. His earliest instruments combined English-style cabinetry with German works. By the time of this instrument he was using English mechanisms. The piano trade was dominated by German and English builders who began coming to America soon after the end of the war in the 1780s. (Photo by Diane L. Nordeck, courtesy of the Smithsonian Institution, Division of Musical History, Washington, D.C.)

musical instruments are finished according to the present taste, and with the latest improvements, as good and cheap as in the City of London. Instruments sold on commission, taken in exchange, reasonable terms. N. B. A good allowance is made to dealers in these articles" (cited in Rita Susswein Gottesman, *The Arts and Crafts in New York, 1777–1799* [New York, 1954], p. 361).

builders was met not many years later by the American development of the one-piece metal frame, which in the nineteenth century became the standard for pianos throughout the world. But where America might excel in technology and industry, American music and musicians were to remain suspect.

PERSISTING PATTERNS

In both the cosmopolitan and provincial traditions, there emerged patterns that exist today. For example, musicians still find it necessary to combine several jobs in order to make a living, with teaching the major source of support. The amateur tradition is still alive in community choral, band, orchestral, and theatrical organizations that have produced not only music but also an audience and financial support for other performance activities. With little of the institutional patronage found in Europe from the court or church, musicians in America, in order to survive, have had to establish a marketplace centered upon music for utilitarian purposes: worship, instruction, entertainment, and participatory recreation.[61]

These competing traditions continue to exist. The vernacular, or provincial, tradition found a more receptive home away from the cultural elite of the eastern cities—on the frontier, where as one writer put it, fine-art music was "the province of females, foreigners or effeminates,"[62] and in communities less trained musically, perhaps, but more relaxed about combining borrowed musical traditions with a fresh creative approach. This tradition is one that led to minstrelsy, ragtime, and jazz, to Stephen Foster, John Philip Sousa, and George Gershwin.

"The pattern had been set" by 1800 for Americans who tried to compete against the tight network of highly trained immigrant musicians. Already William Billings and other

[61] Crawford, *American Musical Landscape*, chap. 2.

[62] H. Wiley Hitchcock, *Music in the United States: A Historical Introduction* (Englewood Cliffs, N.J., 1969), p. 46.

American musicians found they were outsiders.[63] The cultivated tradition, based on European musical taste, continues
to dominate the thinking of most committees who select sym-
phony and opera conductors, of the conductors and managers who select programs and performers, and of music
teachers and university faculties who determine what musical
traditions are to be taught to emerging performers and scholars. America may have declared political independence, but
in musical art, the "endless itch of imitation" of things European has remained strong.[64]

[63]Richard A. Crawford, Record Notes to *Music of the Federal Era*, New
World Records (NW 299), 1978.

[64]Painter John Trumbull to Andrew Elliott, Oct. 16, 1784, cited in Silverman, *Cultural History of the Revolution,* p. 507.

DAVID D. HALL

Books and Reading in Eighteenth-Century America

ROYALL TYLER IS remembered for his play *The Contrast,* which dramatizes the triumph of American simplicity (in the character of Colonel Manley) over decadent European sophistication (in the character of Mr. Dimple). When the work was revived in Boston in the 1970s, a theater critic headlined his unfavorable review "Native American Turkey." Tyler was also a novelist, one of the earliest of the cosmopolitan and enterprising Americans who turned to writing fiction in the new republic. In 1797 a printer in Walpole, New Hampshire, published *The Algerine Captive,* Tyler's first venture in this genre. The fictional author-hero of the novel, a young Yankee who describes his perils as a captive of Algerian pirates, begins the tale by remarking on the changes that have occurred in America in the seven years he has been away:

> When he left New England, books of biography, travel, novels, and modern romances, were confined to our sea-ports; or, if known in the country, were read only in the families of clergymen, physicians, and lawyers: while certain funeral discourses, the last words and dying speeches of Bryan Shaheen, and Levi Ames, and some dreary somebody's Day of Doom, formed the most diverting part of the farmer's library. On his return from captivity, he found a surprising alteration in the public taste. In our inland towns of consequence, social libraries had been instituted, composed of books designed to amuse rather than to instruct; and country booksellers, fostering the new-born taste of the people, had filled the whole land with modern travels, and novels almost as incredible.

After commenting on the high rate of literacy in New England—higher, he declares, than in any other country—he resumes his account of what has changed:

> With one accord, all orders of country life forsook the sober sermons and practical pieties of their fathers, for the gay stories and splendid impieties of the traveller and the novelist. The worthy farmer no longer fatigued himself with Bunyan's Pilgrim . . . but quaffed wine with Brydone in the hermitage of Vesuvius, or sported with Bruce on the fairy-land of Abyssinia; while Dolly, the dairy maid, and Jonathan, the hired man, threw aside the ballad of the cruel step-mother, over which they had so often wept in concert, and now amused themselves into so agreeable a terror with the haunted houses and hobgoblins of Mrs. Ratcliffe, that they were both afraid to sleep alone.[1]

In evoking a sharp change in reading practice, Tyler describes a transition that undoubtedly was under way. Books as a commodity were caught up in a broader transformation that J. H. Plumb and others have labeled the "commercialization of culture."[2]

But at best this was a partial transformation, for it failed to dislodge an older mode of reading to which most literate Americans were accustomed and to which many remained loyal. Nor was it very far advanced in 1797. Case studies of printers and booksellers in the new republic indicate that entrepreneurs of print were still limited to local markets. These same studies demonstrate that the separation of functions well under way in the English book trade had yet to occur in America, where booksellers continued to double as publishers and sometimes as printers. Change was taking place, but its consequences were not fully felt until later in the nineteenth century. And change did not eliminate an older style of reading. New products coexisted in the marketplace with products that had been around for decades, if not centuries. The

---

[1] Royall Tyler, *The Algerine Captive,* Introduction by Jack B. Moore (1802; reprint ed., Gainesville, Fla., 1967), pp. vi–ix.

[2] J. H. Plumb, "The Commericalization of Leisure in Eighteenth-Century England," in Neil McKendrick, John Brewer, and J. H. Plumb, *The Birth of a Consumer Society: The Commercialization of Eighteenth-Century England* (Bloomington, Ind., 1982), pp. 262–85.

persistence of old books was something other than a matter of provincial lag. It reflected deeper cultural patterns that gave books and reading a significance quite different from their meaning to someone like Royall Tyler. These patterns, sketched out in this essay, were competing cultural systems, the very ones that Tyler described in *The Algerine Captive*. The first was a system in which novels figured as the crucial genre, the second was the system that he mocked.

Certainly new relationships between books and readers were emerging in the second half of the eighteenth century, a transition exemplified by the development of the social library. Americans began to copy this English institution in the 1740s, after Benjamin Franklin organized the Library Company of Philadelphia in 1731. The rate of growth was rapid as the number of these libraries doubled from one decade to the next, a pace that continued until 1810 before it slowed. A parallel development was the rise of circulating libraries that were run for profit by individual booksellers. Here, too, the increase was remarkable in the final years of the century.[3] It was also in these years that new themes appeared in the advertising of booksellers. When one of them in Philadelphia in 1798 advertised "sentimental treats for the ladies" as a feature of his inventory, he was one of many who referred increasingly to women readers and their appetite for fiction. The founders of the *Gentlemen and Lady's Town and Country Magazine*, which came into being in Boston in 1784, were typical in boasting that their periodical contained "more fiction than usual, [and] much advice to young ladies . . . about matrimony." Another sales device—applied in particular to fiction—was to condemn old reading matter and to highlight the new. Thus a Philadelphia bookseller advertised in 1769 that his stock included "New Novels in 1768" along with "New Plays and Farces," and in 1766 another referred to "useful Modern books."[4] Let us recall that Royall Tyler de-

[3] A convenient enumeration, though limited to New England, appears in Jesse H. Shera, *Foundations of the Public Library* (Chicago, 1949). See also Robert B. Winans, "The Growth of a Novel-Reading Public in Late Eighteenth-Century America," *Early American Literature* 9 (1975):267–75.

[4] Robert B. Winans, *A Descriptive Checklist of Book Catalogues Separately Printed in America, 1693–1800* (Worcester, Mass., 1981), pp. 95, 46, 60;

scribed the present generation as forsaking "the sober sermons and practical pieties of their fathers" for the pleasures of fiction. This taste for the up-to-date is seen by J. H. Plumb as one of the characteristics of the consumer revolution. The imperative to consume, he declares, was stimulated by the tyranny of fashion and its principle that taste must change each season.

Fiction seems peculiarly suited to this principle. Not only did it emerge in the eighteenth century as the consumer revolution was getting under way, and in quantities that steadily increased, but it seems also to have displaced other genres in the market. Tyler says as much, and Plumb identifies it, along with children's literature, as especially important to the broader change he is describing. Certainly Americans in the late eighteenth century were producing and buying more books than ever before, and the rate of growth was much greater than the growth of population. Americans were also reading far more newspapers; and 23 papers of 1764 had become 58 by 1783, and 150 by 1800; ten years later, the number had soared to 350.[5] Children's literature is more elusive to define and therefore to count, and it may not make much sense to compare the situation before 1750 or 1775 with what happened thereafter since we cannot distinguish the children who may have read adult books in the eighteenth century from those who preferred John Newberry's productions, seen by some as the first true children's books. The "little books for children" that Newberry began to print in London in the 1750s would achieve sales as high as 25,000 copies per title in England, a figure Plumb describes as "vast."[6]

Royall Tyler was not alone in discerning signs of change, or in thinking they betokened a real turning point. In 1803 Sam-

Frank Luther Mott, *A History of American Magazines*, 5 vols. (Cambridge, Mass., 1930–68), 1:29.

[5]G. Thomas Tanselle, "Some Statistics on American Printing, 1764–83," in Bernard Bailyn and John Hench, eds., *The Press and the American Revolution* (Boston, 1981), pp. 315–63; Isaiah Thomas, *The History of Printing in America*, ed. Marcus McCorison, 2d ed. (1810; reprint ed., New York, 1970), pp. 14–16.

[6]Plumb, "Commercialization of Lesiure," p. 305.

uel Miller, a Princeton academic-cum-Presbyterian minister, saluted the eighteenth century as "pre-eminently entitled to the character of THE AGE OF PRINTING." Miller happened to dislike the trends of his day, but his uneasiness with the "mass of new, hastily composed and superficial works" that "crowded out of view the stores of ancient learning and even many of the best works of the preceding century" amounts to the perception that the kinds of books he liked were giving way to different types of reading.[7] Two entrepreneurs of print in Jacksonian America, Samuel Goodrich and Joseph Buckingham, remembered the book market they knew as children at the end of the eighteenth century as limited to a few pious items, a situation wholly different from the market they helped to create. "It is difficult now, in this era of literary affluence, almost amounting to surfeit," Goodrich declared in his autobiography, "to conceive of the poverty of books suited to children in the days of which I write. Except the New England Primer . . . I remember none that were in general use among my companions." To his contemporaries at midcentury, Goodrich offered the contrasting spectacle of "such a juvenile bookstore as that of C. S. Francis, in Broadway, New York," with its "teeming shelves."[8]

The more we look for signs of change, the more they seem to multiply. Some of these trends may signify a "reading revolution," a term that historians of reading and the book trade in Germany and America have applied to the final years of the eighteenth century and the opening decades of the nineteenth. Describing the German situation, Rolf Engelsing suggests that in traditional literary culture, books were printed in small editions and sold at prices that limited their availability. In this other world of print, religious subject matter predominated, all age groups shared the same books, and reading, which often occurred in family or social settings, retained its connections with oral culture and the practice of

[7]Samuel Miller, *A Brief Retrospect of the Eighteenth Century*, 2 vols. (New York, 1803), 2:417, 424–28.

[8]Samuel Goodrich, *Recollections of a Lifetime*, 2 vols. (New York, 1857), 1:165–66, 174; see also David D. Hall, "The Uses of Literacy in New England, 1600–1850," in William L. Joyce et al., eds., *Printing and Society in Early America* (Worcester, Mass., 1983), pp. 1–47.

memorization. But the emergence of fiction and children's literature, genres that usually were issued in larger editions that sold at lower prices than before, helped initiate a new mode of "extensive" reading that was private rather than communal and that fed on change. What Engelsing has described as occurring in Germany others have detected in America.[9]

But if the "commercialization of culture" and a "reading revolution" both seem to follow from what Tyler says of the late eighteenth century in the preface to *The Algerine Captive,* the text of that novel and its own publishing history contain other lessons that do not coincide so easily with the hypothesis of change. Issued by a printer named David Carlisle, *The Algerine Captive* was reprinted twice by other printers before vanishing from sight. If we ask what other books and pamphlets Carlisle printed in the 1790s, we discover that this eager businessman, who began his career as one of Isaiah Thomas's many regional associates, devoted most of his workdays to issuing schoolbooks, ordination sermons, Fourth of July orations, and such delicious ephemera as *A Wonderful Dream,* a twelve-page pamphlet attributed to Isaac Watts that was reprinted eleven times by regional (but never metropolitan) printing offices in the last forty years of the century.

Did *A Wonderful Dream* appeal to the same readers who bought *The Algerine Captive?* Tyler did not seem to think so; his scorn for the "funeral discourses, the last words and dying speeches," and "dreary somebody's Day of Doom" that were of a kind with *A Wonderful Dream* suggests a distinction between readers who preferred the new, sophisticated fiction and those who enjoyed the prophetic, evangelical texts that had, in some cases, originated in the seventeenth century. Were there many readers of this second kind in the early republic, and did the book trade cater to them?

[9]Rolf Engelsing, *Der Bürger als Leser: Lesergeschichte in Deutschland, 1500–1800* (Stuttgart, 1974); the argument is summarized in Engelsing, "Die Perioden der Leseforschung in der Neuzeit: Das statistische Ausmass und die soziokulturelle Bedeutung der Lektüre," *Archiv für Geschichte des Buchwesens* 10 (1969):945–1002. The case for a "reading revolution" in antebellum America is argued by Willliam T. Gilmore in *Reading Becomes a Necessity of Life: Material and Cultural Life in Rural New England, 1780–1835* (Knoxville, Tenn., 1989). I am grateful to Robert Darnton for providing me with notes on Engelsing's essay.

The answer to this question emerges from a series of case studies: the Merriam printing office in Brookfield, Massachusetts, the Concord, Massachusetts, Charitable Library Association, the career of Mason Locke Weems, and the ownership of books in Virginia in the early nineteenth century.

Ebenezer and Daniel Merriam opened a printing office in Brookfield in 1798. Ebenezer and another brother had apprenticed under Isaiah Thomas in Worcester. They hoped to make their way by publishing a newspaper, but gave it up within four years for want of subscribers. Shifting entirely to book production, the Merriams found buyers in an arc of towns and cities—Boston, New York, Philadelphia, Worcester, Hartford, and Albany—from which they received other books in exchange. "Devotional works, readers, spellers, and pocket dictionaries went to city publisher-booksellers by the hundreds. Back came almanacs by the thousands, and assortments of other books in lots ranging from two to two hundred items." The Merriams also distributed their products (and those received from elsewhere) through a network of rural merchants in some twenty-six towns in adjoining counties. Here the process of exchange consisted of books for goods. Cash played little part in either network of exchange, though after 1824 the Merriams paid cash or its equivalent for their supplies of paper. Yet, at best, they were participating in an imperfectly integrated distribution system that limited them to editions of no more than three thousand copies of any book, that required only modest sums of cash or credit to finance, and that called for little long-range planning and nothing in the way of double-entry bookkeeping.

The traditional quality of these business practices was matched by the kinds of books that the firm printed and distributed. Schoolbooks accounted for three-fifths of total sales. By contrast, sales of fiction out of the Merriams' own store "averaged between three and four volumes per year." Only once did the firm attempt a novel on its own, the tried-and-true *Charlotte Temple,* only to find that half of their edition never sold. Keeping back for sale a mere sixteen copies of another novel done for someone else, the Merriams managed to get rid of three copies in the space of four years! As for children's literature, "there was nothing besides the toy books, which were tiny, extremely rudimentary, and sold for a few cents each."[10]

To judge by what the Merriams chose to publish, their customers (other than schoolchildren) preferred devotional and evangelical literature. Four times in the first twenty years of business the firm issued the *Psalms and Hymns* of Isaac Watts, the early eighteenth-century English Nonconformist minister who enjoyed remarkable popularity as a poet and hymnist. Philip Doddridge was another eighteenth-century writer whose work was reprinted. The firm reached back to the seventeenth century for Richard Baxter's *Call to the Unconverted* and *The Saints Everlasting Rest,* Thomas Shearman's *Divine Breathings,* Mary Rowlandson's captivity narrative (it also reprinted John Williams's *The Redeemed Captive* of 1707), and Robert Russell's *Seven Sermons.* The Merriams were not unusual in supposing that such books would find buyers. It may be proposed as a general rule that any local printer in New England in the late eighteenth and early nineteenth centuries issued these same titles or their kin. A handful of authors turn up time and time again—Baxter, Doddridge, Watts, Russell, Joseph Alleine, Thomas Vincent, James Janeway. Books by these writers had been "popular" (in the sense of selling widely and almost continuously) since their initial publication; they were steady sellers that attracted several generations of readers. What they had in common was an evangelical message of judgment and deliverance. Some of these writers were more emphatic than others in describing the terrors of hell, but all of them spoke directly to their readers about life and death and how to be saved. In doing so, they deliberately sidestepped the elaborate reasoning that was suited to a theological treatise, and they were silent on controversial issues of church order, perhaps because, as English Nonconformists (as most of them were), they aspired to reach people who belonged to other groups, including the state church.[11]

[10]Jack Larkin, "The Merriams of Brookfield: Printing in the Economy and Culture of Rural Massachusetts in the Early Nineteenth Century," American Antiquarian Society *Proceedings* 96 (1986):39–73, quotations from pp. 42, 47, 56, 68.

[11]Hall, "Uses of Literacy"; C. John Sommerville, *Popular Religion in Restoration England* (Gainesville, Fla., 1977).

Several of these steady sellers were purchased by the organizers of the Charitable Library Society in Concord, Massachusetts. In 1795, three years before the Merriams arrived in
Brookfield, fifteen Concord men and women formed a social
or subscription library and began to order books not only for
themselves but also for others in the town to read. The
charge-out ledgers of the Charitable Library Society inform
us that the collection consisted largely of European, and especially British, books (more than half of the total). By subject,
religious books constituted 40 percent of the whole, and it
was a book that fell within this category that Concord readers
borrowed more than any other during the last five years of
the century, Henry Grove's *Discourse concerning . . . the Lord's
Supper.* Contrary to Royall Tyler and his vision of such institutions as chock full of "gay stories," the Concord collection included a mere handful of novels. True, it embraced "modern
histories, biographies, and travels as well as poetry, natural
philosophy, and religion." It included Pope and Johnson,
Goldsmith, Addison and Steele. Yet it also included Isaac
Watts and Elizabeth Rowe, two poets who were piously (or
sentimentally) religious, and the great eighteenth-century
steady seller, Doddridge's *Rise and Progress of Religion in the
Soul.*[12] In this regard the creators of the Charitable Library
Society were manifesting the same preferences, pro and con,
as the creators of other social libraries in New England. David
Lundberg has identified ninety-four titles that turn up five
times or more in the catalogs of twelve such libraries. These
"core readings," as he terms them, were predominantly works
of history and religion, with fiction trailing far behind at 5
percent of the total.[13]

Social libraries made books more available because most

[12]Robert A. Gross, "Books and Libraries in Thoreau's Concord," American Antiquarian Society *Proceedings* 97 (1987):129–88. Gross differentiates
the religious books in the Charitable Library from those I described in
"Uses of Literacy" on the grounds that the Concord collection was nonde-
nominational and theologically moderate. But as the presence of Doddridge indicates, the distinction is relative, not absolute.

[13]David Lundberg, "New England Soceity Libraries and the Common
Reader of the 1790s" (Paper presented at the Seventy-Eighth Annual Meeting of the Organization of American Historians, Minneapolis, Apr. 1985).

people in eighteenth-century America never owned or bought more than a few books during the whole of their lives, and some (an unknown percentage but perhaps two-fifths of all adults) bought none at all. The regular customers of American and European booksellers were invariably either the professional classes—clergy, doctors, lawyers, public officials, and the rare scientist—or men of wealth who found pleasure in collecting books. They participated in a learned culture that was nurtured on the wisdom of the past—the Greek and Latin classics, historic controversies in religion, and interpretation of the Bible—though it also occupied itself with theories of the moment in religion, science, and statecraft. But if learned culture thrived on books, the situation was quite different for most farmers, artisans, and merchants, who bought little more than almanacs and Bibles—if that.[14]

These different patterns of consumption emerge from that classic source of evidence for goods, the probate inventories. The eighteenth-century South was a region where, according to this evidence, books were scarce commodities. The leading Virginia printer-bookseller was issuing 6,000 almanacs a year at a time when a *single* northern almanac had annual sales of 50,000 copies. A recent study of 2,400 inventories from Virginia towns and counties for the period 1790–1840 is particularly revealing because it indicates that only half the inventoried Virginians owned books, and that no increase occurred in this proportion over time. Not only did Virginians fail to acquire more books, but they also preferred Bibles (by far the most widely owned volume), religious literature, and history, with novels making only a "modest showing."[15]

[14]Lucien Febvre and Henri-Jean Martin, *The Coming of the Book: The Impact of Printing, 1450–1800,* trans. David Gerard (1958; reprint ed., London, 1984), pp. 216, 221. The limited availability of books is described in Cynthia Z. Stiverson and Gregory A. Stiverson, "The Colonial Retail Book Trade: Availability and Affordability of Reading Material in Mid-Eighteenth-Century Virginia," in Joyce et al., eds., *Printing and Society,* pp. 132–73. Learned readers as active patrons of the book trade are described in Elizabeth Carroll Reilly, "The Wages of Piety: The Boston Book Trade of Jeremy Condy," ibid., pp. 83–131.

[15]Joseph F. Kett and Patricia A. McClung, "Book Culture in Post-Revolutionary Virginia," *American Antiquarian Society Proceedings* 94

An inventory study of equal importance and scope, covering four towns in western Massachusetts, has turned up similar results. Little more than half (54 percent) of all probated estates included books, and, of these, half "contained fewer than five volumes." In other words, three-fourths of the people whose estates went into probate owned either no books or so few that we must infer their essential inactivity as buyers. In Massachusetts, as in Virginia, fiction was strikingly absent except in the "libraries of a few men, almost all of whom were in the top 10 percent of probated wealth." What people bought or inherited were Bibles, religious and devotional works, and schoolbooks.[16]

The structure of the book trade mirrored the limited demand for books. Individual booksellers distributed their products to a local clientele. A national market, one that promised greater sales for a given book, did not yet exist. The Merriams were typical in disposing of the books they printed through exchange with other printers. This system—and an endemic shortage of capital that left printers hesitant to tie up funds in unsold books—made for small press runs. Short of capital and buyers, American printers and booksellers preferred to import from London the more learned books that professionals or the wealthy liked to own. Rarely were these reprinted in America. Instead, American printers published the steady sellers or such local items as sermons.[17]

Winds of change began to blow in the 1790s when an enterprising Philadelphia bookseller, Mathew Carey, joined forces with a legendary salesman-writer, Parson Weems. Carey forged a network of distributors that enabled him to reach a wider reading public. But his business success must not obscure the taste of his customers, a taste that Weems interpre-

---

(1984):97–138. Their analysis is consistent with other inventory studies, including Joseph Towne Wheeler, "Literary Culture in Eighteenth-Century Maryland, 1700–1776," *Maryland Historical Magazine* 38 (1943):273–76; Minor Myers, Jr., "Letters, Learning, and Politics in Lyme: 1760–1800," in George Willauer, Jr., ed., *A Lyme Miscellany, 1776–1976* (Middletown, Conn., 1977), pp. 48–80.

[16]Larkin, "Merriams of Brookfield," pp. 71–72.

[17]Ibid.

ted in his letters and that he tried to satisfy by producing hackwork of his own.

Weems was not what he sometimes said he was, the rector of George Washington's parish, though he could legitimately claim that he was an ordained Episcopal clergyman. Be that as it may, we remember him as the author of *The Life and Memorable Actions of George Washington,* a short work that flouted the ordinary boundaries between truth and fiction. We should know him also as a remarkable salesman, a peripatetic traveler and bookseller in Virginia, Maryland, Pennsylvania, New Jersey, and North Carolina. During his trips, he collected orders for volumes that the Philadelphia entrepreneur Mathew Carey had already printed or proposed to publish. But Weems also peddled books he carried with him, and he played an active role in creating books for the market that he galvanized.

Weems sold lots of books. He fantasized about the prospect of selling "millions," an astonishing word to use around 1800 for any cultural product. Certainly he succeeded in disposing of a quantity that must have numbered in the hundreds of thousands. His success should make us less inclined to use such adjectives as "vast" in describing the sale of 25,000 copies of a Newberry title. Of more importance, Weems's achievement suggests that demand existed, but that price and distribution inhibited consumption. Weems broke the limitations of the system of supply in two ways: he took books directly to consumers, staging, in effect, his private version of the "transportation revolution," and he kept his prices low. In his letters back to Carey he repeatedly insisted on the importance of maintaining prices in the range of 20 to 25 cents. At that level he could make a profit on a forty-page, illustrated, unbound book. In these letters Weems also emphasized the preference of his customers for illustrations. Cheap books, he declared, should look "pretty" and contain "images."

Weems may have sensed that many of his clients had to "see" the meaning of a verbal text before they understood it. These same clients wanted short books and cared little for the hierarchy of learned values that moved Samuel Miller to complain of what was being printed. Indifferent to the authenticity of texts, Weems saw no harm in reducing *The Vicar of Wakefield* to the proportions of a chapbook. In creating books himself, he drew on older literary traditions—the gallows speech, the tale of sensational judgments against sinners. Astonishingly, he borrowed the title and formula of a book published in mid-seventeenth-century England, *God's Revenge against Murder,* by John Reynolds, for a series of chapbooks all of which bear the title, *God's Revenge against . . .* , completed by a variety of moral topics. As in the traditions on which he drew, so in these productions there is room for violence, visions (he also wrote a dream book), and sexuality.[18]

Bearing in mind that Mathew Carey was the principal publisher of the bestselling American novel *Charlotte Temple* (he told a correspondent in 1812 that Americans had bought at least 50,000 copies), that by 1800 the number of libraries, periodicals, and imprints of all categories was increasing, and that fiction was intruding into bookshops and households with much greater frequency, we may nonetheless conclude that the common reader and the book trade were not yet transformed by the "commercialization of culture." The case histories I have sketched suggest the persistence of older patterns of consumption and production. In these shops and households, the brave new world of fiction seems scarcely evident.[19]

These older patterns deserve a closer look. It is all too easy

[18]The essential source on Weems is E. E. F. Skeel, *Mason Locke Weems,* 3 vols. (New York, 1929); the quotations are from 2:167, 186, 109, and see also 1:209. Relevant is James Gilreath, "Mason Weems, Mathew Carey, and the Southern Booktrade, 1794–1810," *Publishing History* 10 (1981):27–49, and James N. Green, "From Printer to Publisher: Mathew Carey and the Origins of Nineteenth-Century Book Publishing," in Michael Hackenberg, ed., *Getting the Books Out: Papers of the Chicago Conference on the Book in 19th-Century America* (Washington, D.C., 1987), pp. 26–44.

[19]There is reason to suppose that reading patterns in eighteenth-century England were not so different from those in America. The borrowers and buyers who came to Samuel Clay's bookshop in Warwick "did not borrow novels with the addictive frenzy lamented by moralists in their attacks on novel-reading. Of the sixty novels withdrawn, thirty-one were borrowed by only one reader each" (Jean Fergus, "Eighteenth-Century Readers in Provincial England: The Customers of Samuel Clay's Circulating Library and Bookshop in Warwick, 1770–72," Bibliographical Society of America *Publications* 78 [1984]:155–92, quotation p. 180).

to assume that the people who owned no books other than Watts's *Psalms and Hymns* and the Bible were constrained from being more active consumers—buyers, say, of the new fiction—by such factors as poverty, illiteracy, and the structure of the book trade. An alternative interpretation is to recognize the role of choice or, better, of participation in a cultural tradition in which books had a quite different significance than they had in the emerging world of fiction. Apart from the learned culture, the prevailing cultural tradition in early eighteenth-century America was what we might term the Protestant vernacular. Originating in the Reformation and gaining sharper focus in the prolonged struggle between factions in the Church of England, the vernacular tradition rested on the premise that everyone must have access to Scripture. From this followed the insistence on literacy that figured so strongly in the Puritan movement, a surge of publications destined for the common reader (primers, psalm books, and translations of the Bible into English), a conception of authorship that denied the role of individual talent (good writers spoke the Truth), and a widespread facility with figural language. The last of these characteristics accounts for the ease with which lay writers such as Mary Rowlandson composed prose and poetry that readers found compelling. The writers, readers, and printers who participated in the vernacular tradition constituted an interpretive community. Hostile to ungodly books and preferring those I have described as steady sellers, they did not need *new* books at all. Within the terms of this tradition, it was sufficient to consult the Bible or its spiritual equivalents.[20]

Many people abstained from the world of fiction or did not bother to acquire books precisely because of their participation in this tradition. Royall Tyler knew quite well that most Americans continued to enjoy "Days of Doom." He was scorn-

[20]This paragraph summarizes my description of this reading community in *Worlds of Wonder, Days of Judgment: Popular Religious Belief in Early New England* (New York, 1989), chap. 1. In an essay written subsequent to this one, I qualify more fully, and from a different vantage, the concept of a "reading revolution" (Hall, "Readers and Reading in History and Theory" [Paris, 1993], in a collection of essays edited by Roger Chartier and Olivier Corpet).

ful of such readers and their culture, a culture he mocked throughout *The Algerine Captive*. Early on, the plot revolves around the education of a young rustic, Updike Underhill. He has a yen for learning, and when his parents consult the town minister for advice, he suggests that Updike leave the family farm and go off to college where he will train for the ministry. This advice pleases the mother. "She did not doubt, when he came to preach, he would be as much run after as the great Mr. Whitefield. 'I always thought,' continued she, 'the child was a genius. . . . The boy loves books. He has read Valentine and Orson, and Robinson Crusoe. I went, the other day, three miles to borrow Pilgrim's Progress for him. He has read it through every bit; ay, and understands it too. Why, he stuck a skewer through Apollyon's eye in the picture, to help Christian beat him.'" Updike's father is no less naive. When the son has to give up college and study on his own, his father gives him "some of the prime books in the several sciences" that he must read to find out which of the professions he wants to enter. "In divinity, I read ten funeral, five election, three ordination, and seventeen farewell, sermons, Bunyan's Holy War, the Life of Colonel Gardner, and the Religious Courtship. In law, the Statutes of New Hampshire, and Burn's Justice abridged. In physic, Buchan's Family Physician, Culpepper's Midwifery, and Turner's Surgery." Having settled on medicine, our hero takes up practice in a town where none of the men who call themselves doctors know anything about their craft, and the satire plays itself out in tales of how they deal with someone who is ill.[21]

Royall Tyler was angered by this naive culture—angered, like the Harvard man he was, by indifference to hierarchy. Yet what Tyler rejected, Mason Weems embraced in his endless retellings of the marvels of "God's Revenge against" sins and in his radical abridgments of famous (we might even say, "serious") books. For that matter, Tyler's own printer-publisher was abetting this culture by reprinting Isaac Watts's *Wonderful Dream*. So also were the writers of most almanacs and the many printer-publishers who kept in circulation such classics of the evangelical tradition as Joseph Alleine's *Alarm* and Rob-

---

[21]Tyler, *Algerine Captive*, pp. 32, 55–56.

ert Russell's *Seven Sermons*—which Weems chose to reprint as his first independent publication.

Tom Paine, who was raised a Quaker and who worked briefly as an itinerant preacher, knew the motifs of this culture, and spoke to and out of it in *Common Sense*. Gordon S. Wood has argued that

> part of the remarkable effect created by Thomas Paine's *Common Sense* . . . resulted from its obvious deepening of the layers of audience to whom it was directed. . . . some of the awe and consternation the pamphlet aroused came from its deliberate elimination of the usual elitist apparatus of persuasion and its acknowledged appeal to a wider reading public. . . . There are few of the traditional gentlemanly references to learned authorities and few of the subtleties of literary allusions and techniques known to the Augustans. Paine scorned "words of sound" that only "amuse the ear" and relied on a simple and direct idiom; he used concrete, even coarse and vulgar, imagery drawn from the commonplace world that could be understood even by the unlearned, and he counted on his audience being familiar with only one literary source, the Bible—all of which worked to heighten the pamphlet's potency and to broaden its readership, pointing the way toward a new kind of public literature.

Though I do not see this literature as so new, the important point is how *Common Sense* departs from other writings of this period that were directed at a "restricted and aristocratic" audience. To quote Wood again, "A large amount of the Revolutionary literature was extraordinarily learned, filled with Latin quotations . . . multitudes of references to every conceivable figure in the heritage of Western culture. . . . Or even more indicative of the limited elitist conception of the audience was the extraordinary reliance on personal correspondence for the circulation of ideas." He reasons, too, that the mode of satire employed by these writers presumes a common set of standards and cultural "intimacy." [22]

Wood has differentiated two interpretive communities, the

[22] Gordon S. Wood, "The Democratization of Mind in the American Revolution," in *Leadership in the American Revolution* (Papers presented at the Third Library of Congress Symposium on the American Revolution, May 1974, Washington, D.C., 1974, pp. 70–71, 68–69).

one "aristocratic," the other "democratic." These labels are oddly apropos, though I do not use them in this essay. What matters more is to discern how each cultural mode encompassed assumptions about the acts of reading and writing and the relationship between authors and a general audience, and to recognize the strength and persistence of the vernacular tradition. Its strength may be measured by the sales of books like Alleine's *Plea for Unconverted Sinners* and the chapbooks Weems assembled, sales that far exceeded those of *Charlotte Temple* and Newberry's fiction for young children. Its persistence may be demonstrated by a glance at the titles favored by the New England (later, the American) Tract Society. Another case in point is the extraordinary history of *Uncle Tom's Cabin,* for the readers of this novel came to it with expectations about truth and fiction that originated in the vernacular tradition.[23]

Persistence, strength, and conflict: the scorn that Royall Tyler expressed for the "country" reader had been voiced by Benjamin Franklin at the outset of his literary career in the "Silence Do-Good" essays and was present well into the nineteenth century among writers who aspired to participate in a different literary tradition, one less tied to democratic piety. Joseph Buckingham and Samuel Goodrich remembered from their childhood having been immersed in the vernacular tradition. They grew up on books like the *New England Primer,* the *Psalms and Hymns* of Watts, and tales of supernatural judgments. When they looked back upon these books and the general "scarcity" of print, they felt a sense of alienation. Thus Goodrich on the Primer: "The 'New England Primer'— the main contents of which were the Westminster Catechism—and some rhymes, embellished with hideous cuts of Adam's Fall, in which 'we sinned all': the apostle and a cock crowing at his side, to show that 'Peter denies his Lord and cries'; Nebuchadnezzar crawling about like a hog, the bristles sticking out of his back, and the like."[24] Here we sense a longing for gentility that, if lacking in the country towns of

[23]Jane Tompkins, *Sensational Designs: The Cultural Work of American Fiction, 1790–1860* (New York, 1985).

[24]Goodrich, *Recollections,* 1:165.

eighteenth-century Connecticut, was within reach in cities like New York and Boston. This was a world view that John Newberry helped encourage, for in his children's stories Newberry replaced the supernatural and the sensual with scenes of nature as benevolent and ordered.[25] His American heirs included Goodrich, whose Peter Parley stories would similarly attack older attitudes, and Noah Webster, who wanted to make uniform the practices of speech and writing. The function of Webster's famous *Dictionary* and *Spelling Book* was not to provide the historical meanings of words, but to establish correct usage and correct spellings. Webster was a cosmopolitan and, like Newberry and Goodrich, a rationalist who condemned "superstition."[26]

We may round out this brief sketch of cultural imperialism (though it may also be perceived as withdrawal from a common culture) by noting what it involved as a mode of reading and writing. Goodrich, who helped create the vogue for gift books in the 1830s, viewed books as commodities in a vast marketplace. Like the novelists of his day, he divested the printed word of its sacramental aura. In its place he put the authority of authors—that is, of individual taste and talent. The format of the gift book, with its vivid binding and variety of contents, corresponds to the marketplace ideal of book buyers who, emancipated from tradition, welcome change and look to books as temporary pleasures. Gift books were expendable. But great authors were permanent. It is marvelously ironic that an ideal of the writer as uniquely gifted— as creative genius—arose in tandem with the triumph of the marketplace.

Similarly, it was in keeping with the marketplace mentality that publishers and critics began early in the nineteenth century to discern a craze for reading. Joseph F. Kett has astutely noted that this observation was self-serving. According to his data, it was also false. That is, the critics who described their times as a new age of reading were proposing that Americans

[25] I base this statement on a reading of a number of the Newberry tales.

[26] The aphorisms that Webster included in his spellers are a case in point; see, for example, the portions quoted in Clifton Johnson, *Old-Time Schools and School-Books* (New York, 1904), p. 183.

should read certain kinds of books; what they ignored was the fact that fiction and its kin appealed only to a small percentage of the reading public.[27]

Thus we come to realize that books and their readers in eighteenth-century America were embedded in a complex web of institutions and assumptions. I have hinted at a few of these relationships in sketching the broad outlines of the conflict between genteel culture and the vernacular tradition. Were we to look closely at the novels written in the early years of the republic, we would find that they embody these and other contests. To speak of the "rise" of fiction as though novels were a mere commodity is therefore to ignore the meanings of the act of reading, meanings that were multiple and varied in response to texts that in themselves were richly dialectical.[28]

Consumers, writers, publishers, and the organizers of libraries all participated in a politics of reading. As so often happens, these politics were mediated by brokers sympathetic to all sides, in this case the printers and booksellers who provided products for whoever wanted books. Yet conflict did not vanish. We have only to remember the turmoil that surrounded novel reading in the first half of the nineteenth century. Recalling this turmoil, it seems right to insist that the history of books and their readers take account not only of mere numbers or a shift in genres but also of the context of these events.

[27] Kett and McClung, "Book Culture," pp. 137–38.

[28] Cathy N. Davidson, *Revolution and the Word: The Rise of the Novel in America* (New York, 1986).

BARBARA G. CARSON

Early American Tourists and the Commercialization of Leisure

AN OLD FORM of personal pleasure—a holiday away from home—took a new twist in England in the eighteenth century. The wealthy and well-born had always traveled for their own amusement; most others had stayed at home. Then, starting roughly three hundred years ago, commercial promoters began developing and offering for sale products, services, and "packaged" activities that opened the world of recreational travel to a mass market. The details of this story fit into the broader patterns of change that current scholars call the consumer revolution and describe as the commercialization of leisure. The social history of early English tourism becomes better known year by year. By contrast, except for specific studies of later nineteenth- and twentieth-century hotels and resorts, the topic hardly has been addressed by students of American history. Did American colonists travel for pleasure? Who were the first tourists? Where did they go? What commercial services and facilities were available to them? Was the traveler's experience in America similar to that in England? How can the growth and development of the commercial travel industry in America be explained?

In one sense, American colonization is quintessentially a story of travel and transportation, but exploration, immigration, conquest, and settlement were not anyone's idea of leisure. Almost no Americans traveled for pleasure in the seventeenth and early eighteenth centuries. Before the 1760s the few exceptions were isolated individuals, families, or friends. Hardy souls, they tolerated a tremendous variety of quality in the facilities and services that they encountered along the road, and they had to be prepared to fend for themselves. Something like organized tourism developed in three stages starting in the third quarter of the century. The first phase was ushered in by the prosperity that followed the Treaty of Paris in 1763. A flush of new money was spent to improve the number and quality of roads, provide public vehicles, and build and expand taverns. Although not specifically intended for tourist trade, such amenities made traveling easier and more comfortable for everyone. Pleasure travel increased modestly but noticeably, and the owners of a few colonial springs took the first tentative steps toward promoting their recreational potential. The Revolution interrupted these developments. The second phase came with the resumption of peace and the founding of the new nation, and despite its uneven economic course, encouraged rapid growth in all aspects of what might be called the travel system. The dissemination of information, improvements in transportation and accommodations, and the creation and development of recognized destinations in this half century paved the way for a third phase, from the 1830s to the Civil War, when the tourist industry assumed its modern character with capitalized investment, large hotels and resorts, and a complex network of interdependent advertisers, suppliers, entertainers, and service personnel.

An aspect of the larger subjects of the consumer revolution and the commercialization of leisure, the history of travel in early America requires more than an account of new facilities and improved services. Taken together, the separate histories of roads, vehicles, taverns, hotels, and tourist attractions constitute less than a full social history of tourism. It is essential to consider people's attitudes toward leisure-time travel, which give us insights into their ways of thinking about time and space, culturally relative concepts whose development historians, anthropologists, and sociologists are only beginning to explore. Modern ideas about vacations and recreational travel evolved out of earlier views on work and leisure, which represented part of the cultural transformation of traditional, preindustrial societies into fully industrialized consumer societies. Just as ordinary Britons and Americans had to put aside their inhibitions about buying goods traditionally considered inappropriate for their social class, so they also gave up older, preindustrial ideas about allocating time to recreational activities. Few Americans thought they had a birthright to leisure. Most would have shared Benjamin Franklin's view that it was a wasteful drain on productive enterprises: "He that can earn ten shillings a day by labor, and goes abroad or sits idle one half of that day, though he spends but sixpence during his diversion and idleness, ought not to reckon that the only expense; he has really spent, or rather thrown away, five shillings besides."[1] Before significant numbers of Americans could feel comfortable about traveling for pleasure, the right to leisure had to lose its privileged status and, like ownership of fancy clothing, tablewares, and other consumer goods, it had to become something that ordinary people felt entitled to, if they could afford it.

Today travel specialists distinguish between day trippers and long-distance tourists; the same categories are useful historically. This essay will focus on the latter, to those who packed their bags and headed off for several days, weeks, or months at a time—in short, Americans away from home, *in* another place but not *of* that place. Business travelers and foreign visitors to America are not central figures in the study of domestic tourism, except occasionally as valuable sources of information about conditions. Similarly, the perspectives of foreign visitors who published so many accounts of their experiences must be carefully distinguished from those of American citizens. However, because foreigners tended to describe an unfamiliar land more fully than American tourists, their accented voices must sometimes be heard in the narrative. The essay will discuss the initial lack of commercialized vacation promotion, contrast early conditions with developments during the first two phases of tourist activity, and compare American improvements in facilities and services and

---

[1] Quoted in Michael R. Marrus, ed., *The Emergence of Leisure in Industrial Society* (New York, 1974), p. 2.

changes in people's attitudes with similar but earlier English practices, the models that Americans modified to satisfy their different setting and different social order.

Dr. Alexander Hamilton, a thirty-two-year-old bachelor and a prosperous physician of Annapolis, set out on a journey in 1744 "intended only for health and recreation."[2] His well-known *Itinerarium* provides the best account of traveling conditions in America in an age when virtually everyone who traveled did so on business. It offers indisputable evidence that in the 1740s almost no one had begun to develop commercial establishments aimed at tourists. Although Hamilton's pleasure trip may not have been unique in early America, it certainly was most unusual. His experience is worth examining closely.

Hamilton and a black servant left Annapolis at the end of May and traveled for four months. They rode Hamilton's own horses because the roads were not always suitable for private chairs or carriages and because New Jersey was the only colony they could cross by public stage coach.[3] They could not buy a road map, per se, because none were available, although conceivably Hamilton could have referred to an early traveler's aid published in 1731. Thomas Prince's *Vade-Mecum for America; or, A Companion for Traders and Travellers*, was a slim volume, nothing more than a bare list of towns and taverns from Maine to Virginia and the mileage between them.[4] Hamilton followed this well-traveled, if not well-mapped, overland coastal route to Philadelphia and New York City, then sailed up the Hudson to Albany. After returning to New York, he pushed on, again by land, to Newport, Boston, and as far north as York, Maine, from which he essentially retraced his steps to Annapolis.

If the roads were poor, the routes were usually—but not always—obvious. Hamilton occasionally lost his way and had

[2]Carl Bridenbaugh, ed., *Gentleman's Progress: The Itenerarium of Dr. Alexander Hamilton, 1744* (Chapel Hill, N.C., 1948), p. 3.

[3]Oliver W. Holmes and Peter T. Rohrbach, *Stagecoach East: Stagecoach Days in the East from the Colonial Period to the Civil War* (Washington, D.C., 1983), pp. 7–8.

[4]Boston, 1731.

to hire a guide. He made at least fifty ferry crossings (compared to the only seven bridges he encountered), spent approximately half of his 122 nights in taverns, and whenever possible in cities took private lodgings.[5] Few of the tavern beds were bug- or flea-ridden.[6] Some may have been luxurious. For instance, at The Sign of the Dragon in Marblehead, Hamilton does not describe his room, but writes that his servant Dromo slept in a bedroom furnished with "tables, chairs, a fine feather bed with quilted counterpine, white callicoe canopy or tester, and curtains."[7] When he returned home four months later on September 29, Hamilton reported with satisfaction that he had "compleated, by land and water together, a course of 1624 miles" and that he had accomplished his purpose and obtained "a better state of health."[8]

Several points in the *Itinerarium* deserve emphasis. First, the travel journal contains no hint of any commercial tourist activity. Although Hamilton was a physician traveling to improve his health, he did not seek out springs or spas. He did not even mention the springs at Bristol, Pennsylvania, where he spent one night and paused to describe the pleasant prospect of the town in some detail.[9] Twenty years hence Bristol Springs would become a fledgling resort. Hamilton said nothing about the potential development of such sites, a significant omission because later physicians were among the principal investors and promoters of health resorts for travelers.[10] Except for his detour up the Hudson, Hamilton stayed near the coast. Although he visited Newport twice for a total of seven days in both July and August, he did not observe or at least

[5] Bridenbaugh, ed., *Gentleman's Progress*, p. xxvii.

[6] Ibid.

[7] Ibid., p. 119.

[8] Ibid., p. 199.

[9] Ibid., p. 30.

[10] Carl Bridenbaugh, "Baths and Watering Places of Colonial America," *William and Mary Quarterly*, 3d ser. 3 (1946):151–81; Janice Zita Grover, "Luxury and Leisure in Early Nineteenth-Century America: Saratoga Springs and the Rise of the Resort," Ph.D. diss., University of California, Davis, 1973.

did not comment on any seasonal visitors.[11] He enjoyed the company of many business travelers, but he did not mention meeting a single individual or family group traveling, like himself, purely for health and recreation.

Similarly, most of the sights he enjoyed along the road were free for the looking. Several houses of prominent citizens he referred to as "pritty boxes."[12] Only two, Malbone near Newport and Mount Burnett near Salem, Massachusetts, inspired more complete descriptions. Although his wording is unclear, it is probable that Hamilton and a friend toured Malbone in the absence of the owner, whom Hamilton met later on his return visit. Viewing the house was a matter of courtesy. It was not, as in England, an American traveler's customary activity to engage servants to give tours of local worthies' houses and grounds.[13] Hamilton did pay admission to a few concerts and presumably paid to see the performing baboon in a tavern at Newtown, Maryland, but these events were scheduled for local residents, not wayfarers.[14] At midcentury, tourist travel in America was still an unexploited economic opportunity.

Second, it is worth noting that the sights that caught Hamilton's attention were very much like those upon which early English travelers commented. Hamilton had been in Scotland before emigrating to Maryland. His superior knowledge, cultivated interests, and well-developed powers of observation are clearly revealed in the pages of his diary. For example, he paid close attention to fortifications and to all evidence of seafaring, perhaps because news that the French and English had declared war reached Philadelphia in June when Hamilton was beginning his journey. Signs of industry were scanty.[15] Hamilton described and admired many public buildings, es-

[11] Bridenbaugh, ed., *Gentleman's Progress,* pp. 101–3, 150–58.

[12] Ibid., pp. 31, 52.

[13] Ibid., pp. 103, 151, 120–21.

[14] Ibid., p. 11.

[15] Ibid. In addition to several ironworks (pp. 9, 103, 149, 158, and 188), Hamilton observed a slate quarry (p. 34), spinning (pp. 12, 94), and itinerant weavers (p. 93).

pecially churches. He found cupolas displaying town clocks noteworthy, particularly in small communities where perhaps he did not expect to see them.[16]

Hamilton's notes on farming practices reveal his interest and training in natural science. Ginseng root and the odor of skunks were new to him, but he was well informed about the use of a friend's sun microscope.[17] Although he showed no particular sensibility for the appearance of landscapes that later travelers called picturesque, he had some appreciation for scenery he passed through. On a side trip that he and Stephen Van Rensselaer took to Cohoes Falls, New York, Hamilton was decidedly lukewarm about the eighty-foot drop and wild gorge they viewed from the heights.[18] On his return trip south from Albany, he noted the Catskill Mountains in the distance but expressed no desire to see them at closer hand.[19] By and large, in describing the scenery, he used conventional language to describe how "the eye [was entertained] with variety of landskips."[20]

Hamilton's journal tells historians one more thing about early recreational travel. Sociability was an important part of the experience. Hamilton wrote mostly about people. His character sketches show the close attention he paid to their visual appearance and their polite or vulgar conversations. He delighted in the company of young women of his social class, and he was not blind to either the charms or shortcomings of girls of lesser status. When he overtook other travelers, he joined them, and in towns he sought out people with whom he could share outings and special events. Most were simple affairs. Hamilton reveled with a "company that came in chairs and on horseback" to a public house four miles outside Boston on fine summer evenings.[21] In Newport the event was a promenade—near town, on foot, the ladies sang, and

[16]Ibid., pp. 22, 51, 102, 119, 123, 142.

[17]Ibid., pp. 63, 158.

[18]Ibid., pp. 63–64.

[19]Ibid., pp. 59, 75–76.

[20]Ibid., p. 59.

[21]Ibid., p. 139.

the whole group numbered only six.[22] Like his observations of buildings, industry, and scenery, his social activities were spontaneous and informal, not packaged entertainment organized by guides or spa proprietors. Hamilton made his own way and participated in activities to which he, as a leisured gentleman, felt fully entitled. He did not need and did not have commercialized facilities to help him enjoy his leisure.

Dr. Hamilton did not remark on any seasonal visitors to Newport. Nevertheless, evidence that southerners and islanders occasionally came by boat to spend the summer at the seaport appears in records as early as the 1730s. Evidence is more abundant in the "society pages" of the *Newport Mercury* from 1767 to 1775. Along with shipping news, the publisher regularly printed announcements about the arrivals and departures of notable visitors. They were identified by government office, military rank, and reputation for wealth, and divided accordingly into two categories, those whose names appeared in capital letters and those for whom lower case was good enough.[23]

Most of Newport's summer visitors came from Charleston. Next most numerous were those from Philadelphia, followed by Jamaicans. The sea voyage took thirty days from Jamaica, ten from Charleston, and five from Philadelphia.[24] No Virginians appear on these published lists, and even though packet boats ran regularly between Newport and New York, no New Yorkers can be identified either. Parties were mostly family groups, often accompanied by servants. Newspaper advertisements for lodgings reveal that they rented furnished houses or suites of rooms. Tavern accommodations were available, but probably the occasional single man, not whole families,

---

[22] Ibid., p. 155.

[23] Carl Bridenbaugh, "Colonial Newport as a Summer Resort," Rhode Island Historical Society *Collections* 26 (1933):3. These American listings seem to imitate more extensive lists of visitors published in the English *Bath Journal* that began to appear in 1744 and continued at least until 1800. See Sylvia McIntyre, "Bath: The Rise of a Resort Town, 1660–1800," in Peter Clark, ed., *Country Towns in Pre-Industrial England* (New York, 1981), p. 208.

[24] Bridenbaugh, "Colonial Newport," p. 5.

slept in these. The season for summer visitors was a long one. Many arrived as early as May and stayed on until October or even November.[25]

The travelers' pleasures were diverse. Concerts, an occasional play, access to the best lending library in America, walks by the water at dusk, a pleasure boat for hire, tea in a nearby town, horse races on the beach, conversations over dinner with friends, picnics, dances, shopping for artificial teeth, complexion cream, hair cushions, and books, instruction in fencing, and lessons in French were diversions to while away the summer.[26] Aside from the single pleasure boat offered for hire, there is no evidence of commercial service specifically intended for visitors. Seasonal residents seem to have moved easily in the social circles of the local squirearchy. They enjoyed each other's company and generally were admired by Newport's other permanent residents.[27] All the same, few of the town's 7,000 to 9,000 inhabitants can have earned a living by catering to the summer trade. The *Newport Mercury* records the arrival of hardly more than 400 tourists over nine years. Admittedly, that total may be low. Although it averages only some 45 visitors per year, numbers varied from season to season, as few as 4 or as many as 99—that is, from one to twelve families. Clearly Newport was not a major commercialized travel destination in America in the 1760s and the early 1770s.[28]

The outbreak of the Revolution shattered the network of business relationships that had brought islanders and southerners to Newport. While the town never recovered its trading prosperity, it retained its reputation as a place to summer. Remembering the Newport of his boyhood between 1792 and 1811, George Gibbs Channing recalled that affluent southerners continued to bring their families not only for the summer months but year round "because of the private school

[25] Ibid., p. 8.

[26] Ibid., pp. 12–17.

[27] Ibid., p. 12.

[28] Ibid., p. 23.

kept there."[29] They made no attempt, he remembered, "at outward display, no building of extravagant residences, and no costly equipages." The one and only concession to the comforts of home was an occasional sailing ship "freighted with Southern edibles, and fitted with elegant accommodations for passengers."[30] It was not until the 1830s that Newport began smartening up as a fashionable watering place with large hotels, handsome private residences, opulent carriages, elegant stores, and a holiday air of prosperity.[31] By 1840 locals were beginning to look on tourism as a mixed blessing. They welcomed the good incomes some earned, but they also were quick to condemn imitation of an "expensive style of living, and too great fondness for convivial entertainments."[32]

Newport residents and visitors had been slower to respond to commercial tourist opportunities than many others in America. Although development elsewhere was very limited in the 1760s and early 1770s, a groundwork was being laid for greater activity from the 1780s to 1830. Thereafter, business boomed all over the United States until the Civil War. These developments take the story beyond the limits of this essay. In both the colonial and Federal periods most urban hotels and rural resorts had similar characteristics and a fairly uniform sequence of growth. A few influential projects stand out for their technological innovations or their levels of capitalization and scale for greater profit. Generally, however, the impression of change during the Federal period was simply a matter of a numerical increase in facilities. Visitors flocked to cities in ever greater numbers, but most excursions to Philadelphia, New York, and Boston combined business and pleasure in ways that confuse the topic of leisure travel. More and more

[29]George Gibbs Channing, *Early Recollections of Newport, R.I.: From the Year 1793 to 1811* (Boston, 1868), p. 42.

[30]Ibid., p. 43.

[31]George C. Mason, *A Hand-Book of Newport and Rhode Island* (Newport, 1852), p. 20.

[32]Sarah S. Cahoone, *Visit to Grand-Papa; or, A Week at Newport* (New York, 1840), p. 178. Also published in New York in 1842 under the title *Sketches of Newport and Its Vicinity.*

destinations suitable for day tripping may have encouraged more people to experiment, however briefly, with a vacation away from home, but these places were not developed to accommodate leisure travelers for extended visits. It makes sense, therefore, after a brief summary of progress in transportation and information systems and a quick glance at urban hotels, to devote the rest of this essay to rural destinations promoted by commercial developers.

A combination of population growth, agricultural improvements, industrial progress, and commercial developments altered the economic climate in late eighteenth-century America in ways that stimulated growth in the travel industry, however indirectly. Urban centers in the East grew as rapidly as the agricultural areas that spread westward. In the newly opened lands the improved plow, the harvester, and the cotton gin increased grain and cotton production and greatly enhanced the value of American agricultural exports. Industry and commerce, concentrated in the Northeast, yielded additional surplus capital. In the dynamic, if unsteady, economy, significantly more people earned incomes and made profits large enough to reinvest in the continuing development of the United States and to spend in the pursuit of leisure.

Pleasure travelers sought destinations with adequate—sometimes even luxurious—amenities. On the way to and from resorts and other attractions, they required ever better meals, lodgings, and a wide range of transportation facilities and services, including improved roads, turnpikes, ferries, bridges, wagons, carriages, stagecoaches, horses, stables, and blacksmiths' repair shops. They also needed travel information, particularly maps and guidebooks. To list these requirements one by one ignores their interrelationship. In reality, they were all mutually dependent components in a travel industry that began to develop in the late colonial era.

While their simultaneous appearance was necessary to effect change, the only way to talk about these developments is one at a time. The design of two- and four-wheeled carriages is as good a place to start as any. Design improved steadily throughout the eighteenth century. Advertisements describe carriages and identify their makers, while personal property tax records and probate inventories record their growing numbers and rising values.[33] Between 1769 and 1772, Pierre Du Simitière, an artist on the lookout for portrait commissions among the carriage trade, compiled careful lists of Philadelphians, New Yorkers, and Bostonians who owned coaches, coach-wagons, and chariots or post chaises.[34] Using these and other sources, historians learn that ownership increased steadily from midcentury to the Revolution. With the coming of peace and independence the numbers of privately owned vehicles grew even more.[35]

Public stage and wagon service also developed in the decade before the Revolution. The principal routes connected the major cities of Boston, New York, and Philadelphia with secondary lines reaching north to Portsmouth, New Hampshire, and south to Wilmington, Baltimore, and Annapolis. In addition to passenger service, the drivers moved goods, carried mail and newspapers, and ran errands.[36] There is no way to estimate the volume of for-hire passenger transportation, but considering that sometimes newspaper advertisements for projected new routes were followed quickly by advertisements for expanded services, demand must have been significant in certain parts of the country. When George Washington supported the new federal government's mail service by stage rather than by horseback, he deliberately endorsed "the means of traveling for strangers, and of intercourse for citizens."[37] Stagecoach operators earned regular incomes for the first time. They could afford

[33]The Museums at Stony Brook, *Nineteenth-Century American Carriages: Their Manufacture, Decoration, and Use* (Stony Brook, N.Y., 1987); Mary Goodwin, "Wheeled Carriages in Eighteenth-Century Virginia," unpublished report, 1959, Colonial Williamsburg Foundation, Williamsburg.

[34]Robert F. Oaks, "Big Wheels in Philadelphia: Du Simitière's List of Carriage Owners," *Pennsylvania Magazine of History and Biography* 95 (1971):351–62.

[35]Holmes and Rohrbach, *Stagecoast East*, pp. 6, 14.

[36]Ibid., p. 13.

[37]Ibid., p. 31.

to improve their facilities and services and could pay tolls on the new turnpikes.[38]

River crossings were the weak link in any early land transportation system. The significance of bridges can easily be underestimated. Ferries consumed time and could be dangerous. For example, on his frequent trips between Williamsburg and his plantation, William Byrd of Westover needed at least five hours to travel twenty-five miles and to cross the Chickahominy River. Because the ferry had to make two crossings to transport his carriage and the four horses that pulled it, Byrd usually sent the carriage ahead and rode to the ferry for the second crossing.[39] Another ferry service, this one across Virginia's York River, boasted a good boat, sufficient hands to run it, a canoe for transporting footmen or others who did not want to travel with the horses, a public house on one side of the river, and the watchful eye of the proprietor who would quickly spot fires or "Smoak on the other side of the River" that signaled waiting passengers.[40] No wonder early travelers noted bridges with care and considered them marvels. Although vital to increased speed and safety, few large bridges were built before the Revolution. Shortly thereafter, spans were laid across the Schuykill, Connecticut, Charles, Mystic, and other rivers, both wide and narrow.[41]

While bridges could speed people overland, steamboats provided more comfortable travel. Although almost twenty years passed between the maiden voyage of a passenger steamboat in America and Robert Fulton and Robert R. Livingston's successful commercial operation on the Hudson River in 1807, steamboats thereafter quickly penetrated the

[38] John Allen Krout and Dixon R. Fox, *The Completion of Independence, 1790–1830* (New York, 1958), pp. 74–91.

[39] Patricia A. Gibbs, memo concerning travel conditions in eighteenth-century Virginia based on the diaries of William Byrd of Westover, Nov. 25, 1985. Research Department, Col. Williamsburg Found.

[40] *Virginia Gazette*, Mar. 28, 1751, reprinted in *William and Mary College Quarterly* 12 (1903):78. I am grateful to Patricia A. Gibbs for this reference.

[41] Krout and Fox, *Completion of Independence*, pp. 82–83; Holmes and Rohrbach, *Stagecoach East*, p. 56.

new nation's inland waterways. The pace of travel quickened further with the advent of the railroad in the 1830s. By 1860 over 30,000 miles of track had been laid.[42] The march of transportation technology reduced travel time literally from weeks to hours. In the 1790s travelers going from Montreal to New York City spent sixteen days in private carriages and boats. By 1809 a combination of stage, ferry, and steamer more than halved the number of days to seven. By 1853 use of railroads and steamboats brought it down to twenty-six and a half hours, and direct trains saved another fifteen hours by 1891. In the space of a century, a journey that once had taken two weeks could be completed overnight and in comfort.[43]

Travelers in the colonies were always eager for information about the road ahead and about the frequency and types of accommodations and services. Towns, taverns, and the distances between them were listed in the 1731 *Vade-Mecum* that Hamilton might have used. Before the Revolution a few enterprising printers and booksellers had published regional road maps showing useful landmarks, roads, ferry crossings, and taverns. They came two ways, "either with rollers or for the pocket."[44] Although strip maps had been available in England since the late seventeenth century, Christopher Colles did not publish the first road map of the United States until 1789.[45]

Many experienced early travelers resorted to the expedient of keeping their own notes for future journeys or relied on information from friends. Harriett Horry's opinions about Virginia and North Carolina taverns are summarized at the beginning of her account of a trip she made north in 1793. She listed distances covered, crossroads or towns she passed

[42]Brooke Hindle and Steven Lubar, *Engines of Change: The American Industrial Revolution, 1790–1860* (Washington, D.C., 1986), p. 146.

[43]H. Walworth, *Four Eras in the History of Travelling between Montreal and New York: From 1793 to 1892* (Plattsburg, N.Y., 1892).

[44]Walter W. Ristow, *American Maps and Mapmakers: Commercial Cartography in the Nineteenth Century* (Detroit, 1985), p. 157.

[45]Christopher Colles, *A Survey of the Roads of the United States of America* (1789; reprint ed., Cambridge, Mass., 1961).

through, names of tavern keepers, the services they provided, their charges, and the quality of meals and accommodations. Her judgments ranged from excellent, good, clean and cold, to tolerable, makeshift, very bad, miserable, and vile.[46] In 1797 George Washington carefully wrote out "an account of the stages on the road" on the 170 miles between Philadelphia and Mount Vernon so that his friend Elizabeth Powell could avoid the worst when she visited. He toted up distances and told her what to expect at sixteen stops. Only a few received his highest rating. At one "the lodging is bad—the eating tolerable"; another was "better for lodging than for eating"; elsewhere, he warned, "the chances are equal whether you get something or nothing." One formerly good house had been sold recently, and he could "give no acct of the present occupant."[47]

Printed, although less detailed, guides became available by the early nineteenth century. In 1802 Mathew Carey of Philadelphia published *The Traveller's Directory,* a hybrid volume covering the main route from New York to Washington with strip maps and accounts "of such remarkable objects as are generally interesting to travellers."[48] Although it was not strictly speaking an aid of this sort, Jedidiah Morse's geography text, the first in America, written for students at his New Haven girls' school, was published in 1783.[49] In 1812 George Temple cribbed its thumbnail descriptions of various New York and New England towns and other landmarks along the routes he described in *The American Tourist's Pocket Companion;*

[46]Harriett Horry, Travel Diary, 1793, South Carolina Historical Society, Charleston. I am grateful to Kym S. Rice for this and the following reference.

[47]George Washington to Elizabeth Powell, Mar. 26, 1797, Mount Vernon Collection, Ladies' Association of the Union, Mt. Vernon, Va.

[48]S. S. Moore and T. W. Jones, *The Traveller's Directory; or, A Pocket Companion: Shewing the Course of the Main Road from Philadelphia to New York, and from Philadelphia to Washington . . . From Actual Survey* (Philadelphia, 1802).

[49]Jedidiah Morse, *The American Geography; or, A View of the Present Situation of the United States of America. Containing Astronomical Geography, Geographical Definitions . . .* (Elizabethtown, [N.J.?], 1789).

or, A Guide to the Springs, and Trip to the Lakes.[50] These books and
several early ones about the Virginia circuit were among the
first American publications to give critical guidance to discriminating travelers.[51]

Most travelers found their accommodations in taverns such
as those Harriett Horry and George Washington patronized.
Two general observations about these buildings and their
furnishings go a long way toward explaining their variable
amenities. First, most taverns looked like, and in fact were,
domestic residences. Paying guests often were obliged to
share family quarters where living space was limited to one or
two rooms with or without lofts. Frequently these were undifferentiated, unspecialized spaces. On the other hand, as standards of living and room use changed and the dwellings of
well-to-do homeowners became larger, prominent taverns, especially those in cities, were sometimes also built on a larger
scale—one that offered private parlors, ballrooms, and less
crowded sleeping chambers to visitors. The City Tavern in
Philadelphia and Fraunces Tavern in New York were two of
the best pre-Revolutionary examples.[52]

Second, tavern financing at this time was a relatively simple
matter of individually owned real and personal property,
rarely the result of complex partnerships or corporate
agreements. The proprietors were solely responsible for the
facilities and services offered to the public, whether they
owned or leased the premises, were solvent or heavily in-

[50]George Temple, *The American Tourist's Pocket Companion; or, A Guide to the Springs, and Trip to the Lakes; Comprising Objects Worthy the Attention of Tourists; Hints for Travelling in Various Manners, Adapted Equally for Those Who May Wish to Combine a Tour for Health and Pleasure with Economy* (New York, 1812).

[51][John Edwards Caldwell], *A Tour through Part of Virginia, in the Summer of 1808, in a Series of Letters, Including an Account of Harper's Ferry, the Natural Bridge, the New Discovery Called Weir's Cave, Monticello, and the Different Medici-nal Springs, Hot and Cold Baths, Visited by the Author* (New York, 1809); James K. Paulding, *Letters from the South, Written during an Excursion in the Summer of 1816* (New York, 1817); idem, *The New Mirror for Travellers and Guide to the Springs by an Amateur* (New York, 1828).

[52]Kym S. Rice, *Early American Taverns: For the Entertainment of Friends and Strangers* (Chicago, 1983), pp. 31–41.

debted.[53] To supply basic creatures comforts for customers, tavern keepers needed to own a minimum stock of domestic goods—beds and bedsteads, sheets, blankets, tables, chairs, tablewares, and utensils. Only as the eighteenth century progressed was this household equipment generally acquired by the sorts of people who ran commercial establishments.[54] Boardinghouses, it should be noted here, also were important in cities. Although they did not offer a full range of services, they were cheaper and quieter than taverns. Perhaps more importantly, because lodgers rented rooms, not sleeping space, some privacy was guaranteed.[55]

While many taverns were slow to change, others grew out of domestic-scaled establishments into ones with characteristics that by 1827 were associated with the new "first class" hotels. Generally, these hotels were larger, more grandly designed, equipped with more and more modern conveniences, backed by complex financial arrangements, promoted by investors and proprietors, and boosted by proud citizens in the communities where they were built.[56]

Earlier hotels were not always moneymakers for investors, but by the 1820s the probability of profits seems to have increased. New York's Tontine Coffee House of 1792 was the success of that decade. Blodget's Hotel, begun the following year in Washington, D.C., brought ruin to its chief advocate and was never finished. Benjamin Latrobe's ambitious proposal in 1797 for a Richmond hotel complete with theater and assembly rooms remained unrealized. The Boston Exchange

[53] Ibid., pp. 31, 37, 39–40.

[54] Lorena S. Walsh, Gloria L. Main, Lois Green Carr, et al., "Toward a History of the Standard of Living in British North America," *William and Mary Quarterly*, 3d ser. 45 (1988):116–70.

[55] Rice, *Early American Taverns*, p. 42.

[56] Doris King first detailed the history of "first-class" hotels in the 1950s. Her work is summarized in Daniel J. Boorstin, "Palaces of the Public," in *The Americans: The National Experience* (New York, 1965), pp. 134–47. For the following summary I have relied more on Janice Boyle Knowles, "Luxury Hotels in American Cities, 1810–1860," Ph.D. diss., University of Pennsylvania, 1972.

Hotel, begun in 1806, plunged its first investor into bank-ruptcy. This eight-story building, with nearly 600 rooms, cost $400,000 and was sold at auction to a joint-stock company. Under David Barnum's skillful management it flourished briefly until it burned in 1818. Barnum moved to Baltimore where, by 1826, leading citizens put together a complicated financial package to build the Baltimore City Hotel with six stories, two hundred rooms, a barbershop, and street-level stores. Boston's Tremont House, designed by Isaiah Rogers, the premier American hotel architect of his era, opened with fanfare in 1829 and operated profitably.

City taverns, boardinghouses, and brand new hotels con-tributed to the growth of urban business, regional economic development, political life, and civic pride. They also signifi-cantly promoted the development of tourism, but, unfortu-nately, historians cannot distinguish between those customers who traveled on business and those who were pleasure trip-pers. For that purpose it is necessary to look closely at destina-tions associated with the idea of a vacation. Both before and after the Revolution, these were invariably rural places where travelers sought to improve their health.

Spas located near major cities—such as Newton Springs, Massachusetts, ten miles from Boston, and Yellow Springs and Bristol Springs, Pennsylvania—twenty and thirty miles, respectively, outside Philadelphia—attracted day trippers. They were among the first American tourist destinations to be commercialized and advertised. Although some affluent patrons traveled to nearby spas in their own carriages, usually public transportation was important to the success of these ventures. John Wood ran two daily round trips from Boston to Newton Springs by 1767. Bristol Springs, lying on the main route south from New York, was well serviced by public ve-hicles. Beginning in 1763 a triweekly stage-wagon carried visitors from Philadelphia to Yellow Springs.[57] The advertise-ments for Yellow Springs are among the first to describe the amenities offered by these early resorts. A number of enter-tainments—dining, dancing, bathing, and drinking the healthful waters—were equally available to overnight lodgers

---

[57]Bridenbaugh, "Baths and Watering Places," pp. 156, 165, 170.

and day trippers. The latter accounted for most of the business, probably outnumbering the longer-term guests by about ten to one. Advertisements also made perfectly clear that the colonial facilities were far from lavish; what we think of as basic amenities usually came with improvements in the nineteenth century. The proprietor of Yellow Springs maintained the two most elaborate bathhouses at any colonial spa. Even so, each was only thirty-five by sixteen feet, and was divided into a bathing room and a drawing room. There were glass windows front and back. Only one was heated by a fireplace.[58]

More distant spas offer a more instructive contrast between tourist travel in the pre-Revolutionary period and its growth in the Federal era. In the winter of 1776, Philip Vickers Fithian, riding circuit in the Blue Ridge Mountains of Virginia, paused to wash his face and hands in the very warm clear water flowing from one of the natural springs found in the valleys throughout western Virginia. Fithian knew from personal experience that two or three hundred people bathed in the pool in the summer but reported that it was utterly deserted in winter. He explained that it was not better known and more extensively developed because of the great distance between its remote location and settled areas, the poor quality of the stony mountain road, and "the little Leisure which the greatest Number of the Americans yet have."[59] Fithian could not imagine that fifty years later thousands would make the circuit of the Virginia springs and equally large numbers would travel widely to seaside and mountain resorts and to other spas.

Stafford Springs, Connecticut, located northeast of Hartford, was seventy miles from Boston and too far from any other population center to have catered to daily travelers. The sequence and scale of its development were typical of rural resorts. Although small numbers of travelers visited there in the colonial period, investment, promotion, and expansion

[58]Carol Shiels Roark, "Historic Yellow Springs: The Restoration of an American Spa," *Pennsylvania Folklife* 24 (1974):28–38.

[59]Robert Greenhalgh Albion and Leonidas Dodson, eds., *Philip Vickers Fithian: Journal, 1775–1776. Written on the Virginia-Pennsylvania Frontier and in the Army around New York* (Princeton, 1934), p. 162.

came only in the early nineteenth century. In the same year that he was running two daily round trips to Newton Springs, John Wood offered to send a stage-wagon to the more distant Stafford Springs on those occasions when he had "a full company."[60] No records tell how frequently he made the extra trip, but John Adams's diary gives some clue as to the few travelers using private transportation. Traveling for his own health in early June 1771, he reported a "naked, barren journey." On his way home he passed three couples that he knew, traveling with relatives and servants in five chaises, presumably on their way to the spa. He wrote, "This week and the next would have brought together a curious collection of characters from all parts of New England, and some, perhaps, from the southern Provinces, and some from the West Indies."[61] The description he provides suggests that a Mr. Child, who owned the springs, had not developed them extensively. Adams drank the waters "with a glass mug broken to pieces and puttied together again." He bathed in "a little reservoir made of wood, about three feet deep," which was covered with a "shed." Nearby he noted "a small house . . . [where] some of the lame and infirm people keep." Mrs. Child sent him to lodge in the village where he spent two nights.[62] Clearly, Adams did not think much of the place.

By 1810 the road from Hartford to Worcester had been turnpiked, which improved business at Stafford Springs. "For a number of years this spring has been neglected for want of convenient accommodations," George Temple wrote in 1812, "but lately buildings are erected, and the visitants have increased." Temple specifically mentioned several boardinghouses that occasionally accommodated as many as a hundred guests.[63] An aquatint of the period shows the three-story hotel built by the physician Dr. S. Willard. Rooms opened onto porches on one gabled end, and there were two small build-

[60] Bridenbaugh, "Baths and Watering Places," p. 156.

[61] Charles Francis Adams, ed., *The Works of John Adams,* 10 vols. (Boston, 1850–56), 2:277.

[62] Ibid., p. 267.

[63] George Temple, *Tourist's Pocket Companion,* p. 66.

ings that may have been bathing facilities. Other nearby structures, shown in another print, were an old ironworks, a
fenced lawn, and tables and benches under a clump of trees
in a rocky glen.[64]

Ballston Spa and nearby Saratoga Springs in upstate New
York were unknown in the colonial era. The first rude tavern
went up in Ballston in 1787. Another twenty years went by
before a New York City investor built and aggressively promoted the Sans Souci Hotel, which could lodge 150 guests.
By then other entrepreneurs were pushing similar schemes.[65]
Farther south the famous Catskill Mountain House took its
earliest form about 1819 as a small refreshment stand outfit-
ted with a few bunks. A short time later entrepreneurs added
a dormitory with separate wings for men and women, and in
1822 they enlarged it into a ten-room hotel to which they
soon added forty more rooms.[66]

This sequence, familiar elsewhere in the North, had its
southern counterpart in Virginia's Blue Ridge Mountains.
The attraction of convivial society, the desire to escape from
the hot and humid Tidewater climate, and the everlasting
search for good health brought many well-to-do travelers to
the mountains, especially to Berkeley Springs, which Lord
Fairfax had given the colony in 1756. Some travelers rode
their own horses while others took their carriages and sent
their luggage on ahead in wagons. No public stagecoach traveled the road until after the Revolution. The House of Burgesses first proposed a lottery to improve the mountain road
in 1763, but not until 1772 was £900 raised.[67] Three years
later the "good Coach-Road" impressed circuit rider Fithian.[68] Because Berkeley Warm Springs was too far way ever

[64]Gerald W. R. Ward and William N. Hosley, Jr., eds., *The Great River: Art and Society of the Connecticut Valley, 1635–1820* (Hartford, 1985), pp.465–67.

[65]Nancy Goyne Evans, "The Sans Souci: A Fashionable Resort Hotel in Ballston Spa," *Winterthur Portfolio* 6 (1970):111–26.

[66]Roland Van Zandt, *The Catskill Mountain House* (Cornwallville, N.Y., 1982), pp. 28–44.

[67]Bridenbaugh, "Baths and Watering Places," p. 164.

[68]Albion and Dodson, eds., *Fithian Journal*, p. 163.

to become a day trip, George Washington's 1761 estimate of a "Company" of two hundred and Philip Fithian's 1775 estimate of four hundred, about half of whom were "visibly indisposed," are noteworthy.[69]

Facilities at Berkeley were modest, to say the least. Through the 1760s and 1770s, visitors bathed in privacy behind a pine stockade. In 1761 George Washington reported food in abundance but lodgings could "be had on no terms but building for them. . . . Had we not succeeded in getting a tent and marquee at Winchester, we should have been in a most miserable situation here." He made family trips with Mrs. Washington and then with her and Patsy Custis in 1767 and 1769. On both occasions he had to repair the rented accommodations and devote much time to securing supplies and services.[70]

Fithian had less to say about Berkeley's development than about the activities he observed there in 1775. His few paragraphs suggest that it was a most curious place. Distinguished individuals are described as "white, feeble, weak," "the Picture of Decrepitude," or "much disordered with the Rheumatism." They were living in a "little bush Village" but on Friday nights one could dance at "a splendid Ball," play all sorts of fast gambling card games in the "dining Room," or listen to a Methodist preacher "haranguing the People." From twelve to four in the morning gentlemen serenaded softly "at different Houses where the Ladies lodge[d]." A visiting Scot, over whom Fithian lost all Presbyterian restraint, was "stimulated by a plentiful Use of these Vigor-giving Waters" and broke into the "Lodging Room of buxom Kate"—with what consequences Fithian dared not speculate.[71] Life at the springs was certainly rustic, but it was not dull. Long before commercial development provided visitors with the comforts of home, they put up with considerable inconvenience for the pleasure of a frolic together in the woods. Southerners and a few afflicted northerners were very ready to exercise the preroga-

[69] Ibid., p. 125.

[70] Bridenbaugh, "Baths and Watering Places," p. 161.

[71] Albion and Dodson, eds., *Fithian Journal*, pp. 126–27.

tives of their class and to buy their leisure as they would any other commodity.

Commercial development at the Virginia springs clearly was led by demand, but as events at Berkeley Springs demonstrated, success was not a foregone conclusion. A Virginia legislative act set aside fifty acres for a proper town in 1776, with the place to be named "Bath." A board of trustees would supervise development, and citizens were "to build convenient houses for accommodating numbers of infirm persons, who frequent these springs yearly."[72] But although various inns and resort cottages were eventually built there, Berkeley Springs, or Bath, never lived up to its early promise.[73] It was located too far north of the Virginia springs circuit that became fashionable in the nineteenth century.

In the immediate postwar years a group of springs extending some seventy-five miles through the valleys of western Virginia were developed into spas. Some were warm, others hot, still others sulphurous, and a few "sweet." Pilgrims traveled from one to another sampling the remedies and enjoying the variety of entertainments at different but not too distant destinations. Four spas made up the earliest circuit, three more soon were added, and by the mid-nineteenth century dozens more were scattered through the mountains and out into the Piedmont closer to Richmond and Washington. The success of the spas was sustained by the growing economic and political importance of the region.

The first spa was Sweet Springs, where in the 1780s a former soldier built a cluster of log cabins "rendered as comfortable as such buildings made in haste will admit." A hotel there had only eight lodging rooms in 1792. Business improved when the fledging spa became the site of the county court. It flourished modestly and briefly when a well-known gambler arrived.[74]

White Sulphur Springs, today's Greenbriar, soon surpassed

[72]Bridenbaugh, "Baths and Watering Places," p. 164.

[73]Percival Reniers, *The Springs of Virginia: Life, Love, and Death at the Waters, 1775–1900* (Chapel Hill, N.C., 1941), pp. 33–41.

[74]Ibid., pp. 41–47.

Sweet Springs in popularity. The aging Thomas Jefferson visited three of the four springs in August 1818. He noted 18 visitors at Warm Springs, 20 at "the Hot," and 150 at White Sulphur. The throngs of visitors probably were attracted by the heavy investment its owner had made in the previous year. James Calwell had built a small tavern on the site in 1809. It grew slowly until 1817 when Calwell borrowed $20,000 to expand his facilities. He continued to borrow for decades to come until, at his death in 1851, his debts totaled $400,000. Calwell's investment attracted attention, but he was overextended and the resort was poorly run. Still, it anticipated a scale of activity that became much more common in the 1830s.[75]

Development at Hot Springs, now Homewood, was less dramatic. Its slower growth was more characteristic of the scale of operations at most early nineteenth-century health spas. One Hezekiah Daggs began peddling in the area about 1814. He opened a general store and a blacksmith shop and in 1817 was hired at an annual salary to keep a tavern at the site. He subsequently leased it. From 1822 to 1827 he was never out of debt, but from 1828 to 1833, years for which no lease agreements survive, business must have improved because in December 1833 he bought Botetourt Springs and ran it for the next two years. Within the years around 1830 the number of visitors to the tavern at Hot Springs doubled. Between May 1 and October 10, 1828, Daggs accommodated 218 visitors; the number for 1833 was 445. Most parties stayed less than a week; very few stayed more than two. Using Jefferson's figure of 20 visitors in August 1818 to project estimates of visitation over a ten-week season from late June to early September, it appears that business was only moderately good during the 1820s, but improved thereafter.[76]

General economic conditions go a long way toward ex-

[75]Ibid., pp. 48–66; Stan Cohen, *Historic Springs of the Virginias* (Charleston, W.Va., 1981), pp. 170–86; Marshall W. Fishwick, *Springlore in Virginia* (Bowling Green, Ohio, 1978), pp. 114–21.

[76]Olive Blair Graffam, "The Commercialization of Leisure at the Antebellum Springs of Virginia: Studies of Hot Springs and Fauquier White Sulphur Springs," M.A. thesis, George Washington University, 1988, pp. 55–75.

plaining the measured pace of spa development in Virginia. Ventures begun after the Revolution were slowed by the War of 1812, hard hit by the panic of 1819, and recovered gradually through the 1820s. Prosperity increased and business began to boom in the 1830s. From then until the Civil War many routes were well supplied with relatively speedy service and reliable accommodations, although travelers still had to accept a wide range of conditions. Veritable "palaces for the public" sprang up. Writing in the 1860s, Anthony Trollope noted "in the States of America the first sign of an incipient settlement is an hotel five stories high, with an office, a bar, a cloak-room, three gentlemen's parlours, two ladies' parlours, a ladies' entrance, and two hundred bedrooms."[77] Mountain and seaside resorts throughout the country were equally well developed, as shown in Edward Beyer's 1858 *Album of Virginia,* which illustrates the impressive buildings of most of the mountain spas and the Hygeia Hotel at Point Comfort on the Chesapeake Bay.[78] By the 1850s, the American tourist industry was firmly launched.

In the first decades of the new republic, men, women, and children began to travel in unprecedented numbers. The discussion of tourist travel in America has focused so far on improved facilities and services and on the growing numbers of travel publications. But even these new levels of comfort, convenience, and information cannot entirely explain why people chose to use their leisure for pleasure travel. No doubt travelers set out on their journeys for a variety of reasons. Some of these were as new as the new republic and deserve closer examination.

Adequate discretionary income was essential, of course, but discovering who had the money, where it came from, and in what years people of different wealth categories began to spend it on travel lies well beyond the scope of this paper.[79]

[77] Anthony Trollope, "American Hotels," in *North America* (1862), quoted in Boorstin, *The Americans: The National Experience,* p. 141.

[78] Edward Beyer, *Album of Virginia* (Richmond, 1858).

[79] In *Springs of Virginia,* pp. 89–95, Reniers details how much pleasure travel could be derived from the sale of a bale of upland cotton in the 1830s.

There is no question that travel cost more than many other forms of commercialized leisure. Elizabeth Drinker's travel accounts in 1771 show just how expensive it could be. She, her young son, and a maid visited Bristol Springs on the Delaware River from late June to early August. They lodged with a widow in what was essentially a rooming house. Mr. Drinker and two more of the couple's children visited at least once during the six weeks. The cost of the visits in Pennsylvania currency was £88.3.8, approximately the annual income of a laboring Philadelphian.[80] Four years later Philip Fithian spent 12 s. 8 d. for two nights at Virginia's Warm Springs.[81] By comparison, decorated teacups, saucers, and nine-inch plates were priced at 5 to 8 d. apiece.[82] Clearly, it was less expensive to buy goods, to bet on a local horse race, to pay for admission to a scientific demonstration at a tavern, or to buy a book or a newspaper than it was to travel in style.

Other explanations for the increase in travel involve changing mental attitudes that, although noticeable enough over a broad time span to merit attention, are not susceptible to measurement and are difficult to prove. The development of modern notions of time and work discipline, the wish for better health, the greater awareness of a broader world, the appreciation of landscape, the desire for sociability with people beyond one's immediate neighborhood, the pursuit of fashion, and the self-confidence to try something new cannot be measured. However, if pleasure travel required both a pull toward a distant destination and a push away from home, these factors provided the momentum.

Pleasure travel differs from many other leisure-time activities in another way. It requires spare time. Time and money to spend on recreational pursuits mark two important differ-

[80]Bridenbaugh, "Baths and Watering Places," p. 176; Billy G. Smith, "The Material Lives of Laboring Philadelphians, 1750–1800," *William and Mary Quarterly*, 3d ser. 38 (1981):185.

[81]Albion and Dodson, eds., *Fithian Journal*, p. 127.

[82]George L. Miller, "Classification and Economic Scaling of Nineteenth-Century Ceramics," *Historical Archaeology* 14 (1980):1–40; idem, "Prices and Index Values for English Ceramics from 1787 to 1880," unpublished manuscript, 1988, Department of Archaeological Research, Col. Williamsburg Found.

ences between the leisured class and working people and between traditional and modern concepts of work time and
playtime. Preindustrial ideas about class-bound uses of leisure
time are easier to describe at the top and the bottom of the
social order than they are for the "middling sort." People in
the middle ranks of society are, of course, our prime interest.
Today wage earners and salaried employees are entitled to
paid vacations, a benefit introduced for middle managers in
industry in the second half of the nineteenth century and extended, despite union and worker resistance, to hourly laborers during World War II.[83] In the eighteenth and early
nineteenth centuries most Americans depended for their livelihood either on their own labor or on regular, if not daily,
attention to business. For them, as Benjamin Franklin made
clear, there was a one-to-one relationship between time and
income. Most eighteenth-century Americans could not afford
leisure time to travel for purely personal pleasure. Merchants
and tradesmen, politicians and military men traveled for business. Occasionally, members of their families accompanied
them.[84]

Many ordinary people could participate in simple forms of
commercialized leisure without varying the rhythm of pre-
industrial life or consciously accepting new concepts of enti-
tlement to leisure time. A few hours here and there or even a
day or two were often available when people needed them.
One theorist contrasts the modern idea of free time, which he
refers to as "a lump of concentrated nothingness," with the
traditional workday, which most resembles "a jellylike substance, [which] could hardly be called a notion, much less a
concept."[85] Working according to preindustrial rhythms,
farmers, craftsmen, tradesmen, their neighbors, and their

[83]The National Industrial Conference Board, *Time Off with Pay* (New
York, 1957), and Donna Allen, *Fringe Benefits: Wages or Social Obligation? An
Analysis with Historical Perspectives from Paid Vacations*, rev. ed. (Ithaca, N.Y.,
1969).

[84]George Washington frequently mentions in his diary that his wife accompanied him on business to Williamsburg. Elizabeth Drinker traveled
with her husband.

[85]Sebastian de Grazia, *Of Time, Work, and Leisure* (New York, 1962), pp.
200–201.

customers rose when they liked and began work when they liked. If anything of interest came their way, they stopped to watch or to take part. This is not to say they were lazy or had forgotten the Protestant work ethic. Nor does it deny the obedience apprentices, journeymen, wives, and children owed their masters, husbands, and fathers. But the time they spent one day gossiping with neighbors, drinking small beer, or indulging in one of the new forms of commercialized leisure, they could make up the next by working longer and harder. Intermingled with the work they had to do was a good deal of spare time, so much that some historians speculate that over an entire calendar year people in traditional communities actually worked fewer days and fewer hours than people today. Some unoccupied time was devoted to religious holidays and public ceremonies. Much spare time was simply unplanned—the random appearances of peddlers or visits by neighbors, for example. The rhythms of industry, where a factory bell called people to work, changed ideas about the relationship of work time and free time among the laboring classes.[86] Historians have had much to say about work discipline and time. Almost nothing has been written, however, to describe how attitudes toward time began to change among people who made up the new class of travelers.

How did people justify spending time pleasing themselves away from home? Frequently travelers told themselves and others that their trips were necessary for the sake of their health. But social critics and moralists ruthlessly stripped away this self-deception and underneath found love of sociability and a yen for fashion. In the history of commercialized leisure and travel, spas were the first and most important destinations. People unaccustomed to the idea of travel for its own sake justified diverting time and money from other pursuits under a supposed need for medical attention. Poor health often caused genuine distress, and medical knowledge was primitive. Those who could afford it preferred preven-

[86]Keith Thomas, "Work and Leisure in Pre-Industrial Society," *Past and Present* 29 (1964):50–66; Neil McKendrick, "Josiah Wedgwood and Factory Discipline," *Historical Journal* 4 (1961):3–28.

tion to treatment. This was especially true for southerners who lived in malarial regions and for city dwellers who feared the outbreak of yellow fever. Of course, one person's desire to take the waters offered ample excuse for other family members to take their pleasure.[87]

Whatever justification they offered for their journeys, most travelers in the period were adamant that leisure should not be taken as a license for laziness. Josiah Tucker, writing in 1757, criticized those who traveled for no better reason than to alleviate boredom at home. "It would be Loss of Time to take any other notice of them, than just to observe, That they are sure of returning Home as Wise as they went out, but much more Impertinent, less Wealthy, and Less Innocent." He thought the frivolous traveler was to be found only in England, "a Country of universal Freedom and Opulence." Reasons for travel that Tucker accepted as sound were as stern and dogmatic as a dictionary definition for leisure—a freedom or opportunity to do something useful, afforded by unoccupied time. People fortunate enough to have leisure at their disposal were expected to use it for self-improvement. By the eighteenth century an improved temperament was associated less with private meditation on the hereafter and more with acquisitions and activities visible to or discussed with one's neighbors. Tucker mentioned collecting antiquities or works of nature, acquiring a taste for music, developing skill at drawing or painting, or taking on foreign mannerisms and new conversational phrases. To him the most commendable motive of all for travel was "to rub off local Prejudices" and to gain an "enlarged and impartial View of Men and Things."[88]

American travel journals and diaries suggest that more and more travelers agreed with Tucker and took to the road to satisfy their curiosity about the world beyond home. Elizabeth Drinker, writing in the 1760s and 1770s about trips she took

[87] Grover, "Magic Fountains: Saratoga and Physical Health," in "Luxury and Leisure," pp. 130–68; Reniers, "The Plague Lends a Hand," in *Springs of Virginia,* pp. 67–74.

[88] Josiah Tucker, *Instructions for Travellers* (1757; reprint ed., n.d.), p. 3.

with her husband, noted their visits to ironworks, a copper mine, and a glass house.[89] In an early nineteenth-century diary Harriet Horry professed interest in devices for cooling food and also in brickmaking.[90] Such observations sometimes led, Tucker advised, to discoveries "which may with Advantage be naturalized at Home" or invested in for profit.[91]

To see landscapes as unexploited sites for economic development or simply as beautiful places is not an innate human response to the environment. Both points of view have a recent history. The market economies of sixteenth- and seventeenth-century Europe required people to make business decisions based on new ways of looking at the world. The promoters of industry and commerce objectified natural resources as commodities to be bought and sold. Their appreciation of the picturesque in painting and literature had a similar basis in their ability to see landscape as a commodity. Perhaps more importantly for the growth of pleasure travel, the concept of the picturesque gave knowledgeable tourists a mental framework in which to take visual pleasure in scenery and talk with others about it.[92]

Novice travelers needed more than basic information about routes and hotels. They needed travel tips, not to mention reassurances that they would have a good time. A new breed of magazine and new novels of social realism were crammed with vivid portrayals of people traveling for pleasure. Fictional characters served as role models for readers unsure of how to behave.[93] Other publications—textbooks on geography, for instance, and writing manuals—may have en-

[89] Henry D. Biddle, ed., *Extracts from the Journal of Elizabeth Drinker, from 1759 to 1807* (Philadelphia, 1889), pp. 21, 31, 36.

[90] Harriett Horry, Travel Diary, 1815, entry for May 28, 1815, S.C. Hist. Soc. I am grateful to Kym S. Rice for suggesting this diary.

[91] Tucker, *Instructions for Travellers*, p. 4.

[92] Bruce Robertson, "The Picturesque Traveler in America," in Edward J. Mygren with Bruce Robertson, *Views and Visions: American Landscape before 1830* (Washington, D.C., 1986); Kenneth Myers, *The Catskills: Painters, Writers, and Tourists in the Mountains, 1820–1895* (Yonkers, N.Y., 1987).

[93] Two of the best examples are Tobias Smollett's *Humphrey Clinker* and Jane Austen's *Pride and Prejudice*.

couraged travel indirectly by stimulating curiosity and by suggesting "If I have done it, you can too." Caleb Bingham's *Juvenile Letters* presented its instructions on letter writing as an account of a young girl's trip from Boston to Mount Vernon.[94]

Around the turn of the century significant numbers of Europeans began traveling to this new United States to see it for themselves. Many described their experiences in print. No matter what their judgments—as disapproving as Mrs. Trollope's or more favorable like Basil Hall's—their published journals opened Americans' eyes to the sights their country offered and taught them how they, too, could see it for themselves. The native-born writer Anne Newport Royall unabashedly imitated these Europeans in hopes that her books would rival their success. Her volumes, published between 1826 and 1831, overflow with enough energy, enthusiasm, and personal prejudice to titillate the most stay-at-home reader.[95] Royall wrote travel books for a living. As a practical businesswoman she pressed owners of stagecoaches, steamboats, and hotels for free services and accommodations in return for promotion in her books. Her unsophisticated, straightforward curiosity and pride in America capitalized on the equally unsophisticated patriotism of her reading public. The United States was expanding and changing rapidly. People who wanted to see it for themselves followed Anne Royall's example, flocked into cities, and journeyed to mountain and seaside resorts.

Despite moralists' condemnations, the enthusiasm for pleasure tripping in the early nineteenth century owes something to fashion. Fashion in appearance and behavior may seem trifling, but it is a sign of a society that is restless, innovative, and

---

[94]Caleb Bingham, *Juvenile Letters, Being a Correspondence between Children from Eight to Fifteen Years of Age* (Boston, 1803).

[95]Anne Newport Royall, *Sketches of History, Life, and Manners in the United States* (1826); *The Tennesseean* (1827); *The Black Book* (1828–29); *Mrs. Royall's Pennsylvania* (1829); *Letters from Alabama* (1830); and *Mrs. Royall's Southern Tour* (1830–31). Mrs. Royall's interest in travel and tourism was probably encouraged by the years she spent near the developing Sweet Springs in western Virginia.

willing to change.[96] Public display is said to have inspired social emulation, encouraged competition, and set off a chain reaction of spending. In traditional societies people were more likely to accept their birthplace in the social order; they acquired suitable possessions and engaged in social activities accordingly. The narrowing of social distance and the spreading of social emulation are considered contributors to the consumer and commercial revolutions of the eighteenth century. These demand-side spurs to the supply-side Industrial Revolution were inspired largely by changing habits in the acquisition of personal property—clothes and adornment, teapots, forks, and tablewares, bedding, and other furniture. The desire to own and display these objects and to experiment with new kinds of leisure activities is evidence that the inhibiting, conservative ideas about appropriate behavior for members of social classes below the very top were undergoing fundamental changes.[97]

The English traveler Robert Southey was among the first to comment on the changing character of touring soon after the turn of the nineteenth century. Mineral springs, he observed, had been the only destinations early in the eighteenth century. But in recent times health concerns "almost ceased to be the pretext." Increasingly, people traveled to seaside resorts for bathing and to the mountains and lakes to study picturesque landscapes, "a new science . . . which assuredly was not possessed by their fathers." According to him, they were inspired by the desire to hobnob with society, by the ambition to find husbands for their daughters, and by fashion. "For the

[96] Fernand Braudel, *Civilization and Capitalism, 15th-18th Century,* vol. 1, *The Structures of Everyday Life: The Limits of the Possible,* trans. Siân Reynolds (New York, 1981), p. 323.

[97] Neil McKendrick, John Brewer, and J. H. Plumb, *The Birth of a Consumer Society: The Commercialization of Eighteenth-Century England* (Bloomington, Ind., 1982), pp. 20–21. See also Chandra Muckerji, *From Graven Images: Patterns of Modern Materialism* (New York, 1983); Colin Campbell, *The Romantic Ethic and the Spirit of Modern Consumerism* (London, 1987); Grant McCracken, *Culture and Consumption: New Approaches to the Symbolic Character of Consumer Goods and Activities* (Bloomington, Ind., 1988).

pride of wealth is as ostentatious in this country as ever the pride of birth has been elsewhere."[98]

Southey emphasized opportunities for courtship and sociability to be enjoyed away from home. Travel was for everyone, women as well as men, the young no less than the old. It brought together people of more or less the same class who otherwise lacked the connections that were established through neighborhood, kinship, or everyday business or professional associations. Opportunities to socialize may have been especially attractive to bourgeois women. As men and their income-earning activities were increasingly removed from the home, women's lives focused around the "cult of domesticity." Family travel could vary home-centered activity without threatening its fundamental importance.

Simultaneous improvements in facilities and services appeared everywhere in the United States by the early nineteenth century. They mirrored deeper transformations in people's self-perceptions and worldview. Scenery was objectified and appreciated, sometimes for profit, but also for visual pleasure. Money seemingly frittered away on fashions and social events may also be regarded as investment in experimental forms of social interaction and the acquisition of new kinds of self-confidence. The search for better health was both a real quest and a pretext that combined self-indulgence with self-improvement. Taken together, these changes comprise the social history of early tourism in America. The increase in vacation travel was more than a temporary change of address for a few well-to-do ladies and gentlemen. It signified the more generally widespread feeling of optimism and opportunity shared by many citizens in the new republic.

[98] Robert Southey, *Letters from England* (1807; reprint ed., London, 1951), pp. 164–65.

NANCY L. STRUNA

Sport and the
Awareness of Leisure

A CONSUMER REVOLUTION in sports involving both men and
women came later to Americans than it did to Britons. Not
until the 1820s did citizens of the United States experience
the highly commercialized and specialized sporting forms and
opportunities that English historians have discovered in late
eighteenth-century Britain. Only then did unabashed commercialized events exist. Equipment manufacturers and retailers sold specialized sporting goods. The middle and upper
ranks of society, particularly in towns and cities, exercised
their hegemony over American sporting styles and mores.[1]

Many of the central features of this eventual consumer revolution—its sports, its facilities, its performers, even its rhetoric—flowed directly from changes in the sporting culture in
the century before the 1820s. Early Americans developed spe-

[1] J. H. Plumb, "The Commercialization of Leisure in Eighteenth-Century
England," in Neil McKendrick, John Brewer, and J. H. Plumb, *The Birth of
a Consumer Society: The Commercialization of Eighteenth-Century England*
(Bloomington, Ind., 1982), pp. 265–85; idem, *Georgian Delights* (Boston,
1980), pp. 40–45, 112–27. See also Robert W. Malcolmson, *Popular Recreations in English Society, 1700–1850* (Cambridge, 1973); Hugh Cunningham,
Leisure in the Industrial Revolution (New York, 1980); John K. Walton and
James Walvin, eds., *Leisure in Britain, 1780–1939* (Manchester, 1983); Michael R. Marrus, ed., *The Emergence of Leisure in Industrial Society* (St. Louis,
1974). No comparable works on American leisure in the eighteenth or nineteenth centuries exist. The most recent and satisfactory discussion of the
1820s as the beginning of a new, commercializing period in the social history of American sport appears in Melvin L. Adelman, *A Sporting Time: New
York City and the Rise of Modern Athletics, 1820–70* (Urbana, Ill., 1985); see also
John Dizikes, *Sportsmen and Gamesmen* (New York, 1981). Earlier and less
complete descriptions of the pivotal nature of the 1820s include John R.
Betts, *America's Sporting Heritage* (Reading, Mass., 1974), and Jennie Holli-
man, *American Sports, 1785–1835* (Durham, N.C., 1931).

cific forms of sport out of more general ones, and they used
and acquired equipment and facilities expressly designed for
sport.[2] Sometimes practiced by only the few, and at other
times shared by many colonists, the sport forms that took
shape and the facilities that were utilized emerged from two
sporting traditions, genteel and folk. Clubs and other less
highly structured groups also formed, and some of them standardized and rationalized particular sports in ways that incorporated both traditions. Eventually some competitive
recreations came to be associated with leisure time, even as
other forms of sport remained tied to ordinary tasks and traditional gatherings. Clearly distinct from either work time or
idle time, but not yet equivalent to the British conception of
free time, this particular sense of early American leisure fostered activities that improved, enlightened, and cultivated,
and it was in leisure time that some forms of sport ultimately
came to be enjoyed on a revolutionary scale.

In 1700 the sporting life of Anglo-Americans resembled that
of seventeenth-century English provincials more than it did
that of either contemporary Londoners or late eighteenth-
and early nineteenth-century Americans. Many forms of
sport, like hunting and fishing, remained general ones. One
either aimed a weapon or cast a line, and in the process the
distinctions between necessary or supplemental food gathering and sport blurred. Other activities were associated with
locally meaningful residual rituals, such as Shrove Tuesday in
Boston where laborers leashed a cock to a pole and shailed
(struck) at it with sticks. In nearby Marblehead a man arranged a bull bait for November 5 (Pope's Day or Guy Fawkes
Day), and, in the Chesapeake, harvest festivals included feats
of physical strength and agility. Competitive recreations also
occurred in the context of ordinary communal life. In the
South, common planters boxed and drank at the ordinaries
(taverns) and "burnt their clothes to save the Mending," and

[2]Throughout this paper I use the term *sport* as an inclusive, descriptive
one. It embraces games, field contests, baits, races, athletic contests, and
diversions and pastimes requiring physical action and prowess. Seven-
teenth- and eighteenth-century Britons and American colonists used the
term far more broadly than do twentieth-century Americans.

boat races took place on the rivers and sounds of New York. Black slaves, naked and armed with knives, dived after sharks in the Carolinas, and throughout the colonies provincials played ninepins and cards at taverns and displayed their shooting skills at trainings. Integrated within and integral to the lives of many colonists, these contests, as had English sport for centuries, provided opportunities for enjoyment, gambling, and physical display.[3]

This brief description leaves out much of the variety of colonial sporting life but not its fundamental experiences. As the eighteenth century began, Anglo-American sport was tied more closely to labor and acts of necessity than to conscious and patterned leisure, and to the affairs of local, public, group life than to private, individual lives. But some colonists had begun to alter residual forms, literally from the ground up. During the 1660s and 1670s, in New York, Massachusetts, and Virginia, racemen had moved their contests from main thoroughfares to unused or unusable grounds.[4] Early eighteenth-century sporting venues also appeared as specialized areas. Within a decade after the first printing of a news-

[3]Samuel Sewall, *The Diary of Samuel Sewall*, 3 vols. (1878–82; reprint ed., New York, 1972), 1:167; Robert E. Moody, ed., *The Saltonstall Papers, 1607–1815* (Boston, 1972), p. 271; "Narrative of a Voyage to Maryland, 1705–6," *American Historical Review* 12 (1907):334–35; William J. Hinke, trans. and ed., "Report of the Journey of Francis Louis Michel from Berne, Switzerland, to Virginia, October 2, 1701–December 1, 1702," *Virginia Magazine of History and Biography* 24 (1916):129; Ebenezer Cook, "The Sot-Weed Factor: Or a Voyage to Maryland. A Satyr," in Bernard C. Steiner, ed., *Early Maryland Poetry: The Works of Ebenezer Cook, Gent., Laureat of Maryland* (Baltimore, 1900), p. 23; John Lawson, *A New Voyage to Carolina* (1709; reprint ed., Chapel Hill, N.C., 1967), p. 158; Louis B. Wright and Marion Tinling, eds., *The Secret Diary of William Byrd of Westover, 1709–1712* (Richmond, 1941), pp. 414–15. Discussions of British sport appear in Malcolmson, *Popular Recreations;* Dennis Brailsford, *Sport and Society: Elizabeth to Anne* (London, 1969); William Strutt, *The Sports and Pastimes of the People of England* (London, 1803).

[4]John Hervey, *Racing in America*, 2 vols. (New York, 1944), 1:6–8, 19–20, 29–31; W. G. Stanard, "Racing in Colonial Virginia," *Virginia Magazine of History and Biography* 2 (1895):293–305; Jane Carson, *Colonial Virginians at Play* (Charlottesville, Va., 1965), pp. 108–9; *Boston News-Letter*, Nov. 11–18, 1717.

paper in Boston in 1704, the *News-Letter* announced off-the-road horse races and a privately owned bowling green open to "all Gentlemen, Merchants, and others, that have a mind to Recreate themselves."[5] In 1712 Harvard College officials purchased a Cambridge orchard, "lately fenced," that they designated as a "place of recreation & exercise for the Scholars."[6] Specialized areas such as these reduced the possibility of accidents to either participants or passers-by. They also secured either a measure of privacy or rank separation when the events were public.

Soon colonists began to develop sporting grounds. In the 1730s and 1740s tavern owners launched a new era in facility building, constructing cockpits, rings for boxers, and ninepins areas in the front or the rear of ordinaries, buildings already advantageously located in towns or at the crossroads that might become towns.[7] By midcentury planters and merchants had also begun to devise structures that merged commerce and style, practicality and symbolism, as befit their desire for gentility. Stables housed the newly imported and, eventually, provincially bred thoroughbreds that improved one's stock, earned stud fees and gambling victories, and transported the owner quickly and gracefully from place to place. Bowling greens, which were sites for entertainment and parts of the symmetrical pattern of the outdoors, spread across expanses of grass between estate entrances and great houses. Game preserves stocked with deer engrossed hun-

---

[5] *Boston News-Letter,* Apr. 26-May 3, 1714.

[6] *Harvard College Records,* 3 vols. (Boston, 1955), 1:401.

[7] *South Carolina Gazette,* Nov. 29, 1735, Feb. 5, 1736, Feb. 19, 1756; *Virginia Gazette,* Feb. 14, 1756, Feb. 27, 1752; *Maryland Gazette,* Feb. 7, 1754; Daniel Fisher, "Journal, 1750–1755," in Louise Pecquet du Bellet, *Some Prominent Virginia Families,* 4 vols. (Lynchburg, Va., 1907), 2:708; Ebenezer Hazard, Journal of Journeys to the South, 1777–78, June 10, 1777, Historical Society of Pennsylvania, Philadelphia; *Boston Evening Post,* Jan. 11, 1773; Mary de Witt Freeland, *The Records of Oxford, Massachusetts* (Albany, 1894), p. 267; Patricia A. Gibbs, "Taverns in Tidewater Virginia, 1700–1774," M. A. thesis, College of William and Mary, 1968; Julia C. Spruill, *Women's Life and Work in the Southern Colonies* (Chapel Hill, N.C., 1938), pp. 293–313; Alice Morse Earle, *Stage-Coach and Tavern Days* (New York, 1900).

dreds of acres of meadow and woods and served as experiments in land conservation and arenas for the chase.[8]

Nowhere were the physical changes, and in fact the relationship between physical and social structures, more evident than at the most nearly universal of eighteenth-century sporting sites, the racecourses. Throughout towns and counties in the middle and southern colonies in the 1740s and later, merchants and planters moved their matches once more, from race paths and fields to mile-long circular or oval tracks. Usually laid out on the outskirts of a town or on an already established race field, these courses tested the endurance—the "bottom"—of the thoroughbreds, and they included the spectators in most un-British ways. In the mother country the racecourses stretched out and back over heaths, plains, and roadways, with few accommodations for any spectators except the rich. The placement and design of colonial tracks, however, displayed none of the British elites' ambivalence, or perhaps even antipathy, toward the observers.[9] Instead, provincial courses took into account the common planters and yeomen who came to see the prime stock that might, with a few shillings "for the leap" or a few pounds "for the season," improve their own animals. The courses suited the freemen and servants who expressed their support with wagers on the

[8] Robert Carter, Letterbook, 1764–68, Dec. 22, 1767, microfilm, Colonial Williamsburg Foundation, Williamsburg; Thomas Anburey, *Travels through the Interior Parts of America,* 2 vols. (1789; reprint ed., Boston, 1923), 2:208–9; William Byrd, *The London Diary (1717–1721) and Other Writings,* ed. Louis B. Wright and Marion Tinling (New York, 1958), pp. 507, 510, 527; John H. Best, ed., *Benjamin Franklin on Education* (New York, 1962), p. 115; Jack P. Greene, ed., *The Diary of Colonel Landon Carter of Sabine Hall, 1752–1778,* 2 vols. (Charlottesville, Va., 1965), 1:71; Louis Morton, "Robert Wormeley Carter of Sabine Hall," *Journal of Southern History* 12 (1946):355; Hervey, *Racing in America,* 1:90. For a discussion of the Georgian emphasis on symmetry, see James J. F. Deetz, *In Small Things Forgotten: The Archaeology of Early American Life* (Garden City, N. Y., 1977).

[9] For the most part, British courses extended over sections of heaths and roads. A few were broad, ovallike "tracks" of up to four miles in circumference. Roger Longrigg, *The History of Horse Racing* (New York, 1972), pp. 86–88; Malcolmson, *Popular Recreations,* p. 51; Cunningham, *Leisure in the Industrial Revolution,* pp. 19–20. Today, Newmarket remains an expansive heath course with accommodations for spectators only where the races begin and end.

local colonel, the patroon, or the merchant. And they provided for those who came just to visit and to enjoy themselves.
Easily accessible, the tracks bound genteel and ordinary colonists together. They ensured that all could see and that the
few could be seen.[10]

As the case of racing suggests, the development of facilities
occasionally coincided with, and may even have been encouraged by, the introduction of new animals or devices. Certainly
equipment and animals for sport became more specialized
and available over the course of the eighteenth century. In
1700 virtually no equipment specific to sport, except for gambling in a few homes and many taverns, existed in the colonies. Guns, sleighs, and horses, of course, served many
purposes, only one of which was recreation. Even before midcentury, however, imports and local artisans changed the picture. "Very fine London" billiard tables were available, as
were battledores and shuttlecocks.[11] By 1751 the Boston merchant Daniel Gairdner advertised "plain and gilded Bibles,
common prayer books . . . and playing cards" at his warehouse on Belcher's Wharf.[12] In the next decade the Philadelphia firm of Rivington and Brown offered its customers a
"complete assortment" of mostly imported side arms, swords,
foils, cribbage boards, quail and dog calls for fowling, par-
tridge and quail nets, cock spurs or gaffs, and fishing tackle.[13]

In the final third of the century, the variety of sporting
goods and animals increased, even though the Revolution interrupted the trade in British imports. Local leather crafts-

[10]*Virginia Gazette*, Mar. 27, Aug. 7, 1752; *Maryland Gazette*, Apr. 25, 1754;
Hunter Dickinson Farish, ed., *Journal and Letters of Philip Vickers Fithian,
1773–1774: A Plantation Tutor of the Old Dominion* (Williamsburg, 1943), p.
32; *New York Gazette*, Nov. 26, 1739; *South Carolina Gazette*, Feb. 14, July 25,
Sept. 12, Oct. 10, 1743, Apr. 10, 1755, Mar. 4, 1756; Hervey, *Racing in
America*, 1:31–32, 42; John Austin Stevens, "Early New York Racing History," *Wallace's Monthly Magazine* 3 (1977):782–88; Carson, *Virginians at Play*,
pp. 118–19; Stanard, "Racing in Virginia," pp. 301–2.

[11]*Virginia Gazette*, Sept. 12, Nov. 28, 1745; John Gibson to Mrs. John
Ross, July 14, 1741, Gibson-Maynadier Papers, Maryland Historical Society, Baltimore; *Maryland Gazette*, Dec. 6, 1745.

[12]*Boston Gazette*, Oct. 15, 1751.

[13]*Maryland Gazette*, Oct. 20, 1763.

men produced sidesaddles. Farmers and planters inbred and trained their own horses to produce hunters, pacers, and trotters. In Williamsburg one could obtain a copy of *Hoyle's Games* at the post office, and in Norfolk a colonist could purchase "billiard balls, all sizes at 10 sh. a pair" from Hardress Waller, who shaped them from the ivory he had on hand.[14] By 1790 a Baltimore harness maker offered for sale an item that illustrated, perhaps more clearly than anything else, the extent of both specialization and fashion among patrons of racing in the young nation: the jockey cap.[15]

Maryland estate inventories for the years between 1770 and 1810 present a picture of the distribution of equipment and animals available for sport and confirm the increasing number and variety of goods (table 1). In 1770 only 6 percent of the estates contained sporting goods, most of which were furniture for gambling and equipment for riding, hunting, and fishing. The numbers were small: one billiard and one backgammon table, three fowling pieces, seven entries for fishing hooks and lines, and two hunting saddles. Twenty years later, 18 percent of the inventories listed sporting equipment, including nine card tables, five packs of cards, and six backgammon tables and boxes. By 1810, 27 percent of the inventories contained equipment, and both the types and the quantities of items had expanded. Not only were there forty-five card tables and fifteen fowling pieces, but there were also shuffleboard and checker sets, sulkeys, dice, and a "pleasure" boat.

The Maryland inventories also suggest trends in the ownership of sporting goods. With the exception of fowling pieces in 1790, very few items appropriate for sport appeared in the poorest 30 percent of estates during the forty-year period (table 2).[16] The percentages of horses registered in these same

[14] *Virginia Gazette*, Sept. 24, 1772.

[15] *Virginia Gazette and Alexandria Advertiser*, Oct. 7, 1790.

[16] Across the period from 1770 to 1810, I maintained a constant percentage of estates within each rank: 30 percent, lower, 60 percent, middle, and 10 percent, upper. Although most analyses of colonial inventories present estate data in constant pounds, the rank demarcations that result (£49–50, £225–26, and £490–91) appeared to be inappropriate for the post-

Table 1. Sporting goods in Maryland estate inventories, 1770–1810

Equipment	1770	1790	1810
Backgammon tables	1	6	5
Billiard tables	1	0	3
Card tables	0	9	45
Dice / box	0	0	1
Fishing hooks / lines	7	4	9
Fowling pieces	3	6	15
Hunting saddles	2	2	2
Packs of cards	0	5	2
Pleasure boat	0	0	1
Shuffleboard / checkers	0	0	4
Sleighs	1	5	7
Sulkeys	0	0	4
Total	15	37	98
Percent of estates with goods	6%	18%	27%
Estate N =	239	206	361

SOURCES: 1770 inventories, Prerogative Court Records, vols. 104–5; Anne Arundel County Inventories, 1787–90, 1808–13; Baltimore County Inventories, 1789–95, 1809–11; Frederick County Inventories, 1786–97, 1808–10; Prince George's County Inventories, 1787–91, 1798–1815; Talbot County Inventories, 1788–92, 1809–11; Worcester County Inventories, 1783–90, 1804–10, Maryland State Archives, Annapolis.

NOTE: The inventories in 1770 came from across the colony; those from 1790 and 1810 were registered by county. Consequently, inventories in the latter two decades represent a cross-section of the state's counties (Anne Arundel, Baltimore, Frederick, Prince George's, Talbot, and Worcester).

Revolutionary decades, when estate values rose and currency values fluctuated. These studies, however, suggest that inventory percentages derived from constant pounds fall between 25–30 percent for the lowest rank and about 10 percent for the most affluent decedents. The precise estate value ranges per rank varied over time: poorest 30 percent: 1770, £1–£59; 1790, £1–£83; 1810, £1–£133; wealthiest 10 percent: 1770, £600+; 1790, £1000+; 1810, £1500+; middle 60 percent: 1770, £60–£599; 1790, £84–£999; 1810, £134–£1,499. When dollars had to be converted into pounds (1810), I used the conversion factor of seven and one-half shillings per dollar.

On analysis of colonial probate records, see Lois Green Carr and Lorena S. Walsh, "Inventories and the Analysis of Wealth and Consumption Patterns in St. Mary's County, Maryland, 1658–1777," *Historical Methods* 13 (1980):81–104; Gloria L. Main, *Tobacco Colony: Life in Early Maryland, 1650–*

Table 2. Percentage of total selected sporting goods in Maryland inventories, by estate range

Estate range	1770	1790	1810
Lower rank	15%	12%	14%
Middle rank	77	46	51
Lower middle	23	15	12
Upper middle	54	31	39
Upper rank	8	42	35

SOURCES: 1770 inventories, Prerogative Court Records, vols. 104–5; Anne Arundel County Inventories, 1787–90, 1808–13; Baltimore County Inventories, 1789–95, 1809–11; Frederick County Inventories, 1786–97, 1808–10; Prince George's County Inventories, 1787–91, 1798–1815; Talbot County Inventories, 1788–92, 1809–11; Worcester County Inventories, 1783–90, 1804–10, Maryland State Archives, Annapolis.

NOTE: Items inventoried were billiard and card tables, fishing goods, fowling pieces, hunting saddles, packs of cards, sulkeys, and horses.

estates actually declined, from 10 percent in 1770 to 6 percent in 1810 (table 3).[17] On the other hand, the wealthiest 10 percent of estates enlarged their holdings of goods over time (table 2). Within these estates, card tables, for example, increased from zero in 1770 to twenty in 1810 (44 percent of the total), and the numbers of horses rose from 178 (25 percent) in 1770 to 260 (31 percent) in 1810 (table 3). In short, the poorest estates persistently owned very little equipment specifically appropriate for sport, while the holdings of the most affluent minority increased.

Goods and animals available for sport were most concentrated in the middle rank estates (table 2). Forty percent of

---

1720 (Princeton, 1982), pp. 274–92; idem, "Inequality in Early America: The Evidence from Probate Records of Massachusetts and Maryland," *Journal of Interdisciplinary History* 7 (1977):559–81; Alice Hanson Jones, *American Colonial Wealth: Documents and Methods,* 3 vols. (New York, 1977), esp. vol. 3.

[17]The decline in the percentage of horses registered in the poorest estates is quite steep, perhaps for reasons other than loss of purchasing power by poor colonists. Changes in record keeping and the increasing number of urban estates (in which, regardless of rank, colonists owned fewer horses compared to rural ones) may also have contributed to this dramatic decline.

Table 3. Percentage of selected sporting goods in Maryland inventories, by estate range

Equipment	1770	1790	1810
Card tables			
Lower rank	0%	0%	16%
Middle rank	0	0	40
Upper rank	0	100	44
Fishing goods			
Lower rank	14	0	22
Middle rank	86	100	67
Upper rank	0	0	11
Fowling pieces			
Lower rank	0	50	7
Middle rank	67	50	53
Upper rank	33	0	40
Packs of cards			
Lower rank	0	0	0
Middle rank	0	60	100
Upper rank	0	40	0
Horses			
Lower rank	10	9	6
Middle rank	65	57	63
Upper rank	25	34	31

SOURCES: 1770 inventories, Prerogative Court Records, vols. 104–5; Anne Arundel County Inventories, 1787–90, 1808–13; Baltimore County Inventories, 1789–95, 1809–11; Frederick County Inventories, 1786–97, 1808–10; Prince George's County Inventories, 1787–91, 1798–1815; Talbot County Inventories, 1788–92, 1809–11; Worcester County Inventories, 1783–90, 1804–10, Maryland State Archives, Annapolis.

the card tables and a majority of the fowling pieces registered in all of the inventories in 1770, 1790, and 1810 appeared in this rank (table 3). So, too, did all of the hunting saddles and more than two thirds of the fishing equipment (67 percent). Still, the dispersion of goods was not uniform throughout this group (table 2). Between 1770 and 1810 estates in the upper middle rank registered more fowling pieces, packs of cards, fishing hooks and lines, and horses than did estates in the lower middle segment. In 1810 alone estates in this range accounted for 39 percent of the total number of selected goods available for sport, compared to 12 percent in the lower middle rank estates. This pattern, along with the increased numbers of goods registered in the wealthiest estates between

1790 and 1810, suggests that real increases in sporting goods and animals over the forty-year period were related directly to wealth.

The values of sporting goods and animals help to sharpen this correlation between ownership and estate worth. The varying ages and conditions of equipment, as well as inflation and the variations of values assigned to goods, do not, of course, enable one to determine absolute values. Average and comparable values suggest, however, that equipment and animals did not become less expensive as they became more varied and numerous. The average value of card tables doubled during this forty-year period, and for the same sum one could purchase a fine mahogany dining table.[18] The average value of horses more than doubled, and in 1810, as in 1770, one could spend an equivalent amount on several cows and calves. A "good" horse, a potential racer, was even more expensive, about the value of a young female slave.[19] Like the jockey cap, then, many of the items useful for sport were initially and remained relatively expensive, perhaps even luxury items registered primarily in middle- and upper-rank estates.

The Maryland estate inventories encourage one other conclusion about late eighteenth- and early nineteenth-century sporting goods: no consumer revolution occurred. More estates did, of course, list such items. By 1810 four and a half times as many inventories had them than had been the case in 1770, but still this represented less than a third of the total number of estates, an unrevolutionary total. Further, the fifty-four card tables, twenty-four fowling pieces, and twenty fishing hooks and lines enumerated in 806 inventories across forty years do not, by any standards, indicate rampant buying. Nor does the average number of horses per estate (table 4) suggest that Marylanders either bred or purchased many

[18] Values of card tables ranged from $2.00 apiece to $40.00 a pair (average value = $8.76; mahogany dining tables = $8.00) in 1810. Backgammon tables ranged in value from seven and one-half shillings in 1770, the same as a spinning wheel, to $3.00 in 1810.

[19] The value range for a "good" horse was probably lower than that for a superb racer, especially a "full blood." Yet the value, as much as $75, was still high enough to restrict ownership.

Table 4. Numbers and values of horses

	1770		1790		1810	
Total horses (valued)	727		698		846	
Total estates (valued)	239		206		361	
Total value, horses	£3,626		£4,563		£10,261	
Average value, horses	£5		£6.5		£12.1	
Average no. horses per estate	3		3.4		2.3	
No. estates with horses	190	(79%)	153	(74%)	208	(58%)
No. estates, 1 horse	34	(14%)	28	(14%)	48	(13%)
No. estates, 0 horses	49	(21%)	56	(27%)	157	(43%)*

SOURCES: 1770 inventories, Prerogative Court Records, vols. 104–5; Anne Arundel County Inventories, 1787–90, 1808–13; Baltimore County Inventories, 1789–95, 1809–11; Frederick County Inventories, 1786–97, 1808–10; Prince George's County Inventories, 1787–91, 1798–1815; Talbot County Inventories, 1788–92, 1809–11; Worcester County Inventories, 1783–90, 1804–10, Maryland State Archives, Annapolis.

*Of these 157 estates without horses, 107 (68 percent) were in Baltimore County.

more of the animals than were essential. That average, in fact, actually declined, from three horses per estate in 1770 to 2.3 in 1810.[20] In short, then, citizens of the young nation had before them greater varieties and numbers of sporting goods and animals than had their early eighteenth-century ancestors. They did not face a flooded market, however, nor did many more people own significantly larger amounts of equipment than earlier generations.

No mass sporting goods market had emerged in the United States by 1810. This is not a surprising conclusion, given that there was neither a large consumer demand nor a supply of standardized and relatively inexpensive goods. Many forms of sport did not require manufactured items, and for those contests that employed some kind of equipment—balls, cock spurs, or guns, for example—substitutes for specialized, standardized sporting goods existed. Bladders and rounded nubbens of wood sufficed as balls, any table could become a card table, and small pieces of metal attached to leather bands served as cock spurs.

Nor is it surprising that holdings of sporting goods were concentrated in the estates of upper middle- and upper-rank colonists. Early and dramatically, these people laid the foundation for a particular style of sport, a gentry tradition, that reflected the colonial social structure by defining rules, conventions, and modes of performance. The most nearly complete and understood picture of the changes in genteel sport forms and provincial rank relations comes from the Chesapeake where, before the 1730s, a native-born squirearchy

---

[20] If one removes Baltimore County estates from this analysis, the average number of horses per estate actually rises slightly, to 3.3. The difference exists, I suggest, because of Baltimore City. Estates that can be identified as city ones register fewer horses (at higher values) than do rural ones. Once Baltimore City estates are removed from the analysis, Baltimore County estates approximate the pattern found in the other counties. (A preliminary analysis of inventories in Suffolk County [Boston], Massachusetts, over the same period [1770–1810] suggests a similar pattern: few horses and more card tables.) Even by 1810, then, the urban-rural differences that other historians have explored in later decades of the nineteenth century apparently had begun to develop.

played, quite literally, by a different set of rules.[21] Such planters did not compete, publicly at least, in brutal and ill-ordered
sports such as cudgeling and fire hunting, forms classified as
plebeian by sixteenth- and seventeenth-century courtesy
manuals. Instead, they fenced in pairs, played established
card and dice games, and raced over predetermined distances
in matches among themselves. Genteel horsemen pledged
themselves to observe the principles of "faire Rideing," and a
racing squire could prosecute an opponent who failed to ad-
here to such an agreement.[22] Further, affluent sportsmen imposed limits on the quantity of game killed and on gambling
wagers, limits beyond which "wantonness" and excess occurred.[23] In short, within a framework of separate events, the
evolving gentry of the Chesapeake developed a set of "right"
actions, an embryonic sporting code, that specified what was
a useful, competitive recreation and what was something else.

The gentry's model of hunting for sport and their
agreements for "faire Rideing" emerged as the Chesapeake
was changing dramatically from a relatively open society to a
hierarchical, biracial one. Regularized and bound in time and
space, their sporting competitions influenced three sets of
relations, all of which were important to their emergence as
an upper rank and to the redefinition of Chesapeake society. First, these contests, governed by particular rules and
conventions, became activities shared and valued among the
planters themselves—for health, for entertainment, for displays of prowess, and, as T. H. Breen has maintained, for
gambling-linked "joking relationships."[24] Second, participa-

[21]This summary draws from Nancy L. Struna, "The Formalizing of Sport
and the Formation of an Elite: The Chesapeake Gentry, 1650–1720s," *Journal of Sport History* 13 (1986):212–34.

[22]Apr. 1, 1698, Henrico County Deeds, Orders, Wills, 3 (1694–1701),
Virginia State Library, Richmond, p. 181; Stanard, "Racing in Virginia,"
pp. 296–97.

[23]Louis B. Wright, ed., *The Prose Works of William Byrd of Westover* (Cambridge, Mass., 1966), pp. 278–79, 373–74.

[24]T. H. Breen, "Horses and Gentlemen: The Cultural Significance of
Gambling among the Gentry of Virginia," *William and Mary Quarterly,* 3d
ser. 34 (1977):257.

tion in sport, the purchase of British books and equipment, and the practice of patronage expanded connections between colonial gentry and the gentry in the mother country, and augmented the provincials' perceptions of their own Britishness. Finally, the gentry's sports in particular and their support for sport more generally reinforced their relations—anchored in land and slaveholding—with smaller local planters. The major planters arranged and provided prizes for contests among smaller landowners, and their own quarter-mile match races became communal festivals. Such acts enhanced the personal prestige and reputation of the large landowners.[25]

We do not yet know whether early eighteenth-century sportsmen in other regions altered sporting forms and styles in the same ways and as extensively as did the native-born squires in the Chesapeake. Groups of men of wealth and influence did race horses, hunt, and sail pleasure boats in the middle colonies and in the Carolinas.[26] In Massachusetts, as well as in other areas in New England, men of similar backgrounds and interests also organized races and played bil-

[25] Louis B. Wright, *The First Gentlemen of Virginia: Intellectual Qualities of the Early Colonial Ruling Class* (San Marino, Calif., 1940), pp. 149–53, 206, 210, 335; Hugh Jones, *The Present State of Virginia* (1724), ed. Richard L. Morton (Chapel Hill, N. C., 1956), pp. 32–43; "Voyage to Maryland," pp. 334–35; Hinke, trans. and ed., "Journal of Francis Michel," p. 129; Wright and Tinling, eds., *Secret Diary of Byrd*, pp. 414–15; Philip Alexander Bruce, *Social Life of Virginia in the Seventeenth Century* (New York, 1907), p. 242; Main, *Tobacco Colony*, pp. 206–39; Jack P. Greene, "Search for Identity: An Interpretation of the Meaning of Selected Patterns of Social Response in Eighteenth-Century America," *Journal of Social History* 3 (1970):189–220; Struna, "Formalizing of Sport," pp. 229–33. For gentry relations later in the eighteenth century, see Charles S. Sydnor, *American Revolutionaries in the Making: Political Practices in Washington's Virginia* (New York, 1965); Rhys Isaac, *The Transformation of Virginia, 1740–1790* (Chapel Hill, N. C., 1982). See also Raymond Williams, *The Sociology of Culture* (New York, 1981), esp. pp. 57–86.

[26] "Journal of Rev. John Sharpe," *Pennsylvania Magazine of History and Biography* 40 (1916):283, 286, 395, 420; Carl Bridenbaugh, *Myths and Realities: Societies of the Colonial South* (New York, 1963), pp. 80–81; James G. Wilson, ed., *Memorial History of New York*, 4 vols. (New York, 1892–93), 2:161, 458.

liards and bowls. Here sport forms became standardized among the "Gentlemen, Merchants, and others," but the contests did not become public events comparable to those in the Chesapeake. A number of factors—the more fully developed and specialized tavern sporting life, an economy less dependent on agriculture and less inclined to residual patron-client relationships, widespread literacy, and the diverse and still vital religious and civil public rituals—may have precluded the development of Chesapeake-like public sporting events.[27]

Regional differences and our lack of knowledge notwithstanding, the early eighteenth-century networks of genteel sportsmen appear as transitional structures. More formal and permanent organizations emerged during the middle third of the eighteenth century when colonists formed many voluntary associations. Among the first, if not the first, of the sport-specific clubs was the Schuylkill Fishing "Colony." Organized outside of Philadelphia by 1732, its members drew up "rules and regulations" for the sport of fishing, which they defined

[27]"Extracts from the Diary of Rev. Samuel Dexter, of Dedham," *New England Historical and Genealogical Register* 13 (1859):308; Francis G. Walett, ed., "The Diary of Ebenezer Parkman, 1719–1728," *Proceedings of the American Antiquarian Society* 71 (1961):99, 105, 118; "James Jeffry's Journal for the Year 1724," *Essex Institute Historical Collections* 36 (1900):331–38; Joshua Gee, Jr., College Memorandum Book, 1714–15, Davis Papers, 11, 1681–1747, Massachusetts Historical Society, Boston; *Boston News-Letter*, Aug. 22–29, 1715, Nov. 11–18, 1717, May 22–29, 1721; *New England Courant*, Apr. 30, 1722; *Boston Gazette*, Apr. 19–26, 1725, June 10–17, 1734; Sewall, *Diary*, 3:193; Fitch E. Oliver, ed., *The Diaries of Benjamin Lynde and of Benjamin Lynde, Jr.* (Boston, 1880), pp. 132–33. About religious rituals, see Charles Hambrick-Stowe, *The Practice of Piety* (Chapel Hill, N. C., 1982); W. DeLoss Love, Jr., *The Fast and Thanksgiving Days of New England* (Boston, 1895); David Stannard, *The Puritan Way of Death: A Study in Religion, Culture and Social Change* (New York, 1977); David D. Hall, *The Faithful Shepherd: A History of the New England Ministry in the Seventeenth Century* (Chapel Hill, N. C., 1972); idem, "Religion and Society: Problems and Reconsiderations," in Jack P. Greene and J. R. Pole, eds., *Colonial British America: Essays in the New History of the Early Modern Era* (Baltimore, 1984), pp. 334–38. I have begun to examine the relationships between sporting events and changes in religious rituals in "Eighteenth-Century Massachusetts; A Physically Expressive Popular Culture" (Paper presented at the Thirteenth Annual Meeting of the North American Society for Sport History, LaCrosse, Wis., May 1985).

as the "handmaiden" to other endeavors.[28] By 1744 Bostonians, too, had formed a club, the Physical Club. During the 1750s and 1760s hunt clubs in South Carolina and the earliest of many southern jockey clubs also appeared.[29]

The upper-rank clubs linked sport and Anglo-American high culture in a way not seen earlier in the colonies. For several generations Britons had recognized the "cultivated" gentleman who, among his other qualities, projected physical strength, grace, and bodily symmetry. Riding, fishing, dancing, fencing, and hunting developed these attributes, as even provincials had long recognized. Before 1730, however, Americans had essentially learned about and come to value these qualities and activities through the lessons of individual experience, as well as books and letters. Thereafter, the expanding interest in and information about human science, as well as the desire to participate more fully in metropolitan culture, encouraged them to communicate more broadly. Like other products of the associational movement—local po-

[28] William Milnor, Jr., *An Authentic Historical Memoir of the Schuylkill Fishing Company of the State in Schuylkill* (Philadelphia, 1830), p. 2; *A History of the Schuylkill Fishing Company of the State in Schuylkill, 1732–1888* (Philadelphia, 1889); Carl Bridenbaugh, *Cities in the Wilderness: The First Century of Urban Life in America, 1625–1742* (New York, 1938), p. 440.

[29] William Douglass, *A Summary, Historical and Political, of the First Planting, Progressive Improvements, and Present State of the British Settlements in North America*, 2 vols. (London, 1755), 2:216; Carl Bridenbaugh, ed., *Gentleman's Progress: The Itinerarium of Dr. Alexander Hamilton, 1744* (Chapel Hill, N. C., 1948), pp. 115–16. Another club, the South River Club, near Annapolis, may have existed before the 1740s. However, I have not found any direct evidence to confirm (or deny) its existence. See South River Club Collection, Md. Hist. Soc., Baltimore; Swepson Earle, *The Chesapeake Bay Country* (Baltimore, 1924), p. 180. The club did play cricket against men from other counties by 1754 (*Maryland Gazette*, Nov. 14, 1754). For Carolina jockey clubs, see *South Carolina Gazette*, Mar. 17, 1757, June 20, 1761; Fairfax Harrison, *John's Island Stud* (Richmond, 1931), pp. 101–31; John B. Irving, *History of the Turf in South Carolina* (Charleston, 1857), pp. 33–36. The jockey club in Charleston actually had formed by 1734, but apparently it did not survive; it was refounded in the 1750s (*South Carolina Gazette*, June 1, Aug. 16, 1734). A Maryland jockey club may also have organized in the 1730s, but it endured only after midcentury. Virginians formed many jockey clubs, and their race announcements appeared frequently and quite regularly in the *Virginia Gazette*. See note 32 below.

litical clubs, subscription theaters, and literary societies—the Schuylkill Fishing "Colony" and the Boston Physical Club encouraged information-sharing about topics important to "cultivated" gentlemen.[30] They were forums for discussions about equipment, ways of playing, knowledge about the body, and all "sundry physical matters" that were meaningful to men who sought to "strengthen and render active their Bodies."[31]

In the South the development of refinement had a public dimension not as evident in the North, and it produced sport clubs whose business became the improvement of both horses and riders: the jockey clubs. Shortly after midcentury members of these clubs devised and publicized a fairly complex system of handicapping based on the age and degree of bloodedness of the horse and on the weight of the rider, a system that complicated wagering and encouraged different events. The clubs also popularized subscriptions (events to which all contributed) and sweepstakes (winner-take-all events) as alternatives to matches. These contests enlarged the field of competitors and produced a pool of money to finance the large purses, commonly £30-£50, but sometimes as high as £500.[32]

---

[30] Richard L. Bushman, "American High-Style and Vernacular Cultures," in Greene and Pole, eds., *Colonial British America*, pp. 345–83; John E. Mason, *Gentlefolk in the Making: Studies in the History of English Courtesy Literature and Related Topics from 1531 to 1774* (Philadelphia, 1935); Virgil B. Heltzel, *Chesterfield and the Tradition of the Ideal Gentleman* (Chicago, 1925); Edwin H. Cady, *The Gentleman in America: A Literary Study in American Culture* (Syracuse, N. Y., 1949); Howard Mumford Jones, *O Strange New World: American Culture: The Formative Years* (New York, 1967); Stow Persons, *The Decline of American Gentility* (New York, 1973).

[31] Bridenbaugh, ed., *Gentleman's Progress*, p. 116; *Benjamin Franklin's Proposals for the Education of Youth in Pennsylvania, 1749* (Ann Arbor, Mich., 1927), p. 10.

[32] About the races, jockey clubs, and contemporary impressions, see *South Carolina Gazette*, Mar. 24, 1764; *South Carolina Gazette and Country Journal*, Feb. 11, 1772; *Maryland Gazette*, Sept. 30, 1747, Oct. 4, 1749, Oct. 29, 1761, May 5, 12, 1768, May 9, 1771; *Virginia Gazette*, Aug. 7, 1752, Mar. 3, May 12, 1774; *Virginia Gazette and Alexandria Advertiser*, Sept. 23, Oct. 7, 1790; Farish, ed., *Journal and Letters of Fithian*, pp. 32, 126; John C. Fitzpatrick, ed., *The Diaries of George Washington*, 4 vols. (Boston, 1925), 3:124; William Eddis, *Letters from America*, ed. Aubrey C. Land (Cambridge, Mass., 1969),

As it was in Britain, thoroughbred racing became and remained the most visible, highly specialized form of sport during the middle and later decades of the eighteenth century and into the next. Events initially arranged to coincide with legislative, court, and election meetings became sufficiently popular in and of themselves to last a week and to double and triple the populations of towns like Annapolis, Williamsburg, and Charleston during and after the 1740s. Even some New Englanders, who, if they raced, favored pacing contests over thoroughbred events, knew enough about the sport to attend contests in towns in other regions—and to criticize a victorious rider who "assumed the airs of a hero or German potentate."[33] Newspapers and the continental "posts" helped to spread news of the races.[34] So did another institution of the upper and, in the final decades of the century, upper-middle ranks of society—the assemblies.

Assemblies were part of the same associational movement that produced the sport clubs, but they were not specifically organized for sport. Over time, however, they did incorporate certain sports within programs for cultivation and entertain-

pp. 54–55; J. F. D. Smyth, *A Tour in the United States of America*, 2 vols. (London, 1784), 1:20; Herbert A. Johnson, ed., *The Papers of John Marshall*, 3 vols. (Chapel Hill, N. C., 1974), 1:315, 362, 383, 411, 2:382. The handicapping system appeared in *Maryland Gazette*, Jan. 13, 1763, Aug. 8, 1765, Sept. 29, 1774. Individuals and fair organizers also sponsored races; see, for example, *Virginia Gazette*, Apr. 21, 28, 1774; Edward M. Riley, ed., *The Journal of John Harrower, an Indentured Servant in the Colony of Virginia* (Williamsburg, 1963), p. 40. See also Isaac, *Transformation of Virginia*, pp. 98–101; Carson, *Virginians at Play*, pp. 120–32, 257–60; John Thomas Scharf, *History of Maryland*, 3 vols. (Baltimore, 1897), 3:73; Fairfax Harrison, "Early Racing Colours in Virginia," *Virginia Magazine of History and Biography* 37 (1929):54–55.

[33] Mark A. DeWolf Howe, ed., "Journal of Josiah Quincy, Junior, 1773," Massachusetts Historical Society *Proceedings* 49 (1915–16):467. For racing in Massachusetts, see Peter Kimball, Journal, 1760–67, Apr. 22, 1760, Essex Institute, Salem, Mass.; *Boston Gazette*, Oct. 20, 1760; *Essex Journal*, May 18, 1774.

[34] See note 32 above. Newspapers covered local races as well as the intercolonial contests, especially between Marylanders and Virginians, or New Yorkers and Virginians, when they occurred.

ment that varied little from place to place.[35] Attend the races, sail, or fish during the day. Enjoy exercise, in other words, that "invigorates, and enlivens all the Faculties of Body and of mind."[36] At night devote oneself to "noble and elegant" amusements: balls and card games.[37] By the 1780s the assemblies had reduced the constricting effects of gender— although not to the extent of engaging in aggressive head-to-head male-female physical competition—and of geography. As foreign and American travelers suggested, an intercolonial sporting life flourished after the Revolution. In towns up and down the Atlantic seaboard, one could enjoy—or criticize— day-long recreations and the evening card parties and balls.[38]

For genteel women, the assemblies capped what had been a gradual movement away from their positions as onlookers at the rail of the primarily male public sporting domain. Dur-

[35] For example, see Joseph Bennett, "History of New England" (1740), Massachusetts Historical Society *Proceedings* 5 (1861):125–26; Jonathan Green, Diary, 1738–52, Feb. 27, 1740, Mar. 1, 1741, Linscott Papers, 1653–1922, Mass. Hist. Soc., Boston; "Extracts from Capt. Francis Goelet's Journal, Relative to Boston, Salem, and Marblehead, &c., 1746–1750," *New England Historical and Genealogical Register* 24 (1870):53; *Virginia Gazette*, Feb. 27, Mar. 5, 1752; *South Carolina Gazette*, Nov. 13, 1755, Oct. 12, 1767, Mar. 7, 1774; Alice Morse Earle, ed., *Diary of Anna Green Winslow* (Boston, 1894), pp. 16–17; "Boyle's Journal of Occurrences in Boston, 1759–1778," *New England Historical and Genealogical Register* 84 (1930):364; Farish, ed., *Journal and Letters of Fithian*, pp. 44, 75, 198; Anburey, *Travels through America*, 2:57. See also Bridenbaugh, *Cities in the Wilderness*, pp. 435–41; James D. Phillips, *Salem in the Eighteenth Century* (Boston, 1937), pp. 179–80; Bridenbaugh, *Myths and Realities*, pp. 86–88.

[36] Lyman H. Butterfield, ed., *Diary and Autobiography of John Adams*, 4 vols. (Cambridge, Mass., 1961), 1:27.

[37] Lyman H. Butterfield, ed., *Adams Family Correspondence*, 4 vols. to date (Cambridge, Mass., 1963–), 1:44–45.

[38] Elizabeth Cometti, ed., *The American Journals of John Enys* (Syracuse, N. Y., 1976), pp. 194, 204, 218, 234, 244; marquis de Chastellux, *Travels in North America in the Years 1780, 1781, and 1782*, ed. Howard C. Rice, Jr., 2 vols. (Chapel Hill, N. C., 1963), 1:176–77, 2:506–7; Evelyn M. Acomb, ed., "The Journal of Baron von Closen," *William and Mary Quarterly*, 3d ser. 10 (1953):213. For an intriguing discussion of the limiting effects of gentility on male-female relationships, see Jan Lewis, *The Pursuit of Happiness: Family and Values in Jefferson's Virginia* (New York, 1983).

ing the middle third of the eighteenth century, some members of the colonial "distaff" side had begun to fish with their husbands, to ride "to take air," and to acquire cards and other equipment for their taverns and homes.[39] Like their male counterparts, most of these female participants belonged to the upper and upper middle ranks in which the declining mortality rate, the increasingly youthful colonial population, the individualization of religious experience, and the economy elevated the maternal and wifely responsibilities of women. The assemblies accommodated the physical skills of some colonial women as well as their public roles as moral arbiters, teachers, and friends.[40]

During the eighteenth century the physical sporting skills of women were not, to be sure, the same as those of men. Women never competed publicly in horse races or in ball games. Still, a few tested the "strength and vigor" of their dancing partners, while others prepared to "make a better Figure in the elegant and necessary Accomplishment" of card play.[41] And, after the 1760s, some townswomen began to shape a separate sphere of sporting competition by transforming the domestic activity of spinning into competitive matches, in much the same way as late seventeenth-century males had formalized horse racing.[42] After the Revolution the informal networks of sporting women evident in the spinning

[39] Bennett, "History of New England," pp. 124–25; "Jeffry's Journal," p. 335; York County Wills and Inventories, 18 (1732–40), Va. St. Libr., Richmond, p. 58.

[40] This paragraph and the succeeding one draw from Nancy L. Struna, "'Good Wives and Gardeners, Spinners and Fearless Riders': Middling and Upper Rank Women in the Early American Sporting Culture," in James A. Mangan and Roberta J. Park, eds., *From "Fair Sex" to Feminism: Sport and the Socialization of Women in the Industrial and Post-Industrial Eras* (London, 1987), pp. 235–55.

[41] "Journal of William Black, 1744," ed. R. Alonzo Brock, *Pennsylvania Magazine of History and Biography* 1 (1877):130–31; Butterfield, ed., *Adams Family Correspondence*, 1:45.

[42] *Essex Gazette*, Aug. 2, 1768; *Boston Gazette and Country Journal*, Oct. 16, 1769; Mary Cooper, Dairy, Feb. 3, Mar. 17, Nov. 14, 1769, New York Public Library; Joseph E. A. Smith, *The History of Pittsfield, Massachusetts, from the Year 1734 to the Year 1800* (Boston, 1869), pp. 205–6; "Extracts from the

contests continued, even as these particular matches themselves ceased. As the century closed, "skillful and fearless riders" challenged one another to horse races, swimmers dived off platforms, and card players gambled.[43] By the 1820s women's interest in physical performance, linked to the goal of health, would become entwined with the cult of domesticity.[44]

Thus both women and men in the colonial upper and, gradually, middle ranks were visible agents in the formalizing of sport in early American society. As in the mother country, and in part because of their ties to the British upper class, these provincials translated expectations of behavior into rules and conventions that set apart particular sports from more general ones. The effect was twofold. Not only did they influence styles of sport, even establishing particular ones as fashions, but they also adopted sport as a part of their style of living. Card tables, bowling greens, pleasure boats, sleek stallions, and smooth pacers, among other things, were becoming attractive to refined Americans. To some extent also, perhaps, it was in connection with such things a man and woman came to be regarded as genteel.

But as thoroughbred racing in particular and gentrification in general suggest, early American sport was not the unique preserve of the rich and well-born. Ordinary Americans—small farmers, tavern keepers, seamen, servants, hunters, and

---

Dairy of James Parker of Shirley, Mass.," *New England Historical and Genealogical Register* 69 (1915):10, 14, 121; Struna, "'Good Wives and Gardeners,'" pp. 249–51.

[43] Ferdinand M. Bayard, *Travels of a Frenchman in Maryland and Virginia with a Description of Philadelphia and Baltimore in 1791*, trans. and ed. Ben C. McCray (Ann Arbor, Mich., 1950), p. 40; Mary Palmer Tyler, *Recollections, 1775–1866*, ed. Frederick Tupper and Helen Tyler Brown (New York, 1925), p. 124.

[44] Struna, "'Good Wives and Gardeners,'" pp. 253–55; Nancy F. Cott, *The Bonds of Womanhood: "Women's Sphere" in New England, 1780–1835* (New Haven, 1977); Deborah Gorham, *The Victorian Girl and the Feminine Ideal* (Bloomington, Ind., 1982); Kathryn Kish Sklar, *Catherine Beecher: A Study in American Domesticity* (New York, 1973); Roberta J. Park, "'Embodied Selves': The Rise and Development of Concern for Physical Education, Active Games, and Recreation for American Women, 1776–1865," *Journal of Sport History* 5 (1978):5–41.

artisans—also molded particular forms of sport. Target shooting, not just at vague marks but at nails in boards and candle
flames and in indoor contests, emerged among men for whom
the development of riflery skills could be a matter of life and
death and for whom the event was an affair of honor and
manliness. Foot racing formalized as "pedestrianism" among
farmers, tradesmen, and artisans; and New York seamen pro-
fessionalized boat racing. Itinerant "exhibition" givers, both
black and white, performed tumbling and acrobatic stunts before the paying, or wagering, crowds in towns and at crossroads. And clearly there were games that many colonists
derived primarily from the experiences of childhood, the still
amorphous bat-and-ball contests.[45]

Elliott J. Gorn has provided us with the only detailed examination of the development of a particular sport form and its
significance among ordinary Americans. Fistfighting had
engaged many ranks of southerners during much of the eighteenth century. As the century progressed, however, gentlemen withdrew, and the physical hand-to-hand combats
became contests found primarily in the western regions of the

[45] *New York Magazine* 5 (1794):287–89; Joseph Doddridge, *Notes on the Set-
tlement and Indian Wars of the Western Parts of Virginia and Pennsylvania, from
1763 to 1783,* ed. Alfred Williams (1876; reprint ed., New York, 1973), pp.
122–25; "Extracts from the Diary of James Parker of Shirley, Mass.," *New
England Historical and Genealogical Register* 70 (1916):13, 15; *Boston Evening
Post,* Jan. 11, 1773; J. E. Norris, ed., *History of the Lower Shenandoah Valley*
(Chicago, 1890), p. 326; John Cumming, *Runners and Walkers: A Nineteenth-
Century Sports Chronicle* (Chicago, 1981); Margaret Woodhouse, "A History
of Amateur Club Rowing in the New York Metropolitan Area, 1830–1870,"
Canadian Journal of History of Sport 11 (1980):73–92; Adelman, *Sporting Time;*
Anne R. Cunningham, ed., *Letters and Diary of John Rowe, Boston Merchant,
1759–1762, 1764–1779* (Boston, 1903), p. 249; Butterfield, ed., *Diary of
John Adams,* 1:172–73; "Boyle's Journal," p. 253; *Virginia Gazette,* Oct. 22,
1772; *The Columbian Mirror and Alexandria Gazette,* Oct. 22, 1795; *Records of
the City of Baltimore (Special Commissioners), 1782–1797* (Baltimore, 1909), pp.
288, 296, 330. For activities associated with children, see *The Diary of William
Bentley, D. D., Pastor of the East Church, Salem, Massachusetts,* 4 vols. (1905–14;
reprint ed., Gloucester, Mass., 1962), 1:254; *A Little Pretty Pocket-Book: Intended for the Instruction and Amusement of Little Master Tommy, and Pretty Miss
Polly* (Worcester, Mass., 1787). See also William Clarke, *The Boy's Own Book:
A Complete Encyclopedia of All the Diversions, Athletic, Scientific, and Recreative, of
Boyhood and Youth* (Boston, 1829); Robin Carver, *The Book of Sports* (Boston,
1834); Horatio Smith, *Children's Amusements* (New York, 1820).

South among farmers, trappers, and itinerant laborers. These men gave fistfighting "rules" and a particular reason for occurring. The rules were simple. The contestants used any and all of their skills—gouging, kicking, slugging. For abelarding, gouging to sever one's vital organs, a few men even prepared themselves: they allowed their fingernails to grow long and then hardened them in wax. The reasons for this form of "rough and tumbling" were straightforward: this was an affair of honor among fiercely competitive individuals.[46]

Like thoroughbred racing, rough and tumbling took place in a distinct facility, one that embraced both the displays of physical prowess and the spectators who were important to the fighters' realization of honor. This was the tavern, ordinary, or inn—the location for many sporting contests during the eighteenth and early nineteenth centuries. The central figure in the tavern was the owner, the man or woman who, having located sport in commercial experience, truly exploited it. Occasionally taverners did this in striking ways, as two figures suggest. In 1732 a South Carolina innkeeper named Eldridge built a "good Pit" for cockfighting. He arranged for seven pairs of cocks to fight any challengers, at the handsome sum of £40 per contest, and he charged each of the spectators ten shillings for the right to wager.[47] By the middle of the eighteenth century, another astute innkeeper, Benjamin Berry, had set up his business at a crossroads in west-central Virginia. Berry dug a bear pit, laid out a ring for fighting, stocked both facilities with his own animals and hangers-on, and arranged events for his customers to enter, wager on, and watch as they drank his liquor. His influence, if not his pit and ring, was lasting: members of a later generation changed the name of the crossroads from Battletown to Berryville.[48]

Eldridge and Berry may not have typified the eighteenth-

[46]Elliott J. Gorn, "'Gouge and Bite, Pull Hair and Scratch': The Social Significance of Fighting in the Southern Backcountry," *American Historical Review* 90 (1985):18–43.

[47]*South Carolina Gazette*, Feb. 24, May 13, 1732.

[48]Alvin Dohme, *The Shenandoah: The Valley Story* (Washington, D. C., 1972), pp. 27–28.

century taverner's approach to sport. But many innkeepers, men and women alike, did provide equipment and space for a variety of contests—cards, dice, ninepins, cockfighting, and billiards. At the taverns these forms of sport became standardized and more complex. And there, also, despite the nearly universal but often ill-enforced laws and licensing regulations, colonists could usually find the "real" contest for which these sports existed: gambling or gaming.[49]

Gambling drew men and, to a lesser extent apparently, women from all ranks. In the 1770s Landon Carter's sons and grandson spent days and weeks gambling with common planters and ministers throughout the northern Virginia countryside. Their contemporary, William Byrd III, accumulated what were, even by Chesapeake standards, excessive gaming debts ranging from £1,000 to as much as £10,000. On a smaller scale, other members of the colonial gentry, at least those outside New England, wagered on their horses, at cards, and on their own athletic prowess. Southern backcountry fistfights involved gambling, as did street contests in Charleston, Boston, New York, and Philadelphia. George Washington's militia units gambled in their Pennsylvania and Virginia encampments in the late 1750s; Continentals continued the practice in the 1770s. Even colonial legislative assemblies and citizen groups, which tried in many ways to limit gambling, actually contributed to its institutionalization— through their lotteries.[50]

Gambling also drew criticisms. In 1752 William Stith, the president of the College of William and Mary, implored the

[49]See note 7, above, and *Maryland Gazette*, Feb. 7, 1754; *Virginia Gazette*, Sept. 12, 1745, Feb. 14, 1751, Feb. 27, 1752; York County Wills and Inventories, 15 (1716–20), p. 207; 18:57; 20 (1745–49), pp. 46–49; 22 (1771–83), pp. 19–24; *Pennsylvania Gazette*, Mar. 1, 1739, May 22, 1740; "Journal of Black," p. 404. See also Stephen Longstreet, *Win or Lose: A Social History of Gambling in America* (Indianapolis, Ind., 1977); W. J. Rorabaugh, *The Alcoholic Republic* (New York, 1979); Henry Chafetz, *Play the Devil: A History of Gambling in the United States from 1492 to 1955* (New York, 1960); Ruth E. Painter, "Tavern Amusements in Eighteenth-Century America," *Americana* 11 (1916):92–115.

[50]Greene, ed., *Diary of Landon Carter,* 1:505, 2:630, 638, 640–41, 703, 755, 850, 870, 996; Robert Wormeley Carter, Almanac Diary, 1768, May 2–7, 1768, College of William and Mary, Williamsburg; Morton, "Robert

members of the Virginia assembly to limit their gambling activities before they lost "all their weight and influence with the
Generality of the People."[51] A decade later Jasper Mauduit
recorded the response of the metropolitan commissioners for
trade about the lotteries set up by the General Assembly in
Massachusetts to finance the colony's war debt. Taking the
stance that lotteries were "destructive to labour, and industry," the commissioners recommended their "total disuse."[52]

Not all of the antagonism derived from institutional
sources. Individuals also censured gamesters. John Adams
identified them as "rakes and fools," people whose gaming
habits would lead to other crimes, even to "debaucheries of
young girls."[53] His Virginia contemporary, William Nelson,
actually saw the "Dissipation & Expence" to which "all kinds
of Gambling" by a "young wild raw lad" could lead. Deeply

Wormeley Carter," pp. 357–58; David Meade, "Recollections of William
Byrd III," *Virginia Magazine of History and Biography* 37 (1929):310; "Journal
of a French Traveller in the Colonies, 1765," *American Historical Review* 26
(1921):741–42; J. Hector St. John de Crèvecoeur, *Letters from an American
Farmer* (1782), ed. Warren Barton Blake (New York, 1957), p. 159; Peter
Wood, *Black Majority: Negroes in South Carolina from 1670 through the Stono
Rebellion* (New York, 1974), p. 34; John C. Fitzpatrick, ed., *The Writings of
George Washington from the Original Manuscript Sources, 1745–1799,* 39 vols.
(Washington, D. C., 1931–44), 1:295, 317; "Orderly Book of the Regiment
of Artillery Raised for the Defense of the Town of Boston in 1776," *Essex
Institute Historical Collections* 14 (1877):68; John M. Findlay, *People of Chance:
Gambling in American Society from Jamestown to Las Vegas* (New York, 1986),
pp. 30–43; John S. Ezell, *Fortune's Merry Wheel: The Lottery in America* (Cam-
bridge, Mass., 1960); U.S. Department of Justice, Law Enforcement Assis-
tance Administration, National Institute of Law Enforcement and Criminal
Justice, *The Development of the Law of Gambling: 1776–1976* (Washington,
D. C., 1977).

[51] William Stith, *The Sinfulness and Pernicious Nature of Gaming: A Sermon
Preached before the General Assembly of Virginia, at Williamsburg, March 1st 1752*
(Williamsburg, 1752), pp. 6–10.

[52] *Jasper Mauduit: Agent in London for the Province of the Massachusetts-Bay,
1762–1765* (Boston, 1918), pp. 15–17. In 1769 the British government ordered the legislatures in the royal colonies to seek permission before au-
thorizing any lotteries (Leonard W. Labaree, ed., *Royal Instructions to British
Colonial Governors,* 2 vols. [New York, 1935], 1:200).

[53] Butterfield, ed., *Diary of John Adams,* 1:14.

in debt, Nelson's neighbor, Jeffrey Grisley, went to jail.[54] But it was Landon Carter who registered some of the most vituperative criticism found in the record of opponents—and victims—of gambling. In terms no planter could have misunderstood, Carter condemned gamblers: "No affrican is so great a Slave, as such are to their Passion for gaming."[55]

In eighteenth- and early nineteenth-century America, gambling may have been the most common—and most controversial—activity associated with sport. It cut clearly across rank lines and linked genteel and vernacular sporting traditions. Unfortunately, however, historians still do not fully understand gambling behaviors. Neither quantifiable nor impressionistic accounts have enabled us to determine whether gambling became more pervasive over time, whether the division between gamblers and their critics deepened or merely changed in type, or even precisely how and why gaming transcended other cultural differences. Nor have we adequately described and explained probable regional patterns. The gambling experience and its locus in human affairs may have varied considerably from place to place and over time.[56]

The published literature does, however, encourage one tentative conclusion about the relationship of gambling to early American life, at least in the South. T. H. Breen, Rhys Isaac, and Bertram Wyatt-Brown, in particular, have demonstrated how gambling incorporated and derived from the values, the relationships, and the patterns of living of particular social groups. In the late seventeenth- and early eighteenth-century Chesapeake, it enabled native-born gentlemen to express core cultural values and to do so in contests that united rather than divided them.[57] Among later Virginia colonists, gambling "was inseparable from the ubiquitous competition

[54]William Nelson to Samuel Athawes, May 16, 1771, William Nelson Letterbook, microfilm, Col. Williamsburg Found.

[55]Greene, ed., *Diary of Landon Carter,* 2:870.

[56]New Englanders gambled, but not to the extent or as frequently as did other colonists. We have not adequately addressed this difference.

[57]Breen, "Horses and Gentlemen," pp. 243, 256. For a fuller treatment of the relationships between gambling (and sport more generally) and the translation of values, see Struna, "Formalizing of Sport," pp. 227–34.

in politics and high living."[58] Even in the nineteenth-century South, it persisted as an important mechanism by which individuals "brought the code of honor into very serious play."[59] So integral to and, in fact, so thoroughly integrated in life, gambling was congruent with, rather than compensatory for, life. It was not irrelevant; it did not provide missing elements. Formalized and conventional, gambling was another means of dealing with the competitiveness of life.[60]

By the time the colonies had become an independent nation, their sporting culture was quite different from what it had been in 1700. Facilities were varied and numerous: racetracks, cock pits, "playing pastures," assembly rooms, and bowling greens existed where once there had been only fields, woods, and one-room buildings. Sporting goods, too, had become relatively more common, although in type and dispersion they lagged behind those in the mother country. Clubs and assemblies sponsored participation for entertainment and self-improvement among rank-conscious citizens. Many sport forms had acquired rules and conventions that both ordered the events and gatherings and differentiated types of activities common either to the gentry and would-be gentry from those of ordinary Americans.

Still, a consumer boom comparable to that evident in eighteenth-century British sporting life did not occur in the United States. In part at least, American sporting consumption, commercialization, and standardization revealed a set of underlying conditions different from those in the mother country. Neither commercially nor intellectually were late eighteenth- and early nineteenth-century Americans as ready, or as able, to manufacture and buy goods, to participate, or

---

[58] Isaac, *Transformation of Virginia*, p. 119.

[59] Bertram Wyatt-Brown, *Southern Honor: Ethics and Behavior in the Old South* (Oxford, 1982), p. 344.

[60] This argument draws especially upon Steven Gelber, "'Their Hands Are All Out Playing': Business and Amateur Baseball, 1845–1917," *Journal of Sport History* 11 (1984):5–27; idem, "Working at Playing: The Culture of the Workplace and the Rise of Baseball," *Journal of Social History* 16 (1983):3–21.

to attend events as were Britons. Citizens of the New World remained nascent capitalists, ethnically and religiously diverse and often firmly rooted in their own locality. Geographical distances and the vagaries and expense of travel compounded the difficulties of social intercourse and marketing, and there was no single colonial center or national press. Even after the Revolution, as political debates and local conflicts suggest, Americans remained localized, a fact reflected in and affecting the lagging standardization and large-scale commercialization of the sporting culture.[61]

Early Americans were unlike Britons in another way as well. They had not defined, exploited, or emulated so fully what was central to the consumer revolution in British sport: the emergent modern concept of leisure. No longer conceived of as an unpredictable break from a task or an interlude contingent on a residual holiday among middle- and upper-class Britons, leisure had acquired particular modern attributes: free disposable time, to be employed in enjoyment, entertainment, and self-improvement. It was conceived of as a separate sphere of life, and much of the production and consumption of metropolitan men and women was directed at such time and the activities that people arranged within it: china, books, fine and fashionable clothing, musical instruments, cricket bats, and racehorses. It was leisure that British manufacturers exploited and that British purchasers demanded and consumed. It was a leisure revolution that underlay the rapid and

[61] Joyce Oldham Appleby, "Commercial Farming and the 'Agrarian Myth' in the Early Republic," *Journal of American History* 68 (1982):833–49; idem, *Capitalism and a New Social Order: The Republican Vision of the 1790s* (New York, 1984); Thomas M. Doerflinger, *A Vigorous Spirit of Enterprise: Merchants and Economic Development in Revolutionary Philadelphia* (Chapel Hill, N. C., 1986); Robert D. Mitchell, *Commercialism and Frontier: Perspectives on the Early Shenandoah Valley* (Charlottesville, Va., 1977); Carville V. Earle and Ronald Hoffman, "Staple Crops and Urban Development in the Eighteenth-Century South," *Perspectives in American History* 10 (1976):7–80; Billy G. Smith, "The Material Lives of Laboring Philadelphians, 1750 to 1800," *William and Mary Quarterly,* 3d ser. 38 (1981):163–202; Richard R. Beeman, *The Evolution of the Southern Backcountry: A Case Study of Lunenberg County, Virginia, 1746–1832* (Philadelphia, 1984); Thomas P. Slaughter, *The Whiskey Rebellion: Frontier Epilogue to the American Revolution* (New York, 1986); David P. Szatmary, *Shays's Rebellion: The Making of an Agrarian Insurrection* (Amherst, Mass., 1980).

commercialized eighteenth-century transformation of luxuries into staples, of fashions into styles, of emulation of the rich and well-born into middle-class consumption.[62]

This leisure revolution was the context in which the consumer boom in British sport occurred. Many men and women located competitive recreations in this now separable sphere of life, and particular sports came to acquire patterns of play, skills, and times of occurrence that bore little resemblance to labor-derived tasks or traditional community games and rituals. Cricket and horse racing had governing bodies and contests no longer associated with older holidays, and both sports, as well as rugby, football, bowling, and hunting, were standardized and filled the free time of middle- and upper-class players and observers. In fact, many sports were bounded in time and space in ways quite different from earlier years. Cricket matches ran for two days on centrally located pitches, and horse races for several hours on the increasing number of flat courses constructed on the outskirts of towns. Both sports supported paid participants, ever-larger crowds, and gambling with money, generally at the beginning and, eventually, the end of the business week.[63]

Even sports of British workingmen underwent significant

[62] Historians who have focused on leisure primarily as the modern, a priori concept of free time include Cunningham, *Leisure in the Industrial Revolution*, pp. 15–51; Plumb, "Commercialization of Leisure," pp. 265–85. McKendrick, Brewer, and Plumb, *Birth of a Consumer Society*, is the only complete work that connects leisure and eighteenth-century consumerism, but its primary concern is consumerism rather than leisure. An alternative historiography is developing in Britain among the "radical" scholars, who stress the historical specificity of leisure. See John Clarke and Chas Critcher, *The Devil Makes Work: Leisure in Capitalist Britain* (Urbana, Ill., 1985); Eileen Yeo and Stephen Yeo, eds., *Popular Culture and Class Conflict, 1590–1914: Explorations in the History of Labour and Leisure* (Atlantic Highlands, N. J., 1981); Walton and Walvin, eds., *Leisure in Britain*.

[63] See note 9, above, and Dennis Brailsford, "Sporting Days in Eighteenth-Century England," *Journal of Sport History* 9 (1982):41–54; Allen Guttmann, *Sports Spectators* (New York, 1986), pp. 53–82; Plumb, "Commercialization of Leisure," pp. 280–82; John Ford, *This Sporting Land* (London, 1977); idem, *Cricket: A Social History, 1700–1835* (Plymouth, 1972); Christopher Brookes, *English Cricket* (London, 1978); David C. Itzkowitz, *Peculiar Privilege: A Social History of English Foxhunting, 1753–1885* (Sussex, 1977); Carl P. Cone, *Hounds in the Morning* (Lexington, Ky., 1981); Wray

change as the revolution in free and disposable time became a force with which they had to reckon. Cockfights, for example, had occurred primarily at Shrovetide, but this ritual connection was broken as the mains became commercialized entertainments in the eighteenth century. Fistfights became prizefights, and combatants became pugilists as the sport acquired upper-rank patrons and professional athletes from the ranks of the working class. Pugilism also acquired a moral code that deterred the stark brutality of traditional fistfighting and made it less of a target for the proponents of "rational recreation."[64]

In the United States in 1800, neither cricket nor horse racing—let alone cockfighting and fistfighting—was as standardized, specialized, and commercialized as each was in Britain. And none of them would become so before the 1820s, when the pursuit of leisure had matured and presented opportunities for commercial exploitation similar to those evident in late eighteenth-century Britain. Up to that point, leisure time was not a subject for an American revolution; it was not an abstract and independent sphere of life. Unlike their British contemporaries, early Americans had but an awareness of leisure.

Vamplew, *The Turf: A Social and Economic History of Horse Racing* (London, 1976); James Walvin, *The People's Game* (London, 1975); Eric Dunning and Ken Sheard, *Barbarians, Gentlemen, and Players* (Oxford, 1979).

[64]Malcomson, *Popular Recreations*, pp. 89–171; James Turner, *Reckoning with the Beast* (Baltimore, 1980); Dennis Brailsford, "Morals and Maulers: The Ethics of Early Pugilism," *Journal of Sport History* 12 (1985):126–42; Peter Bailey, *Leisure and Class in Victorian England: Rational Recreation and the Contests for Control, 1830–1885* (London, 1978). For discussions of nineteenth-century British workingmen's sports and their actions and reactions to modern leisure, see Alan Metcalfe, "Organized Sport in the Mining Communities of South Northumberland," *Victorian Studies* 25 (1982):469–95; Robert D. Storch, "The Problem of Working-Class Leisure," in A. P. Donajgrodzki, ed., *Social Control in Nineteenth-Century Britain* (Totowa, N. J., 1977); Clarke and Critcher, *The Devil Makes Work*, pp. 56–71; Anthony Delves, "Popular Recreation and Social Conflict in Derby, 1800–1850," in Yeo and Yeo, eds., *Popular Culture and Class Conflict*, pp. 89–117; Tony Mason, *Association Football and English Society, 1863–1915* (Sussex, 1980); J. M. Golby and A. W. Purdue, *The Civilisation of the Crowd: Popular Culture in England, 1750–1900* (London, 1984).

Time, especially the manner in which one employed it, had long been a concern of educated colonists. They had even associated some sports—especially baits and games in which they associated dulled moral senses, material loss, and social disorder—with waste of time. Such wasted time did not mean inactivity; instead it involved acts that consumed energy and effort purposelessly and that squandered, or at least failed to increase, money or other material possessions. And for such a waste of time, educated colonists had a specific term—*idleness*.[65]

This association of some sports with idleness persisted through the middle of the eighteenth century, but it acquired a fundamentally secular rather than a religious basis as its proponents observed the "most unhappy Consequences" of time ill-spent among two groups of people.[66] The first were ordinary colonists, whose linkage of sport with community events occasionally resulted in destructive public behaviors: Pope's Day marches that left some servants and laborers "for dead," the "Cudgelling and breaking of heads" after a disputed election, and the harassing of a minister by using, for card play, the stage on which he was to speak.[67] Taverns also bred the waste of time and money and drew strident criticisms. In 1750, for example, a writer to the *Boston Weekly*

[65] Many laws, sermons, and letters illustrate the importance of time and the association of some sports with time and money. In the seventeenth century unlawful sports were even designated as such primarily because they occurred both at inappropriate times, as defined by civil and religious leaders, and with the risk of loss of time, money, or goods. Among the persisting, perceived habits of idlers, too, was gambling. For general discussions of time (and sports associated with its waste, idleness), see James P. Walsh, "Holy Time and Sacred Space in Puritan New England," *American Quarterly* 32 (1980):79–95; Winton U. Solberg, *Redeem the Time: The Puritan Sabbath in Early America* (Cambridge, Mass., 1977); Malcolmson, *Popular Recreations*.

[66] *Boston Weekly News-Letter,* July 5, 1750.

[67] James Freeman, Notebook, 1745–65, Nov. 5, 1745, Nov. 5, 1764, Mass. Hist. Soc., Boston; *Boston Gazette and Country Journal*, Oct. 30, 1769; Cunningham, ed., *Diary of John Rowe*, p. 67; Dr. Alexander Hamilton, Letterbook, 1739–43, Box 2, Dulany Papers, Md. Hist. Soc., Baltimore; Robert B. Semple, *A History of the Rise and Progress of the Baptists in Virginia* (Richmond, 1894), p. 36.

News-Letter noted that taverns "seduced" servants "from their Masters' Business, and many Times are tempted to cheat and rob them," and that young people and apprentices were left "entirely useless or rather a Burden to the Community."[68] Nearly twenty years later, Charles Woodmason, an ordained Anglican minister in South Carolina, concluded that "in and about Charlestown, the Taverns have more Visitants than the Churches." Elsewhere he saw "Drinking Bouts and Card Playing" and "Women in frolicing and Wantoness."[69]

If the public culture of ordinary colonists was a source of concern for an educated, business-oriented minority, so, too, were the actions of some in their own class. At the beginning of the French and Indian War, Washington wrote to Virginia's governor Robert Dinwiddie about the less-than-ideal conduct of some of the officers under his command. They gambled, they drank, and they swore; and, Washington concluded, too many of them "have the seeds of idleness very strongly ingrafted in their natures."[70] In 1762 James C. Maury, a cleric-educator in Louisa County, Virginia, noted the "undistinguishing" effect of these "seeds of idleness" in gentlemen who "consumed too much time" in racing and cockfighting and clearly wasted "their Time & constitutions to very little Purpose."[71] Ten years later the *Virginia Gazette* criticized men who ignored the "tacit obligation" of every member of society "to contribute to the general Good." It maintained that anyone "who spends his whole Time in his stable, and on the Course; . . . who is ever found with Cards, or a Dice Box in his Hand"; and who "flies to the Bottle, or a Strumpet, to kill Thought, and prevent Time's lying heavy on his Hands . . . ought to be looked on as a burthensome member" of society.[72]

[68] *Boston Weekly News-Letter,* July 5, 1750.

[69] Richard J. Hooker, ed., *The Carolina Backcountry on the Eve of the Revolution: The Journal and Other Writings of Charles Woodmason, Anglican Itinerant* (Chapel Hill, N. C., 1953), p. 47.

[70] Fitzpatrick, ed., *Writings of Washington,* 1:317.

[71] James C. Maury, "A Dissertation on Education in the Form of a Letter from James Maury to Robert Jackson, July 17, 1762," ed. Helen D. Bullock (Charlottesville, Va., 1942), p. 42.

[72] *Virginia Gazette,* Oct. 15, 1772.

Thus idlers, whatever their position in society, were condemned by the educated minority. They threatened the public peace and economy, and they were readily identifiable, although probably not because their actions were more disorderly or their numbers larger than had been the case earlier. Like excessive gambling, with which waste of time was often associated, idleness may simply have become understood differently among upper-rank colonists. For such men—rational men who had begun to juxtapose slavery and freedom, monarchy and republicanism—idleness stood in stark contrast to another kind of time, the "Time which is really occupied." Unlike the moments put to "very little Purpose," the latter was that spent in necessary and productive tasks.[73] It was work time.

Besides idle time and "occupied" time, educated colonists had begun to acknowledge a third kind of time in the latter half of the century—leisure. Not unprescribed free time, these "hours which . . . Employment leaves Unengaged" were for "new Advantages, new Schemes of Utility," and for "Relaxation and Diversion" that the "Imbecility of Nature obliges."[74] It was time for writing letters of inquiry and information and time for whatever else "may amuse, instruct, or improve," including "Sketchley's New invented Conversational Cards."[75] Ornamented with forty-eight copper-plate cuts, these cards were wonders to behold. "The more they are played with the more they will improve and instruct," claimed the advertisement. "They will exercise the Imagination, enlarge the Understanding, and every one that plays with them are sure to be gainers."[76]

"Sketchley's New invented Conversational Cards" were not for everyone, and neither the cards nor the sense of leisure in which they were rooted was broadly imposed upon or emulated by ordinary men and women. They were not for southern backwoodsmen, New York boatsmen, or many other early

[73] Ibid., Jan. 24, 1752.

[74] Ibid., Dec. 27, 1751, Dec. 8, 1752.

[75] *Pennsylvania Gazette*, Apr. 23, 1752; *Virginia Gazette*, Nov. 4, 1775.

[76] *Virginia Gazette*, Nov. 4, 1775.

Americans for whom sport forms and opportunities remained closely tied to work, to the rhythms of a still uncompartmentalized life, to the spaces and places in which much of the rest of their life was lived. Nor were they for colonists who competed at Benjamin Berry's pit and ring, provincials who continued, as E. P. Thompson concluded about eighteenth-century British workingmen, to "alternate bouts of intense labour and idleness."[77] Instead, they were for the people who purchased jockey caps and card tables, formed clubs, and laid out bowling greens and thoroughbred racetracks. They were for "gainers," for colonists who had become conscious of the need for personal improvement and cultural refinement and who accepted and shaped particular forms of sport as sources of that cultivation.

It was with this sense of leisure that some early Americans associated particular forms of sport. Fishing occurred in "unengaged" hours as a "handmaiden" to other endeavors. Subscription races secured "Diversion," profit, and status. The assemblies encouraged "Relaxation" with exercise that "invigorates, and enlivens." Leisure was the positive corollary to idleness; it was concrete, productive, and ordered, attributes prized by many colonists.[78] It was also an appropriate time for the now useful competitive recreations that formed the core of the genteel and, eventually, the Victorian sporting experiences.

The designation of leisure as time for "new Schemes of Utility" and "Relaxation and Diversion" was a significant change in early America. It signaled a different way of viewing how one could and should behave, how one might spend the day. It permitted activities that had earlier been secondary ones, dependent on work and church-going but were now both

---

[77] E. P. Thompson, "Time, Work-Discipline, and Industrial Capitalism," *Past and Present* 38 (1967):73.

[78] For changing values and behaviors of late eighteenth- and early nineteenth-century Americans, see Philip Greven, *The Protestant Temperament: Patterns of Child-Rearing, Religious Experience, and the Self in Early America* (New York, 1977), esp. pp. 335–61; Edmund S. Morgan, *American Slavery, American Freedom: The Ordeal of Colonial Virginia* (New York, 1975), pp. 293–387; Isaac, *Transformation of Virginia*, pp. 299–322; Stephanie Grauman Wolf, *Urban Village: Population, Community, and Family Structure in Germantown,*

necessary and enjoyable in their own right: music, dance, reading, sport. It allowed social relations to change and develop: parents with children, farmers and planters with lawyers, merchants with manufacturers, neighbors with friends. It encouraged learning, correspondence, health-seeking, play, even politics, and it stimulated the British style of consumption that underlay true cultivation and improvement. Books, self-help manuals, jockey caps, card tables, eight-day clocks, and china dishes were the instruments of leisure.

The association of sport with this notion of leisure also altered the traditional bases and places for sport. It eroded the ties that sport forms had had to ordinary tasks, ties that had linked the movements within the contests as well as the contests themselves with those experienced in labor and older rituals. Sport in leisure incorporated, even concocted, a different variety of action and competition; in fact, leisure encouraged the creation of new sport forms, as subscription races, bowling on greens, the sailing of "pleasure" boats, and, eventually, baseball suggest. The linkage of sport and leisure, as time distinct from either "really occupied" or idle times, also altered the occasions, as well as the social settings, for sport. No longer did sport occur primarily in the context of older festivals and community gatherings; instead, matches and contests consumed evenings, race weeks, and Saturdays. Finally, insofar as men and women rationalized leisure and assigned to it expectations—especially of beneficial outcomes and productive, efficient ways of behaving—they also projected goals and codes of conduct for sport. Sport was to provide exercise that "invigorates, and enlivens all the Faculties of Body and of mind," all manner of "Recreation and Diver-

---

Pennsylvania, 1683–1800 (Princeton, 1976); Lewis, *Pursuit of Happiness*; William Cronon, *Changes in the Land: Indians, Colonists, and the Ecology of New England* (New York, 1983); T. H. Breen, *Tobacco Culture: The Mentality of the Great Tidewater Planters on the Eve of Revolution* (Princeton, 1985), pp. 160–210; Richard L. Bushman, *King and People in Provincial Massachusetts* (Chapel Hill, N. C., 1985), pp. 226–52; Stuart M. Blumin, "The Hypothesis of Middle-Class Formation in Nineteenth-Century America: A Critique and Some Proposals," *American Historical Review* 90 (1985):299–338; Daniel A. Cohen, "Arthur Mervyn and His Elders: The Ambivalence of Youth in the Early Republic," *William and Mary Quarterly,* 3d. ser. 43 (1986):362–80.

sion," rather than the social disruption and physical excess, even violence, that resulted from cock shailing, mass boxing, and bull baits. Not coincidentally, too, it was the post-Revolutionary War generation that first used the word *sports-man* in ordinary conversation, a term that drew from and reinforced refined manners and gentility. A sportsman was one who was courteous, brave, and generous, who killed only "one brace of woodcocks and two of partridges—missing only two shots," and who dismissed an "unqualified sportsman" as a "most ignorant and conceited pupp[y] or a coward."[79]

The term *sportsman* survived long into the nineteenth century, but it did so primarily as a rhetorical device among southern romantics like John Stuart Skinner and William Ransom Johnson. The eighteenth-century conditions and expectations that had spawned and supported both the genteel sporting tradition and the fashions of ordinary colonists had altered significantly as the Republic matured. So, too, did the older notion of leisure as time for "new Advantages, new Schemes of Utility." In a rapidly urbanizing America, ranks became classes, classes undertook business, and business transformed leisure. What had once been a distinct kind of time observed by gentlemen and gentlewomen became a distinct sphere of life that could both nurture industry and be exploited by industrious men and women, whether rich or poor.

During and after the 1820s the revolution in leisure changed the face of American sporting life. The sports engaged in during leisure became businesslike, a consumer boom involving both men and women took place, and their participation expanded American industry and social relations, as well as the nation's repertoire of values and myths. The "great" thoroughbred contests on Long Island's Union track drew crowds of 70,000 spectators and more from all walks of life as long as that form of horse racing remained profitable. Journalists published sporting magazines in New York and Baltimore, and equipment manufacturers operated

[79]See, for example, *Letters of John Randolph to a Young Relative* (Philadelphia, 1834), pp. 15, 26, 109, 128–29.

in several eastern and midwestern cities and towns. Money drew farmers, artisans, and laborers into the ranks of professional prizefighters and pedestrians, some of whom sought competition in Britain. Educators constructed or purchased equipment for games for boys and girls.[80] In the middle of the nineteenth century, too, some middle-class sportsmen imported the British concept of amateurism as yet another code of conduct to govern some leisure sports. It never rooted. The pretenses of anticommercial and nonutilitarian sport were incongruous not only with the reality of mid-nineteenth century urban sporting life but also with the historical styles that influenced both middle- and working-class fashions, the genteel and folk strains of the eighteenth century.[81] Without realizing it, early Americans had doomed amateurism.

[80]About the races, see Adelman, *Sporting Time*, pp. 31–54; Nancy L. Struna, "The North-South Races: The Transformation of American Thoroughbred Racing, 1823–1850," *Journal of Sport History* 8 (1981):28–57. The first lasting sporting journal, the *American Turf Register and Sporting Magazine* (1829), evolved out of the *American Farmer* (1819), published by John Stuart Skinner in Baltimore. William T. Porter edited the other major journal, *The Spirit of the Times* (1831), in New York. For equipment manufacturers and retailers, see Stephen Hardy, "The Sporting Goods Industry and the Rise of Sport, 1800–1900," unpublished paper, 1987; Betts, *America's Sporting Heritage*, pp. 43–48. See also Peter Levine, "The Promise of Sport in Antebellum America," *Journal of American Culture* 2 (1980):623–34; Cumming, *Runners and Walkers;* George Moss, "The Long Distance Runners of Ante-Bellum America," *Journal of Popular Culture* 8 (1974):371–82; Elliott J. Gorn, *The Manly Art: Bare-Knuckle Prize Fighting in America* (Ithaca, N. Y., 1986); John R. Betts, "Sporting Journalism in Nineteenth-Century America," *American Quarterly* 5 (1953):39–64; idem, "Public Recreation, Public Parks, and Public Health before the Civil War," in Bruce L. Bennett, ed., *History of Physical Education and Sport* (Chicago, 1972), pp. 33–52; Park, "'Embodied Selves,'" pp. 7–18; Harvey Green, *Fit for America: Health, Fitness, Sport, and American Society* (New York, 1986), pp. 1–29.

[81]Ronald A. Smith has explored both the ideology of amateurism and the practices of amateurs in a number of articles and papers. He has argued that the code never described or governed actual practices. His argument appears concisely in "The Historic Amateur-Professional Dilemma in American College Sport," *British Journal of Sports History* 2 (1985):221–31.

T. H. BREEN

"Baubles of Britain": The American and Consumer Revolutions of the Eighteenth Century

SOMETHING EXTRAORDINARY OCCURRED in 1774. Thousands of ordinary people responded as they had never done before to an urban political crisis. Events in Boston mobilized a nation, uniting for the first time artisans and farmers, yeomen and gentlemen, and within only a few months colonists who had earlier expressed neutrality or indifference about the confrontation with Great Britain suddenly found themselves supporting bold actions that led almost inevitably to independence.

At midcentury almost no one would have predicted such an occurrence. Some two million people had scattered themselves over an immense territory. They seemed to have little in common. In fact, contemporary observers concluded that should the colonists ever achieve political independence, they would immediately turn on each other. "In short," declared one English traveler in 1759, "such is the difference of character, of manners, of religion, of interest, of the different colo-

This article first appeared in *Past and Present* 119 (1988):73–104. World Copyright: The Past and Present Society, 175 Banbury Road, Oxford, England. Earlier drafts of the essay were presented at the United States Capitol Historical Society's 1986 symposium and at a workshop for the Anthropology Department, University of Chicago, January 1987. I would especially like to acknowledge the suggestions of Marshall Sahlins, Michael Silverstein, Bernard S. Cohn, James Oakes, and Josef Barton.

nies, that I think . . . were they left to themselves, there would soon be a civil war from one end of the continent to the other."[1] John Adams agreed. Reflecting in 1818 on the coming of revolution, he marveled that the Americans had ever managed to unite. Their own separate histories seemed to have conspired against the formation of a new nation. The colonies, Adams explained, had evolved different constitutions of government. They had experienced "so great a variety of religions, they were composed of so many different nations, their customs, manners, and habits had so little resemblance, and their intercourse had been so rare, and their knowledge of each other so imperfect, that to unite them in . . . the same system of action, was certainly a very difficult enterprise."

Very difficult indeed! And yet in 1776 these colonists surprised the world by successfully forming a new nation. In Adams's words, "Thirteen clocks were made to strike together."[2] Somehow Americans had found a means to communicate effectively with each other, to develop a shared sense of political purpose, to transcend what at midcentury had appeared insurmountable cultural and geographic divisions. The mobilization of strangers in a revolutionary cause eroded the stubborn localism of an earlier period. In other words, it was a process that heightened awareness of a larger social identity. In Benedict Anderson's wonderful phrase, these men and women "imagined" a "community," a national consciousness that, while not yet the full-blown nationalism of the nineteenth century, was nevertheless essential to the achievement of political independence.[3]

[1]Andrew Burnaby, *Travels through North America* (New York, 1904), pp. 152–53.

[2]John Adams to Hezekiah Niles, Feb. 13, 1818, Charles Francis Adams, ed., *The Works of John Adams,* 10 vols. (Boston, 1850–56), 10:283.

[3]Benedict Anderson, *Imagined Communities: Reflections on the Origin and Spread of Nationalism* (London, 1983); Linda Colley, "Whose Nation? Class and National Consciousness in Britain, 1750–1830," *Past and Present* 113 (1986):97–117; Goeff Eley, "Nationalism and Social History," *Social History* 6 (1981):83–107; Richard L. Merritt, *Symbols of American Community, 1735–1775* (New Haven, 1966). Also see T. H. Breen, "A Ploughjogger's Complaint: Ideology and Nationalism in Anglo-American Context, 1740–90"

Efforts to explain this political mobilization have foundered on an attempt to establish the primacy of ideology over material interest.[4] This is not a debate in which the truth lies somewhere between two extremes. Neither the intellectual nor the economic historian can tell us how Americans of different classes and backgrounds and living in very different physical environments achieved political solidarity, at least sufficient solidarity to make good their claim to independence. Economic explanations—those that analyze an individual's political loyalties in terms of poverty or profits, absence of business opportunities or decline of soil fertility—are not only reductionist in character but also narrowly focused upon the experiences of specific, often numerically small groups in colonial society. Though we learn, for example, why certain urban workers in Boston or Philadelphia might have been unhappy with parliamentary taxation, we never discover how such people managed to reach out to—indeed even to communicate with—northern farmers and southern planters. In other words, the more we know about the pocketbook concerns of any particular eighteenth-century American community, the more difficult it becomes to understand a spreading national consciousness that accompanied political mobilization.

Intellectual historians encounter a different, though equally thorny set of problems. They transform the American Revolution into a mental event. From this perspective, it does not matter much whether the ideas the colonists espoused are classic liberal concepts of rights and property, radical country notions of power and virtue, or evangelical Calvinist beliefs about sin and covenants. Whatever the dominant ideology may have been, we find that a bundle of political abstractions

---

(Paper presented at the One hundred seventh Annual Meeting of the American Historical Association, Washington, D.C., Dec. 1992).

[4]I discuss this historiographic debate in *Tobacco Culture: The Mentality of the Great Tidewater Planters on the Eve of Revolution* (Princeton, 1985), chap. 1, and expand the analysis in "Narrative of Commercial Life: Consumption, Ideology, and Community on the Eve of the American Revolution," *William and Mary Quarterly*, 3d ser. 50 (1993): 471–501. See also Gordon S. Wood, "Rhetoric and Reality in the American Revolution," *William and Mary Quarterly*, 3d ser. 23 (1966):3–32.

has persuaded colonists living in scattered regions of America of the righteousness of their cause, driving them during the 1760s and 1770s to take ever more radical positions until eventually they were forced by the logic of their original assumptions to break with Great Britain. Unfortunately, intellectual historians provide no clear link between the everyday world of the men and women who actually became patriots and the ideas that they articulated. We are thus hard-pressed to comprehend how in 1774 wealthy Chesapeake planters and poor Boston artisans—to cite two obvious examples—could possibly have come to share a political mentality. We do not know how these ideas were transmitted through colonial society, from class to class, from community to community.

These interpretive issues—those that currently separate the materialists from the idealists—may be resolved by casting the historical debate in different terms. Eighteenth-century Americans, I shall argue, communicated perceptions of status and politics to other people through items of everyday material culture, through a symbolic universe of commonplace "things" that modern scholars usually take for granted but that for their original possessors were objects of great significance.[5] By focusing attention on the meanings of things, on the semiotics of daily life, we gain fresh insight into the formation of a national consciousness as well as the coming of the American Revolution.[6]

The imported British manufactures that flooded American society during the eighteenth century acquired cultural significance largely within local communities. Their meanings were bound up with a customary world of face-to-face relations. Within these localities Americans began to define social status in relation to commodities. This was, of course, an expression of a much larger, long-term transformation of the

[5] See Mihaly Csikszentmihalyi and Eugene Rochberg-Halton, *The Meaning of Things: Domestic Symbols and the Self* (Cambridge, 1981). Although this is a study of contemporary society, it provides historians with valuable insight into how people interpret the material objects of daily life.

[6] See Lynn A. Hunt, *Politics, Culture, and Class in the French Revolution* (Berkeley and Los Angeles, 1984); Anthony Giddens, *The Constitution of Society: Outline of the Theory of Structuration* (Berkeley and Los Angeles, 1984); Marshall Sahlins, *Islands of History* (Chicago, 1985).

Atlantic world. And though this process differentiated men and women in new ways, it also provided them with a common framework of experience, a shared language of consumption.

But in America something unusual occurred during the 1760s and 1770s. Parliament managed to politicize these consumer goods, and when it did so, manufactured items suddenly took on a radical, new, symbolic function. In this particular colonial setting the very commodities that were everywhere beginning to transform social relations provided a language for revolution. People living in scattered parts of America began to communicate their political grievances *through* common imports. A shared framework of consumer experience not only allowed them to reach out to distant strangers, to perceive, however dimly, the existence of an "imagined community," but also to situate a universal political discourse about rights and liberties, virtue and power, within a familiar material culture. In this context the boycott became a powerful social metaphor of resistance, joining Carolinians and New Englanders, small farmers and powerful merchants, men and women in common cause.[7]

This interpretive scheme gives priority neither to ideas nor experience. Some Americans undoubtedly boycotted British imports because of political principle. By denying themselves

[7]The swadeshi movement in late nineteenth-century and early twentieth-century India provides some intriguing parallels to the American experience. As C. A. Bayly explains, "After 1905, the import of British-made cloth into India and the ensuing destruction of Indian handicraft production became the key theme of Indian nationalism. In the hands first of Bengali leaders and later of Mahatma Gandhi and his supporters, the need to support *swadeshi* (home industries) and boycott foreign goods was woven through with notions of neighborliness, patriotism, purity, and sacrifice, all of which provided unifying ideologies more powerful than any single call for political representation or independence" (C. A. Bayly, "The Origins of Swadeshi [Home Industry]: Cloth and Indian Society, 1700–1930," in Arjun Appadurai, ed., *The Social Life of Things: Commodities in Cultural Perspective* [Cambridge, 1986], p. 285. Also Sumit Sarkar, *The Swadeshi Movement in Bengal, 1903–1908* [New Delhi, 1973]; Bernard S. Cohn, "Cloth, Clothes, and Colonialism: India in the 19th Century," [Paper presented at the Wenner-Gren Foundation Symposium, 1983]).

these goods they expressed a deep ideological commitment. Other colonists, however, gave up consumer items because their neighbors compelled them to do so. They were not necessarily motivated by high principle, at least not initially. But the very experience of participating in these boycotts, of taking part in increasingly elaborate rituals of nonconsumption, had an unintended effect. It served inevitably to heighten popular awareness of the larger constitutional issues at stake. In this sense, the boycott for many Americans was an act of ideological discovery. These particular colonists may not have destroyed tea because they were republicans, but surely they learned something fundamental about republican ideas by their participation in such events. Questions about the use of tea in one's household forced ordinary men and women to choose sides, to consider exactly where they stood. And, over time, pledges of support for nonimportation publicly linked patriotic individuals to other, like-minded individuals. Decisions about consumer goods tied local communities to other communities, to regional movements, and, after 1774, to a national association. Neither the consumer revolution nor the boycott movement can in itself explain an occurrence so complex as the American Revolution. That argument would amount to a new form of reductionism. The aim here is more limited: to explore the relation between the growth of national consciousness and the American rejection of the "Baubles of Britain."

The eighteenth century witnessed the birth of an Anglo-American "consumer society." Though the Industrial Revolution was still far in the future, the pace of the British economy picked up dramatically after 1690. Small manufacturing concerns scattered throughout England began turning out huge quantities of consumer goods—cloth, ceramics, glassware, paper, cutlery—items that transformed the character of everyday life. Merchants could hardly keep up with expanding demand. The domestic market hummed with activity. People went shopping, gawking at the wares displayed in the "bow-windows" that appeared for the first time along urban streets. Advertisements in the provincial English journals fueled the consumer desire, and to those middling sorts who wanted to participate in the market but who did not possess sufficient cash, tradesmen offered generous credit.[8]

Americans were quickly swept up in this consumer economy. These were not the self-sufficient yeomen of Jeffersonian mythology. Eighteenth-century colonists demanded the latest British manufactures. Few would have disagreed with the members of the Maryland general assembly who once announced, "We want the British Manufactures."[9] In order to pay for what they imported, the Americans harvested ever-larger crops of tobacco, rice, and indigo. Northern farmers supplied the West Indian plantations with foodstuffs. Economic historians have traditionally concentrated on this flow of American exports or, more precisely, on the production of staple commodities in response to European market conditions. The problem with this perspective is that it depreciates the role of consumer demand in shaping the colonial economy. At a time when the American population was growing at an extraordinary rate, per capita consumption of British imports was actually rising. In other words, more colonists purchased more manufactured goods every year. Since this

---

[8]The literature on the development of an Anglo-American consumer society during the eighteenth century is quite large. Works that were particularly helpful for this investigation include Charles Wilson, *England's Apprenticeship, 1603–1763* (New York, 1965); Ralph Davis, *A Commercial Revolution in English Overseas Trade in the Seventeenth and Eighteenth Centuries* (London, 1967); Roy Porter, *English Society in the Eighteenth Century* (Harmondsworth, 1982); Harold J. Perkin, *The Origins of Modern English Society* (London, 1969); Neil McKendrick, John Brewer, and J. H. Plumb, *The Birth of a Consumer Society: The Commercialization of Eighteenth-Century England* (Bloomington, Ind., 1982); Paul Langford, *A Polite and Commercial People: England, 1727–1783* (Oxford, 1989), chaps. 2 and 3; Eric L. Jones, "The Fashion Manipulators: Consumer Tastes and British Industries, 1660–1800," in Louis P. Cain and Paul J. Uselding, eds., *Business Enterprise and Economic Change: Essays in Honor of Harold F. Williamson* (Kent, Ohio, 1973), pp. 198–226; Lorna Weatherill, "A Possession of One's Own: Women and Consumer Behavior in England, 1660–1740," *Journal of British Studies* 25 (1986):131–56; Hoh-Cheung Mui and Lorna H. Mui, *Shops and Shopkeeping in Eighteenth-Century England* (London, 1989).

[9]"Proceedings and Acts of the General Assembly of Maryland, 1764–1765," William Hand Browne et al., eds., *Archives of Maryland*, 72 vols. to date (Baltimore, 1883–), 59:210.

was a young population—half of the colonists were under the age of sixteen—one must assume that adults were responsible for this exploding demand. Their consumption raised per capita rates for the entire society. After midcentury the American market for imported goods took off, rising 120 percent between 1750 and 1773. Throughout the colonies the crude, somewhat impoverished material culture of the seventeenth century—a pioneer world of homespun cloth and wooden dishes—was swept away by a flood of store-bought sundries.[10]

These ubiquitous items transformed the texture of everyday life in provincial America. Even in the most inaccessible regions people came increasingly to rely on imports. One English traveler discovered to her surprise that in rural North Carolina women seldom bothered to produce soap. It was not a question of the availability of raw materials. Good ashes could be had at no expense. But these rural women were consumers, and they preferred to purchase Irish soap "at the store at a monstrous price."[11] In more cosmopolitan environments, the imports were even more conspicuous. Eighteenth-century Americans situated other men and women within a rich context of British manufactures. John Adams betrayed this habit of mind when he visited the home of a successful Boston merchant: "Went over [to] the House to view the Fur-

---

[10]I have reviewed the literature of consumer behavior in eighteenth-century America in "An Empire of Goods: The Anglicization of Colonial America, 1690–1776," *Journal of British Studies* 25 (1986):467–99. Also see John J. McCusker and Russell R. Menard, *The Economy of British America, 1607–1789* (Chapel Hill, N. C., 1985), chap. 13; Carole Shammas, "How Self-Sufficient Was Early America?" *Journal of Interdisciplinary History* 13 (1982):247–72; Gloria L. Main, "The Standard of Living in Colonial Massachusetts," *Journal of Economic History* 43 (1983):101–8; Lorena S. Walsh, "Urban Amenities and Rural Sufficiency: Living Standards and Consumer Behavior in the Colonial Chesapeake, 1643–1777," *Journal of Economic History* 43 (1983):109–17; Elizabeth A. Perkins, "The Consumer Frontier: Household Consumption in Early Kentucky," *Journal of American History* 78 (1991):486–510. An interpretation of the character of the eighteenth-century American economy that differs substantially from the one advanced here can be found in James A. Henretta, "Families and Farms: *Mentalité* in Pre-Industrial America," *William and Mary Quarterly*, 3d ser. 35 (1978):3–32.

[11][Janet Schaw], *Journal of a Lady of Quality*, ed. Evangeline Walker Andrews and Charles M. Andrews (New Haven, 1921), p. 204.

niture, which alone cost a thousand Pounds sterling. A seat it is for a noble Man, a Prince. The Turkey Carpets, the painted Hangings, the Marble Table, the rich Beds with crimson Damask Curtains and Counterpins, the beautiful Chimny Clock, the Spacious Garden, are the most magnificent of any Thing I have ever seen."[12] Like other Americans, Adams had obviously developed a taste for British imports.

How does one make sense out of this vast consumer society? There is much that we do not know about eighteenth-century colonial merchandizing. Still, even at this preliminary stage of investigation, it is possible to discern certain general characteristics that distinguished the colonial marketplace at mid-century: an exceptionally rapid expansion of consumer *choice,* an increasing *standardization* of consumer behavior, and a pervasive *Anglicization* of the American market.

Of these three, the proliferation of choice is the most difficult to interpret. We simply do not know what it meant to colonial consumers to find themselves suddenly confronted by an unprecedented level of variety in the marketplace. Perhaps it was a liberating experience? Perhaps the very act of making choices between competing goods of different color, texture, and quality heightened the individual's sense of personal independence? After all, the colonial buyers were actively participating in the consumer economy, demanding what they wanted rather than merely taking what was offered.

Whatever the psychological impact of this change may have been, there is no question that Americans at midcentury confronted a range of choice that would have amazed earlier generations. A survey of New York City newspapers revealed, for example, that during the 1720s merchants seldom mentioned more than fifteen different imported items per month in their advertisements. The descriptions were generic: cloth, paper, ceramics. But by the 1770s it was not unusual during some busy months for New York journals specifically to list over nine thousand different manufactured goods. And as the number of items expanded, the descriptive categories became

[12]Lyman H. Butterfield, ed., *Diary and Autobiography of John Adams,* 4 vols. (Cambridge, Mass., 1961), 1:294. Also see Carole Shammas, *The Pre-Industrial Consumer in England and America* (Oxford, 1990).

more elaborate. In the 1740s New York merchants simply advertised "paper." By the 1760s they listed seventeen varieties distinguished by color, function, and quality. In the 1730s a customer might have requested satin, hoping apparently that the merchant had some in stock. By the 1760s merchants advertised a dozen different types of satin. No carpets were mentioned in the New York advertisements before the 1750s, but by the 1760s certain stores carried carpets labeled Axminster, Milton, Persian, Scotch, Turkey, Weston, and Wilton. One could purchase after the 1750s purple gloves, flowered gloves, orange gloves, white gloves, rough gloves, chamois gloves, buff gloves, "Maid's Black Silk" gloves, "Maid's Lamb Gloves," and even "Men's Dog Skin Gloves." There is no need to continue. Everywhere one looks, one encounters an explosion of choices.

If, as many scholars currently argue, human beings constitute external reality through language, then the proliferation of manufactures during the eighteenth century may have radically altered how Americans made sense out of everyday activities. The consumer market provided them with an impressive new vocabulary, thousands of words that allowed them not only to describe a changing material culture but also to interpret their place within it. Adams demonstrated this point when in his diary he recorded his reactions to the possessions of the wealthy Boston merchant. This language of goods was shared by all who participated in the market. It was not the product of a particular region or class, and thus furnished colonists with a means of transmitting experience across social and geographic boundaries. As we have seen, a visitor could engage the women of North Carolina in a discourse about imported soap. It was a conversation that the women of Virginia and Massachusetts would also have understood.

An example of this kind of cultural exchange occurred in a Maryland tavern in 1744. A traveling physician from Annapolis witnessed a quarrel between an innkeeper and an individual who by his external appearance seemed "a rough spun, forward, clownish blade." The proprietor apparently shared this impression, because she served this person who wore "a greasy jacket and breeches and a dirty worsted cap" a break-

453

fast fit "for some ploughman or carman." The offended customer vehemently protested that he, too, was a gentleman
and to prove his status, pulled a linen hat out of his pocket.
He then informed the embarrassed assembly that "he was
able to afford better than many who went finer: he had good
linnen in his bags, a pair of silver buckles, silver clasps, and
gold sleeve buttons, two Holland shirts, and some neat night
caps; and that his little woman att home drank tea twice a
day." What catches our attention is not the man's clumsy attempt to negotiate status through possessions—people have
been doing that for centuries—but rather that he bragged of
owning specific manufactured goods, the very articles that
were just then beginning to transform American society. He
assumed—correctly, in this case—that the well-appointed
stranger he encountered in a country tavern understood the
language of shirts, buckles, and tea.[13]

This expanding consumer world of the mid-eighteenth
century led almost inevitably to a *standardization* of the marketplace. To be sure, as the previous anecdote suggests,
Americans had begun to define status in relation to commodities. In this they were not unique. Throughout the Atlantic
world, choice created greater, more visible marks of distinction. Nevertheless, by actually purchasing manufactured imports as opposed to making do with locally produced objects,
by participating in an expanding credit network, and by finding themselves confronted with basically the same types of
goods that were now on sale in other, distant communities,
Americans developed a common element of personal experience.

One can only speculate, of course, why colonial shoppers
purchased certain items. They may have been looking for status, beauty, convenience, or price. Whatever the justification

[13]Carl Bridenbaugh, ed., *Gentleman's Progress: The Itinerarium of Dr. Alexander Hamilton, 1744* (Chapel Hill, N. C., 1948), pp. 13–14. I explore the ideological implications of choice and suggest the limitations of republican
thought in developing an understanding of colonial American political culture on the eve of the Revolution in "The Meaning of Things: Interpreting
the Consumer Economy in the Eighteenth Century," in John Brewer and
Roy Porter, eds., *Consumption and the World of Goods* (London, 1993), pp.
249–60.

may have been, the fact remains that people living in different parts of America were exposed to an almost identical range of imported goods. In part, this standardization of the marketplace resulted from the manufacturing process; after all, there were only so many dyes and glazes and finishes available during this period. The Staffordshire ceramics, for example, that sold in Charleston were of the same general shapes and colors of the Staffordshireware that sold in the shops of Philadelphia, New York, and Boston. Indeed, an examination of newspaper advertisements in these colonial ports reveals no evidence of the development of regional consumer taste.[14] British merchants sent to America what they could obtain from the manufacturers; the colonists bought whatever the merchants shipped. It is not surprising, therefore, to discover a Virginian in 1766 exclaiming, "Now nothing are so common as Turkey or Wilton Carpetts."[15] As we have already discovered, carpets of the same description had just made their appearance in the newspaper advertisements in New York and in the home of the Boston merchant described by John Adams.

The standardization of taste affected all colonial consumers. This is an important point. It is easy for modern historians to concentrate on the buying habits of the gentry.[16] Their beautiful houses—many of which are now preserved as museums—dominate our understanding of the character of daily life in eighteenth-century America. This interpretive bias is not a problem peculiar to the colonial period. The consumer behavior of the wealthy has always been more fully documented than that of more humble buyers. But however much we are drawn to the material culture of the colonial elite, we should

[14]Observations about the character and content of eighteenth-century American advertising found in this essay are based on extensive research in the newspapers of Boston, New York, Philadelphia, Williamsburg, and Charleston carried out by the author and Rebecca Becker of Northwestern University.

[15]John Hemphill, "John Wayles Rates His Neighbors," *Virginia Magazine of History and Biography* 66 (1958):305.

[16]See Richard L. Bushman, "American High-Style and Vernacular Cultures," in Jack P. Greene and J. R. Pole, eds., *Colonial British America: Essays in the New History of the Early Modern Era* (Baltimore, 1984), pp. 345–83.

realize that the spread of the consumer market transformed the lives of ordinary men and women as fundamentally as it did those of their more affluent neighbors. Though wealthy Americans purchased goods of superior quality, poorer buyers demanded the same general range of imports. Rural peddlers, urban hawkers, and Scottish factors responded to this eager clientele, providing farmers and artisans with easy credit, the ticket to participation in this consumer society. These people became reliant on imported manufactures, so much so in fact that Francis Fauquier, lieutenant-governor of Virginia, could note in 1763, "These imports daily encrease, the common planters usually dressing themselves in the manufactures of Great Brittain altogether." [17]

Tea provides an instructive example of the standardization of consumer taste. Early in the eighteenth century this hot drink became the preferred beverage in gentry households. Polite women—perhaps as a device to lure gentlemen away from tavern society—organized elaborate household rituals around the tea service. In fact the purchase of tea necessitated the acquisition of pots, bowls, strainers, sugar tongs, cups, and slop dishes. One writer in a New York newspaper suggested the need for a school of tea etiquette. The young men of the city, finding themselves "utterly ignorant in the Ceremony of the Tea-Table," were advised to employ a knowledgeable woman "to teach them the Laws, Rules, Customs, Phrases and Names of Tea Utensils." [18]

Though less well-to-do Americans did not possess the entire range of social props, they demanded tea. As early as 1734 one New Yorker reported: "I am credibly informed that tea and china ware cost the province, yearly, near the sum of £10,000; and people that are least able to go to the expence, must have their tea tho' their families want bread. Nay, I am told, they often pawn their rings and plate to gratifie them-

[17] P.R.O., C.O. 5/1330, Francis Fauquier, "Answers to the Queries Sent to Me by the Right Honourable the Lords Commissioners for Trade and Plantation Affairs," Jan. 30, 1763. Also see Breen, "Empire of Goods," pp. 485–96; and David Jaffee, "Peddlers of Progress and the Transformation of the Rural North, 1760–1860," *Journal of American History* 78 (1991):511–35.

[18] Cited in Esther Singleton, *Social New York under the Georges, 1714–1776* (New York, 1902), p. 380–81.

selves in that piece of extravagance."[19] It did not take long for this particular luxury to become a necessity. "Our people," wrote another New York gentleman in 1762, "both in town and country, are shamefully gone into the habit of tea-drinking."[20] And when Israel Acrelius visited the old Swedish settlements of Delaware at midcentury, he discovered people consuming tea "in the most remote cabins."[21] During the 1750s even the inmates of the public hospital of Philadelphia, the city poorhouse, insisted on having bohea.[22] All these colonists drank their tea out of imported cups, not necessarily china ones, but rather ceramics that had originated in the English Midlands where they had been fired at very high temperature and thus made resistant to the heat of America's new favorite drink.

Ordinary Americans adopted tea for reasons other than social emulation. After all, it was a mild stimulant, and a hot cup of tea probably helped the laboring poor endure hard work and insubstantial housing. Nevertheless, in some isolated country villages the desire to keep up with the latest consumer fads led to bizarre results, the kind of gross cultural misunderstanding that anthropologists encounter in places where products of an alien technology have been introduced into a seemingly less developed society.[23] In 1794 a historian living in East Hampton, New York, interviewed a seventy-eight-year-old woman. "Mrs. Miller," he discovered, "remembers well when they first began to drink tea on the east end of Long Island." She explained that none of the local farmers knew what to do with the dry leaves: "One family boiled it in

[19] Ibid., p. 375.

[20] William Smith, Jr., *The History of the Late Province of New York . . . to . . . 1762*, New-York Historical Society *Collections*, vol. 4, pt. 2 (1829), p. 281.

[21] Cited in Rodris Roth, *Tea Drinking in Eighteenth-Century America: Its Etiquette and Equipage*, U.S. National Museum Bulletin 225 (Washington, D.C., 1961), p. 66.

[22] Billy G. Smith, "The Material Lives of Laboring Philadelphians, 1750 to 1800," *William and Mary Quarterly*, 3d ser. 38 (1981):168.

[23] See, for example, H. A. Powell, "Cricket in Kiriwina," *Listener* 48 (1952):384–85.

a pot and ate it like samp-porridge. Another spread tea leaves on his bread and butter, and bragged of his having ate half a pound at a meal, to his neighbor, who was informing him how long a time a pound of tea lasted him." According to Mrs. Miller, the arrival of the first teakettle was a particularly memorable day in the community: "It came ashore at Montauk in a ship, (the *Captain Bell*). The farmers came down there on business with their cattle, and could not find out how to use the tea-kettle, which was then brought up to old 'Governor Hedges.' Some said it was for one thing, and some said it was for another. At length one, the more knowing than his neighbors, affirmed it to be the ship's lamp, to which they all assented." Mrs. Miller may have been pulling the historian's leg, but whatever the truth of her story, it reveals the symbolic importance of tea in this remote eighteenth-century village.[24]

Standardization of consumer goods created a paradoxical situation. As Americans purchased the same general range of British manufactures—in other words, as they had similar consumer experiences—they became increasingly Anglicized. Historians sometimes refer to this cultural process as "the colonization of taste."[25] The Anglo-American consumer society of the eighteenth century drew the mainland colonists closer to the culture of the mother country. In part, this was a result of the Navigation Acts that channeled American commerce through Great Britain, a legislative constraint that made it difficult as well as expensive for Americans to purchase goods from the Continent. There is no reason to believe, however, that Parliament passed these acts in a conscious attempt to "colonize American taste." That just happened. And during the eighteenth century this process is easy to trace. For most people, articles imported from the mother country carried positive associations. They introduced color and excitement

[24] Henry P. Hedges, *A History of the Town of East-Hampton, N. Y.* (Sag-Harbor, N. Y., 1897), p. 142; T. H. Breen, *Imagining the Past: East Hampton Histories* (Reading, Mass., 1989), chaps. 2 and 3.

[25] Bayly, "Origins of Swadeshi," pp. 303–11. See also Nicholas Phillipson, "Politics, Politeness, and the Anglicisation of Early Eighteenth-Century Scottish Culture," in R. A. Mason, ed., *Scotland and England, 1286–1815* (Edinburgh, 1987), pp. 226–46.

into the lives of the colonists. Their quality was superior to that of locally made goods, silverware and furniture being two notable exceptions. It is not surprising that the demand for British manufactures escalated so quickly after midcentury. The market itself created new converts. Advertisements, merchants' displays, and news of other people's acquisitions stoked consumer desire and thereby accelerated the spread of Anglicization. Booksellers—just to note one example—discovered that colonial readers preferred an English imprint to an American edition of the same title. "Their estimate of things English was so high," reports one historian, "that a false London imprint could seem an effective way to sell a local publication."[26]

Anglicized provincials insisted on receiving the "latest" English goods. They were remarkably attuned to even subtle changes in metropolitan fashion. "And you may believe me," a young Virginia planter named George Washington lectured a British merchant in 1760, "when I tell you that instead of getting things good and fashionable in their several kinds we often have Articles sent Us that coud only have been usd by our Forefathers in the days of yore."[27] Washington may have envied his neighbors in Maryland. According to one visitor to Annapolis: "The quick importation of fashions from the mother country is really astonishing. I am almost inclined to believe that a new fashion is adopted earlier by the polished and affluent American than by many opulent persons in the great metropolis [London]. . . . In short, very little difference is, in reality, observable in the manners of the wealthy colonist and the wealthy Briton."[28] No doubt this man exaggerated, but as he well understood, after midcentury American consumers took their cues from the mother country. Certainly

[26] Stephen Botein, "The Anglo-American Book Trade before 1776: Personnel and Strategies," in William L. Joyce et al., eds., *Printing and Society in Early America* (Worcester, Mass., 1983), p. 79.

[27] George Washington to Robert Cary and Co., Sept. 28, 1760, John C. Fitzpatrick, ed., *The Writings of George Washington from the Original Manuscript Sources, 1745–1799,* 39 vols. (Washington, D.C., 1931–44), 2:350.

[28] William Eddis, *Letters from America,* ed. Aubrey C. Land (Cambridge, Mass., 1969), pp. 57–58.

that was the case of the people whom William Smith observed in New York. "In the city of New-York," he wrote in 1762, "through the intercourse with the Europeans, we follow the London fashions." [29] Benjamin Franklin saw this development in a favorable light; at least he did so in 1751. "A vast Demand is growing for British Manufactures," he marveled, "a glorious market wholly in the Power of Britain." [30] The colonists belonged to an empire of goods. The rulers of the mother country could well afford to let the Americans drift politically for much of the eighteenth century, following a policy that has sometimes been labeled "salutary neglect." Like Franklin, the ablest British administrators must have sensed that the bonds of loyalty depended upon commerce, upon the free flow of goods, and not upon coercion. [31]

Let me summarize the argument to this point. Before the 1760s most Americans would not have been conscious of the profound impact of consumption upon their society. They were like foot soldiers who witness great battles only from a narrow, personal perspective and thus cannot appreciate the larger implications of thousands of separate engagements. Of course the colonists were aware of the proliferation of choice, but for most of them the acquisition of British imports was a private act, one primarily associated with one's own social status within a community or household. Manufactured goods shaped family routines; they influenced relationships within a particular neighborhood. In symbolic terms these articles possessed local meanings. Certainly before the Stamp Act crisis—a few extreme evangelicals like James Davenport to the contrary notwithstanding—the Americans developed no sustained public discourse about goods. [32]

[29] Smith, *History of New-York*, p. 277.

[30] "Observations concerning the Increase of Mankind" (1751), in Leonard W. Labaree et al., eds., *The Papers of Benjamin Franklin*, 28 vols. to date (New Haven, 1959–), 4:229.

[31] See Breen, "Empire of Goods"; T. H. Breen, " The Meaning of 'Likeness': American Portrait Painting in an Eighteenth-Century Consumer Society," *Word and Image* 6 (1990):325–50.

[32] David D. Hall, "Religion and Society: Problems and Reconsiderations," in Greene and Pole, eds., *Colonial British America*, pp. 337–38. The most

Nevertheless the totality of these private consumer experiences deeply affected the character of eighteenth-century provincial society, for in a relatively short period following 1740 this flood of British manufactures created an indispensable foundation for the later political mobilization of the American people. Though these highly Anglicized men and women were not fully aware of this shared experiential framework, it would soon provide them with a means to communicate across social and spatial boundaries. Only after political events beyond their control forced them to form larger human collectivities—as was the case after 1765—did they discover that a shared language of goods was already in place.

The importation of British goods on such a vast scale created social tensions that the colonists were slow to appreciate. The very act of purchasing these articles—making free choices from among competing possibilities—heightened the Americans' already well developed sense of their own personal independence. The acquisition of manufactures also liberated them from a drab, impoverished, even insanitary folk culture of an earlier period. But consumption inevitably involved dependency. The colonists came increasingly to rely upon British merchants not only for what they now perceived as the necessities of daily life but also for a continued supply of credit. So long as the Anglo-American economy remained relatively prosperous and stable, it was possible to maintain the fiction of personal independence in a market system that in fact spawned dependence. But those days were numbered. An increasingly volatile international economy coupled with

famous evangelical of the period, George Whitefield, embraced the latest merchandising techniques, literally selling the revival to the American people. The crowds flocked to hear Whitefield, while his critics grumbled about the commercialization of religion. One anonymous writer in Massachusetts noted that there is "a very wholesome law of the province to discourage Pedlars in Trade," and that it seemed high time "to enact something for the discouragement of Pedlars in Divinity also" (*Boston Weekly News-Letter*, Apr. 22, 1742). For connections between the consumer revolution and the Great Awakening, see Frank Lambert, "'Pedlar in Divinity': George Whitefield and the Great Awakening, 1737–1745," *Journal of American History* 77 (1990):812–37.

Parliament's apparent determination to tax the colonists sparked an unprecedented debate about the role of commerce within the empire. Comfortable relations and familiar meanings were no longer secure. That was the burden of John Dickinson's troubled remark in 1765, "Under all these restraints and some others that have been imposed on us, we have not *till lately* been unhappy. Our spirits were not depressed."[33]

As Dickinson's observation suggests, the colonists' experiences as consumers no longer yielded the satisfaction that they had at an earlier time. The rising level of personal debt made the Americans' growing dependence upon British merchants increasingly manifest, and in this context of growing consumer "disappointment" the meaning of imported goods began to shift.[34] A semiotic order was changing. Articles that had been bound up with local cultures, with individual decisions within households, were gradually thrust into public discourse, and during the constitutional crisis with Great Britain these "baubles" were gradually and powerfully incorporated into a general moral critique of colonial society that traced its origins in part to radical country pamphleteers such as John Trenchard and Thomas Gordon and in part to the evangelical preachers of the Great Awakening.[35] In other words, a constitutional crisis transformed private consumer acts into public political statements. Britain's rulers inadvertently activated a vast circuit of private experience and in the process created in the American colonies what they least desired, the first stirrings of national consciousness.

[33] "The Late Regulations Respecting the British Colonies" (1765), in Paul Leicester Ford, ed., *The Writings of John Dickinson*, 2 vols. (Philadelphia, 1895), 1:217 (my emphasis).

[34] The psychological implications of economic "disappointment" are imaginatively discussed in Albert O. Hirschman, *Shifting Involvements: Private Interest and Public Action* (Princeton, 1982). Also see Tibor Scitovsky, *The Joyless Economy: An Inquiry into Human Satisfaction and Consumer Dissatisfaction* (New York, 1976).

[35] Bernard Bailyn, *The Ideological Origins of the American Revolution* (Cambridge, Mass., 1967); Gordon S. Wood, *The Creation of the American Republic, 1776–1787* (Chapel Hill, N. C., 1969); Edmund S. Morgan, "The Puritan Ethic and the American Revolution," *William and Mary Quarterly*, 3d ser. 24 (1967):3–43; and T. H. Breen, "Narrative of Commercial Life."

To understand the process of symbolic redefinition one must remember that the merchants of the mother country bore as much responsibility as the members of Parliament for the growing unhappiness of the American consumers. To be sure, during the Stamp Act crisis British merchants petitioned the House of Commons in support of the colonists. But at the same time these businessmen pushed upon the American market more goods and credit than it could possibly absorb. Indeed, their aggressive, though short-sighted, drive to maximize returns not only substantially increased colonial indebtedness but also alienated American wholesalers who had traditionally served as middlemen between the large British houses and the American shopkeepers.[36] As Gov. Francis Bernard of Massachusetts explained to the earl of Shelburne in 1768: "For some years past the London merchants, for the sake of increasing their profits, have got into dealing immediately [directly] with the retailers. . . . Instead of dealing with respectable houses the London merchants are engaged in a great number of little shops, and for the sake of advantages derived from trading with people who cannot dispute the terms . . . they have extended their credit beyond all bounds of prudence, and have . . . glutted this country with goods."[37]

Parliament exacerbated these structural tensions within the American market. Though its efforts to raise new revenues after 1764 did not cripple the colonists' ability to purchase imported goods, Parliament did remind the Americans of their dependence. If the colonists continued to purchase items such as glass, paper, and paint from British merchants—which seemed quite likely since they could not produce these articles themselves—then the Americans would inevitably have to pay unconstitutional taxes. As Dickinson noted sarcastically in his influential *Letters from a Farmer in Pennsylvania,* "I think it evident, that we *must* use paper and

---

[36] William T. Baxter, *The House of Hancock: Business in Boston, 1724–1775* (Cambridge, Mass., 1945), pp. 239–42; Marc Egnal and Joseph A. Ernst, "An Economic Interpretation of the American Revolution," *William and Mary Quarterly,* 3d ser. 29 (1972): 3–32; Breen, *Tobacco Culture,* chaps. 3–5.

[37] Cited in William Pencak, *War, Politics, and Revolution in Provincial Massachusetts* (Boston, 1981), p. 164.

glass; that what we use *must* be *British*; and that we *must* pay the duties imposed, unless those who sell these articles are so generous as to make us presents of the duties they pay."[38]

Considering the growing ambivalence of the colonists toward consumer goods—these items were immensely desirable, but also raised unsettling questions about economic dependency—it is not surprising that the Stamp Act crisis sparked a boycott of British manufactures.[39] During the anxious months of 1764 and 1765 urban Americans endorsed nonimportation as the most likely means to bring about the Stamp Act's repeal and alleviate the burden of personal debt. As "Philo Publicus" explained to the readers of the *Boston Gazette*, "We have taken wide Steps to Ruin, and as we have grown more Luxurious every Year, so we run deeper and deeper in Debt to our Mother Country." After observing how extravagantly the people of Boston decorated their parlors, how they piled their sideboards high with silver plate and how they collected costly china, this writer concluded, "I wonder not that my Country is so poor, I wonder not when I hear of frequent Bankruptcies."[40]

The boycott seemed an almost reflexive reaction to constitutional crisis. Of course, in 1765 angry Americans had little other choice. After all, there was no colonial Bastille for them to storm; George III and his hated ministers lived in safety on the other side of the Atlantic. But however circumscribed the range of responses may have been, the boycott served the colonists well. Participation in these protests provided Americans with opportunities to vent outrage against the policies of a distant government—much as Americans and others who

[38]"Letters from a Farmer in Pennsylvania" (1768), in Ford, ed., *Writings of Dickinson*, 1:355. Also William Pitkin to Richard Jackson, Feb. 14, 1767, "The Pitkin Papers," Connecticut Historical Society *Collections* 19 (1921):74.

[39]See Edmund S. Morgan and Helen M. Morgan, *The Stamp Act Crisis: Prologue to Revolution* (Chapel Hill, N. C., 1953).

[40]*Boston Gazette*, Oct. 1, 1764. Also Arthur M. Schlesinger, Sr., *The Colonial Merchants and the American Revolution, 1763–1776* (New York, 1918), pp. 63–65; Charles M. Andrews, "Boston Merchants and the Non-Importation Movement," Colonial Society of Massachusetts *Transactions* 19 (1916–17):182–91. For a discussion of the cultural meaning of debt in this period, see Breen, *Tobacco Culture*.

boycott South African goods do today—and though it was not clear whether anyone in the mother country actually listened, the very act of publicly denying themselves these familiar imports began to mobilize colonists of different regions and backgrounds in common cause.

The success of this first boycott should not be exaggerated. Most activities were restricted to urban centers and though nonimportation momentarily upset the flow of Anglo-American trade, it did not bring the British economy to its knees. Nevertheless, however limited its economic impact may have been, this initial confrontation reveals a mental process at work that in time would acquire extraordinary significance. As early as 1765 many colonists had begun to realize that patterns of consumption provided them with an effective language of political protest. In that sense, Americans discovered political ideology through a discussion of the meaning of goods, through observances of nonconsumption that forced ordinary men and women to declare exactly where they stood on the great constitutional issues of the day. British manufactures thus took on a new symbolic function, and the boycott became a social metaphor of political resistance. If the mainland colonies had not already been transformed into a consumer society, the Stamp Act protesters would have found it extremely difficult to communicate effectively with each other at this moment of political crisis. The purchase of British manufactures was the one experience that most of them shared, and by raising the possibility that they could do without these goods, patriotic Americans strained the bonds of Anglicization.

Revolution did not occur in 1765. The bonds of empire withstood the challenge, and as soon as Parliament repealed the Stamp Act the Americans returned to the import shops. The confrontation with the mother country had eroded but not destroyed the traditional meaning of consumer goods. Newspaper advertisements carried the familiar words "just imported from England," a clear indication that many colonists still took their cultural cues from Great Britain. Until that connection could be severed, independence was out of the question. This does not mean that Americans deserted the political principles that they had mouthed during the Stamp

Act protest; most certainly they were not hypocrites. The boycott had provided colonists with a behavioral link between a
political ideology and local experience, and when it was abandoned, ideas about liberty and representation, slavery and
virtue were temporarily dissociated from the affairs of daily
life.

The Townshend Acts of 1767 returned consumer goods to
the center of American political discourse. These ill-conceived
statutes levied a duty upon imported glass, paper, tea, lead,
and paint.[41] Patriotic leaders throughout the colonies advo-
cated a campaign of nonconsumption, and though this boycott would ultimately disappoint some of its more fervent
organizers, it revealed the powerful capacity of goods in this
society not only to recruit people into a political movement
but also to push them—often when they were unaware of
what was happening—to take ever more radical positions. As
in the Stamp Act crisis, imported British manufactures provided a framework in which many colonists learned about
rights and liberties.

During the period of protest against the Townshend Acts,
roughly between 1767 and 1770, colonists began to speak of
consumer goods in a highly charged moral language. Of
course, these Americans were not the first people to condemn
the pernicious effects of luxury and self-indulgence. That
concern had vexed moralists for centuries. Nevertheless, during the Stamp Act crisis a dominant theme of the political discourse had been debt. The purchase of British manufactures
undermined the personal independence of the American
consumers and thus made them fit targets for tyrannical con-
spirators. But after 1767 the thrust of patriotic rhetoric
shifted from *private* debt to *public* virtue. By acquiring needless British imports the colonial consumer threatened the liberties of other men and women. "Every Man who will take
Pains to cultivate the Cost of Homespun," advised a writer in
the *Boston Gazette,* "may easily convince himself that his private

[41]Merrill Jensen, *The Founding of a Nation: A History of the American Revolution, 1763–1776* (New York, 1968), pp. 237–344; Andrews, "Boston Merchants," pp. 191–252.

466

Interest, as well as [that of] the Publick, will be promoted by it."[42] In other words, how one spent one's own money became a matter deserving public scrutiny.

Consumer artifacts took on new symbolic meaning within a fluid political discourse, and before long it was nearly impossible for Americans to speak of imported goods without making reference to constitutional rights. The politicization of consumption was clearly evident in the December 22, 1767, instructions of the Boston town meeting to its representatives in the general assembly. We, your constituents, they announced, are worried about "the distressed Circumstances of this Town, by means of the amazing growth of Luxury, and the Embarrassments of our Trade; & having also the strongest apprehensions that our invaluable Rights & Liberties as Men and British Subjects, are greatly affected by a late Act of the British Parliament," they urged their representatives "to encourage a spirit of Industry and Frugality among the People."[43] Colonists living in different parts of America called for a boycott not just of those few imports specifically taxed by the Townshend Acts, but, rather, a long list of British manufactures, everything from clocks to carriages, hats to house furniture, even mustard.[44] The lists contained scores of items, a virtual inventory of the major articles of the midcentury consumer culture. The colonists seemed determined to undo patterns of consumption that had taken root in the 1740s, to return perhaps to a simpler period of self-sufficiency, which in fact had never existed but which in this political crisis seemed the best strategy for preserving liberty. In this social context it made sense for colonial writers to declare: "Save your money and you can save your country."[45]

The Townshend boycotts—ineffective though they may

[42]*Boston Gazette,* Jan. 11, 1768.

[43]*A Report of the Record Commissioners of the City of Boston Containing the Boston Town Records, 1758 to 1769* (Boston, 1886), pp. 227–28.

[44]Ibid., p. 221. Also "Virginia Nonimportation Resolutions, 1769," in Julian P. Boyd et al., eds., *The Papers of Thomas Jefferson,* 24 vols. to date (Princeton, 1950–), 1:28–29.

[45]Cited in Andrews, "Boston Merchants," p. 92.

have been in forcing Parliament to back down—helped radical colonists to distinguish friends from enemies. Strangers
communicated ideology through the denial of consumer
goods. Rhetoric was not enough. One had to reveal where
one stood. The nonconsumption movement forced individuals to alter the character of their daily lives, and as they did
so, they formed collectives of like-minded colonists, acts that
inevitably reinforced their own commitment to radical politics. The leaders of Windham, a small village in southeastern
Connecticut, scheduled a town meeting in response to correspondence they had received from Boston. This letter from
the outside urged the people of Windham to join in a boycott;
in other words, to think of politics in terms that extended far
beyond the boundaries of the community. This invitation
caused the villagers to take note of their "surprising fondness
. . . for the use and consumption of foreign and British manufactures." After a full discussion of the issues, they publicly
pledged "to each other that we will discourage and discounte-
nance to the utmost of our power the excessive use of all foreign teas, china ware, spices and black pepper, all British and
foreign superfluities and manufactures." This covenant
helped the townspeople to sort themselves out. One group of
Windham inhabitants was now prepared to expose another
group as "Enemies to their Country," and once this decision
had been taken, both sides probably thought more deeply
about political loyalties than they had ever done before. And
the villagers spread word of their resolution, appointing a
committee "to correspond with committees from the several
towns in the County in order to render the fore-going proposals as extensive and effectual as may be." The confrontation with British imports was extending the political horizons
of ordinary people in this small Connecticut village. Though
they could not possibly correspond directly with distant
Americans, they expressed their "earnest desire that every
town in this Colony and in every Colony in America would
explicitly and publicly disclose their sentiments relating to the
Non-importation Agreement and the violations thereof."[46]

[46]Cited in Ellen D. Larned, *History of Windham County, Connecticut,* 2 vols.
(Worcester, Mass., 1880), 2:116–19.

Without question, one encounters in Windham the makings of an "imagined community," the seeds of national consciousness.

By mobilizing people ordinarily excluded from colonial politics, the nonconsumption movement of this period greatly expanded the base of revolutionary activities. The Townshend boycott politicized even the most mundane items of the household economy and thereby politicized American women. Decisions about consumption could not be separated from decisions about politics. Within this electric atmosphere mothers and wives and daughters monitored the ideological commitment of the family. Throughout the colonies women altered styles of dress, wove homespun cloth, and stopped drinking tea. At one wedding in Connecticut, countrywomen appeared in garments of their own making and insisted upon having "Labrador tea," a concoction brewed from indigenous herbs. Other women in New England participated in spinning and weaving competitions, community rituals of great symbolic complexity. The actual homespun was invested with political significance. But so, too, were the women themselves. Their efforts at the wheel, like those of Mahatma Ghandi in another era, became local representations of a general ideology that connected the people of these communities—at least in their political imaginations—to unseen men and women in other American communities.[47]

The boycott of consumer goods also drew young people into the political debate. The students of Harvard, Yale, and the College of Rhode Island, for example, appeared at commencement during the late 1760s wearing homespun suits.[48] Though such displays irritated royal officials—that was the fun of it—they also transmitted political meanings through nonconsumption to other young people. This was an important element in the process of developing a national consciousness. In a society in which the average age was about sixteen, the young could not be taken for granted. A large

---

[47]Andrews, "Boston Merchants," pp. 193–94. Also Linda K. Kerber, *Women of the Republic: Intellect and Ideology in Revolutionary America* (Chapel Hill, N. C., 1980), pp. 38–41.

[48]Andrews, "Boston Merchants," pp. 195–97.

percentage of the American population in 1776 had not even been born at the time of the Stamp Act crisis, and if college students had not been recruited into the boycott movement, they might not later as adults have appeared at Bunker Hill.

The circle of participation widened to include even the poorer members of colonial society, the kinds of people who were as dependent upon the consumer society as were their gentry neighbors. They collected rags required for the manufacture of "patriotic" paper. Goods—or in this case the denial of goods—were mobilizing an entire populace. Peter Oliver, the Boston loyalist who later wrote an acerbic history of the Revolution, noted that during the protest against the Townshend duties, the city's radicals circulated "a Subscription Paper ... Enumerating a great Variety of Articles not to be imported from *England,* which they supposed would muster the Manufacturers in *England* into a national Mob to support their Interests. Among the various prohibited Articles, were *Silks, Velvets, Clocks, Watches, Coaches & Chariots;* & it was highly diverting, to see the names & marks, to the Subscription, of Porters & Washing Women."[49] Oliver found the incident amusing, an example of how a few troublemakers had duped the poorer sorts. But the porters and washerwomen of Boston knew what they were doing.[50] Affixing one's signature or mark to a document of this sort was a personal risk that they were willing to accept. Like the village women and the graduating students, these people had been mobilized through goods; it is difficult to see how independence could have been achieved without them.

The protest against the Townshend duties generated group activities that might best be called "rituals of nonconsumption." These were focused moments in the life of a community during which continuing social relations were often, quite suddenly, politicized. The spark for these events was usually

[49]Ibid., p. 197; Douglass Adair and John A. Schutz, eds., *Peter Oliver's Origin & Progress of the American Rebellion: A Tory View* (Stanford, 1961), p. 61.

[50]See Alfred F. Young, "George Robert Twelves Hewes (1742–1840): A Boston Shoemaker and the Memory of the American Revolution," *William and Mary Quarterly,* 3d ser. 38 (1981):561–623.

a letter sent by some external body urging the villagers to support the boycott. In some towns large numbers of men and women took oaths before their neighbors swearing not to purchase certain items until Parliament repealed the obnoxious taxes. These ceremonies possessed a curious religious character, much like the covenant renewals in the early Congregational churches of New England. In other communities specially selected committeemen carried subscription papers from house to house.[51] In Boston the "Subscription Rolls, for encouraging Oeconomy, Industry, our own Manufactures, and the disuse of foreign Superfluities" were kept in the office of the town clerk. According to a notice in the *Boston Gazette,* "The Selectmen strongly recommend this Measure to Persons of *all ranks,* as the most honorable and effectual way of giving *public* Testimony of their Love to their Country, and of endeavoring to save it from ruin."[52] Whether they lived in Boston or an inland village, ordinary colonists were obviously under considerable pressure to sign. But the decision was theirs to make. By pledging to support nonconsumption they reaffirmed their moral standing in the community. They demonstrated that they were not "enemies to their country"—a country that in fact they were only just beginning to define.

Perhaps the most effective political ritual associated with nonconsumption, at least in New England, was the funeral. More than any other event connected with the life cycle, the funeral in eighteenth-century America had become an occasion of conspicuous consumption. Wealthy families distributed commemorative rings. Gloves were given out, and custom mandated that all attendants wear mourning dress made of the best imported cloth they could afford. Indeed, opulent funerals were in themselves an indication of the spread of the consumer society. "Such was the fashion," one colonist explained, that bereaved families imagined that if they disappointed their friends and neighbors, "they should

[51]Andrews, "Boston Merchants," pp. 209–14; Schlesinger, *Colonial Merchants,* chap. 3.

[52]*Boston Gazette,* Nov. 30, 1767 (my emphasis).

have made themselves obnoxious to the censures of an ill-natured and malicious world, who would have construed their frugality into niggardliness."[53]

During the protest against the Townshend duties, such extravagant displays suddenly seemed inappropriate. A shift in the symbolic meaning of British imports called forth a change in funeral etiquette. And since these were highly visible events, they inevitably confronted those persons who had not thought deeply about imperial politics with an ideological message. The freeholders and inhabitants of Boston agreed "not to use any Gloves but what are manufactured here, nor any new Garments upon which Occasion but what shall be absolutely necessary."[54] Everywhere one saw signs of retrenchment at funerals, a trend that one anonymous writer declared "affected every true patriot with particular satisfaction."[55] As might be expected, the loyalist historian Peter Oliver denounced the politicization of funerals. He saw the hand of the radicals behind these restrictions. "Under Pretence of Oeconomy," he announced, "the Faction undertook to regulate Funerals, that there might be less Demand for English Manufactures." Oliver recognized that expensive funerals had at an earlier time "ruined some Families of moderate Fortune," but from his perspective the patriot funeral raised even greater problems. "One Extreme was exchanged for another. A Funeral now seemed more like a Procession to a *May Fair;* and Processions were lengthened, especially by the Ladies, who figured a way . . . to exhibit their Share of Spite, & their Silk Gowns."[56] Funerals had moved from the private to the public realm, and as was recently the case in the black townships of South Africa, they became powerful political statements. It is perhaps not surprising, therefore, that the members of the Continental Congress enthusiastically endorsed this particular means of mobilizing mass support,

[53] *Massachusetts Spy,* Jan. 6, 1774. Also Robert A. Gross, *The Minutemen and Their World* (New York, 1976), p. 33.

[54] *Report of the Record Commissioners,* p. 224. Also Andrews, "Boston Merchants," p. 196; Morgan and Morgan, *Stamp Act Crisis,* pp. 247–48.

[55] *Massachusetts Spy,* Jan. 6, 1774.

[56] Adair and Schutz, eds., *Origin & Progress,* p. 62.

pledging in September 1774 that "on the death of any relation or friend, none of us, or any of our families will go into any further mourning-dress, than a black crape or ribbon on the arm or hat, for gentlemen, and a black ribbon and necklace for ladies, and we will discontinue the giving of gloves and scarves at funerals."[57]

The repeal of the Townshend Acts in 1770 retarded the growth of national consciousness in the American colonies. Parliament's apparent retreat on the issue of taxation revealed the symbolic function that consumer goods had played in the constitutional discourse. As political tensions within the empire eased, these articles no longer carried such clear ideological meanings. Repeal, in fact, unloosed a frenzy of consumption. Though the tax on tea remained, the colonists could not be deterred from buying British manufactures. Between 1770 and 1772 they set records for the importation of foreign goods. Radical leaders such as Samuel Adams warned the Americans that the threat to their political liberties had not been removed. He begged them to continue their resistance, to maintain the boycott. But few listened. Commerce returned to the old channels, and as it did so, goods again became associated with the Anglicization of American society. It is no wonder that Adams grumbled in a letter to his friend Arthur Lee that the colonial newspapers were once again filled with advertisements for "the Baubles of Britain."[58]

The nonimportation movement of the late 1760s had in fact been only a partial success. The merchants of Philadelphia accused the merchants of Boston of cheating. People everywhere found it more difficult than they had anticipated to do without the thousands of items imported from the mother country. The most notable successes of the period had been local, something that had occurred within regionally clustered communities. For all the rhetoric, it had proved hard to communicate to very distant strangers.[59] George Mason un-

[57] "The Association," Oct. 20, 1774, in Henry Steele Commager, ed., *Documents of American History* (New York, 1949), p. 86.

[58] Samuel Adams to Arthur Lee, Oct. 31, 1771, Harry Alonzo Cushing, ed., *The Writings of Samuel Adams*, 4 vols. (New York, 1904–8), 2:267.

[59] Jensen, *Founding of a Nation*, chaps. 10–12.

derstood the problem. "The [nonimportation] associations," he explained, "almost from one end of this continent to the other, were drawn up in a hurry and formed upon erroneous principles." The organizers of these boycotts had expected Parliament to back down quickly, certainly within a year or two, but that had not happened. The results did not discourage Mason, however, for as he explained in December 1770, "had one general plan been formed exactly the same for all colonies (so as to have removed all cause of jealousy or danger of interfering with each other) in the nature of a sumptuary law, restraining only articles of luxury and ostentation together with the goods at any time taxed," the results might have been different.[60] Americans had not yet discovered how to communicate continentally.

In 1773 Parliament stumbled upon an element of mass political mobilization that had been missing during the Townshend protest. By passing the Tea Act, it united the colonists as they had never been before. The reason for this new solidarity was not so much that the Americans shared a common political ideology, but rather that the statute affected an item of popular consumption found in virtually every colonial household. It was perhaps *the* major article in the development of an eighteenth-century consumer society, a beverage which, as we have seen, appeared on the tables of the wealthiest merchants and the poorest laborers. For Americans, therefore, it was not difficult to transmit perceptions of liberty and rights through a discourse on tea. By transforming this ubiquitous element of daily life into a symbol of political oppression, Parliament inadvertently boosted the growth of national consciousness. "Considering the article of tea as the detestable instrument which laid the foundation of the present sufferings of our distressed friends in the town of Boston," the members of the Virginia House of Burgesses declared in August 1774, "we view it with horror, and therefore resolve that we will not, from this day, either import tea of any kind whatever, nor will we use or suffer, even such of it as is now at

[60]George Mason to [George Brent?], Dec. 6, 1770, Kate Mason Rowland, *The Life of George Mason, 1725–1792,* 2 vols. (New York, 1892), 1:148–49.

hand, to be used in any of our families."[61] And in the northern colonies, people now spoke of tea drinkers not simply as enemies of our country—a term that in the 1760s had referred to one's colony or region—but as enemies "to the liberties of America."[62]

The public discourse over tea raised issues about the political effects of consumption that had been absent or muted during the previous decade. The language of goods became more shrill and hyperbolic. During the Stamp Act crisis, colonists associated consumption chiefly with personal debt. After Parliament passed the Townshend duties, they talked more frequently in a moral vocabulary. By denying themselves the "Baubles" of the mother country, they might thereby preserve their virtue. But in 1774 they spoke of tea as a badge of slavery, as a political instrument designed by distant tyrants to seize their property. "A WOMAN" argued in the *Massachusetts Spy* that "in the present case the use of tea is considered not as a *private* but as a *public* evil . . . we are not to consider it merely as the herb tea, or what has an ill-tendency as to health, but as it is made a handle to introduce a variety of public grievances and oppressions amongst us." Tea, the writer concluded, is a sign of "enslaving our country."[63] In an impassioned appeal to the citizens of Charleston, South Carolina, one speaker—probably Christopher Gadsden—insisted that a nonimportation agreement would "prove a means of restoring our liberty." "Who that has the spirit of a man," he asked, "but would rather forego the elegancies and luxuries of life, then entail slavery on his unborn posterity to the end of time? . . . Nothing but custom makes the curl-pated beau a more agreeable sight with his powder and pomatum, than the tawney savage with his paint and bear's grease. Too long has luxury reigned amongst us, enervating our constitu-

[61]"Virginia Non-Importation Agreement," Aug. 1, 1774, in Commager, ed., *Documents*, p. 80.

[62]"New York Sons of Liberty Resolutions on Tea," Nov. 29, 1773, ibid., p. 70.

[63]*Massachusetts Spy*, Jan. 6, 13, 20, and Aug. 25, 1774.

tions and shrinking the human race into pigmies."[64] And, finally, another writer in this period bluntly reminded newspaper readers in New England that "the use of Tea is a political evil in this country."[65]

Throughout America the ceremonial destruction of tea strengthened the bonds of political solidarity. Once again, we must look to local communities for the embryonic stirrings of national consciousness. It was in these settings that a common commodity was transformed into the overarching symbol of political corruption. By purging the community of tea leaves—an import that could be found in almost every American home—the colonists reinforced their own commitment to certain political principles. But they did more. The destruction of the tea transmitted an unmistakable ideological message to distant communities: we stand together. The Boston Tea Party is an event familiar to anyone who has heard of the Revolution.[66] In many villages, however, the inhabitants publicly burned their tea. Everyone was expected to contribute some leaves—perhaps a canister of tea hidden away in a pantry, a few ounces, tea purchased long before Parliament passed the hated legislation—all of it to be destroyed in flames that purged the town of ideological sin. "We hear from [the town of] Montague," reported the *Massachusetts Spy,* "that one of the inhabitants having inadvertently purchased a small quantity of tea of a pedlar, several of the neighbours being made acquainted therewith, went to his house and endeavoured to convince him of the impropriety of making any use of that article for the present, while it continues to be a badge of slavery." The visiting committee easily persuaded the man "to commit it to the flames." The group then ferreted the peddler out of the local tavern, seized his entire stock of tea and "carried [it] into the road, where it was burnt to ashes."[67] In Charlestown, Massachusetts, the town clerk announced

[64]"To the Inhabitants of the Province of South Carolina, About to Assemble on the 6th of July," July 4, 1774, Peter Force, comp., *American Archives,* 4th ser., 6 vols. (Washington, D.C., 1837–53), 1:511.

[65]*Massachusetts Spy,* Dec. 23, 1773.

[66]See Benjamin Woods Labaree, *The Boston Tea Party* (New York, 1964).

[67]*Massachusetts Spy,* Feb. 17, 1774.

that he would oversee the collection of all tea in the community "and that the tea so collected, be destroyed by fire, on Friday next at noon day, in the market place." He declared that any persons who failed to participate in this activity "are not only inimicable to the liberty of America in general, but also show a daring disrespect to this town in particular."[68] From Northampton County on Virginia's Eastern Shore came news that a committee had collected 416 pounds of tea. Moreover, "some gentlemen also brought their Tea to the Court House, and desired it might be publickly burnt, in which reasonable request they were instantly gratified."[69] And from Wilmington, North Carolina, a traveler reported, "the Ladies have burnt their tea in a solemn procession."[70]

The seizure and destruction of tea became an effective instrument of political indoctrination, forcing the ignorant or indifferent people of these communities publicly to commit themselves to the cause of liberty while at the same time reinforcing the patriots' commitment to a radical ideology. The individuals involved were often ordinary men and women. Had they not become associated with tea, they might have remained anonymous colonists, going about their business and keeping their political opinions to themselves. But they were not so lucky. Early in 1774 Ebenezer Withington, a "labourer" living in Dorchester, allegedly found some tea on a road that ran along the ocean. Soon thereafter he was called before a meeting of "Freeholders and other Inhabitants" where Withington confessed in writing before his neighbors that "I found said Tea on Saturday, on going round the Marshes; brought off the same thinking no Harm; returning I met some Gentlemen belonging to the Castle [the British fort in Boston harbor], who asked me if I had been picking up the Ruins? I asked them if there was any Harm; they said no except from my Neighbours. Accordingly, I brought Home the same, part of which I Disposed of, and the Remainder took from me since." The townspeople decided that Withington had not realized the political significance of his act.

[68] Ibid., Jan. 6, 1774.

[69] Force, comp., *American Archives*, 4th ser., 1:1045–46.

[70] [Schaw], *Journal of a Lady*, p. 155.

The people who had purchased tea from him were warned to bring it to the village authorities immediately for destruction or risk having their names published as enemies of the country.[71] The Dorchester committee—and committees in other towns as well—performed the same political function that local militia units would serve during the Revolution. They provided ideological instruction, and by so doing made it difficult even for the poorest persons either to remain neutral or retain old loyalties.[72]

Sometimes tea sparked an incident that mobilized an entire village. By their own admission, the inhabitants of Truro, an isolated village on Cape Cod, had not kept informed about the gathering political storm in Boston. Then, one day, some tea apparently washed ashore near Provincetown, and the men who discovered it sold small quantities to a few Truro farmers. That purchase precipitated a crisis. A town committee questioned these persons and concluded "that their buying this noxious Tea was through ignorance and inadvertence, and they were induced thereto by the base and villainous example and artful persuasions of some noted pretended friends to government from the neighbouring towns; and therefore this meeting thinks them excusable with acknowledgement."

But individual confession was not sufficient to exonerate the community. The people of Truro had failed to educate themselves about the dangers to their constitutional liberties and, of course, had left themselves vulnerable to scheming persons who peddled tea, the symbol of oppression. The town meeting decided, therefore, to form a special committee that would draft a resolve "respecting the introduction of Tea from Great Britain subject to a duty, payable in America." After deliberating for half an hour, the members of this committee returned with a statement which was at once defensive and radical: "WE the inhabitants of the town of Truro, though by our remote situation from the centre of public news, we

[71] *Massachusetts Spy*, Jan. 13, 1774.

[72] On the responsibility of the colonial militias to indoctrinate citizens, see John W. Shy, *A People Numerous and Armed: Reflections on the Military Struggle for American Independence* (New York, 1976), pp. 193–224.

are deprived of opportunities of gaining so thorough a knowledge in the unhappy disputes that subsist between us and the parent state as we could wish; yet as our love of liberty and dread of slavery is not inferior (perhaps) to that of our brethren in any part of the province, we think it our indispensable duty to contribute our mite in the glorious cause of liberty and our country." People asked immediately what in fact they could do to demonstrate that their ideological hearts were in the right place. "We think," the committee responded, "that most likely method that we can take to aid in frustrating those inhuman designs of administration is a disuse of that baneful dutied article Tea."[73] The inhabitants of this village communicated their political beliefs not only to the radical leaders of Boston and to the members of the Massachusetts General Assembly but also to themselves through tea. By dropping this popular import they overcame the peculiarities of local experience and linked up with other Americans, distant strangers whose crucial common bond with the farmers of Truro at this moment was their participation in an eighteenth-century consumer society.

During the summer of 1774 patriot spokesmen throughout America called for some form of boycott. Boston's leaders, for example, urged the people of Massachusetts to sign a Solemn League and Covenant pledging to break off "all commercial connection with a country whose political Councils tend only to enslave them."[74] Loyalists castigated this "infernal Scheme." In this atmosphere almost any manufactured article could spark a dispute. The league in fact threatened to bring the political battles of the street into the home, "raising a most unnatural Enmity between Parents & Children & Husbands & Wives."[75] People living in other parts of America now looked to the Continental Congress for guidance. As George Mason had recognized in 1770, a successful boycott required the united and coordinated efforts of all the colo-

[73] *Massachusetts Spy*, Mar. 31, 1774.

[74] Force, comp., *American Archives*, 4th ser., 1:397–98; Jensen, *Founding of a Nation*, pp. 468–75; Schlesinger, *Colonial Merchants*, pp. 319–26; Gross, *Minutemen*, pp. 47, 50–51.

[75] Adair and Schutz, eds., *Origin & Progress*, p. 104.

nists. When the congressional delegates convened in September 1774, they almost immediately passed legislation creating the Association, a vast network of local committees charged with enforcing nonimportation. This was a truly radical act. In an attempt to halt further commerce with Great Britain, Congress authorized every county, city, and town in America to establish a revolutionary government.[76] As Henry Laurens explained in September 1774: "From the best intelligence that I have received, my conclusions are, that So. Carolina, No. Carolina, Virginia, Maryland, Pensylvania, New Jersey, New York, Connecticut, Rhode Island, Massachusets, New Hampshire, one Chain of Colonies extending upwards of 1,200 Miles & containing about three Millions of White Inhabitants of whom upwards of 500,000 [are] Men capable of bearing Arms, will unite in an agreement to Import no goods from Great Britain, the West India Islands, or Africa until those Acts of Parliament which Strike at our Liberties are Repealed."[77]

The colonists responded enthusiastically to the call. The committees monitored consumption, identifying local patriots by the garments they wore and by the beverages they drank, and demanding public confessions from those who erred. In Virginia counties everyone was expected to sign the Association, a promise before one's neighbors—almost a statement of one's new birth as a consumer—not to purchase the despised manufactures of the mother country. According to James Madison, these signings were "the method used among us to distinguish friends from foes and to oblige the Common people to a more strict observance of it [the Association]."[78] As in earlier boycotts, people sorted themselves out politically through goods. A committee in Prince George's County announced "that to be clothed in manufactures fabricated in the

[76] Jensen, *Founding of a Nation,* pp. 506–7.

[77] Henry Laurens to Peter Petrie, Sept. 7, 1774, Philip M. Hamer et al., eds., *The Papers of Henry Laurens,* 12 vols. to date (Columbia, S. C., 1968–), 9:552.

[78] James Madison to William Bradford, Jan. 20, 1775, William T. Hutchinson et al., eds., *The Papers of James Madison,* 16 vols. to date (Chicago and Charlottesville, Va., 1962–), 1:135.

Colonies ought to be considered as a badge and distinction of respect and true patriotism."[79] The local associations also educated ordinary men and women about the relation between consumer goods and constitutional rights, in other words, about the relation between experience and ideology. A committee in Anne Arundel County, Maryland, helped Thomas Charles Williams understand that by importing tea he had "endangered the rights and liberties of America." Proceedings against Williams were dropped after he proclaimed that he was "sincerely sorry for his offense."[80] Silas Newcomb of Cumberland, New Jersey, was more stubborn. The members of the local Association failed to convince the man of his error in drinking "East-India Tea in his family," and they were finally compelled "to break off all dealings with him, and in this manner publish the truth of the case, that he may be distinguished from the friends of American liberty."[81]

The colonists who responded to Boston's call in 1774 were consciously repudiating the empire of goods. Within barely a generation the meaning of the items of everyday consumption had changed substantially. At midcentury imported articles—the cloth, the ceramics, the buttons—had served as vehicles of Anglicization, and as they flooded into the homes of yeomen and gentry alike they linked ordinary men and women with the distant, exciting culture of the metropolis. By participating in the marketplace, by making choices among competing manufactures, the colonists became in some important sense English people who happened to live in the provinces. By taxing these goods, however, Parliament set in motion a process of symbolic redefinition, slow and painful at first, punctuated by lulls that encouraged the false hope that the empire of goods could survive, but ultimately straining Anglicization to the breaking point. Americans who had never dealt with one another, who lived thousands of miles apart, found that they could communicate their political grievances through goods or, more precisely, through the denial of goods

[79] Force, comp., *American Archives*, 4th ser., 1:494.

[80] Ibid., p. 1061.

[81] Ibid., 2:34.

that had held the empire together. Private consumer experiences were transformed into public rituals. Indeed, many colonists learned about rights and liberties through these common consumer items, articles that in themselves were politically neutral but that in the explosive atmosphere of the 1760s and 1770s became the medium through which ideological abstractions acquired concrete meaning.

When the colonists finally and reluctantly decided that they could do without the "Baubles of Britain," they destroyed a vital cultural bond with the mother country. "The country," explained James Lovell to his friend Joseph Trumbull in December 1774, "seems determined to let England know that in the present struggle, commerce has lost all the temptations of a bait to catch the American farmer."[82] Lovell may have exaggerated, but he helps us to understand why in 1774 the countryside supported the cities. Consumer goods had made it possible for the colonists to imagine a nation; the Association made it easier for Americans to imagine independence.

[82]Cited in Jensen, *Founding of a Nation,* p. 561.

CARY CARSON

The Consumer Revolution in Colonial British America: Why Demand?

HEAR TELL THE familiar story of the Industrial Revolution in England and America. Textbook after textbook intones the standard recitation. Once upon a time in the reign of George III a "string of important inventions in a few industries began a profound alteration of the British economy."[1] Steam en-

The author is grateful to many friends and colleagues for donated information and free advice. Those whose suggestions have helped shape the argument presented in the essay include Robert Birney, Marley R. Brown III, Lois Green Carr, Edward A. Chappell, Patricia A. Gibbs, William Graham, Ronald Hoffman, Ivor Noël Hume, Robert Hunter, Rhys Isaac, Carl R. Lounsbury, Ann Smart Martin, George L. Miller, Fraser D. Neiman, Charles Saumarez Smith, Lorena S. Walsh, Mark R. Wenger, and Barbara G. Carson most of all.

[1] R. K. Webb, *Modern England: From the Eighteenth Century to the Present* (New York, 1968), p. 102, is typical of many other surveys that could be cited. Textbook writers in the last twenty years have frequently acknowledged that historians have greatly extended the period of the Industrial Revolution backwards and forwards from 1760, but few have called into question the basic sequence of events in which major technological and organizational innovations vastly increased the productive capacity of industry, thus flooding a mass market with popular goods and services in every price range. Harold J. Perkin, *Origins of Modern English Society* (London, 1969), was about the first survey text to argue strongly that "the most important economic factor in the genesis of industrialism [was] consumer demand" (p. 91). Textbooks in the 1970s began to pick up the theme, often

gines, flying shuttles, water frames, and power looms, operated by men, women, and children summoned to work by a
factory bell, produced prodigious quantities of inexpensive
personal and household goods. Machine-made textiles, pottery, ironmongery, and a multitude of other "necessities," "decencies," and affordable "luxuries" were transported over
improved roads and along newly built canals to markets in
every corner of the realm. There, they were snapped up by a
rapidly growing population of eager consumers, who waxed
healthier, wealthier, and happier than ever before on rising
wages, falling death rates, and a diet of roast beef and white
bread supplied by model farmers and progressive stockbreeders. Echoing the modern corporate slogan Better Things for
Better Living, the orthodox histories endorse a supply-side
explanation for the events that led to industrial and commercial expansion. Consumer demand is presented as a universal
given, as immutable as mankind's quest for a dry cave and a
square meal. Mechanization, the factory system, faster,
cheaper transportation, and new banking and credit facilities
were simply those English-made miracles that finally in the
eighteenth century drove down the cost and increased the
supply of goods and services that everyone had always wanted
and that ordinary people could now afford.

Industrial progress, the schoolbooks imply, thrived on freedom and waited on genius. Histories of the United States provide the classic example. Because Old World mercantilists had
frowned on colonial manufacturers, Americans first had to
win independence, then steal British industrial secrets, to
bring the factory system to these shores. Soon thereafter the
wheels began to turn and the spindles spin, and the rest was
textbook history: "A great change in American ways of making
things soon reshaped American ways of living." The colonists
"had made the things they needed in their own homes and

---

tentatively, as in J. H. Plumb, Frederic A. Youngs, Jr., et al., *The English
Heritage* (St. Louis, 1978), p. 247, where a single sentence—"strong domestic demand, fueled by wealth derived from trade and agriculture, stimulated new methods for increased production of goods"—introduces a
discussion of industrialization along traditional lines. See also Clayton Roberts and David Roberts, *A History of England, 1688 to the Present* (Englewood
Cliffs, N. J., 1980), pp. 464–65.

for their own use. Now goods were produced in factories and by machines for sale to anybody willing to pay for them." "Eventually this would create an American Standard of Living."[2] This version is even more supply driven than the one in which the Industrial Revolution gratifies a universal natural appetite for consumer goods. Mass production in the United States not only met existing demand, aggressive merchandisers deliberately created a market of "new customers needed to buy the masses of goods now produced in the factories."[3]

Either way, the main lines of the cause-and-effect, supply-and-demand argument stand largely uncontested. Moreover, they seem confirmed by the observations of numerous eyewitnesses from the eighteenth century. Listen, for example, to only one of many contemporary voices, this one Henry Fielding's, heard not in his fiction, but in the pages of a pamphlet on public policy.[4] "Nothing," he observed, "hath wrought such an Alteration in this Order of People, as the Introduction of Trade." He explained: "This hath indeed given a new Face to the whole Nation, hath in a great measure subverted the former State of Affairs, and hath almost totally changed the Manners, Customs, and Habits of the People, more especially of the lower Sort. The Narrowness of their Fortune is changed into Wealth; the Simplicity of their Manners into Craft; their Frugality into Luxury; their Humility into Pride, and their Subjugation into Equality." Prosperity, equality, luxury, and pride—the virtues and vices of modern life, the blessings and blights of mass production and mass marketing. Two hundred years have done little to alter history's verdict. The Industrial Revolution awakened an enormous unquenchable appetite for material goods. It sired the race of getters and spenders that we all have become, we Americans nonpariel. The essential truth of supply-side economics stands unchallenged as the incontrovertible central

[2] Daniel J. Boorstin and Brooks Mather Kelley, *A History of the United States* (Lexington, Mass., 1971), pp. 214–15.

[3] Ibid., p. 215.

[4] Henry Fielding, *An Enquiry into the Causes of the Late Increase in Robbers* (London, 1751), p. xi.

thesis that explains the genesis of our consumer societies in the industrialized nations of the West.

Incontrovertible except for one little problem, one awkward fact: *demand came first.*

Henry Fielding was writing in 1750. Already what he called "the former state of affairs" was a memory. Already the manners, customs, habits, and possessions of the most ordinary people had "almost totally changed." Nor was his polemic the earliest one of its kind. The downward and outward spread of luxury had been a favorite target of preachers and pamphleteers for going on fifty years. Before Arkwright, before Watt, before Hargreaves, Wedgwood, Boulton, and Kay, almost before even Abraham Darby, people up and down the social order had discovered and were indulging the most extraordinary passion for consumer goods in quantities and varieties that were unknown, even unimaginable, to their fathers and grandfathers. It was indeed a revolution, but a *consumer* revolution in the beginning. The better known Industrial Revolution followed in response.[5]

The problem of chronology is not a significant issue in its own right. Chicken-or-egg propositions are seldom useful starting points for historical research, and certainly not for students of industrialization. Revisionists who set out along that path will stumble over ample evidence to support the conventional and entirely accurate view that eighteenth-century manufacturers and retailers deliberately created markets for products and services where none had existed before. I would have little success trying to deny that, *once people began thinking and behaving like consumers,* they became fair game to a

---

[5]The literature in which this thesis is advanced is cited in notes 8–17, below. Recently Carole Shammas, one of the earliest and most original writers on the subject, has had second thoughts, which she airs in "Explaining Past Changes in Consumption and Consumer Behavior," *Historical Methods* 22 (1989):61–67. Her argument against a transforming consumer revolution is hard to refute strictly by the numbers. But like other historians who make little distinction between very gradual improvements in living standards and the thoroughgoing changes in lifestyle that ensued when individuals learned to take their social identity from goods, she undervalues the importance of consumerism as a cultural revolution in the values, attitudes, and needs that governed consumption. This essay tries to make that case with some of the precision that economic historians bring to theirs.

swarm of entrepreneurs who quickly spotted markets to exploit and expand.

There is a more important purpose to be served by paying careful attention to the timing of these events and recognizing that a dramatic rise in consumer demand after 1690 or so was sustained for decades by workbench artisans using old-fashioned, seventeenth-century technologies improved in a few minor ways at best. Putting a demand-driven consumer revolution before power-driven industrialization forces historians to ask questions that they have seldom addressed until very recently. It shifts their perspective from the means of production to the consumption of the goods produced. It challenges them to reexamine the economists' premise that demand is a constant that has remained strangely impervious to the forces of historical change that alter other aspects of culture. Initially, it requires attention to answering certain basic questions: What goods did people really acquire? How did they use them? How have people's everyday lives been changed by their possession of newfangled artifacts and the things they can do with them? Who has shared in the wealth of material possessions? How evenly or unevenly have they been distributed, and how have those differences rearranged the social order? Descriptions of material life eventually send historians in search of explanations: What has caused ordinary people at certain times in the past to spend their sometimes small earnings on expendable goods and services in preference to longer lasting investments? Why is there demand for some things at one time and different things at others? Why did the pace of consumption quicken so dramatically in the eighteenth century?

Ultimately, historians who pursue this line of inquiry end up exploring a set of fundamental relationships in modern society. These are social relationships, to be sure, but with this difference: they require the intercession of inanimate agents, namely, the household goods and personal possessions whose ownership and use first became widespread among northern Europeans and North Americans in the eighteenth century. Artifacts and the activities to which they were instrumental defined group identities and mediated relations between individuals and the social worlds they inhabited. We ourselves take the facilitating role of material things for granted. Competence in understanding and using the "language" of artifacts is learned along with the ability to speak, read, and write, although actually it is a far more general form of literacy than the latter two. Ours has become a very complex material culture. Two hundred years ago it was simpler; three hundred years ago very much simpler almost everywhere the world around. Only small groups of affluent courtiers, prelates, merchant princes, and other elites had always led well-furnished lives of luxury. The *consumer revolution* changed all that. That is the term historians now give to that great transformation when whole nations learned to use a rich and complicated medium of communications to conduct social relations that were no longer adequately served by parochial repertories of words, gestures, and folk customs alone. Artifacts expanded the vocabulary of an international language that was learned and understood wherever fashion and gentility spread.

For a time the old handcraft industries supplied the needs of the first new consumers. But they could not keep pace, and, as venture capitalists came to see the tremendous potential for growth in home markets, the search began for new technologies to increase production and new sales strategies to enlarge those markets. Consumer revolution and Industrial Revolution were mutually necessary and complementary sides to events that our textbooks must put back together again—the right way round—before we can appreciate the full significance of one of the great divides in the chronicle of human experience. When one looks back on the whole history of material life, it exaggerates nothing to say that the mass of humanity were only rudimentary tool users before the eighteenth century. A bare hundred years later, by 1800, everyday life for many people in England, continental Europe, and North America was scarcely liveable without a cupboard or a chest of drawers full of things that they used in their dealings with virtually everyone they encountered everyday—family, friends, neighbors, fellow workers, business associates, and perfect strangers.

Why? Historians want reasons to explain why material things became so essential to the conduct of social relations starting only two or three centuries ago. They see it as a historical problem, of course, but the issue draws its intellectual vitality (as good scholarship in history should) from something that concerns a larger body of thoughtful citizens. Recent events in our national life have reopened a debate about the celebrated American standard of living and our persistent belief in a beneficent materialism. For some time now the poor in this country have been getting poorer, absolutely poorer in terms of real disposable per capita income.[6] There have been other periods when the value of wages declined, but this recent impoverishment coincides with an unparalled glut in new consumer goods and services available to those higher up the economic ladder whose buying power has remained constant. The growing disparity between rich and poor, or more accurately and significantly, between rich and middle, puts at risk a basic element in the American dream, the promise of almost universal access to a shared material culture, which for so long helped unite a nation of immigrants into a democracy of fellow consumers.[7] Compared to the rest of a world deeply divided between haves and have-nots,

[6] *Washington Post* editorial, "From Poor to Poorer," Feb. 1, 1986, reviewing two 1985 reports on income distribution issued by the Joint Economic Committee of Congress: Sheldon Danziger and Peter Gottschalk's "How Have Families with Children Been Faring?" and Frank Levy and Richard Michel's "Economic Future of the Baby Boom." Four years later Peter Passell took the nation's pulse again and found "Forces in Society, and Reaganism, Helped Dig Deeper Hole for Poor," *New York Times,* July 16, 1989.

[7] A central theme from George Santayana to Daniel J. Boorstin. Theirs is a view of American history that has been dismissed too easily by the current crop of social historians whose well-placed efforts to recapture the ethnic, regional, and social diversities of American life have at the same time neglected the fact that our history is also a true story of nation-making. Boorstin's permanent exhibit at the Smithsonian Institution, "A Nation of Nations" (National Museum of American History, 1976), and the third volume in *The Americans* trilogy, *The Democratic Experience* (New York, 1973), make an eloquent case in words and images for the unifying influence of a *nineteenth-century* consumer revolution. Boorstin, like other writers on the subject, deals more with consequences than causes, partly because he accepts the myth that "in the older world"—that is, America before 1800—"almost everything a man owned was one-of-a-kind" (p. 90) and partly

Americans are fortunate always to have been a nation of haves and not-yets. That could change. Therefore we need to second-guess what consequences might follow were the wages of hardworking men and women to deteriorate to such a low level that they and their children lost all hope of eventually participating in the consumer culture that has served as one of the great equalizing influences in American life.

Practical solutions are the province of policymakers. We look to historians for the hindsight that helps sort out the real issues from the specious ones and, in this case, to learn how it happened that Americans more than any people on earth have come to require such an orgy of goods and gadgets just to keep them steady on their daily course.

That history—the rise of a consumer society—has finally begun to be written.[8] Not surprisingly, given the newness of

---

because he chooses not to see that consumer goods have always been used to separate and exclude as well as to join and unify.

[8]Compared with supply-side studies of the Industrial Revolution, the literature on home demand and the consumer revolution is puny. The few canonical works start with Elizabeth Waterman Gilboy, "Demand as a Factor in the Industrial Revolution," in R. M. Hartwell, ed., *The Causes of the Industrial Revolution* (London, 1967), pp. 121–38; Joel Mokyr reformulates the "Gilboy thesis" in testable form in "Demand vs. Supply in the Industrial Revolution," *Journal of Economic History* 37 (1977):981–1008; Eric L. Jones, "The Fashion Manipulators: Consumer Tastes and British Industries, 1660–1800," in Louis P. Cain and Paul J. Uselding, eds., *Business Enterprise and Economic Change: Essays in Honor of Harold F. Williamson* (Kent, Ohio, 1973), pp. 198–226; Joan Thirsk, *Economic Policy and Projects: The Development of a Consumer Society in Early Modern England* (Oxford, 1978); and Joel Mokyr, "The Industrial Revolution and the New Economic History," in Mokyr, ed., *The Economics of the Industrial Revolution* (Totowa, N. J., 1985), pp. 1–51. Jan de Vries synthesized much of this discussion and advanced his own explanation for the role of consumption in the process of economic growth in "Between Purchasing Power and the World of Goods: Understanding the Household Economy in Early Modern Europe," which I was privileged to read in advance of its publication in John Brewer and Roy Porter, eds., *Consumption and the World of Goods* (London and New York, 1993), pp. 85–132. This major book of essays appeared too late to consider in my article. The broader cultural dimensions of the subject were treated first in Neil McKendrick, John Brewer, and J. H. Plumb, *The Birth of a Consumer Society: The Commercialization of Eighteenth-Century England* (Bloomington, Ind., 1982). Books and articles that factor consumer demand into the

the subject, the authors have set out from different academic disciplines and are only now arriving at their common destination after traveling along separate intellectual paths. There are, first of all, economic historians who study the wealth of nations and have discovered a notable increase in people's consumption of durable goods around 1700.[9] There are political economists who believe that that shift was reflected in the importance that economic theorists began giving to home markets from the 1690s onwards.[10] There are literary scholars

---

colonial economy include Carole Shammas, *The Pre-Industrial Consumer in England and America* (Oxford, 1990); idem, "Consumer Behavior in Colonial America," *Social Science History* 6 (1982):67–86; idem, "How Self-Sufficient Was Early America?" *Journal of Interdisciplinary History* 13 (1982):247–72; John J. McCusker and Russell R. Menard, *The Economy of British America, 1607–1789* (Chapel Hill, N. C., 1985), chap. 13. Richard L. Bushman, *The Refinement of America: Persons, Houses, Cities* (New York, 1992). Complementary studies of consumer behavior in northern Europe are cited in n. 30, below.

[9] The monographs that provide a database for the broader works cited above include, for England, D. E. C. Eversley, "The Home Market and Economic Growth in England, 1750–1780," in Eric L. Jones and G. E. Mingay, eds., *Land, Labour, and Population in the Industrial Revolution: Essays Presented to J. D. Chambers* (London, 1967), pp. 206–59; Neil McKendrick, "Home Demand and Economic Growth: A New View of the Role of Women and Children in the Industrial Revolution," in McKendrick, ed., *Historical Perspectives: Studies in English Thought and Society in Honour of J. H. Plumb* (London, 1974), pp. 152–210; Lorna Weatherill, *Consumer Behaviour and Material Culture in Britain, 1660–1760* (London, 1988); and, for England's American colonies, Alice Hanson Jones, *Wealth of a Nation to Be: The American Colonies on the Eve of the Revolution* (New York, 1980); Gloria L. Main, *Tobacco Colony: Life in Early Maryland, 1650–1720* (Princeton, 1982), pp. 140–236; Lois Green Carr and Lorena S. Walsh, "Inventories and the Analysis of Wealth and Consumption Patterns in St. Mary's County, Maryland, 1658–1777," *Historical Methods* 13 (1980):81–104; Gloria L. Main and Jackson T. Main, "Economic Growth and the Standard of Living in Southern New England, 1640–1774," *Journal of Economic History* 48 (1988):27–46; Lorena S. Walsh, Gloria L. Main, and Lois Green Carr, "Toward a History of the Standard of Living in British North America," *William and Mary Quarterly,* 3d ser. 45 (1988):116–66, which footnotes other recent useful studies. See also Lois Green Carr and Lorena S. Walsh, "Changing Lifestyles and Consumer Behavior in the Colonial Chesapeake," in this volume.

[10] Joyce Oldham Appleby, "Ideology and Theory: The Tension between Political and Economic Liberalism in Seventeenth-Century England," *Amer-*

and intellectual historians who note an extraordinary out-
pouring of eighteenth-century books, pamphlets, and sermons on the subject of luxury and decadence.[11] Art historians
see the middle and upper middle classes portrayed in countless paintings and prints that are both product and record of a
new affluence and leisured lifestyle.[12] Cultural historians have
started to chart the spread of gentility and etiquette book
manners.[13] Pattern books also interest architectural historians, who see more than coincidence in the appearance of numerous inexpensive handbooks popularizing a standardized
classical architecture at just the time when vernacular building traditions were losing their hold on the folk imagination.[14]

ican Historical Review 81 (1976):499–515; idem, *Economic Thought and Ideology in Seventeenth-Century England* (Princeton, 1978), pp. 163–98. Drew R.
McCoy explores the subject in late eighteenth-century American thought
in *The Elusive Republic: Political Economy in Jeffersonian America* (Chapel Hill,
N. C., 1980).

[11] John Sekora, *Luxury: The Concept in Western Thought, Eden to Smollett*
(Baltimore, 1977), pp. 23–131; Simeon Wade, "The Idea of Luxury in
Eighteenth-Century England," Ph.D. diss., Harvard University, 1969; Neil
McKendrick, "The Cultural Response to a Consumer Society: Coming to
Terms with the Idea of Luxury in Eighteenth-Century England" (Paper
presented at a conference on comparative English and American social his-
tory sponsored by the Institute of Early American History and Culture,
Williamsburg, Sept. 1985). For the American literature on the subject see
Robert Micklus, "'The History of the Tuesday Club': A Mock-Jeremiad of
the Colonial South," *William and Mary Quarterly*, 3d ser. 40 (1983):42–61.

[12] J. H. Plumb, *The Pursuit of Happiness: A View of Life in Georgian England*
(New Haven, 1977); Ellen G. D'Oench, *The Conversation Piece: Arthur Devis
and His Contemporaries* (New Haven, 1980); Stephen Deuchar, *Sporting Art in
Eighteenth-Century England: A Social and Political History* (New Haven, 1988);
Karin Calvert, "Children in American Family Portraiture, 1670 to 1810,"
William and Mary Quarterly, 3d ser. 39 (1982):87–113; idem, *Children in the
House: The Material Culture of Early Childhood, 1600–1900* (Boston, 1992).

[13] Norbert Elias, *The Civilizing Process: The Development of Manners*, vol. 1,
trans. Edmund Jephcott (New York, 1978), pp. 51–217; J. H. Plumb, *Georgian Delights* (Boston, 1980), pt. 1 and introductions to portfolios; Richard
L. Bushman, "American High-Style and Vernacular Cultures," in Jack P.
Greene and J. R. Pole, eds., *Colonial British America: Essays in the New History
of the Early Modern Era* (Baltimore, 1984), pp. 345–83; Christina D. Hemphill, "Manners for Americans: Interaction, Ritual, and the Social Order,
1620–1860," Ph.D. diss., Brandeis University, 1988.

And so it goes among other historical disciplines. The history of technology,[15] business history,[16] and even political history[17] have responded to the sense historians have that people's basic attitudes toward themselves as individuals and their place

[14]The authoritative recent work is John Archer, *The Literature of British Domestic Architecture, 1715–1842* (Cambridge, Mass., 1985), which is mainly a study of the book trade. Nevertheless, his sections on audiences, the format and content of building manuals, and treatises on the classical orders (pp. 20–28) show how "good taste" in architecture was sold to a mass market. The extent to which the American colonies figured in that market is documented from library catalogues and booksellers' lists in Helen Park, *A List of Architectural Books Available in America before the Revolution,* new and enlarged ed. (Los Angeles, 1973). American scholars have yet to explain the inroads that pattern books made on vernacular building traditions in the eighteenth century, most having preferred to demonstrate the influence of specific publications on specific large houses as in Mario di Valmarana, ed., *Building by the Book,* 2 vols. (Charlottesville, Va., 1984–86). Dell Upton addresses the issue directly, but for a later period, in "Pattern Books and Professionalism: Aspects of the Transformation of Domestic Architecture in America, 1800–1860," *Winterthur Portfolio* 19 (1984):107–50. The best treatment of the subject for the seventeenth and early eighteenth centuries is strictly English: M. W. Barley, *The English Farmhouse and Cottage* (London, 1961), pt. 5.

[15]Maxine Berg, *The Age of Manufactures: Industry, Innovation, and Work in Britain, 1700–1820* (Oxford, 1985); Christine MacLeod, *Inventing the Industrial Revolution: The English Patent System, 1660–1800* (Cambridge, 1988).

[16]Besides Neil McKendrick's chapters on Josiah Wedgwood and George Packwood in McKendrick, Brewer, and Plumb, *Birth of a Consumer Society,* pp. 100–194, see his articles "Josiah Wedgwood: An Eighteenth-Century Entrepreneur in Salesmanship and Marketing Techniques," *Economic History Review,* 2d ser. 12 (1960):408–33, and "Josiah Wedgwood and Thomas Bentley: An Inventor-Entrepreneur Partnership in the Industrial Revolution," *Transactions of the Royal Historical Society,* 5th ser. 14 (1964):1–33. Also Lorna Weatherill, *The Pottery Trade and North Staffordshire, 1660–1760* (Manchester, 1971), and idem, "The Business of Middleman in the English Pottery Trade before 1780," *Business History* 28 (July 1986):51–76.

[17]T. H. Breen, "An Empire of Goods: The Anglicization of Colonial America, 1690–1776," *Journal of British Studies* 25 (1986):467–99, and his essay "'Baubles of Britain': The American and Consumer Revolutions of the Eighteenth Century," in this volume. Also John Brewer, "Commercialization and Politics," in McKendrick, Brewer, and Plumb, *Birth of a Consumer Society,* pp. 197–262, and idem, *Party Ideology and Popular Politics at the Accession of George III* (Cambridge, 1976), pp. 159–60, and 173–74 for John Wilkes's sophisticated marketing of propaganda.

in the social order underwent a fundamental change in the years immediately before and after the turn of the seventeenth century. Among the many consequences, none was more novel or conspicuous than the pleasure that men and women took in their physical well-being and the value they placed on material things.

Something new was in the air. About that historians are sure. *What* it was they find easier to say than *why*. A few have attempted explanations, but the reasons they give tell us less about the origins of demand than about the preconditions that they argue had to be present before consumers could finally fulfill the ambitions that they tell us had long been burning holes in their pockets. If anything, arguments based on propitious circumstances only strengthen the simplistic view that these new wants were intrinsic to the human condition, that they awaited only the lifting of demographic, economic, and commercial restraints to achieve some inevitable, natural fulfillment. What is mostly missing in the literature so far are any serious attempts to explain the mainsprings of demand in terms of the commodities that eighteenth-century consumers consumed. There had always been Joneses to keep up with, even in peasant communities. Social upsmanship was nothing new. The real question is why social standing was so suddenly measured not by the number of cows a man owned or his acres of plowland but by the cut of his coat and the fashionableness of his wife's tea table. We ourselves are so used to reading status into objects that it takes a conscious effort of imagination to see an older, unfamiliar world through the eyes of a man like William Cobbett and understand the outrage he felt toward the forces of change that were encouraging plain ordinary farmers to turn themselves into "mock gentlefolks" by furnishing their sturdy, old-fashioned farmhouses with mahogany tables, fine chairs, and woven carpets—"all," he wrote contemptuously, "as bare-faced upstart as any stockjobber in the kingdom can boast of."[18] Who can dismiss his incredulity? If historians would but stop and think

[18]William Cobbett, *Rural Rides* (London, 1932), pp. 190–94. The consumption mania had spread widely throughout lowland England by the time Cobbett wrote this passage in 1825.

494

about it, the pursuit of fashion is indeed surpassing strange. What reasons can be offered to explain the extraordinary meteoric demand for commodities that finally took an Industrial Revolution to supply?

It is too early to expect a definitive answer.[19] Nevertheless, as historians from several contributing disciplines investigate people's overt behavior as consumers, they are discovering where changing living conditions expanded the boundaries of human experience in the eighteenth century. Their scholarship has developed lines of force that arguably follow deeper realities which, although still hidden from view, begin little by little to define the shape of explanations that one day we will see much more clearly. For the time being it is safe only to hazard an answer to the question—Why demand?— by stating it in the form of assumptions and propositions to be tested by research, most of it not yet finished, much of it not yet begun. The body of this essay is therefore organized around seven summary propositions that seem to me to add up to a broad historical interpretation of this central theme in modern life. From them we may also speculate why circumstances peculiar to the American colonies may have favored the ready acceptance and rapid spread of the highly developed materialistic culture that seems so characteristic of this country. Because the ground that this interpretation covers is still such unfamiliar terrain, there are good reasons to arrive at these propositions one at a time by considering those aspects of the subject that historians have already begun to explore.

As so often happens, the first discoveries were largely serendipitous. Beachcombing through records as seemingly dissimilar as probate inventories, storekeepers' accounts, vernacular buildings, and faunal remains from archaeological

[19]Describing the current state of consumer-revolution studies in recent scholarship, Lawrence Stone writes: "It can plausibly be argued that all this was man's first big step to modern consumerism. . . . If this is so, then the three key questions are who were the consumers, what were their motives, and what were the effects of the new demand for luxuries. The first two, unfortunately, remain wrapped in obscurity" ("The New Eighteenth Century," *New York Review of Books,* Mar. 29, 1984).

sites, historians and anthropologists began to see related patterns in both the physical and the documentary evidence. The story they tell goes something like this: Beginning in England as early as the sixteenth century and soon thereafter in England's newly settled North American colonies, people gradually became better furnished, better clothed, better fed, and better sheltered than ordinary folk had ever been before. W. G. Hoskins first called attention to the "rebuilding of rural England" over thirty years ago.[20] Subsequent research has adjusted his dates and refined his conclusions, but the idea that medieval peasant houses were almost everywhere rebuilt or extensively remodeled during the two centuries before 1700 is now accepted orthodoxy.[21] Periods of widespread rebuilding can be recognized in the history of early American architecture as well, the earliest one being largely completed within a single generation by the most affluent settlers in New England, whereas rebuilding was prolonged in the Chesapeake colonies for almost two centuries.[22] Everywhere the conse-

[20]W. G. Hoskins, "The Rebuilding of Rural England, 1570–1640," *Past and Present* 4 (1953):44–59, reprinted in Hoskins, *Provincial England: Essays in Social and Economic History* (London, 1964), pp. 131–48.

[21]R. Machin, "The Great Rebuilding: A Reassessment," *Past and Present* 77 (1977):33–56; J. T. Smith, "The Evolution of the English Peasant House to the Late Seventeenth Century: The Evidence of Buildings," *Journal of the British Archaeological Association,* 3d ser. 33 (1970):122–47; R. W. Brunskill, *Illustrated Handbook of Vernacular Architecture* (London, 1971), pp. 25–29; Eric Mercer, *English Vernacular Houses: A Study of Traditional Farmhouses and Cottages* (London, 1975), pp. 1–7, 23.

[22]Abbott Lowell Cummings, "Massachusetts and Its First Period Houses: A Statistical Survey," in *Architecture in Colonial Massachusetts* (Boston, 1979), pp. 113–221; Kevin M. Sweeney, "Mansion People: Kinship, Class, and Architecture in Western Massachusetts in the Mid-Eighteenth Century," *Winterthur Portfolio* 19 (1984):231–55; William N. Hosley, Jr., "Architecture," in Gerald W. R. Ward and William N. Hosley, Jr., eds., *The Great River: Art and Society of the Connecticut River Valley, 1635–1820* (Hartford, Conn., 1985), pp. 63–72, esp. p. 65; Michael Steinitz, "Rethinking Geographical Approaches to the Common House: The Evidence from Eighteenth-Century Massachusetts," in Thomas Carter and Bernard L. Herman, eds., *Perspectives in Vernacular Architecture, III* (Columbia, Mo., 1989), pp. 16–26; Cary Carson, Norman F. Barka, William M. Kelso, Garry Wheeler Stone, and Dell Upton, "Impermanent Architecture in the Southern American Colonies," *Win-*

quences were similar for the occupants of improved dwellings. Where poor, impermanent buildings were replaced by
houses built with durable, weather-tight materials, the lives of
their inhabitants became warmer, drier, and more comfortable. Innovations in the arrangement of interior space had
even more far-reaching effects on domestic life, in small
houses as well as large. The building of chimneys, upper
floors, and connecting passages partitioned old-fashioned
open halls and cavernous multipurpose rooms into warrens
of smaller, warmer compartments conducive to social segregation, specialization, and privacy.[23] Built-in ovens put new
foods on the dinner table. Glazed windows brought in light
and kept out cold. The evolution of the modern house as we
know it—one big box containing many little boxes inhabited
exclusively by humans and not shared any longer with farm
animals—was largely complete *before* the end of the seventeenth century, *before* the consumer revolution really began.

Further improvements followed from a general increase in
the use of furniture and household equipment. There is sufficient antiquaries' testimony to document a "great (although
not general) amendment in lodging" in Britain going back to
the middle of the sixteenth century.[24] But it has been left to
historians of early America (with a few British and European
exceptions) to explore basic standards of living among ordinary people by making systematic use of probate inventories.
By and large they find little evidence of fashion-conscious
consumers before the eighteenth century. These still were
men and women who were acquiring and learning to use,
often for the first time, tools that we consider essential to
everyday life—tables, bedsteads, frying pans, forks, and
individualized drinking vessels. Many small planters in

---

terthur Portfolio 16 (1981):135–96. See also Edward A. Chappell's essay in
this volume.

[23]Cary Carson, "Segregation in Vernacular Buildings," *Vernacular Architecture* 7 (1976):24–29; Hoskins, *Provincial England,* pp. 138–39. See also
David H. Flaherty, *Privacy in Colonial New England* (Charlottesville, Va.,
1972), pp. 33–84.

[24]William Harrison, *The Description of England* (1577), ed. Georges Edelen
(Ithaca, N. Y., 1968), p. 201.

seventeenth-century Maryland and Virginia, which scholars have studied most thoroughly, lived all their lives almost as unfurnished as aborigines.[25] They slept on mattresses laid on dirt floors, ate pot-boiled stews and hominies prepared in the only available cooking utensil in the house, and sat on boxes and storage chests or just squatted on their haunches for want of stools, chairs, or benches. Middling farmers, who were marginally better off than their poorer neighbors, usually provided themselves first with pans and spits to prepare more varied meals, then with additional sheets and blankets and perhaps a bedstead, and only thereafter with tables and chairs. Beyond these basic necessities, wealthier householders accumulated more goods of the same kind, plus a few such traditional amenities as candles, extra linen, and silver plate. But their inventories reveal that there were no agreed-upon luxuries that upper-class planters acquired in order to assume a distinctively affluent lifestyle. A traveler to Virginia in 1715 was surprised to find that one of the colony's most prominent gentlemen, "though rich . . . has nothing in or about his house but what is necessary." There were "good beds," but no

[25] Early work was confined to St. Mary's County, Maryland, but it established the fact of remarkably primitive living conditions, which later research substantiated and extended to other regions of the Chesapeake. See Barbara G. Carson and Cary Carson, "Styles and Standards of Living in Southern Maryland, 1670–1752" (Paper presented at the Forty-second Annual Meeting of the Southern Historical Association, Atlanta, Nov. 1976), and a companion piece by Carr and Walsh, "Inventories and Wealth." The larger picture that emerged from subsequent research is summarized in Walsh, Main, and Carr, "Toward a History," and Carr and Walsh, "Changing Lifestyles and Consumer Behavior," in this volume. Systematic study of archaeological assemblages from early domestic sites in Maryland and Virginia has produced data that correct for underrepresentation of ceramics, tools, and table utensils in probate inventories. See Dennis Pogue, "Standards of Living in the Seventeenth-Century Chesapeake: Patterns of Variability between Artifact Assemblages," in Council of Virginia Archaeologists, proceedings of Symposium V, 1991 (forthcoming). The issue of living standards is interpreted against broader economic and social backgrounds in Main, *Tobacco Colony*, chaps. 4–7, and Cary Carson and Lorena S. Walsh, "The Material Life of the Early American Housewife," *Winterthur Portfolio*, forthcoming.

bed curtains, "and instead of cane chairs," the traveler noted, "he hath stools made of wood."[26]

Preliminary inventory studies in New England and Pennsylvania paint a sketchy but similar picture of ill-furnished farmer-settlers who eventually were satisfied to achieve a modicum of comfort and convenience.[27] The choice to build inexpensive temporary buildings and furnish them sparingly was an immigrant's and frontiersman's deliberate decision to allocate his limited resources to capital-productive land, labor, and livestock.[28] Homesteading, then and later, meant skimping at first to reap greater rewards afterwards. The noteworthy point to observe, therefore, is not the substandard living endured by newcomers to North America and by those who only eked out a livelihood but the very modest and relatively unsophisticated material life enjoyed by prosperous Ameri-

[26]John Fontaine, "Memoirs of a Huguenot Family," quoted in *Virginia Magazine of History and Biography* 3 (1895):171. The gentleman in question, Robert Beverley of Beverley Park, may have been more eccentric in his tastes than Fontaine implied in this often-cited passage. A probate inventory of the estate of Beverley's father came to light in a private collection in 1992. When Maj. Robert Beverley died in 1686, he left a hall-and-parlor house full of expensive fashionable furniture, including callico bed curtains and twenty-three leather chairs. His son's back-to-basics lifestyle in 1715, whatever the explanation, was not for lack of parental example.

[27]Abbott Lowell Cummings, ed., *Rural Household Inventories [Suffolk, Massachusetts]: Establishing the Names, Uses, and Furnishings of Rooms in the Colonial New England House, 1625-1775* (Boston, 1964); John Demos, *A Little Commonwealth: Family Life in Plymouth Colony* (New York, 1970), chap. 2; Carole Shammas, "The Domestic Environment in Early Modern England and America," *Journal of Social History* 14 (1980):3–24; Jackson Turner Main, *Society and Economy in Colonial Connecticut* (Princeton, 1985), pp. 89–114, 142–73; Peter Benes, "Sleeping Arrangements in Early Massachusetts: The Newbury Household of Henry Lunt, Hatter," and Gloria L. Main, "The Distribution of Consumer Goods in Colonial New England: A Subregional Approach," in Benes, ed., *Early American Probate Inventories* (Boston, 1989), pp. 140–68; Gloria L. Main, "The Standard of Living in Southern New England, 1640–1773," *William and Mary Quarterly*, 3d ser. 45 (1988):124–34; Jack Michel, "'In a Manner and Fashion Suitable to Their Degree': A Preliminary Investigation of Material Culture of Early Rural Pennsylvania," *Working Papers from the Regional Economic History Research Center* 5 (1981).

[28]Cary Carson et al., "Impermanent Architecture," pp. 135–48, 160–78; Main and Main, "Economic Growth," pp. 37–39.

cans throughout most of the seventeenth century.[29]

The general picture, which homesteaders' hardships distort, can be corrected by looking carefully at Old World household inventories, as a few English and European historians now have.[30] They find somewhat larger houses and

[29]Similarly, Patricia Trautman finds that quality and quantity, not the cut of people's clothing, distinguished rich from poor in seventeenth-century Massachusetts. The colony's sumptuary laws notwithstanding, "differences between upper- and lower-class men's suits lay in fabric quality and number of coordinated pieces" (pp. 57–58). Likewise, women's accessories "were owned and worn by all classes of Cambridge residents." Those of higher standing simply had more of them (pp. 61–62). See her "Dress in Seventeenth-Century Cambridge, Massachusetts: An Inventory-Based Reconstruction," in Benes, ed., *Early American Probate Inventories,* pp. 51–73.

[30]The most recent and ambitious use of English probate inventories to study standards of living are Weatherill, *Consumer Behaviour and Material Culture,* and Shammas, *Pre-Industrial Consumer.* James P. P. Horn applies American research strategies to Anglo-American comparative studies in "Social and Economic Aspects of Local Society in England and the Chesapeake: A Comparative Study of the Vale of Berkeley, Gloucestershire, and the Lower Western Shore of Maryland, c. 1660–1700," D.Phil. diss., University of Sussex, 1982, published as "Adapting to a New World: A Comparative Study of Local Society in England and Maryland, 1650–1700," in Lois Green Carr, Philip D. Morgan, and Jean B. Russo, eds., *Colonial Chesapeake Society* (Chapel Hill, N. C., 1988), pp. 133–75, esp. sec. 4; James P. P. Horn, "'The Bare Necessities': Standards of Living in England and the Chesapeake, 1650–1700," *Historical Archaeology* 22 (1988):74–91. Valuable Dutch, French, and German studies give a wider view of living conditions across northern Europe. See Jan de Vries, "Peasant Demand Patterns and Economic Development: Friesland, 1550–1750," in William N. Parker and Eric L. Jones, eds., *European Peasants and Their Markets: Essays in Agrarian Economic History* (Princeton, 1975), pp. 205–66; Micheline Baulant, "Niveaux de Vie Paysans Autour de Meaux en 1700 et 1750," *Annales: économies, sociétés, civilisations* 30 (1975):505–18; Jan de Vries, *The Economy of Europe in an Age of Crisis, 1600–1750* (Cambridge, 1976), pp. 176–92; Ad van der Woude and Anton Schuurman, eds., *Probate Inventories* (Wageningen, Netherlands, 1980); Daniel Roche, *The People of Paris: An Essay in Popular Culture in the 18th Century,* trans. Marie Evans (Berkeley, 1987), esp. pts. 1 and 2. Some of the most recent research is presented in papers compiled and circulated in the proceedings of the Ninth International Economic History Congress, Bern 1986, *Inventaires Après-Deces et Ventes de Meubles: Apports à une histoire de la vie économique et quotidienne, XIVe-XIXe siécle* (Louvain-la-Neuve, 1988); Simon Schama, *The Embarrassment of Riches: An Interpretation of Dutch Culture in the Golden Age* (New York, 1987); and Peter Burke, "*Res et Verba*: Conspicuous Consumption in the Early Modern World," in Brewer and Porter, eds., *Consumption and the World of Goods,* pp. 148–61.

higher levels of furnishing almost everywhere along the social scale, as one would expect in long-established communities where fewer things had to be purchased new or built from scratch. It is also true that these and other records show a steady increase in domestic amenities over the long haul from 1500 to 1700. Likewise, the food ordinary people ate and the beverages they drank were more varied and more nourishing.[31] The clothes they wore became more plentiful, sortable, and warmer.[32]

[31]J. C. Drummond and Anne Wilbraham, *The Englishman's Food: A History of Five Centuries of English Diet* (London, 1939); Christopher Dyer, "English Diet in the Later Middle Ages," in T. H. Aston, P. R. Cross, Christopher Dyer, and Joan Thirsk, eds., *Social Relations and Ideas* (London, 1983), pp. 191–216; Jay Allan Anderson, "'A Solid Sufficiency': An Ethnography of Yeoman Foodways in Stuart England," Ph.D. diss., University of Pennsylvania, 1971; Stephen Mennell, *All Manners of Food: Eating and Taste in England and France from the Middle Ages to the Present* (Oxford, 1985); Carole Shammas, "The Eighteenth-Century English Diet and Economic Change," *Explorations in Economic History* 21 (1984):254–69. For early America, see James T. Lemon, "Household Consumption in Eighteenth-Century America and Its Relationship to Production and Trade: The Situation among Farmers in Southeastern Pennsylvania [1740–1790]," *Agricultural History* 41 (1967):59–70; Audrey Noël Hume, *Food* (Williamsburg, 1978); Peter Benes, ed., *Foodways in the Northeast* (Boston, 1984); Sarah F. McMahon, "Provisions Laid Up for the Family: Towards a History of Diet in New England, 1650–1850," *Historical Methods* 14 (1981):4–21; idem, "A Comfortable Subsistance: The Changing Composition of Diet in Rural New England, 1620–1840," *William and Mary Quarterly*, 3d ser. 42 (1985):26–65; Henry M. Miller, "An Archaeological Perspective on the Evolution of Diet in the Colonial Chesapeake," in Carr, Morgan, and Russo, eds., *Colonial Chesapeake Society*, pp. 176–99; Shammas, *Pre-Industrial Consumer*, pp. 121–57.

[32]This statement about clothing is more a matter of inference from published scholarship than a matter of fact. Margaret Spufford, *The Great Reclothing of Rural England: Petty Chapmen and Their Wares in the Seventeenth Century* (London, 1984), and Beverly Lemire, *Fashion's Favourite: The Cotton Trade and the Consumer in Britain, 1660–1800* (Oxford, 1991), are the only economic histories of ordinary people's clothing, English or American. See also Lemire, "Consumerism in Preindustrial and Early Industrial England: The Trade in Secondhand Clothes," *Journal of British Studies* 27 (1988):1–24. The rest are exclusively costume histories, including Alice Morse Earle, *Two Centuries of Costume in America, 1620–1820*, 2 vols. (New York, 1903), and Edward Warwick, Henry C. Pitz, and Alexander Wyckoff, *Early American Dress: The Colonial and Revolutionary Periods* (New York, 1965). The subject

While the facts are beginning to fall into place, the explanations remain elusive.[33] Yet the one certain lesson to be learned from inventory research is that there was still a decided sameness to people's material lives. Some had more of the same, others less, and accordingly their lives were more or less tolerable. But before the second half of the seventeenth century most people living in the same locality shared the same material culture despite individual differences in the quantity and value of their household goods. Buildings, furnishings, diet, and clothing, all evermore improved and widely enjoyed, partook thoroughly of local custom. Variations were greatest between regions, not between groups within the same region. A century later the reverse was true. The consumer revolution would make comrades of ladies and gentlemen half a world away while leaving near but unequal neighbors worlds apart.[34]

Saying even that much anticipates later developments in a story that starts with a few simple observations drawn from recent research. They can be summarized this way: *Ordinary people all across England and northern Europe enjoyed a rising standard of living in the hundred years or so before the end of the seventeenth century. These were basic improvements affecting diet, dress,*

---

of "clothingways" awaits the same attention that social historians and folklorists have been giving to foodways. Mary Ellen Roach and Kathleen Ehle Musa present a prospectus for such work in *New Perspectives on the History of Western Dress: A Handbook* (New York, 1980). For a small but promising beginning, see Trautman, "Dress in Massachusetts," pp. 51–73.

[33] For example, Fernand Braudel in *Civilization and Capitalism, 15th-18th Century*, vol. 1, *The Structures of Everyday Life: The Limits of the Possible*, trans. Siân Reynolds (New York, 1981), writes broadly on these subjects and with great originality, but large external events—climates, new crops, international markets—are the agents of change in his history. He never questions the assumption that all peoples in all times and places always desire to raise their standards of living. Yet anthropologists argue that material standards are subject to the same cultural influences that shape a people's other values, and that therefore differences and changes in those standards require cultural explanations as well.

[34] This important difference between folk and popular culture, so familiar to geographers, is the organizing concept in Henry Glassie, *Pattern in the Material Folk Culture of the Eastern United States* (Philadelphia, 1969), pp. 33–36.

shelter, and furnishings. American colonists aspired to these higher standards as well and used them as benchmarks against which to measure their success in overcoming the hardships of homesteading. Notwithstanding, folkways everywhere were still thoroughly parochial.

They did not long remain so, not exclusively. The same richly descriptive historical and archaeological research that has established these facts of everyday life in traditional communities in England and the colonies has gone on to show that the quality of that life underwent profound and fundamental alterations after the turn of the century. To understand the difference, a useful distinction must be drawn between standards, styles, and what some call modes or fashions.[35] When we speak of living standards, we refer to a people's level of creature comforts. Either they do or they do not sleep on the floor, can or cannot heat more rooms than a kitchen, and have or do not have a second change of clothes. Lifestyle is something else. Anthropologists use that term to mean a culture's characteristic manner of doing something. Style results from a common understanding that pervades and invigorates everything a people does. As accepted convention, style uses a restricted vocabulary of words, forms, and actions to create a perceptible coherence in which self-acknowledged communities find consensus. Style is a cohesive force. It draws like-minded groups of people together and reaffirms their similarities.

By contrast, mode or fashion accentuates differences in society. It is the outlandish look adopted by individuals or groups who want to set themselves apart from their fellows. Fashion, if you will, is the style of subgroups. Often these have been wealthy or privileged elites, but not always. Religious sects and racial minorities sometimes prefer and sometimes

[35] I owe my appreciation for these distinctions to Dell Upton and Fraser Neiman, who called my attention to Meyer Schapiro, "Style," in A. L. Kroeber, ed., *Anthropology Today: An Encyclopedic Inventory* (Chicago, 1953), p. 287, and James R. Sackett, "The Meaning of Style in Archaeology: A General Model," *American Antiquity* 42 (1977):370–79. Upton describes how style and mode worked in eighteenth-century Virginia churches in *Holy Things and Profane: Anglican Parish Churches in Colonial Virginia* (Cambridge, Mass., 1986), pp. 101–96.

are forced to assume distinguishing modes of dress and behavior.

No people and no period have been devoid of style in this sense, certainly not the Anglo-American folk cultures whose standards of living had been improving steadily throughout the seventeenth century. What historians find so surprising is the suddenness and speed with which fashion entered their lives in the first half of the eighteenth century. A grandson of the old Virginia stick whose unadorned lifestyle had been cause for comment fifty years earlier wrote to a correspondent in London that "I w[oul]d willingly consult the present Fashion for you know that foolish Passion has made its bray, even into this remote region."[36] To some it seemed that the colonies were almost as à la mode as London itself. "The quick importation of fashions from the mother country is really astonishing," an English traveler wrote from Annapolis in 1771. "I am almost inclined to believe that a new fashion is adopted earlier by the polished and affluent American than by many opulent persons in the great metropolis." The good life was not just city life either. In rural areas he had also seen "elegance as well as comfort . . . in very many of the habitations."[37]

Such statements are exaggerated views from the top of society, but probate inventory studies and analyses of archaeological evidence bear out their diminished but essential truth further down the social scale. Wealthy families were the trendsetters, of course. But by the 1730s and 1740s people in the middle ranks of society were purchasing many newly imported "elegances" as well. By the Revolution even some of the poorer sort had made "necessities" of goods that were their fathers' "decencies," their grandfathers' "luxuries," and before that were simply unheard of. All classes continued to acquire basic equipment—better beds and more bed linen most of all, but also tables and chairs, extra cooking utensils, lighting devices, and more. Yet, significantly, by midcentury

[36] Robert Beverley to [John Bland], Dec. 27, 1762; Beverley to Samuel Athawes, Apr. 15, July 16, 1771, Robert Beverley Letterbook, 1761–93, Library of Congress.

[37] William Eddis, *Letters from America*, ed. Aubrey C. Land (Cambridge, Mass., 1969), pp. 19, 57–58.

many poor-to-middling householders forwent ordinary comforts in favor of equipment for specialized social activities—teawares preeminently, but also knives and forks, and some tasteful ceramic and glass tablewares, although usually in odd-lot assortments, not sets, among the less well-off consumers. For the privilege of taking tea in the parlor, more than a few families were content to continue pissing in the barn.

But less and less content after 1760, archaeologists tell us. Their investigations of eighteenth-century trash pits bring us one step closer to understanding people's motives for wanting certain kinds of artifacts, including, it appears, chamber pots in greater numbers as time wore on.[38] Where probate inventories usually only count "6 earthenware dishes" or lump together "a parcel of cracked china," archaeologists recover the actual broken pieces. From them they have learned that many people increasingly took care to provide themselves, their families, and their social equals with individualized artifacts, that is, a plate, a fork and spoon, and a drinking vessel for everyone. Moreover, they insisted that all match. Sets of dishes, sets of chairs, suites of rooms, all fashioned alike, carried two messages: first, that only a certain number of individuals could participate in the event for which the objects were needed and, second, that members of that exclusive company could be known by the similar appearance of the artifacts they used. The traditional, more-the-merrier, vernacular lifestyles were superseded—or, better, *overlaid*—by a fashionableness that divided society into finely calibrated user groups. For, as archaeologists clearly demonstrate, fashion attached itself to some everyday activities more than others. Almost without exception these were those daily, weekly, and seasonal occasions when people consorted together in circumstances where ac-

[38] James J. F. Deetz, "Ceramics from Plymouth, 1635–1835: The Archaeological Evidence," Marley R. Brown III, "Ceramics from Plymouth, 1621–1800: The Documentary Evidence," Garry Wheeler Stone, "Ceramics from the John Hicks Site, 1723–43: The Material Culture," and several somewhat less instructive but still useful essays in Ian M. G. Quimby, ed., *Ceramics in America* (Charlottesville, Va., 1973). See also James J. F. Deetz, *In Small Things Forgotten: The Archaeology of Early American Life* (Garden City, N. Y., 1977), chap. 3; William M. Kelso, *Kingsmill Plantations, 1619–1800: Archaeology of Country Life in Colonial Virginia* (Orlando, Fla., 1984), pp. 176–79, 204–6.

cepted behavior was governed by an implicit knowledge of everyone's place in the social order. Those were mainly meal-times, group entertainments, public ceremonies, outings, and encounters among travelers. Written records, archaeological evidence, antique furnishings, and surviving eighteenth-century buildings all show the same thing, an extraordinary proliferation of goods and an efflorescence of forms in pre-cisely those product lines that were instrumental to the performance of status-conscious social activities. One under-stands why many American householders were spending more on tablewares by midcentury than on the pots and pans used in the kitchen when one reads their orders to England for dinner sets "of the most fashionable sort . . . sufficient for 2 genteel Courses of Victuals."[39]

Here then is one of the main conjunctions in the consumer revolution scholarship. Here is the point where questions about consumer preferences merge with questions first posed by J. H. Plumb and his followers in England and now increas-ingly by American scholars, questions about consumer behav-ior. This literature is growing too. In essence, students of the English scene argue that men, women, and children experi-enced a dramatic expansion in the arts of social living in the eighteenth century. In larger numbers than ever before, ordi-nary middle- and upper middle-class people engaged in en-tertaining and instructional activities that only the aristocracy had enjoyed before, if at all. Popular entertainments included everything from pleasure tripping, theatergoing, ballroom dancing, and attending horse races, circuses, and freak shows to reading novels, buying prints, cultivating flower gardens, dabbling in science, collecting antiquities, and joining clubs. The list of diversions goes on and on.[40]

They were tastes that some Americans acquired as well—more of them after 1800 than before and townspeople sooner than country gentlemen, however much foreign travelers re-membered otherwise. Social historians have recently begun

[39]Beverley to [Bland], Dec. 27, 1762, Beverley Letterbook.

[40]Plumb, *Georgian Delights*, pt. 1 and introductions to portfolios; Peter Clark, *The English Alehouse: A Social History, 1200–1830* (New York, 1983), pp. 222–332.

writing about early American pastimes, some of them in this volume. They find a few colonists beginning to indulge the passions of mind, heart, and body that sought fulfillment in social activities, self-improvements, organized sports, and recreational travel as early as the middle decades of the eighteenth century. At first such pleasant diversions found outlet in purely personal recreations or in activities that were easily organized by small groups of friends or confederates. Men and women with leisure time on their hands bought books for light reading, sheet music and artists' colors, dancing lessons, newspaper subscriptions, sporting gear for fishing, fowling, hunting, and racing, card and billiard tables, and books of rules for the games they played on them. Likewise, and again starting in the 1720s or 1730s, the smart set clubbed together in their pursuit of "Common Amusements," men in eating and drinking societies and sporting associations and both sexes at dancing schools, assemblies and balls, card parties, and concerts.[41]

Wherever leisured Americans could engage in playful activities with little specialized equipment and without extensive supporting services, their recreations resembled those enjoyed by their upper middle-class English brethren at about the same time. What the colonies were slow to develop until the end of the century or later was a significant leisure industry in the service and manufacturing sectors of the economy. Commercial entertainments of the sort that British consumers spent vast sums on throughout much of the eighteenth century were relatively few and far between in the colonies. Heavy capital investment in playhouses, race tracks, assembly

[41]The earliest documented social club in Maryland or Virginia was the Tuesday Club of Annapolis, made famous by Dr. Alexander Hamilton in *The History of the Ancient and Honorable Tuesday Club* (1745–56), ed. Robert Micklus, 3 vols. (Chapel Hill, N. C., 1990). Freemasons and college fraternities clubbed together in taverns and coffeehouses in Williamsburg and Fredericksburg in the 1750s and 1760s, according to Jane Carson, *James Innes and His Brothers of the F. H. C.* (Williamsburg, 1965), pp. 1–2, and Patricia A. Gibbs, "Taverns in Tidewater Virginia, 1700–1774," M.A. thesis, College of William and Mary, 1968. See also Kym S. Rice, *Early American Taverns: For the Entertainment of Friends and Strangers* (Chicago, 1983), and Jane Carson, *Colonial Virginians at Play* (Williamsburg, 1965), pp. 102–270.

rooms, mineral baths, and resort lodgings attracted few American entrepreneurs until the 1790s at the earliest and not significantly for another twenty or thirty years (fig. 1).[42] Similarly, printers and booksellers only discovered a sustaining market for novels, children's books, fiction magazines, 150 newspapers, and circulating libraries at the end of the century. Popular sheet music printed in the United States and American-made musical instruments also became readily available for the first time after the Revolution.[43]

The reason that the commercialization of leisure-time activities in the colonies lagged behind Britain was basically a matter of numbers. Before the end of the century, playgoers, travelers for health and pleasure, library patrons, and sportsmen and sportswomen were often too few in absolute numbers and too small a proportion of the whole population to tempt potential entrepreneurs to invest in the production of recreational goods or supply leisure-time services. Just as successful storekeeping required minimum population densities in the regions from which customers were drawn, so likewise the development of commercialized pastimes appears to have waited, first of all, on the growth of population, urban centers being the first to reach the necessary minimum numbers.[44]

America's small population relative to Great Britain's exaggerated the effect of another obstacle to the growth of leisure industries in North America. Historians of popular culture have been at pains to remind students of modernization that folk customs and traditional lifestyles still flourished in the eighteenth century. When scholars look very closely at the book trade, for instance, or at popular sporting events, or at folk music and country dancing, they find that old favorites and old forms not only persisted throughout the century, but resilient folkways even invaded genteel and learned culture to create distinctive American forms of polite behavior.[45] For

[42]See essay in this volume by Barbara G. Carson.

[43]See essays in this volume by David D. Hall, Cynthia Adams Hoover, and Nancy L. Struna.

[44]See essays in this volume by Richard L. Bushman and Carr and Walsh.

[45]Bushman, "American High-Style," pp. 373–76. The peculiar process by which localities did or did not modernize is worked out with remarkable

example, four important social occasions at which a Virginia gentleman's social skills were put to the test included high society balls, but also lower-brow horse races, cockfights, and fish feasts. Even balls combined "minuets danced with great ease and propriety" with "country-dances," some in the English manner and others without manners at all. "Then came the reels," one Virginian recalled of an official ball held in 1774 at which only "the finest gentleman" and the mayor dared dance with three visiting English noblewomen until the musicians struck up a favorite country tune. "And here our Norfolk lads and lasses turned in with all their hearts and heels."[46] The seaboard American colonies were no more rustic than large parts of rural England. But, the population of North America being comparatively small and dispersed, the veneer of genteel culture was necessarily thinner. Vernacular culture bulked larger proportionately, a check on the commercial success of high-style entertainments until the end of the century.

Be that as it may, folk sports, folk music, and even the almanacs and chapbooks so popular with country readers developed in the course of the century in ways that lent themselves to commercial exploitation when eventually the marketplace grew large enough. Gradually, traditional sporting events began to be held in permanent arenas and on custom-made playing fields. Jockeys left off drag racing on open roads in favor of oval tracks. Tavernkeepers built cockpits, boxing rings, and bowling alleys (fig. 2). Little by little, contests and games that once were open to the whole community were removed from public view, a necessary first step in converting onlookers into paying customers. So too with popular music. Folksinging continued to thrive alongside formal choral music, but increasingly both were learned "by Rule" in singing schools from tunebooks and music teachers and performed in concert. The popular press, historians tell us, printed and

---

subtlety in William T. Gilmore, *Reading Becomes a Necessity of Life: Material and Cultural Life in Rural New England, 1780–1835* (Knoxville, Tenn., 1989).

[46]Hunter Dickinson Farish, ed., *Journal and Letters of Philip Vickers Fithian, 1773–1774: A Plantation Tutor of the Old Dominion*, new ed. (Williamsburg, 1957), pp. 33, 168; *Lower Norfolk Antiquary* 5 (1906):33–35.

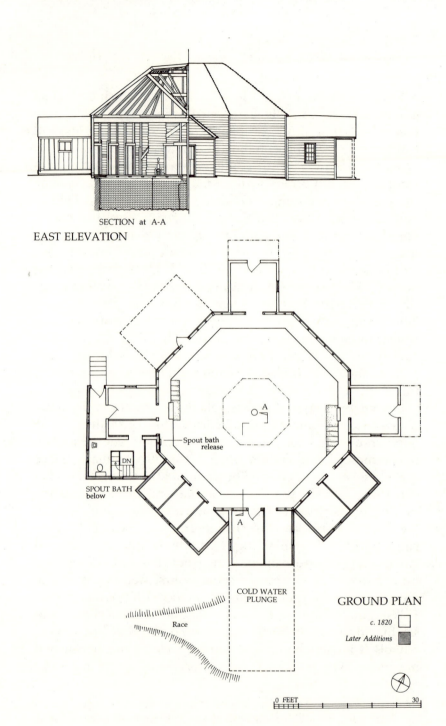

SECTION at A-A

EAST ELEVATION

Spout bath
release

SPOUT BATH
below

DN

A

A

COLD WATER
PLUNGE

Race

GROUND PLAN

c. 1820

Later Additions

0 FEET   30

510

Figure 1. Gentlemen's bathhouse, Warm Springs, Virginia. Local entrepreneurs were already turning the healing waters of Warm Springs to commercial advantage by the 1760s. This oldest surviving bathhouse was built over the principal mineral pool sometime between about 1810 and 1835, probably in the teens or twenties to judge from the moldings and other datable architectural features. As first built, the clapboard-covered octagonal structure was entered through four identical porches, which also served as changing rooms. Sophie du Pont described it in 1837 as "a wooden building having an opening at the top, & four neat & comfortable rooms on as many sides for the accommodation of bathing [obviously for both men and women although separately]. This bath is thirty-eight feet in diameter. . . . It is one of the most curious & beautiful objects I have seen, the water is pure and translucent to an almost dazzling degree, & rises in ceaseless flow, accompanied by showers of bright gleaming air bubbles." Later, as competition among spas promoted the development of special attractions, the west porch was enlarged to accommodate a spout bath after its invention by Dr. Thomas Goode in the 1830s, and the south porch was largely rebuilt to provide a cold water plunge, which was being advertised after 1850. Additional dressing rooms and a solarium or sun deck filled in three other sides of the octagon in the second half of the nineteenth century. A separate and larger bathhouse for women and a three-story hotel, complete with public dining room and ballroom, added to the popularity of Warm Springs in the years before and after the Civil War. (Drawing, Cary Carson and Margaret Mulroony)

Figure 2. Genre painting of fighting gamecocks and brawling cockers allegedly at Berkeley Springs, Virginia, c. 1845–50. Unsigned, but probably by Christian Mayr (d. 1851), a German immigrant painter with a keen eye for the travesty of manners he observed at hillbilly spa towns in western Virginia. His works include Kitchen Ball at White Sulphur Springs *(1838) and perhaps this cockfighting scene attended by ruffians dressed better than they behaved. The painting shows a simple outdoor ring enclosed behind a high fence that excluded all nonpaying customers except agile boys. The legitimate cocking clientele inside the yard lays bets on the birds and perhaps on the impromptu wrestling match as well. The painting was plagiarized by an illustrator for* Harper's New Monthly Magazine *(1857), which claimed that the scene was drawn from life at a cockpit on the outskirts of Greenville, North Carolina. (Private collection; photo, Colonial Williamsburg Foundation)*

sold far more sermons, primers, almanacs, and Doomsday books than travels or fiction throughout the eighteenth century. Yet the remarkable careers of such bookmen as Parson Weems showed the shape of things to come—aggressive merchandizing, abridgments, and cheap "pretty" books crammed with "images." As in provincial England, although perhaps not so rapidly, ordinary country people discovered that middlemen were increasingly eager to help them enjoy their traditional pastimes and introduce them to new ones, always at a price.

The observation that men and women in England and the colonies created for themselves an earthly paradise with goods that modern archaeologists rediscover in fragments, curators collect in museums, and historians quantify from probate inventories brings my argument about an American consumer society to another useful point of summary. My recapitulation of recent scholarship on the seventeenth century described a people who were enjoying a slowly rising standard of living well before 1700. We recognize in these eighteenth-century studies a qualitative difference in material life. Thus my second set of observations takes into account that *sometime toward the end of the seventeenth century and extending into the next, many people began acquiring goods, using services, and engaging in social, recreational, and educational activities that went far beyond meeting or improving basic physical needs. For the first time in Western history considerable numbers of ordinary people deliberately assumed a personal appearance and demeanor and behaved themselves in ways that were more class-bound than culture-bound.*

J. H. Plumb borrowed Thomas Jefferson's phrase "the pursuit of happiness" to describe the pleasures that many took in their new pastimes. Its ring of rights inalienable has not, however, deterred other historians from grubbing in matters of fact to discover the economic roots of consumer demand. Numerous reasons have been offered to explain the extraordinary phenomenon of eighteenth-century consumerism. The problem is that the English explanations are so different from those proposed by historians of colonial America that the answers are not easily reconciled. British historians have asked themselves why that country was so economically and socially ripe for a consumer revolution. They give several an-

swers. Careful study of eighteenth-century political economists, for instance, has revealed an important shift away from
outright opposition to the spread of luxury and even from
the modified view that it was a necessary evil. By the third
quarter of the century, by the time Adam Smith published
The Wealth of Nations, theorists were of a mind to embrace a
"doctrine of beneficial luxury" and admit that domestic consumption operated as a powerful stimulus to industriousness
in all ranks of society.[47] Here social historians make their contribution. They argue that England was prepared socially as
well as intellectually for a consumer boom. They set great
store by the fact that the structure of English society was composed of closely packed strata that bred competition, excited
emulation, and encouraged upward mobility.[48] Contemporaries remarked on the "gradual and easy transition from rank
to rank," a characteristic that made English society very different from others in which consumption of luxuries was confined to an exclusive upper-class market far beyond the reach
of the masses.[49] The commercial opportunities inherent in a
many-layered social order were not lost on entrepreneurs eager to spur on class competition and the spread of new fashions by making goods of different qualities and selling them
over a broad price range.[50] English historians take account of
other factors as well: the size and magnetism of London, the
growth of population, easy access to cheap money, women's
and children's extra earnings as a supplement to family income, rapidly expanding markets, improved food supplies,
the division of labor for mass production, and so on and on
in a recitation of "causes" that is reminiscent of textbook ex-

[47]A. W. Coates, "Changing Attitudes to Labour in the Mid-Eighteenth
Century," *Economic History Review,* 2d ser. 11 (1958):35–51.

[48]Harold J. Perkin, "The Social Causes of the British Industrial Revolution," *Transactions of the Royal Historical Society,* 5th ser. 18 (1968):123–43;
idem, *Origins of English Society,* pp. 73–98; Jones, "Fashion Manipulators,"
pp. 210–16.

[49]Joseph Harris, *An Essay upon Money and Coins* (N.p., 1757), pt. 1, p. 70.
Until recently few questioned that Britain led the consumer world in the
eighteenth century and that aristocratic France, by contrast, remained
mired in tradition. Not so, argues Cissie Fairchilds in "A Comparison of
the Consumer Revolutions in Britain and France" (Paper presented to the
Meeting of the Economic History Association, Boston, Sept. 1992). Her research shows high levels of consumption of domestic amenities, clothing,

planations for the coming of the Industrial Revolution.[51]
There is nothing wrong with the notion that a happy combination of many circumstances conspired to create an ideal
breeding ground for England's embryonic consumer society.
But it does not show how and why it happened, and Plumb's
quip that "there was no simple causative factor—no trigger
that released change, and so moved society into a higher gear,
as a clutch does a motor" is no excuse for not trying to understand the operation of the engine that powered consumerism.[52]

Good historians seldom expect to find single causes for anything. Those who study consumer behavior in North
America, especially in New England and the Chesapeake colonies of Maryland and Virginia, have isolated and investigated
several "triggers." Their work shows that, within the broad
time limits that bracket the advent of consumerism everywhere, close attention to the timing of its appearance in one
region or another can help historians distinguish primary
preconditions from those that were only contributing factors.[53] The key determinants in the upper South turn out to
have been density of settlement and agricultural diversification. At first Chesapeake tobacco planters were too thin on the
ground to keep stores in business year round. Instead English
merchants shipped only such necessities as planters bought
in bulk once a year in trade for their annual crop. As rural
neighborhoods became more densely populated after 1700,
storekeepers could afford to stock a larger inventory and a

---

and foodstuffs among town dwellers in France from 1680 to 1720. French
peasants lagged behind prosperous English tenant farmers at first, but began catching up after 1730 or so.

[50]Neil McKendrick, "The Commercialization of Fashion," in McKendrick, Brewer, and Plumb, *Birth of a Consumer Society*, pp. 34–99.

[51]Ibid., pp. 13–33; McKendrick, "Home Demand," pp. 152–210; Eversley, "Home Market and Economic Growth."

[52]Plumb, *Georgian Delights*, p. 10.

[53]The causal relationships described here are most clearly laid out in
Carr and Walsh, "Changing Lifestyles and Consumer Behavior."

wider selection of goods. Customers, thus protected against
shortages, felt easier about spending discretionary income on
nonessentials, especially as competition among a growing
number of rival storekeepers kept the lid on prices.

The spread of mixed farming was a second factor that
helped to stabilize the local economy. Planting a variety of
cash crops provided a hedge against the unpredictable ups
and downs of the tobacco trade. The more reliable income
they earned from the sale of foods and forest products gave
southern farmers confidence to invest in the tools and materials needed to start home industries such as shoemaking,
weaving, and blacksmithing. The result was not greater self-
sufficiency but a livelier local exchange in homemade manufactures and homegrown foodstuffs. Surpluses were sold
locally. The profits augmented farm incomes. With ready
money in their pockets, planters were willing to spend an extra shilling or two on a chocolate pot or a Gothic novel. One
thing led to another until by midcentury many Virginians
were well launched as consumers of English luxury goods.
In the words of the colony's governor, "These imports daily
increase"—he was writing in 1763—"the common planters
usually dressing themselves in the manufactures of Great
Britain altogether."[54]

Local history research in Maryland and Virginia has counterparts in studies of New England and the middle colonies.
Northern farmers practiced various mixed agricultures from
the very first. The component essential to the development of
a capitalist economy in each locality was the capacity to accumulate liquid financial assets. Many northern farmers and
stockbreeders bought and sold produce on the local market,
and many were favorably situated to export grain and beef
overseas and later also to supply the voracious appetites of
the country's fastest-growing cities. The income they received
from the sale of agricultural commodities not only supported
consumer spending, it also provided venture capital to invest
in new and more lucrative business enterprises. Shipbuilding,

[54]P.R.O., C.O. 5/1330, Francis Fauquier, "Answers to the Queries Sent
to Me by the Right Honourable the Lords Commissioners for Trade and
Plantation Affairs," Jan. 30, 1763.

shipping, coopering, chandlering, milling, and manufacturing in turn gave work to thousands of wage-earning sailors, clerks, artisans, and laborers. They all required additional goods and services, which further expanded the market for English and American manufactures.[55]

When regional comparisons are drawn, they demonstrate that different local circumstances differently shaped the social and economic environments where consumer cultures took root. Everywhere, not one, but a number of interconnected triggers released changes that either slowed down or sped up the spread of consumer habits. Regional studies go far to explain a people's readiness to participate in an international consumer culture. In that sense they parallel the British research that has identified elements in the national economy that created a climate favorable to increased consumption of goods. Difficult as it still is to mesh explanations on both the micro- and macroeconomic levels, both describe developments that had to take place before growing demand for consumer goods could be met. In the last analysis neither the American regional approach nor the larger treatment the subject has received from British scholars can tell us why so many ordinary people chose to spend discretionary income the way they did—not unless historians fall back on the view that the real revolution in consumers' ambitions occurred in some earlier age and that a frustrated demand for consumer goods remained bottled up until events in the eighteenth century finally popped the cork. Some have indeed advanced this case, arguing with Neil McKendrick that "the novel feature of

[55] James A. Henretta, *The Evolution of American Society, 1700–1815: An Interdisciplinary Analysis* (Lexington, Mass., 1973), chap. 2; McCusker and Menard, *Economy of British America*, chaps. 5, 9, 13; Shammas, "Consumer Behavior," pp. 67–86; Breen, "Empire of Goods," pp. 478–85. Main and Main, "Economic Growth," pp. 36–39, note that, while the economic experience of New Englanders varied widely by locality and their stock of assets fluctuated with the ups and downs of the economy, the value of land and its improvements rose fairly steadily in the region as a whole. By comparison the value of consumer goods declined early in the eighteenth century and remained relatively constant thereafter, although the Mains firmly believe that the number of purchases increased and the makeup of these eighteenth-century household goods and personal possessions drove New Englanders' standards of living steadily upwards.

the eighteenth century was not its desire to pursue fashion, but its ability to do so."[56] Later on in this essay I will try to show that proponents of this view misunderstand such evidence of fashionable living in earlier centuries as there most certainly is. In any case, the problem of explaining rising demand will not go away merely by pushing it off on historians of another period. On the contrary, the weight of evidence already presented strongly suggests that, whatever examples of conspicuous consumption may be traced back to the sixteenth century or earlier, responsibility for explaining how ordinary household goods and personal possessions became indispensable tools to the conduct of everyday social relations rests squarely on the shoulders of those who make the late seventeenth and eighteenth centuries their speciality.

To understand the origins of consumer demand is still our quest. Before pursuing it in one last body of published scholarship, the important background research just reviewed first needs to be restated as a third set of assumptions, namely these: *A combination of social, economic, and intellectual circumstances came into play in eighteenth-century England, parts of northern Europe, and North America that enabled the consumer revolution to get started. Thereafter its reception and progress from region to region depended primarily on the wealth and stability of local communities.* This is the most guarded statement so far, because it must not imply that scholars have adequately addressed themselves to Plumb's admonition that "what are so frequently . . . omitted from any discussion of one of the most momentous changes ever achieved in social living are the will, the desires, the ambitions, and the cravings of the men and women who wanted change and promoted it."[57]

Has nothing been written that throws light on the prime motives of those men and women who wanted change? Actually that is the oldest literature of all, and by far the largest. The debate for and against the spread of luxury goes back as far as the consumer revolution itself. It produced a prodi-

[56]McKendrick, "Home Demand," p. 198; Lois Green Carr and Lorena S. Walsh second his statement in "The Standard of Living in the Colonial Chesapeake," *William and Mary Quarterly*, 3d ser. 45 (1988):142.

[57]Plumb, *Georgian Delights*, p. 10.

gious number of tracts and countertracts. Four-hundred-and-sixty catalogued books and pamphlets in the half century between publication of Bernard Mandeville's *Fable of the Bees* (1724) and Smith's *Wealth of Nations* (1776) are but a fraction of the total; it was said at the time that over 500 pamphlets were printed in the 1760s alone.[58] There is a pattern in this tidal wave of ephemera. Scholars say that clear chronological stages can be discerned in the argument. Some have no bearing on our inquiry into consumer demand because sometimes the disputants were less concerned with causes than consequences. Not so when the debate turned to social analyses. Critics feared that "the vast Torrent of Luxury which of late Years hath poured itself into this Nation" would spawn a dangerous insubordination in society.[59] There was no disagreement about the reason behind conspicuous consumption. The new consumers were social climbers. Emulative spending was the engine that drove the fashion trade. Listen once again to Henry Fielding: "While the Nobleman will emulate the Grandeur of a Prince; and the Gentleman will aspire to the proper State of the Nobleman; the Tradesman steps from behind his Counter into the vacant place of the Gentleman. Nor doth the Confusion end here: It reaches the very Dregs of the People, who [are] aspiring still to a Degree beyond that which belongs to them." The "frenzy of Fashion" was deplored from the pulpit, the stage, and the Houses of Parliament.

Similar jeremiads appeared in American newspapers. Many were reprinted from British journals, but there was no shortage of homegrown polemicists who found special reason to decry extravagance in the colonies. "All other Nations have their favorite luxury," wrote one, but in the American catch basin "our Taste is universal," a potent distillation of all the sumptuary excesses of other countries put together.[60] In the

[58]This part of my account draws heavily on McKendrick, "Response to a Consumer Society."

[59]This and the following quotation, cited by McKendrick, are from Fielding, *Enquiry into the Causes of Robbers*, pp. 3-4.

[60]"The Prevalence of Luxury: With a Burgo-Master's Excellent Admonition against It," *Maryland Gazette,* Mar. 9, 1748, cited in Micklus, "'The Tuesday Club,'" p. 46.

colonies no less than in Britain unbridled ambition was un-questionably taken to be the social climber's motive and high living his unearned reward. The familiar refrain sounded ex-actly the same here as it did there: "The wife of the laboring man wishes to vie in dress with the wife of the merchant, and the latter does not wish to be inferior to the wealthy women of Europe."[61] The English-born physician, Dr. Alexander Hamilton, a resident of Annapolis, had no quarrel with "ex-travagant Living in general; I only say," he wrote in defense of privilege, "that if Luxury was to be confined to the Rich alone, it might prove a great national good, and a Public ben-efit to Mankind." Shared with the poor, however, it led to no end of mischief. The doctor may have been remembering an incident that had occurred while he was making his famous *Itinerarium* to New England two years earlier in 1744. He and a gentleman traveling companion had stopped at a poor cot-tage outside New York, "clean and neat but poorly fur-nished." Yet even there they observed "an inclination to finery" in the presence of a looking glass, some pewter spoons and plates, and a teapot. Hamilton's scandalized friend pro-nounced them "superfluous and too splendid for such a cot-tage." "They ought to be sold to buy wool to make yarn," he blustered, adding "that a little water in a wooden pail might serve for a looking glass, and wooden plates and spoons would be as good for use and, when clean, would be almost as ornamental. As for the tea equipage it was quite unnec-essary."[62]

The luxury debate produced more heat than light. Propo-nents and critics took their opposing stands largely with re-gard to the effects they presumed consumption would have on a social order they perceived in traditional terms. There were those who feared creeping egalitarianism most of all. Samuel Adams was alarmed lest affordable consumer goods

[61] Ferdinand-M. Bayard, *Travels of a Frenchman in Maryland and Virginia with a Description of Philadelphia and Baltimore in 1791*, trans. and ed. Ben C. McCary (Ann Arbor, Mich., 1950), p. 130.

[62] *Maryland Gazette*, Dec. 23, 1746; Carl Bridenbaugh, ed., *Gentleman's Progress: The Itinerarium of Dr. Alexander Hamilton, 1744* (Chapel Hill, N. C., 1948), pp. 54–55.

erase "every Distinction between the Poor and the Rich."[63] Others saw greater danger in widespread poverty and unemployment unless the production of luxuries put the lower classes to work and gave them something to work for. Only now, two centuries later, are scholars taking a longer view. They see that English society was undergoing a realignment that not so much overturned the traditional order as it imbued the leisured squirearchy with certain cultural attributes that set them apart from the working classes below them. Known to contemporaries as "genteel taste," this code of conduct modern historians call by various names: civility, sociability, cultivated living, polite society. It was something men and women had to take time to learn, time that working people could not spare. It required the mastery of prescribed social skills, which, when practiced, transformed the activities of everyday life into the arts of genteel living. Old-fashioned folkways followed rules too—implicit rules—but these were different from the artificial rules of etiquette. Folkways were second nature to people born into the fold. Gentility was a taste sought after and acquired only with diligent application. Its validity was certified by open demonstration. It was theater; consequently it needed settings, costumes, props, and (not least of all) audiences. Those audiences were full of aspiring imitators. Often they saw only what was visual, missing the genuine refinements of thought and character underneath. For many looks were enough. The trappings could be purchased in every price range. The consumer revolution put gentility up for sale.

Historians have made considerable headway in recent years in studying this realignment and cultural redefinition of Anglo-American society. Their findings, as I have just described them, can be summarized as a proposition that advances the argument of this essay an important step further:

---

[63] Harry Alonzo Cushing, ed., *The Writings of Samuel Adams*, 4 vols. (New York, 1904–8), 4:315–16. The letter to John Adams, written from Boston on July 2, 1785, lashed out against the "unmeaning & fantastick Extravagance" flaunted by the uppity poor. "You would be surprizd," the writer wagered, "to see the Equipage, the Furniture & expensive Living of too many, the Pride & Vanity of Dress which pervades thro every class."

Fashion became a badge of membership (or a declaration of aspirations to membership) in class-conscious social groups. As the outward signs of status, consumer goods and the social arts they were used to perform served, first, as shared symbols of group identity and, second, as devices that social climbers imitated in hopes of ascending the social ladder.

This fourth statement, presented in the form of a working hypothesis, brings me to the end of the bookshelf that holds current publications dealing directly with the subject. The most recent literature carries the search for an answer to the question—Why consumer demand?—thus far and no further. True, we now better understand some of the factors that created a climate favorable to the spread of fashion in the eighteenth century and enabled ordinary people in ever greater numbers to satisfy their ambitions to acquire material goods. But, as I began by asking, why those ambitions in the first place? Why the late seventeenth and eighteenth centuries specifically? Why household goods and personal possessions instead of some other more intrinsically valuable measures of status? The halfhearted answer that a few historians have offered is that old saw about English and early American society transformed from age-old, collective, peasant communities into a dynamic, cosmopolitan, modern world order in which individuals, cut adrift from their traditional moorings, needed personal status symbols to compete in a social free-for-all for position, power, and prestige. The error is not in believing that such a transformation never occurred but in taking the fact of modernization as its own adequate explanation.[64]

What consumer-revolution studies need now are explanations grounded in circumstances peculiar to the decades immediately before and after 1700. Furthermore, these ex-

---

[64]Richard D. Brown, *Modernization: The Transformation of American Life, 1600–1865* (New York, 1976). Among writers on American material life, a thinly disguised modernization model has found favor with Deetz, *Small Things Forgotten*, pp. 36–43; Henry Glassie, *Folk Housing in Middle Virginia: A Structural Analysis of Historic Artifacts* (Knoxville, Tenn., 1975), pp. 88–113, 188–93, and some of their protégés. For a critical discussion of historians' uses and abuses of the modernization concept, see Christopher Lasch, "The Family and History," serialized in *New York Review of Books,* Nov. 13 and 27, and Dec. 11, 1975.

planations must apply to all those regions and countries where fashion flourished, regardless of their different stages of economic development. Finally, genuinely useful historical explanations will have to demonstrate that fashion-bearing consumer goods solved specific social problems better than any other conceivable form of expenditure.

To present my argument in full, I must advance my thesis three steps further, but without supporting research, at least not research undertaken by students working directly on the subject. The first four summary statements were deduced from a body of clearly relevant evidence. The three remaining propositions can be offered only as hypotheses in need of testing, as blueprints for future research.

These hypotheses stem from the last substantiated statement, that consumer goods and services became the currency of social emulation. This much more may also be asserted: the need for individuals to communicate information about their status was nothing new. Traditionally, most people had lived their entire lives well within the compass of their local reputations. The estimation of a man's standing in his community was based on his family connections, his wealth in land and labor, and the offices he held and through which he exercised authority. All were rooted in a particular place. Social emulation in traditional societies was literally a contest among neighbors. It did not remain so forever. Beginning in the sixteenth century and accelerating rapidly after 1660, significant numbers of people in Britain and northern Europe began moving far beyond the reach of reputation, to neighboring counties, to big cities, to foreign countries, and to overseas colonies. There newcomers and travelers inevitably found themselves measured against perfect strangers. Alas, the old yardsticks were nowhere near at hand.

These statements of fact are appropriated from historical scholarship on subjects altogether unrelated to consumer behavior. They are linked together here to throw a bridge over the chasm of our present ignorance to a proposition that contains the central argument of this essay: *In a world in motion, migrants and travelers needed a standardized system of social communications. They required a set of conventions they could not carry with them that signified anywhere they went the status they enjoyed at home.*

So ordinary people adopted and then adapted to their own various special needs a system of courtly behavior borrowed ultimately from a protocol developed in France and disseminated through Amsterdam and London to provincial England and the colonies. Standardized architectural spaces equipped with fashionable furnishings became universally recognized settings for social performances that were governed by internationally accepted rules of etiquette.

If future research substantiates the main points of this hypothesis, historians can explain the consumer revolution in terms that meet the four required criteria of *time:* the mid- to late seventeenth century onwards; *place:* Britain and northern Europe generally and their overseas colonies as each locality achieved social equilibrium and developed a sustaining economy; *class:* the "middling sort" principally, but eventually even the working poor when they could afford small indulgences; and finally *means:* a large selection of highly standardized, affordable, and widely distributed consumer goods and a comprehensive set of easily learned rules governing their use.

To call this basic alteration in people's use of everyday objects a revolution implies a fundamental contrast between the meaning they attached to material things before the events in question and the meaning ascribed to consumer goods afterwards. It is surprising therefore that almost no one has attempted to explain how personal possessions and ordinary household equipment figured in the lives of traditional peoples before England and its colonies began to respond to the consumer impulse. The question is not what goods they owned or how people used them. That *has* been studied. The problem is knowing what importance people assigned to artifacts, especially how their possessions defined status and how their use intervened and mediated in the users' dealings with others. If goods eventually became high marks of esteem and essential tools necessary to perform activities of great social consequence, what had they been before?

As bad luck would have it, folklorists who have tried to explain the meaning of material culture have written mostly at cross-purposes to another group of sociologists and anthropologists whose principal interest lies in exploring the significance of material possessions in modern industrialized societies. The folklorists start out usefully by making traditional peoples the subjects of their research. Unfortunately for us, their agenda has been dominated almost exclusively by a structuralist search for subconscious assumptions they call "mental templates" that imparted to artifacts their distinctive culturally determined forms. By and large the structuralists have not inquired about the significance that ordinary people consciously or unconsciously bestowed on the artifacts that furnished their everyday lives.[65] The sociologists, on the other hand, have, but, again unfortunately for our purposes, their answers pertain to men and women who long ago became thoroughgoing consumers.[66] Historians are left high and dry. Their only recourse is to take a stab themselves at drawing distinctions between the different meanings of material things before and after the transforming event we are

[65] Henry Glassie is the exemplar among folklorists, and his *Folk Housing* is the archetype of the genre. He has had many imitators. The best of them, Dell Upton and Robert Blair St. George, have pushed the study of material culture beyond the limitations of structuralism. The rest continue gnawing on the indigestible "Georgian Worldview" in books like Mark P. Leone and Parker B. Potter, Jr., eds., *The Recovery of Meaning: Historical Archaeology in the Eastern United States* (Washington, D.C., 1988).

[66] Mary Douglas and Baron Isherwood, *The World of Goods: Towards an Anthropology of Consumption* (New York, 1979); Mihaly Csikszentmihalyi and Eugene Rochberg-Halton, *The Meaning of Things: Domestic Symbols and the Self* (Cambridge, 1981); T. J. Jackson Lears, *No Place of Grace: Antimodernism and the Transformation of American Culture, 1880–1920* (New York, 1981); Richard Wightman Fox and T. J. Jackson Lears, eds., *The Culture of Consumption: Critical Essays in American History, 1880–1980* (New York, 1983); Daniel Horowitz, *The Morality of Spending: Attitudes toward the Consumer Society in America, 1875–1940* (Baltimore, 1985); Simon J. Bronner, ed., *Consuming Visions: Accumulation and Display of Goods in America, 1880–1920* (New York, 1989); and Susan Strasser, *Satisfaction Guaranteed: The Making of the American Mass Market* (New York, 1989). Three recent works provide a longer historical perspective on the subject: Chandra Mukerji, *From Graven Images: Patterns of Modern Materialism* (New York, 1983); Colin Campbell, *The Romantic Ethic and the Spirit of Modern Consumerism* (Oxford, 1987); and Grant McCracken, *Culture and Consumption: New Approaches to the Symbolic Character of Consumer Goods and Activities* (Bloomington, Ind., 1988). Despite shortcomings in each of these histories written by social scientists, their work serves notice that modern consumer behavior was not the creation of department stores, world's fairs, mail-order houses, and advertising agencies.

calling the consumer revolution. Because its timing and progress responded to so many complicated influences after the
middle of the seventeenth century, historians are well advised
to look as far back as the late Middle Ages to find English
folk culture unalloyed. A backward glance at the attitudes of
ordinary people toward their personal possessions in the two
or three centuries preceding American colonization is justified because the profound differences to be observed are instructive in understanding why consumer behavior in the
eighteenth century took the surprising forms it did. Considering that my fifth proposition turns on a correlation between
geographical mobility and the spread of consumer habits,
the following account of material life in fourteenth- and
fifteenth-century Britain starts by making connections between a medieval villager's neighborhood and the social order in which he fit, between his social status and his
reputation, and finally between his standing in the community and the value of his personal possessions.

Scholarship since the 1950s has punctured many sentimental stereotypes about medieval peasants and their descendants
under the Tudors and Stuarts. The legendary English village,
immutable, self-contained, and largely self-sufficient, now lies
discarded on the spoilheap of history. In its place medievalists
have reconstructed a picture of peasant communities ordered
in a familiar hierarchy of yeomen, husbandmen and craftsmen, and poor laborers, but at the same time open to social
conflicts, far-flung market forces, outside cultural influences,
and a never-ending turnover of inhabitants. As early as the
fourteenth century more than a third of all peasant families in
villages in the East Midlands died out or moved away within a
single generation. Native sons and daughters left home in
ever-larger numbers after 1400, especially servants, craftsmen, and laborers in search of work. The pace of resettlement
continued to grow at such a rapid rate in the sixteenth century that only one in four married men and one woman
in three raised their children in the same village where they
themselves had grown up. Staying put had become the exception for a majority of English villagers and moving around
the rule.[67]

The homebound, hidebound swain of days gone by has

now been superseded in the literature by the footloose migrant worker. All the same, scholars who have carefully examined the geography of the social worlds in which medieval villagers lived and moved have discovered that the mobility of these men and women was usually confined to a fairly small area and involved propertyholding yeomen and husbandmen much less than young craftsmen and farm laborers. Those roles were later reversed in the great overseas migrations of the seventeenth century, but before 1600 the most substantial villagers were also the most settled. Furthermore, their extravillage relationships took the forms of marriages, court battles, ownership of property in nearby parishes, and various kin connections that reaffirmed an individual's roots in the greater locality. They were the kinds of ties that expanded the range of a man's or woman's local reputation.[68] For most peasants the village of their birth was still the center of the universe, however much they orbited around it. Relatively few escaped its gravitational pull altogether. Those who did, those who took themselves off to market towns, county seats, and sometimes even London, were responding, it should be noted, to forces of change that were to grow more powerful as the sixteenth century drew to a close. These few were forerunners of the genuine pioneers who became much more numerous after 1600. For the time being, though, and despite its ever-changing cast of characters, the English village and its neighborhood retained its ancient integrity as a vital community center.

Status, wealth, and power ran together in such face-to-face societies. And they ran principally to those same proper-

[67] J. Ambrose Raftis, *Tenure and Mobility: Studies in the Social History of the Medieval English Village* (Toronto, 1964), pp. 173–75; Edwin B. DeWindt, *Land and People in Holywell-cum-Nedingworth [Huntingdonshire]: Structures of Tenure and Patterns of Social Organization in an East Midlands Village, 1252–1457* (Toronto, 1972), pp. 166–205; Rodney H. Hilton, *The English Peasantry in the Later Middle Ages* (Oxford, 1975), pp. 15, 76–94; Keith Wrightson and David Levine, *Poverty and Piety in an English Village, Terling [Essex], 1525–1700* (New York, 1979), pp. 73–91, 102–9; Peter McClure, "Patterns of Migration in the Late Middle Ages: The Evidence of English Place-Name Surnames," *Economic History Review*, 2d ser. 32 (1979):167–82.

[68] Wrightson and Levine, *Poverty and Piety*, pp. 74–82.

tyholders with the oldest and deepest roots. That tended to exclude those on the top as well as those at the bottom of the social ladder—the wealthiest gentlemen landowners because, being players in a larger county social scene, they were the most migratory of all, and landless laborers and craftsmen, of course, because they had small stake anywhere and frequently wandered off in search of employment. The larger farmers and husbandmen formed the bedrock of village society. They settled down, they prospered, they sank their wealth into the land, they married back and forth, and they dominated local affairs. They also opened their ranks and shared their offices with newcomers of comparable social standing from neighboring villages, people whom they knew by reputation. Medieval and early modern communities were not closed, just close.[69]

Status among such village worthies was literally a matter of common knowledge. A man's reputation (or "estate," to use their word) resided in his neighbors' estimation of his worth measured in the only terms that mattered—in land, labor, livestock, precious plate, and capital improvements (such as barns and mills) among his property, reputable kinfolk and creditable neighbors among his relations, and the offices he held and the largess he dispensed in the exercise of his authority. All but plate were indivisible from their locality, and gold and silver objects were safest locked away or else displayed in the stronghold of the owner's own house. A peasant's reputation was his letter of credit beyond the village boundaries. As we have seen, that network of acquaintances might extend some miles roundabout, but seldom farther.

Material things that lacked intrinsic value counted for next to nothing in establishing their possessor's social standing. Well-off yeoman farmers were, of course, likely to enjoy the convenience of larger dwellings to accommodate their larger households. They furnished them likewise—that is, according to need, which meant scarcely at all in the late Middle Ages. Everyday domestic life required relatively few pieces of furniture, cooking equipment, and tablewares among all classes of

[69] Ibid., pp. 82–109; Hilton, *English Peasantry*, pp. 20–36; Keith Wrightson, *English Society, 1580–1680* (London, 1982), pp. 17–65.

men and women from princes to peasants. The household goods of typical fourteenth- and fifteenth-century farmers included chests, tables, stools, ale stands, and an occasional cupboard, plus cooking pots and other kitchen gear, as well as plates and drinking vessels of wood, horn, earthenware, and leather. Chairs were far from numerous and bedsteads evidently rarer still in ordinary farmhouses.[70] Men of greater estate might own an aumbry (a food locker) or a bedstead with curtains. But by and large, as we already noted about living standards among American colonists in the seventeenth century, rich and poor lived fundamentally alike, the only difference being that the one generally enjoyed more of the same than the other.

That is the first point worth remembering about household goods in traditional English village communities, that since no one's social standing was judged by the quality of his furniture, no one saw advantage in acquiring more or better pieces than use and convenience required. Before the seventeenth

---

[70] Information about ordinary farmers' domestic furnishings is extraordinarily scarce before the middle sixteenth century. The most revealing evidence is presented by R. K. Field, "Worcestershire Peasant Buildings, Household Goods, and Farming Equipment in the Later Middle Ages," *Medieval Archaeology* 9 (1965):105–45, and discussed in Penelope Eames, "Inventories as Sources of Evidence for Domestic Furnishings in the Fourteenth and Fifteenth Centuries," *Furniture History* 9 (1973):33–40. On the absence of bedsteads Eames concluded that either they were built-in or not inventoried, but the American evidence (see n. 25 above) reopens the strong possibility that many ordinary men and women in England may have slept directly on the floor as colonists still were doing three hundred years after the Worcestershire survey was made. Christopher Dyer treats peasants' possessions in the context of *Standards of Living in the Later Middle Ages: Social Change in England, c. 1200–1500* (Cambridge, 1989), pp. 160–77. See also Nat Alcock, "A Medieval Kitchen," *Vernacular Architecture Group Newsletter* (1987):6–7; Carole A. Morris, "Anglo-Saxon and Medieval Woodworking Crafts: The Manufacture and Use of Domestic and Utilitarian Wooden Artifacts in the British Isles, 400–1500 A.D.," D. Phil. diss., Cambridge University, 1984; Rosemary Weinstein, "Kitchen Chattels: The Evolution of Familiar Objects, 1200–1700," *Oxford Symposium on Food and Cookery, 1988 Proceedings: The Cooking Pot* (London, 1989), pp. 168–82. Weinstein offers the useful reminder that medieval cookery and cookwares have a changing history too and that "by the 16th century the variety of wares had increased beyond useful classification, so much so that students consider the period ca. 1480–1500 a ceramic revolution" (p. 171).

century, furniture was largely exempt from social pressures to conform to changing tastes.

Heavy wooden furniture and coarse earthenware vessels that had little value in themselves nevertheless were used in two distinctive ways as accessories to the display of real wealth and the affirmation of social precedence. Both are worth considering briefly because they stand in marked contrast to later uses of consumer goods as status symbols in their own right. Affluence took material form in articles of three or four kinds in medieval households: exotic and expensive foodstuffs, jewelry and plate, and textiles made into clothing or used as napery, upholstery, bedclothes, and wall hangings. Many quite modest householders could count a silver spoon or two among their liquid assets, spread the trestle boards with a tablecloth, or deck the hall with "pentyt clothes," a poor man's tapestries. Furniture and ceramic tablewares were important principally as objects needed to store, display, and serve those few articles of conspicuous consumption. Valuables of all kinds, but especially plate, cash, and yardgoods, were locked away, for instance, in the most common containers to be found in houses everywhere, chests and boxes in the larger sizes and less frequently such smaller "cases of boxes" and cabinets "as Ladyes keepe their rings, necklaces, Braclett[s], and Jewells In."[71] Notice that the contents usually far exceeded the value of the container. There were other medieval forms which persisted well into the seventeenth century that functioned principally as display stands for plate or as sideboards for serving dishes and drinking vessels used at table. Cupboards (literally *cup boards*) were essentially open shelves on wooden frames, the prefix referring not to china teacups, but to goblets that sometimes appear in ones and twos even in quite humble householders' inventories, at least by the first half of the sixteenth century. Once again, such pieces of furniture were usually wooden structures of only small importance compared to the objects they displayed. As a matter of fact, much medieval furniture literally had to be dressed before it

---

[71] Randle Holme, *The Academy of Armory; or, A Storehouse of Armory and Blazon,* vol. 2 ed. I. H. Jeayes, 2 vols. (Chester, 1688, London, 1905), 2:bk. 3, chap. 14, p. 14. Holme compiled his manuscript before 1649.

was ready to use, that is, it was draped with status-bearing textiles. Carpets and cloths covered rough cupboards and tables, curtains and testors concealed bare bed frames, and upholstery and cushions softened hard wooden stools, chairs, and benches.

Furniture and tablewares that became showpieces by the eighteenth century were still show*cases* in medieval times. They were auxiliary equipment useful for displaying, presenting, and safekeeping other objects and substances of much greater account because precious metals could be cashed in on a rainy day and expensive perishables could be shared with friends and neighbors as proof of the host's reputation for hospitality. That was the first use of medieval furniture.

There was another. Certain kinds of household equipment could sometimes be used to assert and reinforce an individual's degree of estate. In particular, seating furniture, bed hangings, standing salts, and various covered table vessels expressed social realities very precisely. Always the controlling factor was *precedence* rather than rank based strictly on such immutable qualities as occupation, officeholding, or other preferment. Status defined in those terms is inalienable from its holder. Its perquisites go wherever the rank-holder goes unless modified by something else. Rules of precedence were the modifiers in medieval society. The status that precedence conferred on an individual was relative to the estates of everyone else who was present on occasions where social formalities were observed. Thus, in practice, a yeoman farmer might sit in an armchair in his own hall and drink from a covered cup at his own table, but he would expect to occupy a stool or form located below the salt and drink from a tankard in the house of his seignorial lord. Precedence overruled all other measures of rank in the use of objects that had ceremonial significance. Not even ownership, let alone conversance with ritual furniture and utensils, entitled a person to use them in every situation.[72] Let us note in anticipation of later events

[72]This and the preceding discussion are the very original contributions of Penelope Eames, *Medieval Furniture: Furniture in England, France, and the Netherlands from the Twelfth to the Fifteenth Century* (London, 1977), and idem, "Documentary Evidence concerning the Character and Use of Domestic Furnishings in England in the Fourteenth and Fifteenth Centuries," *Furni-*

that the rule of precedence was to be thoroughly swept away, except on state occasions, by the scramblers after luxury in the centuries still to come. Little by little, gentility would supersede precedence as the chief regulator of men's and women's social interactions.

Every peasant household was also equipped with utilitarian objects seemingly too mundane to be adjuncts to ceremony. The historical sources that tell us what meaning people attached to furniture of estate throw no light at all on their attitudes toward all the other things recorded in a probate inventory. If there were some way to discover how English folk cultures accounted for commonplace artifacts in the experience of everyday living, we might better understand how completely the consumer revolution altered the traditional relationship between men and women and their tools in favor of the rank-conscious uses to which fashionable goods came to be applied in later times. Some documents have a little to say, but the most explicit and revealing information on this aspect of popular culture comes curiously from artifacts that quite literally speak for themselves.

In the long ages before empirical thinking invaded the realm of folklore, the belief was nearly universal that the cosmos was an organic unity in which every part—physical as well as spiritual—bore a harmonic correspondence to every other part. The difference between matter and spirit was blurred. The elements themselves, ordinary people believed, were literally alive. Trees, rocks, rivers, and animals were endowed with supernatural properties. Some held truly magical powers, which could be enlisted on a man's or woman's behalf or turned against them. Others, it seems safest to say, were simply felt to embody humanlike qualities over and above their natural attributes. Sometimes they were given personalities and the gift of speech, as well as limbs, wings, and anthropomorphic faces in visual representations.[73]

ture History 7 (1971):41–57. Eames's study of late medieval furniture and her interpretation of its meaning are important advances on the older but still useful Eric Mercer, _Furniture, 700–1700_ (New York, 1969).

[73]Animism is poorly studied in English sources. What little is known has been said by Keith Thomas, _Religion and the Decline of Magic_ (New York,

The doctrine of correspondences among all physical things in the animistic world of premodern England, and, it should be said, its earliest colonies, also extended to manmade houses and everyday objects. Dwellings were likened to the human body. The analogy was not just a literary metaphor invented by the seventeenth-century poets and sermon writers who were the first to set down in print these ancient superstitions. To the folk imagination the similarities between windows and eyes, doors and mouths, and roofs and heads were plausible beyond all question. Just as the body's orifices were the weak points in its defenses against witchcraft and disease, the corresponding openings in a house were prudently fortified against evil spirits by burying "witches bottles" under doorsteps and hearths, concealing horse skulls behind walls, and mounting cherubs' heads on gate posts.[74]

Spirits and other personifications lived indoors as well as out. From antiquity the hearth had always been a place where the presence of the domestic genie was strongly felt. Folklorists might suspect that the table was another. Eating and drinking are often activities where important social exchanges take place. Vessels for food and drink assist in that interchange. Therefore the possibility must be entertained that, where commonplace objects meddled in the affairs of

---

1971), pp. 222–31, and Charles Pythian-Adams, *Local History and Folklore: A New Framework* (London, 1975), pp. 12–17. See also Peter Burke, *Popular Culture in Early Modern Europe* (New York, 1978). Jon Butler discusses the use of magical charms in American occult practices in *Awash in a Sea of Faith: Christianizing the American People* (Cambridge, Mass., 1990), pp. 72–74, and Mechal Sobel writes about the African-American spirit world in *The World They Made Together: Black and White Values in Eighteenth-Century Virginia* (Princeton, 1987), pp. 96–98. On spiritualism in American folk pottery specifically, see John M. Vlach's chapter on African influences in face vessels from Edgefield, South Carolina, in Catherine Wilson Horne, ed., *Crossroads of Clay: The Southern Alkaline-Glazed Tradition* (Columbia, S. C., 1990), pp. 26–36.

[74]Robert Blair St. George discusses "architectural pathology" in Old and New England at length in a work in progress. A curious assortment of horse bones excavated on a late seventeenth-century site in Virginia is interpreted as a possible talisman by Kelso, *Kingsmill Plantations*, pp. 182–83. Amulets to "keep de witches away," occasionally excavated on slave sites, are described in Theresa A. Singleton, "The Archaeology of Slave Life," in Edward D. C. Campbell, Jr., with Kym S. Rice, eds., *Before Freedom Came: African-American Life in the Antebellum South* (Richmond, 1991), pp. 155–75.

men and women anyway, tablewares were welcomed into the company of eaters and drinkers perhaps little differently from the other commensals who sat around a peasant table.

Written records remain noncommittal on this point. Fortunately, their silence is uproariously broken by testimony from a multitude of garrulous artifacts. Most major collections of English ceramics contain at least a few slipware and saltglaze bottles, jugs, and pitchers bearing inscriptions that give the vessels actual speaking parts: "I by my Master heare am Sent / to make You merrey is my Intent"—to cite one example among many.[75] Such pot laureates were meant to be droll, no doubt about it. But humor is culture-bound too, and full of insights. If historians are prepared to collect evidence from these gallipot informants, they will observe several qualities in them that say worlds about English and American folk material culture before the consumer revolution (fig. 3).

First of all, most were communal drinking vessels, usually harvest pitchers, puzzle jugs, or stoneware bottles. They were brought out at those times of day and seasons of the year when peasants regularly consorted together in activities that reinforced their solidarity. The vessels addressed their users

[75] Slipware harvest jug (1764), Barnstable, Devon (Colonial Williamsburg Foundation, Williamsburg, acc. no. 1963-658). Vessels that use the personal pronoun should not be confused with a larger number that bear political slogans or repeat popular doggerel of the day. Ceramic collections surveyed for this section include those at the Colonial Williamsburg Foundation, the Henry Francis du Pont Winterthur Museum, Winterthur, Del., and the Burnap Collection at the William Rockhill Nelson Gallery, Kansas City, Mo. For specimens in tin-glazed earthenware see also Louis L. Lipski and Michael Archer, *Dated English Delftware: Tin-Glazed Earthenware, 1600–1800* (London, 1984), esp. pp. 228–34. Inscribed ceramics are preceded by a long line of English facejugs and figure vessels going back to the fourteenth century at least. See Ross E. Taggart, ed., *The Frank P. and Harriet C. Burnap Collection of English Pottery in the William Rockhill Nelson Gallery* (Kansas City, Mo., 1967), p. 17, nos. 1–2; John G. Hurst, David S. Neal, and H. J. E. van Beuningen, *Pottery Produced and Traded in North-West Europe, 1350–1650* (Rotterdam, 1986), pp. 93–94, 142–46, 210–21, 255; and Bernard Rackham, *Medieval English Pottery* (London, 1948). Puzzle jugs, fuddling cups, pitchers in the shape of cats, and other inscribed drinking vessels used in merrymaking were given a new lease on life by the tin-glazed or delftware potters who supplied both folk and up-scale markets in England and the colonies after 1600, according to Lipski and Archer (*Dated English Delftware,* pp. 156–235).

Figure 3. Face vessels and other anthropomorphic objects had frequented all levels of European society since the Middle Ages. It was only natural therefore that favorite drinking bottles, tablewares, clay pipes, and tobacco cans were stowed away to the American colonies in immigrants' personal baggage. Others came in trade. In North America they met and mingled with ceremonial and everyday objects used by other folk cultures, African and native American, where beliefs in animism also had deep roots. (a) Aachen (Germany) stoneware bottle, made c. 1475–1525 in the form of a bagpiper, is similar to one found in a pre-1538 context in Canterbury, England. German and Belgian jugs and bottles were widely exported and fragments turn up frequently on early Tudor archaeological sites from palaces to peasant houses. Immigrants to the colonies left behind a host of personable face vessels like these. (Van Beuningen–de Vriese Collection, Boymans–van Beuningen Museum, Rotterdam; drawing after David S. Neal.) (b) Saintonge (France) figurine bottle used in the second quarter of the seventeenth century in the household of Walter Aston, "Gentleman," militia colonel, and first owner of Causey's Care in Charles City County, Virginia. Made after c. 1610 and discarded before c. 1640. (Virginia Historic Landmarks Commission.) (c) Polychrome chafing dish from southwest France, probably exported through La Rochelle, the chief supplier to the Arcadian fur trade post at Fort Pentagoet, Castine, Maine. Not a brazier for cooking, the basin contained steaming water to warm food in dishes supported on the knobs above the relief molded masks. Stylistically c. 1550–1650, but from the table of the garrison commander Charles d' Aulnay, 1635–54. (New Brunswick Museum, Maine; drawing after Cathy Brann.)

(d) Bartmann stoneware bottle with a double mask (Germany), dated 1661. It remained in use in a fashionable Jamestown rowhouse (structure 17) until c. 1720. (National Park Service.) (e) Copper tobacco can, punch-decorated with the figure of an owl smoking a 1620–60-style pipe. Its unknown owner lived at Littletown Plantation, James City County, Virginia, the home of Col. Thomas Pettus, a native of Essex and a member of the governor's council in Virginia. The farmstead was occupied c. 1640–1700. (Virginia Historic Landmarks Commission.) (f) Indian effigy tobacco pipe, probably made by a Piscataway potter using a gear wheel from a watch to roulette the human face. Discovered at St. Mary's City, Maryland, probably from a deposit of c. 1650. (Historic St. Mary's City.) Face vessels gradually disappeared from polite company after 1700. Commercial potteries in Britain went on producing Toby jugs and puzzle pots for taverns and other vernacular haunts, although none has turned up on American sites. Folk potters in this country continued to find ready markets for face vessels wherever folk customs persisted. (g) Stoneware pitcher, made locally at Alexandria, Virginia, possibly by John Swann, 1813–21, and thrown into a privy behind an artisan's shop near the Market Square. (Alexandria Archaeology.) (h) Stoneware face cup with Kaolin teeth and eyes made by slaves working at the Thomas Davies Pottery, Bath, South Carolina, c. 1860. Davies explained that "weird-looking" vessels made by his black potters were "modeled in the front in the form of a grotesque human face evidently intended to portray the African features." This cup was recovered from one of the pottery's Civil War period waster dumps. (Augusta Richmond County Museum, Augusta, Ga.; drawings, Nancy Kurtz)

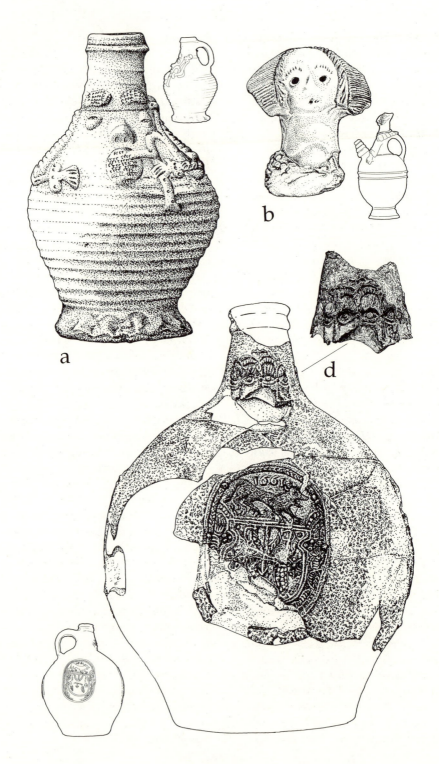

a

b

d

c

f

e

g

h

0 INCHES 3 a : c : d : g : h

2 e

2 b : f

537

as they would good neighbors, sometimes as they paused from work ("Now I am Com for to Suply / the Harvismen when they are Dray") and other times when the village lads were wiling away empty hours tippling and gaming ("Gentlemen now try your Skill / Ill hould you sixpence if you Will / That you dont drink unless you Spill").[76] Jug and Bottle were just two more good old boys who helped with the harvest and afterwards joined the merrymaking that included all villagers regardless of rank.

They were not, however, unconscious of rank. The act of eating and drinking together was always an occasion to acknowledge the village social order. Harvest jugs could show great social acumen when paying the respects of their "Masters" to the recipients of their proffered hospitality. One North Devon pitcher, which was imported into Sussex County, Delaware, after 1698 (fig. 4), recites a pretty little speech: "Kind Sr: i Com to . . . Sarue youre table with Strong beare / for this intent i was sent heare." The sender, however, anticipated that "Kind Sr" might prefer to share his gift with his own lower ranking fieldhands. So the vessel was further instructed to say, "or if you pleas i will Supply / youre workmen when in haruist dry / when thy doe Labour hard and Sweate / good drinke is better far then Meate."[77] Pots—like other peasants—knew their place and everybody else's in the intimate, face-to-facejug, village communities they all inhabited together.

Their testimony is sufficient to support at least a strong presumption that these and probably a larger menagerie of unlettered domestic utensils were part of an animated world that we moderns know only as children. It was a small world, as we have seen, larger than a village, but usually not wider than the circle of acquaintances that a person could meet or know by reputation in a lifetime of moving around its environs. Its

[76]Harvest jug (1764), Col. Williamsburg Found.; slip decorated puzzle jug (c. 1800), possibly Sussex (Nelson Gall., acc. no. B-756 [BI. 33]).

[77]Sgraffito harvest jug (1698), North Devon (Winterthur Museum, acc. no. 64.25); illustrated (but verse incorrectly transcribed) in C. Malcolm Watkins, *North Devon Pottery and Its Export to America in the 17th Century* (Washington, D.C., 1960), p. 39.

landscape—real, imagined, and blurry in between—was as crowded as a canvas by Hieronymus Bosch. Like his paintings, its denizens included a fantastical fellowship of human beings, spirits, animals, artifacts, and a veritable zoo of halfling hybrid combinations. Animal, mineral, or vegetable—all were inseparably linked in a harmonic, though often not harmonious, unity. In the long ages before ordinary men and women learned to give notional values to utilitarian objects according to their capacity to reflect flatteringly on their owners, the material world was an infinitely lively place where cats played fiddles and little dogs laughed and a dish could elope with a spoon.

This patchwork quilt of commonplaces that covered the British Isles in the Middle Ages began to come unraveled, and the local colors run together, as economic pressures further accelerated the movement of people and expanded their cultural horizons in the sixteenth century. Folklife and folklore, including traditional ideas about material things, persisted centuries longer, of course, surviving well into our own times in pockets of rural England and in the hills and hollows of backwoods America. All the same, it is also fair to say that the singular habits of personal acquisitiveness that later came to characterize consumer behavior can already be detected by the second half of the sixteenth century. The complex causes are much studied by historians of early modern Europe. Some emphasize the pressure of a rapidly growing English population on food resources after about 1520. Higher prices and lower wages pushed the unemployed and underemployed off the land toward cities and colonies where opportunities looked brighter.[78] Other historians prefer to see the impetus to these events coming from the opposite direction, pulling people away from their ancestral homes more than pushing them. These historians understand the expansion of Europe in the sixteenth century to have been an expansion in the capitalistic mode of production. Capitalism required a

---

[78] J. D. Chambers, *Population, Economy, and Society in Pre-Industrial England* (Oxford, 1972); R. B. Outhwaite, *Inflation in Tudor and Stuart England* (London, 1969); Margaret Spufford, *Contrasting Communities: English Villages in the Sixteenth and Seventeenth Centuries* (Cambridge, 1974).

0 INCHES   4   8

Figure 4. Sgraffito-ware harvest jug (1698), North Devon, England, with a history of ownership in Sussex County, Delaware. Inscribed "Kinde Sr. i Com to Gratifiey youre Kindness Love and and [sic] Courtisey: and Sarue youre table with Strong beare for this intent i was sent heare: or if you pleas i will Supply youre workmen which in haruist dry: When they doe Labour hard and Sweate: good drinke is better far then Meate." Such vessels (and verses) continued to perform their original functions for at least another generation in rural Delaware where it was still common practice in the 1720s for smallholders and gentlemen to work side by side helping each other bring in the harvest, repair barns, and whitewash houses. No one worked for wages in these circumstances, it was said. Caesar Rodney, one of the region's prominent shirtsleeve gentlemen, often recorded that a shared pipe and a draught of rum were his neighbors' only reward for helping out— that and the "old Seremony of fidling and Danceing" in the evening. The decoration of the 1698 Devon pitcher catches the last rays of one era and the first of another in its schizophrenic combination of folk elements—the birds, ponies, and tulips—with a stylish baroque portrait medallion enclosed in a wreath of fruit. Even the ancient spout effigy now wears a fashionable hat and periwig. (Winterthur Museum; drawing, Nancy Kurtz)

global redistribution of labor to cities at the commercial centers of the system and to overseas colonies at the peripheries, there to be populated by suppliers of raw materials and buyers of finished goods.[79]

Proponents of both explanations identify two consequences of these events that bear on our search for the origins of consumer demand. Each left its mark on village life. Rising prices filled the pockets of the growers of agricultural commodities while at the same time emptying the pockets of those with only their labor to sell in a crowded labor market. A social gap opened between landholders and wage earners, which the spread of international Protestantism and formal education widened into divergent and distinctly different cultural outlooks between parish notables and their poorer neighbors. To Marxist historians, the polarization of two cultures resembles nothing so much as the division of society into separate classes of employers and proles. Either way, the much older rule of precedence began giving way in the sixteenth century to differences based on lifestyles.

The second consequence could be seen everywhere on tracks and highways leading from villages to provincial towns and from towns to the great metropolis. The ceaseless movement of people that historians now know began centuries earlier accelerated still more in the sixteenth century. Besides landless farm workers looking for employment in nearby parishes and the ever-circulating population of young men and women in local service, the roads filled up with others traveling longer distances. Younger sons of established country families journeyed to larger towns to seek apprenticeships and follow trades that seldom brought them home again. Migration that removed people from their immediate localities was further swelled in the sixteenth and early seventeenth centuries by a stream that became a torrent of desperately poor wage laborers unable to find work in the countryside and forced to wander far and wide to eke out a bare living.[80]

[79]Immanuel Wallerstein, *The Modern World System,* 2 vols. (New York, 1974–80), 1:esp. chaps. 5–6.

[80]Alan Everitt, "Social Mobility in Early Modern England," *Past and Present* 33 (1966):56–73, deals with geographical mobility as well; Julian Corn-

Better poor relief and increased food production reduced the number of tramping poor after the English Civil War, but aggregate mobility rates remained high. Furthermore, and of greater importance for the study of material life, movers in the latter half of the seventeenth century tended to be more affluent and respectable—lesser gentry families drawn to the bright lights of provincial towns, apprentices to the professional and higher-status crafts, skilled artisan refugees from the Continent to the safety of tolerant England, and women to domestic service in the town houses of merchants, gentlemen, and professionals.[81]

Throughout the entire period the magnetism of London exerted a tremendous influence on local and regional migration patterns. The metropolis grew enormously, sometimes it seemed exponentially, from 60,000 inhabitants in the early sixteenth century to 200,000 by 1600, 350,000 by 1650, and more than half a million by the end of the seventeenth century.[82] Reliable estimates make 11 percent of the total popula-

wall, "Evidence of Population Mobility in the Seventeenth Century," *Bulletin of the Institute of Historical Research* 40 (1967):143–52; John H. C. Patten, *Rural-Urban Migration in Pre-Industrial England* (Oxford, 1973); Peter Laslett, "Clayworth and Cogenhoe," in Laslett, ed., *Family Life and Illicit Love in Earlier Generations* (Cambridge, 1977), pp. 50–101; E. A. Wrigley and R. S. Schofield, *The Population History of England, 1541–1871: A Reconstruction* (Cambridge, Mass., 1981), pp. 219–28; David Souden, "Migrants and the Population Structure of Later Seventeenth-Century Provincial Cities and Market Towns," in Peter Clark, ed., *The Transformation of English Provincial Towns, 1600–1800* (London, 1984), pp. 133–68; Peter Clark and David Souden, eds., *Migration and Society in Early Modern England* (Totowa, N. J., 1987).

[81] Introduction to Clark and Souden, eds., *Migration and Society,* pp. 28–38, and Peter Clark, "Migration in England during the Late Seventeenth and Early Eighteenth Centuries," ibid., pp. 213–52.

[82] Bernard Bailyn, *The Peopling of British North America: An Introduction* (New York, 1986), p. 24, is my source of information for estimates of London's population and the other figures cited in the following discussion, although even more recently calculated population estimates for sixteenth-century London are presented in Steven Rappaport, *Worlds within Worlds: Structures of Life in Sixteenth-Century London* (Cambridge, 1989), pp. 61–86. Also see Lawrence Stone, "Social Mobility in England, 1500–1700," *Past and Present* 33 (1966):16–55, esp. pp. 29–33 for population movement to towns,

tion of England and Wales resident in greater London by 1700. The capital was a catch basin for tens of thousands of migrants, who may not have left home intending to move far but, not finding opportunities nearby, drifted from place to place and eventually gravitated into the sprawling London labor market. Bernard Bailyn has described early modern England and northern Europe as "a world in motion." It can be added that it was a centrifugal motion expanding the tight little circles in which medieval migrants had moved mostly from neighborhood to neighborhood. That was one difference. The movers themselves were another. They ceased to be principally the poorest people in society after the Restoration. A better class of migrants was not long discovering that they needed an altogether new approach to integrate themselves into the unfamiliar communities they joined.

At first the colonization of North America was simply a spillover from these local and regional movements of people across England, Scotland, and Wales and eventually large parts of Holland, Flanders, Scandinavia, the German states, and Switzerland as well.[83] Bailyn, whose multivolume treatment of the subject provides a framework for understanding these national migrations as parts of a global resettlement of British and European peoples, identifies two categories of emigrants. They came from different backgrounds and sought different fortunes overseas in ways that were to bear

and pp. 51–55 for the rise of a "pseudo-gentry" whose names were prefixed by "Mr."

[83] Bailyn, *Peopling of British North America*, chap. 1; David W. Galenson, *White Servitude in Colonial America: An Economic Analysis* (Cambridge, 1981); David Souden, "'Rogues, Whores, and Vagabonds'? Indentured Servant Emigration to North America and the Case of Mid-Seventeenth-Century Bristol," in Clark and Souden, eds., *Migration and Society*, pp. 150–71; Bernard Bailyn, *Voyagers to the West: A Passage in the Peopling of America on the Eve of the Revolution* (New York, 1986); idem, "From Protestant Peasants to Jewish Intellectuals: The Germans in the Peopling of America," *German Historical Institute Annual Lecture Series* 1 (Oxford, 1988), pp. 1–12; Henry A. Gemery, "Emigration from the British Isles to the New World, 1630–1700: Inference from Colonial Populations," *Research in Economic History* 5 (1980):179–213; and idem, "European Emigration to North America, 1700–1820: Numbers and Quasi-Numbers," *Perspectives in American History*, new ser. 1 (1984):283–342.

directly on their material living standards in America. One group consisted mainly of young, unmarried men, frequently in the seventeenth century the sons of yeomen and husbandmen or rural craftsmen. A hundred years later their ranks were swelled by disappointed artisans and runaway apprentices from urban employers. Usually impecunious, they earned their passage across the Atlantic by indenturing themselves to American masters who badly needed their labor and specialized skills. They tended therefore to settle first in the older agricultural regions and somewhat later in the growing seaport cities. As bondsmen, they earned little income during the period of their service, which had the effect of delaying for four years or more their entry into the market as consumers of anything beyond the maintenance and freedom dues owed by their masters. On the other hand, coming originally from London or from one of the larger provincial English cities, as many of them had by the middle of the eighteenth century, freedmen were seldom unacquainted with the "decensies" and "luxuries" that poverty and servitude had long denied them.

The other group of emigrants was older and more prosperous. They paid their own passage to North America in family groups that included women and children. Most of them were farmers. The English among them came at first from the Home Counties and the south generally. Their destination was overwhelmingly New England before 1650, although some ended up in the proprietary colony of Maryland. A hundred years later the center of family emigration from Britain shifted northward to Yorkshire and Scotland, again in response, it seems, to changing patterns of internal migration caused in part by commercialized farming and the breakup of the Scottish clans. In America the lure of cheap, empty land drew these British farmers to the vast backcountry tracts of Nova Scotia, New York, Pennsylvania, and North Carolina. There they were thrown together with individuals and families from lower Germany, Switzerland, Ulster, and Holland, many of whom, like themselves, had been uprooted by dislocations at home that predisposed them to the blandishments of recruiting agents working for American speculators in western lands.

Few families were wealthy, but, being free, they contributed immediately to the American economy, not only the foodstuffs and handcrafts they sold at market, but, after their initial investment in necessary capital improvements, also the durable goods they purchased for their own consumption. Country people may not have been fashion setters by city standards, even those of artisans, but many of the middling sort had already developed a taste for certain genteel practices before emigrating. They transmitted that virus from their homelands to the hinterlands of America. Travelers' journals are replete with accounts of backwoodsmen who served a proper English tea in the howling wilderness. As one intrepid Englishwoman reported, it was "droll enough to eat out of China and be served in plate" in the hovel of a mere sawmill operator in the wilds of North Carolina, for the "house [was] no house" and hardly bigger or better than one of the man's slave cabins. Yet, she conceded, "the master and the furniture made you ample amends."[84] Drawing room manners, however watered down, were no mystery to many immigrant families who flooded into the backcountry that began filling up after 1763. Meanwhile in the cities, skilled indentured servants marked time until they too would be free to set up as journeymen, tradesmen, or clerks and share in the world of goods they saw all around them.

I have let this moving picture of uprooted peoples roll forward 200 years from the sixteenth century to the eighteenth to show how the settlement of colonies was but one episode in a massive global redistribution and relocation of British and European populations. Without doubt here was an event in Western history that reshaped the lives of a multitude of the same "middling sort" of people who by the eighteenth century were becoming participants in an emerging transatlantic consumer society. Here at last are the highly mobile, ordinary people who must be present to sustain our hypothesis about a standardized and widely distributed mass material culture. Moreover, their journeys start and end in precisely those loca-

[84][Janet Schaw] *Journal of a Lady of Quality,* ed. Evangeline Walker Andrews and Charles M. Andrews (New Haven, 1921), p. 185. The year was 1775.

tions where the drama took place—northern Europe, the British Isles, and North America—the same places where consumer spending and fashionable living reached epidemic proportions by the closing decades of the eighteenth century.

The strands of the argument played out in the fifth proposition are drawing together. If mobility data were more complete and if the most sensitive evidence of early consumer behavior could be reduced to a headcount, we would almost certainly see a pair of trend lines rising suggestively in parallel tracks. A burst of population growth during the period of initial settlement followed by a diminished but consistently strong stream of English immigration into mainland North America through the 1680s would coincide with the earliest measures of fashionable consumption among American elites. Migration rates fell off sharply in the 1690s but recovered again after 1700. Both indicators would then veer sharply upwards, the number of free white immigrants from the 1710s onwards and consumption levels from the 1720s. Both skyrocketed to 1740.[85] The correlations invite speculation about possible explanatory connections, but they are suggestive and no more. These trends might also correlate merely by coincidence or might perhaps be better explained by some third factor—by the growth of wealth, for instance, or by growing extremes in wealth, or, as some scholars have argued on the American side, by a re-Anglicizing of colonial culture. If there really is a case to be made that geographical mobility, as it became an ever more commonplace experience, diluted and eventually dissolved the traditional links between neighborhood, personal reputation, status, and power and in their place substituted an altogether novel system of values that measured reputation and social standing by the possession and prescribed use of relatively inexpensive and socially significant consumer goods—if that is the case that has to hold water—then it must be demonstrated that the meaning of material things and the uses to which they were put changed, not just for the migrants and movers, but for the stay-behinds

[85]Gemery, "European Emigration," table 3, pp. 303, 317–20; Galenson, *White Servitude*, table H.3, pp. 216–17; McCusker and Menard, *Economy of British America*, fig. 10.2, p. 220. The consumption indicators are discussed below.

and stay-at-homes as well. The thesis presented here cannot be confined to a mobile population alone, if for no other reason than because participation in the new consumer culture clearly was not limited to peripatetics exclusively, however many they may have been. The argument applies more broadly than that. The fifth proposition is addressed to Anglo-American, even Euro-colonial, society as a whole. It holds that the sheer volume of increased travel and migration reshaped basic cultural norms throughout northern Europe and its overseas colonies. The fact of geographical mobility, if not always the personal experience of it, enforced on virtually everyone to some degree or other new standards and practices of social intercourse.

The immediate beneficiaries were the travelers themselves, the merchants, itinerant tradesmen, immigrants, colonists, army officers, crown officials, churchmen, tourists, scientists, sportsmen, convalescents, and a host of other footloose men and women, especially those of some little reputation, whose journeys nevertheless carried them outside the effective range of their reputations. In their need to make themselves known in strange places they adopted a different system of social communication. For it to work, the information they transmitted had to be received, understood, and heeded. Increasingly it was. The presence of travelers and migrants altered the chemistry of everyday life in the settled communities into which they and their affairs intruded. Their traffic, whether for business or pleasure, brought advantage to the settled individuals with whom they necessarily had dealings. The locals soon discovered that they could advance their own fame and fortune by welcoming outsiders into their circle of acquaintances on these new terms. Thus a value system prized initially for its portability spread far and wide among peoples who were less traveled and otherwise appear little different from the inhabitants of the medieval villages that we looked at earlier except that now some of their affairs and some of their associates were farther flung.

The old-fashioned measures of personal reputation were not immediately thrown over. But they were no longer enough by themselves. The chiefest men and women in any particular locality where those who possessed the wherewithal and wielded the influence that usually brought them to the attention of strangers in the first place. Their accommodation to fashionable living therefore often merely reaffirmed the old pecking order based on landholding and lineage. Indeed the good manners that newcomers offered as their principal letters of credit were honored in no small part precisely because local worthies had already been observed to behave after the same fashion. Gentility was like paper money. It was presumed to stand for tangible social assets that unfamiliar bearers kept stashed away at home, and it was generally accepted at face value because it was currency that homegrown ladies and gentlemen traded in as well. In short, gentility and the consumer goods required to practice the arts of fashionable living were a social compact into which more and more covenanters were drawn as they perceived that the opportunities for personal betterment in a more open society outweighed any advantage to be gained from stubborn adherence to tradition. Visual literacy was as much a prerequisite to getting a piece of action in the expanding world 300 years ago as computer literacy is our entré to a shrinking world today.

Neither events nor inventions precipitate cultural changes so fundamental and so far-reaching. They happen cumulatively, occurring slowly and haphazardly at first and only gaining momentum as time goes by. Assigning a starting date to the consumer revolution is, therefore, much less instructive than narrowing to two or three generations the era when consumer culture became a pervasive social force. This essay proposes that that moment occurred throughout large parts of provincial England and North America in the hundred years or so between, say, the Restoration and 1760. To test the validity of the fifth proposition—and to sharpen the focus of our search for the origins of demand—we must therefore look most carefully for evidence of this transformation in consumer behavior in the several decades around 1700.

First, though, we need to take account of a body of recent scholarship that would push the dating of these developments back to Tudor times, a century or more before the period where we will concentrate our search. Some historians have argued that the ambition to cut a fashionable figure was widely felt among even commonfolk not later than the six-teenth century.[86] They are not talking about an improving standard of living, which we have already acknowledged to be an important consequence of Elizabethan prosperity. These historians have in mind out-and-out conspicuous consumption, and they point to a flurry of Tudor sumptuary laws as proof that Phillip Stubbes wrote the truth in 1595 when he said that "no other nations take such pride in apparel as Eng-land."[87] His evidence is undeniable. But when historians ask *what* was consumed and *why,* the village jack-a-dandies who so excited the displeasure of their Elizabethan superiors turn out to resemble only remotely their descendants in the eigh-teenth century for whom gentility with its wardrobe of fash-ionable clothing and toolbox of newfangled housewares would eventually become a total way of life. The hallmarks of the consumer revolution, we must keep in mind, were not just a profusion of attractive and affordable personal possessions but also a code of easily learned rules governing their use.

The importance that people in Tudor and Stuart times attached to clothing appears on close inspection to have been decidedly more traditional than innovative. Sumptuary laws were aimed overwhelmingly at excesses in dress, at what Stubbes called "pride of apparel." Such "new fangles" of-fended propriety in two ways, by extravagant use of expen-sive materials by those who could ill afford them and by misuse of fashionable clothing reserved for those who could.

---

[86]McKendrick, "Commercialization of Fashion," pp. 34–42. Idem, "Home Demand," pp. 197–98, borrows its argument from Joan Thirsk, "The Fantastical Folly of Fashion: The English Stocking Knitting Industry, 1500–1700," in N. B. Harte and K. G. Ponting, eds., *Textile History and Economic History* (Manchester, 1973), pp. 50–73, and Wilfrid Hooper, "The Tudor Sumptuary Laws," *English Historical Review* 30 (1915):433–49. Fashion in clothing is Grant McCracken's starting point in *Culture and Consumption,* pp. 11–16. See also F. J. Fisher, "The Development of London as a Center of Conspicuous Consumption in the Sixteenth and Seventeenth Centuries," *Transactions of the Royal Historical Society,* 4th ser. 30 (1948):37–50. American sumptuary legislation is discussed in Patricia Trautman, "When Gentlemen Wore Lace: Sumptuary Legislation and Dress in Seventeenth-Century New England," *Journal of Regional Cultures* 2 (1983):9–21.

[87]Phillip Stubbes, *The Anatomie of Abuses,* 4th ed. (London, 1595), pp. 9–10.

A lowly collier's wife in Jamestown, Virginia, broke both rules in 1618 by wearing a "rough bever hatt with a faire perle hatband, and a silken suite thereto correspondent."[88] Her higher-ranking neighbor, William Harwood, was measured by a different yardstick. As "governor" of nearby Martin's Hundred, he was entitled by executive order of the Virginia Company to wear the woven gold garter points that archaeologists found on the site of his house.[89] Statute law in Massachusetts expressly forbade persons worth less than £200 to buy or wear "gold or silver girdles, hatbands, belts, ruffs, [or] beaverhats" as well as "any slashed clothes other than one slash in each sleeve and another in the back."[90]

In Old and New World alike there was a rising tide of infractions against decorum. Its magnitude *was* new. But the forms extravagance took were not. Woven textiles, precious metals, jewelry, and exotic furs and feathers had always marked the high status of their owners and wearers. Made into clothing, often styled with cutwork and slashes to show off wasteful consumption, textiles were the most ancient personal status symbols of all. Why did coxcombs spend every farthing on such frippery? Was it a bold stroke to launch themselves into polite society? Not in 1600, not according to William Vaughan, who had interviewed numerous servants who, he said, had bestowed "all the money they had in the world on sumptuous garments." When he had asked these men "how they would live hereafter," they invariably replied that "a good marriage will one day make amends for all."[91] Here was self-advancement accomplished the old-fashioned way, by making advantageous family alliances. Both dress and success were still viewed in very traditional terms. As a matter

[88]Susan M. Kingsbury, ed., *The Records of the Virginia Company of London,* 4 vols. (Washington, D.C., 1906–35), 3:221; Lyon Gardiner Tyler, ed., *Narratives of Early Virginia* (New York, 1907), p. 285. John Pory was equally scandalized to report that "our cowekeeper here of James citty on Sundays goes accowtered all in freshe flaming silke" (ibid.).

[89]Ivor Noël Hume, "First Look at a Lost Virginia Settlement," *National Geographic* 155 (June 1979), illustrated on p. 746.

[90]Quoted in Earle, *Costume in America,* 1:61.

[91]William Vaughan, *The Golden Grove* (London, 1600), n.p.

of fact, sumptuary laws were medieval legal instruments for the defense of privilege by precedence, despite their apparent obsession with rank alone. Precedence, as we saw in connection with ceremonial furniture and tablewares, entitled individuals to use certain objects, or disallowed their use, depending on specific social circumstances. That was the trouble with clothing and the reason it had to be strictly controlled. Clothing was too portable and too inseparable from the wearer. A man could not remove or change his clothes—except to doff his hat—at the sudden appearance of social superiors. So there had to be laws to prevent commonfolk from ever wearing articles of clothing that might conceivably—somewhere, sometime—give offense to someone who had greater precedence. Sumptuary laws provided those blanket proscriptions. They were not intended primarily to check the spread of fashionable living.

To answer the historians who detect consumer impulses as early as the sixteenth century, it can be said in summary that *standards of living* were indeed improving rapidly on the eve of American colonization. *Lifestyles* changed more slowly where they challenged traditional attitudes about the value and use of material things.

But challenged they were. There is no question that the identification of individuals with their personal possessions grew closer in the sixteenth and seventeenth centuries. Nothing in earlier times resembles the remarkable variety of affordable haberdashery that flooded popular markets fully 200 years before the appearance of machine-made textiles. Studies of the stocking knitting industry in the sixteenth century estimate that a work force of maybe 200,000 part-time cottage knitters produced upwards of 20 million pairs of stockings annually. The selection of colors, qualities, and styles was so "wanton" that "no sober chaste Christian" could put on some of the really tawdry pairs of hosiery offered for sale without risking eternal damnation—again the opinion of the censorious Stubbes. Pretty gloves, ribbons, hats, and caps became plentiful as well, all at prices to suit every purse.[92]

[92] Discussed in Thirsk, "Folly of Fashion," pp. 55–60; idem, *Economic Policy and Projects,* pp. 106–32.

Sensitivity to customers' personal preferences and attention to price points anticipated market strategies that Josiah Wedgwood and others made famous in the eighteenth century.[93] Variety and affordability both show concern for something else that had to happen before the meaning of material things could change. Englishmen had to develop the modern notion of the individual's right to property ownership. This is no place to blunder unwarily into the thicket of historical controversy surrounding the origins of English individualism.[94] My particular interest in showing that expanding consumer choices went along with an enhanced regard for personal property need only take passing notice of work by political economists who find that a key prerequisite to England's maturing market economy was recognition of the fact that individuals were the sole owners of their resources to be employed however they saw fit.[95]

Usually when historians write on this subject they cite heavyweight authorities like Hobbes and Locke. I would simply observe that far beneath the notice of those erudite philosophers a kind of rough-and-ready possessive individualism spread rapidly throughout Anglo-American society, leaving its signatures written all over the everyday objects that individuals possessed. Personalized marks of ownership appear everywhere starting quite abruptly in the 1580s and 1590s. House-proud men and women carved, stitched, stamped,

[93] Neil McKendrick, "Josiah Wedgwood and the Commercialization of the Potteries," and "George Packwood and the Commercialization of Sharing: The Art of Eighteenth-Century Advertising; or, 'The Way to Get Money and Be Happy,'" in McKendrick, Brewer, and Plumb, *Birth of a Consumer Society,* pp. 99–194.

[94] Alan Macfarlane, *The Origins of English Individualism: The Family, Property, and Social Transition* (New York, 1978). A review by Lawrence Stone in the *New York Review of Books,* Apr. 19, 1979, draws the battle lines for the fracas that has followed.

[95] C. B. Macpherson, *The Political Theory of Possessive Individualism: Hobbes to Locke* (Oxford, 1962), pp. 46–70. Joyce Oldham Appleby discusses the clash of interests and philosophies between old-fashioned mercantilists who saw England as a giant workhouse and a new breed who viewed the economy as an aggregation of self-interested individual producer-consumers in "Ideology and Theory" and *Economic Thought and Ideology.*

chased, and painted their initials, names, significant dates, and other identifying devices on personal possessions in the seventeenth century as never before or since.[96] Name plaques and datestones, mounted on houses and barns, broadcast to every passerby facts of village life that previously had been common knowledge. Indoors, householders carved their initials on cupboards, cabinets, and expensive armchairs as if the forms by themselves no longer confirmed unequivocally their users' importance.[97] Chests identified by names or initials the owners of their increasingly valuable contents, and more and more were fitted with locks to secure a little bit of personal storage space in what were otherwise still communal rooms.[98] Actually, some rooms were becoming less communal. For the first time inventory takers were shown into chambers known

[96]The practice descended the social scale in the eighteenth and nineteenth centuries as consumers' ambitions invaded traditional communities and as ethnic subgroups accommodated their material culture to mainstream English taste. For examples in many media, see Scott T. Swank et al., *Arts of the Pennsylvania Germans* (New York, 1983).

[97]My confidence in these unsupported statements comes from many years of fieldwork recording English vernacular buildings and from observations drawn from the study of museum collections. It remains for someone to do a systematic frequency distribution study of dated and personalized buildings and domestic artifacts in Britain and America. Their starting point should be Machin, "Great Rebuilding," pp. 33–56; idem, *The Houses of Yetminster (Dorset)* (Bristol, 1978), table 17, p. 144; Raymond B. Wood-Jones, *Traditional Domestic Architecture of the Banbury Region* (Manchester, 1963), fig. 83 and Appendix 1; [Sarah Pearson], *Rural Houses of the Lancashire Pennines, 1560 to 1760* (London, 1985), pp. 185–93; Patricia E. Kane, "The Seventeenth-Century Furniture of the Connecticut Valley: The Hadley Chest Reappraised," in Ian M. G. Quimby, ed., *Arts of the Anglo-American Community in the Seventeenth Century* (Charlottesville, Va., 1975), pp. 79–122; and Patricia E. Kane, "The Joiners of Seventeenth-Century Hartford County," *Connecticut Historical Society Bulletin* 35 (1970):82–85. The practice of personalizing furniture is discussed briefly in [Barbara McLean Ward et al.], *A Place for Everything: Chests and Boxes in Early Colonial America* (Winterthur, Del., 1986), pp. 5–7.

[98]Locked chests became an obsession for Virginia planters who shared their dwellings with an ever-changing population of indentured servants and slaves; inventory takers in York County, Virginia, meticulously recorded trunks and chests with locks and keys. See York County Deeds, Orders, Wills, 1–6 (1637–84), Virginia State Library, Richmond.

not by their location over, behind, or within other rooms, but by the personal name of their principal occupant, which they dutifully recorded as the "roome called Mr. Wm ffarvar['s] roome," to take one Virginia example from many hundreds.[99] Coats of arms, family devices, and still more initials were engraved on silver plate and pewter, embroidered on bed hangings, etched in glass, pressed into bottle seals, and scrolled into stumpwork pictures. The bond between owner and object grew closer, but at the same time the social distance between them widened into a gulf. Facejugs and vessels carrying first-person inscriptions remained imprisoned in unregenerate folk culture (fig. 3). One senses that more worldly users were fast learning the modern practice of treating inanimate objects strictly as possessions, mere goods and chattels, one more resource to be employed, as the economists said, however their owners saw fit. Artifacts ceased to be actors in their own right. Instead they were acted upon by makers and users. Inscriptions on ordinary utilitarian objects bespeak not comradeship but ownership. They sound more and more like dog tags—"Roger Smith his Bottle," "Mrs. Mary Sandbach her Cup"—or, alternatively, like shopkeepers' receipts—"Made for Mrs. Hugs by Jos. Hollamore, Barnstable."[100]

A transformation was taking place, as mundane as it was also profound and far-reaching. A few household goods and articles of personal apparel had always been highly valued because they were made of precious materials, were hard to get, or represented their owner's ability to pay lavishly for other people's labor. Now little by little that small assortment of prized possessions was supplemented and expanded by whole categories of things whose worth was more notional—ascribed—than real. The fact of ownership became evermore its own reward. In life and death alike a man's or woman's estate came to be regarded as the sum total of old wealth and

[99] Henrico County Deeds, Orders, Wills, 2 (1678–93), Va. St. Libr., inventory (1677/8) of Col. William Farrar, p. 51.

[100] Slipware bottle (1752), Staffordshire (Col. Williamsburg Found., acc. no. 1952-408); posset bowl (1720), England (Nelson Gall., acc. no. B675 [BI.123]); slipware harvest jug (1764), Devon (Col. Williamsburg Found.).

new, of land, its products and improvements, cash, plate, and uncollected debts, but, as probate inventories attest by the hundreds of thousands starting in precisely this period, of household gear as well and personal possessions often itemized down to the last linen handkerchief and appraised to the final ha'penny. Quality and quantity became twin ladders to greater reputation and upward social mobility. "Gentry or gentilitie is taken two waies," wrote Francis Markham in 1625, "that is to say, either by acquisition or descent."[101] The old way was tried and true, the other strictly parvenu. Yet to many men and women who set out on the road to Bristol or London or set sail for Massachusetts or Maryland, the brave new world of material goods offered an irresistible shortcut to the good name they lacked at home or left behind.

Looked at backwards in historical perspective, the contrast between material life in medieval times and the early modern period appears so striking that the term *revolution* seems well deserved. Certainly the eighteenth-century critics of luxury saw their era as the dawn of a new age, for better or worse. In reality the course of change was evolutionary. It only seemed otherwise because its pace sped up so dramatically after 1700. It burst on people's consciousness all of a sudden in the eighteenth century when it was already well advanced. Consequently, explicit discussion of fashionable living appears relatively late in conventional literary sources, and usually they describe the phenomenon in its maturer stages of development. It follows that historians who seek the earliest ancestors of *Homo gentilis* must undertake a kind of paleontological research among the fossil tools they left behind to discover a story that is largely unrecorded in the standard texts. The analogy is not so far-fetched as it may sound. Our quarry from the beginning of this essay has been man the modern tool user. What earlier states he evolved from and what new uses and meanings for material things he discovered along the way were usually not matters that he—or she—put in writing. These can, however, be strongly inferred from careful study of obsolescent tools, which, when new made, were full of uses, but, gradually aging into junk, were eventually

[101] *The Booke of Honour* (London, 1625), p. 58.

discarded into trash pits, attics, and museums and replaced by later models. The replacements performed their tasks better in a utilitarian sense, or else they better equipped their users to compete successfully in a faster social swim. To understand demand is still the goal. To succeed, written-record historians must pay a little attention to the very artifacts that in their day satisfied that demand. Their materials, forms, ornamentation, and especially their uses are a *pre*historian's earliest clues to the evolutionary history of consumer behavior.

The story early American artifacts tell about the origins of demand picks up where the foregoing account of material life in provincial England left off in the sixteenth century. The landscape that English and European immigrants and African slaves roughed out of the North American wilderness appears remarkably traditional at first glance. Farmers in New England sited their barns alongside public roads, usually well forward of the house, in an age-old demonstration of wealth and status that no one in agricultural communities mistook (fig. 5).[102] Likewise, early tobacco plantations in the Chesapeake colonies were conspicuous for buildings that emphasized their productive capacity, not the owner's claims to gentility. A planter's own dwelling often nestled in a litter of nearly identical clapboard-covered structures, one hardly distinguishable from the others.[103] Besides their own house, planters frequently built numerous outbuildings and quarters, the most typical of which one early traveler in Virginia itemized as "a separate kitchen, a separate house for the Christian slaves [that is, indentured servants], one for the negro slaves, and several to dry the tobacco, so that when you come to the home of a person of some means," he said, "you think you are entering a fairly large village"—and in 1686 he still meant an old-fashioned village. Buildings everywhere in the colonies were so thoroughly vernacular that today archi-

[102] Robert Blair St. George, " 'Set Thine House in Order': The Domestication of the Yeomanry in Seventeenth-Century New England," in Jonathan L. Fairbanks and Robert F. Trent, eds., *New England Begins: The Seventeenth Century*, 3 vols. (Boston, 1982), 2:162–63.

[103] Durand de Dauphiné, *A Huguenot Exile in Virginia*, ed. Gilbert Chinard (New York, 1934), pp. 119–20.

tectural historians can often trace them back to specific regions in England. Most exhibited no fashionable pretensions
whatsoever. Contemporaries used words like *homely* and *slight*
to describe cottages that people back home best understood
when correspondents likened them to barns.[104] There were a
few larger and better-built houses, some substantial and commodious enough to remain serviceable for 300 years. But, as
we have seen, even they provided only such amenities as were
already transforming late medieval houses in England,
namely, chimneys, upper floors usually given over to bedchambers, and various arrangements of ground floor rooms
that had hardly begun to separate work spaces from those
increasingly reserved for dining, sitting, socializing, and re-
tiring.

Material life in the earliest American colonies remained
rooted in the traditions of the English countryside and to an
unknown extent the folkways of African villages. Only when
architectural and furniture historians add up the cumulative
effect of many small improvements and innovations is it possible to detect an unmistakable drift toward true fashion consciousness, that radically new way of thinking that deployed
personal possessions in support of social hierarchies built not
upon precedence but on manners. The popularity of mono-
grams is a tip-off to students of material culture to look for
other attributes of everyday objects that refined them into
symbols of class consciousness. There is an intelligible pattern
in their development. And while it admits many exceptions,
it exhibits notable congruences between furniture history and
the history of gentility starting approximately in the middle
decades of the seventeenth century. Several features of furniture in this period bear looking into one at a time—a tendency toward greater use of costly and exotic materials, the
standardization of ornament, a proliferation of new forms,
and eventually the combination of furnishings into sets and
suites intended for use by ladies and gentlemen who regularly
engaged in well-rehearsed social activities.

I am not the first to attach significance to these novelties,
nor will I be the last to concede that buyers found newfangled
goods desirable for a host of strictly personal reasons, includ-

---

[104]Quoted in Carson et al., "Impermanent Architecture," pp. 146, 153.

Figure 5. Cushing farmstead, Hingham, Massachusetts. House built July 1679 (diary), enlarged with lean-to addition and modernized c. 1740–62 (inscription) and perhaps again shortly before c. 1800, enlarged for the last time and restored 1936; aisled grain and cattle barn c. 1679–93 (will), lengthened soon afterwards, heightened early nineteenth-century; corn house, seventeenth or eighteenth century, but standing by 1783 (inventory). Daniel Cushing, Sr., a well-to-do South Shore farmer, bought this property in 1675, built his "Dwelling house" four summers later, and a "Barne and all other Buildings standing there upon" by the time of his death in 1693. Originally, the hall-and-parlor house rose only one and a half stories high although two large front-facing gables gave extra headroom to the attic bedchambers. A cooking hearth and built-in oven equipped the hall. Cellar stairs in the lobby led down to a cool storeroom for foodstuffs and dairy products underneath the parlor. The unusually large and handsome parlor must have held the best bed as well as seat furniture and perhaps a dining table considering the size of the room. Upstairs, those who slept in the bedchamber over the parlor enjoyed warmth from a fireplace; lodgers in the hall chamber shivered. Despite differences in the status and uses of the four rooms, the exposed ceiling frames in all were expensively embellished with quarter-round chamfers, and the fireplace walls were sheathed with planed boards heavily shadow-molded along the joints. Incised lines on a lintel coverboard (surviving in the hall) imitate denticulation. In the same room black marbleized beams and yellow walls spotted with brown polka dots were probably painted c. 1700–1725. Above average in their day, such refinements failed to meet the tastes and social requirements of later Cushings. One or more renovations, starting c. 1740–62, removed the gables, raised the roof to two full stories, and added a lean-to kitchen across the back. A fashionably renewed staircase installed in the lobby and raised panels mounted on the fireplace walls in the parlor and former hall (a sleeping and dressing room by 1783) marked these as genteel spaces suitable for company. Farmhands and domestics could be restricted to the back rooms, coming and going to the cellar and the lean-to chambers via a service stair constructed with sheathing reused from the parlor. Reference to a "back new kitchen" in 1803 suggests the addition of a summer kitchen and perhaps other service rooms in a shed, which was much altered in the 1936 restoration. Daniel Cushing's farmyard lay 160 feet along the road leading into town. There he built a five-bay, plank-sided barn with an aisle or lean-to along the south side perhaps for a stable, a porch too narrow for carts, and a gable on the rear roof to provide light for threshing and air for winnowing. An oak planked threshing floor divided the barn between storage space for harvested crops and open stalls for dairy cows. That combination was a new development in mixed farming regions in seventeenth-century England as well. Stalls used for milking and feeding were floored for cleanliness; those for bedding cattle had dirt floors for easy mucking. Soon after the barn was built, Cushing lengthened it by another three bays, perhaps to store larger harvests. A surviving corn house, standing on staddle stones and fitted with two adjustable corn bins, is undatable, but may have numbered among "all other Buildings" on the farmstead in 1693. Sometime after c. 1800 a later owner raised the barn roof and removed the porch and gable. (Drawing, Cary Carson and Jeffrey Bostetter)

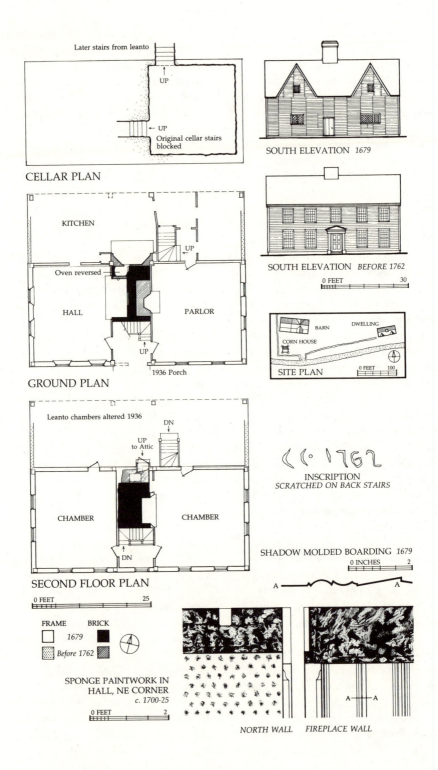

Later stairs from leanto

UP

← UP

Original cellar stairs blocked

CELLAR PLAN

SOUTH ELEVATION *1679*

KITCHEN

UP →

Oven reversed

HALL

PARLOR

UP

1936 Porch

GROUND PLAN

SOUTH ELEVATION *BEFORE 1762*

0 FEET   30

BARN   DWELLING

CORN HOUSE

SITE PLAN   0 FEET   100

Leanto chambers altered 1936

DN

UP to Attic

CHAMBER

CHAMBER

DN

SECOND FLOOR PLAN

INSCRIPTION
SCRATCHED ON BACK STAIRS

SHADOW MOLDED BOARDING *1679*

0 INCHES   2

A   A

0 FEET   25

FRAME   BRICK

1679

Before 1762

SPONGE PAINTWORK IN
HALL, NE CORNER
c. 1700-25

0 FEET   2

NORTH WALL   FIREPLACE WALL

560

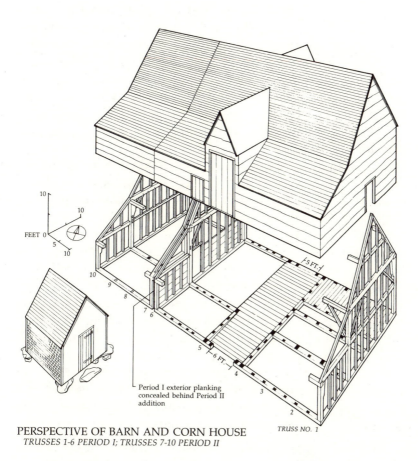

10
10
FEET 0
5
10

5 FT.

10
9
8
7 6
6 FT.
5
4
3
2

Period I exterior planking
concealed behind Period II
addition

TRUSS NO. 1

PERSPECTIVE OF BARN AND CORN HOUSE
TRUSSES 1-6 PERIOD I; TRUSSES 7-10 PERIOD II

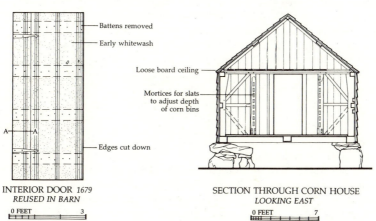

Battens removed

Early whitewash

Loose board ceiling

Mortices for slats
to adjust depth
of corn bins

A — A

Edges cut down

INTERIOR DOOR *1679*
REUSED IN BARN

0 FEET   3

SECTION THROUGH CORN HOUSE
LOOKING EAST

0 FEET   7

561

ing their beauty, convenience, comfort, utility, and sometimes good value.[105] As the saying goes, there is no accounting for taste. What most certainly must be accounted for was the growing disposition of clients and craftsmen to prefer those design innovations that refashioned household artifacts to enhance their recognition and shared use by a universe of gentlefolk. By the same token, consumer choices reflected a spreading dissatisfaction with things that were meaningful only locally. Modernity gradually superseded memory where social sorting took place. Canon challenged custom. Brand names banished folk art to the cultural boondocks.

The first signs of fashion were nowhere visible on the rural American landscape or along the colonies' earliest city streets.[106] Outwardly, neither farmhouse nor town house revealed the first stirrings of the consumer impulse that incubated in the innermost sanctum of a yeoman's or merchant's physical world, namely, his domestic parlor. Parlors still retained their ancient functions as ground floor strongrooms and sleeping chambers, but, given hearths of their own, they were becoming withdrawing rooms and sitting rooms as well (fig. 5). Here, behind closed doors, master and mistress felt most at home. Here, removed from the lesser inmates of the house, they entertained their social equals. Here, not surprisingly, they amassed those material things they prized above all else.[107] It is here, then, in the early American parlor that

[105]When T. H. Breen writes that historians "can only speculate about the motivation of the colonial buyer," he is dealing with consumer psychology on a personal level—that is, "each person entered the market for slightly different reasons." He reaches for a deeper explanation when he goes on to say, "In addition, consumer goods provided socially mobile Americans with boundary markers, an increasingly recognized way to distinguish betters from their inferiors, for . . . in whatever group one traveled . . . one knew that consumer goods mediated social status" ("Empire of Goods," pp. 495–96).

[106]The first fashionable buildings in North America (as I am using that term in this essay) appeared in Boston and Virginia in the 1660s and 1670s and made no inroads on vernacular building tradition for another generation. See Abbott Lowell Cummings, "The Beginnings of Provincial Renaissance Architecture in Boston, 1690–1725," *Journal of the Society of Architectural Historians* 42 (1983):43–53; and Cary Carson, "The Public Face of Architecture in the American Colonies" (Paper presented at the Fortieth Williamsburg Antiques Forum, Williamsburg, Feb. 1988).

historians should look for the first telltale signs of fashion transformed into a total way of life.

Let us open the door into a parlor chosen at random from households in rural Massachusetts whose contents were inventoried by order of the Suffolk County court in the last quarter of the seventeenth century.[108] Random, of course, does not mean typical, and John Weld, a yeoman farmer of Roxbury, left a slightly larger estate than many of his neighbors when he died in 1691. But his was not the largest, not by far. Most of the furnishings that the inventory takers recorded in Weld's parlor were in no way extraordinary for the time or place. The most valuable piece in the room was "a fether bed." As we saw earlier, good beds had once been an uncommon luxury among ordinary farmers, but, ever since the sixteenth century, they were becoming favorite acquisitions for English and American householders who could afford to improve their standard of living. Weld's parlor featherbed was well supplied with "a pair of sheets, Rugg, Coverlid, Blanket, Curtaines and Valines, Bolster, Pillows, and [a] Bedsted" (or frame) to raise the whole affair off the ground. The many textiles, not the plain, wooden bedstead, brought the total valuation to £6, a tidy sum, but nothing that other farmers could not match. "One standing Cupbord" was worth another pound (a fairly standard valuation for such a piece) and "a pair of tongs and a pair of small Andirons" on the hearth five shillings more. Everything else in the room came to £1 10s. inclusive for "A table, 5 Joynt stools, a wicker Chair, two other Chairs, 2 wrought stools, a wrought Chair, and a Glass-Case."

A furniture historian, thus admitted vicariously into John Weld's parlor, recognizes first of all its ancient use as the principal sleeping chamber in the house.[109] But no longer was it

---

[107] Dramatically demonstrated by Robert Blair St. George in ratios showing furniture value per square foot of floor space in Fairbanks and Trent, eds., *New England Begins*, 2:171–72. Parlor furniture was worth almost two and a half times as much as the next best furnished rooms in the Dedham and Saugus houses he studied.

[108] Cummings, ed., *Rural Household Inventories,* pp. 62–64.

[109] Actually John Weld kept another, even more valuable, featherbed and a chest of drawers filled with sheets and napkins in his kitchen chamber, an

merely an "inner room" partitioned off the hall, a cold retreat
come end of day. A fireplace equipped with tongs and "small
Andirons" (not the larger kind cooks needed) made the parlor a comfortable gathering place for family and friends to
share their leisure time. Leaving servants and hired hands to
eat at the "old Table" and sit on an "old setle Bench" in the
hall alongside a cheese press and skeins of linen yarn, the
parlor-users seem to have taken their meals seated around a
newer table. It was set with glass and other tablewares (unrecorded but presumably) stored in the "Glass-Case" and the
"standing Cupbord." There were stools and chairs enough
for a company of eleven. All the same, the parlor seating furniture was a motley assortment that reveals Weld's disinclina-
tion to provide the occupants of his parlor with matching
chairs that accorded every sitter equal status. The one upholstered "wrought" chair, if it was his own, may indicate that the
senior Weld observed the old rules of table to his dying day.

Much can be read into this one room in one house in one
village in rural Massachusetts that applies to furnishings and
fashions in comfortably well-off households all over the American colonies toward the close of the seventeenth century.
Prestige was still conspicuously attached to expensive textiles
like Weld's bed hangings and to cupboard plate. Textiles still
imparted most of the value to the joined furniture they covered or cushioned. Other important distinctions were observed as well between the men and women entitled to sit on
chairs and those consigned to stools and benches. These all
were backward-looking customs. The Roxbury parlor also incorporated some of the innovations that had begun to alter
everyday house life in the preceding hundred years and were
becoming fairly commonplace by the end of the century. The
householder's high table had removed into the privacy of
the parlor, physically segregating persons of quality from the
"mess" left behind in the hall. The display furniture had lum-
bered after, and some of the newer pieces were curiously
"wrought" or otherwise embellished in ways that so excited
the admiration of beholders that a proud owner, such as John

---

atypical arrangement that might be explained if we knew the inmates of
the house.

Weld may have been, might instruct his joiner to carve "IW" on a drawer front or on the cresting rail of a chair.

What else can we learn about ordinary household gear in this period? What can a thorough knowledge of artifacts tell us about the way class consciousness eroded the old rules of precedence and laid the groundwork for that exclusionary aesthetic we call fashion? To examine the materials from which everyday objects were made is one useful place to start. Although the neighbors who compiled Weld's inventory saw no need to say so, we may safely assume that his furniture was oak, the favorite building material of joiners going back hundreds of years. Oak did not necessarily mean clumsy or plain. The "wrought" stools and chair, upholstered with needlework or turkeywork seats, might just as likely have been carved with a flat, leafy, strapwork decoration that was also popular throughout the seventeenth century. The case pieces in Weld's parlor, the cupboard and the glass case, although not exceptionally valuable, are hard to imagine without at least a smattering of another common variety of mannerist-influenced ornament concocted of turned spindles, bosses, and applied architectural moldings. Such elements, glued and nailed to the oak carcasses of a farmer's cupboards and chests, were usually dabbed with black paint in imitation of ebony. Sometimes real ebony was used, one of several exotic woods from South America, Africa, and the Far East imported by timber merchants into Amsterdam and London and transshipped to joiners' shops in the colonies.[110]

[110]This statement and the following general account of household furniture draw on a remarkable body of new scholarship by Benno M. Forman and several exceptional students he trained at the Winterthur Museum. Their work, in which connoisseurship is informed by historical research, has begun to reach publication. The books and articles that I borrow from here, usually without further citation, are Benno M. Forman, *American Seating Furniture, 1630–1730* (New York, 1988); idem, "The Chest of Drawers in America, 1635–1730: The Origins of the Joined Chest of Drawers," *Winterthur Portfolio* 20 (1985):1–30; Robert F. Trent, "The Chest of Drawers in America, 1635–1730: A Postscript," ibid., pp. 31–48; Benno M. Forman, "Furniture for Dressing in Early America, 1650–1730: Forms, Nomenclature, and Use," *Winterthur Portfolio* 22 (1987):149–64; Robert F. Trent, "New England Joinery and Turning before 1700," Fairbanks and Trent, eds., *New England Begins*, 3:501–50. The approach they follow and many of their

For the first time ever, familiar pieces of farmhouse furniture were turned into eyecatchers before so much as a "cuberd cloth" was draped over top or the family plate put on display. Livery cupboards, court cupboards, chests, and boxes were deliberately made to look expensive by the extra workmanship they received and by the use of rare and unusual materials. As a matter of fact, relatively speaking, they *were* expensive. True, John Weld's bed hangings were worth six times more than the standard cupboard in his parlor, but he was a traditionalist. Even so, at £1 the cupboard represented two-fifths of the total value of all the parlor furniture used for dining, sitting, and storage. Elsewhere, even among some of his Roxbury neighbors, it was not uncommon for cupboards to be appraised for two, three, and four times as much. In settled communities everywhere, the price and value of good furniture were going up.

More importantly, imported woods and jazzy paintwork represented a different kind of value from investments in silver plate, gold threads, or latten spoons. Fancy furniture had little intrinsic value. It was not readily negotiable. It stood for money spent and gone forever. It implied reserves of wealth only marginally depleted by "wasteful" expenditures on property that did not appreciate in value or possessions that could not be melted down and coined. In that respect fine furniture resembled sumptuous garments. Costly ornament lavished on otherwise mundane stands and storage boxes advertised the owner's superior ability to squander his wealth, to use it frivolously, literally to consume his assets. Social symbolism that once resided in the things that case and seating furniture displayed or stored came to be attached to the furniture itself, indeed at first to the selfsame pieces that had long assisted in public demonstrations of social precedence, namely, open cupboards, storage containers, and chairs of state.

The observation that such formerly utilitarian fittings acquired trappings that were aimed deliberately at impressing

ideas about contemporary uses of furniture were drawn from the work of English and European curators and architectural historians, superbly brought together in Peter Thornton, *Seventeenth-Century Interior Decoration in England, France, and Holland* (New Haven, 1978).

denizens of the parlor directs attention to this audience of privileged spectators. Who were they? Obviously those with eyes to see and minds to comprehend. But see and understand what? The literal answer, of course, is the physical appearance of the artifacts they looked at, the visual components and overall composition that formed the design. Furniture historians have made an interesting discovery about the design of household articles in the seventeenth century. Craftsmen then, like medieval craftsmen earlier, used geometry to lay out their work. The difference was that this geometry was based on a system of proportions derived from classical architecture. It was the brand of northern European classicism that art historians call mannerism.[111] First Antwerp and Germany and then Amsterdam after 1590 had been the principal artistic centers from which prototypes, patterns, and publications had spread the mannerist aesthetic throughout northern Europe and across the English Channel to become the dominant taste of the seventeenth century. Popular initially in court circles, this extravagantly decorative style was picked up and purveyed to bourgeois merchants and affluent yeomen by countless joiners, weavers, metalworkers, printers, and potters, many of whom were religious refugees from France and the Low Countries. Others, mostly English, joined the Protestant migrations to North America.

Artisans were not aestheticians. They did not have to be. Mannerist motifs were easily reduced to formulas that craftsmen could learn by rote and then replicate over and over again by using a simple rule and compass. Careful examination of pieces of American-made furniture reveals the lightly scribed lines and compass arcs that joiners scored across the surface of their work as they laid out mannerist-inspired strapwork, S-scrolls, and decoration in the applied molding style.[112] Tools and templates took the guesswork out of crafts-

---

[111]Robert F. Trent, "The Concept of Mannerism," in Fairbanks and Trent, eds., *New England Begins*, 3:368–79, and Trent, "New England Joinery," pp. 504–6.

[112]Robert Blair St. George, "Style and Structure in the Joinery of Dedham and Medfield, Massachusetts, 1635–1685," *Winterthur Portfolio* 13 (1979):1–46, esp. pp. 20–24; idem, *The Wrought Covenant: Source Material for*

manship.[113] Not only could artisans make more objects in less time to meet the growing demand for quality household furnishings, jigs also guaranteed clients a higher degree of design consistency. Without consistency there can be no standardization. Mannerist geometry gave artisans a compositional strategy that they could follow using ordinary hand tools to create look-alike products for sale to what was already becoming a mass market without boundaries. Mannerism was the first international style to impress its image on city and village cultures alike. It was expressed in a thousand different forms and motifs because individual shop masters still controlled the design process.[114] But the look was recognizable the world over because the work all proceeded from the same principles. Mannerism did not impart meaning to the artifacts it adorned per se.[115] It simply made their meaning—whatever that was—intelligible to a larger audience, the audience of urbane and knowledgeable parlor users. Mannerism was a new communications medium in the service of a message that historians can understand a little better by inquiring further into the uses to which people put their ever more numerous and newly valuable possessions.

There will be some who object that a functional analysis of household goods belabors the obvious. This essay set out to explain consumer behavior. Why make the problem more complicated than it has to be? Why not simply recognize that, as divisions in English and American society became more pronounced for reasons having little or nothing to do with

the Study of Craftsmen and Community in Southeastern New England, 1620–1700 (Brockton, Mass., 1979), fig. 41a.

[113]David Pye, The Nature and Art of Workmanship (Cambridge, 1968), pp. 13–24.

[114]Benno M. Forman describes how ideas about style traveled from one country to another in "The Chest of Drawers," p. 13.

[115]True enough in the context of the events that I am describing here, although elsewhere I have argued that architecture in the mannerist style ballyhooed its novelty in deliberately provocative acts of message-sending (see Carson, "Public Face of Architecture"). In yet another context, Robert F. Trent makes a convincing case that mannerism held great meaning as a badge of solidarity among radical Protestants in the courts of Elizabeth and James I ("Concept of Mannerism," p. 376).

consumption, the upper classes deployed consumer goods along a broad front to mark the social boundaries between themselves and those below them? Why not accept the obvious explanation that this passion for domestic paraphernalia was just the newest wrinkle in the age-old contest between the haves and the have-nots?

I tried earlier to rebut this commonsense assertion that the rich always have more toys by looking back at the fourteenth and fifteenth centuries and discovering that that statement is not a very useful way to understand material life in the Middle Ages. Four hundred years later a fuller historical record supports another observation, that by the eighteenth century, however much wealthy consumers outspent their social inferiors, it is more important to recognize that the things they bought were significantly different in kind from the things other people had. Ownership qualified them to participate in activities that were barred to the dispossessed. Inasmuch as these were choices freely made by men and women who could afford to buy and learn to use the necessary accoutrements to fashionable living, artifacts are a faithful record of activities willingly engaged in, and their uses are a guide to motivations more complex than the desire merely to outspend the competition.[116]

[116]Attentive students of material culture can read between these lines the logic that underlies the research strategy I employ throughout this section of the essay. Like any other historian's set of working assumptions, mine too require some leaps of faith. All are consistent with my understanding of human nature. The line of my reasoning starts with the function of artifacts: the functions they were designed to perform indicate the primary uses to which they were put; uses imply choices; choices imply motives; and so it logically follows that the reasons people chose to acquire certain goods and use them as they did are as close as historians can usually come to understanding the meaning they attached to material things. The trick, of course, is to identify correctly the use, the user, and the period of use. The attention my approach gives to deliberate choices is not meant to dismiss structural anthropologists' valid observation that every culture perceives a narrower range of possible designs and uses for artifacts than their tools could make or the human mind imagine. Nor does it deny that there are distinctive cultural patterns to be observed in people's selections from the limited repertory of alternatives they perceived and that in those patterns can be found many meanings that *we attach* to their material things. That simply is not my assignment. To answer the question, Why demand?, I need

Had the old rules of precedence remained fully in force, we would expect few additions to the inventory of ceremonial furniture and tablewares that had served adequately for several centuries. Indeed, as we have already seen, traditional pieces of status-displaying furniture enjoyed continued high favor long enough to receive a thorough face-lifting in the mannerist style in the seventeenth century. So did the glass and ceramic vessels customarily used to establish protocol at table. Archaeologists working at Jamestown, St. Mary's City, and other early seventeenth-century sites in the Chesapeake region have found fragments of exquisitely delicate standing cups made in Venice or by Venetian-trained glassblowers working in London or the Netherlands. The elongated stems were twisted into mythological animal shapes or molded into swollen balusters and grotesque lion masks (fig. 6).[117] The Jamestown excavations also yielded pieces of two rare Rhenish stoneware jugs, one with biblical scenes, the other decorated with the seven electors of the Holy Roman Empire, the figures on both set in an arcaded mannerist frieze (fig. 6).[118]

to explain *their* motives. The men and women whose lifestyles are described in this part of the essay acquired and learned to use household goods that they already knew would help them achieve whatever result they sought or that they hoped would. Things that worked, they kept and used again; unsuccessful products and unacceptable behavior were forgotten. Popular artifacts (in the sense of socially successful artifacts) can therefore be regarded as individual choices that happily conformed to lifestyles that found favor with some larger number of people in society. For students of material culture, popular artifacts thus become evidence from which it is reasonable to infer generally the motivations of the lifestyle group as a whole.

[117] John L. Cotter, *Archaeological Excavations at Jamestown, Virginia* (Washington, D.C., 1958), p. 188; John L. Cotter and J. Paul Hudson, *New Discoveries at Jamestown* (Washington, D.C., 1957), pp. 44–45.

[118] Illustrated in Cotter, *Excavations at Jamestown*, p. 183, but only correctly identified and knowledgeably discussed in Ivor Noël Hume, *Here Lies Virginia: An Archaeologist's View of Colonial Life and History* (New York, 1963), p. 289 and figs. 20, 121, and idem, "Rhenish Grey Stonewares in Colonial America," *Antiques* 92 (1967):349–53 and fig. 2. For the specific attribution of the seven electors jug, see Hurst, Neal, and van Bueningen, *Pottery in North-West Europe*, p. 204. The fragments (J7037/1–2 and J33,868) were recovered from fill deposited in Refuse Pit 1 (Zone B) circa 1650–60 (catalog card, Jamestown Archaeological Collection, Colonial National Historical

Made about 1610, these magnificent drinking vessels were probably covered with lids befitting their superior size and status and may have been "tipped" with silver or pewter mounts, a technique much employed by mannerist craftsmen to enhance the preciousness of objects made of baser materials.[119] Heirlooms by the time they were broken, they must have been cherished like the "old fashioned guilt Canne [tankard] with a lidd" that was still one of the proudest possessions of a neighboring York County planter in 1659.[120]

Sherds found on archaeological sites from Pemaquid to Poquoson tell the same story.[121] Cloisonné enameled knife handles, polychrome delftware platters and drug pots, imported Chinese porcelain curios, colorful Spanish and Portuguese majolica, slip-decorated serving dishes, sgraffito wares from the west of England, Rhenish and Flemish stoneware jugs and

Park, Jamestown, Va.). The jugs were therefore half a century old when they were finally broken and thrown away.

[119]Trent, "Concept of Mannerism," p. 377, and Joy Kenseth, "'A World of Wonders in One Closet Shut,'" in Joy Kenseth, ed., *The Age of the Marvelous* (Hanover, N. H., 1991), pp. 81–101 and entries 29–39. Such objects were owned in the neighborhood of Jamestown, for example, William Hughes's "small black jack [a leather tankard] tipp'd with Silver" (York County Deeds, Orders, Wills, 3 [1657–62], inventory dated 1661, p. 154). Hughes was a planter and a merchant.

[120]York County Deeds, Orders, Wills, 3, inventory (1659) of Francis Wheeler, a merchant, p. 77. The can was valued at £3 10s.

[121]Kelso, *Kingsmill Plantations,* p. 183 and fig. 129; Julia B. Curtis, "Chinese Ceramics and the Dutch Connection in Early Seventeenth-Century Virginia," *Vereniging van Vrienden der Asiatische Kunst* 15 (1985):6–13; Cotter, *Excavations at Jamestown,* pp. 182–85; Cotter and Hudson, *Discoveries at Jamestown,* pp. 34–45; Henry M. Miller, *A Search for the "Citty of Saint Maries": Report on the 1981 Excavations in St. Mary's City, Maryland* (St. Mary's City, 1983), pp. 74–107; idem, *Discovering Maryland's First City: A Summary Report on the 1981–1984 Archaeological Excavations in St. Mary's City, Maryland* (St. Mary's City, 1986), pp. 16–18, 61, 83–92, and 111–13; Ivor Noël Hume, *A Guide to Artifacts of Colonial America* (New York, 1970), is full of accurately dated specimens, but it does not always name the American sites where similar sherds have been found; C. Malcolm Watkins, "Ceramics in the Seventeenth-Century English Colonies," in Quimby, ed., *Arts of the Anglo-American Community,* pp. 275–99; Alaric Faulkner and Gretchen Fearon Faulkner, *The French at Pentagoet, 1635–1674: An Archaeological Portrait of the Acadian Frontier* (Augusta, Maine, 1987), pp. 196–97, 208–16, 237–42.

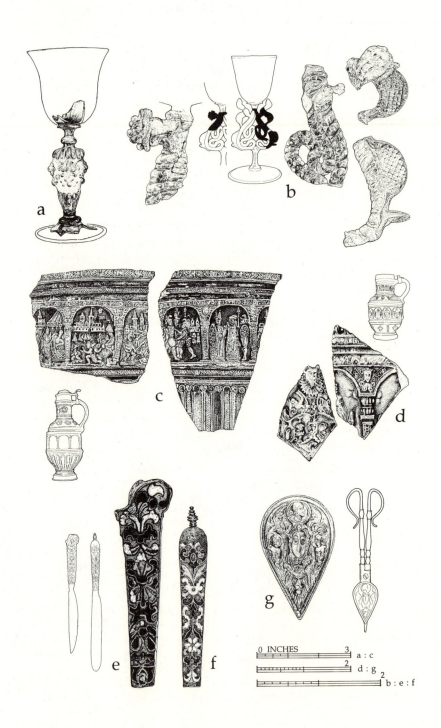

a

b

c

d

e   f   g

Figure 6. High-quality mannerist table-wares and domestic utensils excavated on American sites. (a) One of several identical wine glasses recovered from the c. 1676 wreckage of structure 112 at Jamestown, Virginia. The swollen baluster stem, molded with lion masks, floral swags, and heavy gadroons, was a widely used element for Venetian and Venetian look-alike cups, goblets, bowls, and tazzas. Netherlands or possibly England, c. late sixteenth or early seventeenth century. (National Park Service.) (b) Stem fragments from two or more delicate Venetian-style flügelglas wineglasses. They probably set Gov. Charles Calvert's table at St. John's, St. Mary's City, Maryland, at the end of the seventeenth century. The serpentine twist stems, intertwined with threads of blue glass and pincered into wings along the back, terminate in butterflies and raspberry prunts instead of the usual dragon heads. Excavations at St. Mary's City have yielded large quantities of refined façon de Venise table glass, most of it probably Dutch, from the households of prominent officials and gentlemen lawyers, but not from the city's taverns. Last quarter of seventeenth century. (Historic St. Mary's City.) (c) Two pieces of a large, Westerwald-type, blue and gray stoneware jug excavated at Jamestown from a c. 1650–60 context. A frieze of arcaded panels depicts scenes from the biblical story of Judith and Holofernes. Besides the tapered columns paneled with scales and winged cherub heads in the spandrels, mannerist elements include rosettes and medallions on the shoulders and neck band of this 13-inch drinking vessel. C. 1610–20. (National Park Service.) (d) Body fragments of a Westerwald stoneware panel jug discarded at Jamestown c. 1650–60. Busts and strapwork shields of the Seven Electors of the Holy Roman Empire appear in an arcaded frieze supported on mannerist tapered columns with lobed baluster capitals. The smaller sherd depicts the "Römisher Kaiser." Identical jugs in other collections are dated 1602 and 1603. (National Park Service.) (e) Table knife handle of brass and black and white cloisonné enamel found at Jamestown in a context that indicates that the knife remained in use to the middle of the eighteenth century. Probably Dutch, c. 1650. (National Park Service.) (f) Brass fruit knife handle with cloisonné decoration in green, black, white, and blue enamel. Excavated at Kingsmill Tenement, James City County, Virginia, a farmstead belonging to tenants or servants of Richard Kingsmill, a resident of Jamestown. Principal occupation 1625–50. English or Dutch, c. 1575–1650. (Virginia Historic Landmarks Commission.) The similar floral festoon and strapwork decoration on handles of different shapes shows how ingeniously mannerist designers adapted standard motifs to meet customer demand for overloaded ornament. (g) Brass cover to a pair of snuffer scissors (originally tinned to resemble silver) from Causey's Care, Charles City County, Virginia. The snuffer may have been owned by gentleman Walter Aston as early as the 1620s, eventually passing into the possession of his lower-status son, who used it until his death in 1665. A well modeled and finely cast head of Mercury makes the centerpiece of a sophisticated composition incorporating a lion mask, two elongated human figures, and a profile Roman head in medallion. Germany, Holland, or Belgium, late sixteenth century. (Virginia Historic Landmarks Commission.) Faces, figures, and animal heads—realistic, mythical, and grotesque—appear on these and other objects in the mannerist idiom. While the convention and even many motifs can be traced directly to the high-style sources that inspired serious mannerist artists and decorators, the run-away popularity of the style with lower-brow consumers must have owed much to its affinity to the age-old anthropomorphic character of animistic folk art. (Drawings, Nancy Kurtz)

pitchers emblazoned with fantastical human masks and spotted with the usual mannerist bumps and bosses—all these treasures were brought to America by first- and second-generation colonists (figs. 6–8). They tell archaeologists what historians only guess at from later probate inventory references to such tantalizing curiosities as "one painted Dish," a "Chaney [China] saltcellar," "Holand juggs," "portingale [Portugal] ware," and a "white cupp with a silver tip" that belonged to one of John Weld's Roxbury relatives. These were not everyday utensils. They were showpieces. One Virginia inventory described the location of "two glasses and whyte Earthen Ware"; they were displayed on the planter-owner's "Cupboardshead," the cupboard itself being a "Court Cupboard with Drawers" worth a whopping £5.[122] Sherds and inventories bring us to the same conclusion. Up-to-the-minute status symbols were present in American homes from the very beginning and were treasured for years thereafter. Furthermore, they were the same covered drinking cups, standing salts, knives and spoons, platters, chargers, drug jars, and assorted freakish knicknacks that had customarily set peasant tables and garnished their cupboards going back a long, long time. In short, there were already status symbols aplenty in the colonies, enough, it would seem, to satisfy even the ambitious social climbers whose success by the second half of the seventeenth century propelled them far above their less fortunate neighbors.

How very curious, then, that they wanted more. How inexplicable is the sudden appearance of so many new and different household goods in the middle decades of the seventeenth century if their insatiable buyers only sought to acquire things that signified their superior ability to spend with abandon. Those things already existed. They were still the height of fashion. The demand for more things, different things—*many more and different things*—must therefore be owing to something besides social competition. Inescapably the search for an explanation of consumer behavior comes down to understanding how a whole host of new inventions

[122]York County Deeds, Orders, and Wills, 3, inventory (1657) of Gyles Mode, a planter and physician, p. 23.

574

equipped their owners and users to meet social needs and solve social problems that had arisen more or less recently. Demand has seldom been satisfied merely by ownership or possession. Ultimately historians must ask specifically what new housewares were "needed" and acquired, and specifically how they altered age-old habits and household routines.

To list all the furniture forms and ceramic- and glass-vessel types that were created brand-new or entered mainstream popular culture between approximately 1650 and 1750 is to demonstrate with astonishing clarity precisely when the modern domestic environment was born. These are pieces of furniture and tablewares that have been taken so much for granted by those who could afford them since the eighteenth century that a house without them mocks the very meaning of the word *furnished*.

Among the earliest inventions it is worthy of note that many were accessories to people's dressing activities and toilet preparations. That is hardly surprising considering that the human body, when it came to clothing, had long been treated like a medieval cupboard, a bare frame to be draped and adorned before it reflected the glory of him or her to whom the face belonged. Faces became the ultimate insignia of the possessive individual consumer. They bore endless looking at and looking after. Among the new furniture forms that appear in inventories of 1660–90 are *chamber tables* and *dressing boxes*, both accessories to the serious work of self-beautification.[123] The one was less a table than a chest raised on a frame, the container too small to store textiles and the legs too tall to use conveniently except while standing. Furniture historians believe that chamber tables held the innumerable "basons and ewers" that are listed in inventories and were used for washing hands and face. They may also have

[123]The following discussion takes its facts from Forman, "Furniture for Dressing," pp. 149–60. Closely parallel developments in English upper-class circles are summarized in Edward T. Joy, *Getting Dressed* (London, 1981), pp. 8–27. The earliest English publication devoted exclusively to cosmetics was *Beauties Treasury; or, The Ladies Vade Mecum* (London, 1705). Recipes for facial preparations had been included in numerous cookbooks since the 1660s.

Figure 7. Containers for new beverages enjoyed by sociable colonists. (a) Chinese porcelain wine cup from an unprovinced site at Kingsmill, Virginia. Others exactly like it have been found at several very early sites along the James River, including the Maine on the Governor's Land (1618–25), Wolstenholme Town (1620–22), and Causey's Care (1620s). Identical Wan Li export wares were also salvaged from two Dutch East Indiamen, the Witte Leeuw, shipwrecked in 1613, and the Banda, which sank two years later. C. 1610–40. (National Park Service.) (b) Sgraffito-ware drinking cup was a top-of-the-line version of many otherwise undecorated earthenware cups used to serve imported wine at Jamestown tables. This and other brightly colored North Devon slipwares, stored in service rooms in structure 112, were destroyed in a fire c. 1676. (National Park Service.) (c) Stem from a lead crystal goblet showing English glassmakers' modifications to a German form known as a roemer. English consumers were told in 1662 that roemers were specifically intended for "Rhenish wine, for Sake, Claret, Beer." This one found its way into a fine Jamestown rowhouse (structure 17) before it was broken about 1720. C. 1680–90. (National Park Service.) (d) Early lead crystal wineglass from the household goods of Lt. Gov. Francis Nicholson, whose house

g   h

i

0 INCHES   3

in the up-and-coming capital city of Williamsburg burned c. 1705–
10 or a little later. The baluster stem, raised foot, and small bowl gave
new delicacy and elegance to the wine and punch parties where such
glasses were used. English, c. 1690–1710. (Colonial Williamsburg
Foundation.) (e) Chinese porcelain teabowl probably used at Jamestown structure 19, one of the largest and best taverns serving the capital c. 1665–1700. C. 1645–65. (National Park Service.) (f) Blue-
and-white faience drinking cup with two handles, known as an "ear'd
coffee" in London in 1699. This one was traded to Seneca Indians
and recovered from one of their village sites in western New York.
Dutch, c. 1665–80. (Rochester Museum and Science Center; drawing, Patricia Miller.) (g) Tin-glaze drinking cup with one handle, for
coffee, cappuccine, or maybe chocolate. Presumably one of a set, this
very fashionable drinking vessel belonged to John Brush, a social-
climbing Williamsburg artisan, as early as the 1710s. Brush's china
closet contained other specialized drink wares as well, including (h)
tin-glaze teabowls—a step down from porcelain, but still very smart—
and (i) a delftware punch bowl. All his blue-and-white beverage vessels were English-made and imported soon after 1700. They were broken and discarded by c. 1717–27. (Colonial Williamsburg
Foundation; drawings, Nancy Kurtz, except as noted)

577

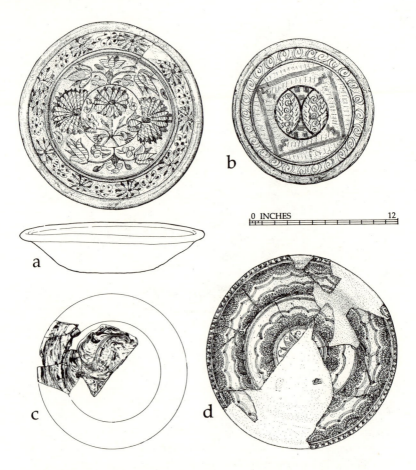

Figure 8. Imported serving dishes used to set Virginia tables. (a–b)
*North-Devon sgraffito-decorated slipware dishes discarded c. 1695 on
the site of gentleman Henry Harwood's house at Jamestown (structure
86). C. 1640–70. (National Park Service.)* (c) *Italian marbleized
slipware dish (possibly Pisa), excavated at Newport News, resembles
sherds from William Harwood's farmstead at Martin's Hundred, occupied c. 1625–50. (Knowles Collection, Colonial Williamsburg
Foundation.)* (d) *Blue-and-white, tin-glaze, earthenware dish, probably Portuguese, excavated at Jamestown near the site of a small dwelling or workshop (structure 21) occupied in the last quarter of the
seventeenth century. C. 1670. (National Park Service; drawings,
Nancy Kurtz)*

been a place to put away the handsome new *barber bowls* that were available by the 1680s.[124]

Dressing boxes, sometimes worth as much as £5, were divided up inside into tiny compartments for the cosmetics, powders, and unguents needed to improve on nature. Sometimes they were fitted with a "Myrour" under the lid to assist the user in performing the kind of close-up facial renovations that old-fashioned country people had little time or use for.[125] Dressing boxes first appear in New England inventories in the 1670s among the belongings of Bostonians, men as often as women, significantly. Well-off Philadelphians had them by the last quarter of the century. Frequently the trendsetters were sea captains, mariners, and merchants, the very men whose affairs were advanced not so much by a familiar honest face as a fashionably pretty one. Just outside Boston in Roxbury, on the other hand, the one and only dressing box in John Weld's village belonged to the neighborhood's one and only gentleman, a man of considerable estate and, judging from his "Goods in the House," no stranger to high living.[126] These containers for cosmetics, combs, and brushes were usually placed on top of another piece of furniture low enough to permit the user to sit before the glass. The term *dressing table* was not used in Boston inventories until the year 1700 and then in reference to a table so modestly valued that it seems likely that stands for dressing boxes were undecorated at first. Instead they were draped with a piece of cloth called by the borrowed French term *toilet*, which the English defined as "a Kind of Table-Cloth, or Carpet, made of fine Linnen,

[124]The earliest dated delftware barber bowl is 1681 (Lipski and Archer, *Dated English Delftware*, p. 295).

[125]To earlier generations grooming meant shaving and beard trimming for men and haircuts for both sexes, but seldom the application of facial cosmetics. Early inventories are likely to list looking glasses in association with razors, scissors, combs, and wash bowls, the whole kit occasionally described as a "barbers case with some instruments and a small looking glasse to it." See York County Deeds, Orders, Wills, 3, inventories of Hugh Stanford (1657), John Goslings (1658), Thomas Bucke (1659), and John Heyward (1661), pp. 23–24, 69, 135.

[126]Cummings, *Rural Household Inventories*, pp. 54–57, inventory of John Bowles (1691).

Sattin, Velvet, or Tissue, spread upon a Table in a Bed-Chamber, where Persons of Quality dress themselves; a Dressing-cloth."[127] Sure enough, "twilights" show up in probated New England estates in 1711 and a "table & twilight" by 1718, once again in each case the property of a cosmopolitan Bostonian with connections abroad. Dressing furniture reached maturity with the appearance of "twilight tables" in the 1720s, progenitors of the long line of *toilet tables* that continues to the present day.

A companion piece to the dressing table and another commonplace furniture form with an unusual history in this period was the *chest of drawers*.[128] It was destined to become the principal storage container for clothing and other textiles in fashionable Anglo-American households in the second half of the seventeenth century. In so doing, it sent the long-lived family of chests, trunks, and coffers into permanent retirement in the attic after centuries of loyal service.[129] Extra and unseasonable wearing apparel had previously been stowed away inside chests underneath yardgoods, table linens, or whatever else was piled on top. Chests were hard to use. A person had to crouch alongside them or paw through their contents from a stooped position overhead. But their immense popularity testifies that such inconveniences had long been tolerable to men and women who changed their clothes infrequently by later standards and, when they did, were accustomed to hang idle garments on pegs rather than fold them and lay them away flat. Chests and trunks best stored stuff that was seldom needed. Yet their poor design for daily use only became an inconvenience when people began wearing clothes made from thinner, lighter, linen and cotton materials and when advancing fashion required a greater assortment of such garments. In England urban aristocrats and rural gentlemen with plenty of houseroom to spare could

[127] Quoted in Forman, "Furniture for Dressing," p. 158.

[128] For most of what follows, see Forman, "The Chest of Drawers," pp. 1–17.

[129] No chests are listed in rural Suffolk County, Massachusetts, garrets or cellars until after 1700, then with increasing frequency throughout the eighteenth century (Ward et al., *A Place for Everything*, p. 6).

accommodate the towering clothes presses that joiners began building about 1625 and were fitting with sliding shelves and drawers by midcentury. The lower, smaller chest of drawers was preferred by wealthy middle-class town dwellers who valued compactness and yet desired the convenience of drawer storage for the seasonable clothing they were putting on and off more frequently. Chests of drawers appeared almost simultaneously in London and New England in the late 1630s and 1640s. The earliest documented American pieces came over, the evidence suggests, in the baggage of immigrants from the metropolis. London-quality pieces were made in Boston and sold at London prices to the leading commercial families of that town by the third quarter of the century. Farther south in Maryland and Virginia they first show up in inventories in the 1660s.[130] Thereafter chests of drawers, the expensive kind as well as plainer, cheaper models, became steady sellers for town and country joiners throughout the colonies. Some conservative buyers initially combined old habits and new in a hybrid form, an old-fashioned lid-top chest with drawers underneath, but by 1760 drawer storage had become the norm almost without exception among middling householders of English descent even in the countryside.

What was stored in a chest of drawers depended on its location. In a hall it was likely to hold textiles for laying a table or making a bed. "Cases," or slipcovers, for sets of upholstered dining chairs were put away in drawers out of season in one fashionable Boston hall as early as 1658, a reminder that the proliferation of new furniture forms was partly its own spur to greater storage needs. Despite the variety of uses to which chests of drawers were put, their invention and spread were principally a response to people's growing attention to their personal appearance. When these new case pieces stood in

[130]Testamentary Proceedings, 3:127–59, Maryland State Archives, Annapolis, inventory of Capt. William Smith (1668). Smith, though a wealthy innkeeper, leased a residence formerly owned by the governor of the colony. York County Deeds, Orders, Wills, 4 (1665–68), inventories of Adam Miles (1668) and John Hubberd (1667), pp. 212–13, 230. Hubberd was a merchant and Miles may have dabbled in trade. Both chests of drawers were valued at £1 10s.

chambers or parlors, the drawers were crammed with fresh linens, assorted seasonal garments, and ribbons, buttons, jewelry, and other accessories.

By the 1690s fine ladies and gentlemen were coming to regard a chest of drawers as an important component in a set of dressing furniture that included the table, box, and occasionally even *stands* on which they placed pots and basins for convenience or candles to shed light full face on their toilet preparations.[131] Sometimes *looking glasses* came en suite too. The small, hand-held mirrors of earlier times were superseded in fashionable circles by larger glasses. After 1660 they were often fitted with rings to hang them on the wall or struts to stand them on a table top, thereby providing fastidious users with a still reflection and giving beauticians use of both hands. Upright rectangular looking glasses joined the kit of dressing chamber paraphernalia as English mirror glass manufacturers (holding patents since 1663) found ways just before 1700 to elongate the squarish face glass into a three-quarter-length living portrait of face and figure fashionably united. Never before in human history had people seen themselves "from top to toe," as one delighted English woman described the first experience of seeing her reflection at full length.[132]

Silvered reflections and painted "effigies" were the quintessential expression of the personal identity that men and women concocted with the things they kept in drawers and dressing boxes to create the artificial self-images that they then saw mirrored back at them from looking glasses in the parlor chamber and from oil canvases on the parlor wall. *Painted portraits* were yet another new addition to the furnishings of prosperous American homes in the second half of the seventeenth century.[133] As such they appropriated and do-

---

[131] *Wash basins* developed wide rims to prevent water damage to the wooden stands they stood on or fit into. The earliest dated example of an improved wash basin in delftware is 1680 (Lipski and Archer, *Dated English Delftware*, p. 297).

[132] Christopher Morris, ed., *The Journeys of Celia Fiennes* (London, 1949), p. 154. She was visiting Chippenham Park, Cambridgeshire, in 1698.

[133] Jonathan L. Fairbanks, "Portrait Painting in Seventeenth-Century

mesticated a category of artifacts that earlier ages had reserved for church and state officials and others of great estate.
Painters and limners (miniaturists) worked in the prevailing
mannerist idiom. Mannerist art theory held that the purpose
of "pikture-making" was to "record and perpetuate the Effigies of Famous Men."[134] That justification was widely accepted by Americans in the seventeenth century, a point that
Samuel Sewell was making when he recorded in his diary in
1685 that "Govr. Bradstreet's Effigies [are] hung up in his best
Room."[135] The earliest pictures painted abroad and imported
into the colonies were often portraits of religious leaders and
civilian officials, like the "Judge Richardson to the wast in a
picture" inventoried in 1660 among the possessions of a Virginia planter who appears to have been no relation to the
judge.[136] Soon the likenesses of unexceptional householders
were added to the gallery of famous men. For the living, portraits advertised an individual's place in society. Men often
held gloves, canes, books, documents, and other recognized
badges of office; gentlewomen posed with fans, Bibles, and

Boston: Its History, Methods, and Materials," in Fairbanks and Trent, eds.,
New England Begins, 3:413–79; E. P. Richardson, *Painting in America* (New
York, 1956), pp. 23–29.

[134] John Elsum, *The Art of Painting after the Italian Manner* (London, 1704),
p. 9.

[135] Quoted in Fairbanks, "Portrait Painting in Boston," pp. 413, 421.

[136] York County Deeds, Orders, Wills, 3, inventory (1660) of Lt. Col.
Thomas Ludlowe, p.108. Among the earliest surviving paintings are those
of John Winthrop (English portrait and miniature imported 1631), Puritan
divine Dr. William Ames (Dutch portrait imported by his widow 1637), Gov.
Pieter Stuyvesant (several family portraits painted in Breda and imported
to New Amsterdam 1647), Gov. Edward Winslow (portrait painted on a
return visit to London in 1651), and the Rev. Increase Mather (portrait by
a Dutch painter working in London for whom Mather sat on a trip to England in 1688) (see Fairbanks and Trent, eds., *New England Begins*, 1:10–13,
2:157–58, 304–6, 3:413–15, 455; Richardson, *Painting in America*, p. 25).
Wayne Craven dates the earliest locally painted portraits in Virginia to the
1690s in *Colonial American Portraiture: The Economic, Religious, Social, Cultural,
Philosophical, Scientific, and Aesthetic Foundations* (Cambridge, Mass., 1986),
pp. 178–95. See also Richard H. Saunders, "The Portrait in America, 1700–
1750," in Richard H. Saunders and Ellen G. Miles, *American Colonial Portraits, 1700–1776* (Washington, D.C., 1987), pp. 1–27.

bouquets of flowers. Not a few portraits spelled out the sub-ject's name or initials or inserted the family's crest so that viewers could not fail to be duly impressed. After death, por-traits honored the memory of the sitter and celebrated the family's genealogy no less than funerary monuments immor-talized its reputation in the churchyard. The medium lived on to enjoy even greater popularity in the baroque-style por-traiture introduced into the colonies after the turn of the cen-tury by John Smibert, Peter Pelham, Gustavus Hesselius, and Charles Bridges.[137] Their mastery of the Italian chiaroscuro technique of modeling light and shade relied less on explicit signs and symbols to indicate social standing. Instead it re-vealed the inner refinements of a genteel character through an integrated composition of costume, carriage, and com-plexion. By the 1730s or so the portrait habit had been thor-oughly ingrained. Painted faces conferred respectability on their subjects by proxy. Framed portraits bore witness to the good taste and well-deserved reputations of those whose walls they adorned.

It is not inaccurate to see in this related group of seven-teenth-century household artifacts associated with the activi-ties of dressing, grooming, and imagemaking a continuation of a venerable and nearly universal preoccupation with self-adornment as an individual's most explicit expression of so-cial eminence. There was little new in that. It can even be argued that the mannerist ornament that embellished these otherwise utilitarian objects merely corrupted classical motifs into a superficial decorator style whose separate elements imi-tated in baser materials the rare gems and precious baubles that had always encrusted sacred and ceremonial objects, in-cluding the sumptuous garments that men and women of great estate had long bespangled with ruffles, jewels, and fili-gree. The ambition was an old one—to look the part.

Notwithstanding, there is also something new and different to be observed in these pieces of dressing furniture, articles of clothing, cosmetics, and artificial likenesses. First, it was all

[137] Fairbanks and Trent, eds., *New England Begins*, 3:420–21; Richardson, *Painting in America*, pp. 30–48; Graham Hood, *Charles Bridges and William Dering: Two Virginia Painters, 1735–1750* (Williamsburg, 1978).

equipment necessary to achieve a calculated effect. The results—fresh-smelling clothes, a pretty face, a fashionable figure—were unattainable without the gear. Its use required
learned skills and careful practice. Of course that much may
be said about tools of any kind. The difference worth noting
is the sheer number of new tools invented or popularized in
the second half of the seventeenth century to perform basic
everyday chores. Washing, dressing, and making oneself presentable all reached new heights of elaboration and refinement by 1700. Second, it should not be overlooked that the
act of using the new equipment, the preparations themselves,
assumed an importance it had never had before in bourgeois
circles. The rich ornament and fine workmanship lavished on
lowly toilet kits and storage boxes are one indication. So are
the many popular depictions of ladies and gentlemen ensconced in their dressing chambers and busy at their toilet
seen in prints, performed in comedies, and described in light
literature of the period. Such scenes illustrate one final observation to be drawn from examination of dressing furniture
and corroborated by probate inventories. The equipment
needed for dressing and grooming was increasingly regarded
as a suite of furnishings to be encountered in a specific place
within the house. Inventory takers in Boston began using the
verbal formula "chest of drawers, table, and dressing box"
with great frequency after 1690. By the 1710s they confirm
what we see with our own eyes in museum collections, that
separate pieces in these sets were made to match: one chest
of drawers of "black walnut, 1 table . . . , 1 black frame looking
glass, . . . [and] 2 Black sconces" all worth £14 in 1711 or the
"black Japand [gilded gesso] Chest of Drawers £2:10:00; ditto
Table and dressing boxes, £1:5:00" that belonged to another
Bostonian in 1716.[138] Albeit these were objects intended for
personal use and the storage of personal possessions, they
nevertheless joined a growing list of domestic goods that genteel householders everywhere regarded as pieces belonging
to sets that users could expect to find in public rooms reserved for the activities in which they assisted. It was another
step in the process of converting the many folkways that had

[138] Forman, "Furniture for Dressing," pp. 159–60.

governed people's private ablutions and informal dressing habits into a standardized system of polite public behavior. Where fashion could coerce a man at his washstand, there was no telling how it would refurnish the rooms of his house where he displayed all his resplendence to neighbors and strangers.

These numerous self-centered artifacts, however prosaic and traditional their uses, are important to understand the argument about geographical mobility advanced in the fifth proposition. All contributed to overhauling and standardizing people's personal appearance. No longer was it enough to be expensively dressed. To cut a respectable figure abroad or to command respect at home from those with experience abroad it was increasingly necessary to dress according to an acknowledged formula. Gentility put on a uniform; it wore a stock expression; it prescribed universal good manners. Drawers and dressing boxes contained the essential costumes and makeup. Mirrors imaged rehearsals. Prints popularized role models, and portraits immortalized successful performers. Bedchambers became actors' and actresses' dressing rooms, and parlors and public spaces the stages on which they appeared.

All these preparations culminated in formal performances that began now to reshape fundamentally the daily routines of quite ordinary people. Burghers and a few country gentlemen were usually first, but others followed soon enough. These were social events by definition, occasions when men and women consorted together in activities that, whatever their ostensible purposes, served deep down to reaffirm and regulate the established social order. Communities everywhere have always practiced such observances, be they traditional societies or modern. Sometimes the sorting mechanisms take the form of ceremonies and rituals, other times contests. The social behavior that fashion-conscious ladies and gentlemen began to exhibit in the seventeenth century is more accurately understood as performance than as ritual, because it involved real win-or-lose tests of social skills, not merely the repetition of symbolic formulas. If the performer met the prevailing standard of behavior in the judgment of peers, he or she was entitled to their company however slightly acquainted they may have been beforehand. The occasions when such formalities were observed were frequently events that brought together people from outside the immediate family. They could be friends, neighbors, or business associates. Often they were complete strangers. Because such displays of hospitality had traditionally involved the sharing of food and drink, it is not surprising that the earliest genteel performances took place at table and radically altered the design of furniture and utensils used at mealtimes. Fashion found many other venues as the eighteenth century progressed, and it attached itself to many other artifacts later employed in these additional genteel pursuits. But our search in this essay for the origins of consumer demand in the half century before 1700 requires that we look no further than that already familiar fashion center in early American homes, the formal parlor. Its furniture and other equipment used to seat, serve, feed, and entertain a householder's family and guests numbered among the earliest mass-produced consumer goods that can be called genuine inventions.

Even John Weld of Roxbury owned one such novelty despite his conservative taste. His *glass case* was an object utterly unknown to earlier generations. The form has recently been identified as a small case piece used to store drinking glasses, galley pots, and other refined table garnitures, which, when not in use, were exhibited behind an open grillwork of turned spindles.[139] The whole contraption was set up prominently on a cupboard or table top. It probably contained the English, German, Dutch, or possibly Venetian-made beer and wine-glasses that archaeologists commonly find on colonial sites of the period 1670–85.[140] Had Weld lived a few years longer, he might have added to its contents the sturdy, less expensive, lead crystal *drinking glasses* perfected by English glassmakers after 1675 and widely marketed in the American colonies by the 1690s.[141] Their design, not just their affordability, re-

[139] Identified in Fairbanks and Trent, eds., *New England Begins,* 2:279–80, and discussed p. 377.

[140] Noël Hume, *Guide to Artifacts,* pp. 184–92.

[141] G. Bernard Hughes, *English, Scottish, and Irish Table Glass: From the Sixteenth Century to 1820* (London, 1956), pp. 41–59. The origins of the lead-

sponded to changing tastes in table manners. The earlier style
table glasses, while usually delicate, were often studded with
prunts or ringed with trailed-glass bands applied partly as
decoration in the mannerist idiom and partly to give users
a hefty grip. The newer wines supported the bowl on an
inverted baluster stem raised on a generous spreading foot
(fig. 7). Not only were they intentionally one-handed vessels,
they were designed to be elegantly held by pinching either
the stem or the foot between the thumb and forefingers, as
depicted in many prints and paintings of the period.[142] That
left the other hand completely free to engage in the practiced
gestures that accompanied genteel conversations, which were
the real substance of the dinner table performance. Two-fisted
drinkers, as imbibers from old-fashioned fuddle cups and
puzzle jugs had often been, were looked upon askance by
those cognizant of refined dining etiquette. A tobacco inspector in Virginia, for instance, a guest at Robert Carter's table
in 1774, was dismissed as "Dull" and "unacquainted with
company" when, drinking his host's health, "he held the Glass
of Porter fast with both his Hands, and then gave an insignificant nod to each one at the Table, in hast, & with fear, &
then drank like an Ox." In civilized company thirst quench-
ing took second place to observing the proper forms, so that
"the Good Inspector" was further faulted for being "better
pleased with the Liquor than with the manner in which he
was at this Time obliged to use it."[143] Such offenses against the
rules of table had become embarrassing in gentry circles by
the third quarter of the eighteenth century.

A hundred years earlier the nabobs themselves were only
half initiated to the arts and artifacts of formal dining. When

crystal industry in England have recently received renewed attention, summarized in Christine MacLeod, "Accident or Design? George Ravencroft's
Patent and the Invention of Lead-Crystal Glass," *Technology and Culture* 28
(1987):776–803. For table glass used in Virginia see Ivor Noël Hume, *Glass
in Colonial Williamsburg's Archaeological Collections* (Williamsburg, 1969), pp.
9–28.

[142] Both techniques are shown, for example, in Kneller's portrait of the
duke of Newcastle (c. 1718) illustrated in Hughes, *Table Glass*, fig. 32.

[143] Farish, ed., *Journal and Letters of Fithian*, p. 138.

William Fitzhugh ordered from England a fabulous assortment of silver tablewares in 1688, his reasons recalled the values of an old-fashioned hoarder: "I esteem it as well politic as reputable, to furnish my self with an handsom Cupboard of plate which gives my self the present use & Credit, [and] is a sure friend at a dead lift without much loss, or is a certain portion for a Child after my decease."[144] His order included a single three-quart tankard, no doubt to be prominently displayed on the cupboard when the ham-fisted grandee was not wielding it himself. Otherwise his expensive new table service included all the necessary place settings for a company of fashionable diners. There were knives, forks, and spoons for twelve and a dozen plates to match. A "small silver basin" may have been the same "Monteeth Bason" later recorded in Fitzhugh's will. *Monteiths* were a type of deep container said to have been invented in the year 1683.[145] Fitzhugh's must have been one of the earliest in the colonies. They were used to rinse and chill stemmed wineglasses between courses, which servants then refilled and returned to their respective users on a *salver* (Fitzhugh called his a "Salvator plate"). Salvers were another novel utensil described in 1661 as "a new fashioned peece of wrought plate . . . used in giving Beer or other liquid thing, to save the [table] Carpit and Cloathes from drops."[146] Here again special equipment was desired to prevent the spills and spots that stained reputations more indelibly than clothes. Fitzhugh rounded out his new table service with a pair of candlesticks, a set of sugar, pepper, and mustard casters, and four serving dishes, including two "pretty large" ones "for a good joint of meat," a clear indication that these were wares sufficient to lay a formal table in two or three

[144]Richard Beale Davis, ed., *William Fitzhugh and His Chesapeake World, 1676–1701: The Fitzhugh Letters and Other Documents* (Chapel Hill, N. C., 1963), pp. 244–46, 249–50, 258–59, 382.

[145]Thornton, *Seventeenth-Century Interior Decoration*, p. 391 n. 13. He describes the use of monteiths on p. 284.

[146]Thomas Blount, *Glossographia; A Dictionary, Interpreting All . . . Words . . . Now Used in Our Refined English Tongue*, 2d ed. (London, 1661), s.v. "Salver." A recipe for "Taking Spots and Stains Out of Garments, Linnen, etc." was important enough to include in *The Family Dictionary; or, Household Companion*, published in London in 1695.

courses.[147] The likes of that had seldom been seen in the colonies. No wonder he instructed his purchasing agent to have "W F S & [my] coat of Arms put upon all pieces that are proper, especially the Dishes, plates, and Tankards, etc."

In their different ways Fitzhugh's invoice and Weld's inventory catch the march of table fashions at half stride. Neither the Virginia grandee nor the New England farmer had set aside all his old assumptions about tablewares and the order of company at mealtimes. Yet the one had acquired many tablewares and the other one or two that anticipated the idea that diners at the same table, although not necessarily equal in rank, were a miniature meritocracy based on each person's knowledge and practice of good manners.

Fashionable dining arbitrated even the shape of *oval tables*. Always tables had been four-sided before, square or rectangular, large or small, but always four corners had marked the metes and bounds between the head, the foot, and the two sides in between. Each was a distinct social territory. Protocol placed the most important male diner at the head or top of the table, usually located at one of the ends, but sometimes midway along one side. His dependents took their places to the right and left in descending order of precedence according to gender, estate, age, and servility. Hence William Cobbett's recollection of days gone by when a typical English farmer used "to sit at the head of the oak table along with his men, say grace to them, and cut up the meat and the pudding."[148] Wives (according to prints and paintings showing upper-class dining scenes) appear to have sat next to their husbands at the head of the table or, alternatively, opposite at the foot. It is harder to say where custom assigned seats to more ordinary housewives, if indeed their traditional duties as cooks and servers gave them leisure to sit at all at mealtimes.[149]

[147]Mark R. Wenger sets Fitzhugh's table in "The Dining Room in Early Virginia," in Carter and Herman, eds., *Perspectives in Architecture, III*, pp. 149–59, although he draws somewhat different conclusions from mine.

[148]Cobbett, *Rural Rides*, p. 192.

[149]Despite much recent interest in culinary history, nothing authoritative has been written about common people's table customs before the eigh-

The advent of fashionable dining changed everything, not least of all the shape of four-sided tables. They became round or oval. Tables without corners made a closed circle of men and women whose shared commitment to the arts of civility outweighed any real differences in their rank. Master and mistress were replaced by host and hostess, and so thorough was the revolution in manners that husbands and wives actually traded places. The meat carving and soup ladling duties were reassigned to the hostess, who was ensconced in the place of honor. The host, seated at the foot, was responsible for the guests' "entertainment," that is, the company's exchange of pleasantries.[150] That, too, was said to happen more easily at round tables. "It is the custom here in England," wrote a knowledgeable housekeeper in 1758, "to eat off square or long Tables; the French in general eat on round or oval," thus giving them "vastly the advantage in the disposing and placing their Entertainment." Companions seated in a circle enjoyed greater informality, what the housekeeper called "this French fashion of perfect ease."[151]

Although many a staunch Englishman was happier square than French, the Gallic-inspired oblong tables with hinged or "falling" leaves had in fact captured the fancy of some English noblemen as early as the 1630s and 1640s.[152] Their space-saving convenience and showy stylishness had recommended

teenth century. The best one can do is work backwards from such statements as Alice Smith's in the *Art of Cookery; or, The Compleat-Housewife* (London, 1758), that "in the old way, when there was but a tolerably large company, it was almost impossible the Mistress of the house should taste a bit of any thing" because she was so busy waiting on others. If such was true for gentlewomen when they entertained guests, a hypothesis worth testing might hold that serving at table was a gender-specific chore expected of all classes of women.

[150]"The John Trot Fault: An English Dinner Table in the 1750s," *Petits Propos Culinaires* 15 (1983): 55–59; [John Trusler], *The Honours of the Table; or, Rules for Behaviour during Meals* (Dublin, 1791), pp. 4–5. I am grateful to Patricia A. Gibbs for these obscure but illuminating references.

[151]Smith, *Art of Cookery*. The convenience of round tables is discussed in Thornton, *Seventeenth-Century Interior Decoration*, p. 226.

[152]Thornton, *Seventeenth-Century Interior Decoration*, pp. 378 n. 10, 391 n. 6.

them to cosmopolitan London merchants by the 1650s and 1660s. Americans were no laggards either. Maryland merchant Thomas Cornwaleys owned a splendid round table by 1645, almost as early as anyone in England. "One Ovall table with bolt & catches" for the gate legs and leaves numbered among other expensive and fashionable furnishings in a Virginia hall in 1667. Another one valued at a staggering £3 10s. furnished the first true "dyning Roome" owned by a great Boston merchant in 1669.[153] A generation later the use of such tables, often specified as walnut, was no longer confined to the colonies' advanced tastemakers. Rounded tables became increasingly commonplace in gentlemen's houses over the next half century.[154]

Mealtime performances required *matching dining chairs* whether the table was oval or not. These too made their first appearance in American parlors in the second half of the seventeenth century. Socially differentiated seating furniture had been one way that precedence-minded diners had known their place around old-fashioned tables. Where chairs had been scarce, usually they were reserved for the householder himself, sometimes his wife, and on occasion honored guests. Children, servants, hired hands, and other social inferiors had often sat on stools, forms, benches, and makeshift chests and boxes, or might even have stood. In New England where inexpensive turned chairs had been almost as common as stools in England, the "chair-man's" seat of authority was frequently distinguished by arms or "elbows," needlework cushions, extra turnings, or decorative carving. Few, however,

---

[153] P.R.O., Court of Chancery: Thomas Cornwaleys vs. Richard Ingle, examination of Cuthbert Fenwick, Oct. 20, 1646, C24 690/14. The very fine table, standing in the parlor, was worth £3. York County Deeds, Orders, Wills, 4, inventory (1667) of Mathew Hubberd, a planter, pp. 330–35. His neighbor, Maj. Joseph Croshaw, another large planter, owned the other earliest oval table in 1668 and a round one as well (ibid., p. 190). Robert F. Trent, *Historic Furnishings Report: Saugus Iron Works National Historic Site* (Harpers Ferry, W.Va., 1982), pp. 33, 46, 60–61.

[154] As early as 1710 on the Eastern Shore of Maryland, for example (Somerset County Court Records, EB 14/365, Md. State Arch., inventory of Col. Francis Jenkins), or as late as 1745 in conservative Suffolk County, Massachusetts (Cummings, *Rural Household Inventories*, p. 130).

rivaled the imposing "wainscot great chairs" that furniture historians have discovered were owned exclusively by a small number of country gentlemen, merchants, and divines.[155]

This ancient seating plan was subverted by the invention of the *upholstered back-stool* about 1615.[156] Literally joint stools with stuffed seats and backrests, they gained great popularity simultaneously in London and Boston in the 1640s and elsewhere in the ensuing half century.[157] In Virginia "Chair stooles" were owned early enough to have worn out by the 1670s, and yet some still considered them "new Fashion" in Maryland as late as 1710.[158] Three features recommended their use in polite society. Their sometimes lower height, armless sides, and open back were a convenience especially to women who wore fashionable farthingale skirts; indeed the French term for them translated as "farthingale chair." Second, they usually came en suite, often in sets of six or a dozen. An additional single matching "elbow chair" conferred the traditional chairman's symbolic authority on a host or hostess, but otherwise each diner was shown to an individual and identical seat. The third feature, their coordinated upholstery, reinforced this impression of sameness and, not coincidentally, conferred on the whole assembled company the superior status long attached to rich textiles. A covering of expensive-looking fabric, trimmed with fringe and garnished with brass nails, literally clothed the new furniture form in a familiar status symbol of great antiquity. Dining chairs upholstered in Russia leather and woven turkeywork (the former were imported from London to Boston by the late 1640s and the latter by 1654) are a historian's clue that back stools were not intended for the whole universe of trenchermen who had

[155] Forman, *American Seating Furniture,* pp. 84–88, 145–46.

[156] Thornton, *Seventeenth-Century Interior Decoration,* pp. 185–92; idem, "Back-Stools and Chaises à Demoiselles," *Connoisseur* 185 (1974):99–105.

[157] Forman, *American Seating Furniture,* pp. 195–213.

[158] York County Deeds, Orders, Wills, 8 (1687–91), inventory of Josias Moody (1676), pp. 37–38; Somerset County Court Records, EB 14/365, inventory (1710) of Col. Francis Jenkins. Moody, a planter, was called a "Gentleman"; Jenkins was a very wealthy merchant and shipowner.

formerly bellied up to supper tables set round with communal benches and assorted stools without backs. Matching sets of dining chairs were reserved for the new breed of parlor users. They were the colonies' most prominent citizens at first, men like the councillors for whom the governor of New Amsterdam ordered from Holland in 1660 "8 Spanish chairs for the gentlemen," adding parenthetically that "at present we use only pine benches."[159] By 1700 numerous references to "Rushy leather" and "Turkie workt" chairs in American inventories give ample proof that many middle-class colonists were importing a fair share of the "5000 dozen" such chairs that were said to be produced in England every year, not to mention those they bought from American joiners and upholsterers as early as 1662.[160]

Yet even before the popularity of turkeywork and leather chairs had peaked, artisans in London developed a line of high-backed *cane chairs* that were mass produced in such astonishing numbers and enjoyed such tremendous success in the marketplace that they revolutionized the furniture industry and made genteel dining affordable to large numbers of middling consumers on both sides of the Atlantic.[161] They also took an important step away from the medieval tradition of covering sturdy oak furniture with costly textiles. These chair frames were built either of walnut or other fine woods for the gentry or, less expensively, of beech stained brown or black in imitation of walnut and ebony. What their caned bottoms and backs lacked in splendor, they more than made up for (their makers explained in 1688) by "their Durableness, Lightness, and Cleanness from Dust, Worms and Moths, which inseparably attended Turkey-work, Serge, and other Stuff-Chairs and

[159]Quoted in Forman, *American Seating Furniture*, p. 197.

[160]R. W. Symonds, "Turkey Work, Beech, and Japanned Chairs," *Connoisseur* 93 (1934):221–27. Forman believes that the first immigrant upholsterer was at work in Boston by 1662.

[161]R. W. Symonds, "Charles II: Couches, Chairs, and Stools," pt. 1 (1660–70) and pt. 2 (1670–80), *Connoisseur* 93 (1934):15–23, 86–95; idem, "Cane Chairs of the Late 17th and Early 18th Centuries," *Connoisseur* 93 (1934):173–81; idem, "English Cane Chairs," pts. 1 and 2, *Connoisseur* 127 (1951):8–15, 83–91; Forman, *American Seating Furniture*, pp. 229–80.

Couches."[162] Here was clean modern furniture for the same persnickety people who turned up their noses at spotted tablecloths and ripe-smelling linens.

For everyday use it hardly mattered that cane chairs lacked coordinated upholstery, which sitters always covered up anyway. Sets of high-backed chairs had something better. Their identical carved crest rails towered above the tallest users in unobscured affirmation of every diner's equal right to occupy one piece in the set. Crested chair frames communicated other subliminal messages as well. We have already noted the resemblance between picture frames and looking glasses of the period. Similarly, many late seventeenth-century mirrors were surmounted by fretted crests that reappeared in almost identical form atop high-backed chairs. Thus the correspondence was complete from model to rehearsal to performance. Ebonized high-backed chairs enframed a person's fashionable face and figure in the same image that he or she had composed it earlier at the dressing table and could further study its idealized form in the prints and portraits that lined the parlor walls. En suite meant more than chairs by the dozen or rooms decorated with color-coordinated curtains, upholstery fabrics, and paintwork. More fundamentally, en suite was a state of mind made manifest in a pervasive and unified aesthetic and a corresponding system of artificial good manners.

Cane chairs date and document very precisely the spread of those manners to mass markets throughout the English-speaking world. The first ones were made in London in 1664. Their popularity caught hold in provincial England and in the colonies in the early 1680s. By 1688 it was said that they were "much used in England, and sent to all parts of the World"; specifically "above Two thousand Dozens [were] yearly Transported into almost all the Hot Parts of the World" where upholstered furniture fared poorly.[163] Immigrant metropolitan chair-frame makers had set up shop in Boston by 1690 and Philadelphia by 1700. Less than ten years later Boston's craftsmen were supplying a huge export market

[162] Company of Joyners petition, quoted in Forman, *American Seating Furniture*, p. 238.

[163] Quoted in Symonds, "English Cane Chairs," pp. 13–14.

throughout New England, New York, and farther south with a cheaper, leather-covered, high-backed chair in a "plain" turned style that sold six times faster than the carved variety.[164] The demand for them was so great that chairmakers could not manufacture them "so fast as they were bespoke."[165]

The customers for such sets of new chairs and the parties that gathered round the new walnut tables sat down to meals that were not mere "yeoman's fare." That was the term applied to the one-course menu of boiled meat, beans, or porridge, plus bread, cheese, and beer or milk, that traditionally had given "solid sufficiency" to the Englishman's midday meal.[166] Polite dining produced a more *elaborate cuisine* eaten with tools and following rules designed to sort out the initiated from the uninitiated. True dining, it was said, "was a thing lately sprung up" in Elizabethan times when "pampering of the belly began to take hold, occasioned by idleness and great abundance of riches."[167] One-course meals yielded to two, three, and more, each with several standing dishes. Cooks and guests alike increasingly needed special instruction not only to prepare but even to recognize the "variety of many severall Dishes, that in the former Service were neglected"— that, in the not-so-humble opinion of the first English cookery book writer (1609) to set himself up as a culinary arbiter of "the Name and Kindes of all ["Meates and Drinks" lately] disputed of."[168] *Cookbooks* published in England in the sixteenth century had been few and mostly medicinal. Starting in the 1590s recipes began to rival remedies. For the first time housewives were introduced to "proper Sauces" (1591), the "newest fashion of cutting up any Fowle" (1617), and "the or-

---

[164]Forman, *American Seating Furniture*, pp. 281–356.

[165]Quoted ibid., p. 283.

[166]Anderson, "'Solid Sufficiency,'" pp. 234–73.

[167]Harrison, *Description of England*, pp. 142, 144. Barbara Ketcham Wheaton, *Savoring the Past: The French Kitchen and Table from 1300 to 1789* (Philadelphia, 1983), chap. 6, dates the rise of French cuisine "governed by accepted rules" to the middle of the seventeenth century.

[168]W. E. Esquire, *The Philosophers Banquet . . .* (London, 1614), title page. There is no known copy of the first edition.

derly serving [of meat and fish dishes] to the Table" (1594).[169] One little book addressed to "all ladies and gentlewomen and others whatsoever" was the first English publication (1621) to contain engraved diagrams illustrating the preferred placement of sweets on the table.[170] By 1653 such hostess lore had become "very necessary for all Ladies and Gentlewomen," a social obligation in which cookbook writers and their printers were eager to assist.[171] Forty-six new titles and many reprints appeared in the second half of the seventeenth century (compared to sixteen in the first), and ten more were issued by 1710 before the numbers dwindled again.[172] One ingenious English publisher sold *The Genteel House-Keepers' Pastime* (1693) with "a pack of Playing Cards," which an inexperienced hostess could keep in her pocket to sneak a look at when she set the table or carved the roast.[173] A few English cookbooks found their way into American kitchens before the end of the century. Already by 1705 it was observed that the Virginia "Gentry pretend to have their Victuals drest, and serv'd up as Nicely, as at the best Tables in London."[174] The prescriptive cookbook literature neatly brackets the freshman years of this new Epicurean age.

New foods begot a bewildering array of new tablewares. Traditional "country fare" had usually been served in wooden bowls and trenchers before the sixteenth century. Thereafter, improving standards of living and rising expectations had set

---

[169]Arnold Whitaker Oxford, *English Cookery Books to the Year 1850* (1913; reprint ed., London, 1977), pp. 9–10, 17.

[170]John Murrell, *A Delightful Daily Exercise for Ladies and Gentlewomen* (London, 1621), preface.

[171]W. J., Gent., *A True Gentlewomans Delight . . .* (London, 1653), title page.

[172]Oxford, *English Cookery Books*. These should be regarded as minimums. Other titles have been located since 1913.

[173]*The Genteel House-Keeper's Pastime* (London, 1693), title page.

[174]Robert Beverley, *The History and Present State of Virginia* (1705), ed. Louis B. Wright (Chapel Hill, N.C., 1947), p. 291; Louise Conway Belden, *The Festive Tradition: Table Decoration and Desserts in America, 1650–1900* (New York, 1983), p. 97.

many farmers' tables with pewter and earthenware as well.[175] Still and all, eating and drinking vessels had been as few as need be and strictly utilitarian—bowls and deep dishes for everyday stews and pottages, a few plates and platters for roasted meats, and sundry jugs, bottles, tankards, and flagons to pass around home-brewed beverages. Cutlery had been confined to horn and base-metal spoons and to pointed knives for cutting and spearing. Hands and fingers substituted for nonexistent forks. When meat was eaten, for example, a person displaying good table manners had anchored it to the bowl or plate with one hand while cutting it into pieces with a knife held in the other. Napkins cleaned up sticky fingers afterwards. Such customs prevailed universally at polite American tables. Inventories routinely record piles of napkins and motley assortments of wood, pewter, tin, and pottery hollow wares. What later struck Dr. Alexander Hamilton as "a picture of that primitive simplicity practiced by our forefathers" (he had just witnessed a ferrykeeper and his family eating their unsauced vittles from "a dirty, deep, wooden dish which they evacuated with their hands, cramming down skins, scales, and all") had not so many years before been the unremarkable custom of all diners.[176]

Those were the days (Hamilton concluded) before "the mechanic arts" had supplied men like him "with instruments for the luxury and elegance of life." Such eating tools accompanied the multiple-course meals that first appeared on fashionable dining tables after about 1650. Flatwares (that is, plates and platters) begin showing up on American archaeological sites in greater proportion to hollow ware bowls and deep dishes after the 1670s.[177] Culinary historians are still learning

---

[175]The best account of ordinary table furnishings in Tudor and Stuart England is Anderson, "'Solid Sufficiency,'" pp. 236–40; Gerard Brett, *Dinner Is Served: A Study in Manners* (London, 1969), presents an admirably concise assessment of the alterations in tablewares brought about by changing table customs after 1600. For later American practice, see Jane Carson, *Colonial Virginia Cookery* (Williamsburg, 1968), pp. 6–13; Helen Sprackling, *Customs of Table Top: How New England Housewives Set Out Their Tables* (Sturbridge, Mass., 1958).

[176]Bridenbaugh, ed., *Gentleman's Progress*, p. 8.

how such tablewares were arranged and how those arrangements assisted in the observance of the new table proprieties.
A table setting for a "variety of messes" must certainly have
required more numerous *large serving dishes* like the two for
"a good joint of meat" that William Fitzhugh ordered in silver
in 1688 or like the colorful sgraffito-decorated dishes made
in North Devon, traded by the hundredweight to Ireland and
North America, and excavated at Jamestown and other Virginia and Maryland sites in contexts seldom earlier than 1675
(fig. 8). Fancy serving dishes found their way onto American
tables from potteries in Germany, Holland, Italy, Spain, and
Portugal, including a matched pair of lobed dishes found in
the ruins of Capt. Thomas Pettus's plantation house along the
James.[178] Many platters were pewter. "Three large pewter
dishes marked on the outside with W" set Virginia planter
Richard Watkins's table in the 1660s, along with five "middling dishes" and another small one, all in pewter and all
proudly monogrammed with his initial.[179]

[177]Deetz, "Ceramics from Plymouth," pp. 28–29; Brown, "Ceramics from
Plymouth," p. 56; Kelso, *Kingsmill Plantations*, pp. 177–79; Fraser Neiman,
The "Manner House" before Stratford: Discovering the Clifts Plantation (Stratford,
Va., 1980), pp. 36–47; Anne Yentsch, "Minimum Vessel Lists as Evidence
of Change in Folk and Courtly Traditions of Food Use," *Historical Archaeol-
ogy* 24 (1990): 24–53.

[178]Alison Grant, *North Devon Pottery: The Seventeenth Century* (Exeter,
1983), pp. 114–30; Linda Blanchard, ed., *Archaeology in Barnstable, 1987–88*
(Barnstable, n.d.); Watkins, *North Devon Pottery*, for the archaeological dat-
ing evidence, pp. 34–41; Miller, *Search for "Saint Maries*," pp. 87, 97–98.
Sgraffito-ware appears somewhat earlier on the site of Maryland's capital
and earlier by fifty years—before 1622—at Wolstenholme Town along the
James River, but the bulk of excavated sherds in the Chesapeake date from
the fourth quarter of the century. See also Leslie B. Grigsby, *English Slip-
Decorated Earthenware at Williamsburg* (Williamsburg, 1993), pp. 28–37. New
England archaeologists have excavated sgraffito-decorated ware on a Plymouth Colony site occupied c. 1635–50 (see Deetz, "Ceramics from Plymouth," pp. 24–25). Pettus's "valuable Chinese porcelain and matched
dinnerware sets" are briefly mentioned in Kelso, *Kingsmill Plantations*, p.
178, and the marbleized tin-glazed earthenware is illustrated in Kelso,
"1973 Interim Report on the Excavations at Kingsmill Plantation," Virginia
Historic Landmarks Commission (Richmond, 1974), plate 3.

[179]York County Deeds, Orders, Wills, 4, p. 323. A hundred years later
pewter still set many fashionable tables despite the availability of fine china.
See Ann Smart Martin, "The Role of Pewter as Missing Artifact: Consumer

Hostesses who followed the cookery books that came with "Pictures curiously Ingraven displaying the whole Arts" of table setting were instructed to place such platters symmetrically in the middle of the table. They might elevate the centerpiece above the lesser dishes on a *dish ring* like the one a Virginian ordered from London in 1728, describing it as "a fashionable ring to set a dish upon in the middle of the table." Less fancy "wicker rings to set under dishes" were used to display cooks' handiwork as early as 1677 in Massachusetts and by 1668 in Virginia. Everywhere their purpose was "to make the feast look full and noble."[180] The savories, sauces, and sweetmeats that accompanied the main dishes were served in accessory bowls, dishes, and porringers. All these were old standbys. Now they were joined by newly invented *sugar boxes* (earliest American reference 1638), *fruit dishes* (1667), *covered mustard pots* (1674), and even *sauce boats,* which potters were supplying in affordable delftware by the 1660s (fig. 9).[181]

An acquired taste for imported wine and a genius for concocting other beverages and palliatives using wine as an ingredient set artisans to experimenting with many special-purpose drinking vessels. The earliest were sometimes made in silver for the custom trade, but were soon copied in pewter and earthenware for broader markets. Among them delftware and slip-decorated ceramic beverage containers are uniquely

Attitudes toward Tablewares in Late 18th-Century Virginia," *Historical Archaeology* 23 (1989):1–27.

[180] Belden, *Festive Tradition,* pp. 41–45; York County Deeds, Orders, Wills, 4, inventory (1668) of Maj. Joseph Croshaw, pp. 190–91. He had "weeker rings for dishes seaven," equipment to mount a splendid meal.

[181] Giles Rose, *A Perfect School of Instructions for the Officers of the Mouth* (London, 1682), title page; Albert S. Roe and Robert F. Trent, "Robert Sanderson and the Founding of the Boston Silversmiths' Trade," in Fairbanks and Trent, ed., *New England Begins,* 3:481–82; Edward J. Nygren, "Edward Winslow's Sugar Boxes: Colonial Echoes of Courtly Love," *Yale University Art Gallery Bulletin* 33 (1971):39–52; York County Deeds, Orders, Wills, 4, inventory (1667) of Edward Lockey (occupation uncertain, but related by blood and marriage to London shopkeepers and merchants), pp. 191–92; Lipski and Archer, *Dated English Delftware,* p. 235. If no. 1036 was not intended for sauce, it certainly appears to be a container for some other table delicacy.

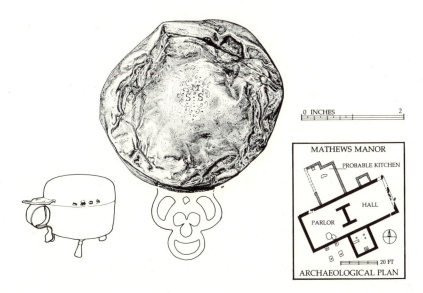

MATHEWS MANOR

PROBABLE KITCHEN

HALL

PARLOR

20 FT

ARCHAEOLOGICAL PLAN

Figure 9. Silver skillet or saucepan lid, hallmarked London 1638, excavated at Mathews Manor, Denbigh, Virginia, in a c. 1650 context. The pounced initials SSM stand for Capt. Samuel Mathews and his second wife, a daughter of English nobleman Sir Thomas Hinton. Mathews was a planter-trader who earned a reputation in Virginia as a "most deserving common-wealthsman" before his final return to England in 1652. Utensils such as these—another one was described in a wealthy Plymouth Colony merchant's inventory (1674) as a "skillett with a siluer porring dish [porringer] as a Couer to it"—were just beginning to bring new refinements to English dining tables in the 1630s. Candied fruits, sugared nuts, and other sweetmeats, which cooks prepared over kitchen fires in long-handled "ladle skillets" (also known as "stew pans" or "sauce pans"), must then have been transferred to these smaller covered skillets intended for table use. Their short legs kept them standing upright on a warm hearth until they were carried to the table and served to the guests, who not only were meant to savor their contents, but also to appreciate the precious metal containers and the engraved ornament that embellishes many surviving specimens. The wonder is that such dainties were being cooked in Mathews's kitchen and served in this fashionable skillet in his dining parlor (inset) almost as soon as such utensils graced London tables. There is a simple explanation. Mathews was sent back to England to stand trial for treason in 1637. The charges eventually were dropped, and he returned to Virginia two years later, but not before he acquired a second wife, a silver skillet, and a cultivated sweet tooth. (L. B. Weber Collection, Colonial Williamsburg Foundation; drawing, Nancy Kurtz)

instructive to historians because numerous dated specimens record the onset of new vessel types and the periods of their greatest popularity while archaeological sherds verify their use on American sites. The roster starts with tin-glazed earthenware *posset pots,* first dated 1631 and much in vogue from 1650 to about 1710. *Caudle cups,* the earliest inscribed 1646, drove delftware tankards off the market from approximately 1650 to 1680 during the same period when sgraffito-ware wine cups appeared on gentry tables in Jamestown (fig. 7). The tin-glazed caudle cups were more or less abruptly superseded in turn by *punch bowls,* which began their long reign around 1681 (the earliest dated delftware example) as accessories first to Venetian-style wineglasses and then to improved lead crystal stemwares after about 1690.[182] Common to all the new cups and glasses was their small size. These were individualized drinking containers, a world removed from the belching great bottles and flagons that had formerly passed from grip to grip.[183]

Tablewares in matching sets signified each diner's provisional membership in the dinner table company. At the same time they provided each individual with the personal tools that he or she needed to demonstrate the polite skills that validated claims to gentility. The kit evolved from the middle decades of the seventeenth century to include individualized dinner plates and drinking vessels and eventually forks as well as knives and spoons. One of the greatest merchant-planters of Maryland owned a whole "Boxe of Purslayn China dishes [and] two Boxes of drinkinge glasses" within the first decade of that colony's settlement.[184] *Matched plates* in sets of dozens

[182]Lipski and Archer, *Dated English Delftware,* pp. 156–218, 235–306; Watkins, *North Devon Pottery,* figs. 12, 14.

[183]More than one American archaeologist has observed an "increase in the absolute numbers of ceramic drinking vessels" on sites occupied during the first quarter through the first half of the eighteenth century (Deetz, "Ceramics from Plymouth," p. 29). Teacups account for many of them. Probably so does the trend toward individualized food serving, although that correlation is harder to demonstrate. See Kelso, *Kingsmill Plantations,* pp. 178–79 n. 27 and fig. 124; Neiman, *The "Manner House,"* pp. 36–40.

[184]P.R.O., Chancery, Cornwaleys vs. Ingle, C24 690/14. The earliest por-

and half dozens were also sold in pewter and earthenware at more reasonable prices. The earliest delftware set is dated 1661. An inscription painted on each identical plate advertises the host's reputation for civility (and by implication acknowledges his guests' ability to read if not spell) in the greeting "Weilcom my Freinds.[185] Here was the forerunner of "company china." Pewter plates inventoried in multiples of twelve hint at the appearance of flatware sets on a few affluent gentry tables in Virginia as early as 1659. Matched tin-glazed dishes were used in the capital of Maryland before 1668 if "several peeces of blew Earthen ware" were in fact dinner plates.[186] Like the dozen silver plates that came with Fitzhugh's dinner service, plates in sets were intended as accessories to the new cuisine. Sometimes that connection had to be spelled out. One inscribed set of dinner plates dated 1712 (and still "speaking" in the first-person voice of folk pottery) gave untutored users explicit versified instructions, "On me to Eat Both sauce & meat."[187]

New-style *cutlery* presented novices with other daunting challenges. The test was not simply which fork to lift first, but how to use a table fork at all. Bluffing was difficult without going hungry, because just when forks were introduced into wider social circles in the third quarter of the seventeenth century, table knives were redesigned with blunt points. Not by accident was it no longer possible to bayonet pieces of food with the same tool used to cut them up. The new-model forks and knives found their way onto American tables very slowly

---

celain tablewares recovered on James River sites are wine cups dating from the first quarter of the seventeenth century. Enormous quantities of utilitarian tea bowls and dinnerwares were imported at the end of the century and in evermore standardized forms after 1712. See Julia B. Curtis, "Perceptions of an Artifact: Chinese Porcelain in Colonial Tidewater Virginia," in Mary C. Beaudry, ed., *Documentary Archaeology in the New World* (Cambridge, 1989), pp. 20–31.

[185] Lipski and Archer, *Dated English Delftware*, p. 43.

[186] York County Deeds, Orders, Wills, 3, inventory (1659) of William White, a clerk, p. 60; Md. State Arch., Testamentary Proc., 3:127–59, inventory of Capt. William Smith, a wealthy innkeeper.

[187] Lipski and Archer, *Dated English Delftware*, p. 72.

before the 1690s, but after that their popularity paralleled the cane chair's.[188]

Archaeologists and curators can now furnish quite accurately this seventeenth-century parlor dining scene that I have described at considerable length. Likewise, costume historians can dress authentically a fashionable company of men and women diners, and culinary historians can spread their table with a reconstructed banquet of cookbook foods and imported beverages. By contrast, social historians still have much to learn about the event itself, the dinner table performance that became the earliest fully developed and most frequently practiced form of social interaction among genteel friends and acquaintances. Slow as that scholarship may be in coming, careful attention to the material evidence presented here supports two or three observations about fine dining, which shed light on the nature of consumer culture generally. First, fashion as always was inherently exclusionary, a point that almost every writer on the subject has been quick to make. Fewer have remarked on a second equally important quality, that fashionable living was also extraordinarily accessible, not just open to the obviously qualified, but almost evangelical in the enthusiasm with which proponents extended a helping hand to promising aspirants, however rigorously they enforced the initiation rites and upheld the rules of membership afterwards.

Both observations, and a third one as well, are superbly illustrated by the group of decorated tin-glazed tablewares that holds the all-time record for longest popularity. Seventy years separate the first dated specimen in 1682 from the last in 1752.[189] Curators and collectors call these dinnerwares

---

[188] In Fernand Braudel's often-cited discourse on the use of forks (*Structures of Everyday Life*, pp. 203–9), he makes the unsubstantiated claim that "there is no mention of table forks in any [English] inventory before 1660." Reaching the same conclusion, but with more evidence to show for it are G. Bernard Hughes, "Evolution of the Silver Table Fork," *Country Life*, Sept. 24, 1959, pp. 364–65, and Noël Hume, *Guide to Artifacts*, pp. 177–84. For evidence on American use see Carr and Walsh, "Changing Lifestyles and Consumer Behavior," tables 1–6, this volume, and Main and Main, "Economic Growth," table 5.

[189] Lipski and Archer, *Dated English Delftware*, pp. 52–126.

"Merryman plates," because the set of six is always inscribed with a rhyme that poses the question What is a merry man? and proceeds line by line and plate by plate to instruct a would-be host "To entertain his Guests / With wine and merry Jests" (fig. 10). Was such fun-loving crockery actually used at formal tables? Each piece in the series is always conspicuously numbered "1" through "6," probably to assist illiterate servants—increasingly a class apart—to set the plates around the table in the correct sequence. Why? Perhaps so that the educated guests could recite the verses aloud as one of their "merry Jests" in an evening's entertainment. No one knows for certain. But in that robust age when sophisticated tastes and refined table manners were still newly learned from cookbooks, crib cards, and instructions painted on the dinnerwares themselves, it was not unheard of for a Merryman and his tipsy friends to backslide into their former state of bucolic revelry. The last two plates in the series warned him and them that on those occasions that "if his wife Do frown," then "All merryment Goes Down." The verse takes a tiresome dig at scolding wives, but in fact the real butt of the joke was the relapsed Merryman whose spouse was no mere party pooper but a new-model hostess performing her appointed duties. Less than a hundred years after Shakespeare rued that "It was never merrie worlde in England since Gentlemen came up," wives too had assumed no small share of responsibility for policing the dinner table, a portent of bigger things to come. Frowning Mrs. Merryman demonstrates the point about accessibility. Women had been beneficiaries of their father's or husband's status in the Middle Ages, legally and socially. The rise of a consumer culture gave them access to a little social status that they earned themselves.[190]

The years between the first and last Merryman plates, 1682 and 1752, encompass the time period in which I have set about in this essay to pull together scattered evidence from a variety of sometimes unlikely sources to create a picture of material life that is recognizably the forerunner of the fashionableness about which so much was being said and written later in the eighteenth century. I have paid very close at-

---

[190]This story will be told in Carson and Walsh, "Material Life."

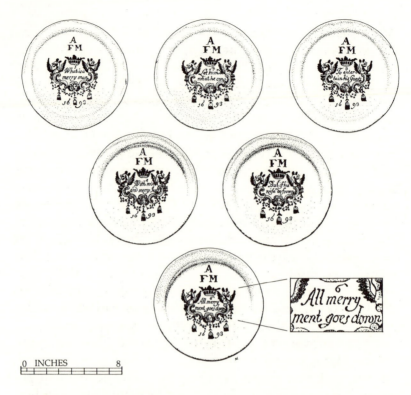

0 INCHES 8

Figure 10. Full set of six "Merryman plates," English tin-glaze earthenware, dated 1693, probably made and monogrammed for the Arbuthnott family of Scotland. Each plate is sequentially numbered above the verse. Few knife scratches in the glaze of these and similar plates in the Winterthur Museum and Colonial Williamsburg collections strengthen the suggestion that such wares were intended only for occasional use at table, and, then, perhaps as the fruit plates that are often pictured in Dutch genre paintings. Merryman plates seldom have holes in the footrings common to decorative plates hung up for display. (Delhom Collection, Mint Museum of Art, Charlotte, N.C.; drawing, Nancy Kurtz)

tention to the earliest dated appearance of newfangled housewares and foodstuffs as authenticated by documents, stratified archaeological assemblages, and the hallmarks and dates affixed to artifacts in museum collections. That evidence shows conclusively that the seventeenth century was a time of lively innovation. A trickle of new products in the 1630s, 1640s, and 1650s became a steady stream after the Restoration and swelled into a torrent by 1720. As we told ourselves when we began this long cross-examination of the artifactual record, timing is one crucial factor in substantiating the central proposition of this essay. Consumer behavior was an evolving form of social interaction resorted to by people whom events had scattered far beyond their birthplaces or, alternatively, homebodies who nevertheless regularly consorted with strangers. Historians have never before demonstrated that the invention and introduction of standardized, fashion-bearing consumer goods coincided very closely with accelerated, short-distance, inland movement among the professional classes and landed gentry in England after 1660 and increased long-distance migration to the colonies by a new breed of post-Restoration entrepreneurs. Careful attention to dated artifacts confirms that correlation.

Inception is one way to apply the time factor. Pace is the other. How rapidly did fashionable living penetrate to lower levels in English and American society? Two other variables used to test my hypothesis bear on this second measure of timing, namely, class and place.[191] The speed of spreading consumer demand varied appreciably from town to country and from class to class as defined by wealth and occupation. Therefore, wherever possible my account of genteel consumption in the seventeenth century has identified tastemakers and fashion centers as well as new inventions. London, Boston, New York, and early Philadelphia have recurred again and again in reference to cities and towns at the forefront of the new bourgeois taste. So have tiny Jamestown, scraggly St. Mary's City, Maryland, and even a few rural coun-

[191] On this point historians who are happiest when history-writing tips its hat to systems theory should see O. A. Spratt, "The Analysis of Innovative Processes," *Journal of Archaeological Sciences* 9 (1982):79–94.

ties on the lower Virginia peninsula where a consistently profitable sweet-scented tobacco was grown. Their prominence, along with the much larger northern seaports, seems surprising until one remembers that all these places were home to the same class of wealthy merchants for whom the Navigation Acts opened an empire to commercial exploitation. For the thesis advanced in my fifth proposition to hold water, it has to be shown that consumer goods answered needs that these men felt first and foremost.

Great merchants were travelers and townspeople by definition. They did business with others like themselves. Their success served as a cultural model for their lesser neighbors no less displaced. Townspeople were rootless people, never more so than the citizens of the boomtowns that sprang up in North America.[192] Far more so than most countryfolk, urban dwellers needed a universal and portable system of social communications simply to signal to others who they were and to recognize birds of the same feather. Townspeople were therefore especially eager to learn the rules and acquire the goods that made the new system work.[193] Where they settled

[192] Not unexpectedly, American towns and cities continued in the eighteenth century to collect immigrants in proportionally larger concentrations than did rural populations. See Gary B. Nash, *The Urban Crucible: Social Change, Political Consciousness, and the Origins of the American Revolution* (Cambridge, Mass., 1979), pp. 103–11. It is perhaps a little surprising that even in such small towns as Williamsburg, foreign-born residents still accounted for almost half the population as late as 1770, by then four times the number of immigrants to be found in the countryside outside the town. See Lorena S. Walsh, "York County Urban and Rural Residents Compared," in "Urbanization in the Tidewater South, Part II: The Growth and Development of Williamsburg and Yorktown," final York County Project report to the National Endowment for the Humanities, grant no. RO-20869-85, 1989, pp. 12–13.

[193] Fisher, "Development of London"; E. A. Wrigley, "A Simple Model of London's Importance in Changing English Society and Economy, 1650–1750," *Past and Present* 37 (1967):44–70; Weatherhill, *Consumer Behaviour and Material Culture*, pp. 70–90; Peter Borsay, "The English Urban Renaissance: The Development of Provincial Urban Culture, c. 1680–1760," *Social History* 5 (1977):581–603; Peter Clark and Paul Slack, *English Towns in Transition, 1500–1700* (Oxford, 1976), pp. 141–57; Penelope J. Corfield, *The Impact of English Towns, 1700–1800* (Oxford, 1982); Susan Mackiewicz, "Philadelphia Flourishing: The Material World of Philadelphians, 1682–

densely, their patronage attracted and sustained communities of luxury craftsmen, traders and retailers, and suppliers of genteel services. Townspeople developed a distinctive lifestyle. At first it was not shared even with those nearby country gentlemen who were rich enough to join them, but, having less occasion for polite intercourse among their all-too-familiar neighbors, had less need for fancy clothes, toiletries, tablewares, dining and seating furniture, and later tea sets, gaming tables, and other pieces of specialized social equipment. Those were precisely the things that townspeople spent ever greater proportions of their noncapital wealth to acquire. Even artisans and tradesmen living in towns consumed luxuries that country gentlemen had little use for initially.[194]

1760," Ph.D. diss., University of Delaware, 1988; Main and Main, "Economic Growth," pp. 40–41; Lorena S. Walsh, "Urban Amenities and Rural Sufficiency: Living Standards and Consumer Behavior in the Colonial Chesapeake, 1643–1777," *Journal of Economic History* 43 (1983):109–17; specifically for Williamsburg and Yorktown, see Walsh, "York County Residents," pp. 1–20; and Carr and Walsh, "Changing Lifestyles and Consumer Behavior," tables 5–6; Kathleen Warden Manning, "Two Studies of North Carolina Material Culture in the Eighteenth Century," pt. 2, M.A. thesis, University of North Carolina at Greensboro, 1978. Ann Smart Martin, "'Fashionable Sugar Dishes, Latest Fashion Ware': The Creamware Revolution in the Eighteenth-Century Chesapeake," in Paul A. Shackle and Barbara J. Little, eds., *The Historic Chesapeake: Archaeological Contributions* (Washington, D.C., forthcoming), demonstrates from her study of storekeepers' records that urban consumers enjoyed a much larger selection of fashionable tea and tablewares than country buyers were offered. Her earlier work has shown that the contrast between Williamsburg and most York County consumers was still significant in 1815 (Ann Morgan Smart, "The Urban / Rural Dichotomy of Status Consumption: Tidewater Virginia, 1815," M.A. thesis, College of William and Mary, 1986).

[194]Lorna Weatherill (*Consumer Behaviour and Material Culture*, pp. 79–90) asks the right question—"Why should living in a town result in a greater likelihood of owning domestic goods?"—and she steers clear of the most commonly given wrong answer by correctly asserting that "there was more to individual consumption than social competition, fashion, and emulation." Yet her own explanation ultimately falls short of the mark too. It may be true that "material goods could compensate for some of the inconveniences of town life" and that overcrowding might cause urban dwellers "to look inwardly to the living space and make this as aesthetically pleasing and comforting as possible." But the proximity argument not only fails to explain consumption in places where crowding was not a problem; its empha-

When landed families finally succumbed to fashion, often their first destination was a county town or watering hole where they too could sample urban amenities for a whole social season and hobnob with other butterflies from round about.

In cases where trade and commerce took gentlemen to such town-forsaken ends of the earth as the Chesapeake colonies, many were careful to keep up not just appearances but imperial connections as well. The same Maryland and Virginia households in which we have already noted unusually early ownership of fashionable furnishings for grooming and dining were oftentimes also supplied with maps, charts, globes, clocks, secular books, portraits of the king and queen, and prints of London landmarks.[195] In other words, wherever the earliest new consumers were located, even on remote plantations, almost always they appear to have plugged themselves into commercial and cultural networks with links back to England and the metropolis. Over and over again the earliest documented users of dressing boxes and chests of drawers, for instance, or the first importers of refined tablewares have turned out to be town-dwelling merchants, sea captains, colonial officials, and various hangers-on, or in the rural South,

---

sis on goods that provided greater privacy (window curtains) and prettiness (pictures) ignores the more important social uses of most new consumer goods and the activities in which they assisted. Weatherill comes closer to a real explanation when she writes that people in towns "were liable to meet others and to learn about consumption and to have the opportunity to present themselves in a variety of different situations" (p. 89). Consumer goods appeared first and most frequently in the possession of citizens with the farthest-flung connections because town house parlors and dining rooms were the venues where such people exchanged their social credentials.

[195]The 1710 inventory of Col. Francis Jenkins of Somerset County, Maryland, provides one of the best examples. Jenkins owned sixteen maps, all presumably mounted, including "3 maps of the quarters of the World," "1 Map of the Celestial and Terestrial Globe," a London map, and another of Virginia. His walls also displayed "4 Small Draughts of Pauls Monument Exchange," "2 large heads of K Wm and Q Mary in frames," and four more unidentified "Heads." I am grateful to Paul Touart and Willie Graham for bringing this inventory to my attention and to Lorena S. Walsh for identifying Jenkins.

large planter-capitalists. In virtually every case, they were men and their wives who were entitled to a considerable reputation but were deprived of a landholder's traditional means of showing it.

Other immigrants, of course, also needed help to assimilate themselves socially into their New World homes. Why were so many not quicker to adopt the city dweller's shortcuts to respectability? Many simply could not afford goods that were still very expensive in the seventeenth century or the leisure time to learn and practice their use. For others old integrative channels still worked tolerably well.[196] Seventy percent of the farmers and rural artisans who settled in the Massachusetts Bay colony migrated in company with families, neighbors, or members of the same church. Former village elders in England often became town fathers in New England. The largest landowners in one place frequently were first in line to acquire comparable holdings in the next. The continuities between Old and New England must not be exaggerated, and, indeed, I will have something to say shortly about the discontinuities that were inherent in the American experience. Nevertheless, the fact remains that the agricultural communities that grew up in the northern colonies retained and observed many customary measures of status and reputation that helped countryfolk find a familiar niche. Similarly, the apprenticeship system gave immigrant artisans an immediately recognizable place in society with a master and shopmates to serve as a newcomer's ready-made social world. In another way, indentured servitude and even slavery, while hardly providing traditional channels of access to the social order, nevertheless assigned status to hundreds of thousands of unattached men and women who landed everywhere in North

[196] Few historians of this period have asked how immigrants were received, by whom, and what strategies they adopted to assimilate themselves into new communities. It is the missing chapter in David Cressy, *Coming Over: Migration and Communication between England and New England in the Seventeenth Century* (Cambridge, 1987). The most suggestive work is Peter Clark, "Migrants in the City: The Process of Social Adaptation in English Towns, 1500–1800," in Clark and Souden, eds., *Migration and Society*, pp. 267–91. Bailyn has something to say about the sale and distribution of servants and convicts in *Voyagers to the West*, pp. 324–52.

America but labored in the largest numbers in the southern colonies and on the islands.

As long as tried-and-true paths of access into unfamiliar social surroundings worked for most free migrants, the impetus to adopt the manners and trappings of gentility was mainly restricted to urban elites, the same class of trendsetters that figured prominently in our survey of dated artifacts. The problem was that those channels worked less and less well as the seventeenth century wore on, both here and at home. New arrivals in English towns and cities found fewer kin to lodge and look after them and fewer brides with family, friends, and position to bestow as dowry. Charities that once dispensed hospitality to strangers were swamped by the tide of vagrants that surged through the English provinces before 1640. In New England as well, the initial settlements were followed by innumerable dislocations and out-migrations as new towns hived off old ones, land-poor grandsons went searching for greener pastures, and individual wageworkers followed wherever opportunities beckoned. North America was seldom a one-stop final destination. "Wandering about," said one astonished English observer of Americans' peripatetic habits, "seems engrafted in their Nature."[197] Seen in the broader course of events, pulling up stakes and moving on in the New World were episodic events in the continuing resettlement of northern Europe.

The swelling volume of this ceaseless moving around in the colonies becomes just as important to the argument of this essay as the continued arrival of new immigrants, maybe even

[197]Clark, "Migrants in the City," pp. 269–76. Kin ties may again have smoothed the reception of urban newcomers in the eighteenth century as townspeople's living standards continued to rise. For internal migration in preindustrial England, see E. J. Buckatzch, "The Constancy of the Local Populations and Migration in England before 1800," *Population Studies* 5 (1951–52):62–69; Cornwall, "Evidence of Population Mobility," pp. 143–52; and more recent works cited in Clark, "Migration in England." A useful comparative study is W. R. Prest, "Stability and Change in Old and New England: Clayworth and Dedham," *Journal of Interdisciplinary History* 6 (1976):359–74. John Murray, earl of Dunmore, to the earl of Dartmouth, in Reuben G. Thwaites and Louise P. Kellogg, eds., *Documentary History of Dunmore's War, 1774* (Madison, Wis., 1905), pp. 368–95.

more so.[198] Turnover migration is the hardest of all population movement to track or measure. Historians' picture of it in the colonies, fractured though it is, nevertheless suggests that these perpetual pioneers were sufficiently numerous and some of them prosperous enough to have contributed significantly to the continued downward and outward spread of consumer culture even when the flow of overseas immigrants flattened out from 1650 to 1710.[199] The raw numbers can only be approximated, and then most reliably for those empty frontiers that were just filling up. Yet even informed guesswork hints at droves of old and new settlers who were forever on the lookout for better prospects: 1,000 homesteaders in the Albemarle region of North Carolina in 1660 became 10,000 by 1700. In just half that time the population of Penn-

[198] Especially when the population of mainland North America began to grow faster by natural increase than by immigration from abroad. Compare table H.3 in Galenson, *White Servitude,* pp. 216–17, and table 3 in J. Potter, "The Growth of Population in America, 1700–1860," in D. V. Glass and D. E. C. Eversley, eds., *Population in History: Essays in Historical Demography* (London, 1965), p. 642. Between 1710 and 1740 free white immigrants accounted for upwards of twelve percent of the population, but much less after the middle of the century.

[199] The complex subject and imperfect literature are deftly summarized by James P. P. Horn in an essay that examines a wider area than the title suggests: "Moving On in the New World: Migration and Out-Migration in the Seventeenth-Century Chesapeake," in Clark and Souden, eds., *Migration and Society,* pp. 172–212. The key regional studies include Daniel Scott Smith, "The Demographic History of Colonial New England," *Journal of Economic History* 32 (1972):165–83; T. H. Breen and Stephen Foster, "Moving to the New World: The Character of Early Massachusetts Immigration," *William and Mary Quarterly,* 3d ser. 30 (1973):189–222; Ralph J. Crandall, "New England's Second Great Migration: The First Three Generations of Settlement, 1630–1700," *New England Historical and Genealogical Register* 129 (1975):347–60; Douglas Lamar Jones, *Village and Seaport: Migration and Society in Eighteenth-Century Massachusetts* (Hanover, N.H., 1981), pp. 40–69, 103–13, and a useful bibliographic note, pp. 124–33; Lorena S. Walsh, "Staying Put or Getting Out: Findings for Charles County, Maryland, 1650–1720," *William and Mary Quarterly,* 3d ser. 44 (1987):89–103; Allan Kulikoff, *Tobacco and Slaves: The Development of Southern Cultures in the Chesapeake, 1680–1800* (Chapel Hill, N.C., 1986), pp. 76–77, 145–57, for eighteenth-century migration. See also idem, "Migration and Cultural Diffusion in Early America, 1600–1860: A Review Essay," *Historical Methods* 19 (1986):153–69.

sylvania jumped from 700 to 18,000.[200] Some of these were new arrivals. Others were drifters from the economically depressed Chesapeake colonies. Former servants and landless sharecroppers swelled the ranks of "Loose and vagrant persons, That have not any Settled Residence."[201] Like the miserable subsistence migrants who wandered through the English countryside before the Civil War, the "scumme and refuse of America" who tramped the roads in the decades before 1700 were indeed homeless, but also much too poor to spend their way to respectability by acquiring status-giving personal possessions.[202] Still they were free laborers, and work in the colonies was plentiful. Not a few got lucky eventually. In time some of them purchased the trifling "superfluities" that, modest though they were, often attracted unfavorable notice from those who condemned them as "altogether unsuitable to their poverty."[203] At the very least, able-bodied men and women in labor-scarce North America were always *potential* consumers.

Not all turnover migrants were poor. Small planters in Virginia moved whole families to the Eastern Shore of Maryland in the 1660s and 1670s and to Pennsylvania after 1680 where larger tracts of empty land could be had more cheaply in districts newly opened. Similarly, refugees from the earliest New England settlements began dispersing along the coast from Maine to Long Island and far into the interior almost from the moment of arrival in a settling-out process that never ceased in the generations that followed. Persistence rates, which measure the stability of stay-at-home populations, began to decline in New England towns in the 1730s from which they never recovered. While many movers came from the lower social ranks, they were joined by significant numbers of middle- and upper-class fortune seekers as well. Except for the longer distances everyone traveled in the colonies, these more substantial migrants resembled their counterparts in

[200] McCusker and Menard, *Economy of British America*, pp. 172, 203. Other new colonies grew even faster.

[201] W. P. Palmer, ed., *Calendar of Virginia State Papers*, 11 vols. (Richmond, 1875–93), 1:52.

[202] Cited in Horn, "Migration in the Chesapeake," p. 198.

[203] Cited in Trautman, "Dress in Massachusetts," p. 52.

Restoration England who changed addresses not so much from necessity as to improve their already favorable circumstances still further. Their optimism and readiness to act on their ambitions sometimes disposed these betterment movers to consider the advantages that might be gained by acquiring the consumer goods that could launch them into polite society. Often they brought along inherited capital or at least the labor to produce the capital needed to buy instant respectability to replace the reputations that their forefathers had earned the old-fashioned way in the towns and neighborhoods the younger generation left behind. Inventory studies of the upland counties they settled in central Massachusetts and Connecticut indicate that they made heavy investments in material goods once the hardships of homesteading were past, at the same time that the relative value of such assets was declining in the older settlements.[204]

To contemporaries blinkered by older ways of thinking, it surpassed understanding that people would voluntarily "abandon their friends and families and their ancient connections" to gamble on an unknown future.[205] "Emigration is a form of suicide," wrote one dismayed correspondent to a Bavarian newspaper, because, he said, "it separates a person from all that life gives except the material wants of simple animal existence."[206] He was right about the separation and, actually, he was not wrong in predicting that many of his emigrating countrymen would indeed lead impoverished, violent, animallike lives on the margins of North American civilization. What he could not appreciate from his Old World vantage point, even as late as 1816, was the prospect of some emigrants for doing better than that. Early nineteenth-century America had already become the proverbial "best poor man's country" where ordinary, hardworking men and

---

[204] Main and Main, "Economic Growth," pp. 37–39; Kevin M. Sweeney, "From Wilderness to Arcadian Vale: Material Life in the Connecticut River Valley, 1635–1760," in Ward and Hosley, eds., *The Great River,* pp. 17–27.

[205] Eddis, *Letters,* pp. 37–38.

[206] *Allgemeine Zeitung* (Augsburg), Dec. 9, 1816, trans. Marcus Lee Hansen, *The Atlantic Migration, 1607–1860* (1940; reprint ed., New York, 1961), p. 3.

women could satisfy a good deal more than simple material wants. By then inexpensive consumer goods and easygoing gentility were fast replacing severed ancient connections. They were cauterizing the wounds of separation. They were, in effect, the key to life after suicide.

The first signs of the consumer revolution appeared almost simultaneously among the freest-wheeling participants in the British and American economy in the latter half of the seventeenth century. Proving that was one reason to date precisely the earliest appearance of diagnostic consumer goods. Ownership of such things spread rapidly to other groups in provincial England and colonial America in the decades after 1690 as more and more people saw the social advantage to be gained by identifying closely with their goods. Evidence for that is everywhere scholars look. Furniture historians tell us that almost £5,000 worth of (mostly cane) chairs—more than "sixteen hundred dozen"—were shipped from England to mainland America between 1697 and 1704.[207] Zooarchaeologists find microscopic pollen grains in early privy pits showing that up-and-coming artisans were dining on the same broccoli, parsley, and other haute cusine vegetables in the 1720s that it was said gentlemen themselves had only "very lately tryed" ten years later.[208] Counting and cataloging ceramic sherds, archaeologists also report "a marked increase of fine imported wares" in the closing decades of the seventeenth century.[209]

[207]The figures exclude 1698. See R. W. Symonds, "The Export Trade of Furniture to Colonial America," *Burlington Magazine*, Nov. 1940, pp. 152–63.

[208]John Brush, a Williamsburg gunsmith worth a modest £90 when he died in 1727, ate well, but he or someone else in his household also suffered from whipworm and intestinal roundworm. Parasite eggs were abundant in the same latrine fill (Karl J. Reinhard, "Analysis of Latrine Soils from the Brush-Everard Site, Colonial Williamsburg, Virginia," unpublished report, 1989, Col. Williamsburg Found.). Gregory A. Stiverson and Patrick H. Butler, eds., "Virginia in 1732: The Travel Journal of William Hugh Grove," *Virginia Magazine of History and Biography* 85 (1977):34. It was said that the broccoli-eating gentlemen "at Their Tables have commonly 5 dishes or plates" (p. 29).

[209]Brown, "Ceramics from Plymouth," p. 45. Demonstrated in the con-

Most persuasive of all are the social historians who use a so-called amenities index to analyze probate inventories.[210] They can detect consumer goods in minuscule quantities—a table fork here or a teapot there—and then can add all the evidence together to reveal broad chronological trends, sorted according to regions, wealth groups, and town and country residence. There is no arguing with their conclusions. Among rural buyers, goods that indicate some degree of fashion consciousness began appearing in 10 percent or more of the poorer households (those estates valued at less than £100) by the 1720s and 1730s. That seems to be the moment that economists call the "takeoff point." At least one in ten wealthholders worth less than £49 (the poorest group) owned table forks by the 1730s; one in ten was drinking tea by the 1740s and 1750s; and his one-in-ten wife was setting the table with a few pieces of refined earthenware by midcentury in some localities and from the 1760s and 1770s in others. Generally speaking, the wealthier they were, the higher and sooner rural consumers score on the amenities index. Item by item they approach the consumption levels achieved earlier, faster, and more completely by townspeople and a few prominent country gentlemen. Quantitative historians who have developed this valuable indicator are quick to remind us that one in ten consumers still means nine of ten who were not. They also caution that mere possession of a table fork or a teacup is

----

text of a single, early eighteenth-century town in Ivor Noël Hume, *Pottery and Porcelain in Colonial Williamsburg's Archaeological Collections* (Williamsburg, 1969); also Julia B. Curtis, "Chinese Export Porcelain in Eighteenth-Century Tidewater Virginia," in John Yolton and Leslie Ellen Brown, eds., *Studies in Eighteenth-Century Culture* vol. 17 (East Lansing, Mich., 1987), pp. 119–44.

[210]Carr and Walsh, "Changing Lifestyles and Consumer Behavior"; Main, "Standard of Living in New England," table 7; and, for Britain, Weatherill, *Consumer Behaviour and Material Culture*, pp. 201–7. Unfortunately, English and American scholars have not used the same market basket of goods or employed the same social and economic categories to define wealth groups, thus making direct comparisons impossible. Nevertheless, Weatherill's tables 8.2, 8.3, and 8.4 show that yeomen and husbandmen in the countryside and most urban-dwelling artisans not engaged in the luxury trades were still making almost no use of forks, saucepans, fine china, or tewares by 1725, the last year for which she presents quantitative data.

617

never proof positive that the owner fully embraced or even fully understood etiquette-book culture. The woman who "drank the remains of [her] tea from the spout of the tea-pot, saying 'it tasted better so,'" would receive the same score for that amenity as Norborne Berkeley, baron de Botetourt, governor of Virginia and a renowned "man of parade," who doubtless gave smashing tea parties using his "2 red china teapots" set out on a "Scollop'd claw tea table" and served in "29 bleu & white tea cups & 64 saucers."[211] Such reminders aside, it is impossible to deny the essential truth of the quantifiers' bottom line, that "a rising standard of consumption was underway on both sides of the Atlantic" by 1770, bringing with it a lifestyle that "penetrated . . . all but perhaps the poorest levels of rural . . . society."[212]

The further conclusion does not logically follow, however, that these eager new consumers were inspired to ape their betters by nothing more than envy. Amenity scores tell us how far consumer behavior spread and how fast, but not how come. To answer that was the second reason I examined so exhaustively the activities and artifacts of grooming, dressing, image making, and formal dining in seventeenth-century American parlors. When historians take the trouble to trace modern consumer behavior back to its origins and use the evidence of artifacts to ask how fashionable living really worked for those engaged in it, their actions appear to require a more complicated historical explanation than one that merely makes consumption a footrace between gentlefolk and a pack of impertinent social climbers nipping at their heels. When the goods that consumers consumed are used to refurnish the intimate social spaces that their users once inhabited, the effect is to magnify genteel domestic activities to

[211]Mary Clavers, *A New Home—Who'll Follow! or, Glimpses of Western Life* (New York, 1850), p. 82, recalling what passed for gentility on the Michigan frontier twenty years earlier; *William and Mary Quarterly*, 1st ser. 22 (1914): 252; *An Inventory of the Contents of the Governor's Palace Taken after the Death of Lord Botetourt* (1770) (Williamsburg, 1981), p. 6. The governor's tea things were stored in a "Closet to the little Room."

[212]Carr and Walsh, "Changing Lifestyles and Consumer Behavior," Main and Main, "Economic Growth," p. 44.

a large enough scale to reveal their composition of separate elements, including instruction, preparation, rehearsal, performance, acclamation (or not), and acceptance (or rejection). Those components leave little doubt that there was more to a formalized lifestyle than can be adequately explained by what sociologists and anthropologists like to call "elite group boundary maintenance." As a regulator of social interaction, gentility worked better as a maze than a wall.

The interrelated parlor activities that I have anatomized one utensil at a time were enlarged upon and elaborated in the course of the eighteenth century until they ruled over a fashionable gentleman's entire house as completely as they ruled his whole life. Having now discovered their origins in the second half of the seventeenth century, I need comment further on the gentrification of American homes only so far as to demonstrate how fashionable living became an international code of behavior observed by many of the "middling sort" and eventually known and acknowledged by virtually everyone. Mere possession of enumerated amenities might indeed be mistaken for evidence of nothing more than status display and social emulation were it not so clear that consumer goods also served as an essential medium of social integration. That is something historians find easier to understand when they look beyond possession pure and simple and recognize that the *widespread prescribed use* of such goods was the thing that differentiated them from older status symbols and adapted them for their new role in a modern, interactive, visual communications system.

The rise of formal domestic living can be quickly summarized to highlight those features that met so well the needs of an international community of users. The architectural spaces that consumer goods turned into interchangeable social settings derived ultimately from French interior decoration developed in the salons of Paris after about 1625. There aristocratic designers had relaxed the stiff and formal architectural aesthetic of Renaissance Italy to create interiors that were practical and comfortable by the standards of the day while giving up nothing to elegance and grandeur.[213] They employed two devices to achieve their impressive effect. First, they organized the principal rooms in a house and the dominant pieces of furniture in those rooms in hierarchies of social importance. Second, they subordinated the decoration of public rooms to single harmonious schemes of coordinated colors, forms, and materials. Variations on those two principles have shaped the history of domestic art in the West ever since.

All we need note about the planning of Parisian town houses and noble palaces are those elements—much boiled down—that eventually influenced first English and then American taste, mostly by way of Holland before 1675. The salient features were the division of houses into state rooms and domestic apartments, their arrangement into suites of rooms in ascending order of importance and intimacy as one approached the owner's inner sanctum, the creation of specialized entertaining rooms for use by his family, friends, and closest associates, and the unified decoration of rooms into which this invited public was admitted.[214] Needless to say, neither London merchants nor wealthy colonists built a full complement of great chambers, antechambers, withdrawing chambers, and state bedchambers with adjoining private closets. On the other hand, some were sufficiently attuned to aristocratic fashion to recognize its essential correspondence to those parallel developments in vernacular building practice that already were transforming parlors into sitting rooms and upstairs chambers into best bedrooms. Several leading commercial families in early Boston and Salem built scaled-down versions of formal suites of rooms containing "great" and "little" parlors and corresponding greater and lesser upstairs bedchambers, all as early as the 1660s (fig. 11).[215] Their man-

---

[213]Thornton, *Seventeenth-Century Interior Decoration*, pp. 1–106. Eric Jones describes early Parisian influence on fashion in "Fashion Manipulators," pp. 208–10.

[214]Mark Girouard, *Life in the English Country House: A Social and Architectural History* (New Haven, 1978), pp. 119–62.

[215]Overlooked in Abbott Lowell Cummings, *The Framed Houses of Massachusetts Bay, 1625–1725* (Cambridge, Mass., 1979), the French-via-London

Figure 11. John Turner House, Salem, Massachusetts. Property acquired 1668 (deed), house built soon thereafter (window cames dated 1664), enlarged with a parlor wing and kitchen ell probably by 1680 (inventory presented 1693), modernized c. 1710–30, lean-to and kitchen removed 1794, Victorianized after 1858, restored 1909. Shipowner and merchant John Turner, Sr., amassed the most valuable Essex County estate of his generation (over £6,700) by the time he died in 1680. Twelve years earlier he had built a two-unit, two-story, clapboard-covered frame house with a porch tower and two facade gables overlooking the harbor. At first it resembled other large vernacular houses in the seaport. Soon he added and furnished a spectacular block of downstairs and upstairs rooms that shows how formal living made its entry into the provinces. The principal room in the original structure was a fine large hall, whitewashed and accented in Spanish brown. The other ground floor room may have started as a kitchen (with oven) before its conversion to a retail shop by 1680. The new wing raised the social ante enormously by creating pairs of complementary apartments on each floor. The former "Hall" became exclusively a dining room with a large table, twelve leather chairs, and a glass case full of glasses. The brand-new adjoining "Parlor" was fitted out as a sitting room with seventeen turkeywork chairs and two small tables at which the family could take private meals. All beds were removed to the floors above. There a revamped "Hall Chamber" played withdrawing room to a more private "Parlor Chamber." Besides its expensive curtained bed, the quasi-public room was furnished for socializing as well as sleeping with a round table, a cupboard, eight turkeywork chairs, and three others with cushion seats. By contrast, Turner could find privacy in the splendid new bedchamber over the parlor when he wanted to write at his scriptoire, sleep in a bed hung with a "sute of whit linen curtains & vallens," and safely lock away a rich store of textiles, including an exotic pintado carpet, a rare Indian chintz. Architecturally, the new wing exuded gentility. The rooms were larger and higher than usual; shoulder-level wainscot covered the walls; cased beams and fully plastered ceilings were among the earliest in New England; and a color scheme of gray and white paint coordinated the new suites of rooms. Outside, Turner proclaimed his independence from the vernacular convention of clapboards by sheathing the entire parlor block (and perhaps the rest as well) with wide flush planks shadow-molded along their edges. Other improvements included a "New Kitchen" ell and alongside probably also the "Leanter" rooms (mentioned in 1742) to accommodate a "Brewinghouse" and "Countinghouse." Turner's innovations lasted thirty or forty years until his son reached the zenith of his own career as a merchant, magistrate, and king's councillor. John II replaced the casements with sash and installed smaller, more efficient fireplaces. He also employed a Boston- or London-trained joiner to repanel the lobby and entertaining rooms and build a buffet in the parlor. These alterations further refined the family's use of the apartments in accordance with international gentry practice. Formal dining and tea taking moved from the hall into the parlor, renamed the "Best Room." A long table and the old leather chairs stayed behind in the hall for lesser occasions. The social center of the house removed upstairs to the "Great Chamber," which, besides its lavishly appointed tester bed, contained seating furniture, pictures, garniture, sconces, and other fashionable gear three times more valuable than the similar bed-sitting equipment next door in the hall chamber. Conceivably at the same time a disused flue was ingeniously reconstructed as a tiny back stairs leading directly from the ground floor hall to a servants' or slaves' garret, thereby creating the secret passage that Nathaniel Hawthorne made famous in this, The House of Seven Gables. *(Drawing, Cary Carson and Margaret Mulrooney)*

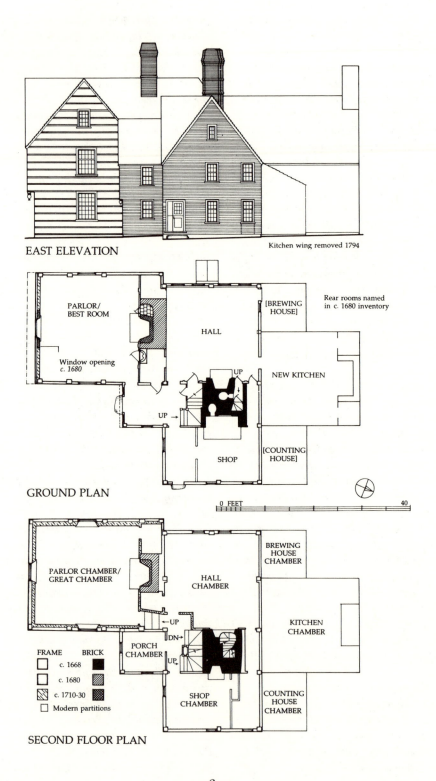

EAST ELEVATION

Kitchen wing removed 1794

PARLOR/
BEST ROOM

HALL

[BREWING
HOUSE]

Rear rooms named
in c. 1680 inventory

Window opening
c. 1680

NEW KITCHEN

UP

UP →

SHOP

[COUNTING
HOUSE]

GROUND PLAN

0 FEET   40

PARLOR CHAMBER/
GREAT CHAMBER

HALL
CHAMBER

BREWING
HOUSE
CHAMBER

KITCHEN
CHAMBER

←UP

DN→

PORCH
CHAMBER

UP

FRAME   BRICK

☐ ◼ c. 1668
☐ ▨ c. 1680
▨ ▨ c. 1710-30
☐ Modern partitions

SHOP
CHAMBER

COUNTING
HOUSE
CHAMBER

SECOND FLOOR PLAN

622

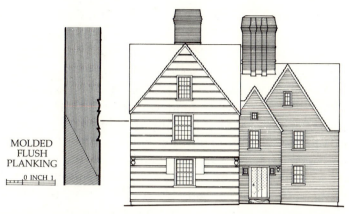

MOLDED
FLUSH
PLANKING

0 INCH 1

SOUTH ELEVATION

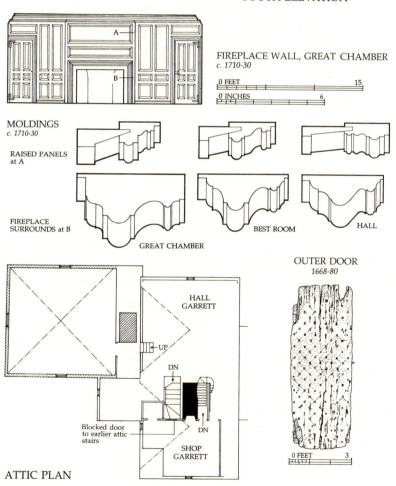

A

B

FIREPLACE WALL, GREAT CHAMBER
c. 1710-30

0 FEET ———————————————————— 15

0 INCHES ———————————— 6

MOLDINGS
c. 1710-30

RAISED PANELS
at A

FIREPLACE
SURROUNDS at B

GREAT CHAMBER

BEST ROOM

HALL

HALL
GARRETT

UP

DN

DN

Blocked door
to earlier attic
stairs

SHOP
GARRETT

ATTIC PLAN

OUTER DOOR
1668-80

0 FEET 3

sions (in contrast to their neighbors' dwellings) set aside special places for entertaining social equals who took meals with them in "dyning rooms," strolled through their picture "galleries," or conferred with them privately in "closets" and "studies."[216] They also may have been the first New Englanders to admit callers into halls that had become vestibules or passages to control access to other parts of the house.[217] Here again a Frenchified design element subsumed another venerable feature of vernacular house plans, the cross passage, and conflated that with a more recent innovation in folk housing, the circulation corridor, to create a stylish entrance hall that functioned as the first receiving room in the sequence that led to the heart of the house. Such corridor waiting rooms were planned into new gentry houses or added to old ones more and more frequently after 1690 in all the colonies.[218]

---

model for advanced house designs and furnishings in mid-seventeenth-century Boston was first recognized by Trent and is discussed in his *Historic Furnishings Report,* pp. 43–64.

[216]The uses to which rare early galleries may have been put is a matter that invites interesting speculation. One was recorded between an unusual lean-to parlor and a lean-to chamber in the inventory of the Rev. John Cotton (died 1652), who acquired his Boston house, built about 1636, from Sir Henry Vane, the son of a nobleman and the governor of the Massachusetts Bay colony. Trent conjectures (*Historic Furnishings Report,* p. 46) that "Vane may have intended the suite of parlor, gallery, and chamber to function as a suite in the grand manner, and accordingly he may have used his gallery for pictures." On the other hand, an immensely wealthy Virginia merchant, Col. Joseph Bridges, kept only odds and ends in a gallery in his three-story house, which also contained one of the earliest dining rooms in 1686 (Isle of Wight County Deeds, Orders, Wills, 2 [1661–1719], Va. St. Libr., pp. 255–63). In neighboring Surry County, a "Shovell Board Roome" listed in George Procter's inventory of 1678/9 was probably provided for patrons of the tavern he ran. (Surry County Deeds, Wills, etc., 2 [1671–84], Va. St. Libr., p. 199). Rooms set aside for purely recreational uses were consistent with new ideas about houses as centers for leisure-time activities.

[217]Discussed in Cummings, "Beginnings of Provincial Architecture," and Carson, "Public Face of Architecture."

[218]Mark R. Wenger, "The Central Passage in Virginia: Evolution of an Eighteenth-Century Living Space," in Camille Wells, ed., *Perspectives in Vernacular Architecture, II* (Columbia, Mo., 1986), p. 137, states that the earliest known inventory reference to a passage in Virginia and earliest house plan showing one date to 1719. But see both a "Passage" and an "Upper Pas-

Even so, changes dictated by foreign fashion made slow headway against the weight of tradition. Innovations were usually undertaken only by the wealthiest builders, and even they seldom embraced new ideas uncritically and without making concessions to local practice. Although a few halls were converted into dining rooms as early as the 1660s, seventy-five years later there was still confusion about whether a ground floor room reserved for public sociability was "hall or entertaining room."[219] The high gentry in Virginia only began calling "passages" by their proper Anglicized French name—saloon—after 1760 or so. And, often as not, they continued using them as "summer halls" in the time-honored manner of the region, a practice that surprised foreign travelers explained was "preferred by the family, on account of [passages] being more airy and spacious than any other [room]." Sometimes saloons also doubled as "an occasional ball-room."[220] Consequently, some entrance halls in southern houses received a higher degree of architectural ornamentation in relation to subsequent rooms than was usually the case in comparable English and French houses.[221] On the

sage" in a 1689 inventory in York County Deeds, Orders, Wills, 8, pp. 362–63, cited in Mary Ann Weiglhofer, "Inventories as a Barometer of Room Function in Colonial York County, Virginia," unpublished report, 1981, Col. Williamsburg Found., p. 9.

[219] In this case, it was the upper-class vestrymen of Truro Parish (Fairfax County, Virginia) who could not decide what to call the new hall in a glebe house they were building in 1737 (*Minutes of the Vestry: Truro Parish, Virginia, 1732–1785* [Lorton, Va., 1974], p. 15).

[220] Isaac Weld, *Travels through the States of North America*, 2 vols. (1800; reprint ed., New York, 1968), 1:207, and Thomas Anburey, *Travels through the Interior Parts of America*, 2 vols. (1789; reprint ed., New York, 1969), 2:359, cited and discussed in Wenger, "The Central Passage," pp. 142–43. It is significant when travelers comment on such American departures from architectural canon. Their surprise betrays their expectation of finding gentlemen's houses laid out in ways to which they were already accustomed.

[221] Mark R. Wenger is the acknowledged American expert on this subject. His articles on "The Central Passage" and "The Dining Room" are the first in a series of essays he is writing on gentry houses in early Virginia. Conversations with him have shaped what I have written here, as have two other essays: Dell Upton, "Vernacular Domestic Architecture in Eighteenth-Century Virginia," *Winterthur Portfolio* 17 (1982):95–119, and Edward A.

other hand, once visitors penetrated beyond these cross-ventilated entry halls in the most ambitious gentry houses being built in the colonies after the middle of the eighteenth century, especially in major cities, they might indeed encounter one or more pairs of high-fashion entertaining rooms: formal parlors communicating with dining rooms on the ground floor, drawing and withdrawing rooms upstairs, dressing rooms equipped with tea tables and replete with side chairs removed from adjacent bedchambers, and here and there even a ballroom coupled with a card or supper room. Always the architectural details and the quality of the furniture were finely calibrated to indicate to trained eyes which was the superior room where the most socially important activities took place (fig. 12).[222]

American prodigy houses containing suites of rooms that gave full play to ladies' and gentlemen's good manners were, of course, few and far between. The lesser gentry had decidedly less to show, often scarcely more than a dining room graced by a formal mantel and chimney piece or a parlor from which the beds had recently been removed. Nevertheless, as Kevin M. Sweeney describes elsewhere in this volume, house plans began to exhibit a greater uniformity from the early eighteenth century on. Variations still abounded where patrons and builders bowed to hardy regional preferences,

---

Chappell, "Looking at Buildings," *Fresh Advices: A Research Supplement to the Colonial Williamsburg Interpreter* 5 (1984):i–vi.

[222] Edward A. Chappell and the staff of architectural historians at Colonial Williamsburg have recorded this neglected social-architectural information in a number of large gentry houses in Virginia, Maryland, Charleston, and Philadelphia. It appears in print only in Chappell, "Reconsidered Splendor: The [Virginia Governor's] Palace Addition of 1751," unpublished report, 1985, Col. Williamsburg Found., and in a forthcoming addendum, "Grand House Interiors of Colonial America." Even the choice of paint colors, the number of coats to be applied, or sometimes the decision to paint at all were matters in which builders and clients took careful account of the relative importance of the rooms or architectural elements to be painted (Edward A. Chappell, Willie Graham, and Carl R. Lounsbury, "The Social Significance of Paint Color Schemes in Eighteenth-Century Public Buildings," memorandum, Oct. 10, 1989, Col. Williamsburg Found.). Orlando Ridout V, *Building the Octagon* (Washington, D.C., 1989), pp. 107–24, discusses the same hierarchy of architectural ornament in the best American house history yet written.

but upper-class houses increasingly incorporated a few of the spacial relationships and visual cues that told persons of taste that genteel behavior in some form or other was known and practiced by the owner (fig. 13).[223] Below the gentry level, the mass of folk housing remained impervious to the advance of fashion until the opening decades of the nineteenth century, as Edward A. Chappell illustrates in his accompanying account of the second "great rebuilding" in North America. Because dwellings were usually people's largest and most valuable possessions, they were often the last to be remodeled or replaced.

For that reason many newcomers to fashion found that it was easier and less expensive to create tasteful interiors in the new style by following Anglo-French models in the appointment and furnishing of rooms. Upholsterers and paperhangers were more affordable than carpenters and masons. Best rooms, of course, had never been utterly devoid of ornament, even in vernacular buildings. Farmers and town dwellers in England and the colonies had long brightened up halls and parlors with painted canvas hangings and with colors liberally brushed and sponged over walls and ceilings (fig. 5).[224] What

---

[223] For the most explicit discussion of these developments among minor gentry builders in the Chesapeake, see Upton, "Vernacular Domestic Architecture"; Carl R. Lounsbury, "The Development of Domestic Architecture in the Albemarle Region," in Doug Swaim, ed., *Carolina Dwelling* (Raleigh, N.C., 1978), pp. 46–61; Camille Wells, "The Eighteenth-Century Landscape of Virginia's Northern Neck," *Northern Neck of Virginia Historical Magazine* 37 (1987):4217–55; and Bernard L. Herman, *Architecture and Rural Life in Central Delaware, 1700–1900* (Knoxville, Tenn., 1987), pp. 14–41. Oddly enough the other middle colonies and New England are still virgin territory for fieldwork-based regional studies of eighteenth-century vernacular architecture. Scholars there know to expect buildings to be "expressions of a complex regional aesthetic" (Ward and Hosley, eds., *Great River*, p. 63), but no one has carefully worked out how "architectural style was negotiated in a way that softened fashion's cutting edge." Ronald D. Clifton, "Forms and Patterns: Room Specialization in Maryland, Massachusetts, and Pennsylvania Family Dwellings, 1725–1834," Ph.D. diss., University of Pennsylvania, 1971, makes a useful start using probate inventories.

[224] Cummings, *Framed Houses of Massachusetts Bay*, pp. 192–201; Abbott Lowell Cummings, "Decorative Painting in Seventeenth-Century New England," in Ian M. G. Quimby, ed., *American Painting to 1776: A Reappraisal* (Charlottesville, Va., 1971), pp. 71–125.

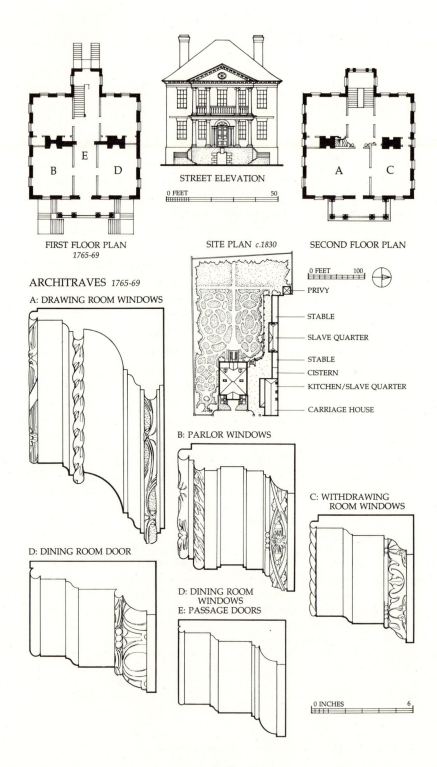

FIRST FLOOR PLAN
1765-69

STREET ELEVATION

0 FEET   50

SITE PLAN *c.1830*

SECOND FLOOR PLAN

ARCHITRAVES *1765-69*

A: DRAWING ROOM WINDOWS

0 FEET   100

PRIVY

STABLE

SLAVE QUARTER

STABLE

CISTERN

KITCHEN/SLAVE QUARTER

CARRIAGE HOUSE

B: PARLOR WINDOWS

C: WITHDRAWING
    ROOM WINDOWS

D: DINING ROOM DOOR

D: DINING ROOM
    WINDOWS
E: PASSAGE DOORS

0 INCHES   6

Figure 12. Trackers through unfamiliar social landscapes knew where they were, what to expect, and how to behave inside well-appointed genteel buildings by using their sixth sense for the subtle indicators of status that were provided by architectural fittings and furnishings in public rooms. Something seemingly as straightforward as the architraves around window jambs and door openings could communicate a wide range of social messages by their various combinations of moldings, carving, materials, and paintwork. Few employed a more sophisticated lexicon than the Miles Brewton House in Charleston, South Carolina, an exceptionally lavish Palladian town house built 1765–69. It openly proclaimed its social pretensions on the outside by its splendid wrought iron gates, two-story porch, and formal walled garden behind the house (the layout of beds, as shown, dates to the 1830s). Inside, visitors encountered suites of rooms on each floor. Like other gentry houses in the town, they were laid out on a double-pile plan organized around a central passage. The relative importance of each social space was a sum of all its parts—pilastered, paneled, papered, or plastered walls, architraves with or without crossettes, marble or wood mantels, chairrails carved or plain, concealed or exposed hinges, and papier-maché ceiling ornaments reserved for the best rooms. The code was also embedded in single elements. Architraves around the windows at the Miles Brewton House perfectly calibrated the pecking order among the publicly important front rooms on each floor. The most splendid was a large ballroom or drawing room (A) entered from the upper passage. Its window jambs were trimmed with giant compound moldings highlighted by rococo and rope carving on the beads. Next most favored was the parlor immediately below (B). The architraves around its windows were smaller but still richly embellished with more cable molding and an ovolo backband carved with flowers and frets. The withdrawing room off the second-floor ballroom (C) appears to have been slightly inferior to the parlor. Accordingly, its three-part architrave lacks the parlor's elegant channel moldings but it still sports a foliated ogee backband with a bead-and-reel astragal. That separates the moldings in the withdrawing room from those used to trim window openings in the dining room downstairs (D), the only front room in which those surrounds were left uncarved. There, only the architrave around the door is embellished with a carved egg-and-dart backband. Moldings in the passage (E) are a simplified variant of the dining room architraves, and those in the back rooms simpler still. Ladies and gentlemen developed a keen eye for meaningful details in the eighteenth century. Josiah Quincy dined with Miles Brewton in 1773 and afterwards made careful notes on the appearance of the drawing room: "The grandest hall I ever beheld, azure blue satin window curtains, a rich blue paper with gilt maschee borders, most elegant pictures, excessive grand and costly looking glasses, &c." His host's new house was finer than any Quincy had seen before, but his discerning taste had been honed in lesser gentlemen's houses built along similar lines. (Drawing, Cary Carson and Jeffrey Bostetter)

French designers introduced was the idea of architectural decoration complemented by a room's upholstered furnishings. The concept of en suite applied not just to furniture in sets but also to wall coverings color-coordinated with bed hangings, window curtains, and upholstery fabrics, all to heighten the effect of luxury and elegance. By now it should come as no surprise to learn that merchant princes in Boston were the first Americans to remodel their sleeping apartments into the kind of penultimate public-private withdrawing rooms so sumptuously appointed that no ordinary functional room names did them justice. Instead they were called the "Green Chamber," "Red Chamber," "Purple Chamber," or just "Painted Chamber" in a telling departure from traditional room naming practices that emphasized the new importance of decor.[225] Appearing first in inventories from the 1660s and 1670s, rooms known by the color of their coordinated textiles and wall coverings increased in popularity throughout the eighteenth century, at first, of course, with the superior class of houseowners who could afford a "Paper Room" (1737) when wallpaper (another French invention) came into fashion or a "Chintz Chamber" (1774) when English printed cottons made into window and bed curtains were by all accounts "the Most Approved Manner now in Vogue."[226] Wallpaper was made in a wider range of qualities than textile wall coverings and sold at lower prices than upholstery fabrics, making "Papering as cheap as Whitewash-

---

[225]Cummings, *Framed Houses of Massachusetts Bay*, p. 192. The earliest Virginia inventory that lists chambers by color—red and green—was taken on the death of Col. Thomas Willoughby of Norfolk County in 1672 (Norfolk County Wills and Deeds E, 4 [1666–75], Va. St. Libr., pp. 124–25). Willoughby, son of a prominent Virginia merchant, was educated at Merchant Taylors School in London before returning to the colony.

[226]The "Paper Room" belonged to John Welland of Boston (Cummings, ed., *Rural Household Inventories*, p. xxxi); the "Chintz Chamber" was one of a suite of rooms including a "Yellow Chamber," "Red Chamber," and "Dressing Chamber" at Belvoir, the home of George William Fairfax of Fairfax County, Virginia (Fairfax Family Papers, 1756–87, Virginia Historical Society, Richmond). See also Catherine Lynn, *Wallpaper in America from the Seventeenth Century to World War I* (New York, 1980), pp. 17–24, and Florence M. Montgomery, *Printed Textiles: English and American Cottons and Linens, 1700–1850* (New York, 1970), pp. 36–82.

Figure 13. Verdmont, Smith's Parish, Bermuda. House c. 1700–1714 (inventory), remodeled c. 1760–82 (inventory) and retrimmed c. 1790–1820, roof replaced before it was blown off again in 1926; kitchen-storeroom-slave quarter eighteenth century (maybe the "Outt Houses" inventoried in 1714) with nineteenth-century improvements; both buildings restored after 1951. Before the end of the seventeenth century the largest houses on Bermuda resembled one on this property (insert) owned by Capt. William Sayle, three times governor of the island and founder of North Carolina. His 1671 inventory describes a two-story vernacular house that bears instructive comparison with the high gentry mansion that John Dickinson built to replace it before 1714. Both were two stories high. Both had about the same number of rooms on each floor. Both named the same three entertaining rooms—hall, parlor, and dining room. The difference lay in the fashionableness, formality, organization of living space, and genteel amenities afforded by the house owned by Dickinson, a merchant and man of affairs with strong royalist sympathies. It resembled Sayle's in only one old-fashioned feature: the front entrance still opened directly into the hall, not into a center passage. Otherwise everything about the new house conformed to the dicta of international taste at the turn of the century: the double-pile plan, the hall turned into a formal sitting room and picture gallery (Sayle's hall had still been an eating room), the parlor bedchamber moved upstairs into a dressing and reception room, convenient access to all rooms from a generous half passage and stair-case, sumptuous Renaissance moldings used to trim mantels and stairs, and the unstopped chamfered beams in the hall and parlor (the penultimate refinement before ceiling beams were cased and beaded). From the front, Dickinson's house represented a balanced composition of centered doorway and windows (almost certainly casements) surmounted, not by the monitor roof of today, but probably by a pair of pitched roofs over the inhabited garret. The formal plan extended to the grounds, located on a leveled hilltop. The house looked out on a garden set about with large stone urns on pedestals and was enclosed behind an ornamental fence running atop a rusticated stone wall. Work buildings—a kitchen (with a smokehood), buttery, storerooms and cellars, "Servants Lodgings," and a "Cabbin," perhaps for Dickinson's house slaves—were grouped together around back, out of sight. So Verdmont remained until c. 1760 when Dickinson's granddaughter and her husband, a prominent customs collector, modernized and redecorated the house in a newer mode. They installed sash windows and interior shutters, wallpapered three front rooms, reduced the size and retrimmed the fireplaces (lavishly in the dressing chamber), added a second-floor passage leading to a balcony, and converted the front rooms downstairs into double parlors for tea, cards, and music. These improvements, topped up with a few neoclassical cornice moldings and architraves a generation later, refitted Verdmont for fashionable living well into the nineteenth century. (Drawing, Jeffrey Bostetter)

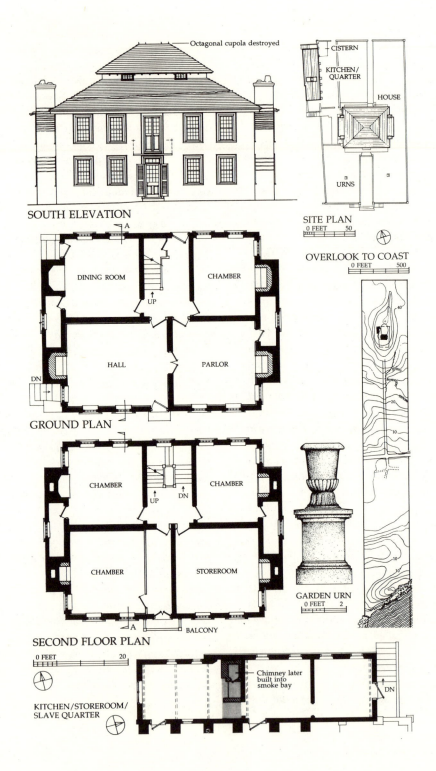

Octagonal cupola destroyed

SOUTH ELEVATION

CISTERN

KITCHEN/
QUARTER

HOUSE

URNS

SITE PLAN

0 FEET 50

OVERLOOK TO COAST

0 FEET 500

DINING ROOM

CHAMBER

UP

HALL

PARLOR

DN

GROUND PLAN

CHAMBER

CHAMBER

UP   DN

CHAMBER

STOREROOM

SECOND FLOOR PLAN

BALCONY

A

GARDEN URN

0 FEET 2

0 FEET 20

KITCHEN/STOREROOM/
SLAVE QUARTER

Chimney later
built into
smoke bay

DN

632

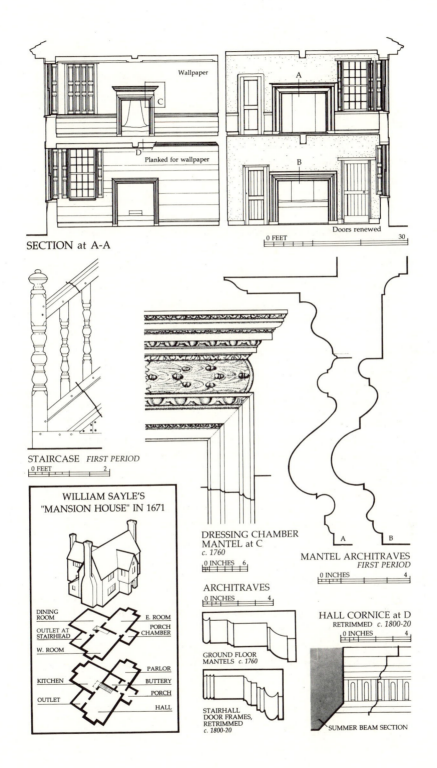

SECTION at A-A

Wallpaper

A

C

D

Planked for wallpaper

B

Doors renewed

0 FEET   30

STAIRCASE   *FIRST PERIOD*

0 FEET   2

**WILLIAM SAYLE'S
"MANSION HOUSE" IN 1671**

DINING ROOM

OUTLET AT STAIRHEAD

W. ROOM

KITCHEN

OUTLET

E. ROOM

PORCH CHAMBER

PARLOR

BUTTERY

PORCH

HALL

**DRESSING CHAMBER
MANTEL at C**
c. 1760

0 INCHES   6

ARCHITRAVES

0 INCHES   4

GROUND FLOOR
MANTELS *c. 1760*

STAIRHALL
DOOR FRAMES,
RETRIMMED
c. 1800-20

MANTEL ARCHITRAVES
FIRST PERIOD

A   B

0 INCHES   4

HALL CORNICE at D
RETRIMMED *c. 1800-20*

0 INCHES   4

SUMMER BEAM SECTION

ing," according to one Philadelphia paperhanger in 1783. Where advertisers claimed that "the expense of papering a room does not amount to more than a middling set of prints," middling sorts of people were literally able to cover old walls with a paper-thin veneer of spanking-new imported elegance (fig. 13). It was observed after the Revolution that houses in Philadelphia were "seldom without paper tapestries, the vestibule especially being so treated." In truth, if one believes paperhangers' advertisements, there was not an entertaining room imaginable for which an appropriate fashionable paper could not be purchased for pennies a roll.[227]

Other architectural features that became standard components in eighteenth-century interiors underwent the same transformation from high-style French to middle-brow English and American. Everywhere the same effects were sought: to achieve greater comfort and convenience, to heighten pomp and ceremony, and to accomplish all by employing a design idiom that was universally recognized and acclaimed. Wall surfaces not covered with real or "mock" paper tapestries were likely to be "wainscotted," not with the small oak panels common to earlier interiors, but with large raised panels set in a framework of stiles and rails and trimmed around with classical moldings. Those and many other architectural elements borrowed from antiquity were concentrated on chimney pieces, ceilings, and the architraves around windows and doors. Often they were brightly colored. Not just the chimney breast received decoration, but the firebox too. Now made smaller and more efficient, it acquired a bolection molded frame (fig. 13), sometimes a mantel shelf to display garniture, and a fascia set with painted tiles that resembled oriental porcelain and were easy to keep clean. Buffets were pulled in behind dining room walls to become built-in cupboards fitted with glass doors to store and show off expensive tablewares. Having so many things worth seeing required more light than unglazed and shuttered openings or case-

[227]These and other advertisements collected in Alfred Coxe Prime, comp., *The Arts and Crafts in Philadelphia, Maryland, and South Carolina, 1721–1785: Gleanings from Newspapers*, 1st ser. (Topsfield, Mass., 1929), pp. 275, 279, 281, are cited in an intelligent discussion of the buyers of wallpaper and where they hung it in Lynn, *Wallpaper in America*, pp. 154–61.

ment windows had admitted into late medieval rooms. Hence, engravings of the 1630s and early 1640s show daylight streaming into Parisian interiors through the earliest known double-hung, sliding-sash windows.[228] After dark, the splendors of French court life were reflected from wall sconces, pier glasses, and mirror plate set into chimney breasts, these too being elements that soon found their way onto the international cultural scene.

To describe this ensemble is to describe the appearance of houses that sprang up in every eighteenth-century English market town and every colonial seaport. The point is that these stock elements were already going together in France by 1650, and soon after that were multiplied a thousand times in Amsterdam, London, Boston, and wherever else fashion traveled. "A Gentleman from London," according to one who was, "would almost think himself at home in Boston, when he observes the numbers of people, their houses, their furniture, their Tables, their dress and conversation." A Bostonian's display of fashion, he said, was "as splendid and showy as that of the most considerable Tradesman in London."[229] That level of perfection had been achieved by 1720, but only just. The elements of the unifying French-Dutch-London aesthetic had still been coalescing in earlier decades. Innkeepers in Maryland's capital village of St. Mary's City used decorative tiles to face fireplaces in new and remodeled taverns starting in the 1670s.[230] A resident of Jamestown built a large brick edifice a few years before or after 1675 containing a domestic parlor with a fourteen-foot ceiling and a highly sophisticated, London-quality molded plaster chimney piece with baroque polychrome decoration incorporating half-sized figures

[228]Thornton, *Seventeenth-Century Interior Decoration*, plates 85 and 131; H. J. Louw, "The Origin of the Sash-Window," *Architectural History* 26 (1983):49–72.

[229]Daniel Neal, *The History of New England*, 2 vols. (London, 1720), 2:590. New fashions leapt across the Atlantic in a matter of months: "There is no Fashion in London, but in three or four Months is to be seen in Boston" (p. 614).

[230]Garry Wheeler Stone, *Seventeenth-Century Wall Tile from the St. Mary's City Excavations, 1971–1985* (St. Mary's City, 1987).

sculptured in high relief.[231] A Boston merchant, Thomas Banister, wrote to his London agent that sliding-sash windows were "the newest Fashion" in that city in the spring of 1701. He had seen "some curious clear glass," which someone told him was called "crown glass." One of his neighbors had "glazed the front of his house with it," and, Banister had to admit, it looked "exceeding well." So well that he too had "a great mind to have one room or two glazed with that glass."[232] A few years later carpenters hired to build a house for a minister who had recently moved from Boston to the north parish of Andover, Massachusetts, were stumped by his request for new-fashioned wainscoting in the parlor and parlor chamber. They were unacquainted with the technique of slotting raised panels into grooved stiles and rails. So they planked the wall in the usual way and simply nailed up mitred moldings like pictures frames to simulate fielded panels.[233] On the other hand, carpenters that Samuel Harrison employed to add a posh new wing to a plantation house south of Annapolis in the 1720s knew all about the new paneling. When they had finished installing several rooms with it for Harrison, he employed skilled painters to marbleize the walls in hues of green, red, and yellow. They were even sufficiently up-to-date to execute French-style overmantel landscapes and the fanciful *dessus-de-porte* paintings that took their name from their location above interior doors.[234] In his new dining room Harrison

---

[231]Recently discovered to have belonged to structure 44/53/138 in a study of the archaeological collections from late seventeenth-century Jamestown by Kathleen J. Bragdon, Cary Carson, Edward A. Chappell, and Willie Graham.

[232]Charles F. Montgomery, "Thomas Banister on the New Sash Windows, Boston, 1701," *Journal of the Society of Architectural Historians* 24 (1965):169–70.

[233]Abbott Lowell Cummings, "The Parson Barnard House," *Old-Time New England* 47 (1956):29–40. The parlor chamber in this house, which Cummings dated circa 1715, is illustrated and discussed in broader context in his *Framed Houses of Massachusetts Bay,* pp. 187–91.

[234]Descriptions of Holly Hill (Anne Arundel County, Maryland) appear in Carson et al., "Impermanent Architecture," p. 178, and idem, "The 'Virginia House' in Maryland," *Maryland Historical Magazine* 69 (1974):186–91.

installed a very early built-in buffet. Its use was almost as foreign as its name was unpronounceable. Among southern inventory takers it often came out "Boofott" or "Beaufett" or (was it?) "Bow-Fatt."[235] Never mind. Owning one was all that counted.

Thus, little by little and piece by piece the standardized formal interior took shape in the American colonies. Its elaborately staged design scheme was considered necessary and appropriate principally for those rooms where important social transactions were expected to take place. The "decoration . . . is only to be found in the rooms which a visitor is likely to see," wrote a Frenchman about houses in Philadelphia in 1798. "Everything else can get along in any old way." Likewise, all that Virginians wanted in a house, it was said, was "a bed, a dining room, and a drawing room for company."[236] House architecture responded to changing routines in house life as more and more everyday activities assumed social significance and were played before audiences of discriminating spectators. The seventeenth-century grooming and dining performances that I described earlier had taken place mostly in undifferentiated parlors. Eventually they became "dining parlors" when bedsteads removed to separate bedchambers, and, sometime after that (by the 1760s in rural New England), when formal dining repossessed the hall, leftover parlors were known as "setting parlors" in recognition of their sole remaining use. Houses and their furnishings became accessories to their inmates' sociability as the beau ideal civilized all manner of formerly mundane household activities and added new ones as well. While no Americans, however self-important, are known to have held levees, gentility attached no little significance to the proprieties of rising, dressing, and breakfasting, all before a day was scarcely begun. Consequently, expensive and fashionable furniture came to be lo-

---

[235] Culled from a typescript survey of "Virginia Room-by-Room Inventories," n.d., Architectural Research Department, Col. Williamsburg Found.

[236] *Moreau de St. Méry's American Journey, 1793–1798,* trans. and ed. Kenneth Roberts and Anna M. Roberts (Garden City, N.Y., 1947), p. 264; marquis de Chastellux, *Travels in North America in the Years 1780, 1781, and 1782,* ed. Howard C. Rice, Jr., 2 vols. (Chapel Hill, N.C., 1963), 2:441.

cated in best bedchambers, habitable closets, and dressing rooms. Beds themselves retained their age-old eminence, dignified occasionally by canopies and commonly by curtains and valances.[237] They were attended increasingly by a swarm of side chairs, high and low stools, couches, and daybeds, all in matching upholstery and perhaps still faintly echoing the status distinctions that the same pieces of chamber furniture had signified in France. Furniture historians guess that they were used to seat companions who had leisure hours to spend lolling about on the overstuffed mattresses and cushions that padded late seventeenth-century seating furniture and that later became an integral part of upholstered sofas and easy chairs.[238]

Leisure was, of course, an indispensable condition of gentility. Many of the new social activities by which ladies and gentlemen earned their reputations were forms of entertainment and play devised to keep them busy without actually working. These obligatory diversions required still more specialized utensils. Cupboards full of paraphernalia were needed, for instance, just to prepare, serve, and consume the exotic beverages that were now taken at set times throughout the day, tea notably, but coffee, chocolate, punch, and probably posset as well (fig. 7).[239] As good manners invaded room after room

[237]Cummings, ed., *Rural Household Inventories*, p. 190; Thornton, *Seventeenth-Century Interior Decoration*, pp. 149–225; Abbott Lowell Cummings, *Bed Hangings: A Treatise on Fabrics and Styles in the Curtaining of Beds, 1650–1850* (Boston, 1961); "Bed Hangings," in Florence M. Montgomery, *Textiles in America: A Dictionary Based on Original Documents* (New York, 1984), pp. 15–47, and "Bed Hangings," in Montgomery, *Printed Textiles*, pp. 49–65.

[238]Sometimes "couches" were light-weight beds and nothing more, as they appear often to have been in the southern colonies. Their otherwise complicated history is told, as far as it is now known, by Thornton, *Seventeenth-Century Interior Decoration*, pp. 149–79, 210–17, and Forman, *American Seating Furniture*, pp. 208–12. The story continues in Edward S. Cooke, Jr., ed., *Upholstery in America and Europe from the Seventeenth Century to World War I* (London, 1987).

[239]Tea drinking is the one most often cited and best studied, starting with Rodris Roth, *Tea Drinking in Eighteenth-Century America: Its Etiquette and Equipage*, U.S. National Museum Bulletin 225 (Washington, D.C., 1961). Curtis, "Chinese Export Porcelain," pp. 121–29, makes the important observation that, while porcelain vessel forms became more standardized after

in the eighteenth century, special-purpose furniture fine-tuned architectural spaces in readiness for the gentlefolk whose social lives were unimaginable without them (fig. 14). Formal behavior spawned the progeny of armchairs, easy chairs, elbow chairs, smoking chairs, and lolling chairs that appear for the first time in eighteenth-century inventories, mostly after 1750. Similarly, among tables, a host of upstart forms were designed specifically for dining, tea, breakfast, cards, dressing, sewing, gaming, drinking, mixing, shaving, in short, every conceivable activity for which a flat surface was desirable. Gone were the days when convenience alone fixed the customary locations of versatile, convertible furniture. Formal living required formal settings. The stage required props in places where the actors could count on finding them from one performance to another (fig. 15). So ensued those furniture forms known only by their place-names—corner chairs and corner tables, end tables, sideboards, side tables, and side chairs.[240] While tea and calico were remembered as "the chief initiating articles" that introduced ordinary people

1712, suggesting a growing consensus about their use, teawares continued to be sold in a wide variety of fashionable patterns. Mary C. Beaudry, "Ceramics in York County, Virginia, Inventories, 1730–1750: The Tea Service" (Paper presented at the Eighth Annual Conference of the Society for Historical Archaeology, Charleston, S. C., Jan. 1975), and Martin, "'Fashionable Sugar Dishes,'" present valuable new evidence about the status of tea drinkers, information corroborated from archaeological sources in Yentsch, "Minimum Vessel Lists." Barbara G. Carson, *Ambitious Appetites: Dining, Behavior, and Patterns of Consumption in Federal Washington* (Washington, D.C., 1990), describes how teawares and tea etiquette continued to respond to changing social customs after the Revolution. Chances are that other beverages inspired other protocols. The fantastical appearance of posset pots is surely owing to some extraordinary custom in their use, which still awaits discovery.

[240]Inventories and newspaper advertisements started using adjectives that referred to the placing of pieces of furniture with some regularity after 1720 and most frequently in the 1760s and 1770s. I am grateful to linguist Karin Goldstein at Colonial Williamsburg for undertaking for me a study of furniture lexemes to corroborate impressions drawn initially and unsystematically from my acquaintance with museum collections (Goldstein, "Locational Lexemes: An Examination of Subgeneric Levels of Categories of Furniture in Eighteenth-Century Documents," unpublished report, 1989, Col. Williamsburg Found.).

Figure 14. **Mr. Peter Manigault and His Friends.** *Ink and wash drawing by George Roupell, Charleston, S.C., c. 1750. The host (on the left, addressing "Howarth") and seven officers and gentlemen friends exchange toasts and show off their clubical manners in a room so architecturally standardized that it could equally be Manigault's parlor or a private entertaining room at a fashionable city tavern. An inscription on the back dispels the mystery. This particular punch party was held "at the House of Mr. Manigault," either his town house or "Steepbrook" at Goose Creek. It hardly mattered. The furnishings alone (including the caged bird and the liveried waiter) defined the event and distinguished the company. Eighteenth-century American scenes seldom depict so comprehensively all the elements necessary to the kind of genteel performance shown in this drawing, including its setting, props, costumes, and gestures. Even the performers' lines— "Pray, less noise Gentlemen" and "Squire Isaac your Wig, you Dog!"—had been scripted by the participants' long instruction in the arts of civility and rehearsed over a lifetime of similar encounters with social equals. (Courtesy, Winterthur Museum)*

PARLOR WINDOWS

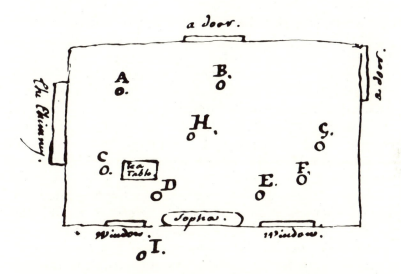

Figure 15. This unusual diagram of tea drinkers fashionably deployed in the parlor of Dr. William Shippen's Philadelphia town house was sketched by one of Nancy Shippen's suitors, who happened to be passing by on a Sunday evening about 8 o'clock. The year was 1780. "I peep'd through the window and saw a considerable Tea Company," he wrote to her later the same evening. "You will see the plan of this Company upon the next page." It shows chairs and a rectangular tea table pulled out from the walls and set up for use. The family and guests are positioned accordingly: an aged grandfather (A) "sitting before the Chimney meditating," an uncle (B) "walking up and down" and entertaining the guests (E, F, G) with "his agreeable conversation," Nancy herself (C) in charge of the tea table, at which her mother (D) was also seated, and Cyrus, the Negro butler, "standing in the middle of the room—half asleep" (H). This occasion was not the first or last time that the amorous "Spy" (I) and presumably other passersby on South Fourth Street observed the Shippens' mannerly parlor activities through the large, uncurtained, street-level windows. Big cities afforded countless instructional opportunities to attentive window shoppers. (Courtesy, Library of Congress)

641

to consumer goods "by imperceptible degrees" after 1750, the famous Philadelphia antiquary John Fanning Watson believed that it was principally household furniture, greatly "added to both in quantity and kind," that "began the marked distinction between rich and poor, or rather between new-fashioned and old-fashioned." He was right to correct himself. Consumption was no longer a prerogative of wealth. By midcentury people of fairly modest means were becoming consumers too, and their purchases were not confined to small comforts and trifling conveniences. Like their betters, they too increasingly resorted to fashion to define their social relationships. To entertain stylishly, even on a limited budget, a householder absolutely needed a few appropriate pieces of furniture. Their specialized forms, standardized ornament, and assigned places provided the essential visual signals needed to cue the newfangled good manners that Watson's "genuine old-fashioned sort of people" were increasingly at pains to learn.[241]

The whole history of Western art can scarcely produce another earlier example of ideas that spread so rapidly and widely from court to countryside. Domestic architectural spaces planned, decorated, and furnished en suite refashioned drawing rooms and parlors around the world little more than a century after their invention in early seventeenth-century Paris. The scale was much reduced, the splendor diminished, the lines simplified, and the materials cheapened. Yet one idea endured. That was the notion that virtually anyone could hold court in their own house by carefully observing prescribed conventions and correctly using a few pieces of standardized equipment. The goods could be purchased at popular prices and the manners learned from plays, prints, and publications.

Instruction in the genteel arts has sometimes been attributed to a tremendous supply-side growth in the etiquette and design book trade. The spread of fashionable living undeniably created worldwide markets for authors and publishers of

[241]John Fanning Watson began collecting oral histories from the oldest inhabitants of Philadelphia in the 1820s for his *Annals of Philadelphia and Pennsylvania*, 3 vols. (1830; reprint ed., Philadelphia, 1898), 2:527–28.

pattern books and self-improvement manuals. We have seen already how a new cuisine rewrote cookbooks. Likewise, handbooks for builders began rolling off the presses from the middle of the seventeenth century. A hundred years later makers of many other fashionable goods had also fallen prey to entrepreneurial printers and booksellers.[242] Cabinetmakers, carvers, silversmiths, and upholsterers became targets for pattern books with hard-sell titles like *Household Furniture in the Genteel Taste for the Year 1760,* with their implication that today's fashions would be gone tomorrow. Some were practical treatises, but many were stylebooks like Thomas Chippendale's *Gentleman and Cabinet-maker's Director* that aimed at patrons as much as craftsmen. Consumers represented a huge market for these writers. Hence it was to their aspirations and anxieties that publishers directed an avalanche of betterment books on every conceivable subject where fashion held sway—on deportment, dressing, dancing, conversing, letter writing, game playing, traveling, gardening, collecting, and, of course, ultimately and inexhaustibly, on etiquette itself (fig. 16).[243]

Did such handbooks really bring the light of civilization to the outer edges of empire and illuminate the benighted cul-de-sacs of the English provinces? They were supposed to. Architectural writers like William Pain and Thomas Rawlins

[242]See works cited in n. 14, above, for bibliographies and studies of builders' manuals. There is no comparable body of work for other kinds of eighteenth-century pattern books although some help may be found in Susan Lambert, ed., *Pattern and Design: Designs for Decorative Arts, 1480–1980* (London, 1983), pp. 39–116.

[243]Advice literature as a genre deserves the same careful study that only courtesy and etiquette books have received so far from Elias, *Civilizing Process;* John E. Mason, *Gentlefolk in the Making: Studies in the History of English Courtesy Literature and Related Topics from 1531 to 1774* (Philadelphia, 1935); Joan Wildeblood, *The Polite World: A Guide to English Manners and Deportment from the Thirteenth to the Nineteenth Century* (London, 1965); and for American manners, Arthur M. Schlesinger, Sr., *Learning How to Behave: A Historical Study of American Etiquette Books* (New York, 1946); and most recently and systematically, Hemphill, "Manners for Americans." Regrettably, even Hemphill can present no evidence to show that readers actually modeled their behavior on these prescriptive conduct books. Cathy N. Davidson assesses the influence of a "reading revolution" in another prescriptive genre, the novel, as it reshaped American attitudes and manners around 1800 in *Revolution and the Word: The Rise of the Novel in America* (New York, 1986).

explicitly addressed readers who lived in "remote Parts of the Country, where little or no Assistance for Designs is to be Procured."[244] Colonial newspaper advertisements, booksellers' accounts, and library lists tell us that design books and manners manuals were indeed imported into North America where the conduct books sold in quantities that required numerous reprintings, new editions, collections, abridgments, and eventually American take-offs.[245] Historians can even point to some evidence that they were read. Parents are known to have urged sons and daughters to consult the likes of *The Lady's Library* and *The Whole Duty of Man* "over and over again" (in Benjamin Franklin's words) whether or not children actually took the advice.[246]

So, can it be said that the revolution in manners was chiefly disseminated in the pages of popular social guides and illustrated pattern books? Was the penny press responsible for teaching craftsmen and their customers the classical orders, the line of beauty, and the rules of etiquette? Recently historians have decided not, not directly. The how-to-behave books

[244] The quotation is from Thomas Rawlins, *Familiar Architecture* (London, 1768). In his preface to *The Practical Builder* (London, 1774), William Pain noted a "very great Revolution (as I may say) which of late has so generally prevailed in the Stile of Architecture, especially in the decorative and ornamental department"; hence his book was intended "to furnish the Ignorant [and] the Uninstructed, with . . . a comprehensive System of Practice."

[245] For American ownership of architectural treatises see Park, *Architectural Books*. Schlesinger, in *Learning How to Behave* (p. 9), makes a start at listing etiquette books that went through multiple printings and editions, which Hemphill enlarges in "Manners for Americans," Appendix, pp. 568–91. For pattern and betterment books as part of a bookseller's total trade, see Gregory A. Stiverson and Cynthia Z. Stiverson, "Books Both Useful and Entertaining: A Study of Book Purchases and Reading Habits of Virginians in the Mid-Eighteenth Century," unpublished report, 1977, Col. Williamsburg Found., and Susan Stromei Berg, "Agent of Change or Trusted Servant: The Eighteenth-Century Williamsburg Press," M. A. thesis, College of William and Mary, 1993.

[246] Albert Henry Smyth, ed., *The Writings of Benjamin Franklin*, 10 vols. (New York, 1905–7), 3:435. Washington composed his own "Rules of Civility" in 1747 at the age of seventeen, probably by borrowing from a pirated English edition of an earlier French courtesy book. See Charles Moore, ed., *George Washington's Rules of Civility and Decent Behavior* (Boston, 1926), pp. x–xiv, 23–65. Kenneth A. Lockridge, *The Diary, and Life, of William Byrd II of Virginia, 1674–1744* (Chapel Hill, N.C.1987), pp. 21–26, argues that, lacking role models, Byrd learned to be a gentleman through books alone.

Figure 16. Purveyors of store-bought culture first had to invent entirely new visual languages to convey through books the knowledge and skills that had formerly always been handed down in person from masters to apprentices, tutors to pupils, and parents to children. Never before had education required that learners first be able to envisage information presented in two-dimensional formats and then translate that book knowledge into practice. Some early illustrations instructed through pictures alone. Table settings, fancy folded napkins, the classical orders of architecture, penmanship, pruning methods, furniture design, and countless other skills were learned by trial and error simply by comparing the practitioners' achievements to the illustrations published in the self-help manuals they consulted. More ambitious authors experimented with graphics that demonstrated the steps involved in achieving the desired results. The English translator of Willem Goeree's An Introduction to the General Art of Drawing *(London, 1674) promised readers that the author had simplified "the secret Mysteries, Power and Propertie of the Art of Painting" to "one easie and rational Method" using a set of reduction grids. An accompanying plate (A) showed the work in three stages of completion. Illustrators soon discovered how to apply the graphics design concept of "small multiples" to help viewers make visual comparisons that showed variations in data from frame to frame, as in (B) John Gunn's* The Theory and Practice of Fingering the Violoncello *(London, 1789). The diagrams in this and other play-by-the-numbers instruction manuals also made innovative combinations of pictures and standard musical notation. All the same, illustrated how-to-do-it books portrayed the subtleties of human movement only imperfectly. Ingenious engravers tried many different ways*

to represent the continuous motion of three-dimensional bodies through space and time. The graceful arts of dancing and deportment posed the greatest challenges to their talents. The Dancing-Master; or, The Art of Dancing Explained *(London, 1744), an English edition of Pierre Rameau's famous work (Paris, 1734), used the engraved text itself to trace the synchronous movements of male and female dancers across the ballroom floor (C). By this "new and familiar Method," the English publisher advertised, "the Manner of Performing all Steps in Ball Dancing is made easy." But self-taught dancers were still confined to the flat plane of the printed page in most books. Less so the readers of Kellom Tomlinson's* The Art of Dancing, Explained by Reading and Figures *(London, 1735). His engraver made sophisticated use of architectural perspective and fully modeled figures to create the illusion of three-dimensional interior space (D). He covered the floor in the foreground and receding middle distance with the shorthand symbols of Tomlinson's dance notation system. The pace was regulated by sequential numbers that not only coordinated the dance partners' separate movements but keyed their progress to a musical score printed overhead. Thus, an entire dance routine—steps, gestures, melody, and tempo combined—was recorded in a single set of "cuts." Three centuries earlier the Gutenberg letterpress, movable type, and oil-based printing inks had provided the fundamental technology for print culture. Scarcely less important advances in the arts of illustration in the seventeenth and eighteenth centuries greatly expanded the number of subjects that could be effectively disseminated in books and opened communications with a vastly larger reading public. (Courtesy, Winterthur Library and the New York Public Library)*

A

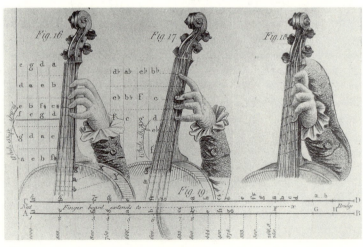

B

The Figure of the Man making a whole Turn, taking Hands, and letting go in Turning

The Figure of y.^e Woman making a whole Turn, Taking Hands, and letting go in Turning

C

K.T. inv.   G. Bickham Sculp.

To James Stanley Esqr. Son & Heir to Sr. Edward Stanley Bar^{t.} & to my much respected Scholar Miſs Elizabeth Stanley his Sister.
This PLATE is humbly inscribed by Their most obliged Servt. Kellom Tomlinson.

D

may or may not have been an exception. How effectively they reformed behavior is a hard thing to gauge. On the other hand, scholars are quite sure that the direct influence of style-books on art and architecture was negligible. While they may have been a source of ideas and inspiration, sometimes a ready reference for proportions, and very occasionally an easy steal for decorative details, almost never were entire buildings or whole pieces of furniture copied cold from English designs. More often new fashions were imported as manufactured goods or were introduced by immigrant craftsmen, who advertised themselves as "late from London." Otherwise, tasteful people were busy keeping an eye on one another. Emulation among the already fashionable was very much the order of the day. A cabinetmaker with "carved Chairs in the newest fashion" to sell in Charleston knew that their acceptability was vouched for by advertising that they were "the same Pattern as those imported by Peter Manigault, Esq.," the city's society lion (fig. 14).[247] Nor did those who wanted to improve their social graces necessarily reach first for *The Friendly Instructor*. Real-life paragons were more immediate and usually more compelling models. Such a man was Col. William Moseley, who, one impressionable resident of Norfolk, Virginia, remembered, "was reckoned the finest gentleman we had" and on special occasions was sent for "express . . . to come to town with his famous wig and shining buckles, to dance the minuet."[248] Young men who were "utterly ignorant of the Ceremony of the Tea-Table" might find some help in books, but their best advice was to employ a knowledgeable hostess "to teach them the Laws, Rules, Customs, Phrases and Names of the Tea Utensils."[249]

Laws, rules, and terminology were the stuff of books. A Beau Nash or an accomplished gentlewoman taught something else besides. Their kind was acquainted with the prevailing customs that the rule books left out. Custom naturalized etiquette and thus produced the indefinable art

[247] *South Carolina Gazette*, July 9, 1772, cited in Prime, comp., *Arts and Crafts in Philadelphia, Maryland, and South Carolina*, p. 176.

[248] *Lower Norfolk County, Virginia, Antiquary* (1906):33–35n. The year was 1774.

[249] Cited in Esther Singleton, *Social New York under the Georges, 1714–1776* (New York, 1902), pp. 380–81.

of gentility that careful instruction and trial and error taught better than book learning. To understand how good manners spread so far and fast in eighteenth-century America, historians must accept the paradox that etiquette was at once a set of rules and a body of inspired improvisation. That quality of spontaneity, bounded but not hobbled by convention, was the spark that ignited fashion's infinite creativity. Cabinetmakers, the avant-garde among tastemaking artisans after 1700, were known to have a "lighter Hand and quicker Eye" than those old dogs, the joiners, and "upon this," it was said, "depends the Invention of new Fashions." It was a byword among cabinetmakers that "he that must always wait for a new Fashion till it comes from Paris, or is hit upon by his Neighbour, is never likely to grow rich or eminent."[250] Consumers as well were disinclined merely to borrow fashions unaltered. Novelties should attract attention, but not appear outlandish. Thus, the gentle arts are everywhere observed to have allowed sufficient latitude in their performance and variation in their accessories to include virtually anyone who respected the essential formalities of standardized design and polite behavior.

There arose, as a result, a new kind of regionalism throughout the beau monde, not to be confused with the parochialisms of folk cultures.[251] Yet it was not entirely dissimilar either,

---

[250]R[obert?] Campbell, *The London Tradesman* (London, 1747), pp. 171–72.

[251]Studies of American furniture have respected geographical boundaries since the 1930s, but only a few furniture historians have tried to explain how these regional differences occurred. About the first was Charles F. Montgomery, *American Furniture: The Federal Period* (New York, 1966), and subsequently his essay "Regional Preferences and Characteristics in American Decorative Arts: 1750–1800," in Charles F. Montgomery and Patricia E. Kane, eds., *American Art, 1750–1800: Towards Independence* (Boston, 1976), pp. 50–66. His explanation, that regional characteristics were mostly owing to craft organization and specialization, is seconded and enlarged upon by Benjamin A. Hewitt in *The Work of Many Hands: Card Tables in Federal America, 1790–1820*, ed. Benjamin A. Hewitt, Patricia E. Kane, and Gerald W. R. Ward (New Haven, 1982), and Forman, *American Seating Furniture*, p. 55. Forman further demonstrates the influence of immigrant craftsmen in transmitting furniture-making practices from one place to another. As Philip D. Zimmerman explains in "Regionalism in American Furniture

at least not in one vital respect. Gentility, for all its worldly ways, was a respecter of ordinary people's stubborn fondness for things reassuringly familiar. It demanded conformity to a few cardinal standards observed and practiced everywhere while at the same time it also tolerated an older form of conformity to local customs and appearances. In a process reminiscent of creolization, gentility absorbed, accepted, and to a certain extent bowed to regional customs. Foreign travelers in eighteenth-century America frequently recorded how the rules were bent one way in this or that city, another way in the countryside, and differently still from colony to colony. Nevertheless, virtually everywhere they went they were usually received politely and shown courtesies they understood. Thus the new system of manners that spurred the consumption of fashionable goods solved major problems of social communications in an age of rapid expansion precisely because it was ecumenical in both senses of that word. To those abroad in the world it offered a universal code of behavior to smooth their reception in faraway places. To those homebodies, who nevertheless had their own reasons to want to appear presentable to outsiders, an all-embracing ecumenical gentility was agreeably forgiving of trifling differences.

Studies," in Gerald W. R. Ward, ed., *Perspectives on American Furniture* (New York, 1988), p. 18, the buyer's preferences are almost wholly unaccounted for in research so far. Consumers played a role in shaping regional styles through purchases that cumulatively ensured the success of certain products (and their makers or sellers) over others deemed less desirable. The theory behind such a process is briefly explained by Fraser Neiman in his review of *The Work of Many Hands* in *Vernacular Architecture Newsletter* 16 (1983):6–11. A furnishings history from the consumer's point of view was promised and described in a still unpublished companion volume to Peter Benes, *Two Towns: Concord and Wethersfield. A Comparative Exhibition of Regional Culture, 1635–1850* (Concord, Mass., 1982), pp. xv–xvi. The only other work that comes close is Edward S. Cooke, Jr.'s, highly original *Fiddlebacks and Crooked-backs: Elijah Booth and Other Joiners in Newtown and Woodbury [Connecticut], 1750–1820* (Waterbury, Conn., 1982), and idem, "Craftsman-Client Relations in the Housatonic Valley [Connecticut], 1720–1800," *Antiques* 125 (1984):272–80. No one yet has recognized, much less explored, the fundamentally different nature of regional customs in folk and polite cultures or tried to explain by what process the one may have led to the other in traditional communities that opened their doors to fashion in the eighteenth century.

Variations in the practice of the gentle arts and localism in the design of American-made artifacts should therefore not be taken as evidence of fashion's impeded progress, as so often they have been.[252] On the contrary, they were the essential conditions that hastened its spread where otherwise it never would have gone. Benjamin Rush was addressing the creole side of etiquette when he implored young women in Philadelphia to "awake from this servility [to British manners]—to study our own character—to examine the age of our country—and to adopt manners in every thing, that shall be accommodated to our state of society, and to the forms of our government."[253] In point of fact, polite behavior among Americans was already displaying notable republican deviations from European norms. Alexis de Tocqueville was not the first to observe that American manners were "neither so tutored nor so uniform" as in France.[254] Were they inferior? Had Americans by insisting on their own preferences seceded from the international community of civilized ladies and gentlemen? Tocqueville thought not. American manners were "frequently more sincere," he believed. His good opinion was echoed a few years later by a Polish traveler, a nobleman's son, who explained that "good breeding prevails, and hearty, intentional politeness marks [Americans'] address and intercourse" despite their inattention to the "minute details and

---

[252]The view used to be that folk art represented "primitive," "naive," or "amateur" misinterpretations of high-style art or was just an inept or ignorant attempt at imitation. Anthropologists disabused art historians of that notion, most of whom now understand that variations from elite models and design-book prototypes occurred all along a continuum from court to country. Artificers who were removed intellectually and geographically from the centers of metropolitan culture selectively appropriated those serviceable parts of elite aesthetics that experience had taught them would please and satisfy their patrons. Research needs to identify which elements were chosen and explain why.

[253]Benjamin Rush's address to the Young Ladies' Academy of Philadelphia, given in 1787, was published as *Thoughts upon Female Education Accommodated to the Present State of Society, Manners, and Government in the United States of America* (Boston, 1791), p. 18.

[254]Alexis de Tocqueville, *Democracy in America*, trans. Henry Reeve, 2 vols. (New York, 1900), 2:229.

rites of courtesy."[255] Gentility went abroad in the new United States attired in formal clothes, but never a straightjacket. Its widespread appeal lay in its uniform standards, and its widespread acceptance in their lenient application.

The refinement of manners and the consumption of fashionable goods that mid-nineteenth-century observers held up as evidence of a "truly American and republican school of politeness" had been set in motion all of two centuries earlier and already were well advanced before the country won independence and declared a republic.[256] We began our search for this emergent American gentleman in John Weld's farmhouse in Roxbury, Massachusetts, and specifically the parlor that his neighbors inventoried in 1691. There can be no more striking measure of fashion's progress among ordinary Americans in the years following Weld's death than to peer in at another doorway in the same village eighty years later.

Stephen Brewer died in 1770 leaving an inventoried estate only slightly larger than Weld's had been.[257] Yet by then Brewer had reason to be called a "Gentleman" despite his occupation as a sometimes blacksmith and barber. His neighbors knew why. Fully half the rooms in his house—no larger than Weld's—were furnished with an eye to their fashionable appearance. Guests who called on Brewer were admitted into an "Entry" lined with thirteen chairs, three tables, and a desk and bookcase, and the walls hung with pictures and a looking glass. Callers who passed muster could then be shown into the principal ground floor entertaining room where nary a bed nor old-fashioned chest was anywhere in sight. This room was reserved exclusively for formal meal taking—for dining

[255]Adam von Gurowski, *America and Europe* (New York, 1857), pp. 375–76.

[256]Quoted by Schlesinger, *Learning How to Behave*, p. 21.

[257]Cummings, *Rural Household Inventories*, pp. 237–40. The inventory takers clearly failed to record the name of a workroom they viewed between the "Entry Below" and the "Kitchen." Stephen Brewer's total estate was appraised at £855.16.7, about £125 greater than the value of John Weld's after adjustment for inflation. His household furnishings were worth £108, plus a £9 chaise and personal clothing appraised at £20; Weld's furnishings had totaled £103. I am grateful to Gloria L. Main for supplying the correct deflators.

at an oval table set with an assortment of pewter plates, glasses, and delftware and also for tea and coffee drinking, for which a special tea table was provided with the requisite pot, salvers, and sugar cannister. An expensive clock chimed the dinner hour and signaled teatime in Brewer's formally regulated household. Another looking glass in this room gave invited company a second chance to adjust a wig or straighten a collar to please the barber gentleman. The third room fashionable enough to warrant yet another looking glass was Brewer's bedchamber upstairs. He not only slept there and stored his clothes in a "Case [of] Draws," but he and family or friends also used it as their withdrawing room. It was furnished with parlor-quality chairs, including an easy chair, and decorated with two large pictures and seven smaller ones hung on the walls.

Brewer's possessions totaled only a few pounds more than the appraised value of Weld's household goods. The real difference was the importance Brewer attached to his furnishings and the ways he put them to use. Weld's greatest treasures had been the dozens and dozens of fine napkins, sheets, pillow beers, and uncut yardgoods locked away in his kitchen chamber. Rarely seen and never all at once, they figured less conspicuously than his cows and oxen in making his reputation as a substantial farmer in the neighborhood. Eighty years later Roxbury residents were spending roughly the same sums to furnish their houses, or even somewhat less, but they were buying many more things, paying less for each, and getting more bang for their bucks besides. Stephen Brewer's teakettle was worth only twenty-one shillings, but a blacksmith who owned one and used it properly could reasonably expect to be called a "Gentleman" at home and abroad.

Not that Brewer traveled abroad frequently or far. He did not have to. The world had come to Roxbury by 1770. It came in books, newspapers, store-bought goods, and cabinetmakers' work. More important, it came in person. Travelers of all sorts crisscrossed the land. Everywhere they went they sought out and consorted with local gentlefolk whose qualifications were certified by their fashionable possessions and refined manners. Historians know that for a fact because travelers said so explicitly in the diaries they kept of their journeys.

Travel journals became an immense literature in the eighteenth century and an immensely valuable primary source for historians who want proof that international-style consumer goods and etiquette-book manners were indispensable prerequisites to people's moving around. Diaries have often been used to document the appearance of luxuries in this place or that. Many record just as faithfully travelers' own use of fashionable things to find their social bearings where other indicators were less easily deciphered. Because the power of artifacts to communicate such information over great distances is central to understanding the nature of modern consumer culture, excerpts from a typical traveler's journal are ultimately the most apposite illustrations I can offer in support of my answer to the question that began this essay: Why the tremendous demand for genteel goods and services in the eighteenth century? *Some Cursory Remarks Made by James Birket in His Voyage to North America* shows us why, page after page.[258]

Birket was a merchant from Antigua. He made an overland trip from Portsmouth, New Hampshire, to Philadelphia in 1750, incidentally passing within a few miles of Roxbury on his way south from Boston. His notes are indeed cursory and wholly devoid of intentional insights. In most of the towns and villages he rode through he tallied up the number of houses that were "of Modern Architecture" or "built after the modern taste which make avery good Apearance" or simply those he called "neat and Genteel." His list had a practical application for him. Invariably these houses were owned by the business associates he called on or those gentlemen to whom he was later introduced and with whom his diary records he then often dined. Invited into their homes, he found "many of the rooms . . . hung with printed Canvas and paper etc. which looks very neat." Others were "well wainscoted and painted," worthy of note not because they were remarkable but precisely the opposite, because they were finished "as in other places." Birket was a man who knew what to look for and was gratified when his expectations were met.

[258]C[harles] M. A[ndrews], ed., *Some Cursory Remarks Made by James Birket in His Voyage to North America, 1750–1751* (New Haven, 1916), pp. 4, 8–9, 21, 24, 27, 30–34.

That applied to people's behavior as well. A new acquaintance could receive no higher accolade in his diary than that he "treated us very kindly And in a very Genteel manner."

Birket divided American society into two parts only. There were the "Country people," whom he characterized as "the rude lazy drones of this Part of the world." They lived in "old," "sorry," and "indifferent" houses. "The better sort of People" were the go-ahead crowd that the traveler recognized by their highly visual lifestyle, to which he attached three adjectives interchangeably—"new," "genteel," and "neat." Those qualities rather than any bankable assets were Birket's guide to sizing up a gentleman's reputation. It was a fine line, which mere spendthrifts could overstep. For instance, some of the leading merchants of Boston furnished their houses "in an Elegant manner" and "Their dress [was] very genteel." But the Antiguan confided to his diary that "In my Opinion both men & Women are too Expensive in that respect." Sometimes tastefulness was missed by inches and the offender's reputation diminished accordingly. Birket was taken to see a prominent sea captain's country house outside Newport, Rhode Island. He thought it made "a good Appearance at a distance," but then found that "when you came to Survay it nearer it does not Answer your expectation." His reason is quite astonishing. He found no fault with the "Hewn Stone and all the Corners and Sides of the windows . . . painted to represent Marble." Or with the "large flight of Steps into the first Story which is very Grand." Or with the "Handsome Garden" walled around the front of the house. All those were splendid and deservedly earned the house and garden's reputation as "the wonder of that part of the Country." No, the terrible problem was something else. It was a matter of a few critical inches. Upon returning from his visit, Birket carefully entered in his journal that "the upper Story is Neither . . . proportionable in the height of the rooms nor Size of the Windows." On further reflection he decided the house also suffered for having no true basement.

Poor Captain Malbone! No amount of elegance, no outlay of wealth could spare him the scorn of this traveling West Indian cognoscente! Can anyone deny that a revolution in cultural values had surely occurred when a man's property, his

herds, his ships, his offices, his gold and silver, even his ancient lineage were betrayed by an ignorance of proportion?
Birket was no petty one-upsman; on the contrary, he was eager to befriend people of good taste. That was just the point.
There had to be rules and standards to tell the genuine article
from the counterfeit.[259] What another traveler said of Virginians was true everywhere: people looked "more at a man's
outside than his inside."[260] Men and women had few other
alternatives in the rapidly expanding world of eighteenth-
century England and its colonies. Their lives were crowded
with too many strangers and recent acquaintances to apply
the traditional measures of respect. Instead gentility assigned
face values to the commonplace artifacts and everyday activities that knowledgeable travelers expected to encounter anywhere worth going.

At home as well as abroad their genteel manners served to
distinguish and dignify the "better sort of People" from the
country drones. Birket's dinner companions were often men
who clearly clubbed together regularly. Sea captains, merchants, slave traders, and other men of the world brought
back home the shared experiences and international outlook
they had acquired in their foreign travels. They also brought
home new wealth, not the only wealth in the region, but the
"Opulant fortunes" that Birket said created "great Reputation." It was hard to argue with conspicuous success even if it
did put on haughty airs and funny clothes. So little by little
other locals less worldly-wise discovered good reasons of their
own to leave off the older customs of their station and place
in favor of borrowed foreign fashions that garnered for them

[259]James Birket was not alone in his criticism. Dr. Alexander Hamilton
had a remarkably similar reaction to Capt. Godfrey Malbone's fabulous
house when he passed through Newport six years earlier in 1744: "It is the
largest and most magnificent dwelling house I have seen in America. It is
built intirely with hewn stone of a reddish colour; the sides of the windows
and corner stones of the house being painted like white marble. . . . This
house makes a grand show att a distance *but is not extraordinary for the architecture, being a clumsy Dutch modell*" (Bridenbaugh, ed., *Gentleman's Progress*, p.
103, my italics). A rule was a rule was a rule!

[260]London merchant Peter Collinson to John Bartram of Pennsylvania,
Feb. 17, 1737, in *William and Mary Quarterly*, 2d ser. 6 (1926):303–5.

a little of their neighbors' reflected splendor and sometimes more than a little of the prosperity that followed the carriage trade. Birket's diary gives honorable mention, for instance, to an innkeeper in New London, Connecticut, who parlayed his "great Politeness & Good Manners to his Guests" into a thriving business aimed at discriminating travelers like those in the merchant's party.

It was no great step down the social ladder from hostelers and others whose services put them directly in touch with outsiders to men like "Gentleman" Stephen Brewer, the barber-blacksmith of Roxbury. Full of get-up-and-go, he may actually never have gone farther than Boston. His customers may only have known fashionable foreigners by second- or third-hand acquaintance through the tavernkeepers who entertained the local gentry who in turn hosted celebrities from far away. Nevertheless, by 1770 many thoroughly ordinary men no better than Brewer saw real gains to be made by learning the rudiments of gentility and purchasing the accessories to fashion. To such an extent had "magnificence in the matter of teapots" challenged the old order and meaning of material things that even men and women who seldom ventured outside the village eagerly acquired from their neighborhood storekeepers the goods that conferred social respectability in an increasingly rank-conscious society.[261]

The great movement of European peoples that achieved a momentum in the eighteenth century that rolls forward into our own times was the definitive force that shaped modern consumer culture eventually for everyone whether migrant or not. The travelers themselves were first "to obtain the Reputation of being Men of Vertu and of an elegant Taste." They most urgently had need "to acquire foreign Airs and adorn their ... Persons with fine Cloaths and new Fashions and their Conversation with new Phrases." They led the way, but their wake washed back on the shores they left behind and passed by. The influence of their example worked inexorably "to rub off local Prejudices" even among the firmly set-

[261]The teapot remark was made by *A Frenchman in England, 1784: Being the Mélanges sur l'Angleterre of François de la Rochefoucault*, ed. Jean Marchand, trans. S. C. Roberts (Cambridge, 1933), p. 24.

tled. Thus, vicariously, homebodies as well gradually acquired some measure of "that enlarged and impartial View of Men and Things, which no one single Country can afford."[262] Then as now—for indeed then *is* now—space travel opened a new view of the world and spun off a wealth of new consumer goods that altered the lives of Earthlings everywhere.

The other essays in this volume all measure from their different historical angles the progress of consumer culture in America immediately before and after the Revolution. Because mine is a different task, to describe the changing meaning of material things and explain the origins of popular demand for fashionable goods, the argument I have advanced so far applies to the North American colonies as one of many regions where migration and resettlement brought these new international cultural forces into play.

It remains to ask what circumstances peculiar to these colonies account for the rampant materialism for which Americans were singled out and praised or damned starting as long ago as the early nineteenth century. Several characteristics of American society encouraged the unusually rapid spread of consumer habits among ordinary people after 1800. These elements bear looking at in a final summing up of the case for consumption as a medium of social communications because they appear to explain Americans' exceptional need for consumer goods in American terms. As we have seen already, fashionable living in the late colonial and early republican years was a mixed blessing. It opened doors to countless thousands at the same time that it barred them to countless others. Taking account of the American evidence therefore leads to two corollary observations—one positive and one negative— to add to the five preceding statements that together summarize my interpretation of this central theme in the nation's cultural history.

Many a commentator on the American scene presumed a connection between the physical mobility of the country's "promiscuous masses" and their eagerness to acquire the trappings of success. Catharine E. Beecher, writing in 1841,

[262] Josiah Tucker, *Instructions for Travellers* (London, 1757), p. 3.

but remembering as far back as the turn of the century, observed that "reverses of fortune are, in this land, so frequent and sudden, and the habits of people so migratory, that there are strangers in every part of the country, many of whom have been suddenly bereft of wonted comforts."[263] There was irony in the way that moving house broke up a family's accumulated possessions and then, shortly afterwards, landed the new arrivals in circumstances that placed a premium on material things that could give some clue to their personal identity and social standing. The man who boasted in 1744 that "his little woman att home drank tea twice a day" might have found sympathy from pioneer housekeepers in Kentucky fifty years later, almost every one of whom, it was said, "had some bowl or dish she brought from the old states . . . as proof of her primitive gentility."[264] The great movement of peoples to and through the colonies in the first century and a half only increased in speed and volume as the new nation spilled over the mountains and flooded across the interior after the Revolution. "Every thing is moving and changing," Beecher later wrote in description of "this migratory and business Nation." Fortune-seeking sons left "the rich mansions of their fathers to dwell in the log cabins of the forest," and they took "the daughters of ease and refinement" with them "to share the privations of a new settlement." Extreme geographical mobility eroded familiar social distinctions. Poor people struck it rich; wealthy ones lost everything. Tocqueville reported that "wealth circulates . . . with incredible rapidity, and experience shows that two successive generations seldom enjoy its favors." A perception grew up that there were "no distinct classes, as in aristocratic lands," no "impassable lines." Even in "the more stationary portions of the community" observers noted "a mingling of all grades of wealth, intellect, and educa-

[263] Catharine E. Beecher, *A Treatise on Domestic Economy for the Use of Young Ladies at Home and at School* (1841; reprint ed., New York, 1970), pp. 17, 264.

[264] Bridenbaugh, ed., *Gentleman's Progress*, pp. 13–14; Maria Daviess, *History of Mercer and Boyle Counties* (Harrodsburg, Ky., 1924), p. 45. I am grateful to Elizabeth A. Perkins for permission to read in manuscript her paper "The Consumer Frontier: Household Consumption in Early Kentucky," *Journal of American History* 78 (1991):486–510.

tion."[265] American storekeepers had long heeded a piece of very un-English advice, to behave "in the same manner to every person altho of different stations in life" and, of course, to sell the same goods to anyone with ready money or sound credit.[266] A yeastier environment for the germination of materialistic values is hard to imagine. So historians should not be surprised to hear an English traveler declare in 1807 that "pride of wealth is as ostentatious in this country as ever the pride of birth has been elsewhere."[267]

American society was exceptionally mobile and fluid, and it became ever more so. Both traits exaggerated people's need for affordable, portable, interchangeable status signifiers. So did another American characteristic. The country's social structure encouraged emulative consumption by its flatness as well. If England's densely layered classes bred competition and made social climbing easy, a foreshortened social hierarchy in America placed an even heavier burden on consumer goods to define differences. Although hardly classless in reality, American society lacked the extremes of wealth and poverty found in Britain and Europe. Its reputation as "a best poor man's country" was deserved. More important, it was believed. Richard Montgomery, a disappointed placeman in his native England, complained in 1772 that "a man with little money cuts a bad figure in this country among Peers, Nabobs, etc., etc." Emigration was his only out. "I have cast my eye on America," he wrote, "where my pride and poverty will be much more at their ease."[268] A man of his breeding did not expect to forsake fashion in the colonies; he simply looked

[265]Beecher, *Treatise on Domestic Economy*, pp. 16–17, 267; Alexis de Tocqueville, *Democracy in America*, ed. J. P. Mayer, trans. George Lawrence (Garden City, N.Y., 1969), p. 54.

[266]William Cuninghame to Bennett Price, Oct. 7, 1767, William Cuninghame and Co. Letter Book, 1767–73, privately owned, inquiries to National Library of Scotland. My thanks to Harold Gill for this reference.

[267]Robert Southey, *Letters from England* (1807; reprint ed., London, 1951), pp. 164–65.

[268]Richard Montgomery to John Montgomery, n.d. [1772], cited in Thomas H. Montgomery, "Ancestry of General Richard Montgomery," *New York Genealogical and Biographical Record* 2 (1871):129.

forward to paying less for it. It was well known that the excessive "luxuries, elegancies & refinements . . . attainable in England . . . no money [could] procure in this country."[269] Having "never known such," Americans were "undoubtedly as happy without." Ignorance was bliss. The new United States was "a glorious country for persons of industrious habits and moderate means," and "the mass of the white population," being a larger proportion of the whole here than elsewhere, was reckoned by those who had traveled or lived on both sides of the Atlantic to "enjoy here decidedly more comfort than in England." Increasingly those comforts were supplied by purveyors of attractive, inexpensive, store-bought goods.

Consumers of British-made wares sold to mass markets in the colonies came to include a significant number of American freeholders by the fourth quarter of the eighteenth century. T. H. Breen argues elsewhere in this volume that buying and using the "baubles of Britain" had become so widespread by the 1760s that consumption was the principal shared experience that overcame sectional differences and made coconspirators of merchants, planters, farmers, and artisans when the call went out to boycott British manufactures. The conflict with Britain was not essentially a dispute over imports, but consumer goods became the instruments, he says, that mobilized a populace and linked abstract ideas to everyday experiences common to a multitude of men and women throughout all the colonies.

Hard numbers are lacking for the decade between the Stamp and Townshend Acts and the Revolution. Yet historians can get some sense of how many ordinary Americans were swept up in the consumer economy in these and the years immediately following Independence by extrapolating backwards from data collected in 1815 for a new tax on luxury goods.[270] It imposed duties on a long list of household furni-

---

[269]This and the following quotations are from an 1832 diary of Ann Maury, a young Englishwoman widely traveled in the United States, published in *Intimate Virginia: A Century of Maury Travels by Land and Sea*, ed. Anne Fontaine Maury (Richmond, 1941), p. 199.

[270]With the important exception of Ann Smart Martin's thesis, "Urban / Rural Dichotomy," the 1815 property tax on household furniture is virtually unknown and almost unused by social historians. Returns survive for

ture, excluding only beds, kitchenwares, family portraits, and things homemade. All households without exception were subject to assessment; those with furniture worth less than two hundred dollars were exempt from payment. Thus, by ranking the estimated total of 800,000 American families in 1815 by the value of their domestic possessions, the lawmakers created an index that historians can use to measure the progress of consumer spending shortly after the turn of the century. Surprisingly, the number of exempt households—those least well furnished—was put at only 259,000. Less than a third of all householders fell below what might be called the poverty level of genteel furnishings. Fully half the number of families in the country, 400,000, owned luxury goods worth two hundred to six hundred dollars. Forty-five thousand more were assessed for clothes presses, dining and tea tables, settees, prints, pianofortes, coffee urns and teapots, chandeliers, epergnes, and other nice things valued up to a thousand dollars. That left a top layer of no more than 76,000 affluent families who furnished their houses five times more expensively than the exempted households. In other words, consumer wealth bulked broadly in the middle ranks of American society by 1815. Moreover, much of it was invested in articles that clearly indicate that the middle classes had joined enthusiastically in the practice of the gentle arts. The great architectural rebuilding that replaced so many colonial structures on

---

Massachusetts, Pennsylvania, Maryland, Virginia, North Carolina, and perhaps other states. Enactment of the statute is recorded in the Records of the Ways and Means Committee, "Report on So Much of the President's Message as Relates to the Finances of the United States," Oct. 10, 1814 (National Archives, HR 13-A D14.4); *Annals of Congress*, 13th Congress, 3d Session, "State of the Treasury," p. 1095, "Proceedings," pp. 132, 254, "Operation of the Direct Tax," pp. 1096–97, "Taxation of the District of Columbia," p. 1098; *U.S. Statutes at Large*, 13th Congress, 3d Session, 1815, pp. 196–98. The assessors went house to house collecting very specific information. They organized the Virginia returns into four categories: (1) major pieces of furniture, down to chairs made of mahogany, plus carpets, window curtains, and venetian blinds, (2) case pieces in other woods, (3) pictures, looking glasses, and musical instruments, and (4) containers for genteel beverages, fancy lighting devices, and wash basins (Tax Records, "Personal Property Tax, 1815," by county, Va. St. Libr.). Taxes were also levied on expensive footwear, horse harness, gold and silver watches, paper, nails, and playing cards.

the American landscape in the 1810s, 1820s, and 1830s was obviously accompanied, maybe slightly led, by a no less thorough refurnishing and refashioning of middling Americans' homes, notably among city dwellers and farmers able to employ hired hands or slaves. Probate inventories, the 1815 property tax, and archaeological excavations on early nineteenth-century domestic sites corroborate the view that the wealth of goods was already widely shared.[271]

This picture of prosperity can be overdrawn, of course. Travelers in the new United States still encountered rustics who used old-fashioned chests for chairs and tables and slept all in one bed like a pile of puppies. The narratives suggest that the most primitive living conditions among whites were to be found in frontier settlements.[272] But even there pack trains, canal boats, and peddlers' wagons caught up with homesteaders remarkably quickly, especially after the first quarter of the nineteenth century.[273] Back East the flow of

[271]As yet only Lorena S. Walsh has pulled together a tentative summary view of consumption patterns in the United States in the early nineteenth century in "Consumer Behavior, Diet, and the Standard of Living in Late Colonial and Early Antebellum America, 1770–1840," in Robert E. Gallman and John Joseph Wallis, eds., *American Economic Growth and Standards of Living before the Civil War* (Chicago, 1992), pp. 217–64. There is other valuable information in Bernard L. Herman, "Multiple Materials, Multiple Meanings: The Fortunes of Thomas Mendenhall," *Winterthur Portfolio* 19 (1984):67–86, as well as several articles on the ceramics market in America in the same issue. Also essays in Suzanne M. Spencer-Wood, ed., *Consumer Choice in Historical Archaeology* (New York, 1987).

[272]See, for example, J. Franklin Jameson, ed., "Diary of Edward Hooker, 1805–8," in *American Historical Association Reports* 1 (1896):895, for a description of a preacher's house in the Carolina mountains; also Louis-Philippe, *Diary of My Travels in America*, trans. Stephen Becker (New York, 1977), pp. 113–14, for a vernacular bedroom scene in Knoxville in 1797 that nonplussed even the sophisticated future king of France.

[273]Besides Elizabeth Perkins's study of Kentucky in "Consumer Frontier," other useful local histories and archaeological site reports that document the westward spread of consumer goods and habits include George L. Miller and Silas D. Hurry, "Ceramic Supply in an Economically Isolated Frontier Community: Portage County of the Ohio Western Reserve, 1800–1825," *Historical Archaeology* 17 (1983):81–92; Mark J. Wagner and Mary R. McCorvie, "Archaeological Investigations at the 'Old Landmark': An Early to Mid-Nineteenth-Century Tavern along the St. Louis–Vincennes Trace,"

manufactures coursed along the nation's growing network of commercial arteries and branched off into the tiniest capillaries of trade to reach remote backcountry hamlets and farmsteads. Ralph Waldo Emerson observed from his own window an "endless procession of wagons loaded with the wealth of all the regions of England, of China, of Turkey, of the Indies which from Boston creep by my gate to all the towns of New Hampshire and Vermont." Summer and winter "the train goes forward at all hours, bearing this cargo of inexhaustible comfort and luxury to every cabin in the hills."[274]

Emerson exaggerated for literary effect, but his words condense on a kernel of truth large enough to substantiate the first of the corollary statements about American consumer culture that refines and extends the general propositions already advanced. I have made a case here for a causal connection between the great European migrations after 1600 and a fundamental alteration in the meaning that people gave to commonplace artifacts. We have already seen ample evidence of both the stimulus and the response at work in the colonies. This much more also seems fair to say, that it was doubly difficult for such a culturally diverse and extraordinarily mobile people to establish and maintain a traditional repertory of place-centered status symbols. Consequently, Americans were exceptionally eager to adopt the international protocol of etiquette-book manners as the Esperanto of their social intercourse. Thus we can say in particular about Americans' experience of materialism that *widespread possession and use of fashion-bearing, status-giving artifacts gave this nation of newcomers unusually easy access to the American social system. Moreover, as the supply of factory-made goods increased and prices dropped, participation in the country's consumer culture acted as a powerful engine of democratization. Specifically, British manufactured goods and fash-*

---

unpublished report, c. 1989, American Resources Group, and Partners in Historic Preservation, Carbondale, Ill.; and David L. Felton and Peter D. Schulz, *The Diaz Collection: Material Culture and Social Change in Mid-Nineteenth-Century Monterey*, California Archaeological Reports, no. 23 (Sacramento, 1983).

[274] William H. Gilman et al., eds., *The Journals and Miscellaneous Notebooks of Ralph Waldo Emerson*, 16 vols. (Cambridge, Mass., 1960–82), 5:296–97. He made the observation in 1837.

ions served additionally to induce many ethnic peoples to accommodate themselves willingly or unwillingly to the dominant English culture.

This final somewhat sour note is a reminder that gentility was sometimes a coercer. Acculturation is always a calculus of gains and losses. Historians of early America, leery of unfashionable consensus history, have bothered to learn almost nothing yet about the multitude of inconspicuous non-English immigrants who lost no time acquiring standardized consumer goods to compensate for the handicaps of language and custom that otherwise excluded them from mainstream popular culture.[275] They know something about a few prominent immigrants and ethnic groups. These, they argue, conformed to English tastes under duress and mostly for show.[276]

German settlers transplanted remarkably complete and cohesive traditions from their various homelands to New York, Pennsylvania, and the southern backcountry. For two or three generations their Old World folkways remained little changed by contact with other colonists. A traveler through Pennsylvania in the early 1780s noted that even at a distance "it could be pretty certainly guessed whether [a] house was that of a German or of an English family" by the number and placement of chimneys: a single off-center stack in the middle of the house was likely to serve a common flue for a German farmer's *Küche* hearth and *Stube* stove (fig. 17) while "two chimneys, one at each gable end, [were usually indication that] there should be fire places, after the English plan."[277]

[275]Unreconstructed consensus historian Daniel Boorstin has amply demonstrated for a later period in American history the price that most students of immigration pay for their neglect of this subject. Ideas that he first presented in *The Americans: The Democratic Experience*, esp. part 2, "Consumption Communities," were further developed in a Smithsonian Institution exhibit, "Suiting Everyone: The Democratization of Clothing in America" (1974), accompanied by an interpretive catalogue of the same title by Claudia B. Kidwell and Margaret C. Christman (Washington, D.C., 1974).

[276]Dell Upton, ed., *America's Architectural Roots: Ethnic Groups That Built America* (Washington, D.C., 1986), more clearly inferred from the illustrations than stated in the text.

[277]Johann David Schoepf, *Travels in the Confederation* (1783–84), trans. and ed. Alfred J. Morrison (1788; reprint ed., New York, 1968), p. 125.

The German settler's "rough country mode of living" was commonly contrasted to the "English family used to living genteelly."[278] The difference, of course, was both one of origins and lifestyles. Germans still followed their customary folkways; "refined" Britons had become gentlefolk, recognizable as such because they declined to "work themselves and must employ servants and day laborers." Germans therefore had two hurdles to overcome to qualify as equals. They had to put aside their distinctively un-English customs, at least those they publicly displayed, and after that, like everybody else, they had to learn leisure-class manners.

Toward the end of the eighteenth century many began making such concessions by Anglicizing family names, learning English, drinking tea, dressing fashionably, and building houses that showed an impeccably conventional facade to passersby (fig. 18).[279] Some, maybe many, conformed thoroughly and enthusiastically. But scholars have conjectured that others knuckled under only where it could be seen. Behind closed doors they were slow to reorganize the traditional living spaces of the *Ernhaus*. More significantly, they embellished those same private interiors and the furnishings they contained with an astonishingly rich, gaudy, flamboyant decora-

[278]*The Notebook of a Colonial Clergyman, Condensed from the Journals of Henry Melchior Muhlenberg*, trans. and ed. Theodore G. Tappert and John W. Doberstein (Philadelphia, 1959), pp. 229–30, from a journal entry dated 1783, the same year of Schoepf's description of German and English houses in the same locality.

[279]Klaus Wust, *The Virginia Germans* (Charlottesville, Va., 1969), pp. 93–199; Henry Glassie, "Eighteenth-Century Cultural Process in Delaware Valley Folk Building," *Winterthur Portfolio* 7 (1972):29–57; Stephanie Grauman Wolf, *Urban Village: Population, Community, and Family Structure in Germantown, Pennsylvania, 1683–1800* (Princeton, 1976), pp. 127–53; Robert D. Mitchell, *Commercialism and Frontier: Perspectives on the Early Shenandoah Valley* (Charlottesville, Va., 1977), pp. 104–9, 122–32; Lonn Taylor, "Fachwerk and Brettstuhl: The Reflection of Traditional Folk Culture," in Ian M. G. Quimby and Scott T. Swank, eds. *Perspectives on American Folk Art* (New York, 1980), pp. 162–76; Elizabeth Augusta Kessel, "Germans on the Maryland Frontier: A Social History of Frederick County, Maryland, 1730–1800," Ph.D. diss., Rice University, 1981, pp. 284–342; Edward A. Chappell, "Acculturation in the Shenandoah Valley: Rhenish Houses of the Massanutten Settlement," *Proceedings of the American Philosophical Society* 124 (1980):55–89.

Figure 17. Hehn-Kershner House, Wernersville vicinity, Berks County, Pa. Probably built 1755 (inscription), modernized after 1803, fell into ruin after interiors were removed to the Winterthur Museum in 1957. George Hehn, Jr., the builder of this exceptionally large limestone farmhouse, was a third generation descendant of Palatine immigrants to New York who later followed Conrad Weiser to Pennsylvania. Hehn, a prosperous farmer, ranked in the top 10 percent of tax-paying landowners in the township. The next owner to acquire the property in 1772, militia captain Conrad Kershner, was also well-off and another immigrant's grandson. Despite their American origins, both men's families practiced conservative German house habits, however grandly. They entered the house directly into a busy Küche; they ate and socialized in an elegant Stube heated by a five-plate iron stove stoked from the kitchen; they retired at night to an equally handsome and heated sleeping Kammer upstairs; they climbed up and down a narrow boxed stair (dimly lit from one or two tiny windows) from cellar to attic; they cooled milk and drew water from a spring in the basement; and they baked bread in a bakehouse located in a separate outbuilding. Clearly the house builders were familiar with German construction methods and materials—dressed stonework, clay tile roofs, and ceilings infilled with mud and straw spread on wattles. The exuberantly molded ceilings and medallions in the Stube and Kammer took inspiration in equal part from German vernacular plasterwork and the German baroque. Be that as it may, Hehn's house made subtle concessions to nonethnic taste as well. The uniform size of the windows and their regular placement gave the front and the roadside gable a more formal appearance than most other German houses in the neighborhood. Likewise inside, the use of stock hardware and conventionally trimmed door and window frames deliberately avoided the flamboyant ironwork and robust moldings still dear to many German builders. Englishisms were hard to keep out. They infiltrated even into rural Pennsylvania in the guise of manufactured goods. The Englishman's architectural ideal was ever-present to Hehns and Kershners who gathered around the iron stove in their Stube or Kammer, for one of its cast-iron plates (later reused in building or rebuilding the nearby bakehouse and thus preserved) depicted the biblical story of Susanna and the Elders in a scene that included her rich husband's pattern-book town house. Kershner sold the house in 1803, and soon afterward (judging from a chair-rail molding) the new owner made changes that further modernized and gentrified the dwelling. He removed the ornamental ceiling in the parlor and pulled out the old stove to make room for a ground floor bedchamber. The room above the kitchen was partitioned into two rooms and seemingly incorporated into a two-story range of rooms built against the east hillside. Large doors at ground level suggest an agricultural use for this addition, but a second staircase communicating with rooms upstairs and the relocation of the attic stairs look like segregated accommodations for farm workers. The kitchen stair, also rebuilt, now led to an open landing and into what had apparently declined into a second-best bedchamber. The reused stove plate suggests that the two-story bakehouse and smokehouse also figured among these early nineteenth-century improvements. A subterranean cellar and a nearby stable and barn may have as well. (Drawing, Cary Carson and Margaret Mulrooney, from salvaged interiors, photographs and measured sketches in Winterthur Archives, and fieldwork by Edward A. Chappell, 1991)

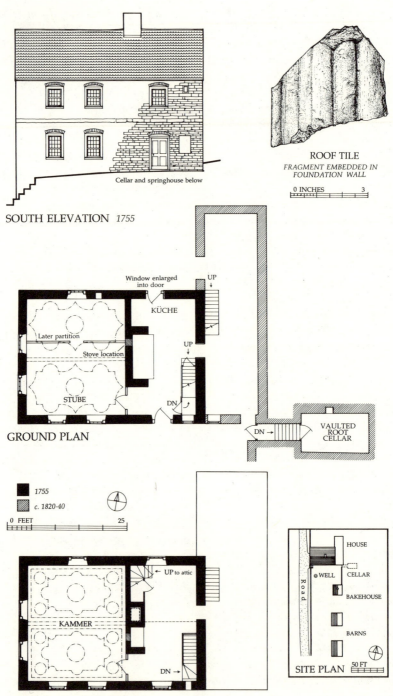

SOUTH ELEVATION *1755*

Cellar and springhouse below

ROOF TILE
*FRAGMENT EMBEDDED IN
FOUNDATION WALL*

0 INCHES   3

Window enlarged
into door

UP

KÜCHE

Later partition

UP

Stove location

DN

STUBE

GROUND PLAN

DN →   VAULTED
ROOT
CELLAR

■ 1755
▨ c. 1820-40

0 FEET   25

UP to attic

KAMMER

DN →

SECOND FLOOR PLAN

HOUSE

WELL

CELLAR

Road

BAKEHOUSE

BARNS

SITE PLAN   50 FT

668

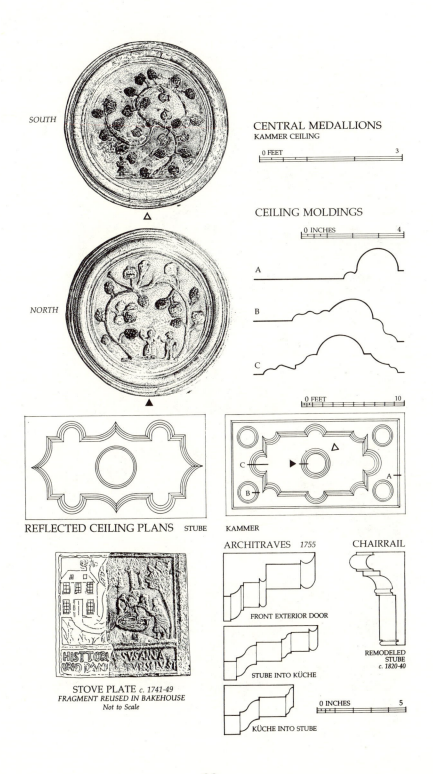

SOUTH

CENTRAL MEDALLIONS
KAMMER CEILING

0 FEET   3

CEILING MOLDINGS

0 INCHES   4

A

NORTH

B

C

0 FEET   10

REFLECTED CEILING PLANS   STUBE   KAMMER

STOVE PLATE *c. 1741-49*
FRAGMENT REUSED IN BAKEHOUSE
Not to Scale

ARCHITRAVES   *1755*   CHAIRRAIL

FRONT EXTERIOR DOOR

STUBE INTO KÜCHE

REMODELED
STUBE
c. 1820-40

KÜCHE INTO STUBE

0 INCHES   5

669

Figure 18. House with Six-Bed Garden, *one of a pair of similar ink and watercolor drawings attributed to David Huebner, Upper Montgomery County, Pa., 1818. Poorly paid schoolmasters in German settlements earned pocket money by making baptismal certificates and other illuminated documents. They also gave small* Fraktur *drawings to diligent pupils as rewards for good work and to ingratiate themselves with the parents who renewed their contracts annually. Such personal and personalized documents became treasured keepsakes. Adolescents and proud new mothers and fathers often kept them in the one piece of furniture that German householders considered their very own, an individual's* Kischt *or dowry chest. Fraktur was primarily a country art. Known prize winners and certificate holders seldom lived in towns or even villages. Cosmopolitan town dwellers were less taken with folk artists' enthusiasm for colorful, playful, stylized flowers, birds, animals, and geometric pinwheels. This drawing of an Anglicized house in a* Fraktur *firmament is therefore an unusual expression of both Id and Ego in the half-acculturated German-American personality. (Courtesy, Schwenkfelder Library, Pennsburg, Pa.)*

tion quite beyond anything recollected from the old country and quite unlike other Americans' artistic expressions in the early nineteenth century.[280] Some have interpreted these dichotomous, outside-inside, public-private aesthetics as evidence of a cultural split personality inflicted on minorities by the overweening hegemony of a master race of English descendants.[281] The incandescent flowering of German-American decorative arts does indeed suggest some little resistance and proudhearted reaction to outside pressures to conform. Chances are that, when historians investigate acculturation among other large, stable ethnic groups as carefully as they have studied the Germans, they will discover comparable cross-currents in the mainstream of taste.

On the other hand, now that we understand how gentility accommodated itself separately, differently, and piecemeal to each traditional culture it encountered, it seems highly likely that the process of Americanizing non-English peoples was also part of the idiosyncratic transformation of folkways into formalities that accounts for regional differences in middle-class culture everywhere after 1800. The dilemma facing Americans of European descent may therefore have been less a choice between ethnic or English than one between folk or formal. By the end of the eighteenth century isolated German, Swiss, Dutch, and Scotch-Irish communities were opening up to the same outside influences that promoted gentility and use of consumer goods among country people everywhere. Under the circumstances even Dunkers, Dutchers, Jocks, and Paddywhacks may have conformed their house habits more or less willingly.

[280]Chappell, "Acculturation," pp. 61–63; Swank et al., *Arts of the Pennsylvania Germans;* Richard Henning Field, "Proxemic Patterns: Eighteenth-Century Lunenburg-German Domestic Furniture and Interiors," *Material History Bulletin* 22 (1985):40–48.

[281]The ethnic argument loses some of its force when historians find references to English-Americans who likewise were careful to keep up exterior appearances, but showed indifference to fashion indoors. A traveler to central Massachusetts in 1760 observed that "the Painting and Utensils and Furniture in the Houses did not equal outward Appearances of their Houses in this part of the Country" (Paul Coffin, "Memoir and Journals: A Tour to the Connecticut River," *Maine Historical Society Collections* 4 [1856]:261–64).

Others had no choice whatsoever. For every ethnic traditionalist forced against his will to accept the majority's tastes, there were probably a hundred whom the system snubbed and excluded. Snobbishness about possessions was noway exclusively American. But it blossomed with special luxuriance here where the color of money outshone the quality of birth and where so many middling sorts jockeyed for position in society's compacted ranks. "True republicanism" was said to ensure "that every man shall have an equal chance—that every man shall be free to become as unequal as he can."[282] In competition where advantage was gained so decidedly by possessing material things, the possessors learned to manipulate and control the unpossessed in ways that again were not unknown elsewhere but reached new heights—or really new depths—of perfection in republican America. The idea of status competition has woven in and out of my account without ever becoming the main thread of the argument. Many other writers on consumption, from the moralists of the eighteenth century to latter-day Veblenites, would have emulation explain virtually everything about the rise of fashion. Others insist that it explains nothing.[283] I lean toward the latter view when it comes to first causes, for what impresses me most about early consumers' behavior is not so much their exclusivity as their love for the rules, conventions, and symbols that identified kindred spirits and gave worthy claimants access to privileged social circles. But how then can historians account for modern consumers' puzzling addiction to novelty? Why the never-ending march of fashions if already fashionable people were happy to welcome successful emulators into their ranks? One recent answer, that consumption actually has little to do with emulation and is better understood as a deep desire to experience the anticipated enjoyment of products and services not yet acquired, takes the subject down an interesting byway.[284] But no matter how widespread the pleasures of

[282] *How to Behave* (New York, 1856), p. 124.

[283] Colin Campbell, a disbeliever, critiques the emulation arguments in his *Romantic Ethic*, pp. 36–57.

[284] Ibid., pp. 88–95.

window-shopping had become by the end of the eighteenth century, this hedonism argument leaves unexplained the undeniable fact that fashionable elites had attracted imitators of their domestic lifestyles before 1700 and imitators of their sartorial styles a hundred years before that. The "epidemical madness" to consume was rampant for decades before the cerebral pleasures of contemplating future purchases became addictive.

Historians who will not dismiss status competition as a driving force behind fashion are obliged to give a better explanation for it than human nature. The goods themselves are one important key to understanding how emulation worked to the advantage of some and the disadvantage of others. Inherent in the household furnishings and personal possessions that became status symbols for an international gentry were two qualities that impeached the lasting value of those symbols: they could be cheapened, and they could be mass produced. The old-fashioned marks of distinction could not. Pasture and plowland were not usually expandable commodities in England, lineage was not usually for sale except by marriage, and labor was something would-be employers could either afford or not. Among the traditional status-bearing artifacts, painted canvas and base metals were shams that fooled no one. Only articles of clothing could be made cheaply, plentifully, and deceptively like the finery they imitated. No wonder sumptuary excesses caused such alarm, and no wonder annual fashions appeared first in the garment trades well before 1600.

When household furniture, tablewares, vehicles, and even buildings were subsequently pressed into service to communicate people's social identities, they opened to manufacturers a multitude of new product lines that could, like clothing, be made in a range of qualities and prices to satisfy a wide marketplace demand. That demand came from two sources. At the low end were those who wanted in, the emulators and "mechanics struggling to be genteel."[285] These lesser social climbers were not the ultimate tastemakers, of course; they only wanted the "latest fashions" already displayed by those

[285]Quoted in Schlesinger, *Learning How to Behave*, p. 17.

they aspired to copy. The demand for new things came from those whose privileged society the imitators desired to join. Because emulators became so numerous by the middle of the eighteenth century and because it was often so difficult on first acquaintance to tell a genuinely cultivated gentleperson from the many fraudulent look-alikes, the in-crowd that paid close attention to such things looked to high fashion as the elusive sine qua non that separated them from the clamorous herd of pretenders who flaunted last year's fads. The desire to bring on board those social equals who were entitled to respect was always counterbalanced by the impulse to pull up the ladder before mock ladies and gentlemen climbed higher than they deserved. The history of consumer culture since the seventeenth century has to be understood as this tug-of-war between two great contending social needs: on the one hand, the need for a new, universally accessible, portable system of status definition and, on the other, an effective means to differentiate and mark off one group from another. Affordable consumer goods used to engage in imitative genteel activities satisfied the first requirement; changing fashions and arcane rules of etiquette served the other. The synergy between them was unusually strong in North America. Where so many strangers in a nation of nations set such great store by a person's possessions, fashionable consumption became an exaggerated symbol of personal worthiness and a dreadful instrument of social control. The new United States had no shortage of true gentlefolk who understood that "the best finished furniture or finest marble will lose half its luster" without the polish of good manners. But the future increasingly belonged to a baser crowd that saw nothing but their own advantage in "Rules for Ladies" that included the advice "Always keep callers waiting, till they have had time to notice the outlay of money in your parlors." Scolding writers of popular etiquette books could say a thousand times a thousand ways that wealth "ought not to be the passport into the higher orders of society," that instead "education should be the test of gentility." But lamentably in wide-open republican America "knaves and fools [were] often more successful than the wise and the good."[286]

Social conflict between well-bred and ill-bred competitors

was modern class warfare waged along new lines and fought with new weapons. The rich and powerful were able to turn the system of manners back in its own defense to gain psychological advantage over their "unworthy" rivals. They cynically employed fashion and ceremony as instruments of intimidation. Dr. Alexander Hamilton of Annapolis was one of the first to describe how it worked. He even illustrated his "History of the Tuesday Club" with sketches showing club members parading their pomp before the hoi polloi of the town (fig. 19). He explained that "this luxurious and effeminate age" required it. Where nature no longer distinguished the upper classes "from the common Rascallion herd," the newly risen "degenerate, puny, pigmy race" of rulers had only "these magnificent trappings and Embelishments . . . [to] keep the great Leviathan of Civil Society under proper discipline and order." Sure enough, when Hamilton and his cronies sallied forth into the town once a year resplendent in their full Tuesday Club regalia, they were "stared at . . . by persons of all Ranks and degrees, who seemed to be as much astonished, as the mob is at a coronation procession, or any such Idle pageantry."[287] Just as kings and queens and ancient nobles once held the rabble in awe by their lavish feasts and stately ceremonies, now a lesser race of merchants, planters, physicians, and lawyers thought well to tranquilize the masses by showing off good manners.

Such display often achieved the desired effect. Men and women whose status was uncertain even to themselves and who therefore sought a firm footing in the lower ranks of genteel society were often rebuffed and cowed by the sheer arrogance of those who preceded them. Little people suffered most sorely the afflictions of a social system governed by annual fashions and mysterious initiations, little people like the artisan who wrote in despair to a Boston newspaper in 1792 that "from my situation in life, I am *virtually* debarred from

[286]*Journal of the Life of Nathanial Luff, M.D., of the State of Delaware* (New York, 1848), pp. 12–13, recalling Philadelphia in the 1770s; Sara Payson (Willis) Parton, *Fern Leaves from Fanny's Port-Folio* (Auburn, N.Y., 1853), pp. 317–19; [Margaret Bayard Smith], *What Is Gentility? A Moral Tale* (Washington, D.C., 1828), p. 4.

[287]Quoted and discussed in Micklus, "The 'Tuesday Club,'" pp. 55–56.

Figure 19. One after another the Tuesday Club's processions through the streets of Annapolis acquired the semblance of semi-official ceremonies. *Dr. Alexander Hamilton's drawings of the first three "Grand Anniversary Processions," those of 1747, 1750, and 1751, and another showing the members rehearsing an ode they performed on the last occasion, record the process by which the pomp and grandeur of private citizens received attention, respect, and finally official sanction from the town fathers. Thus, by degrees, public displays of civility came to reinforce the rule of well-bred gentlemen over the rest of society and the authority they exercised by dint of their superior manners. According to Hamilton's drawing and account of the club members' initial grand procession (a), that first year they simply attracted curious stares from all who happened to be out on the street at the time, most notably "from the Great Collonel Bumbasto, then accidentally passing by," who showed them the courtesy of a "very Low bow." Three years later in 1750 the next outing (b) seems to have been preceded by all the advance publicity of a circus parade: "It was honored with a great number of Spectators of all Ranks from windows, walls, Balconies, and even the Sides of the Streets were lined with Children and other Spectators, nay, the* Patres Conscripti, *or members of the Great provincial Senate, deigned to come forth of the doors of their house and look on this gallant Show." The following year the spectacle came even closer to receiving official recognition (c). The master of ceremonies, ode in hand, actually led the marchers past the club president's house, their ultimate destination, to the council's own chambers at the capitol. In that exalted setting (d) "the music of the anniversary ode . . . was performed on many Instruments accompanied with voices, with great applause, before a grand and Splendid assembly of the prime Gentlemen and Ladies" of the town. The poet laureate came well supplied with "printed Copies of the ode" to pass out to the spectators. Once this public recital was completed, members retraced their steps to the president's house to perform it all over again privately. Participation in this annual event required not only the right clothes and correct comportment, but also fashionable houses with formal reception rooms. Each procession convened at the town house of one pseudonymous "Sir John Oldcastle," in real life a modestly wealthy Annapolis landowner. Notwithstanding, he solemnly received the club brothers in his entry hall and then, "Introducing them into the Antichamber, Entertained them with Rich Lemonian punch and Generous wine." The company moved easily from such public architectural spaces to the outdoor parade route and, at its other end, an outdoor courtyard facing the president's house, which was "strowed with flowers & the Colors displayed as usual." Here the procession halted again, and the marchers spent "sometime sitting in the yard, round a table Garnished with punch bowls, bottles, Glasses and Tobacco pipes." Eventually they "Translated themselves into his honor's great Saloon"—another formal receiving room— "which was beautifully Illuminated with Sconce lights, and set out with various garlands and flowers" as well as the "great Chair of State" occupied by the club president. The fusion of dress, deportment, and display with political authority was openly demonstrated and easily enforced in a culture that still made no hard and fast distinctions between public and private or indoors and out. (Courtesy, John Work Garrett Library, Special Collections Department, The Johns Hopkins University)*

The first grand Anniversary Procession

a: 1747

The Second grand Anniversary Procession.

b: 1750

Third Grand Anniversary Procession

c: 1751

Grand Rehearsal of the Anniversary Ode.

d: 1751

any of the *common amusements* of this town." He explained that there were no actual regulations that excluded mechanics from concerts, assemblies, and public card parties. There did not have to be. "The *distance* that is always observed by those who move in the higher sphere, and the *mortification* which I and my family must inevitably undergo if we were with them, exclude us as much as if there was a solemn *act* of exclusion."[288] Because fashionable consumption was no formulaic ritual, because every occasion for its display was a live performance that tested an individual consumer's social skills, there were always real winners and real losers. They could be found as well in Britain, northern Europe, and indeed wherever consumer culture followed the footsteps of people who moved in wider and wider social circles. But the contest that produced winners and losers in polite society was played by a simplified set of singularly materialistic rules in America where otherwise virtually anybody was free to purchase property from a land office and lineage from a sign painter.[289] Showy material possessions and a passing acquaintance with their use increasingly became the most important measures of Americans' social standing as the country expanded beyond the older east coast settlements and as manners were appropriated by people not to manners born.

So here at last my account of fashionable consumption is brought to the final corollary. However much Americans' enthusiasm for store-bought things created opportunities for social advancement and cultural assimilation, *the excessively materialistic values that attached to social status in the new United States had the effect of sharpening class differences by making them visible, tangible, and inescapable. To accentuate differences is always*

[288]*Columbian Centinel*, Dec. 8, 1792.

[289]It was said, for example, of planter-merchants on Barbados that "they out do the Dutch in Heraldry for every man assumes what coat he pleaseth ... and they are such unthinking Devills here that if two brothers dye the Years one after the other, they generally have different Coates [painted on the funeral hatchments] for the painter has forgott, what he Drew for the first Brother, [or] the family did not like it & makes him design another" (Capt. Thomas Waladuck to James Petiver, Nov. 13, 1710, Sloane mss., British Library). I am grateful to David Shields for bringing this letter to my attention.

the purpose of fashion. It often had sinister applications. In this coun-try more than others it gave an upper class of purveyors and possessors a new kind of social control over an underclass of the less possessed. With this acknowledgment that consumer culture cut both ways in the capitalistic society that the United States was fast becoming after 1800, I rest my case. This account is now brought forward to a point where it meets and engages an impressive body of recent scholarship that explores how nineteenth- and early twentieth-century inventions, events, and institutions made mass consumerism synonymous with the American way of life. The themes running through this literature pull back and forth between the same contending interpretations of the good and evil consequences of material-ism that have animated the luxury debate since the eigh-teenth century, particularly the American version. One scholar's "people of plenty" are another's hapless victims of consumer choices imposed on them by corporate captains and confidence men.[290] The judgment of history mirrors both the dreams and the nightmares of American consumers' own experience.

These writers on consumption in recent times appear to have read little history before the 1880s. Their statements about fundamental shifts from local to national market sys-tems, from an economy of production to one of consumption, and from a clientele of elite customers to a mass market of ordinary buyers—*all supposedly taking place in the latter half of the nineteenth century*—reveal a lack of familiarity with a much

---

[290]The principal works are cited in n. 66, above. Sociologist David M. Potter formulated the benign consumption thesis in *People of Plenty: Eco-nomic Abundance and the American Character* (Chicago, 1954). His critics, com-ing out of the Veblenite and Marxist traditions, include Stuart Ewen, *Captains of Consciousness: Advertising and the Social Roots of the Consumer Culture* (New York, 1976); Lears, *No Place of Grace;* and idem, "The Concept of Cultural Hegemony: Problems and Possibilities," *American Historical Review* 90 (1985):567–93. The power-struggle interpretation has drawn fire from Warren I. Susman, *Culture as History: The Transformation of American Society in the Twentieth Century* (New York, 1984), and Horowitz, *Morality of Spending.* Lears finds historical precedent and cultural significance in the debate itself in "Beyond Veblen: Rethinking Consumer Culture in America," in Bron-ner, ed., *Consuming Visions,* pp. 73–97.

longer chronology of historical events.[291] The value of starting the story at its real beginning three (or even four) hundred years ago is not merely to set the record straight or give early modern historians the first say. Only a longer perspective can provide the focal length needed to perceive differences crucial to understanding the essential nature and complicated development of modern consumer culture. Those instructive differences include important distinctions between improved living standards and changing lifestyles, between gentility and fashion, between the market forces of supply and demand, and, most important of all, between prime causes and the many other factors that contributed to the growth, spread, and acceptance of consumer values. Once again, Americans' eagerness to believe the myth of our own uniqueness obscures the reality of our much older and more tangled ancestry.

Adam Smith was a close student and compulsive explainer of people's economic behavior. He pondered the same question about the origins of demand that historians too have lately decided is worth fuller investigation. "To what purpose is all the toil and bustle of this world?" he asked with regard to the rising tempo of production in England's workshops. A sweeping answer would have come as no surprise from the author of *The Wealth of Nations*. But on this occasion in 1759 he sought a deeper explanation in the psychology of individual consumers. "It is our vanity which urges us on," he concluded. "It is not wealth that men desire, but the consideration and good opinion that wait upon riches."[292] By the middle decades of the eighteenth century men were earning those riches by toiling and bustling harder than ever before. They were earning the consideration and good opinion they desired in new ways

[291] Conveniently summarized in Bronner's introduction to his *Consuming Visions*, pp. 1–4. While Lears is not ready "to abandon my own and other historians' stress on the late nineteenth century as a period of crucial transformation," he has come round to the view that "an understanding of that transformation requires a subtler conceptual framework than simply the notion of a shift from a Protestant 'producer culture' to a secular 'consumer culture'" ("Beyond Veblen," ibid., p. 77 n. 8).

[292] Adam Smith, *The Theory of Moral Sentiments* (London, 1759), p. 108.

as well. Landed property remained the most secure form of wealth in Britain, just as it paid the richest dividends in inflationary North America. But reputation was usually accorded to property owners and other wealthholders only when they used those resources to attain the necessary learning and leisure to participate in genteel society. Vanity was no longer satisfied merely by the good opinion of neighbors. By Smith's day riches spent on fashionable good manners were investments in reputations recognized and honored worldwide.

The decade of the 1750s stands more or less at the centerpoint of events that take on new significance when placed in a chronological narrative that spans all of two centuries between 1650 and 1850. For the first hundred years or so larger and larger numbers of quite ordinary men and women (who were already enjoying a rising standard of living) increasingly found themselves in social circumstances where individuals were rewarded for acquiring and learning to use a variety of domestic goods in ways that resembled the status-defining qualities of fashionable clothing. Between roughly 1650 and 1750 the desire to purchase amenities that distinguished polite society—the genteel orders—from the roughscuff masses gradually exceeded the capacity of workbench craftsmen to meet the demand. Northern Europe's emerging capitalist entrepreneurs were quick to spot the opportunities in these earliest consumer developments to profit from the new inventions, technologies, power sources, labor supplies, distribution links, and sales strategies that already anticipated Adam Smith's busy world of the 1750s. These and other innovations continued to gather greater momentum and over the next hundred years—the hundred years following 1750—precipitated the second great revolution, industrialization. Somewhere along the way consumption and production became so reciprocally interactive that historians lose track of cause and effect. Mass abundance became a universal way of life in nineteenth-century England and America, or, perhaps more accurately, the universally accepted standard by which the good life was measured. By then explanations for it are as complex as modern society itself.

I have tried in this essay to treat the earlier stages of the consumer revolution (when causes can still be distinguished from consequences) with some of the same precision that economic historians bring to their work on the origins of factory production. Unfortunately, cultural events seldom leave behind quantitative evidence of the sort that scholars need to answer definitively the most interesting questions they ask. The sources that best address the questions Why demand? Why 1650 to 1750? Why household goods and personal possessions rather than intrinsically valuable property? must be pieced together from a grab-bag of museum and archaeological collections, vernacular buildings, probate inventories, travel journals, town histories, immigration studies, and folklorists' hindsights. Hodgepodge though it is, the evidence can be used fairly systematically to clarify some of the major unresolved theoretical problems in consumer revolution studies. By supplying answers to questions about new products and their domestic uses, students of material culture can give the revolution definition and identify its leading indicators. By paying attention to the social status of tastemakers and trendsetters and observing where, when, and by whom their example was followed, they can isolate the leading sectors in the emerging consumption economy and date a "takeoff point" when demand for affordable luxuries began reshaping the means of production and supply. Scholars have had trouble distinguishing the central event from its antecedents in sixteenth-century sumptuary practices and also from its remarkable aftermath in the nineteenth century when England and America became vast emporiums. Close attention to artifacts and manuscripts alike reveals recognizable stages in the development of consumer behavior from its ancient practice in courtly circles to its seminal fusion with seventeenth-century notions of gentility, its explosive elaboration into fashion-consciousness by the middle of the eighteenth century, its rambunctious accommodation to popular taste soon after 1800, and finally its wholesale commercialization from the 1880s onwards.

Economic historians are used to analyzing events in just such stages of growth and development. Cultural historians usually are not. That difference leads to an imbalance in colonial American scholarship. Production and trade are almost always discussed in the context of the British mercantile system. Consumption seldom is.[293] Consequently, American historians have been slow to acknowledge that the rise of a consumer society transformed the British Isles and British Empire as one. Indeed its effects were felt throughout all of northern Europe. It is therefore certainly a mistake to interpret American consumers' new lifestyles as evidence of nothing more than the colonies' success at finally catching up to English standards after the hardships of settlement.

The creation and spread of an international gentry culture has figured curiously little in the long-running historical debate about the influence of Americans' European antecedents. This culture-or-environment controversy has warmed up again with the recent publication of two major reinterpretations by David Hackett Fischer and Jack P. Greene. One school examines the English roots of seventeenth-century colonial society and finds the cultural continuities decidedly stronger than the differences.[294] The other stresses the departures from English custom induced by the unusual conditions that colonists encountered in the New World.[295] On one thing they more or less agree, that during the eighteenth century the colonies drew closer to the mother country again, culturally and intellectually as well as administratively. The traditionalists see that as the unexceptional outcome of the colonists' tenacious hold on their old English heritage; those who stress the homesteaders' formative experience explain it as a gradual return to traditional ideals once colonial societies

[293]The point of Breen's argument in "Empire of Goods" and Bushman's point of departure in "American High-Style."

[294]David Hackett Fischer, *Albion's Seed: Four British Folkways in America* (New York, 1989). Taking less extreme positions are David Grayson Allen, *In English Ways: The Movement of Societies and the Transferal of English Local Law and Custom to Massachusetts Bay in the Seventeenth Century* (Chapel Hill, N.C., 1981), and Edmund S. Morgan, *American Slavery, American Freedom: The Ordeal of Colonial Virginia* (New York, 1975).

[295]Jack P. Greene, *Pursuits of Happiness: The Social Development of Early Modern British Colonies and the Formation of American Culture* (Chapel Hill, N.C., 1988); Thad W. Tate, "The Seventeenth-Century Chesapeake and Its Modern Historians," in Thad W. Tate and David L. Ammerman, eds., *The Chesapeake in the Seventeenth Century: Essays on Anglo-American Society* (Chapel Hill, N.C., 1979), pp. 3–50; Sumner Chilton Powell, *Puritan Village: The Formation of a New England Town* (Middletown, Conn., 1963).

became larger, hardier, wealthier, and more socially elaborated. The term *anglicization* (or *reanglicization*) appears frequently in the literature to describe how American culture on
the eve of the Revolution became more English than it had
been since shortly after the initial migrations.[296]

Is that assertion true? The answer is a complicated yes and
no. James Deetz's colorful analogy of a rocket that travels fast-
est as it leaves the launch pad and again when it falls back
to earth is often cited to illustrate the separation and later
reunification of Anglo-American culture. But his further observation is usually omitted, that the rocket reentered an atmosphere in which British culture had profoundly changed
from its seventeenth-century form.[297] Archaeologists call that
change *Georgianization,* a term as awkward as it is inaccurate.
The consumer revolution preceded the rule of Hanover
kings, drew inspiration from sources outside their realm, and
spread its influence far beyond their writ. Its ideology and
energy were overtly internationalist. To overlook that fact,
or to make a mishmash of old-fashioned folkways and newfangled formalities, as Fischer has done, is tantamount to
writing today about earth science in ignorance of plate tecton-
ics. What insight can come from describing the influence of
venerable English traditions when those traditions were undergoing profound transformation in England itself? Of
course a gentleman in eighteenth-century Philadelphia resembled a contemporary Londoner! Who would expect anything else from someone who also shared a common culture
with ladies and gentlemen in Stockholm, Dublin, Brussels,
Paramaribo, and Williamsburg! Their British ancestry was not
in dispute when American writers anxiously explained to
readers back home that "they live in the same manner, dress
after the same fashion, and behave themselves exactly as the
gentry in London." The point at issue was their broader claim
to be inheritors of British *civilization.* That was their real patri-
mony. The British part was taken for granted. Being a *civilized*

[296]Greene, *Pursuits of Happiness,* pp. 174–75. The historiography of this
theme is discussed in Breen, "Empire of Goods," pp. 496–99, and James A.
Henretta, "Wealth and Social Structure," in Greene and Pole, eds., *Colonial
British America,* pp. 279–81.

[297]Deetz, *Small Things Forgotten,* pp. 37–40.

Briton was something else. It raised gentlemen above the endemic barbarism of the real American wilderness and above the vulgarities of those "whose language and manners [were] strange to them" in the cultural wildernesses that could be encountered almost anywhere.[298]

The other economic and social historians, the environmentalists who stress the impact of local conditions in the colonies, can fall into the same trap. Anglicization can be equated too simplistically with the process of becoming more English. Region by region Jack Greene has braided together numerous demographic, social, economic, and environmental variables into a developmental history of the American colonies that is sensitive to differences in timing and variation from place to place. Yet he too reaches the overarching conclusion that all the mainland colonies became increasingly alike in the generations immediately preceding the Revolution. His argument appears unassailable partly because he builds it on bedrock monographic scholarship. The problem with it is the implication it carries that these overseas societies resembled British society, especially its metropolitan culture, *as a consequence* of becoming more populous, more affluent, more settled, and more complex, in a word (the contemporary word for it) more "improved." We have encountered this confusion once before. The same regional historians whose work Greene has summarized so comprehensively include those who hold the view discussed earlier that the desire to acquire consumer goods awaited only the fulfillment of certain social and economic preconditions to achieve satisfaction. The stock character in that scenario was a closet consumer who patiently bided his time until powerful restraints on his ambitions were finally relaxed. The stock character in the anglicization story is a hereditary gentlemen who allegedly always "displayed a strong desire to replicate British society" and, when conditions in the colonies finally allowed after 1690, "took pride in the extent to which those societies were coming increasingly to resemble that of the metropolis."[299]

[298] Hugh Jones, *The Present State of Virginia* (1724), ed. Richard L. Morton (Chapel Hill, N.C., 1956), pp. 81, 102.

[299] Greene, *Pursuits of Happiness,* p. 168.

All that is perfectly true as far as it goes. The trouble is that historians who have argued that Americans "rejoined the Western world" in the eighteenth century have usually thought they were describing only one process of historical change.[300] In fact there were two. There is nothing wrong with Greene's three-stage model in which transplanted British customs and institutions first were simplified, then elaborated by acculturation to local social environments, and finally replicated as "a measure of cultural achievement" by provincial societies far removed from the center of empire.[301] Generally speaking, the histories of most immigrant groups cohesive enough to sustain their remembered traditions probably follow a roughly similar course regardless of time or place. All that notwithstanding, the replication stage in the American colonies coincided with and was fundamentally shaped by the second formative process, international gentrification. The convergence was no historical accident. I have already explained how gentility and materialistic values served the special needs of hundreds of thousands of long-distance movers to North America. On the other hand, I have also shown that the usefulness of a highly elaborated visual communications system was not confined to people or places involved in founding overseas societies. Civilized manners and their fashionable accessories were acquired by at least as many stay-at-home consumers whose enthusiasm for the gentle arts was much more than homage-paying to Mother England. Not one, but two transforming events came together in the hundred years between 1650 and 1750, first to reshape British and European cultural norms and then to impress their indelible hallmark on malleable America.

Most historians have come around to the same conclusion that a traveler in America reached just before the Revolution,

[300]The phrase was first used strictly in reference to the Massachusetts Bay Colony by T. H. Breen and Stephen Foster, "The Puritans' Greatest Achievement: A Study of Social Cohesion in Seventeenth-Century Massachusetts," *Journal of American History* 60 (1973):22. For Jack Greene it aptly describes the convergence of all mainland colonial societies with mainstream social and cultural developments in Great Britain.

[301]Greene, *Pursuits of Happiness*, pp. 166–69.

that "very little difference is, in reality, observable in the manners of the wealthy colonist and the wealthy Briton."[302] Is it therefore splitting hairs to argue over how that happened? I believe not. I think it makes a difference that goes beyond merely satisfying our historical curiosity to find out not only what events took place, but how and why.

First of all, appreciating the true internationalist character of these changes can save historians wasted effort. It defines out of existence a troubling paradox to those who believe that "the Anglicization thesis obviously makes it hard to explain the American Revolution."[303] The colonists' increasing participation in a transatlantic consumer culture did indeed intrude on the developing conflict with Great Britain in several ways. T. H. Breen has shown that many Americans resented the debts they owed to British merchants and the taxes they paid to Crown officials on imported goods that they had come to regard as near necessities. His essay in this volume further describes how consumer goods may also have served symbolically as a common language of resistance creating ties between regions and classes that otherwise had not yet learned to speak with one voice. But to go further than that in search of reasons that explain away Americans' affinity for British culture at the same moment when they were throwing off British rule is an unnecessary exercise. Independence involved no repudiation of the values that both Britons and Americans shared. Moralists damned the excesses of fashionable consumption, patriots temporarily embargoed its products, and republicans later decried its snobbery. But gentility remained secure because the idea of it transcended national boundaries and outlasted international incidents. Americans who developed a taste for French fashions during and after the war were simply switching brand-names and suppliers, and then not for long. The American Revolution made less difference to the consumer revolution than the other way around.

Something else worth knowing about early modern England and the colonies can be learned by observing that gen-

302 Eddis, *Letters*, pp. 57–58.

303 Breen, "Empire of Goods," pp. 497–99.

teel Americans had become citizens of a wider world by the middle of the eighteenth century. Paying attention to consumer behavior has opened another rich field of inquiry to social historians, a field some call material history or the history of material life. These historians recognize that there is a social story to be told about the historical development of our own highly materialistic culture. Because the evidence for its study is so remarkably varied and often so remarkably unfamiliar to historians who usually consult only written records, students of material life have learned to make distinctions and play by rules that other social historians would find useful in their work as well.

Much historical writing on the seventeenth and eighteenth centuries deals one way or another with the events and forces that modernized Western societies. Political and economic historians bring an enviable precision to their accounts of this transformation largely because the official records and statistical evidence they use were written or compiled while performing the activities they seek to explain, for example, buying services, selling goods, paying taxes, collecting customs, making laws, and casting votes. Social historians have accumulated impressive databases as well. But much of their information is culled from tax records, censuses, muster rolls, wills and inventories, and court books that were created in the course of keeping records for purposes very different from those that now interest the scholars who consult them to study social change. Lacking direct evidence, they must infer general explanations from patterns of recorded behavior largely unrelated to the subjects they inquire into. To help themselves interpret those patterns, they have borrowed freely from modern sociology, anthropology, and linguistics. Theories originally designed by social scientists to test hypotheses about living societies often substitute for the directly relevant evidence that historians lack for times past. This reliance on theoretical assumptions about the nature of early modern society and the changes it underwent can lift the art of historical generalizing into the stratosphere, where indeed historians should want to soar, but where high fliers sometimes end up writing fairly windy history. Modernization theory is still frequently called on to provide a framework that many hope will best explain the transformation of early American society and culture from a state of ancient communalism into that modern condition that sets high value on pluralistic individualism. Few scholars question the broad outlines of this thesis or disagree that British and American communities were moving toward greater order, coherence, differentiation, and complexity in the eighteenth century. The challenge for historians is to dig beneath those descriptive generalizations to discover the forces that were pushing social change in that direction.

Hypotheses are only hunches. To demonstrate their validity they must be tested against the complexities of real life. Over the years social historians have been learning to make a functional distinction between the usefulness of much quantitative evidence for the purpose of asking questions and the efficacy of some narrative evidence for testing them. Genuine advances in historical understanding have followed when new hypotheses about social change were carefully framed in terms that genuinely explanatory evidence could answer, notably, for instance, in the lively subfields of women's history, African-American history, and the history of the family, all of which turn out to be subjects that are richly documented in a wide variety of sources.

So also is the social history of material life. It too is well recorded by abundant evidence that historians can use to penetrate social scientific abstractions and explain concretely how and why we moderns begin to recognize ourselves when we hold up a mirror to the seventeenth and eighteenth centuries. Making a case in favor of a history of material life has been the hidden agenda in this interpretive essay on consumer demand. Material history is not to be confused with the histories of material things themselves—we call that art history—or with social history merely illustrated with artifacts. The history of material life tells its own important story, an account of people's growing dependence on inanimate objects to communicate their relationships with one another and mediate their daily progress through the social worlds they inhabited. It has common characteristics with other testable social histories. It can be told as a narrative that is grounded in real places, follows a datable chronology, identifies specific causes, contributing factors, and measurable consequences, and records critical transitions from one stage of development to another. The evidence for past material life includes bodies of quantitative data that *indirectly* suggest their meaning by revealing patterns of ownership, testation, and disposal of goods, from which historians make educated guesses about the uses those objects served. At the same time, there is also much other evidence that speaks *directly* to the question of use: surviving artifacts whose design discloses their function, sherd collections from use-related archaeological contexts, travelers' descriptions of unfamiliar customs, advertisements and prescriptive handbooks, and genre paintings, prints, and other illustrations including eventually photographs.[304] The primary sources that historians of material history can use to test and refine the bigger pictures suggested by the pattern-making evidence go on and on.[305]

An abundant historical record never guarantees that historians will put it to use. Fashions in history writing wait on events. Not by accident have social historians only recently joined forces with other scholars to study the origins of our modern consumer society. Reaganomics in the 1980s launched Americans on a spending spree. At first, the binge appeared to be broadly based. Sales of 62 million microwave ovens, 105 million color television sets, and 31 million cordless telephones, when divided by 91 million U.S. households, suggested that this wealth of consumer goods must have been widely shared by the "Splurge Generation," even allowing for some families' multiple purchases. On closer inspection, however, it also became apparent that large numbers of ordinary people had been left out or left behind. The consumption boom coincided with a record high percentage of people whose incomes fell below the poverty line. Even full-time em-

[304] My use of all these sources throughout this essay should have, I trust, dispelled any suspicion that I trust them uncritically. For a further explanation of the connection I make between the use of artifacts and the meaning that users attached to them, see n. 116, above.

[305] The range is represented in works cited in *Decorative Arts and Household Furnishings in America, 1650–1820: A Bibliography*, ed. Kenneth L. Ames and Gerald W. R. Ward (Winterthur, Del., 1989).

ployment no longer gave many people access to the good life. Workers' wages stagnated while managers' salaries soared. Corporate chief executives' earnings rose 50 to 100 times higher than the average wage-earner's take-home pay.[306] In the aftermath, parents became pessimistic about their children's chances to improve or even equal the living standards they themselves achieved. A younger generation felt cheated out of its American birthright to a brighter future. People of all ages were dismayed that our nation values immediate material gratification above everything else. Americans grew frightened. They wanted to know how we got into this pickle. They groped for perspective. What did it mean? What did it portend? Historians obligingly came forward with a history of American material life.

Meanwhile, other astonishing consumer spectacles unfolded beyond our borders, but not uninfluenced by our example or unchallenged by our power. All across Eastern Europe, the former Soviet Union, China, and the Middle East, people who had been denied amenities that we in the West consider necessities toppled the governments, dissolved the nations, and repudiated the philosophies they blamed for their deprivation. "My countrymen interpret the term 'standard of living' to mean consumer goods," marveled an uncomprehending East German Communist Party official. "They are going West where they can find better and more plentiful goods."[307] An Arab strongman invaded the neighboring oil-rich sheikhdom of Kuwait. An American president won it back, not primarily (he told the public) to defend American strategic interests, not to uphold American democratic principles, but to "maintain America's standard of living." And for millions of approving voters that rationale was a fair trade for the 500,000 sons and daughters and 50 billion dollars dispatched to fight Operation Desert Storm. Iraqi con-

---

[306] Robert J. Samuelson, "The Binge Is Over," *Washington Post*, July 5, 1989; Spencer Rich, "U.S. Poverty Rate Up; Median Income Falls," ibid., Sept. 27, 1991; Robert J. Samuelson, "Trendy Pessimism," ibid., Nov. 13, 1991.

[307] Quoted in Jim Hoagland, "Reunification Qualms: From Western Shops," ibid., Dec. 23, 1989.

voys retreating north from Kuwait City were bombed to smithereens on a highway near Mutlaa. Afterwards the telecasts showed miles and miles of devastated vehicles, body parts, incinerated passengers, and, everywhere strewn over the tarmac, the booty that Iraqi soldiers had looted from the fabled city they sacked before fleeing. What did they plunder? Not the precious treasure that ravaging hoards bore off in ages past. The photographs showed something else, something commonplace, something uncomfortably familiar. The broken suitcases and smashed trunks spewed out a lurid cornucopia of television sets, polyester clothing, nylons, high heels, Nike running shoes, plastic toys, and children's story books.[308] There in the carnage lay ruined not only a dictator's grotesque ambitions, but also, pathetically, the broken dreams of thousands of little people who would stop at nothing and give up life itself just to possess a few pieces of what has become the real wealth of nations in the modern world.

Westerners viewed these scenes with a mixture of revulsion, ambivalence, and shame. Thousands died to keep cheap oil flowing into the economies that sustain our own standard of living. Ironically, ours is a way of life that the vanquished measured by the victor's standards—by the goods that the haves have and the have-nots don't. Americans could not fail to see reflected in the wreckage of Arab lives human aspirations not so different from the dreams that they themselves feared their own children would be denied. They felt torn. Their righteousness was shaken. Their values appeared sullied, their patriotism dishonored. Again, people wanted explanations. How do we and our friends repeatedly get into these messes? Once more historians obligingly come forward, this time with perspectives on a global history of material life.

The time for jeremiads against materialism has passed. The consumer habit is too ingrained in modern culture to renounce and unlearn. Indeed, its utility as a worldwide communications system spreads ever farther, ever faster as the latest alternatives to capitalism are denounced by their own disillusioned citizens. Their rage feeds on many complicated

[308] Steve Coll and William Branigin, "Spin Control on the 'Highway of Death,'" ibid., *National Weekly Edition*, Mar. 18–24, 1991.

frustrations, not least of all the conviction that life is too short to spend queuing up for ordinary amenities and too long to stay cooped up behind iron curtains. They compare their own poverty and restrictions to the affluence and mobility they see elsewhere in the world, and from that they learn a history lesson that we in the West are prone to overlook. Easy access to consumer goods has been, on balance historically, a tremendous liberating force in modern society. Plentiful, affordable goods, far more than belief in political philosophies, have oiled the wheels of democracy. They have also been a potent solvent to dissolve people's murderous loyalties to clans, races, religions, and nation-states. Consumer goods, the things they do, and the harmless human pleasures they can provide have become for millions the fullest expression of their liberal Jeffersonian right to the pursuit of happiness. Materialism has often, of course, been carried to excess. No one knows better than historians that the rise of consumer culture has been attended at every step by greed, discrimination, exploitation, war mongering, environmental degradation, and moral emptiness. On the other hand, few know as well as historians that the answers to the question *Why demand?* should not cause thoughtful people to despair. The answers should instead concentrate their minds on choices still to be made that will determine whether the world's resources in the future can be shared more widely and equitably at the same time that they are more wisely used and responsibly conserved.

Contributors
Index

Contributors

T. H. BREEN is the William Smith Mason Professor of American History and director of the Center for the Humanities at Northwestern University. His publications include *Tobacco Culture: The Mentality of the Great Tidewater Planters on the Eve of Revolution* (1985) and *Imagining the Past: East Hampton Histories* (1989). Breen is currently completing a study of political ideology and market experience on the eve of the American Revolution.

RICHARD L. BUSHMAN, Gouverneur Morris Professor of History at Columbia University, is author of *King and People in Provincial Massachusetts* (1985) and *The Refinement of America: Persons, Houses, Cities.* (1992).

KARIN CALVERT is an assistant professor in the Department of American Civilization at the University of Pennsylvania. She is the author of *Children in the House: The Material Culture of Early Childhood, 1600 to 1900* (1992), and she is presently at work on a study of the process of creating tradition, rituals, and a sense of shared culture in early America.

LOIS GREEN CARR is Historian for Historic St. Mary's City and for the Office of Research, Survey, and Registration of the Division of Historical and Cultural Programs, Department of Housing and Community Development, State of Maryland. She is coauthor of *Maryland's Revolution of Government, 1689–1692* (1974) and *Robert Cole's World: Agriculture and Society in Early Maryland* (1991) and is author and coauthor of many articles on colonial Chesapeake history. She is presently collaborating on a study of the social and economic development of the Chesapeake region over the colonial period.

BARBARA G. CARSON teaches in the Art and American Studies departments of the George Washington University and in the American Studies Program at the College of William and Mary. She has written *The Governor's Palace: The Williamsburg Residence of Virginia's Royal Governor* (1987) and *Ambitious Appetites: Dining, Behavior, and Patterns of Consumption in Federal Washington* (1991). In addition to studying travel in early America, she is writing about interpretive messages at history exhibitions and historic sites and studying changes in the furnishings of public buildings and private dwellings from the colonial period to the Civil War.

CARY CARSON, Vice-President for Research at the Colonial Williamsburg Foundation, works alongside colleagues from most of the disciplines that contribute to consumer-revolution studies—economic and social historians, architectural historians, archaeologists, anthropologists, and curators. Their collaboration and their employment by a museum that generously supports scholarship in the public interest are a continual source of ideas for Carson's own research and writing on early American social history, material culture, and the role of history museums as public educators.

EDWARD A. CHAPPELL is Director of Architectural Research at Colonial Williamsburg, where he is responsible for the care and interpretation of historic buildings. A graduate of the College of William and Mary and the University of Virginia, Chappell is interested in how buildings function socially and how museums employ them politically.

DAVID D. HALL, professor at the Divinity School, Harvard University, is a cultural historian. He has written widely on the seventeenth century, most notably, *Worlds of Wonder, Days of Judgment: Popular Religious Belief in Early New England* (1989). He is general editor of a multivolume "History of the Book in America," to be published by Cambridge University Press.

CYNTHIA ADAMS HOOVER, Curator of Musical Instruments since 1961 at the Smithsonian Institution, studies music and musical instruments in American life. This work has resulted in several exhibitions and related publications on such subjects as *Music in Early Massachusetts* (a collaborative exhibition at the Boston Museum of Fine Arts with a major monograph appearing in the accompanying publication in 1985), *American Ballroom Music and Dance, 1840–60* (a carefully researched live performance of music and dance, later recorded by Nonesuch Records and awarded a *Stereo Review* Record of the Year Award in 1975), and *Music Machines—American Style* (a study showing the impact of science and invention on the performance, reproduction, and dissemination of music in America). On the faculty of Aston Magna Academy, she presented studies of eighteenth-century American theater, chamber music, and patronage. She has served on the editorial boards of the *New Harvard Dictionary of Music*, the *New Grove Dictionary of American Music*, *The Complete Works of William Billings*, and New World Records. She is presently work-

Contributors

ing on two projects—a study of the cultural, social, and technological history of the piano in America, which she began during a Guggenheim Fellowship year, and the editing of a diary kept by William Steinway, 1861–96.

MARGARETTA M. LOVELL is associate professor of History of Art, University of California, Berkeley. She has taught at Yale University and the University of Michigan, has held the Duane A. and Virginia S. Dittman Chair in American Studies at the College of William and Mary, and has curated the American paintings collection of the Fine Arts Museums of San Francisco. She is the author of *A Visitable Past: Views of Venice by American Artists, 1860–1915* (1989) as well as numerous articles on eighteenth-century American artisans and painters. Her current research areas include nineteenth-century landscape painting and further work on eighteenth-century art and its context.

NANCY L. STRUNA is an associate professor in the Department of Kinesiology and an affiliate member of the Department of History at the University of Maryland, College Park. She is currently completing a book about sport and the changing relationship between labor and leisure in early America, which will be published by the University of Illinois Press. Her articles include "Gender and Sporting Practice in Early America, 1750–1810" (1991), "Sport and Society in Early America" (1988), and "The Formalizing of Sport and the Formation of an Elite: The Chesapeake Gentry, 1650–1720s" (1986).

KEVIN M. SWEENEY is associate professor of History and American Studies at Amherst College. His 1986 Yale dissertation and forthcoming book, "River Gods and Related Minor Deities: The Williams Family and the Connecticut River Valley, 1637–1790," was awarded the 1987 Jamestown Prize by the Institute of Early American History and Culture. Currently he is working on a book of essays exploring the material culture of the Connecticut Valley during the seventeenth and eighteenth centuries.

LORENA S. WALSH is a historian with the Colonial Williamsburg Foundation. She is coauthor of *Robert Cole's World: Agriculture and Society in Early Maryland* (1991) and the author of numerous articles on colonial Chesapeake history. She is completing a study of Chesapeake plantation agriculture, 1620–1820.

703

Index

Acrelius, Israel, 457
Adam, Robert, 52, 223
Adams, John, 271, 273, 330, 392, 431, 445, 451–53, 455
Adams, John Quincy, 307–8
Adams, Samuel, 46–47, 473, 520–21
Addison, John, 66
Addison, Thomas, 66
Advertisements, 245–49, 294, 320–21, 411, 449–50, 453, 465; by craftsmen, 347, 648; and consumers, 134, 235, 247, 249, 449–50, 459; and consumer society, 235, 247, 249, 455, 648; and fashionable goods, 244, 634, 648; and imported goods, 452–53, 473; by teachers, 309–10, 339; by tradesmen, 356, 630, 634; and travel, 374, 380, 383–84, 390–91
Agents, 47, 106–10, 456
Agriculture, 120, 212–13, 239, 383, 450, 516
Albrecht, Charles, 349
Album of Virginia (Beyer), 397
Algerine Captive (Tyler), 354–56, 359, 368
Allen, Capt. Bozone, 236
Amenities scores, explanation of, 69–70, 114, 617
Americans: and British goods, 450, 459; and British merchants, 462–63, 466; and debt, 462–64, 466, 475, 691; diversity of, 444–46, 655; emulate mother country, 459–60, 465; independence of, 461, 482; materialism of, 658, 664–65, 682–83; political mobilization of, 446–47,

461, 465; and taxes, 463–64, 471, 481; uniting of, 444–45
Anderson, Benedict, 445
Anglicization, 2, 461, 465, 481, 547, 687–91; through goods, 458–59, 473, 481; of market, 452
Annapolis, 69, 91, 151, 186, 424, 459
Anne Arundel County, Md., 68–69, 118, 129–30, 146, 148–49, 151, 165; diversification in, 122; inventories, 91, 102, 112, 114, 127; and tea, 481
Antes, John, 347
Architecture: Georgian, 2, 11, 16, 38–39, 170–71, 196–97; impermanent, 35, 172, 174–75, 194, 497, 499; permanent, 172–73, 194, 198, 226, 497; vernacular, 208, 223, 492, 557–58, 620, 624, 627. *See also* Housing
—interiors, 38, 216–17, 221–25; classical, 221, 492, 634; finish of, 21, 178, 193, 216–22, 225, 626, 634; ornamental, 16, 28, 40, 225, 625. *See also* Back rooms
Ariss, John, 39
Arlington, 173
Artisans. *See* Craftsmen
Arts, 329–30
Assemblies, 424–26, 433, 440, 507–8
Associations, 480–82
Asylums, 221–22, 227–28
Axson, William, 247

Back rooms, 20–21, 23–24, 66
Bacon's Castle, 172
Bailyn, Bernard, 544

Consumption (*cont.*)
competitive, 28, 31–32, 34–
35, 102, 134, 144; conspicuous, 25, 67, 102, 179, 187,
471, 518–19, 530, 550, 657;
criticized, 46–47; and demographics, 123–24, 126–28;
and dependency, 461, 466;
diversification and, 122–23,
148, 151, 165; and emula-
tion, 660, 673–74; and fashion, 223, 228, 642, 675–76,
682, 691; increase in, 228,
232, 450–51, 473, 491, 513,
617–18, 658, 685; and individual, 214, 460–61, 482;
and industry, 514, 685; and
inheritance, 129, 164; and
mobility, 526, 547, 607, 613,
657–59; patterns of, 51,
58, 144, 148, 227, 284, 539;
politicization of, 462, 465,
467–69, 471, 475; regional,
517–18; rural, 117, 213, 617;
and social communication,
448, 458, 461, 658, 661, 690;
and spending, 112, 653; standard of, 60, 70, 114, 123,
126–27, 618; study of, 515,
618–19; urban, 102–3, 213;
and wealth, 118, 123, 150,
455, 642
Continental Congress, 479–80
Copley, John Singleton, 265, 292–
95, 297, 304
Craftsmen, 189, 240–42, 267,
287, 363, 545; and architectural design, 11, 28, 39–40,
46, 224, 636; books for, 643;
in Chesapeake, 120, 122,
149; as consumers, 102, 546,
609; and demand, 240–41,
487–88; and design, 5–6, 28,
40, 46, 567–68; and furniture
design, 28, 40–41, 46, 54,
567–68, 648–49; goods produced by, 103, 411–12, 568,
595–96, 648; housing of, 35–
36, 183, 187, 189–90, 228;
marketing by, 228, 247–48;
social status of, 611, 676,

682; techniques of, 567–68.
See also Cabinetmakers; Car-
penters; Furniture makers;
Silversmiths; Tradesmen
Crawford, Richard, 321
Credit, 110–11, 238, 450, 454,
456, 461, 463
Crehore, Benjamin, 347–48
Crips, Richard, 191
Cupboards, 22, 63, 128, 529–31,
563–66, 574, 638
Custis, John, 173

Daggs, Hezekiah, 396
Dance, 272–73, 314, 325, 426,
506–9; masters, 242, 273,
275, 309–10; minuet, 273,
509; schools, 310, 339, 507
Deane, Elkanah, 188
Deetz, James, 688
Deference, 253
Delaware, 197, 209, 457
Demographics, 123, 126–29, 145,
150, 164, 509, 515
Destinations, 374, 378, 381–83,
390–91, 397. *See also* Spas
De Vries, Jan, 240
Dickinson, John, 462–64
Dickinson, Jonathan, 183
Dining, 117, 505–6, 590–91; cookbooks offer advice on, 594,
596–97, 600, 604; and furnishings, 587, 589–92,
598–99; as genteel activity, 8,
31, 587, 590, 602, 604; new
equipment for, 8, 589, 594,
597–600, 602–3; proper behavior at, 215–16, 588, 596,
603–5; wares for, 65–68, 505,
593, 595, 602, 653; wares for,
as amenities, 69, 81, 91, 102,
116. *See also* Ceramics; Glassware; Silver
Dining rooms, 21, 23–24, 67,
186–87, 195, 624–26; buffets
in, 634, 636–37; decoration
of, 21, 216, 243, 653
Diversification, 118, 120, 122,
148–51, 164–65; and con-
sumption, 122–23, 148, 151,

McCracken, Grant, 222
McKendrick, Neil, 104, 134, 171, 228, 517–18
MacPherson, John, 25
Madison, James, 480
Maine, 175–76
Manigault, Peter, 49, 648
Mannerism, 565, 567–68, 570–71, 583–84, 588
Manners. *See* Behavior
Maps, 376, 383, 386–87
Market Square Tavern, 192
Marketing, 3, 103, 105–8, 122, 134, 150, 228; strategies, 111, 117, 553; techniques, 26, 106, 110–11, 134, 228
Marketplace, 463, 486–87, 491; colonial, 452, 515–17; growth of, 456, 488, 509, 516–17, 568, 674; standardization of, 452, 454–55; variety of goods in, 452, 674
Markham, Francis, 556
Maryland, 242, 245, 390, 450, 545, 592, 602–3; housing in, 172, 196–97, 204–7, 230; inventories, 65–66, 236–37, 412, 414–16; orphans court records, 180–81, 206; Prince George's County, 147, 207; St. Mary's City, 545, 607–8, 635. *See also* Annapolis; Anne Arundel County, Md.; Chesapeake; St. Mary's County, Md.; Somerset County, Md.
Mason, George, 473–74, 479–80
Massachusetts, 240, 347–48, 360, 362, 364, 431, 478–79, 611; destruction of tea in, 476–78; furnishings in, 563–64, 615; housing in, 175, 180, 207, 209, 636; laws to regulate dress in, 258–59, 551; shops in, 236, 239–40; sports in, 408, 420–21; springs in, 390; tax data on, 207, 239–40. *See also* Boston
Mass production, 228, 587, 594
Mauduit, Jasper, 431
Maury, James C., 438
Maverick, Samuel, 236

Mawdsley, John, 186
Merchants, 235, 237, 265, 360, 363, 449, 592; and advertising, 245–46, 452–53; in Chesapeake, 104, 106–11, 145; and commerce, 106–7, 109–11, 237–38, 608; and consumption, 31–32, 35, 579, 608–11; English, 103, 106, 108–9; housing of, 179, 183, 186–88, 192–93, 197, 231; lifestyle of, 36, 47, 144, 451–52, 655; as models, 25, 608; and portraits, 292; and nonimportation, 473; and sports, 409–10; and travel, 399
Merriam, Daniel, 360–62, 364
Merriam, Ebenezer, 360–62, 364
Middle class, 63, 117, 228, 492, 546, 619; aspirations of, 211, 257, 259–60, 271–72, 275–76; clothing of, 257–60, 275, 278–79, 281; consumption of, 32, 227, 244–45, 435, 450, 504, 524, 546, 594, 642, 662–63; creation of, 189, 227, 251; in Europe, 257–58; furnishings of, 62–63, 66–67, 498; and gentility, 34, 275; and gentry lifestyle, 105, 130, 132, 271; growth of, 214, 231, 257; housing of, 35, 63, 182–83, 187, 189–91, 194–97, 207–8, 211, 220, 229, 231, 634; leisure time of, 399–400; in nineteenth century, 227, 231; resources of, 114, 504–5; and sports, 414–15, 418, 427, 443; as tenants, 189–90; use of objects by, 66, 244–45, 498, 673. *See also* Craftsmen; Merchants; Tradesmen
Miles, Sarah, 275
Miller, Samuel, 358, 365
Montgomery, Charles F., 46
Montgomery, Richard, 660
Morrison, Hugh, 39
Morse, Jedidiah, 387
Moseley, William, 648
Mount Pleasant, 218